ANDERSONVILLE PRISON

UNION SOLDIERS
BURIED HERE

Dorence Atwater

Heritage Books
2024

HERITAGE BOOKS

AN IMPRINT OF HERITAGE BOOKS, INC.

Books, CDs, and more—Worldwide

For our listing of thousands of titles see our website
at
www.HeritageBooks.com

A Facsimile Reprint
Published 2024 by
HERITAGE BOOKS, INC.
Publishing Division
5810 Ruatan Street
Berwyn Heights, MD 20740

2005

International Standard Book Number
Paperbound: 978-0-7884-7741-6

INTRODUCTION

Andersonville Prison is often a term equated with the idea of horror. It was officially known as Camp Sumter when established but has been identified with the small southern Georgia town by the name of Andersonville. As the Union troops pushed deeper into the south, the Confederate Army constructed this prison in the early part of 1864 in order to move more and more of the prisoners into one location. As the war began to turn against the south, the plight of the prisoners became worse with the lack of clothing, food, medical facilities and shelter.

The prison was designed to house 10,000 prisoners, but in the fourteen months it was in existence more than 45,000 prisoners came here. Of these prisoners, more than 13,000 died from disease, poor sanitation, malnutrition, overcrowding or exposure to the weather. The first prisoners came in about February 1864 but by August 1864, the south began to move these prisoners into other areas of the region.

Originally the prison was about 16.5 acres and was enclosed by a fifteen foot high fence make of hewn pine logs. In June of 1864 it was enlarged to cover 26.5 acres. It was about 1620 feet long and 779 feet wide with sentry boxes at each 30 yard interval. There was a "deadline" about 19 feet wide around the inside of the prison. No prisoner was allowed to cross into this area and if they did, they were shot on sight.

There were at least three persons of note involved in this prison. The first was Dorence Atwater, a member of the 2nd New York Cavalry. He was only 19 years old when he was sent to Andersonville, but there he became the 'keeper' of the books to record the deaths of prisoners brought there. It is his list that we include in this set of records. Secondly, there was Clara Barton who was authorized by President Abraham Lincoln to gather information on missing soldiers and to get medical supplies to them. She came to the prison in July of 1865 and was instrumental in identifying and marking the graves of the dead. Third and certainly not the least was Captain Henry A. Wirz of the 4th Louisiana Infanty. He was sent to Andersonville in March 1864 and was put in command of the prisoners. Following the war, he was arrested, tried and hanged as a war criminal.

The material found in the following pages were gleaned from a book, ***THE SOLDIER'S STORY OF HIS CAPTIVITY AT ANDERSONVILLE, BELLE ISLE*** by Warren Lee Goss 2nd Massachusetts Regiment of Heavy Artillery. The engravings were by Thomas Nast, the celebrated American artist. Some of the material were from actual photographs taken by Confederate photographers. Under some of the engravings you will see page references. These refer to the book mentioned above. We left these in place as a better explanation of the image than just a title.

There are other listings of soldiers who died in this prison, but this book takes into account only those on the Atwater listing.

James L. Douthat
Mountain Press 2005

Federal Soldiers who Died at Andersonville, Georgia Confederate Prison

1

****

NAMES

OF THE

Union Soldiers buried at Andersonville.

THE following is a complete list of the names of the Union soldiers who died at Andersonville, Georgia, as far as can be ascertained, together with their rank, the numbers of their graves, the regiments and companies to which they belonged, the dates of their decease, and the diseases of which they died, arranged alphabetically by states and by names.

The numbers prefixed to the names denote the graves. Persons numbered below 12367 died in 1864; those numbered above, in 1865. The rank of sergeant is indicated by a section mark (§), that of a corporal by a double dagger (‡), next after the names; all persons whose names are not so marked were privates, unless otherwise particularly stated.

The diseases of which they died are abbreviated as follows:—

Abscess............abs.	Diarrhœa........dia.	Hemorrhoides....hes.	Pneumonia.......pna.
Anasarca..........ana.	" acute ...dia. a.	Hepatitis..........hep.	Remittent Fever..r. f.
Ascites ....asc.	" chronic.dia. c.	Hydrocele........hye.	Rheumatism......rhm.
Asphyxia..........asa.	Diphtheria ......dip.	Hydrothorax......hyx.	Rubeola..........rua.
Bronchitis........brs.	Dysentery ......dys.	Icterus ....ics.	Scorbutus ....scs.
Catarrh ....cah.	" acute ...dys. a.	Ictus Solis.........i. s.	Small Pox.........s. p.
Cathisnetics.......cas.	" chronic.dys. c.	Intermittent Fever. i. f.	Syphilis..........sys.
Cerebritis ....ces.	Enteritis ....ens.	Laryngitis.........las.	Typhoid Fever...td. f.
Congestive Chill..c. c.	Epilepsy..........epy.	Marasmus.........mas.	Typhus Fever....ts. f.
Congestive Fever..c. f.	Erysipelas..........ers.	Nephritis ....nes.	Ulcus.............uls.
Constipatio........con.	Gangrene..........gae.	Phthisis ....phs.	Vulnus Selop .....v. s.
Debilitas ....des.	Gastritis............gas.	Pleuritis..........pls.	Wounds..........wds

ALABAMA.

No. of Grave.

7524 Barton, Wm, 1 cav, L, Sept 1, scs.
2111 Berry, J M,§ 1 cav, A, May 17, dia. c.
4622 Belle, Robert, 1 cav, A, Aug 3, dys.
5505 Boobur, Wm, 1 cav, E, Aug 13, dia.
8425 Brice, J C, 1 cav, L, Sept 11, scs.

8147 Guthrie, J, 1 cav, I, Sept 8, scs.

2514 Henry, P, 1 cav, F, June 26, pna.

996 Jones, Jno F, 1 cav, K, Mar 15, ana.

No. of Grave.

4715 Mitchel, Jno D, 1, A, Aug 4, scs.

5077 Ponders, J, 1 cav, H, Aug 8, dia.
5763 Panter, R, 1, L, Aug 15, dia. c.
6886 Patterson, W D, 1, K, Aug 25, dia. s.
2504 Prett, J R, 1, F. June 26, dia. a.

10900 Redman, W R. 1 cav, G, Oct 14, scs.

4731 Stubbs, W, 1, I, Aug 4, brs.

CONNECTICUT.

2380 Anderson, A, 14, K, June 23, dia. c.

8461 Batchelder, Benj, 16, C, July 17, dia. a.
3664 Baty, John, 16, C, July 19, dia. c.
7306 Brunkissell, H, 14, D, Aug 30, dys.
2833 Brennon, M, 14, B, July 3, dys. c.
3224 Burns, John, 7, I, July 12, dia.
10414 Blumly, E, 8, D, Oct 6, scs.

545 Bigelow, Wm, 7, B, April 14, dia.
11965 Ball, H A, 3, B, Nov 11, scs.
12089 Brookmeyer, T W, 8, H, Nov 18, scs.
12152 Burke, H, 16, D, Nov 24, scs.
12209 Bone, A, 1, E, Dec 1, scs.
10682 Burnham, F,‡ 14, I, Oct 11, dys. c.
10690 Barlow, O L, 16, E, Oct 11, dys. a.
10876 Bennett, N, 18, H, Oct 13, scs.

****

5806 Brown, C H, 1, H, Aug 15, dys.
5919 Boyce, Wm, 7, B, Aug 17, dys.
6083 Bishop, B H, 1 cav, I, Aug 18, dys.
6184 Bushnell, Wm, 14, D, Aug 19, ces.
1763 Bailey, F, 16, E, Sept 4, dys.
2054 Brewer, G E, 21, A, June 16, dia. c.
5596 Burns, B, 6, G, Aug 14, brs.
5632 Balcomb, 11, B, Aug 14, dia.
5754 Beers, James C, 16, A, Aug 15, dys.
11636 Birdsell, D, 16, D, Oct 28, scs.
4206 Blakeslee, H, 1 cav, L, July 30, ana.
3900 Bishop, A, 18, A, July 24, dys.
1493 Besannon, Peter, 14, B, June 2, dia.
2720 Babcock, R, 30, A, July 1, scs.
2818 Baldwin, Thomas, 1 cav, L, July 3, pna.
2256 Bosworth, A M, 16, D, June 21, dia. c.
5132 Bougin, John, 11, C, Aug 8, dys.
5152 Brooks, Wm D,‡ 16, F, Aug 9, dys.
5308 Bower, John, 16, E, Aug 11, scs.
5452 Bently, F, 6, H, Aug 12, dia.
5464 Bently, James, 1 cav, I, Aug 12, scs.
4830 Blackman, A,‡ 2 art, C, Aug 6, scs.
7742 Banning, J F, 16, E, Sept 3, dys.
8018 Ballentine, Robert, 16, A, Sept 6, dys.
12408 Bassett, J B, 11, B, Jan 6, '65, scs.
12540 Bohine, C, 2, E, Jan 27, '65, rhm.
12620 Bemis, Charles, 7, K, Feb 8, scs.

3707 Chapin, J L, 16, A, July 21, '64, i. f.
3949 Cottrell, P, 7, C, July 25, dia. c.
3941 Clarkson, —, 11, H, July 25, scs.
4367 Culler, M, 7, E, July 31, dia.
4449 Connor, D 18, F, Aug 1, scs.
4848 Carrier, D B, 16, D, Aug 6, dia. c.
6060 Cook, W H, 1 cav, G, Aug 18, ces.
6153 Clark, H H, 16, F, Aug 15, dys.
6846 Clark, W, 6, A, Aug 25, dia.
5799 Champlain, H, 10, F, Aug 15, dys.
336 Cane, John, 9, H, April 2, dia.
620 Christian, A M, 1, A, April 19, dys.
775 Crawford, James, 14, A, April 28, dia. c.
7316 Chapman, M, 16, E, Aug 30, scs.
7343 Cleary, P, 1 cav, B, Aug 31, scs.
7395 Campbell, Rob't, 7, E, Aug 31, dia.
7413 Culler, M, 16, K, Aug 31, dia. a.
7685 Carver, John G, 16, B, Sept 3, dys.
7780 Cain, Thomas, 14, G, Sept 4, dia.
9984 Crossley, B, 8, G, Sept 29, scs.
10272 Coltier, W, 16, B, Oct 3, dia.
11175 Callahan, J, 11, I, Oct 19, scs.
11361 Candee, D M, 2 art, A, Oct 23, scs.

25 Dowd, F, 7, I, March 8, pna.
7325 Davis, W, 1 cav, L, Aug 30, dys.
2813 Davis, W, 10, E, July 3, ana.
3614 Damery, John, 6, A, July 20, dia.
7597 Diebenthal, H, 11, C, Sept 2, dia.
8568 Donoway, J, 1 cav, A, Sept 12, dys.
8769 Dutton, W H, 16, K, Sept 14, dys.
5446 Dugan, Chas, 16, K, Aug 12, scs.
11339 Dean, R, 16, H, Oct 23, scs.
11481 Demmings, G A, 16, I, Oct 24, scs.
11889 Downer, S, 18, C, Nov 7, scs.
11991 Demming, B J, 16, G, Nov 13, dia.

3484 Emmonds, A, 16, K, July 17, td. f.
4437 Easterly, Thomas, 14, G, July 31, dia. c.
4558 Earnest, H C, 6, I, Aug 2, gae.
7346 Ensworth, John, 16, C, Aug 31, scs.
7603 Edwards, O J,‡ 8, G, Sept 2, dia.
8368 Evans, N L, 16, I, Sept 10, scs.
11608 Emmett, W, 16, K, Oct 28, scs.
12442 Eaton, W, 6, F, Jan 12, '65, dia. c.

186 Fluit, C W, 14, G, March 27, dia.
1277 Francell, Otto, 6, C, May 22, dia.
2612 Fry, S, 7, D, June 28, dia. c.
4444 Fibbles, H, 16, G, Aug 1, dia.
4465 Fisher, H, 1, E, Aug 1, dys.
5123 Florence, J J,‡ 16, C, Aug 8, dys.
5382 Fuller, H S, 24, H, Aug 11, scs.
5913 Frisbie, Levi, 1 cav, G, Aug 17, dys.

5556 Fogg, C,§ 7, K, Aug 13, dys.
8028 Feely, M, 7, I, Sept 6, scs.
9089 Filby, A, 14, C, Sept 1x, dia. c.
10255 Frederick, John, 7, A, Oct 3, scs.
12188 Fagan, P D, 11, A, Nov 28, dys.

3028 Gordon, John, 14, G, July 7, dia.
4096 Gray, Pat, 9, H, July 27, phs.
4974 Grammon, Jas, 1 cav, K, Aug 7, scs.
4005 Gulterman, J, mus, 1, E, July 26, des.
5173 Gilmore, J, 16, C, Aug 9, dia.
7057 Gallagher, P, 16, D, Aug 28, dia.
7337 Gott, G, musician, 18, Aug 30, dys.
7592 Goodrich, J W, 16, C, Sept 2, scs.
7646 Graigg, W, 16, B, Sept 3, dys.
9423 Guina, H M, 11, G, Sept 21, dia.
10300 Grady, M, 11, B, Oct 4, scs.
10397 Gladstone, Wm, 6, K, Oct 6, dys.

49 Holt, Thomas, 1 cav, A, March 15, pls.
2336 Hughes, Ed, 14, D, June 22, dia.
3195 Hitchcock, Wm A, 16, C, July 12, dia.
3448 Hall, Wm G, 1, K, July 17, dys.
3559 Holcomb, D, 14, D, July 18, dia.
1350 Hilenthal, Jas, 14, C, May 25, dia.
3033 Haskins, Jas, 16, D, July 8, dia. c.
5029 Hollister, A, 1 cav, L, Aug 8, dia.
5162 Hally, Thomas, 16, F, Aug 9, dia.
5352 Hanson, F A, 15, I, Aug 11, ana.
6695 Hodges, Geo, 1 cav, H, Aug 24, dia. c.
4937 Harwood, G, 15, A, Aug 7, ana.
6964 Hoyt, E S, 17, B, Aug 27, dia.
7012 Hull, M, 16, E, Aug 27, scs.
7380 Holcomb, A A, 16, E, Aug 31, dia.
7642 Haly, W, 16, D, Sept 3, dys.
7757 Hubbard, H D, 16, D, Sept 4, gae.
8148 Hubbard, B, 16, A, Sept 8, dys.
8403 Haywood, 18, E, Sept 11, dia. c.
8613 Heath, J,§ 16, K, Sept 13, scs.
9129 Hall, B, 16, G, Sept 18, ana.
9369 Heart, W, 11, F, Sept 20, scs.
9981 Hurley, R A, 16, I, Sept 29, dia.
12086 Hibbard, A, 18, D, Nov 18, scs.
12117 Hancock, W, 14, G, Nov 22, dys.
12163 Hudson, Chas, 11, C, Nov 26, scs.

9340 Islay, H, 11, Sept 4, scs.

737 Jamieson, Charles, 7, D, April 26, dia.
5221 Johnson, John, 16, E, Aug 10, dys.
7083 Johnson, G W, 11, G, Aug 28, dys.
7365 Jamison, J S, q m s, 1 cav, Aug 31, dia. c
7570 Jones, John J, 16, B, Sept 2, dia.
7961 Jones, James R, 6, G, Sept 6, dia.
8502 Johnson, F, 1, D, Sept 12, gae.
11970 Johnson, C S, 16, E, Nov 12, scs.
12340 Johnson, W, 16, E, Dec 26, scs.

1590 Kingsbury, C, 14, K, June 3, pna.
5186 Klineland, L, 11, C, Aug 9, scs.
6374 Kempton, B F, 8, G, Aug 21, dia. c.
6705 Kershoff, B, 6, H, Aug 25, dia. a.
6748 Kelley, F, 14, I, Aug 25, rhm.
7749 Kalty, J, 1 cav, L, Sept 3, dia. a.
8065 Kimball, H H, 7, H, Sept 7, dia. a.
8866 Kohlenburg, C, 7, D, Sept 15, scs.
10233 Kearn, T, 16, A, Oct 2, dia. a.

3401 Lendon, H, 16, D, July 16, dia. c.
5893 Lastry, J, 10, I, Aug 16, dia. c.
5499 Lewis, J, 8, E, Aug 12, dia. c.
6124 Leonard, W, 14, H, Aug 19, dia. a.
7912 Levanaugh, Wm O,§ 16, C, Sept 5, dys.
7956 Linker, C, 8, G, Sept 6, dia. a.
9219 Lewis, G H, 7, G, Sept 19, scs.
10228 Lee, — farrier, 1 cav, F, Oct 2, dia. c.

74 Mills, W J, 6, D, March 20, rhm.
119 McCaulley, Jas, 14, D, March 20, dia.
2295 Miller, Charles, 14, I, June 21, dia. a.
3516 McCord, P, 16, G, July 18, td. f.
3644 Miller, A, 14, D, July 19, scs.
3410 Mould, James, 11, E, July 16, td. f.

****

3932 McGinnis, J W, 15, E, Aug 17, ens.
4079 Miller, D, 1 cav, E, July 27, dia.
4417 Messenger, A, 16, G, July 31, dia
4492 McLean, Wm, 11, F, Aug 1, scs.
4595 Marshall, B, 8, H, Aug 3, dia.
5238 Mickallis, F, 16, F, Aug 10, dia. a
5328 Miller, H, 16, A, Aug 11, dys.
6342 Malone, John, 16, B, Aug 22, dia.
6426 Messey, M, 7, E, Aug 22, scs.
6451 McGee, Thomas, 11, D, Aug 22, dys.
6570 McDavid, Jas, 1, K, Aug 23, i. s.
6800 Meal, John, 11, D, Aug 25, dys.
6902 Mape, George, 11, B, Aug 25, dia. a.
6240 Marshall, L, 8, H, July 20, scs.
7547 Moore, A P,‡ 1 cav, H, Sept 2, dia. c.
7852 Miller, F D, 16, B, Sept 5, des.
8150 Modger, A, 10, I, Sept 8, wds.
8446 Mathews, S J, 16, K, Sept 11, scs.
8501 Meyers, L, 1 cav, Sept 12, scs.
9170 Merts, C, 11, C, Sept 18, scs.
9321 Milor, W,§ 14, F, Sept 20, dia.
10595 McCreieth, A, 14, H, Oct 10, scs.
10914 McKeon, J, 7, H, Oct 14, scs.
11487 Murphy, W, 16, C, Oct 26, scs.
11538 McDowell, J, 11, D, Oct 27, dys.
12134 Montjoy, T, 5, C, Nov 23, dia.

5044 Nichols, C, 16, G, Aug 8, dys.
6222 Northrop, John, 7, D, Aug 20, ces.
7331 North, S S,§ 1 cav, D, Aug 30, c. f.
10895 Nichols, M, 7, I, Oct 14, scs.

4565 Orton, H C, 6, I, Aug 9, rhm.
7511 Olena, R, 1 cav, E, Sept 1, scs.
8276 Orr, A, 14, H, Sept 14, scs.

2960 Pendalton, W, 14, C, July 6, scs.
3868 Pompey, C, 14, B, July 24, dia.
4356 Parker, S B, 10, B, July 31, dia. a.
3803 Phelps, S G, 1, H, July 22, td. f.
4934 Pimble, A, 16, I, Aug 7, dia. c.
5002 Plum, James, 11, G, Aug 8, des.
5386 Patchey, J, 1 cav, I, Aug 12, dia.
7487 Post, C,‡ 16, K, Sept 1, dia. a.
7688 Potache, A, 7, G, Sept 3, dia. a.
9248 Phillips, J I, 8, B, Sept 19, scs.
9444 Padfrey, Sylvanus, 8, H, Sept 21, dia.
9533 Painter, N P, 7, C, Sept 22, scs.
10676 Puritan, O, 1 cav, L, Oct 11, scs.
11616 Peir, A, 7, D, Oct 28, wds.

2804 Ruther, J,‡ 1 cav, E, July 3, pna.
2871 Reed, H H, 2 art, H, July 4, dia.
3674 Risley, E,‡ 10, B, July 20, dia.
4636 Reins, Wm, 11, I, Aug 3, dia.
5902 Ross, D, 10, K, Aug 16, dia.
6400 Robinson, H, 21, K, Aug 21, scs.
6796 Ringwood, R, 14, J, Aug 25, dia.
8078 Reed, John, 7, B, Sept 7, dia. a.
8170 Richardson, C S, 16, E, Sept 9, scs.
8345 Ray, A, 11, G, Sept 10, scs.
7310 Reed, Robt K, 7, A, Aug 30, dia.
8662 Roper, H, 16, G, Sept 13, ana.
10029 Robinson, J W, 18, D, Sept 29, dia.
10196 Richardson, D T, 16, G, Oct 2, scs.

10416 Reynolds, E, 1, E, Oct 6, dia.
12031 Rathbone, B, 2, A, Nov 15, '64, scs.

4 Stone, H I, 1 cav, A, March 3, dys.
234 Smith, Horace, 7, D, March 29, dys.
2405 Seward, G H, 14, A, June 24, dys. c.
2474 Stephens, E W, 1 cav, L, June 25, ts. f.
3010 Scott, W, 14, D, July 7, scs.
3026 Sutcliff, B, 21, G, July 7, dia. c.
3041 Stuart J, 7, July 8.
3522 Smith, J, 14, I, July 18, dia. c.
3598 Sherwood, D, 1, D, July 18, dia. a.
4212 Smith, C E,‡ 1 cav, L, July 27, dia.
4316 Straubell, L, 11, C, July 30, dia. c.
4555 Straum, James, 2 art, D, Aug 2, dia.
4722 Sullivan, M, 16, D, Aug 4, dia.
4892 Steele, Sam, 14, C, Aug 6, dia. c.
5385 Shults, C T, 14, I, Aug 12, dys.
5563 Stino, P, 16, K, Aug 13, dia.
5712 Steele, Sam, 16, C, Aug 15, dia.
5725 Smith, S, 7 B, Aug 15, scs.
6734 Steele, James M, 16, F, Aug 25, dia.
7070 Stephens, B H, 14, Aug 28, dia.
7975 Smith, Henry, 5, H, Sept 6, scs.
8088 Short, L C, 18, K, Sept 7, scs.
8235 Smally, L, 16, E, Sept 9, scs.
9304 Starkweather, E M, 1 cav, L, Sept 20, dys
9435 Sutliff, J, 16, C, Sept 21, dia.
9648 See, L, 1, G, Sept 24, gae.
9987 Sling, D, 7, F, Sept 29, dia.
10138 Schubert, K, 16, K, Oct 1, dia.
10247 Sparring, T, 7, K, Oct 3, dia.
10476 Steele, H, 16, F, Oct 7, dys.
10787 Stauff, J, 1 cav, L, Oct 12, dia.
12005 Swift, J, 1, K, Nov 14, dia:
12288 Smith, J T, 7, D, Dec 13, scs.

541 Taylor, Moses, 14, E, April 14, brs.
4443 Thompson, Wm T, 14, I, Aug 1, dia.
5427 Thompson, F, 14, A, Aug 12, dia. c.
5479 Tibbels, Wm, 16, G, Aug 12, dia.
7723 Treadway, J H,‡ 15, E, Aug 3, dia. a.
10035 Tisdale, Ed F, 1 cav, B, Sept 29, scs.
10142 Taylor, J, 14, I, Oct 1, scs.
11089 Turner, H, 11, A, Oct 18, scs.

3107 Valter, H, 14, A, July 10, ana.

401 Winship, J H, 18, C, April 6, dys,
2158 Weldon, Henry, 7, E, June 19, dia. a.
2601 Warner, E, 1 cav, E, June 28, dia.
5543 Wikert, Henry, 14, C, Aug 13, dys.
5222 Wright, C, 16, B, Aug 10, dys.
4649 Wheely, James, 10, G, Aug 3, dia.
5675 Wenchell, John L, 16, E, Aug 14, gae.
6138 Way, H C, 16, K, Aug 19, dia.
6918 Wiggleworth, M L, 2 art, H, Aug 26, scs
8024 West, Chas H, 16, I, Sept 6, ts. f.
9028 Williams, H D,‡ 16, F, Sept 17, scs.
9265 Wheeler, J, 1 cav, M, Sept 19, scs.
9512 Ward, Gilbert,§ 11, Sept 22, dys.
10033 Weins, John, 6, K, Sept 29, dip.
12600 Ward, G W, 18, C, Feb 6, '65, scs.

6394 Young, C S,‡ 16, C, Aug 21, '64, pna.

DELAWARE.

8812 Aiken, Wm, 7, G, Sept 15, scs.

5529 Boice, J, 4, Aug 13, dia.
7016 Brown, J H, 2, I, Aug 27, dia. a.

1709 Callihan, Jno, 1, B, June 7, dia. c.
2698 Conoway. F, 1, K, June 30, dia. c.
4394 Conley, J H, 2, F, July 31, dia. a.
2253 Connor, G, 1 cav, D, Dec 9, scs.
10868 Conner, C, 2, F, Oct 13, scs,
11245 Cunningham, K, 1, F, Oct 13, scs.

6217 Donahue, H, 2, D, Aug 20, scs.

6677 Emmett, W, 1, K, Aug 24, ana.

2091 Field, S, 2, D, June 17, ana.

9004 Hanning, H, drum, 2, F, Sept 17, scs.
8346 Hills, W, 2, K, Sept 10, dia. c.
5504 Hobson, W, 1 cav, E, Aug 13, dia. a.
9839 Hudson, G W,§ 2, Sept 27, scs.
11634 Hussey, J R, 1 cav, D, Oct 28, scs.

790 Joseph, W C,‡ 1, E, April 28, dia. c.
5346 Jones, H, 2, B, Aug 11, dia.

11410 Kinney, M, 1, D, Oct 24, scs.

8292 Laughlin, R M, 1, C, Sept 9, scs.
483 Limpkins, J H, 2, D, April 9, dia. c.

5956 Maham, Jas, 2, C, Aug 17, td. f.
8972 Moxworthy, Geo, 2, D, Sept 16, dia.
9580 Martin, J, 1, G, Sept 23, dia.
2943 Manner, C, 2, K, Sept 23, dia.
1671 McCracklin, H, 1, B, June 6, dys.
1570 McKinney, J, 1, F, Oct 27, scs.
12407 McBride, 2, F, Jan 6, '65, scs.

9450 Norris, Clarence, 1 cav, L, Sept 21, dia.

6307 Peterson, P, 4, F, Aug 20, dia.
8743 Piffer, W, 2, F, Aug 14, des.

7551 Reitter, G, 2, F, Sept 2, dys.
11534 Riddlor, H A, 1, H, Oct 27, scs.

6618 Saurot, John, 2, E, Aug 23, dia. a.
6479 Sholder, Ed, 2, H, Aug 22, dia. c.
6393 Simble, Wm, 1 cav, C, Aug 23, dia. a.
12707 Sill, James, 2, K, Feb 23, '65, scs.
5764 Smith, E E, 2, E, Aug 15, dia. a.

276 Taylor, Robt, 1, G, March 31, pna.
8082 Thorn, H I, 2, D, Sept 8, dys.
9324 Tilbrick, E L, 1 cav, L, Sept 20, dia. c

11981 Warner, G, 2, K, Nov 13, scs.
10302 Wilds, J, 2, K, Oct 4, scs.
198 Wilburn, Geo, 2, G, March 27, brs.

DISTRICT OF COLUMBIA.

8449 Boissonnault, F M, 1 cav, H, Sept 11, scs.

11700 Clark, Theodore, 1 cav, I, Oct 31, scs.

11180 Farrell, C, 1 cav, E, Oct 19, scs.

5736 Gray, G S, 1 cav, K, Aug 15, dys.

9463 Pillman, John, 1 cav, D, Sept 21, scs.

6873 Ridley, A C, 1 cav, M, Aug 26, dys.

11716 Russell, T, 1 cav, D, Nov 1, scs.

6847 Stretch, J, 1 cav, G, Aug 25, des.
8189 Sergeant, L,§ 1, G, Sept 8, dys.
11742 Stanhope, W H, 1, I, Nov 2, dia.

12457 Veazie, F, 1 cav, K, Jan 15, '65, dia

8172 Winworth, G, 1 cav, G, Sept 8, dys.
8907 Wiggin, Nat, 1 cav, M, Sept 15, scs.
10301 Wilson, W, 1 cav, E, Oct 3, scs.

ILLINOIS.

8402 Adams, H F,§ 17, E, Sept 11, scs.
12430 Adder, W, 30, C, Jan 4, '65, dia.
3840 Adlet, John, 119, K, July 23, dia. c.
8249 Adrian, F, 9 cav, E, Sept 9, scs.
5876 Akens, C,‡ 78, F, Aug 16, dia.
8381 Albany, D, 22, D, Sept. 10, scs.
1264 Aldridge, A, 16 cav, L, May 20, dia.
8127 Alexander, B, 123, B, Sept 8, scs.
1423 Allen, R C, 17, I, May 28, dia.
10762 Alf, H, 89, A, Oct 12, dys.
2409 Allison, L J, 21, B, June 24, dys.
6710 Anderson, A, 19, K, Aug 24, scs.
10242 Anderson, A, 98, E, Oct 3, scs.
9946 Anderson, W, 89, C, Sept 28, scs.
10271 Anthony, E, 3, E, Oct 3, dia.
7319 Armstrong, R, 89, A, Aug 30, scs.
12792 Arnold, L, 137, I, March 18, '65, scs.
10979 Atkins, E, 6, C, Oct 15, scs.
9733 Atkinson, James, 14 cav, D, Sept 25, dys.
11777 Atwood, A, 23, G, Nov 3, scs.
8046 Augustine, J, 100, I, Sept 6, ana.

3709 Babbitt, John, 7, K, July 21, scs.
2598 Babcock, F, 44, G, June 28, pna.
3783 Bailey, P,§ 38, B, July 22, ana.
12530 Baker, James, 25, H, Jan 26, '65, scs.
2892 Baker, John, 89, B, July 4, pna.
3308 Baker, Thomas, 16 cav, M, July 14, dia.
1934 Bales, Thomas, 2 art, M, May 11, ana.
5848 Barber, C F, 112, I, Aug 16, des.
3329 Barclay, P, 42, I, July 23, dia. c.
12758 Barnard, W, 14, F, March 12, '65, dia. c.
10450 Barnes, Thomas, 125, F, Oct 7, dia.
8458 Barnet, J, 120, I, Sept 11, gne.
8762 Barrett, A,‡ 25, A, Sept 14, dia.
12687 Bass, J, 2 cav, C, Feb 22, '65, dia.
977 Basting, C, 47, B, May 9, dia.
3275 Bathrick, J, 1 cav, A, July 14, dia.
4618 Batsdorf, M, 93, F, Aug 3, i. f.
3603 Bayley, Frank, 16 cav E, July 19, dia. a.
11917 Beaver, M, 29, B, Nov 8, scs.
11652 Beard, J, 14 K, Oct 30, scs.
1870 Beal, John, 78, June 12, dia. c.
6644 Bear, D, 93, B, Aug 28, scs.

4573 Beck, J, 21, G, Aug 2, dys.
411 Beliskey, J, 16 cav, D, April 7, dia.
1260 Bender, George, 12, C, May 20, dia.
5242 Bennet, A, 16, B, Aug 10, dia.
6412 Benning, John, 6 cav, G, Aug 22, dia.
3345 Benstill, John, 27, H, July 15, dia.
10653 Benton, C W, 29, B, Oct 11, scs.
8136 Berlizer, B, 16 cav, F, Sept 8, scs.
10681 Best, William, 88, E, Oct 11, scs.
4315 Black, John,§ 31, A, July 30, wds.
2904 Black, J H, 21, E, July 5, scs.
1665 Blanchard, L,‡ 16 cav, D, June 6, ans.
1983 Blosa, P, 21, A, June 15, pna.
11085 Bodkins, E L, 103, D, Oct 18, scs.
2890 Bogley, J E, 21, D, July 4, dia.
12456 Bohem, J, 14 cav, E, Jan 14, '65, scs.
9899 Boles, William, 89, C, Sept 27, scs.
10795 Bolton, N P, 100, B, Nov 4, scs.
10791 Boman, J, 108, D, Oct 12, scs.
3008 Boorem, O, 64, B, July 7, dia.
12621 Borem, M, 85, G, Feb 9, '65, pls.
11921 Bouser, G, 89, F, Nov 8, scs.
5475 Bowden, W, 9, F, Aug 13, scs.
5046 Bowen, A O, 113, C, Aug 8, dys.
5943 Bowman, E, 123, F, Aug 17, scs.
9328 Boyd, B F, 6 cav, K, Sept 25, dia.
11678 Boyd, H P, 14, I, Oct 31, scs.
1971 Boyd, J E, 84, B, June 15, dia.
10984 Boyer, J,§ 14, H, Oct 16, dia.
11720 Boyle, F, 4, B, Nov 1, scs.
12840 Bradford, D, 85, C, April 25, '65, dia.
4259 Branch, J, 38, C, July 29, scs.
1815 Brandiger, F, 24, K, June 10, dia.
1619 Brannock, C,§ 79, K, June 4, dia.
1578 Brayheyer, H, 7 cav, M, June 3, pna.
3940 Brett, James, 88, K, July 24, scs.
1669 Brewer, Henry,§ 24, C, June 6, dia.
6421 Brewer, H, 78, F, Aug 22, scs.
3264 Bridges, W H, 30, K, July 13, des.
9570 Bridges, W J, 122, F, Sept 23, dia.
1613 Bridewell, H C, 28, D, June 4, dia.
2367 Brinkey, Morris,§ 16 cav, L, June 25, cah
3056 Britsnyder, J, 65, G, July 9, dia.
2927 Brockhill, J, 4 cav, M, July 5, scs.

8717 Brookman, J E,‡ 44, I, July 21, dia.
3911 Brothers, D, 48, H, Sept 16, scs.
9350 Brown, A F,§ 73, C, Sept 20, dia.
12450 Brown, H, 15, F, Jan 14, '65, scs.
5978 Brown, J, 73, B, Aug 17, ces.
9011 Brown, J H, 12, F, Sept 17, dia.
5924 Brown, J M, 29, B, Aug 17, ens.
6836 Brown, William, 1 cav, G, Aug 26, dys.
8962 Brown, William, 16, C, Sept 16, ana.
6256 Bryant, William C, 107, A, Aug 20, scs.
10763 Briden, E, 35, E, Oct 12, dys.
5785 Buck, B F, 30, I, Aug 15, wds.
4963 Buchman, 16 cav, H, Aug 7, dys.
10888 Buckmaster, J, 79, C, Oct 13, scs.
12362 Buffington, B, 74, F, Dec 30, dia.
5457 Burdes, G, 89, A, Aug 12, i. f.
4299 Burrows, J, 90, L, July 30, dia.
7055 Burns, John, 100, K, Aug 28, dia.
5936 Burns, H,§ 16 cav, D, Aug 17, scs.
526 Burr, W B, 112, E, April 13, dia.
1858 Burton, O L, 35, I, Nov 6, scs.
11858 Butler, H J, 89, D, Oct 10, scs.
10362 Butler, N,‡ 89, D, Oct 5, scs.
8776 Butler, J, 89, A, Sept 14, dia.
11668 Button, A R, 79, E, Oct 30, scs.
9824 Butts, John, 22, F, Sept 27, dia.
626 Byres, George, 65, B, April 19, '65, dia.

12348 Cadding, J C, 89, B, Dec 27, scs.
6356 Callahan, C, 39, F, Aug 21, dia.
6505 Campbell, J M, 120, G, Aug 22, '65, dia.
10026 Capell, C, 87, D, Sept 29, dia.
10257 Capsey, J,‡ 90, D, Oct 3, scs.
3556 Carl, C C, 38, H, July 18, dia.
666 Carroll, J, 3, H, April 22, ts. f.
7037 Carroll, J Q,‡ 78, I, Aug 27, dia.
3393 Carren, O, 38, H, July 16, ana.
6693 Carirt, Robert, 113, D, Aug 24, dia.
446 Cault, Albert, 116, A, April 9, pna.
1844 Castle, F, 103, E, June 10, dia.
7502 Center, E R, 115, H, Sept 1, dys.
3907 Charles, R J, 5 cav, M, July 24, dia.
6109 Chase, E S, 23, C, Aug 18, scs.
9095 Chattenay, S, 82, H, Sept 18, scs.
10459 Chenly, S, 79, A, Oct 7, scs.
4319 Chitwood, Thos C, 16 cav, H, July 30, dia.
3205 Chlunworth, Wm, 9, G, July 12, dia.
10551 Choate, Wm, 6 cav, D, Oct 10, scs.
9935 Chunberg, A, 89, G, Sept 28, scs.
6935 Christiansen, J, 82, F, Aug 26, ana.
7868 Clancey, J W, 38, E, Sept 5, gae.
504 Clark, A E, 16 cav, M, April 12, pna.
7760 Clark, C, 51, K, Sept 4, dia.
9560 Clark, C, 29, B, Sept 23, dys.
8834 Clark, F J, 6 cav, B, Sept 15, scs.
12672 Clark, R, 114, F, Feb 13, '65, dia.
5143 Clark, Wm, 14 cav, K, Aug 9, dys.
9925 Cleaver, M, 3 cav, H, Sept 28, scs.
8750 Cleggett, M,‡ 36, I, Sept 14, dys.
5787 Cline, John, 12 cav, I, Aug 15, dia.
12726 Cline, M, 14, B, March 4, '65, dia.
12051 Cline, T, 15, E, Nov 16, scs.
2287 Clusterman, ——, 16 cav, D, June 21, dia. c.
2048 Coalman, H, 16 cav, June 15, dia.
2753 Colbern, M, 73, I, July 1, dia.
2244 Colburn, Thomas, 16 cav, G, June 20, dia.
5597 Colburn, William, 16 cav, G, Aug 14, scs.
300 Cole, John, 112, E, April 1, dia.
7211 Cole, W H, 112, A, Aug 29, dia. c.
6971 Coller, John, 6, B, Aug 27, dia.
256 Collins, Wm, 93, G, March 30, ts. f.
1198 Coddington, M J, 93, G, May 18, dys.
11719 Compton, H H, 21, K, Nov 1, scs.
2933 Cooret, D, 78, F, July 5, dia.
4683 Covey, J, 38, I, Aug 4, scs.
2758 Corey, O C, 106, D, July 1, dia.
6738 Cornelius, Jas, 9 cav, H, Aug 24, dia.
8856 Corwin, J, 7 cav, K, July 24, dia.
3677 Corwin, J V, 6 cav, L, July 20, dys.
6091 Cotton, J,‡ 100, H, Aug 18, i. s.
9704 Craig, G, 23, B, Sept 25, scs.
9307 Craig, J, 38, I, Sept 20, scs.

12506 Craig, J, 2 art, B, Jan 22, 65, dia.
9704 Craig, S, 23, B, Sept 25, scs.
10087 Craig, F, 9, K, Sept 30, scs.
1974 Crandall, W M, 93, A, June 15, dia.
2329 Crane, M, 23, E, June 23, dia. c.
2253 Crawford, Wm, 16 cav, K, June 21, dia.
10912 Crelley, C W, 29, B, Oct 14, ana.
4879 Cook, G P, 16 cav, L, Aug 6, dia.
12433 Crosbey, J, 90, C, Jan 11, '65, scs.
1417 Cross, E, 111, C, May 27, brs.
8859 Cross, J D, 14 cav, I, Sept 15, wds.
7982 Cross, J T, 21, D, Sept 6, scs.
6744 Crouse, J,§ 16, I, Aug 24, dys.
2032 Cruse, J, 79, D, June 15, dia. c.
2179 Creman, George, 24, C, June 19, dia.
10026 Cupell, C, 82, D, Sept 29, dia.
10257 Cupsay, J,‡ 90, D, Oct 3, scs.
3887 Curtis, A, 16, D, July 24, dia.

8626 Dake, G,‡ 100, D, Sept 13, dys.
4663 Dalby, James, 73, H, Aug 3, dys.
1826 Darling, D W, 93, B, June 10, scs.
10961 Darum, J J, 112, I, Oct 15, scs.
356 Davis, And, 112, A, April 2, dia.
8553 Davis, C, 112, E, Sept 12, scs.
10603 Davis, J, 113, D, Oct 10, scs.
4150 Davis, W, 16 cav, M, July 28, dia.
4048 Davis, H,§ 38, A, July 27, dys.
12311 Delancey, L D, 2 art, F, Dec 9, scs.
7013 Day, W F, 111, H, Aug 27, wds.
9073 Decker, C, 7 cav, M, Sept 17, dia.
4608 Decker, J P, 119, C, Aug 3, dys.
7150 Demos, B F, 78, F, Aug 29, dia. c.
2497 Denhart, W, 16 cav, K, June 26, dys.
4422 Denioo, E,§ 79, B, July 31, dia.
7514 Deming, Joseph, 31, D, Sept 1, scs.
12660 Denton, E,‡ 15, B, Feb 16, '65, dia.
2231 Detreeman, D,§ 44, E, June 20, scs.
5165 DePue, J W, 16, C, Aug 9, scs.
352 Derans, G W, 21, B, April 2, dia. a.
2365 Drieks, Henry, 89, C, June 23, dys.
12547 Dilley, A, 15, E, Jan 28, '65, pna.
1314 Dobson, M,§ 3 cav, H, May 23, dia.
8187 Dock, C, 9 cav, H, Sept 8, scs.
3834 Dodd, G W, 21, F, July 23, ts. f.
4207 Dodson, R B, 6 cav, B, July 29, dia.
2867 Dooley, James, 16 cav, L, July 4, r. f.
1441 Doran, W H, 78, I, May 28, ana.
1103 Donen, C, 6, I, May 15, dia.
1727 Dowd, J W, 38, G, June 8, dys.
1343 Dowdy, John, 16, K, May 24, brs.
10143 Dowell, J W, 112, K, Oct 1, scs.
10496 Downer, A, 24, H, Oct 8, scs.
12436 Doyle, P, 65, H, Jan 11, '65, wds.
12476 Doyle, J, 112, I, Jan 17, '65, wds.
5053 Drake, R R, 34, H, Aug 8, dia. c.
10332 Dresser, C, 24, G, Oct 4, dia. c.
9678 Drum, G, 89, Sept 24, scs.
3123 Dudley, J W, 89, F, July 10, ana.
2666 Dumond, P, 35, E, June 29, dia.
9947 Dunn, Alexander, 75, A, Sept 28, scs.
12496 Dunsing, A, 30, C, Jan 21, dia.
9037 Dyer, J C, 30, D, Sept 17, scs.
12686 Drew, E, 53, D, Feb 20, '65, rhm.

209 Eadley, Levi, 26, H, March 28, dys.
8045 Easinbeck, M, 100, D, Sept 6, dia.
10909 Easley, W A,‡ 21, G, Oct 14, scs.
5992 Eastman, Wm, 36, F, Aug 17, mas.
4962 Edwards, C D, 51, K, Aug 7, dys.
8084 Elliott, Ed, 92, B, Sept 7, dia.
9703 Ellis, William, 26, G, Sept 25, dia.
9734 Ellison, W, 14 cav, F, Sept 25, dia.
2249 Elslin, James, 112, E, July 24, ana.
4502 Emery, J, 22, K, Aug 1, dia.
4979 Emerson, J, 16 cav, L, Aug 7, scs.
9717 Erb, J, 9, C, Sept 25, dia.
12628 Ermains, F, 14 cav, M, Feb 14, '65, dia.
214 Errickson, C, 16 cav, M, March 28, cal.
2211 Ench, W, 29, H, June 20, asa.
11727 Enrow, W, 7 cav, M, Nov 1, dys.
2936 Evans, J, 9, C, Sept 25, dia.

3373 Eydroner, R, 74, F, July 15, dia.

6268 Fagan, O, 23, G, Aug 20, mas.
2436 Fandish, S, 1 art, A, June 25, dia.
2230 Farmer, F, 21, A, June 20, dia.
4991 Farnham, C A, 51, D, Aug 7, dia.
10740 Ferguson, Louis,‡ 115, K, Oct 14, dia.
2512 File, R, 11, K, June 26, dia.
12628 Fermer, J, 14, M, Feb 20, '65, dia.
3854 Finch, F M, 21, G, July 24, dia.
10097 Fink, J P, 53, F, Sept 30, scs.
11541 Fish, J, 65, G, Oct 27, scs.
984b Fisher, S F, 123, F, Sept 27, dia.
2129 Fitzgerald, H, 16 cav, I, June 18, pna.
9992 Flanagan, J, 42, H, Sept 29, scs.
6972 Floyd, A, 7, A, Aug 27, dia.
10881 Ford, W J,§ 17, I, Oct 13, dia.
161 Folk, A P, ‡12, G, March 26, td. f.
2564 Forney, D, 93, G, June 27, scs.
8230 Foster, A J, 16 cav, M, Sept 8, dia.
7720 Foster, B B, 112, G, Sept 3, dia.
12473 Foster, E S,‡ 9, A, Jan 17, '65, scs.
531 Fowler, John, 14, D, April 13, dia.
12275 Frame, W, 120, E, Dec 17, dia.
12837 Francis, J F, 12, I, April 19, dia.
5933 Franklin, H, 81, F, Aug 17, ens.
432 Frass, Louis, 16, E, April 8, pna.
4031 Freeman, D, 11 cav, L, July 26, brs.
2089 French, J, 129, B, June 17, '63, dia.
2210 Fritz, P,§ 38, C, June 20, scs.
1055 Fremont, James, 7 cav, B, May 13, dia.
497 Fuller, Ira B, 112, D, April 11, dia.
8114 Funks, Wm, 26, F, Sept 8, scs.
2021 Furlough, H, 23, B, June 15, dia.

9926 Gaines, C, 20, B, Sept 28, wds.
1347 Gallagher, P, 21, C, May 24, dys.
579 Garim, John,§ 59, April 16, dia.
12801 Gerlock, D, 30, C, March 30, '65, rhm.
1340 German, P, 24, G, May 24, dia.
1416 Gibson, H D, 93, K, May 27, dia. c.
4201 Gibson, L F, 78, I, July 29, dys.
4485 Gichma, J,§ 16 cav, G, Aug 1, dys.
1652 Giles, J V, 89, H, June 5, des.
7988 Giles, S P, 112, A, Sept 6, dia.
5144 Gillespie, J W, 84, H, Aug 9, dys.
1499 Gillgrease, J, 16 cav, I, May 30, dia.
1868 Gilmore, J, 16 cav, E, June 12, dia.
12731 Gleason, G M, 14 cav, A, Mar 4, '65, dia. c.
1850 Glidwell, F,‡ 73, K, June 11, dia.
2001 Goffinet, P, 51, D, June 15, dia.
10307 Goddard, H, 89, G, Oct 4, scs.
4203 Gooles, H F,§ 47, B, July 29, scs.
12847 Gordon, I, 114, B, April 25, '65, dia.
7953 Gore, F, 36, I, Sept 5, dys.
7761 Gore, N, 15, C, Sept 4, dia.
6111 Garrig, J, 78, F, Aug 18, scs.
12461 Gott, H, 39, C, Jan 15, '65, scs.
9403 Graber, J, 24, H, Sept 21, dia. c.
9312 Graber, J F, 81, D, Sept 20, dia.
2164 Grace, W, 21, D, June 19, dia.
6617 Graham, M J, 41, E, Aug 23, **dia.**
10998 Gruvel, J, 51, C, Oct 16, scs.
2942 Greadley, H, 20, A, July 6, dys.
4560 Greathouse, J, 6, I, Aug 2, dia.
783 Greaves, George, 16, K, April 28, dia.
12116 Green, C, 79, A, Nov 22, scs.
11155 Green, John, 23, H, Oct 19, scs.
7836 Green, M, 9, C, Sept 4, gae.
3111 Greenwall, B, 16 cav, L, July 11, dia.
11778 Greer, George,‡ 120, D, Nov 3, scs.
10594 Gress, J, 29, B, Oct 10, dia.
12834 Grimmins, M A, 42, H, April 17, '65, dia. c.
4083 Griswold, J P, 79, E, July 27, ts. f.
2501 Grogan, H, 66, B, June 26, dys.
10466 Grower, H, 42, K, Oct 7, dia.
3730 Gulk, P, 79, B, July 21, scs.
5025 Guyen, William, 72, E, Aug 8, dys.
5961 Gonder, H, 16 cav, B, Aug 17, ens.

5074 Hageman, James, 16 cav, E, Aug 8, dia.
4094 Haggard, E, 16 cav, K, July 27, dia.

11959 Hagtnis, W, 89, B, Nov 11, scs.
2825 Haines, Theodore, 14 cav, M, July 3, dia.
63 Haks, William, 16, E, March 19, pna.
11572 Hall, G H, 7 cav, B, Oct 27, scs.
12314 Hall, H C,‡ 41, D, Dec 20, scs.
7194 Hall, J L, 9, C, Aug 29, dys.
12223 Hall, J L, 89, G, Dec 4, scs.
11833 Hall, Peter,‡ 103, D, Nov 5, scs.
10061 Haley, C H, 22, H, Sept 30, scs.
1241 Hallam, Wm, 82, H, May 20, dia. c.
2605 Hanna, P, 21, G, June 28, dia. c.
187 Hannah, H,‡ 107, C, March 24, dia. a.
11188 Hansom, D, 39, E, Oct 19, dia. a.
318 Harken, John, 65, E, April 2, dia.
6684 Harlan, J C, 7, L, Aug 24, scs.
6113 Harrell, G, 120, K, Aug 19, dys.
2633 Harrington, S M, 112, A, June 29, dia. a.
11725 Harris, E K, 79, C, Nov 1, scs.
10447 Harris, G W, 9, G, Oct 7, scs.
8715 Harshman, Peter, 84, H, Sept 14, scs.
2677 Hart, George, 16 cav, K, June 30, ans.
2202 Hart, W, 16 cav, K, June 19, r. f.
1980 Harney, E, 39, B, June 15, pna.
10606 Hathaway, S, 15 cav, B, Oct 10, scs.
12791 Hauch, L, 15, D, March 18, '65, dia.
8608 Hawkins, J W, 79, I, Sept 12, scs.
2326 Hayward, W G,‡ 16, I, June 22, dia.
5192 Hayworth, F, 7 cav, I, Aug 10, scs.
1852 Hegenberg, W, 24, F, June 11, scs.
8798 Helch, S, 77, K, Sept 15, dys.
6489 Hendson, Geo B, 31, C, Aug 22, dia. a.
1162 Henry, Wm P, 23, A, July 17, dia. c.
6035 Herdson, Wm H, 107, C, Aug 18, ces.
8428 Herrell, Wm, 14 cav, K, Sept 11, scs.
2365 Hess, H, 84, G, June 27, dia.
1906 Hester, John, 38, G, June 13, dia. c.
7865 Hicks, George W, 65, F, Sept 5, dia. a.
8303 Hicks, H, 11, G, Sept 10, dys.
1102 Hicks, W, 85, D, May 15, dia.
12070 Highland, C, 14 cav, C, Nov 17, wds.
725 Hilderbrand, N, 24, G, April 25, pna.
8830 Hill, Aaron, 115, C, Sept 15, scs.
67 Hill, David,‡ 36, A, March 19, brs.
8721 Hill, Henry, 11, Sept 14, dia.
4489 Hill, J, 9 cav, F, Aug 1, scs.
12683 Hinchcliff, J, 8, B. Feb 20, '65, dia.
6117 Hoen, Peter, 112, H, Aug 19, dia.
3825 Hoffman, J, 7 cav, I, July 23, dys.
11847 Hofman, R, 35, C, Nov 5, dia.
2098 Hook, Jas J,§ 98, E, June 17, scs.
3255 Hoppock, I, 112, F, July 13, dys.
9880 Horeson, A F, 38, F, Sept 27, dia.
9214 Hormer, J, 38, F, Sept 19, dia.
12090 Horn, T, 86, A, Nov 18, scs.
89 Horseman, W, 16 cav, I, March 21, pna.
5812 Howard, D N,§ 79, E, Aug 16, dia.
10782 Howard, G S,‡ 127, K, Nov 3, scs.
3211 Howell, J W, 78, F, July 12.
11506 Hoye, J, 100, A, Oct 26, dia. c.
5741 Hude, C, 24, F, Aug 15, scs.
6035 Hudson, W H, 107, C, Aug 13, ces.
9962 Hughes, D L, 125, H, Sept 28, dia.
12755 Hulse, A B, 14, D, March 12, '65, uls.
11140 Hungerford, N, 108, I, Oct 19, scs.
6085 Huntley, R, 89, F, Aug 18, ana.
1136 Hurlburt, D, 84, C, May 16, wds.
1162 Hurry, W B, 23, A, May 16, dia.
5019 Hutchins, S, 104, A, Aug 8, scs.
4583 Hustand, B F,§ 92, D, Aug 2, dys.
4091 Hyber, John, 6 cav, A, July 27, dys.

3312 Iverson, J S, 16 cav, I, July 14, dia.

4132 Jaccards, S A,§ 29, E, July 28, ans.
2658 Jackson, H, 51, C, June 29, dia. a.
10287 Jackson, M, 123, F, Oct 4, scs.
12797 Janks, J P, 3 cav, A, March 18, '65, dia
3686 Jarvis, J, 73, K, July 20, r. f.
6733 Jenningsen, G B, 30, E, Aug 24, dia.
1845 Jenny, E H,‡ 79, F, June 11, dia. c.
2135 Jewett, F, 14, A, June 18, dia. c.
1996 Johnson, C W, 7 cav, F, June 15, dia. c

9458 Johnson, Joseph, 125, K, Sept 21, scs.
1412 Johnson, J S, 7, C, May 27, dia. c.
5395 Johnson, Samuel, 100, B, Aug 12, scs.
9827 Jones, G W, 27, E, Sept 27, scs.
8971 Jones, J, 117, E, Sept 16, scs.
4889 Jones, P, 41, G, Aug 6, dys.
644 Jones, Thomas, 112, E, April 12, pna.
2567 Jones, Thomas, 16 cav, F, June 27, dia. c.
2990 Jones, Wm, 27, D, July 7, scs.
1764 Jordan, B W, 84, D, June 9, dys.
9153 Jordan, M, 38, C, Sept 18, dia.
2961 Joy, B, 16, I, July 6, dia.
2241 Joyce, A, 90, D, June 20, ana.
10513 Justice, H, 7 cav, H, Oct 8, dys.

12052 Kane, H, 95, A, Nov 16, scs.
4308 Kappel, H, 29, H, July 30, i. s.
4743 Keefe, James P, 2 art, M, Aug 5, dia.
8348 Kelaze, E, 20, G, Sept 10, dia. c.
18 Kell, M R,‡ 49, D, March 7, pna.
7183 Kelley, John, 75, F, Aug 29, scs.
6795 Kelley, William, 94, I, Aug 25, dia. c.
5518 Kennedy, M, 38, C, Aug 13, scs.
12488 Kent, J, 14, F, Jan 19, '65, pls.
5707 Kerbey, John, 96, H, Aug 15, scs.
396 Kiger, John, 22, E, April 6, pna.
10520 Kilkreath, J, 42, A, Oct 8, scs.
82 Kimball, James, 25 art, L, March 20, ana.
158 Kinkle, John, 16, G, March 25, r. f.
696 Kinderman, G, 82, D, April 26, dys.
7807 Kingham, J, 38, G, Sept 4, scs.
685 Klinehaus, D, 65, G, April 23, dia.
4766 Kenigge, A, 113, C, Aug 5, des.
4908 Knight, J, 9, H, Aug 6, ana.
11891 Knoble, P, 108, E, Nov 7, scs.
4700 Koahl, J, 16 cav, H, Aug 4, dia. c.
2754 Krail, J, 16 cav, I, July 1, scs.
12685 Kreiger, J, 14, E, Feb 20, '65, des.
652 Kaiber, John, 16, D, April 20, ts. f.
1809 Keyser, John, 32, I, June 10, dia.

7927 Lacost, J M, 89, E, Sept 5, ana.
7299 Ladien, J, 100, H, Aug 23, scs.
7155 Lambert, C, 38, D, Aug 29, dia. c.
10419 Lamsden, W H, 78, A, Oct 6, scs.
12044 Lance, V, 59, D, Nov 16, scs.
12270 Langley, G, 14, K, Dec 12, scs.
5906 Lanner, W A, 9 cav, E, Aug 16, dia. c.
1233 Law, Henry, 93, G, May 20, dia. c.
9635 Lawrene, L G, 89, G, Sept 24, scs.
10179 Lape, J, 125, A, Oct 1, dia.
10896 Leatherman, M, 98, E, Oct 14, scs.
8464 Leach, W, 115, B, Sept 11, scs.
4172 Lee, A, 112, B, July 28, dia.
8524 Lee, P,‡ 16, A, Sept 12, scs.
963 Lee, Thomas, 8, E, May 9, dia.
1297 Lee, W E, 16 cav, I, May 23, dys.
11258 Lewis, Charles, 79, A, Oct 21, scs.
6238 Lewis, Thomas, 2, L, Aug 20, ces.
10148 Lickey, J B, 96,§ F, Oct 1, scs.
8295 Liday, J, 113, I, Sept 9, dys.
6295 Liken, John,§ 112, I, Aug 20, scs.
1685 Linday, B, 57, H, June 6, dia.
7768 Linderman, H A, 99, B, Sept 4, dys.
6414 Lindsay, A, 113, D, Aug 22, scs.
1818 Linebergh, I,‡ 16, F, June 10, pna.
11449 Linwood, J, 79, F, Oct 25, scs.
12358 Lipsey, D,‡ 2 cav, C, Dec 30, scs.
10405 Lord, L B,‡ 112, B, Oct 26, des.
11222 Lorsari, C, 89, C, Oct 20, scs.
2268 Loudon, L, 16 cav, D, June 21, dia. c.
1017 Lowry, Frank, 35, E, May 11, dys.
2342 Lusk, John, 29, B, June 23, dia. c.
1456 Lutz, John, 23, H, May 29, pna.
8196 Lyman, J, 100, D, Sept 8, scs.
11467 Lynch, V,‡ 38, C, Oct 26, scs.

10849 Mack, J, 14 cav, G, Oct 13, dys.
5390 Madden, L, 96, D, Aug 12, scs.
11358 Maddock, J W,§ 79, A, Oct 23, scs.
10982 Madrill, A, 12, A, Oct 15, scs.
3935 Malcolm, J R, 38, K, July 25, dia. a.

2868 Manning, A, 215, A, July 4, des
953 Manty, P,§ 16 cav, E, May 8, dia.
2050 Markman, Wm, 16 cav, K, June 16, dia. c
6333 Marritt, H, 16 cav, L, Aug 21, scs.
2762 Marshall, A,‡ 96, C, July 2, dia. c.
8444 Martin, A, 16 cav, L, May 28, pna.
4071 Martin, I, 9, K, July 27, dia.
12757 Masman, S, 42, G, March 12, '65, dia.
863 Mason, Thos B, 93, B, May 3, dys.
1428 Massey, W F, 111, D, May 28, dia. c.
746 Master, Wm, 12, A, April 26, dys.
429 Mathening, A D,§ 79, I, April 8, pna.
12744 Matthews, F M, 32, G, March 7, '65, dia.
1061 Maxem, H C, 19, H, May 13, dia.
3280 Maxwell, S, 8 cav, C, July 13, dys.
10019 May, M H, 89, I, Sept 29, scs.
3100 McCampbell, D, 104, B, July 10, dia. s.
56 McCleary, Thos, 16 cav, L, March 17, pna.
1315 McClusky, James, 16 cav, K, May 27, dia.
4850 McCray, A, 103, A, Aug 6, dys.
1617 McCready, Wm, 96, C, June 4, ana.
6513 McCreary, J, 119, C, Aug 22, pls.
5724 McCone, R, 16 cav, K, Aug 15, scs.
3050 McCunne, H, 13, C, July 8, dia. c.
3470 McEntire, L, 16 cav, K, July 17, dys.
5283 McGee, Wm, 30, D, Aug 11, wds.
11623 McGivens, J, 119, A, Oct 28, scs.
11952 McLarens, B, 89, A, Nov 10, scs.
1634 McLaughlin, B, 90, I, June 5, scs.
3169 McLing, Benj,‡ 23, E, July 11, dia.
4725 McMahon, M, 93, E, Aug 4, dia.
1337 McMillan, W B,‡ 112, E, May 24, pls.
9763 McMiller, W B, 78, D, Sept 25, scs.
692 McShaw, B, 80, B, April 23, dia.
9710 McWorthy, W M, 92, G, Sept 25, dia. c.
3279 Mead, G, 19, H, July 14, brs.
4648 Medler, H, 38, I, Aug 3, scs.
6266 Mee, William, 51, C, Aug 20, i. s.
2177 Meher, Charles, 16 cav, F, June 19, dia. a
2049 Mercenner, Chas, 90, A, June 16, dia. c.
2637 Merritt, F,§ 89, F, June 29, scs.
7464 Merg, F, 44, K, Sept 1, dia. a.
9145 Meyers, A,‡ 24, H, Sept 18, scs.
5608 Meyers, J, 24, K, Aug 14, dia.
2097 Meyers, J K, 116, C, June 17, dia. c.
5432 Meyers, Samuel, 25, A, Aug 12, i. f.
9188 Miller, F,‡ 16, B, Sept 18, scs.
3139 Miller, H, 92, F, July 10, pna.
11721 Miller, J, 21, C, Nov 1, scs.
2257 Miller, J M,§ 31, I, June 21, dia. c.
9795 Miller, M, 92, A, Sept 27, scs.
4515 Miller, Mac, 16 cav, C, Aug 18, dia. a.
3955 Mills, N, 11, K, July 25, scs.
10721 Mills, S, 14 cav, F, Oct 14, wds.
7989 Mind, D, 8, D, Sept 6, dia. a.
381 Mitchan, A, 92, E, April 5, dia.
11617 Mitchell, J R, 89, G, Oct 27, scs.
9753 Mix, C, 22, C, Sept 25, scs.
4680 Mixwell, L B, 38, F, Aug 4, dys.
4526 Monecal, J, 21, G, Aug 2, dia. a.
2646 Morehead, J, 9, E, June 29, dia. c.
2539 Morley, H, 16 cav, M, June 26, dia. c.
9187 Moran, F, 89, C, Sept 18, dia.
7428 Moran, W, 21, C, Aug 31, ana.
10645 Morbly, B, 48, H, Oct 11, dia. a.
6402 Mountz, R, 6, B, Aug 21, dia.
3263 Morris, B, 8 cav, F, July 13, pna.
816 Morris, J, 15, H, April 30, dys.
1320 Morris, James, 66, K, May 23, dia.
12757 Mossman, S, 42, G, March 12, '65, dia. c.
2993 Mulford, W R,§ 23, July 7, dia. c.
2834 Mulkey, D, 89, D, July 3, dys.
11900 Munz, P, 14, I, Nov 7, wds
50 Myers, Charles, 16 cav, B, March 16, pla
3080 Myers, C H,‡ 24, F, July 9, ana.
5038 Myers, F, 16 cav, L, Aug 8, dys.
1407 Meyers, P, 24, F, May 27, dia. c.

438 Nashen, Ed, 65, A, April 8, dia. c.
283 Neal, Joseph, 16, K, April 1, dia.
7439 Needham, L H,§ 42, K, Sept 1, dia.
9531 Nelson, J,‡ 3, K, Sept 22, scs.

8166 Newberg, H, 22, F, Sept 8, dia.
299 Newbery, Wm, 2 art, M, April 1, pna.
5778 Newby, E, 123, A, Aug 15, dia. c.
8129 Newlan, H, 25, B, Sept 8, scs.
4896 Nicely, F, 82, A, Aug 6, dia.
6945 Nichols, L C, 14, F, Aug 26, scs.
7847 Nicholson, R H, 123, B, Sept 4, dia. a.
7086 Nugent, T, 108, E, Aug 28, dia. c.
12460 Nully, C, 120, A, Jan 15, '65, scs.

6519 Obevre, O B,‡ 112, C, Aug 22, dia. a.
10851 O'Brian, D, 88, C, Oct 13, scs.
11274 Ochley, Wm, 24, K, Oct 20, scs.
3847 O'Connor, M, 2, F, July 24, scs.
1921 O'Dean, Thomas, 78, F, June 14, dia. c.
1533 O'David, J H, 9, A, June 1, dia. c.
7751 O'Donnell, 34, I, Sept 3, scs.
3609 Odom, W, 9, G, July 19, scs.
1502 Oglesby, D, 16 cav, M, May 31, dia. c.
1214 O'Keefe, M, 2 art, G, May 19, dia.
7856 Olderfield, J R, 6 cav, B, Sept 5, des.
9196 Oley, O S,‡ 21, I, Sept 18, dia. c.
10042 Oleny, A, 108, K, Sept 29, dia. a.
9885 Olson, J, 112, K, Sept 27, scs.
6098 Olson, J, 89, D, Aug 18, dia. c.
30 O'Neil, D, 16 cav, K, April 19, s. p.
10469 Osborn, J W, 9, H, Oct 7, dia. c.
6774 Oss, 89, D, Aug 25, dia. a.
4123 Ottway, D, 8 cav, A, July 28, dys.
8414 Owens, C, 120, Sept 11, dia.
10279 O'Mine, D J,‡ 9 cav, E, Oct 3, scs.

5541 Padon, C, 12, F, Aug 13, dia.
6095 Paine, S, 88, B, Aug 18, scs.
3408 Paisley, F F, 120, E, July 16, dys.
6301 Parshall, J M, 114, A, Aug 20, dia. c.
6303 Partridge, W J,§ 30, F, Aug 20, wds.
12357 Parkhurst, B, 14, H, Dec 30, scs.
12677 Patterson, F J, 14, F, Feb 19, '65, dia. c.
393 Penny, James, 14 cav, D, April 6, dia. c.
12707 Penny, W, 114, F, Feb 26, '65, dia. c.
7700 Peeter, H M, 107, C, Sept 3, dia.
2621 Perkins, A E, 89, A, June 28, ts. f.
4853 Perry, George, 89, G, Aug 6, i. f.
8313 Perry, J, 9 cav, G, Sept 20, dia. c.
3953 Perry, N, 1 cav, B, July 18, des.
12179 Peterson, J B, 112, I, Nov 27, ana.
1686 Pettas, Wm, 65, I, June 6, dia. c.
5889 Pettijohn, J, 21, F, Aug 16, dia.
12594 Philbrook, A,§ 17 cav, F, Feb 5, '65, dia. c.
410 Phillips, Wm,‡ 16 cav, L, April 6, dia.
4887 Pierce, Charles,‡ 16 cav, H, Aug 6, scs.
1506 Pierce, W B, 8 cav, H, May 31, dia. c.
3764 Place, S, 44, F, July 22, dys.
10059 Plamerly, H, 14, D, Sept 30, scs.
3679 Porterlange, Wm, 24, K, July 24, dia.
1862 Pollard, F, 127, A, June 12, dia. c.
9602 Post, George, 7 cav, L, Sept 23, dia. a.
5783 Powell, A, 122, C, Aug 15, dia.
3058 Powell, D, 16 cav, K, July 9, dia. a.
3422 Powers, James, 44, C, July 16, dia.
23 Preston, C W, 8 cav, M, March 8, pna.
6007 Price, J M, 79, D, Aug 17, dia. c.
9059 Prickett, F, 30, E, Sept 17, scs.
12597 Pratt, W, 16, F, Feb 6, '65, dia. c.
10893 Prime, D, 38, K, Oct 14, scs.
7972 Puck, John, 122, D, Sept 5, scs.
1143 Puhrer, Fred, 27, A, May 16, dia.
10412 Pyner, T, 89, D, Oct 6, scs.

10531 Quinn, P, 52, A, Oct 8, scs.

3039 Ralston, John, 79, I, July 8, r. f.
1011 Ramsay, J C, 21, B, May 10, dia.
1765 Ramsay, A B, 45, K, June 9, dia.
12763 Ramsey, T J, 79, A, March 12, '65, scs.
10772 Randall, C F, 124, I, Oct 12, scs.
8578 Rankin, W A,‡ 3 cav, I, Sept 12, dia. a.
12680 Ransom, J, 4 cav, B, Feb 19, '65, dia. a.
7604 Reany, J H,§ 6 cav, B, Sept 2, dia. c.
5968 Redmont, John, 112, H, Aug 17, dia. a.
8571 Reed, A, 98, I, Sept 12, dys.

3496 Reed, D, 26, H, July 18, scs.
12324 Richardson, T, 34, E, Dec 23, scs.
1616 Richards, H, 79, I, June 4, scs.
3809 Rickold, W, 16, G, July 23, scs.
2836 Rictor, Charles,‡ 82, H, July 3, dia.
8632 Ripley, J, 9, B, Sept 13, gae.
7748 Ritter, D, 14 art, D, Sept 3, dia. a.
2074 Roberts, W W, 16 cav, I, June 17, ana.
8410 Robinson, E H, 36, A, Sept 11, ana.
4460 Robinson, H B,§ 6 cav, B, Aug 1, dia.
6080 Robinson, J B, 79, A, Aug 18, ces.
10751 Roder, F, 16 cav, G, Oct 12, scs.
2596 Rodenberger, N, 96, E, June 29, scs.
10184 Roferty, J C, 6 cav, H, Oct 1, dia. a.
747 Rodgers, O, 12, A, April 26, dys.
1807 Rogers, Silas, 65, D, June 10, dia. c.
7228 Rogers, George, 16 cav, G, June 29, dia
528 Rolla, E J, 103, G, April 13, dia.
4389 Rosecrans, H, 113, A, July 31, ana.
11473 Ross, J W, 45, F, Oct 26, dys.
8465 Ross, Thomas, 113, K, Sept 11, scs.
306 Rudd, Eras,§ 100, K, April 2, dia.
1294 Rudd, F, 16 cav, L, May 23, dia. c.
2557 Ryan, M, 89, A, June 27, phs.

2000 Saddle, M, 27, G, June 15, ana.
9845 Saler, J B,§ 14, F, Sept 20, dia. a.
10512 Sandler, L,‡ 19, D, Oct 8, dia.
11289 Sargeant, M,§ 14, K, Oct 22, scs.
1902 Savage, P P, 13, June 13, dia. c.
9915 Sauin, B, 36, C, Sept 28, scs.
7558 Schrider, D, 23, A, Sept 2, dys.
7163 Schrider, John, 44, K, Aug 29, dia. c.
3493 Schannolter, C, 24, H, July 17, dys.
10359 Schurtz, W, 44, F, Oct 5, scs.
1573 Scitaz, Victor, 16 cav, L, June 3, dys.
11077 Scott, H, 28, G, Oct 17, scs.
4524 Scuyner, N,‡ 64, G, Aug 2, wds.
12034 See, S, 11, G, Oct 15, scs.
1787 Seeley, Charles, 44, G, June 10, dia. c.
9325 Sem, C, 8 cav, D, Sept 20, dia. c.
4872 Serens, R B, 112, I, Aug 6, dys.
1333 Setters, Geo H, 38, G, May 24, dia. c.
12827 Seward, R, 61, E, April 8, '65, dia.
5350 Seybert, A J, 39, E, Aug 11, scs.
9322 Shadrach, G H, 7 cav, C, Sept 20, dia. c.
1661 Shanbach, Ed, 44, E, June 6, ana.
8861 Shark, L F, 113, D, Sept 15, dia. a.
12149 Sharp, A, 7 cav, B, Nov 24, scs.
2579 Sharp, A H, 22, A, June 27, dys.
1899 Sharp, E D T, 89, June 13, dia.
2647 Shaw, J, 89, E, June 29, dys.
7315 Shaw, Joseph, 98, D, Aug 30, scs.
4135 Sheeby, John,§ 42, G, July 28, dia. c.
8386 Sherwood, J F, 16 cav, I, Sept 10, dia. c.
7270 Shields, J A, 6 cav, E, Aug 30, scs.
12046 Siebert, H C, 7 cav, M, Nov 16, scs.
10441 Siffle, H, 7 cav, M, Oct 7, scs.
2430 Silkwood, H M, 89, D, June 24, epy.
1717 Silter, John, 16 cav, I, June 9, ana.
12713 Simmons, W D, 42, H, March 1, '65, dia
7630 Simpson, C, 14, D, Sept 2, dia. c.
12834 Simmons, M A, 42, H, April 17, '65, dia
309 Sipple, A, 107, E, April 2, dia.
12390 Skinner, H, 14, C, Jan 4, '65, dia. c.
10082 Skinner, Wm, 16, G, Sept 30, scs.
2585 Slasher, H,‡ 96, E, June 28, scs.
10663 Slick, P, 9, E, Oct 11, dia. c.
9402 Smith, C W, 16, K, Sept 24, dia.
5960 Smith, George, 53, E, Aug 17, dys.
362 Smith, John B, 7 cav, L, April 2, dia.
12566 Smith, J S, 115, D, Feb 1, '65, des.
10866 Smith, N P, 28, G, Oct 13, scs.
10975 Smith, O, 114, H, Oct 15, scs.
4659 Smith, William, 16 cav, M, Aug 3, gas
8223 Snyder, B, 6 cav, B, Sept 8, dia.
8079 Sommers, W, 40, F, Sept 7, dia.
2165 Soms, C, 82, A, June 19, dia. c.
4283 Spangler, H J, 16 cav, L, July 30, dia.
9092 Spindler, W, 113, F, Sept 18, dia.
11359 Sprulock, A, 79, E, Oct 23, scs.
4598 Sprague, W, 8 cav, K, Aug 3, dia.

1667 Springer, M, 112, E, Jan 6, dia. c.
2132 Steilhoult, A, 92, H, Nov 23, wds.
2532 Standsfield, H, 96, H, June 26, dia.
1718 Stark, F, 78, H, June 8, dys.
1018 Stegall, J, 16 cav, L, May 11, dia.
10737 Stevens, S, 44, D, Oct 11, dia. c.
6292 Stewart, F, 78, I, Aug 20, scs.
4878 Stillwell, F H, 79, L, Aug 6, scs.
1640 Stillwell, James, 38, I, June 5, r. f.
10828 Stine, A, 14, H, Oct 13, scs.
4724 Stopes, S W, 89, E, Aug 4, scs.
8451 Storem, A, 89, D, Sept 11, scs.
12190 Storem, C, 98, C, Nov 28, scs.
10440 Strand, John, 9, H, Oct 6, dia.
8549 Striker, J, 11, K, Sept 12, scs.
12822 Stringer, P, 15, B, April 5, '65, dia.
9013 Strong, S M, 95, B, Sept 17, dia.
855 Stune, S L, 40, G, May 3, dia. c.
8615 Sullivan, J, 16 cav, I, Sept 13, dia.
12482 Sullivan, M, 15, E, Jan 17, '65, des.
9325 Sunn, C, 8 cav, D, Sept 20, dia.
11808 Suter, B F, 4 cav, L, Nov 4, scs.
5515 Sutton, M, 9 cav, M, Aug 13, dia.
4442 Swanson, P, 9, K, July 31, dys.
12725 Steinhaus, J, 15, B, March 3, '65, dia.
6292 Steward, F, 78, I, Aug 20, scs.
12557 Swarts, E,‡ 24, G, Jan 30, '65, scs.
6105 Swartz, A, 7 cav, M, Aug 18, dia.
505 Sweet, Wm, 89, E, April 12, rhm.

10515 Tanner, J, —, A, Oct 8, scs.
502 Taylor, George, 16 cav, M, April 12, pna.
10036 Taylor, H,‡ 7 cav, I, Sept 29, scs.
809 Taylor, James, 4 cav, F, April 30, dia.
12526 Taylor, M P, 14, I, Jan 26, '65, rhm.
1825 Temple, I, 100, H, June 10, dia.
4466 Terry, John, 16 cav, M, Aug 1, dia. c.
12437 Thayer, D, 64, E, Jan 12, '65, rhm.
2415 Thomas, A, 16, A, June 24, des.
10411 Thompson, D, 24, K, Oct 6, scs.
6491 Thompson, F, 10, B, Aug 22, dia.
7128 Thompson, G G, 1 cav, M, Aug 28, '63, scs.
2453 Thompson, John, 16 cav, I, June 25, dia.
6831 Thompson, T, 2, M, Aug 25, scs.
10847 Thomsburg, N C, 79, A, Oct 5, ts. f.
8863 Thorn, J, 16 cav, K, Sept 15, dys.
9833 Thurmain, J, 84, E, Sept 27, scs.
46 Tuiler, W, 16 cav, D, March 15, pna.
3064 Topp, A, 19, C, July 9, ana.
547 Trailer, Van Buren, 16 cav, I, Apl 14, pna.
11550 Trask, J J, 7 cav, B, Oct 27, scs.
751 Trowbridge, L, 16 cav, M, April 26, dia.
1915 Trout, E, 21, F, June 14, dia.
2502 Turnerholm, S H, 19, K, June 26, dia. c.
3032 Tucker, E, 38, B, July 8, dia.
12736 Tucker, J, 7, F, March 6, '65, des.
10832 Tucker, J P, 8 cav, G, Oct 13, scs.
10988 Turner, S, 120, A, Oct 16, gae.

11091 Underwood, D, 11, E, Oct 18, dia.

5183 Vase, ——, 16 cav, H, Aug 9, dys.
1078 Vaugh, James, 16 cav, L, May 14, dia.
7765 Vincent, L D, 7 cav, G, Sept 4, dia.
1026 Voris, Ross, 16 cav, I, May 11, dia. c.

3271 Volter, George, 9, C, July 13, dia. c.
2015 Vought, Wm, 24, H, July 15, dia.
5638 Vox, Wm, 24, E, Aug 14, dia.

6767 Waddle, J,§ 112, C, Aug 24, scs.
2964 Wahl, M, 16 cav, I, July 6, dia. c.
9218 Walker, George, 31, K, Sept 19, scs.
12072 Ward, R S, 15, C, Nov 18, i. f.
11345 Ward, G B, 7 cav, E, Nov 23, scs.
2488 Ward, W J, 16 cav, M, June 26, dia.
12392 Wareck, N, 120, D, Jan 4, '65, scs.
7895 Warkwich, J, 93, C, Sept 5, scs.
5898 Watts, Wm, 16 cav, L, Aug 16, dia.
11619 Waterman, L, 95, D, Nov 28, scs.
6173 Weaver, G, 16 cav, L, Aug 19, scs.
9317 Weaver, Alex, 93, A, Sept 20, dia.
742 Weeks, Benj, 16 cav, L, April 26, dia.
10785 Weedman, J W,‡ 38, I, Oct 12, scs.
4941 Weinmiller, John,§ 56, G, Aug 7, des.
10001 Welch, John, 7, E, Sept 29, dia.
11751 Welch, L, 24, F, Nov 2, scs.
10085 Welch, G,§ 95, A, Sept 30, scs.
4358 Wentworth, Charles, 27, D, July 31, r. f.
7426 Westbrook, B D, 6 cav, B, Aug 31, gae.
3067 Whalin, M, 23, B, July 9, scs.
3910 Wham, T, 21, G, July 24, scs.
9184 Wheeler, J, 61, F, Sept 18, dia.
992 Wheelock, A, 96, H, May 10, ana.
1496 Whitmore, B, 16 cav, D, May 31, ana.
1699 Whitmore, L, 104, I, June 7, dia.
5998 Whitney, J F, 89, G, Aug 17, dia.
8713 Whipp, Charles, 9 cav, E, Sept 14, scs.
5613 Wildberger, P, 6 cav, B, Aug 14, dia.
5158 Wiley, T, 7, M, May 15, dys.
12732 Wiley, W P, 32, C, March 5, '65, scs.
12671 Wilkes, R, 81, A, Feb 18, '65, dia.
7840 Wilhelm, G A, 9, C, Sept 4, gae.
90 Will, Gustavus, 16 cav, E, March 21, pna.
9785 Will, J, 36, B, Sept 26, dia. c.
8310 Williams, A, 22, I, Sept 10, scs.
3254 Williams, E, 49, D, July 13, pna.
10899 Williams, G W, 15 bat, Oct 14, scs.
11497 Williams, G B, 15, B, Oct 26, dia.
12780 Willis, A P, 84, A, March 15, '65, dia.
4737 Wilson, D, 16 cav, M, Aug 4, scs.
9531 Wilson, J,‡ K, Sept 22, scs.
11712 Wilson, W,§ 89, F, Nov 15, dia.
1130 Wimmer, G, 16 cav, I, May 15, pna.
989 Wink, Lewis, 16 cav, C, May 10, r. f.
8755 Winning, D, 125, C, Sept 14, dia.
6079 Winters, Wm, 24, H, Aug 18, scs.
3743 Wismer, J,‡ 74, G, July 21, scs.
2301 Wing, John, 7 cav, H, June 22, dia.
8815 Wood, 21, G, Sept 15, dys.
1042 Woodcock, R, 16 cav, L, May 12, dia.
3695 Workman, James, 7, G, July 21, dia.
10582 Worthy, A A, 21, K, Oct 10, dys.
2664 Wright, J W, 35, C, June 28, dia. c.
5265 Wright, M, 59, E, Aug 10, i. f.

12309 Yates, J, 120, E, Dec 19, dia.
10766 Yagle, C, 24, B, Oct 12, scs.

2391 Zimmerman, Philip, 1 art, June 24, dia.
72 Zoran, Philip, 44, I, March 20, pna.

INDIANA.

571 Allen, Jessie,‡ 116, K, April 15, dys. c.
1917 Adkins, George, 6 cav, D, June 14, scs.
3991 Andrews, E L, 6 cav, K, July 26, ana.
4270 Anderson, D, 76, E, July 29, dia.
5680 Ault, J W, 40, D, Aug 14, dia.
4921 Alexander, S, 93, D, Aug 26, scs.
7124 Alexander, J D, 5 cav, K, Aug 28, scs.
9292 Auburn, C, 65, H, Sept 19, dia.
9445 Atkins, J F, 2 cav, H, Sept 21, dia.
9584 Adams, H, 35, A, Sept 23, dia.
9643 Allen, D B,§ 29, Sept 24, gae.
9759 Alfred, W J, 117, K, Sept 25, scs.

10473 Allyn, D, 88, K, Oct 7, scs.
10793 Atland, C, 32, C, Oct 12, scs.
11186 Albin, I, 89, D, Oct 19, dia.
12183 Austin, Alfred, 5, K, Nov 27, scs.
12513 Amick, W, 93, B, Jan 23, '65, scs.

313 Bush, David, 117, C, April 2, pna.
576 Bee, Thomas, cav, April 16, dys. c.
596 Bock, Samuel, 75, I, April 17, dys. c.
838 Brown, T, 66, D, May 1, dia.
1514 Barrey, Henry, 84, D, May 31, dys.
1600 Boley, A J, 66, C, June 4, dia. c.

****

1759 Barra, John, 65, H, June 9, dia. c.
2016 Burnett, Wm, 6 cav, G, June 15, dia.
2191 Buckhart, E, 27, F, June 19, dia.
2222 Brasier, S, mus, 19, I, June 20, dia.
2299 Bumgardner, 44, D, June 22, dia.
2458 Barrett, E, 42, I, June 25, dia. c.
2874 Bowman, John, 42, C, July 4, dia.
3044 Bruce, J W, 5 cav, M, July 8, dia. c.
3359 Broughton, D, 7 cav, K, July 15, dys.
3366 Bricker, J, 68, C, July 15, dia. c.
4027 Barton, J F, 52, G, July 26, dia. c.
4035 Ballinger, Robert, 39, I, July 26, scs.
4251 Bonly, James, 81, C, July 29, dia.
4479 Baker, J, 9, G, Aug 1, scs.
4563 Baker, D W, 13, B, Aug 2, dia.
4948 Bayer, F, 129, H, Aug 7, dys.
5089 Brenton, J W, 29, I, Aug 8, scs.
5093 Bowlin, Wm, 53, G, Aug 8, wds.
5220 Barton, E, 2 cav, G, Aug 10, scs.
5275 Busick, W A,‡ 101, F, Aug 10, dia.
5442 Bryer, P, 81, K, Aug 12, scs.
5590 Bohems, Philip, 79, A, Aug 14, dia.
5690 Baker, I P, 7 cav, H, Aug 15, dia.
5794 Boom, W P, 31, F, Aug 15, scs.
5981 Barton, George, 130, F, Aug 17, dia. c.
6163 Brookers, J M, 112, E, Aug 19, dys.
6410 Brown, J M, 66, F, Aug 22, scs.
6518 Bartholomew, I, 99, A, Aug 22, dys.
7370 Bamgroover, J A, 101, H, Aug 31, dia.
7794 Barnes, Thomas M, 5 cav, B, Sept 4, dys.
8314 Babbitt, W H, 29, I, Sept 10, dys.
8397 Bassinger, H, 14, C, Sept 10, dia.
8519 Boyd,, W F, 125, F, Sept 12, ana.
9098 Bartley, S, 88, I, Sept 13, scs.
9548 Bray, T E, 79, K, Sept 23, scs.
9708 Brown, J,§ 1 cav, A, Sept 24, dia.
9777 Birch, T A, 58, L, Sept 26, scs.
9793 Bozell, J F, 40, B, Sept 26, scs.
9846 Bixter, D, 5, B, Sept 27, scs.
10350 Blackaber, Wm H, 42, I, Oct 5, scs.
10939 Benton, L, 30, H, Oct 14, scs.
11559 Bennett, R N, 72, D, Oct 27, scs.
11604 Benuis, J M,‡ 87, F, Oct 28, scs.
11919 Brown, D, 128, B, Nov 8, dys.
11930 Bailey, George, 72. A, Nov 8, scs.
12019 Bennet,, A, 29, G, Nov 15, scs.
12128 Booth, J, 32, E, Nov 22, scs.
12294 Bennett, C, 6, H, Dec 15, scs.
12486 Barrey, H, 66, I, Jan 19, '65, scs.
12504 Balstrum, J, 93, F, Jan 22, '65, scs.
12596 Branson, E, 57, A, Feb 6, '65, pna.

301 Charles, James. 6, G, April 1, dia,
625 Connell, P, 6 cav, M, April 19, dys. c.
634 Claycome, S A,§ 66, G, April 20, dia.
1117 Cox, Joseph.§ 42, B, May 15, dia.
1146 Carter, Henry, 2, C, May 16, pna.
1172 Curry, J W, 30, F, May 17, dia. c.
1463 Currier, Wm, 87, K, May 30, dia.
1523 Crest, J D, 31, F, May 31, dia. c.
2254 Carpenter, O C,‡ 29, D, June 21, dia.
2307 Cottrell, M,§ 6 cav, G, June 22, ana.
2776 Cooley, A, 38, C, July 2, pna.
3043 Clark, W, 82, C, July 8, dys.
3922 Connolley, D, 9, I, July 25, dia.
4192 Cox, S, 66, E, July 28, dia.
4917 Clifford, H C, 7 cav, I, Aug 6, scs.
5262 Courtney, J F, 2 cav, L, Aug 10, dys.
5654 Collar, E, 130, G, Aug 14, scs.
5660 Crews, E M, 5 cav, A, Aug 14, dys.
5901 Clark, A, 54, A, Aug 16, dia. c.
6208 Chrichfula, S, 93, A, Aug 19, gae.
6477 Croane, J J, 22, C, Aug 22, scs.
6646 Cornelius, E, 58, B, Aug 23, scs.
6926 Carnahan, A W,§ 6, E, Aug 26, dys.
7383 Carpenter, S, 66, I, Aug 31, scs.
7726 Callings, W, 120, F, Sept 3, dia.
7737 Cramer, A, 30, H, Sept 3, des.
7899 Cheny, James, 7 cav, I, Sept 5, dys.
8051 Crumton, R, 101. I, Sept 6, dia.
8108 Crazen, J, 53, G, Sept 7, scs.
8133 Crager, J, 13, C, Sept 8, c. f.

8144 Cooper, ., 80, E, Sept 8, dia.
9294 Christman, J E, 6 cav, G, Sept 19, scs.
9535 Collins, G, 56, F, Sept 22, dia.
9980 Connett, Daniel, 130, F, Sept 28, scs.
10084 Conel, J, 13, D, Sept 30, dia.
10905 Callan, M, 35, B, Oct 13, dia.
11423 Cafer, J H, 87, K, Oct 24, scs.
11631 Cummings, J W, 93, F, Oct 28, scs.
12062 Clark, M, 101, B, Nov 17, dia.
12173 Cannon, A, 42, F, Nov 26, scs.
12213 Cregs, Wm, 5 cav, E, Dec 3, scs.
12415 Collins, W A,§ 5, G, Jan 8, '65, scs.
12559 Calvert, G F, 8 cav, I, Jan 30, '65, dia.
4234 Curry, W F, 4 cav, I, July 29, dia. c.

426 Dummond, J H, 65, F, April 7, dia. c.
508 Davis, J M, 66, , April 12, dia.
964 Darker, Wm, 12, C, May 8, ana.
2205 Denny, John, 44, E, June 19, dia.
3157 Detrich, C, 29, K, July 11, dia.
3419 Dusan, J, 6, D, July 16, dia. c.
4021 Develin, E, 35, B, July 26, pna.
4029 Decer, P, 32, K, July 26, scs.
4124 Dill, C P, 42, F, July 27, dia.
5255 Davis, K, 13, D, Aug 10, dia.
5367 Dunben, M, 36, E, Aug 11, scs.
5420 Delup, Z S, 13, D, Aug 12, scs.
5681 Dallinger, W C, 38, E, Aug 14, dia.
6147 Denton, Philip, 81, D, Aug 19, '65, scs.
6834 Downey, S M, 116, I, Aug 25, scs.
6944 Dowell, W L, 6, C, Aug 26, dys.
9638 Dunlap, W, 30, A, Sept 24, scs.
10010 Downs, J R, 5 cav, I, Sept 29, dys.
10435 Dane, Andrew, 36, I, Oct 6, scs.
10446 Dignon, L, 35, B, Oct 7, dia.
10916 Dawson, L F, 29, I, Oct 14, scs.
10954 Dial, R, 1, B, Oct 14, dia. c.
12087 Daffendall, P H, 58, D, Nov 18, scs.
12172 Davenport, J, 6 cav, I, Nov 24, scs.
12236 Delashment, F,§ 14, B, Dec 6, scs.
12533 Duckworth, J, 85, F, Jan 27, '65, scs.
12545 Dawley, J, 73, I, Jan 27, '65, rhm.
12580 Dawson, J, 124, D, Feb 3, '65, pls.
9236 Diver, O, 19, F, Sept 19, gas.

916 Evans, G H, 1 cav, A, May 6, dia. c.
917 Edwards, G H, mus, 6, G, May 7, dia. c
1083 Ellis, H C, 6 cav, D, May 14, dia.
1279 Evans, W, 75, I, May 22, r. f.
1346 Eskridge, Oakley, 29, D, May 24, dia. c.
1994 Edwards, J W, 38, G, June 15, dia. c.
2481 Esenthal, F, 5 cav, D, June 25, dia. c.
4075 Eaton, W H, 58, B, July 27, dia. c.
4953 Ecker, J, 39, I, Aug 17, ana.
5076 Evans, J, 6 cav, I, Aug 8, dia.
7917 Ells, D, 20, I, Sept 5, dia. c.
11320 Elston, F, 9, B, Oct 22, scs.
11429 Estelle, E W,§ 2 cav, L, Oct 24, scs.
11712 Eldridge, E, 38, Nov 1, scs.
11774 Earl, D,‡ 2 cav, B, Nov 3, scs.
12285 Emmons, W, 5, D, Dec 14, scs.

1482 Frecks, F, 35, D, May 30, dia.
1808 Fitter, B, 66, I, June 10, dia.
2143 Fike, Tobias, 30, D, June 18, dia.
3014 Fitzgerald, I, 30, D, July 7, dia.
3453 Fescher, D, 32, E, July 17, scs.
3637 Fuget, W, 3 cav, C, July 20, dys.
8379 Fields, N, 6 cav, F, Sept 10, scs.
8547 Fenton, I, 72, D, Sept 12, scs.
8766 Forward, S, 8 cav, I, Sept 14, ana.
9847 Forshua, W, 25, H, Sept 27, scs.
10509 Farmingham, W C, 14 cav, K, Oct 8, scs
11311 Fanier, F, 6 cav, I, Oct 22, scs.
11526 Fish, C, 2 cav, H, Oct 26, scs.
12012 Falkerson, J,§ 93, B, Nov 14, i. f.
12144 Francis, F, mus, 93, Nov 24, scs.
12320 Fross, John,§ 5 cav, D, Dec 24, scs.
12728 Felnich, H, 10, F, March 4, '65, dia. c.

98 Graham, Wm, 6, G, March 22, pna.
322 Gladman, H, 110, B, April 2, pna.

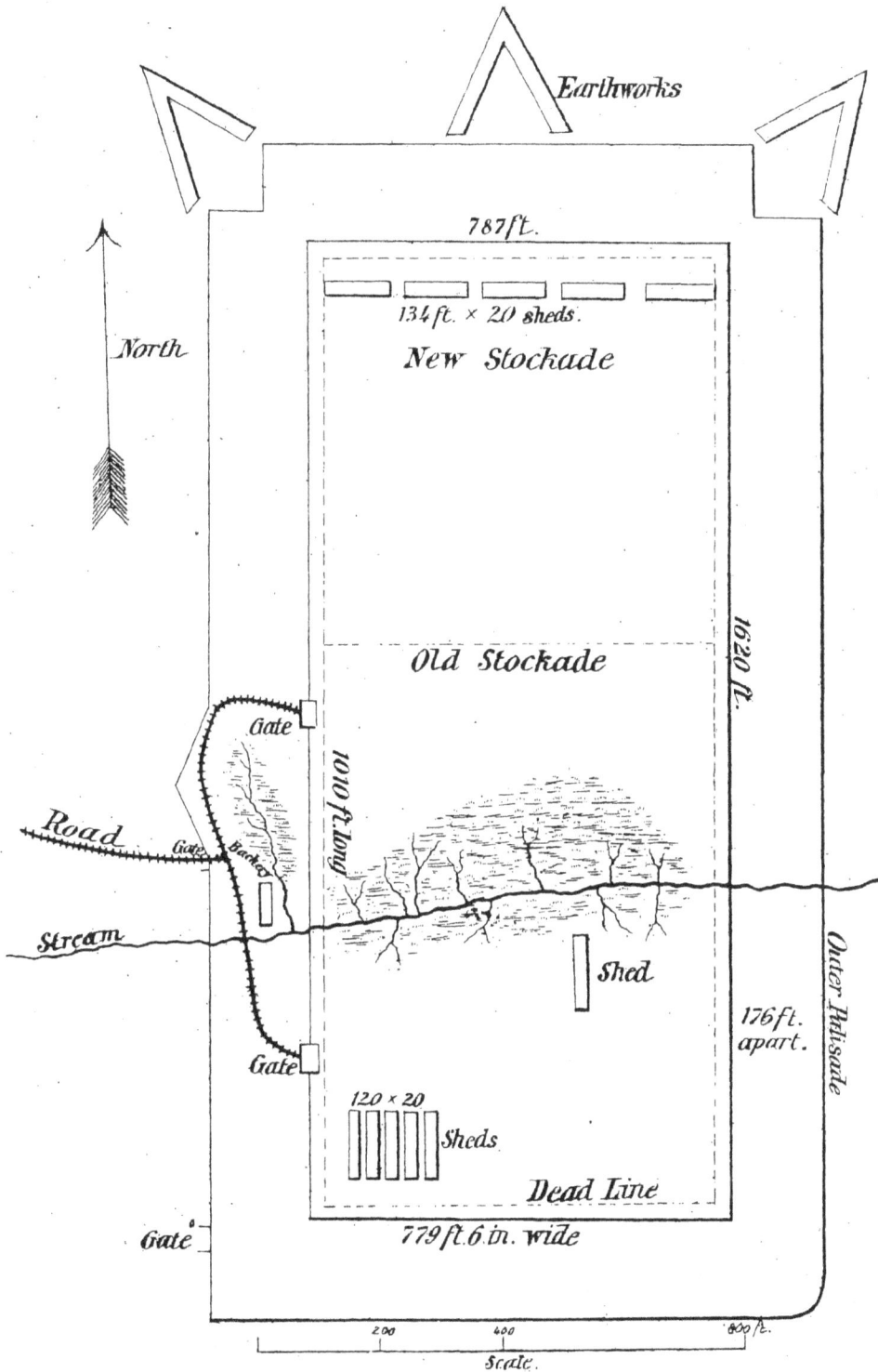

Earthworks

North

787 ft.

134 ft. × 20 sheds.

New Stockade

1620 ft.

Old Stockade

1010 ft. long

Gate

Road

Gate   Banked

Stream

Shed

176 ft.
apart.

Gate

Outer Palisade

120 × 20

Sheds

Dead Line

Gate

779 ft. 6 in. wide

200   400   800 ft.

Scale.

PLAN OF PRISON GROUNDS
ANDERSONVILLE,
Measured by Dr. Hamlin.
Copy Right secured.

1048 Goodwin, Wm, 2 cav, M, May 12, ana.
1165 Grimes, F O, 66, I, May 17, dys.
1215 Garver, John, 29, F, May 19, dia. c.
1312 Gullsen, William, 7 cav, L, May 23, dia. c.
1594 Griffin, William, 6 cav, I, June 3, rhm.
2337 Gray, D L, 22, I, June 22, ts. f.
2386 Guthrie, W B, 80, C, June 24, dia. c.
2418 Gillard, Wm, 120, C, June 24, r. f.
3573 Gibbons, W T, 128, I, July 19, dia.
4179 Gould, Wm, 66, E, July 28, scs.
4273 Gilbert, H A,§ 2 cav, K, July 29, dia.
4347 Galliger, Wm, 7, B, July 31, dia.
4901 Gerard, H, 35, G, Aug 6, ana.
6189 Goodwin, I, 20, F, Aug 19, dia.
6398 Gordon, W M, 74, G, Aug 21, scs.
6493 Goodridge, E,‡ 94, H, Aug 22, dia. c.
7298 Grass, C, 32, H, Aug 30, scs.
7321 Gray, H F, 2 cav, H, Aug 30, scs.
7698 Gerber, I, 30, C, Sept 3, dia.
8546 Galliger, P, 58, C, Sept 12, scs.
8791 Gagham, Wm, 35, K, Sept 14, scs.
9112 Green, S, 72, E, Sept 18, wds.
9114 Gillan, J, 29, F, Sept 18, scs.
10782 Griswold, Thomas, 2, F, Oct 12, scs.
11409 Gordon, J W, 13, D, Oct 24, scs.
11581 Greenwood, W, 3, C, Oct 28, scs.
12216 Grant, H G, 5, G, Dec 3, dia.
12398 Garnett, T, 6, E, Jan 5, '65, scs.
12483 Green, Wm, 39, E, Jan 19, '65, scs.

630 Hollar, John, 5 cav, I, April 19, dia. c.
879 Henick, Wm, 30, F, May 4, dys.
1953 Hall, L S, 117, C, June 14, dys.
2118 Hilliard, J, 116, D, June 17, dia. c.
2130 Hodges, J, 7, C, June 18, pna.
2379 Hustin, James, 74, B, June 23, dia.
2392 Hodges, S, 9, F, June 24, dia.
2629 Humphrey, I, 3, C, June 28, dia.
2768 Hendricks, J, 2 cav, C, July 2, rhm.
2768 Higgins, M P, 3 cav, C, July 2, dys.
2793 Hodges, W J, 5, F, July 2, scs.
2812 Hillman, H, 65, G, July 3, ana.
2974 Hamilton, James, 7, K, July 7, dia.
3289 Hine, S, 68, A, July 14, dia.
3507 Hodgen, J W, 80, G, July 18, des.
4487 Hanger, L S, 65, A, Aug 1, dia.
5362 Hart, J R, 88, H, Aug 11, scs.
5678 Hittle, B, 6 cav, L, Aug 14, scs.
5695 Helville, N C, 20, F, Aug 15, dia.
5872 Heah, Jacob, 20, G, Aug 16, dia.
6076 Hearne, John, 5 cav, F, Aug 18, scs.
6198 Hershton, A, 4, M, Aug 19, dys.
6491 Hendrick, I, 129, H, Aug 22, scs.
7031 Hartsock, I, 30, A, Aug 27, dia.
7790 Hunter, J M, 42, F, Sept 4, des.
7837 Hammond, G W,‡ 65, D, Sept 4, dia.
7903 Halfre, J A, 32, A, Sept 5, dia.
7971 Hamilton, P S, 7, E, Sept 6, scs.
8091 Hughes, W H,‡ 81, D, Sept 7, dys.
8347 Hart, A, 7, A, Sept 10, dia.
8541 Haff, M, 4 bat, Sept 12, ana.
8681 Hunter, H, 42, F, Sept 13, scs.
8778 Haynes, W, 30, G, Sept 14, ana.
8836 Higgins, John W, 3 cav, C, Sept 15, scs.
8967 Holloway, J, 5 cav, M, Sept 16, dia.
9083 Hubbner, F, 4 cav, E, Sept 18, dia. c.
9329 Hurst, R V,‡ 36, B, Sept 20, scs.
9429 Higgins, W E, 53, H, Sept 21, wds.
9911 Haghton, J, 2, D, Sept 28, ana.
9933 Harrington, O, 30, I, Sept 28, dys.
10123 Hoffman, J, 80, C, Oct 1, pna.
10293 Hunstler, W H,§ 38, E, Oct 4, scs.
10522 Hoagler, N C, 39, E, Oct 8, scs.
10613 Harris, W C, 13, D, Oct 10, dia. c.
10820 Hector, E, 13, D, Oct 12, scs.
11231 Haskins, H, 99, A, Oct 20, scs.
11243 Hasfle, J, mus, 1, F, Oct 21, scs.
11790 Hill, R, 14, D, Nov 4, scs.
12249 Hamilton, D, 13, B, Dec 9, scs.
12536 Hall, H H, 2, E, Jan 5, '65, dia.

6444 Ihn, C, 129, B, Aug 22, '64, scs.

8963 Igo, T,‡ 4, H, Sept 16, dia.

670 Johnson, Isaac, 5, C, April 22, dys.
1931 Jennings, C,‡ 6 cav, I, June 14, dia. c.
2212 Jackson, John, 22, C, June 20, dia
2353 Jones, Wm M, 63, D, June 23, dia. c.
3311 Jasper, Wm, 38, I, July 10, scs.
5245 Judd, Henry,§ 2, D, Aug 10, scs.
6172 Julerso, H, 2 cav, D, Aug 19, mas.
6311 Jones, H C, 5, C, Aug 20, scs.
7100 Jones, A, 88, I, Aug 28, dia.
9948 Johnson, J, 7 cav, A, Sept 28, scs.
12517 Jones, J, 120, C, Jan 24, '65, rhm.
12799 Johnson, H, 40, C, March 19, '65, dia. s

417 Kistner, George, 42, B, April 7, des.
618 Kinnan, A, 56, G, April 18, dia.
858 Ketchum, G W,§ 5 cav, I, May 3, dia.
2036 Kelley, John,§ 5 cav, June 15, dia.
2407 Kennedy, Amos, 2, H, June 24, dia. c.
1908 Kelso, E O, 3 cav, C, June 13, dia. c.
2527 Kanga, J, 74, E, June 26, r. f.
3047 Kennedy, J W,‡ 3, I, July 8, dia.
4024 Keys, Wm, 72, E, July 26, des.
5149 Keiler, W J,§ 4 cav, H, Aug 9, dys.
5253 Kocher, T, 29, I, Aug 10, scs.
5722 Kern, W, 25, H, Aug 15, ens.
6596 Kelly, John, 32, C, Aug 23, scs.
7085 Kames, J, 128, F, Aug 28, dia.
8621 King, D, 81, A, Sept 13, scs.
10689 Keller, I, 49, B, Oct 11, dia. c.
12278 Kuling, I, 79, A, Dec 12, scs.
12587 Keef, P,‡ 10 cav, C, Feb 4, '65, dia.

1041 Lewis, J, 6, H, May 12, '64, dia. c.
1229 Lawrence, R J, 30, G, May 20, dia. c.
1261 Lower, N G, 116, I, May 21, dia.
2615 Lewis, James, 65, F, June 28, dia. c.
2745 Luff, C, 58, I, July 1, dia. c.
3029 Lewis, J, 3 cav, C, July 7, scs.
3767 Lannon, J S, 128, F, July 22, des.
3890 Lawrence, D, 80, A, July 24, dia.
4548 Lyons, Wm, 35, A, Aug 2, scs.
5014 Lee, John, 3 cav, C, Aug 8, dys. c.
5585 Lawson, William, 75, A, Aug 14, scs.
5616 Lawyer, James, 80, B, Aug 14, dys.
6775 Lyons, Wm, 1, E, Aug 25, dia.
7162 Lowery, D, 2 cav, G, Aug 29, dia.
8607 Lunger, A, 7 cav, M, Sept 12, scs.
9256 Liggett, ——, 52, G, Sept 10, scs.
10508 Lewis, R, 7 cav, C, Oct 8, dia. c.
11152 Lash, J, 101, B, Oct 18, scs.
11715 Lakin, A, 7 cav, Nov 1, scs.
12250 Lawrence, B T, 42, D, Dec 9, scs.

130 McCarty, John, 66, D, March 23, i. f.
631 Mullen, James, 6 cav, G, April 19, dia.
746 Masters, Wm, 65, G, April 26, dia.
841 Milton, John, 18, C, May 1, dys.
903 Mytinger, Wm, 117, F, May 5, dia. c.
954 Milburn, J, 6, K, May 8, dia.
1090 Moore, Peter, 6, I, May 14, dia. c.
1405 Miller, Jacob, 74, E, May 27, dia.
1516 Martin, George,§ 3 cav, C, May 31, dia
1860 Merritt, H, 30, G, June 12, dia. c.
2240 Mitchell, J J, 30, D, June 20, dia.
2397 Milliken, S L, 1 cav, G, June 24, phs.
2511 Moueyhon, B, 38, D, June 26, dia. c.
2608 Marsh, J, 88, D, June 28, dia. c.
5 Moodie, Z, 117, K, March 31, s. p.
3387 Mank, E, 80, E, July 16, dia. c.
3633 Marlit, J, 80, H, July 20, scs.
3884 Mulchy, J, 35, A, July 24, dia. c.
4010 Mercer, John, 12, F, July 26, dys.
4388 Malshy, F, 14 cav, A, July 31, dia.
4959 McDale, R, 19, A, Aug 7, dia.
5562 Manihan, J, 38, D, Aug 13, dia.
5618 Mageson, J, 7 cav, A, Aug 14, ts. f.
5703 Mensome, S,§ 42, E, Aug 15, dys.
5713 Monroe, S, 33, F, Aug 15, scs.
5767 Montgomery, R, 80, F, Aug 15, dys. s
5863 Michael, S, 7, I, Aug 16, dia.

6461 Mitchell, J H, 30, I, Aug 22, scs.
6521 Monroe, H J,§ 44, G, Aug 22, scs.
6566 Mathews, M, 42, K, Aug 23, i. s.
7043 Milsker, J, 5, D, Aug 27, dia.
7233 Matheny, N,§ 42, A, Aug 29, dia.
7272 McQueston, J O, 13, B, Aug 30, dia.
7510 Myers, A, 29, E, Sept 1, scs.
7820 Moore, G,‡ 101, F, Sept 4, dys. c.
7973 Mine, John N, 2, H, Sept 6, scs.
8007 Miller, W W, 101, B, Sept 6, dia. c.
8176 McCoy, W,§ 66, B, Sept 8, dia.
8389 Murphy, J, 9, E, Sept 10, dia.
8851 McElvain, J, 93, E, Sept 15, dia. c.
8925 Myers, J, 143, D, Sept 16, scs.
9575 Morrison, J, 4, B, Sept 23, dia. c.
9600 Miller, J, 7 cav, G, Sept 23, scs.
9856 Murgu, A, 35, D, Sept 27, scs.
10231 Monay, G W, 7, E, Oct 2, dia.
10245 McFarney, J, 93, B, Oct 3, scs.
10394 Maples, H, 29, H, Oct 6, scs.
10891 Murphy, F, 35, B, Oct 13, scs.
10995 McDonald, I, 74, B, Oct 16, scs.
11166 Mills, Milton, 26, D, Oct 18, scs.
11271 Mitchell, I, 7, K, Oct 21, scs.
11585 McCarty, A, 7, A, Oct 28, scs.
11665 McBeth, I C, 28, K, Oct 30, dia.
11680 Murphy, F, 35, C, Oct 31, scs.
11746 McCarty, A, 7, A, Nov 2, dia.
11857 McCarty, I, 6, A, Nov 6, scs.
11946 Miller, F B, 30, C, Nov 10, scs.
12548 Madlener, L, 12, K, Jan 27, dia. c.
12563 McFall, I, 30, A, Jan 31, scs.
12624 Mainfold, W, 6 cav, I, Feb 9, rhm.
12639 Montgomery, W, 5 cav, G, Feb 17, dia. c.
12709 Maloy, I, 11 cav, G, Feb 28, dia. c.

2007 Nossman, G, 117, G, June 15, dia.
3205 Newcomb, George, 22, A, July 12, ana.
3519 Nucha, S, 3 cav, I, July 18, dia.
4627 Napper, W H,§ 6, I, Aug 3, scs.
6528 Norton, N A, 38, B, Aug 23, dys.
10187 Note, John H, 39, F, Oct 1, scs.
12226 Nichols, J, 38, G, Dec 5, scs.
9494 Newbery, M, 7 cav, L, Sept 21, dia.

342 O'Niel, Thomas, 6, G, April 2, dia. a.
1874 Oliver, John,‡ 42, June 12, dia. c.
2778 Oliver, H H, 5 cav, M, July 2, dia.
5226 Oliver, J, 120, K, Aug 10, scs.
5361 Osborn, J, 73, E, Aug 11, dia.
7863 Oliver, J, 19, D, Sept.5, dia.
7911 O'Conner, Thomas, 5 cav, B, Sept 5, dia.
10940 Olinger, E, 65, A, Oct 14, scs.
12544 Ortell, M, 35, G, Jan 27, scs.
12590 Ousley, W I, 7, A, Feb 5, dia. c.

287 Peache, Cyrus, 66, D, April 1, dia.
559 Pashby, John, 6 cav, C, April 15, dys. c.
3434 Pavy, W, 123, A, July 17, dia.
3738 Palmer, A, 42, F, July 21, dys.
4068 Parker, E,§ 29, A, July 27, dia.
4171 Park, John, 129, B, July 28, r. f.
4551 Pettus, H, 53, C, Aug 2, dys.
4553 Pruitt, H C, 7 cav, K, Aug 2, scs.
5627 Prentice, J M, 22, K, Aug 14, wds.
6159 Penat, Alexander, 38, B, Aug 19, dys.
6278 Patterson, E, 4 cav, G, Aug 20, mas.
6874 Parten, D R, 65, F, Aug 26, dia.
7710 Plough, J W,§ 89, D, Sept 3, scs.
8661 Pratt, William, 29, F, Sept 13, ana.
9196 Plumer, A, 2, D, Sept 18, scs.
9705 Pope, I T,§ 5 cav, G, Sept 24, scs.
9709 Patterson, N S, 93, G, Sept 24, dia.
10128 Packett, T C,§ 39, F, Oct 1, scs.
11880 Pangburn, ——,§ 20, B, Nov 6, gae.
12572 Potts, I, 99, H, Feb 2, scs.
12588 Phepps, A, 30, D, Feb 4, scs.
1249 Packer, Samuel B, 6 cav, G, May 20, dys.

872 Remy, John, 66, B, May 4, r. f.
944 Reed, R, 57, F, May 7, dia.
1065 Remcett, L, 65, H, May 13, dia.

1558 Roll, N C, 117, F, June 2, dia. c.
1696 Reese, L, 116, I, June 7, dia. c.
2140 Robinson, L, 7, I, June 18, r. f.
4039 Rogman, ——, 38, I, July 26, dia.
4165 Reiggs, K N, 39, K, July 28, scs.
4406 Richardson, I, 35, I, July 31, dia.
5180 Rawlings, J W, 117, F, Aug 9, dys.
5259 Rains, G D, 4, G, Aug 10, dys.
5454 Ritter, Benjamin, 29, K, Aug 12, scs.
5542 Ralph, G, 68, F, Aug 13, dys.
6247 Roundbush, Daniel, 6, B, Aug 20, dia.
6383 Redyard, A, 65, F, Aug 21, dia.
6754 Russell, J, 7, K, Aug 24, dia.
7677 Ringold, I, 7 cav, I, Sept 3, dia.
8488 Russmore, E, 2 cav, C, Sept 11, scs.
8577 Redman, N E, 80, F, Sept 12, scs.
9521 Richardson, John, 86, D, Sept 21, dia.
9547 Riggs, L, 19, E, Aug 23, scs.
10829 Reeves, Wm, 42, F, Oct 13, scs.
11416 Rierdon, M D, 5 bat, Oct 24, scs.
11451 Rutger, W,‡ 44, D, Oct 25, scs.
11935 Russell, W H, 13, C, Nov 9, scs.
12454 Robinson, R, 8 G, Jan 14, wds.
12523 Richardson, E, 127, E, Jan 26, scs.
1440 Ryan, Martin, 35, B, May 28, dys. c.
6707 Rawlings, E,§ 66, C, Aug 24, dia.

86 Smilley, ——, 65, I, March 21, dia.
129 Stein, Thomas, 66, D, March 23, dys.
205 Stouts, ——, 65, I, March 28, dia. c.
768 Sanderson, H, 6 cav, G, April 27, dia.
817 Sears, I, 65, I, April 30, dia. c.
901 Shick, Eli, 20, C, May 5, dia. c.
1039 Smith, M C,‡ 24 bat, May 12, ts. f.
1331 Smith, H, 86, A, May 24, dys.
1400 Sapp, A J, 44, H, May 26, ana.
1430 Swindle, T O,§ 82, A, May 28, dia. c.
1501 Smith, L, 116, A, May 31, ana.
1611 Schroder, W, 42, A, June 4, dia.
1690 Sparks, L D, 66, D, June 7, dia.
1732 Search, C, 5 cav, D, June 8, dia.
2079 Shigley, T W, 10, H, June 17, pna.
2083 Stinit, D, 6 cav, L, June 17, pna.
2218 Smudley, W, 5, E, June 20, scs.
2318 Swain, J W, 30, A, June 22, dia. c.
2420 Snow, J, 5 cav, G, June 24, dia. c.
2447 Stafford, J W, 68, I, May 25, dia. c.
2740 Smith, J, 65, H, July 1, dia.
2799 Stanchley, Wm, 5, K, July 2, scs.
2923 Stofer, L,§ 29, B, July 5, dia.
3416 Spencer, M, 80, K, July 16, dia. c.
4014 Shields, J, 128, F, July 26, dys.
4054 Smith, J W, 38, G, July 27, dia.
4062 Smith, H, 79, H, July 27, dia.
4088 Schneider, S A, 3 cav, July 27, dia.
4229 Sollman, C,§ 35, D, July 29, dia.
4418 Stevens, M, 6 cav, M, July 31, dia.
4630 Snider, D, 117, K, Aug 3, scs.
4799 Summersvolt, V, 29, A, Aug 5, scs.
5254 Scott, B, 9, D, Aug 10, scs.
5418 Smith, Samuel E, 9, C, Aug 12, scs.
5513 Shoemaker, E W, 5 cav, I, Aug 13, scs.
5514 Sims, S, 101, B, Aug 13, dia.
5571 Sackett, I, 6 cav, G, Aug 14, ts. f.
5611 Stockman, L M, 68, E, Aug 14, dia.
5884 Standish, M, 66, B, Aug 16, dia. c.
5977 Stockhoff, G, 19, I, Aug 17, dia. c.
6044 Stout, H, 7, G, Aug 18, dia.
6736 Sipe, J, 82, A, Aug 24, dia.
6830 Strong, L, 9, F, Aug 25, scs.
7120 Spellman, J, 80, F, Aug 28, scs.
7264 Shaver, F, 129, I, Aug 30, scs.
7683 Snyder, L, 6 cav, A, Sept 3, dia.
7822 Sanders, D, 7, I, Sept 4, dia.
8058 Suthien, J H, 66, E, Sept 7, dia.
8107 Starkey, I, 6 cav, I, Sept 7, scs.
8262 Sizeman, I, 123, B, Sept 9, scs.
8313 Stegewald, J M,§ 22, K, Sept 10, scs.
8623 Swillenbarger, F, 21, I, Sept 13, scs.
8666 Sylvanus, J J, 35, G, Sept 13, scs.
8727 Shoel, J P, 30, B, Sept 14, scs.
8910 Storm, L M,§ 6, A, Sept 16, scs.

9093 Simmons, J, 84, I, Sept 18, dia.
9252 Sharp, D M, 13, E, Sept 19, scs.
8646 Sharpless, W, 43, G, Sept 23, dia.
9623 Smith, S B, 17, F, Sept 24, dia.
9807 Skeels, W, 65, A, Sept 26, dia.
10790 Smith, George, 131, D, Oct 12, dys.
10949 Smith, I, 39, I, Oct 14, scs.
11006 Sioat, G W,§ 44, B, Oct 16, scs.
11187 Seigferd, G H, 4 cav, I, Oct 19, dia.
11427 Swietzer, J, 2, G, Oct 24, scs.
11842 Shaw, W R, 99, B, Nov 5, wds.
11969 Shoe, G W, 74, E, Nov 12, scs.
11984 Steamer, F, 29, F, Nov 13, scs.
12113 Scarff, F, 6 cav, D, Nov 21, scs.
12381 Starke, M S, 93, D, Jan 2, des.
12492 Salts, H C, 4 cav, F, Jan 20, dia. c.
12582 Smith, D H, 12 cav, H, Feb 3, dia c.
12615 Sides, G, 66, A, Feb 8, pls.
12666 Smure, C, 2 cav, G, Feb 17, dia. c.
12724 Stewart, E B, 38, E, March 3, scs.
12809 Staley, G W, 72, A, March 24, dia. c.
2625 Sattershwait, A, 82, I, June 28, scs.

518 Tenher, James, 117, I, April 13, dia. c.
3778 Tunblora, B, 65, B, July 22, dia.
3791 Thompson, T, 6 cav, C, July 22, dys. a.
4733 Tooley, G W, 42, H, Aug 4, scs.
5065 Truman, L H,§ 6 cav, G, Aug 8, scs.
5403 Taylor, N, 63, I, Aug 12, wds.
6509 Tooley, W R,‡ 42, H, Aug 22, dys.
6719 Todd, T, 6, B, Aug 24, hep.
7096 Thomas, H D, 42, I, Aug 28, ana.
7442 Taylor, George H, 4 cav, M, Sept 1, dia. c.
8495 Trumble, D A, 30, A, Sept 11, dia.
8525 Taylor, E, 25, I, Sept 12, dia.
10438 Thomas, M, 2 cav, A, Oct 6, dys.
12337 Tucer, B, cit, Nov 26, scs.
12609 Terhune, C, 9 cav, A, Feb 7, pls.
10219 Tasnahet, Charles,§ 33, E, Oct 2, scs.

10356 Underwood, P, 7 cav, C, Sept 5, scs.
10760 Upton, F M, 52, A, Oct 12, scs.

1717 Voit, T, 6 cav, K, June 8, dia. c.
5363 Venome, James, 30, K, Aug 11, dia.
6250 Vanose, J, 93, B, Aug 20, ces.
7691 Verhouse, D, 42, A, Sept 3, scs.

135 Windinger, J, 117, G, March 24, r. f.
886 Walters, J H,‡ 6 cav, G, May 5, i. f.

934 Williams, A, 6, G, May 7, dia. c.
1194 Wright, Samuel, 6 cav, I, May 18, dia.
1776 White, P, 6 cav, C, June 9, dia. c.
1812 Wise, Eli, 88, D, June 10, dia.
1918 Warren, E, 65, H, June 14, dia.
2107 Williams, F, 38, F, June 17, dia. c.
2242 West, E, 7 cav, H, June 20, dia.
2363 Woodward, W W, 29, A, June 23, dia. c.
2417 Wilson, J N, 75, G, June 24, dia. c.
2467 Warden, I, 44, B, June 25, dia. a.
2554 Warren, E, 37, I, June 27, pna.
2670 Ward, J, 79, F, June 29, ana.
2900 Wyn, W E, 13, D, July 5, dia.
2929 Wislake, I, 116, I, July 5, dys. c.
2934 Wicks, L, 6 cav, H, July 6, dia.
4528 Whitehead, J, 29, I, Aug 2, dia.
4639 Winship, James, 36, K, Aug 4, scs.
4826 Witt, T, 125, D, Aug 5, dia.
5399 Wade, C, 81, K, Aug 12, dys.
5547 Waynin, J H, 4 cav, I, Aug 13, dia.
6132 Washburn, R H, 6 cav, A, Aug 19, scs.
6405 Winders, A, 120, I, Aug 21, des.
6524 Wagner, M, 5 cav, I, Aug 22, scs.
7184 Winters, F W, 84, C, Aug 29, dia.
7191 Wagoner, E, 42, A, Aug 29, scs.
7349 Witzgall, John, 2, D, Aug 31, scs.
8943 Weiber, Charles, 13, F, Sept 16, scs.
9228 White, W, 7, E, Sept 19, dia.
9316 Watkins, J, 81, A, Sept 20, dia. c.
6418 Wellington, H, 129, I, Sept 21, dia. c.
9501 Wilson, J B, 6, E, Sept 21, dia.
9998 Wagner, F, 7, D, Sept 29, dia.
10648 Ward, J, 29, G, Oct 11, scs.
11141 Whitehead, N B, 5 cav, L, Oct 18, scs.
11424 White, R B, 6, D, Oct 24, scs.
11602 Walters, J, 5, I, Oct 28, scs.
12708 Winebrook, P, 35, B, Nov 18, scs.
12316 Werper, J, 32, E. Dec 20, scs.
12341 White, J, 7, A, Dec 26, scs.
12462 Wells, J M, 13, D, Jan 16, scs.
12497 What, J, 93, B, Jan 21, pls.
12737 Wade, W, 10 cav, M, March 6, dia. c.
3837 Weltz, Ira,§ 4, B, July 23, dia. c.
6000 West, S N,‡ 7, B, Aug 17, dia.
9920 Williams, J A,§ 38, C, Sept 28, scs.

5055 Younce, Charles A, 7 cav, I, Aug 8, dys.
5838 Yorker, Daniel, 28, B, Aug 16, ens.

1540 Zuet, J, 65, H, June 1, des.

IOWA.

5560 Allen, N, 3, K, Aug 13, dia.
8974 Ankobus, L,‡ 6, I, Sept 17, dia. c.
9472 Ashford, A W, 11, C, Sept 21, wds.
11784 Alderman, W W, 31, F, Nov 4, scs.
11896 Austin, Wm, 3 cav, A, Nov 7, dia.

1293 Bartche, C P, 5, K, May 23, dia.
1570 Bingman, W H, 39, H, June 3, dia.
5276 Blanchard, A, 7, A, Aug 10, dia. c.
6164 Bursford, M, 7, F, Aug 19, dia.
7779 Baird, J J, 26, H, Sept 4, dia.
8265 Buckmaster, F, 15, K, Sept 9, dia.
9301 Buell, J, 4, D, Sept 20, dia.
9456 Boylan, C, 14, G, Sept 21, dia.
9691 Boles, M B, —, I, Sept 24, dia.
10749 Bellings, J, 5, B, Oct 12, scs.
11334 Blakely, Geo, 3, G, Oct 23, wds.

167 Collins, Henry,§ 4, G, March 26, dia.
328 Chenworth, Wm, 4, K, April 2, dys.
4582 Cromwell, G W, 27, F, Aug 2, dia.
5101 Cooper, S, 5, B, Aug 9, scs.
5244 Cox, E E,‡ 5, G, Aug 9, dys.
5620 Cox, W A, 5, G, Aug 14, dia.
5999 Coder, E, 31, E, Aug 17, dia.
6378 Cox, H, 5, I, Aug 21, scs.
6604 Clamson, Henry, 26, I, Aug 23, dia. c.

6848 Collins, M, 3, L, Aug 25, dia.
8062 Culbertson, S,‡ 5, H, Sept 7, dia.
8352 Crow, B, 4, E, Sept 10, dys.
9784 Coles, J W,§ K, Sept 26, dia. c.
9820 Cobb, E, 3 cav, C, Sept 26, dia. c.
10037 Cramer, J M, 5 cav, B, Sept 29, dia. c.
10901 Chapman, J, 3, G, Oct 14, gae.
12230 Chamberlain, J B, 8 cav, A, Dec 6, wds.

2903 Davis, S, 3, E, June 30, dia. c.
4206 Davis, J, 15, D, July 29, wds.
9229 Davis, H, 17, A, Sept 19, scs.
4675 Dermott, L, 5, G, Aug 4, scs.
6849 Discol, S, 26, I, Aug 25, dys.
9852 Dingman, W, 31, D, Sept 27, scs.
11098 Denoya, W H, 5, M, Oct 18, des.
11753 Dutlin, S, 6 cav, C, Nov 2, scs.
12245 Durochis, Wm, 12, H, Dec 8, scs.
12657 Derickson, W W,‡ 8 cav, M, Feb 15, dia c

262 Ennis, Wm, 4, B, March 31, dys. a.
11414 England, G, 9, F, Oct 24, scs.

3705 Field, Jacob, 5, K, July 21, dys.
4503 Farnsworth, S, 2, H, Aug 1, ana.
1316 Forney, James M, 10, K, May 23, dia.
7715 Fru', J, 10, Sept 3, dia.

7878 Frederick, J A, 16, C, Sept 5, dia.
8380 Frussell, G W, 6, D, Sept 10, scs.
10048 Fordson, Michael, 16, H, Sept 29, dia.
11078 Fener, J W. 3 cav, B, Oct 17, scs.
12711 Ferguson, A W, 15, A, Feb 28, uls.

750 Gain, L, 6, C, April 26, ts. f.
1484 Gender, Jacob, 5, I, May 30, dia. c.
5004 Gentle, G, 4, G, Aug 8, dia. c.
5836 Gunshaw, C, 26, Aug 16, mas.
10511 Gray, J, 11, C, Oct 7, dys.
10366 Gothard, J, 8, G, Oct 11, scs.

5461 Harris, J, 8 cav, H, Aug 13, dys.
8106 Hastings, J,§ 11, B, Sept 7, dia.
9379 Hird, D,‡ 3, G, Sept 20, wds.
9417 Hudson, M, 16, B, Sept 21, dia.
2168 Huffman, R J, 5, H, June 19, dys.
862 Heeller, A, 5, D, May 3, brs.
1633 Harper, D, 7, K, June 5, des.
1816 Hurlay, J, 8, H, June 11, dia. c.
12749 Hubanks, C,§ 17, H, March 8, des.

10360 Ireland, J S, 5 cav, H, Oct 5, wds.

4461 Jones, C, 4, B, Aug 1, scs.
8656 Jenks, G A,§ 8, C, Sept 13, dia. c.
9401 Jones, J, 5, C, Sept 21, dia. c.

3204 Kolenbrander. H, 17, K, July 12, dia.
7 King, Alexander, 17, H, April 5, s. p.
6464 King, E, 2 cav, C, Aug 22, wds.
3560 Kesler, F, 4, B. July 18, scs.
5378 Kennedy, B, 16, I, Aug 11, wds.
11281 Knight, J H,§ 9, I, Oct 22, gae.

892 Lambert, Chas,‡ 39, K, May 5, brs.
2045 Littleton, J, 5, June 15, dia.
7959 Lord, L, 13, G, Sept 6, des.
8263 Lanning, A, 13, I, Sept 9, scs.
9438 Lowdenbeck, N, 5, B, Sept 21, ana.
10224 Lowelenbuck, D R, 5, B, Oct 2, dia.
10881 Layers, W, 5, E, Oct 14, scs.
11752 Luther, J,‡ 9, B, Nov 2, scs.
12629 Littlejohn, L D, 4 cav, B, Feb 10, dia. c.

257 Moore, John, 39, H, March 31.
307 Myers, M, 4, K, April 2, dia.
450 Moon, James, 39, H, April 9, dys.
1192 McMullen, James, 4, C, May 18, i. f.
1317 Miller, F, 5, H, May 23, dia.
1472 McCameron, W, 4, A, May 30, r. f.
2027 McAllister, A P, 14, E, June 15, dia.
3423 McNeil, J W, 11, I, July 16, dip.
4804 Moore, Wm, 13, A, Aug 5, scs.
5445 Murray, J J, 17, I, Aug 12, scs.
6167 McCall, Thos, 8 cav, M, Aug 19, mas.
6315 Merchant, Wm, 13, G, Aug 25, dia.
6878 Maynard, J D, 4, B, Aug 26, dys.
7143 McDonald, D B,§ 5 cav, M, Aug 29, dia.
8120 McClure, Z,§ 16, C, Sept 8, scs.
9274 Martin, S S, 11, G, Sept 19, scs.
9585 Mann, J, 16, Sept 23, scs.
9113 Miller, J, 5, D, Oct 1, scs.
10827 McCoy, G B,‡ 5, G, Oct 13, dia.
10950 Mercer, John, 4, C, Oct 14, scs.
11745 Miller, E,‡ 31, D, Nov 2, scs.
12484 Martin, J B, 5, B, Jan 19, rhm.
12561 Macy, C S, 8 cav, C, Jan 31, dia.

6959 O'Conner, P, 26, D, Aug 27, dia.
9509 O'Verturf, P W, 5, H, Sept 22, scs.
12169 Osborn, F L, 16, A, Nov 26, scs.

1972 Peterson, J, 76, E, June 15, ana.
2869 Palmer, L H, 9, D, July 4, ana.
6209 Phillpot, C P, 31, B, Aug 19, dia.
9370 Putnam, O, 27, F, Aug 20, scs.
10270 Pitts, J, 16, I, Oct 3, dia.
10297 Pugh, A,‡ 8, M, Oct 3, scs.
10413 Parker, D, 4, I, Oct 6, scs.

18 Rule, Y A, 10, A, April 12, s. p.
1796 Ryan, Charles, 5, G, June 10, pls.
1820 Richardson, John, 2 cav, I, June 11, d
1951 Ratcliff, J, 4, I, June 14, des.
5878 Reed, R, 16, I, Aug 16, dia. c.
6572 Robinson, D, 13, G, Aug 23, wds.
7400 Rice, H M, sut's clerk, 9, Aug 31, scs.
9413 Riley, M, 5, A, Sept 21, ts. f.
9483 Reeves, S J, 9, D, Sept 21, des.
10015 Reed, C, 2, C, Sept 29, scs.
10017 Rogers, L, 4, F, Sept 29, scs.
12264 Russel, E, 4, G, Dec 12, scs.
12287 Raiser, A, 8, C, Dec 14, scs.

451 Stout, John, 5, A, April 9, pna.
599 Shuffleton, J, 5, H, April 17, pus.
641 Seeley, Norman, 9, B, April 20, pna.
2712 Smith, R F,‡ 10, H, July 1, dia.
2845 Shutter, J, 30, K, July 3, dys.
3060 Sparks, M J, 5, K, July 9, dys.
4178 Sutton, S, 5, H, July 28, ana.
4773 Smith, Charles,‡ 20, F, Aug 4, scs.
5410 Starr, C F, 30, H, Aug 12, pna.
5892 Sheddle, G, 16, C, Aug 16, dia. c.
7954 Seins, Wm, 3, D, Sept 6, dia. c.
8200 Smith, J, 13, A, Sept 8, dys.
9209 Smith, O, 5, D, Sept 19, scs.
9125 Sherman, J W, 3, I, Sept 17, dia. c.
9234 Spears, J, 5 cav, H, Sept 19, scs.
9367 Smith, D, 3 cav, B, Sept 20, dia.
11789 Shaw, W W, 5, H, Nov 4, scs.
12729 Snice, W, 16, E, March 4, dia. c.
10884 Sayres, W, 5, E, Oct 14, scs.

1981 Taiping, Wm, 5, K, June 15, pna.
3986 Thopson, M, 5, G, July 25, dys.
6687 Tivis, C, 5, A, Aug 24, scs.
9720 Tonune, B, 4 cav, M, Sept 25, scs.
11708 Thier, A F, 3, Nov 1, scs.

10351 Voke, John C,‡ 5, E, Oct 5, scs.

1674 Whitman, O R,‡ 5, E, June 6, dia. c.
2161 Wells, F,§ 5, I, June 19, dia. c.
2213 Withsrick, A K, 9, K, June 20, scs.
2855 Wolf, B F, 8, E, July 4, dia.
4916 Wolfe, J H, 2, C, Aug 6, scs.
6934 Wheelan, J,§ 26, D, Aug 26, dys.
8101 Walworth, C,§ 5, K, Sept 7, scs.
8131 Woolston, S P,§ 13, H, Sept 8, dia.
9221 Ward, O R, 3, E, Sept 19, ana.
9486 Wagner, Joseph, 13, E, Sept 21, scs.
9727 Wersbrod, Y, 31, A, Sept 25, scs.
10848 Wilson, P D, 10, G, Oct 13, scs.
10942 Woodward, J, sut, 9, Oct 14, scs.
11114 Whiting, J, 5, H, Oct 18, scs.
11141 Whitehead, N B, 5 cav, L, Oct 19, scs.
12741 Wen, C, 57, C, March 6, dys.

KANSAS.

1614 Freeman, F J,§ 8, F, June 4, dia. a.
1935 Gensarde, Thos, 8, A, June 14, dia. c.
12157 Sweeney, M, 1, H, Nov 22, scs.

11139 Weidman, W, 8, B, Oct 19, dia. c.
1663 Williams, C A, 8, A, June 6, dys.

KENTUCKY.

329 Allen, Sam'l S,‡ 13, F, April 2, dia. c.
674 Alford, George, 11 cav, B, April 22, sys.
1575 Anderson, S, 11 cav, D, May 3, dia.
3385 Adams, J D, 1 cav, I, July 16, dia.
3759 Ashley, J M, 1 cav, L, July 22, scs.
4723 Allen, Wm,‡ 11 cav, C, Aug 4, scs.
4894 Atkins, A, 39 cav, H, Aug 6, ana.
6095 Aughlin, J A,‡ 18 cav, B, Aug 18, scs.
6720 Arnett, H S, 13 cav, A, Aug 24, dia.
10514 Adamson, Wm, 15 cav, K, Oct 8, scs.
11759 Adams, J L, 27, G, Nov 3, scs.
12426 Arthur, D, 4, G, Jan 9, dia. c.
12528 Ayers, E, 52, A, Jan 26, pls.
12703 Ayers, S, 52, A, Jan 26, dia. c.
12593 Arnett, T, 4 cav, F, Jan 5, dia. c.

193 Bow, James, 1 cav, March 27, pls.
261 Burrows, Wm, 1 cav, K, March 31, dia. c.
366 Byerly, Wm, 11 cav, E, April 2, rua.
379 Baker, Isaac, 1 cav, H, April 5, dia. c.
413 Basham, S, 12 cav, E, April 7, dia. c.
419 Button, Ed, 11 cav, D, April 7, dia. c.
608 Burritt, B, 6 cav, D, April 13, dia.
609 Bloomer, H, 4 cav, G, April 18, dia.
803 Baker, A W, 3 cav, C, April 29, dia. c.
832 Boley, Peter, 12, L, May 1, dia.
891 Bird, W T, 11 cav, H, May 5, dia.
857 Bailey, A W, 14, G, May 2, dia. c.
1167 Burton, Tillman, 1 cav, F, May 17, scs.
1200 Butner, L B,§ 6 cav, I, May 18, dia.
1263 Bell, P B, 11 cav, I, May 21, dys.
1362 Barnett, James, 8 cav, H, May 25, dys.
1566 Baird, Sam'l J, 12 cav, D, June 2, dia.
1789 Bishop, D L, 11 cav, A, June 10, dia.
2022 Bowman, G, 11 cav, D, June 15, dia. c.
2423 Bray, H N,‡ 9 cav, H, June 24, phs.
2529 Buchanan, S, 12 cav, F, June 26, dia. c.
2760 Ball, David, 11 cav, B, July 2, dia. c.
3087 Beard, John C,§ 1 cav, C, July 9, dia. c.
3228 Brophy, M, 5 cav, L, July 12, dys.
3433 Bailey, F M, 4 cav, G, July 17, scs.
3909 Banner, J, 11 cav, C, July 24, dia. c.
3998 Bridell, S,‡ 3 cav, F, July 26, dys.
4562 Booth, Z,§ 16 cav, E, Aug 2, scs.
4653 Barger, George, 5 cav, I, Aug 3, dia.
4835 Baker, Wm, 3 cav, I, Aug 6, ana.
4971 Bigler, A, 6 cav, B, Aug 7, scs.
5471 Bailey, J H, 11 cav, A, Aug 12, dia. c.
5644 Branan, H, 1 cav, G, Aug 14, dys.
6576 Boston, J, 27 cav, E, Aug 23, scs.
6727 Bottoms, J M, 1 cav, H, Aug 24, dys.
9551 Brinton, W J,§ 11 cav, C, Sept 23, ana.
9563 Barnett, A, 12 cav, K, Sept 23, scs.
9628 Brown, J, 10 cav, I, Sept 24, dia.
9740 Boyd, M, 13 cav, A, Sept 25, dia.
10147 Batt, W, 5, G, Oct 1, dia.
10202 Byron, H M,§ 1 cav, I, Oct 2, scs.
10451 Bill, B S. 1 cav, K, Oct 7, pna.
10816 Bodkins, P,‡ 1 cav, K, Oct 12, dia. c.
10859 Bagley, T, 11 cav, Oct 13, scs.
11052 Brickey, W L, 4, F, Oct 17, gae.
12256 Baldwin, J W, 11, H, Oct 21, dia.
11303 Brown, E W, 4, F, Oct 22, scs.
11491 Barber, T, 4 cav, H, Oct 26, scs.
12006 Brannon, J, 3, B, Nov 13, scs.
12304 Beatty, R, 5, B, Dec 18, dia.
12333 Barnes, J, 11, D, Dec 25, scs.
12360 Brodus, O, 11 cav, A, Dec 30, scs.
12421 Britton, J, 45, F, Jan 9, scs.
5098 Bowman, Henry, 11 cav, F, Aug 9, dia. c.
12777 Balson, L, 12, B, March 15, dia. a.

11483 Cranch, J P, 10, D, Oct 26, scs.
240 Conler, Wm, 14, I, March 30, dia.
484 Caldwell, Wm, 12 cav, I, April 9, dia.
509 Cook, Theod, 12 cav, D, April 12, dia. c.
672 Colvin, George, 11 cav, D, April 22, dia.

877 Christmas J, 11 cav, F, May 4, dia.
966 Collague, M, 12 cav, E, May 8, dia.
1268 Cash, Philip, 1 cav, I, May 21, pna.
1600 Cole, W C, 1 cav, C, June 4, dia.
1676 Christenburg, R I,§ 12 cav, G, June 6, dya
1687 Callihan, Pat, 11 cav, A, June 6, scs.
1856 Clune, H, 11 cav, E, June 12, dia. c.
2152 Clinge, W H, 40, A, June 18, des.
2293 Cox, A B, 6 cav, I, June 21, i. f.
2339 Chippendale, C, 1 cav, B, June 22, dia. a
2446 Carlisle, J, 6 cav, I, June 25, dia. c.
2823 Cummings, J, 11, F, July 3, dia.
2912 Cleming, Thos, 18, I, July 5, dia. c.
3184 Carter, W, 11 cav, H, July D, dys.
60 Cristian, John, 4 cav, C, July 4, s. p.
4044 Clark, A H, 11, I, July 27, dia.
4809 Chapman, 11, H, Aug 5, dia.
6387 Coulter, M, 23, B, Aug 21, pna.
9835 Conrad, R P, 4, B, Sept 27, scs.
11179 Clun, W H, 11 cav, L, Oct 19, scs.
11486 Chatsin, W M, 6 cav, H, Oct 26, scs.
12447 Carcunright, 4, C, Jan 13, scs.
12700 Cook, J P, 4, G, Jan 26, dia.
2223 Corbitt, Thos, 5, A, June 20, dia.
8113 Coyle, C, 11 cav, I, Sept 7, scs.
4740 Chance, A J, 1 cav, C, Aug 5, ana.

421 Dupon, F, 12, G, April 7, pna.
1388 Delaney, M, 11 cav, I, May 26, dia.
1414 Dugean, J R,§ 12 cav, K, May 27, dys.
1568 De Barnes, P M, 11 cav, C, June 2, dia.
1627 Demody, Thos, 1 cav, H, June 4, dia. c.
1867 Drake, J H, 12 cav, G, June 12, ana.
2736 Davis, B, 5, C, July 1, dia. c.
23 Duncan, E, 12 cav, G, April 15, s. p.
3623 Dodson, E, 39, H, July 20, scs.
27 Derine, George, 1 cav, I, April 17, s. p.
3024 Davis, G C, 12 cav, F, July 25, des.
3966 Derringer, H, 11 cav, I, July 25, dia. c.
4510 Dulrebeck, H, 11, E, Aug 1, dia. c.
4556 Delaney, H, 4 cav, H, Aug 2, dys.
5088 Dounty, P, 5, F, Aug 8, dys.
5899 Daniel, R, 9, F, Aug 16, dia. c.
11405 Disque, F,§ 6 cav, G, Oct 24, scs.
12280 Duland, D W, 3, K, Dec 13, scs.
12623 Dannard, W, 4, D, Feb 9, dia. c.
12684 Dipple, S, 4, E, Feb 21, dia. c.
1109 Dinsman, H, 4 cav, E, May 15, dia. c.
2805 Davis, J P, 13, A, July 3, dia.
2117 Davis, C, 6 cav, D, June 31, scs.

639 Eodus, James, 1 cav, F, April 20, dia.
1174 Edmiston, J W, 11 cav, A, May 17, dia. e
1439 Edwards, H S,‡ 8 cav, K, May 27, dia. c
2544 Emery, J, 10, G, June 27, ts. f.
5341 Errbanks, J, 1 cav, A, Aug 11, dia.
12277 Esteff, J, 1 cav, L, Oct 22, dia.
1447 East, R, 1 cav. G, May 29, dia.

384 Falconburg, I K, 1 cav, A, April 5, pna.
2540 Fleming, R, 4 cav, D, June 27, dia. c.
3640 Forteen, John, 8, A, July 20, dia.
4344 Fenkstine, M, 1, D, July 30, dia.
6763 Featherstone, J, 6, C, Aug 25, i. f.
7068 Fritz, J, 4 cav, G, Aug 28, dys.
10280 Funk, L, 1 cav, I, Oct 4, wds.
11549 Frazier, C R, 23, H, Oct 27, wds.
11720 Fletcher, T, 17, E, Nov 1, dia. c.

1612 Gritton, G, 11 cav, D, June 4, dia. c.
1618 Graves, G, 18, C, June 4, dia. c.
1841 Gritton, M, 11 cav, B, June 11, dia. c
2583 Gibson, John, 6 cav, L, June 27, dys.
3630 Griffin, B, 11, E, July 20, dia.
3663 Glassman, P, 4 cav, B, July 20, dia.
3888 Gouns, J M, 4, H, July 24, dia.
4438 Gather, M, 4 cav, F, July 31, dia.

6779 Gullett, A, 45, K, Aug 15, ana.
7197 Green, J B,§ 11, I, Aug 29, dia.
7817 Grabul, B, 1, F, Sept 4, ana.
8049 Gury, J, 4, H, Sept 6, scs.
8903 Gray, C D, 20, G, Sept 18, scs.
9318 Gett, John,§ 40, G, Sept 20, dia.
9950 Gill, W J, 11 cav, H, Sept 28, scs.
10053 Gower, J C, 13, A, Sept 30, scs.
10650 Gibson, A, 8 cav, K, Oct 10, scs.
10831 Grulach, J,§ 4, K, Oct 13, scs.
11910 Grimstead, J R, 1, E, Nov 8, scs.
12022 Griffin, R, 11, E, Nov 15, scs.
1235 Gregory, H, 12 cav, D, May 20, dia.

81 Hanns, J B, 12, K, March 20, pna.
237 Holloway, Richard, 4, I, March 29, ts. f.
289 Harley, Alfred, 40, K, April 1, dia. c.
292 Hood, G, 5 cav, F, April 1, dia.
348 Hammond, J W, 1 cav, G, April 2, dia. e.
376 Harper, J, 1, C, April 5, dia. a.
402 Harlow, Harvey, 13, I, April 6, dys.
614 Hess, Wm F, 12 cav, M, April 18, dys.
643 Hendree, A,§ 11, F, April 20, brs.
1023 Hillard, Geo, 11, D, May 11, ts. f.
1127 Hoffman, C, 11 cav, E, May 15, dys.
1584 Hughes, Thomas,§ 9, G, June 3, ana.
1760 Hennesy, J, 28, D, June 9, dia. c.
1878 Hundly, Geo W, 4 cav, June 12, dia.
1956 Hazlewood, J H, 18, G, June 14, dys.
1990 Hamner, A, 9, B, June 15, dia.
2490 Huison, J W,§ 9, B, June 26, pna.
2705 Hillard, S, 1 cav, I, June 30, dia. c.
3239 Henderson, J, 18, B, July 12, dys.
26 Hooper, Samuel, 11 cav, D, April 16, s. p.
3944 Hooper, J, 1 cav, D, July 25, scs.
3994 Hickworth, J, 45, D, July 26, dia.
4313 Hall, J H, 1 cav, C, July 30, dia.
4420 Hammontius, P, 6 cav, L, June 31, dia. c.
4970 Hayner, E, 1 cav, D, Aug 7, scs.
5059 Haines, J, 12 cav, D, Aug 8, scs.
5091 Harrington, C, 15, K, Aug 8, scs.
5793 Hatfield, L, 1, F, Aug 15, ana.
6193 Hendrie, Wm, 11 cav, F, Aug 19, scs.
6801 Hardison, G, 23, I, Aug 25, r. f.
8032 Hise, P, 4, I, Sept 6, dia.
8111 Hicks, P, 11 cav, F, Sept 7, scs.
8181 Heglen, C, 4 cav, I, Sept 8, dys.
9376 Hanker, R, 18, F, Sept 20, scs.
9599 Hyrommus, Jas, 11 cav, D, Sept 23, dia.
10683 Halton, S M, 2, K, Oct 11, scs.
11054 Halligan, J, 4, A, Oct 17, ana.
11095 Hall, F, 1 cav, F, Oct 18, scs.
11132 Hazer, John, 11, I, Oct 18, scs.
11251 Harter, F, 12 cav, M, Oct 21, dia. c.
12293 Hays, J F, 5, A, Dec 15, scs.
12518 Hasting, J, 4, H, Jan 24, scs.
12638 Hudson, B F, 4, A, Feb 11, dia. c.

5734 Inman, John, 24, A, Aug 15, dia.
9757 Isabell, J M, 3, H, Sept 25, scs.
11392 Inman, W, 11 cav, D, Oct 24, scs.
12203 Isabel, A, 1, K, Dec 1, scs.

649 Jackson, John, 45, D, April 20, ana.
2679 Jeffries, Wm, 1 cav, A, June 30, dia.
5229 Jacobs, John W, 4 cav, I, Aug 10, scs.
7294 Johnson, A, 10, H, Aug 31, scs.
7371 Jenkins, S, 6 cav, A, Aug 31, dia.
7594 Justin, J, 39, F, Sept 2, ana.
7754 James, W, 5, K, Sept 4, dia.
9654 Jarvis, W D, 12, D, Sept 24, dia.
11000 Jordan, J, 5 cav, B, Oct 16, dys. c.
11143 Jones, D, 1 cav, L, Oct 18, scs.
12541 Jones, J, 16, E, Jan 27, dia.

87 Kennedy, Jas, 11 cav, E, March 21, dia. c.
191 Knotts, Fred, 11 cav, E, March 27, ts. f.
926 Kessmer, John, 12 cav, I, May 7, dia.
1045 Kennedy, S B, 39, B, May 12, dia.
1173 Keiling, M, 11 cav, D, May 17, pna.
3928 Keystone, C, 6, E, July 25, dia.
4921 Kennder, A,‡ 1 cav, A, July 6, dia.

5553 Knapp, Thomas, 6 cav, M, July 13, scs.
5925 Kressler, P, 4 cav, K, July 17, d s.
12265 Knapp, J, 5 cav, B, Dec 12, scs.

48 Lenniert, L, 1, K, March 15, brs.
310 Lambert, R, 11 cav, F, April 2, dia.
1135 Lay, Wm, 11 cav, D, May 16, pls.
1726 Lossman, A, 4 cav, E, June 8, dia.
1802 Larger, W, 1 cav, L, June 10, dys.
1912 Ledford, J A, 16, B, June 13, dia. c.
2109 Little, J, 1, D, June 17, c. f.
2352 Lononey, B, 1 cav, K, June 23, ana.
2654 Lutherland, H, 32, G, June 29, dys.
2668 Lasper, Otto, 15, H, June 29, dia. c.
2537 Lublett, M L, 13, E, July 3, ts. f.
3340 Leville, Thomas, 4, D, July 15, dys.
3398 Lee, S, 1 cav, A, July 16, scs.
3658 Loy, W B, 8 cav, L, July 20, ana.
3776 Lanhart, J, 6 cav, G, July 22, dia.
3839 Lowry, Jas W, 12 cav, G, July 23, dia. e.
6024 Lewis, T, 2 cav, C, Aug 18, scs.
7132 Landers, ——,‡ 36, I, Aug 28, dia.
7934 Luster, W, 1 cav, B, Sept 5, dia.
8487 Lutton, Thomas, 6, K, Sept 11, scs.
8634 Little, J F, 12 cav, D, Sept 13, dia.
11870 Lindusky, G, 11, G, Nov 6, scs.
12175 Ledwick, A, 7, C, Nov 27, scs.
9175 Lord, Wm, 20, G, Sept 18, scs.

271 McMannus, Saml, 11, D, March 31, dia. c
369 Miller, John, 3, A, April 5, pls.
525 McDougal, W C, 14, K, April 13, hye.
796 Mills, John, 1, H, April 29, dia. c.
991 McClure, P, 11 cav, C, May 10, dys.
1222 Marshall, Wm, 5 cav, I, May 19, dia. c.
1380 Montgomery, W A, 5 cav, H, May 26, dia. c
1391 Moreland, H, 1 cav, F, May 26, dia. a.
1969 Merix, J, 45 cav, D, June 14, dia. c.
2024 Morton, W, 7 cav, I, June 15, ana.
2137 Meldown, D, 11 cav, E, June 18, dia. a.
2669 Miller, W C, 27 cav, A, June 29, dia.
3152 Mitchell, James, 12 cav, C, July 11, dia.
64 Mullins, W W, 1 cav, H, Aug 8, s. p.
3418 Morgan, J, 4 cav, D, July 17, dia. c.
4513 Masters, J, 11 cav, A, Aug 1, scs.
4550 McDonald, J, 4 cav, I, Aug 2, dys.
4646 Mitchell, R M, 17 cav, E, Aug 3, dys.
5691 Mooney, Pat, 11 cav, G, Aug 15, dia.
7951 McCarty, E, 5 cav, K, Sept 6, dia.
8455 McCarty, John, 6 cav, K, Sept 9, scs.
8685 McCarter, W, 9 cav, B, Sept 13, scs.
9259 Munch, J, 28 cav, F, Sept 19, cah.
9498 Macary, C, 11 cav, M, Sept 21, gae.
9711 Moore, Wm, 12 cav, D, Sept 24, dia.
7336 Martin, F P, 12 cav, D, Aug 30, scs.
10170 Marshall, L, 1 cav, F, Oct 1, dia.
10460 Mills, George, 4 cav, H, Oct 7, scs.
11455 Murphy, W M, 2 cav, H, Oct 25, scs.
11478 Miller, E, 4 cav, I, Oct 26, scs.
12466 Miller, J, 4 cav, K, Jan 16, rhm.
12491 Meyers, J, 4 cav, C, Jan 20, dia.
12720 Meach, A J, 1 cav, s, March 3, des.
12764 Morgan, F,‡ 3, I, March 12, wds.

212 New, Geo W, 1 cav, F, March 28, pna.
447 Neely, B W, 1 cav, G, April 9, dys.
63 Nelson, John, 1 cav, D, July 19, s. p.
7693 Northcraft, J, 6 cav, H, Sept 3, scs.
9230 Newton, A,‡ 4 cav, H, Sept 19, dia. c.

2499 O'Bannon, Wm, 11 cav, B, June 20, dia. s
2513 Oper, L, 4 cav, B, June 26, dia. c.
11943 Owen, W,‡ 1 cav, L, Nov 9, scs.

1178 Pott, J, 7 cav, C, May 17, scs.
1905 Porter, J F, 18 cav, June 13, pna.
3654 Pulliam, J, 2, July 20, dys.
4220 Plyman, Wm, 39, D, July 27, dia. c.
5761 Pally, S C,§ 12 cav, B, Aug 15, dia. c.
6616 Phelps, Wm E, 6 cav, F, Aug 23, dia.
6632 Pruils, W H, 1 cav, F, Aug 23, scs.
7222 Pope, Frank,‡ 5 cav, B, Aug 29, scs.

8070 Pott, Samuel, 4 cav, G, Sept 7, dys.
8207 Patterson, J, 2 cav, B, Sept 8, dys.
9299 Phelps, F M,§ 11 cav, I, Sept 20, dia.
10249 Partis, J R, 1 cav, F, Oct 3, scs.
12220 Pace, John, 3 cav, G, Dec 4, scs.
12327 Purcell, J, 1 cav, G, Dec 23, scs.

2144 Quéata, J, 11 cav, E, June 18, dia.

452 Rurves, E,§ 4 cav, F, April 9, des.
577 Roberts, R, 12 cav, H, April 16, dia.
590 Ramay, Lester, 39 cav, H, April 17, dys.
637 Raberie, Geo, 1 cav, A, April 20, pna.
825 Richardson, M,‡ 3, H, May 1, pna.
1097 Runs, T, 11 cav, H, May 14, dia.
1193 Russell, Jacob, 12 cav, B, May 18, dia.
1355 Ritter, B B, 6 cav, L, May 25, dia.
1555 Rose, R C,‡ 6 cav, B, June 2, scs.
1571 Rogers, W, 1, F, June 3, dia. c.
2463 Reve, F N, 11, F, June 25, dia.
2751 Reilly, Thos, 1, D, July 1, dia. c.
4018 Ramsay, Robert, 45, A, July 26, dys.
4482 Robertson, H, 11 cav, D, Aug 1, des.
4549 Rodes, James, 1 cav, F, Aug 2, dia.
4919 Rockwell, W W,‡ 1 cav, C, Aug 6, ana.
5775 Roberts, L, 1 cav, K, Aug 15, scs.
5967 Rieff, R, 1 art, Aug 17, scs.
5976 Roberts, Andrew, 1 cav, K, Aug 17, dia. c.
6274 Readnian, W, 11 cav, I, Aug 20, mas.
7215 Rogers, Henry, 12 cav, A, Aug 29, dia.
10124 Robuy, F, 15 cav, E, Oct 1, scs.
11369 Racine, P, 12 cav, M, Oct 23, scs.
11583 Ryan, W, 1 cav, I, Oct 28, scs.
11642 Riddle, J H, 1 cav, I, Oct 30, scs.
11644 Rogers, Wm, 2 cav, I, Oct 30, scs..
11873 Rusby, J, 2 cav, F, Nov 6, scs.
12828 Rice, P D,§ 3, I, April 9, dia. c.
1202 Ruble, Leander,‡ 11 cav, D, May 19, dia. c.
4106 Rankin, J H,§ 18 cav, G, July 27, dia.

213 Simpson, W, 1 cav, C, March 28, pna.
277 Sims, Geo,§ 40, I, March 31, pna.
567 Summers, W H, 11 cav, D, April 15, pna.
797 Smith, Geo, 13 cav, G, April 29, ana.
925 Sallac, Geo,‡ 11 cav, C, May 7, dia. c.
995 Smith, Wm A, 4 cav, K, May 10, dia.
1003 Smith, H, 16 cav, B, May 10, dys.
1101 Smith, R C, 1 cav, I, May 14, dys.
1180 Schafer, J E, 4 cav, A, May 18, dia.
1500 Stempf, Lewis, 12 cav, G, May 31, dys.
1659 Sutherland, J E,§ 1 cav, C, June 6, dys.
1681 Sebastian, J W, 45, C, June 6, dia.
1691 Sanders, J S, 12 cav, E, June 7, dia.
1708 Stine, C, 4 cav, K, June 7, dys.
1716 Sandfer, Jno, 11 cav, B, June 8, dia. c.
1811 Summers, Wm, 11 cav, D, June 10, dia.
1827 Sweeney, M, 5 cav, I, June 11, dia.
1952 Shirley, John, 28 cav, E, June 14, dia. a.
1964 Stanley, C O, 17 cav, E, June 14, dia. c.
2063 Salmond, P, 18 cav, H, June 16, scs.
2094 Shanks, W L, 6 cav, B, June 17, dia.
2766 Show, J, 11 cav, I, July 6, dia. c.
44 Smith, John, 2 cav, I, May 13, s. p.
51 Shaggs, I P, 11 cav, G, June 2, s. p.
3402 Shuman, J, 4 cav, A, July 16, dia.
4258 Smith, B,‡ 5 cav, A, July 29, dia. c.
4829 Schmal, Andrew, 4 cav, B, Aug 6, dys.
4831 Schottsman, F,‡ 1 cav, D, Aug 6, dia.
4976 Snyder, H M, 10 cav, B, Aug 7, scs.
5297 Smith, W H,‡ 27, E, Aug 11, dys.
5280 Stevens, P L,§ 12 cav, G, Aug 20, ts. f.

6280 Schrausburg, R, 1 cav, K, Aug 20, scs.
8226 Stimett, J, 6 cav, K, Sept 9, scs.
8437 Sutton, Thomas, 6 cav, A, Sept 1, scs.
8827 Shulds, J, 2 cav, K, Sept 15, scs.
10154 Sanders, B, 4 cav, F, Oct 1, dia.
10673 Sheppard, T L, 5 cav, H, Oct 11, dia.
11456 Sapp, B, 1 cav, B, Oct 25, scs.
11898 Selors, W H, 1 cav, C, Nov 7, scs.
12556 Stewart, E, 4 cav, A, Jan 30, scs.
10197 Sawney, Wm, 5 cav, H, Oct 2, scs.

253 Taylor, Thos,‡ 11 cav, H, March 30, dis.
391 Thrope, H, 1 cav, B, April 6, dia. c.
781 Tucker, Wm, 12 cav, I, April 28, dia. c.
1009 Travis, Geo, 16 cav, E, May 10, dia.
1628 Truney, J, 11 cav, C, June 4, dia. c.
2116 Tutune, J,§ 11 cav, A, June 17, scs.
2371 Tudor, Ab'm,‡ 11 cav, A, June 23, dia. c.
3701 Tullor, G W, 28, A, July 21, cah.
5424 Tabu, Silas, 27, D, Aug 12, dia.
6234 Templeton, W H,‡ 11 cav, B, Aug 20, dys
6257 Tapp, George, 13 cav, I, Aug 20, scs.
6508 Tracy, Jas, 11 cav, L, Aug 22, dia.
6956 Thorp, J, 4 cav, K, Aug 26, scs.
7205 Tucker, Robt, 17 cav, G, Aug 29, scs.
10028 Tucker, J A, 15 cav, A, Sept 29, scs.
10398 Thornburg, R, 2 cav, G, Oct 6, ts. f.
10588 Tussey, E D, 24 cav, A, Oct 10, scs.
10809 Terry, Wm, 1 cav, A, Oct 12, scs.
10892 Thomas, W E,§ 11 cav, G, Oct 14, scs.

10657 Vandevier, J, 11 cav, C, Oct 11, dia.

278 West, John C, 11 cav, E, March 31, ts. f.
494 White, A, 6 cav, K, April 12, dys.
735 Wallar, M R, 16 cav, C, April 24, dys.
1125 White, John, 11 cav, D, May 15, dys. c.
1706 Westfall, J, 4 cav, D, June 7, dys. c.
1734 Wickles, John, 40, K, June 8, dia. c.
1745 Walsh, J E, 6 cav, L, June 8, dia.
1894 Wright, John E,‡ 1 cav, June 13, dia.
2199 Wheelan, Jas, 18 cav, C, June 19, dia.
2584 White, C, 1 cav, H, June 27, ana.
2901 Wiser, R M, 1 cav, B, July 5, dia.
40 Ward, F W, 1 cav, A, May 3, s. p.
4374 Warren, W P, 34 cav, K, July 31, dia.
4624 Wallace, H, 14 cav, E, Aug 3, dys.
4697 West, P H, 6 cav, K, Aug 3, dia.
15057 Webb, J, 6 cav, F, Aug 8, scs.
5762 Welch, T C, 5 cav, G, Aug 15, dia.
5790 Walsh, John, 6 cav, H, Aug 15, scs.
6101 Winter, H, 11 cav, E, Aug 18, dia. c.
6121 Winfries, W S, 3 cav, A, Aug 19, dys.
6893 White, S A, 17 cav, G, Aug 26, dys.
7038 Willser, J, 11 cav, I, Aug 27, scs.
7694 Wells, John W, 12 cav, C, Sept 3, wda.
8533 Wallace, J,§ 11 cav, K, Sept 12, dia.
9258 Warner, D, 12 cav, A, Sept 19, scs.
9541 Wicog, S, 4 cav, I, Sept 23, dia.
9636 Wagoner, H,‡ 4 cav, I, Sept 24, scs.
10770 Warner, Thos, 15 cav, F, Oct 12, scs.
10808 Walton, J J, 8 cav, A, Oct 14, scs.
11749 Willit, M, 4 cav, I, Nov 2, scs.
12279 Weasett, A, 1 cav, D Nov 13, scs.

904 Yocombs, H, 11 cav D, May 5, phs.
1166 Yoam, J, 10 cav, D, May 17, cah.
2689 Yeager, L,§ 11 cav, _, June 30, dia.
3757 Yeast, R, 1 cav, I, July 22, cah.

5257 Zertes, G, 4 cav, G, Aug 10, ana.

LOUISIANA.

6778 Kimball, Jas, 2 cav, A, Aug 25, con.

VIEW OF THE PRISON FROM THE MAIN GATE.

Rebel Photographs which were taken when about 35,000 men were here confined.   Original Picture in possession of the publishers.

last of July, or first of August, an addition was made to the stockade.   This gave to
led into the space of ten acres more room by ten additional acres."

MAINE.

2804 Anderson, John, 19, I, June 28, dia. c.
3093 Allen, A, 32, K, July 10, dia. c.
7024 Arnold, E W, 17, G, Aug 27, dia. c.

  22 Butler, C A, 3, K, March 7, pna.
 269 Brown, E M, 5, G, March 31, dia.
3953 Buner, A E, 31, E, July 25, scs.
6211 Bachelor, P,§ 3, K, Aug 19, dia. c.
9162 Baker, James, 17, H, Sept 18, dia. c.
10669 Ballast, J, 19, G, Oct 11, scs.
7663 Bartlett, H, 17, C, Sept 3, i. s.
7255 Barney, G S, 32, I, Aug 30, scs.
6683 Bean, G W, 8, C, Aug 24, des.
6603 Bennett, L, 1 art, Aug 23, dia.
9097 Berry, C H, 6, H, Sept 18, scs.
7645 Bigelow, C, 19, H, Sept 3, scs.
5290 Blaizdell, H. 8, F, Aug 11, scs.
12055 Boren, W, 16, I, Nov 16, dia.
9408 Bowden, ——, 7, A, Sept 21, dia.
4776 Braley, J, 3, E, Aug 4, dia.
5015 Briggs, J C, 19, F, Aug 8, scs.
8542 Brinkerman, L, 9, D, Sept 11, scs.
8247 Broadstreet, C B, 1 cav, B, Sept 9, dia. c.
6811 Brown, J, 8, G, Aug 25, dia. c.
11980 Bryant, C D, 16, E, Nov 13, dia. c.
5719 Bullsen, E T,§ 5 cav, B, Aug 15, ens.
5757 Bunker, S A, 1 art, A, Aug 15, scs.
8474 Burgen, A, 4, I, Sept 11, scs.

7017 Cardoney, C, 17, G, Aug 27, dia.
7746 Carlen, M, 1 cav, F, Sept 3, dia.
8374 Carr, J, 19, E, Sept 10, scs.
6246 Carlton, J S, 31, D, Aug 19, dia. c.
5989 Chase, F W, I art, D, Aug 17, dia.
2316 Clark, James, 1 cav, C, June 22, dia.
8143 Clark, P M,§ I cav, C, Sept 8, dia. c.
10376 Clark, L, 19, D, Oct 5, dia.
10421 Clayton, E B, 1, F, Oct 6, scs.
  28 Cohan, D, 3, K, March 7, pna.
6950 Conder, W H, 16, G, Aug 26, brs.
8037 Conley, W, 5, F, Sept 6, dia.
3943 Cook, James, 4, D, July 25, ts. f.
8483 Condon, D H, 20, K, Sept 11, scs.
 425 Craw, H, 3, B, April 7, pna.
12061 Cressy, N F, 11, G, Nov 17, scs.
10936 Cromwell, S R,‡ 1 art, M, Sept 14, scs.
11211 Cromwell, W H, 19, D, Oct 20, scs.
8625 Curtiss, John, 16, I, Sept 13, scs.
12367 Cutts, O M, 16, D, Jan 1, scs.
  80 Cutter, A, 20, E, March 20, dys.
5171 Cross, Noah, 1 art, A, Aug 9, i. s.
8581 Crosby, W, 4, A, Sept 12, dys.

8445 Davis, D, 3, C, Sept 11, scs.
 227 Davis, Wm L, 20, E, March 29, dia.
5615 Dougherty, Thomas, 8, G, Aug 14, dys
6612 Donnell, F, 8, E, Aug 23, dia.
9624 Downes, J, 8, G, Sept 23, dia.
1359 Doyle, Wm, 6, D, May 25, dia. c.
5481 Drisdale, F, 1, H, Aug 13, dia.
4425 Duffy, A, 3, G, July 31, ana.
6415 Dugan, D, 32, A, Aug 21, scs.
6438 Dunning, S P, 29, G, Aug 21, dia.
7240 Dunnie, G, 5, G, Aug 29, ana.
6357 Dye, John, 1 cav, E, Aug 21, scs.
5035 Dittener, H, 20, A, Aug 8, scs.

10608 Eckhard, H, 7, C, Sept 10, scs.
7212 Edwards, N S, 1 cav, F, Aug 29, dia.
8538 Ellis, A, 2 art, H. Sept 11, dia.
1877 Emerson, H H, 3, June 12, scs.

2628 Farewell, E, 31, E, June 28, dys.
8401 Ferrell, P, 6, H, Sept 10, scs.
4765 Fish, Wm, 7, A, Aug 5, dys.
5243 Flagg, J B, 5, K, Aug 10, dys.
 69 Flanders, L G, 20, E, March 19, dia.

1989 Foley, John, 19, E, June 15, dia.
2362 Forrest, Thomas, 1 cav, E, June 23, dia
2482 Foster, A,‡ 6, K, June 25, dia. e.
8145 Foster, E R, 16, C, Sept 8, dia.
7073 Foster, Samuel, C, 16, K, Aug 28 r. .
6191 Frisble, L, 7, C, Aug 19.
10957 Fitzgerald, Joseph, 8, E, Oct 14, scs.

5907 Gardner, W H,§ 4, Aug 16, scs.
12515 Gibbs, R, 19, K, Jan 23, dia.
2006 Gilgan, W, 7, C, 5, July 5, dys.
6107 Goodward, A, 1 art, I, Aug 18, dia.
5580 Goodwin, M T, 8, F, Aug 14, dia.
4141 Grant, G, 1 art, F, July 28, dia.
7391 Grant, Frank, 16, F, Aug 30, car.
8392 Griffith, S, 8, G, Sept 10, dia. c.
9190 Gunney, C, 31, A, Sept 18, dia.
10031 Gunney, J F,§ 1, I, Sept 29, scs.
11823 Gilgrist, ——, 31, E, Nov 5, scs.

8306 Hammond, J, 19, G, Sept 10, ana.
12343 Harris, J S, 1, F, Dec 26, dys.
3506 Hassen, H, 7, G, July 18, dia.
3274 Hatch, J S, 3, G, July 13, dys.
6112 Hatch, S,§ 8, F, Aug 19, scs.
9311 Heath, B, 3, F, Sept 20, dia.
4174 Heninger, ——, 19, July 28, des.
12349 Hopes, H, 19, D, Dec 27, scs.
7474 Howard, D H, 17, D, Sept 1, dys.
3844 Howe, Samuel W, 1, K, July 23, dia.
7186 Hoyt, A D, 3, K, Aug 29, dia.
3237 Hudson, W, 17, E, July 12, dia.
8797 Hughes, Wm, 31, K, Sept 15, scs.
9652 Humphrey, ——, 3 cav, L, Sept 24, scs
3484 Hunkey, E B, 1, L, July 17, dia. c.
4703 Henley, D, 8, G, Aug 4, dys.

5355 Ingols, L, 16, H, Aug 11, i. s.
9389 Ingerson, P, 7, J, Sept 20, dia.

11489 Jackson, A J, 17, J, Oct 26, scs.
10619 Jackson, R, 7, B, Oct 10, scs.
10710 Jackson, R W, 7, D, Oct 11, dia.
12602 Jerdan, J, 19, F, Feb 6, rhm.
7385 Johnson, B, 7, K, Aug 30, scs.
5849 Jones, Wm, 19, E, Aug 16, ens.
10243 Jory, G F, 8, F, Oct 3, scs.

11586 Kellar, J, 19, J, Oct 28, scs.
8237 Kelley, L, 11, D, Sept 9, dia.
3313 Kennedy, W, 17, G, July 14, dia.
6169 Kilpatrick, C, 3, C, Aug 19, des.

5366 Ladd, C, 6, I, Aug 11, dia. c.
8350 Lamber, W, 17, K, Sept 10, dia.
11707 Levitt, H, 19, A, Nov 1, scs.
7967 Lincoln, A, 16, I, Sept 6, scs.
10931 Littlefield, C, 1 cav, F, Oct 14, scs.
6340 Lord, Geo H, 3, B, Aug 21, dia.
5549 Ludovice, F, 13, F, Aug 13, scs.
 490 Lowell, B, 4, G, April 12, dia. c.

9426 Macon, L, 8, A, Sept 21, dia.
 709 Malcolm, H M, 16, A, April 24, ers.
6606 Marshall, B F, 1, H, Aug 23, dia.
12122 Maston, A, 19, D, Nov 22, scs.
10392 Mathews, James, 32, F, Oct 14, scs.
12011 Maxwell, J, 8, E, Nov 14, scs.
3679 McFarland, G, 3, G, July 21, ana.
9538 McGinley, J, 7, A, Sept 22, scs.
2200 McKinney, G, 3, I, June 19, dia.
12084 McFarland, E S, 8, I, Nov 18, scs.
4391 Medcalf, Oliver, 8, H, July 31, dia. c.
12768 McFarland, W,‡ 19, K, March 13, scs
5200 Melgar, J, 7, Aug 10, dia.
5614 Messer, C R, 7, F, Aug 14, scs.
9399 Miller, C J, 1 cav, B, Sept 21, scs.

****

2002 Miller, J O, 2, D, June 15, dia.
7573 Mills, M, 1, Sept 2, dia.
2868 Moore, Charles W, 8, B, July 3, dys.
11042 Moore, G, 18, D, Oct 17, scs.
7273 Moore, J D, 1 cav, B, Aug 30, scs.
6940 Moore, W C, 7, A, Aug 26, scs.
8118 Moyes, F, 32, F, Sept 8, dia.

7046 Newton, C, 9, K, Aug 27, ana.
1507 Nickerson, D, 4, F, May 31, dia. c.
8020 Nolton, H, 7, B, Sept 6, ana.

2131 O'Brien, W, 16, A, June 18, dia. c.
6325 Opease, S, 19, Aug 21, des.
143 Osborn, A J, 8, March 24, dys.
10866 Owens, O H, 10, Nov 6, scs.

3710 Parker, A, 1 cav, E, July 21, dia.
7979 Parsons, James W, 16, D, Sept 6, dia.
9362 Patrick, F, 14, F, Sept 20, dia.
2272 Peabody, F S,§ 5, I, June 20, dia.
12543 Pequette, P, 4, G, Jan 28, scs.
1486 Perkins, D, 1 cav, I, May 31, dia.
5197 Perkins, T, 1, H. Aug 10, scs.
6911 Peters, H, 4, E, Aug 26, scs.
12056 Phillbrook, F, 1 art, A, Nov 17, dia.
2064 Phelps, W H, 1 cav, H, June 16, dia.
3436 Pinkham, U W, 1 art, A, July 17, dia.
1361 Pottle, A E, 1 cav, L, May 25, dia.
5698 Pratt, A M, 1 cav, L, Aug 15, wds.
8441 Pulerman, G, 16, D, Sept 11, scs.
12410 Prescott, C, 19, H, Jan 7, dia.

7785 Richardson, C, 31, L, Sept 4, scs.
6762 Richardson, J K, 8, G, Aug 24, scs.
10465 Richardson, W M,‡ 1 cav, B, Oct 7, dys.
5522 Ricker, Wm,‡ 1 cav, D, Aug 13, dys.
8480 Ridlon, N, 7, D, Sept 11, scs.
900 Riseck, R, 3, I, May 5, ana.
3921 Roberts, H, 19, K, July 25, dia.
5236 Rowe, L, 1, A, Aug 10, dia.
166 Rosmer, Frank, 4, C, March 26, dia.
5796 Ruet, H, 2, H, Aug 15, dys.
8557 Russell, G A, 1 cav, E, Sept 12, scs.

5450 Sampson, E, 1, F, Aug 12, scs.
4532 Sawyer, Enos, 1 art, H, Aug 2, dia.
3182 Sawyer, John, 31, K, July 11, i. s.
11462 Shorey, S, 1 cav, K, Oct 20, scs.

2243 Simmons, G F, 6, K, June 20, dia.
3159 Smith, W, 9, K, July 11, dia. c.
3331 Smith, W A, 6, F, July 14, dia.
1782 Snowdale, F, 4, C, June 10, dia. c.
9974 Snower, S C, 19, A, Sept 28, dia.
1998 Springer, H W, 36, A, June 15, dia.
4596 Steward, G, 20, H, Aug 3, dia.
11562 St Peter, F, 19, F, Oct 27, scs.
7001 Swaney, P, 19, F, Aug 27. dia.
199 Swan, H B,‡ 3, F, March 28, dys.
1936 Swan, F, 3, F, June 14, ana.
8682 Thompson, F, 9, E, Sept 13, scs.
10455 Thompson, John, 3, E, Oct 7, dia.
621 Thorn, E, 9, I, April 19, dys.
10928 Toothacre, J, 7, G, Oct 14, scs.
1106 Turner, C C, 4, E, May 15, dia. c.
5090 Tufts, J, 32, C, Aug 8, dia.
11875 Taylor, G, 9, C, Nov 16, scs.
12322 Tuttle, D L, 32, F, Dec 20, scs.
12196 Tuttle, L S,‡ 32, F, Nov 30, dia.
12706 Thorndie, W B,‡ 19, I, March 2, scs.

6245 Valley, F, 32, K, Aug 19, dia.
3335 Venill, C, 32, G, July 15, dia.

7226 Walker, A B,‡ 1, K, Aug 29, dia.
3894 Walker, M C, 5, I, July 24, des.
7722 Wall, A, 1 cav, K, Sept 4, dia.
5942 Walsh, Thomas, 20, H, Aug 17, scs.
6750 Watson, B, 7, K, Aug 24, dys.
10558 Webber, Oliver, 3, A, Oct 9, dia.
4559 Whiteman, A M,‡ 5, I, Aug 2, scs.
1648 Whitcomb, T O, 4, F, June 5, dia. c
6251 Whittier, J K P, 32, C, Aug 19, brs.
10445 Willard, W, 20, B, Oct 7, scs.
7711 Williams, C, 6, G, Sept 3, des.
6900 Wilson, George, 32, C, Aug 26, dia.
3639 Wilson, G W, 16, H, July 20, ana.
3132 Willey, D H, 19, E, July 10, dys.
3860 Winslow, E, 1, 4 B, July 24, scs.
5512 Winslow, N L, 4, K, Aug 13, des.
6372 Wyman, A, 32, C, Aug 21, scs.
2095 Wyman, J, 16, A, June 17, dia.
12470 Wyer, R, 3, K, Jan 16, dia.
12043 Wright, C, 1, G, Nov 16, scs.

178 Young, E W,§ 3, H, March 26, des.
6369 Young, J, 3, H, Aug 21, scs.
8140 Young, J W,‡ 8, I, Sept 8, scs.

MARYLAND.

850 Allen, W H, 1, H, May 3, dys.
1028 Anderson, Wm, 2, C, May 11, dys.
1379 Aikens, A, 1 cav, I, May 26, dia. c.
1928 Adams, Jas T, 6, H, May 14, dia.
10288 Abbott, D E, 2, D, Oct 4, scs.
2325 Archer, H, 1, I, Dec 24, scs.

112 Babb, Samuel, 8, I, March 23, brs.
288 Berlin, Jas, 2 cav, F, April 1, pna.
472 Beltz, W W, 2, H, April 9, dia. c.
1086 Bowers, A, 1, I, May 14, dia. c.
1455 Brown, Augustus, 2, G, May 29, dia. c
1487 Braddock, Wm, 2, D, May 30, dia.
1549 Buck, H, 1 cav, B, June 1, dia. c.
1644 Buckley, Geo, 9, B, June 5, dia. c.
2404 Bennett, C B, 1, D, June 24, dia. c.
3268 Brant, D B, 2, H, July 13, dia. c.
4602 Betson, James, 1 bat, A, Aug 3, scs.
5261 Ball, J A, 2, B, Aug 10, scs.
5525 Brown, J C, 1 art, B, Aug 23, scs.
6540 Brown, E R, 2, C, Aug 13, scs.
7727 Brown, E, 2, D, Sept 3, dys.
8975 Buckley, A M, 1, B, Sept 17, dia.
11184 Beale, R, 1 cav, D, Sept 19, scs.
11761 Buckner, George, 2, K, Nov 3, scs.
11620 Bell, J R, 8, D, Oct 28, scs.
12373 Bloom, J,‡ 7, F, Jan 1, pls.
12679 Book, C, 8, G, Feb 19, dia.

54 Carpenter, Wm, 2 cav, I, March 17, dia.
304 Cook, Lewis, 9, E, April 1, dys.
469 Coombs, E A, 9, I, April 9, dia.
524 Carter, Wm, 2, C, April 13, pna.
728 Cury, W H, 9, F, April 25, dia.
1357 Carl, J M, 6, E, May 25, dia. c.
1371 Cabbage, C H, 2, H, May 25, dys.
2012 Cullin, John, 2, D, June 15, dia.
4182 Crasby, M, 1, G, July 28, dys.
4620 Carter, John, 2, C, Aug 3, dia.
5036 Carr, Wm, 1 cav, D, Aug 8, dia. c.
5063 Childs, G A, 9, I, Aug 8, dia. c.
5826 Crisle, J, 6, G, Aug 16, dys.
8008 Crouse, W A, Coles' cav, E, Sept 6, dia.
8035 Conway, Wm E, 4, E, Sept 6, dia.
8266 Crabb, H, 4, E, Sept 9, dia. c.
8357 Coon, H S, 1, E, Sept 10, dia.
8618 Crouse, J A, 1 cav, A, Sept 13, dia. c.
10600 Collins, D, 1, C, Sept 10, dia. a.
12395 Callahan, P, 1, F, Jan 4, dia.

181 Duff, Chas,‡ 8, A, March 27, pna.
1410 Dunn, John,‡ 9, H, May 27, dia. c.
2396 Davis, Thomas, 9, June 24, scs.
3912 Drew, C, 35, B, July 24, dia.
4138 Dennis, Benj, 2, A, July 28, dia.
4211 Davis, G, 1 cav, F, July 29, scs.
6510 Dickwall, Wm, 2, F, Aug 22, dia.

8199 Deller, F, 1, E, Sept 8, dia.
6788 Dennissen, T, 42, I, Aug 25, dia.

8428 Ellis, C, 4, D, Sept 12, scs.
10410 Eli, W, 7, C, Oct 6, scs.

3849 Fecker, L, 2, I, July 24, scs.
1321 Fairbanks, J E, 9, C, May 23, dia. c.
2559 Francis, J,‡ 2, K, June 27, r. f.
2600 Feage, F J, 2, H, June 28, dia.
2824 Farrass, Jas, 7, G, July 2, dys.
6016 Frantz, F, 2, H, Aug 17, ana.
7404 Fink, L, 2, H, Aug 31, des.
9290 Frederick, J E, 9, I, Sept 19, scs.
12752 Freaere, W, 8, A, March 10, scs.

1271 Gordon, A B, 9, E, May 22, dys.
2138 Gerard, Fred, 1 cav, B, June 18, dia. c.
3013 Green, Thos, 2, D, July 7, dia.
3789 Gregg, F, 2, I, July 22, dia.
6072 Gilson, J E.§ 1 cav, C, Aug 18, scs.
6731 Ganon, J W, 2, K, Aug 24, dia.
12735 Goff, John, 1, I, March 6, dia. c.

1767 Honck, J,‡ 2, H, April 27, dia.
826 Hickley, John, 9, G, May 1, ana.
1625 Howell, L H, 1 cav, M, June 4, dia. c.
1720 Hoop, H, 2, I, June 8, scs.
2357 Hickley, J S, 2, H, June 23, dia. c.
2494 Hidderick, H, 1, I, June 26, dia.
2978 Hite, J E, 2, I, July 7, dia. c.
3864 Hering, P,§ 2, C, July 24, scs.
4767 Hank, Thomas, 1 bat, D, Aug 5, scs.
5292 Hilligar, 1, E, Aug 11, dia.
5408 Hood, John, 8, C, Aug 12, scs.
5917 Holmes, L, 2, H, Aug 17, dys.
6484 Hour, S, 8, E, Aug 22, dia.
6504 Harris, J E, 1, A, Aug 22, dia.
7434 Hazel, J, 9, C, Sept 1, dys.
8165 Himick, F, 1 cav, E, Sept 8, r. f.
8398 Hall, J, 7, D, Sept 10, dia. c.
9932 Holden, J R, 9, C, Sept 28, dys.
11109 Hakaion, F, 2, K, Oct 18, scs.
12422 Hoover, J, 2 cav, C, Jan 9, scs.

2895 Isaac, Henry, 2, H, July 4, dia. c.

93 Jones, David, 1 bat, A, March 22, dia.
669 Jenkins, M, 2, A, April 22, dia. c.

460 Keplinger, J, 2, H, April 9, dia.
544 Keefe, Lewis, 7, F, April 14, pna.
7242 Kirby, J, 9, F, Aug 29, dys.

1019 Laird, Corbin, 1 cav, F, May 11, dia. c.
1756 Lees, W H, 2, C, May 13, i. f.
3913 Louis, J,§ 2, B, July 24, dys.
11385 Little, D, 2 cav, K, Oct 24, scs.
12361 Lebud, J, 1 cav, D, Dec 30, scs.
12667 Lambert, W, 1, I, Feb 17, scs.

206 McCarle, Jas, 1 cav, B, March 28, dia. c.
471 Moland, B, 2, F, April 9, dia. c.
896 Myers, Noah, 9, G, May 5, dia.
1190 McGuigen, S K, 1 bat, D, May 18, dia.
1307 Myers, L S, 1, B, May 23, dia. c.
1797 Moore, Frank, 9, A, June 10, c. c.
1898 Moffitt, Thos, 6, June 13, dia. c.
2059 Martz, G H, 2, H, June 16, ana.
3429 Machler, C S, 1 bat, A, July 17, dia.
3797 McKinsay, Jno, 2, I, July 22, dia.
4051 Miller, F, 6, C, July 27, scs.
4146 Mathews, F, 8, G, July 28, dia.
4881 Macomber, John, 1 cav, B, Aug 6, dia.
5170 Marvin, J, 2, H, Aug 9, scs.
6757 Moon, J J, 1, D, Aug 25, scs.
7281 McCullough, J, 1, I, Aug 30, scs.
7327 McLamas, J, 7, C, Aug 30, dys.
8043 Markell, S, 2, H, Sept 6, dia.
10170 Munroe, J,‡ 4, H, Oct 1, dys.

10861 Markin, W, 1, F, Oct 13, scs.
11547 Mathews, J, 8, Oct 27, scs.
12608 McMiller, J A, 1, E, Feb 7, scs.

91 Nice, Jacob, 5 cav, M, March 2, pna.
371 Nace, Harrison, 9, H, April 5, pna.
9752 Norris, N, 1, I, Sept 25, scs.

153 Pool, Hanson, 2, H, March 25, phs.
7590 Porter, G, 1, I, Sept 2, dia.
7981 Pindiville, M, 7, H, Sept 6, scs.
5069 Papple, D,‡ 2, H, Aug 8, dys.

252 Rusk, John, 9, E, March 30, dia.
918 Russell, A P, 2, C, May 6, dys.
1606 Rodh, Simon, 9, E, June 4, dia.
1901 Robinson, J, 9, June 13, dia. c.
2350 Rynedollar, Wm, 1 cav, D, June 23, dia. c.
6599 Reed, Thos P, 1 art, B, Aug 23, dia. c.

155 Seberger, F, 9, F, March 25, c. f.
317 Scarboro, Rob't, 9, I, April 2, pna.
478 Suffecol, S, 1, I, April 9, dia. c.
718 Sinder, John, 2, H, April 24, dia.
899 Snooks, W, 9, E, May 5, dia. c.
1205 Spence, Levi, 9, D, May 19, ana.
1272 Scarlett, Jas, 1, D, May 22, dys.
1926 Smith, Ed,§ 9, I, June 14, dia. c.
2004 Stafford, John, 9, G, June 15, dia.
2361 Shipley, W, 9, G, June 23, dia. c.
2489 Schneder, J, 1 bat, B, June 26, dia.
5797 Smith, John, 1 cav, B, Aug 15, dys.
6751 Shelley, B, 2, F, Aug 24, scs.
6818 Shiver, G H,‡ 1, C, Aug 25, scs.
6919 Stull, G E, 1 cav, D, Aug 26, dia. c.
7580 Shiling, Wm, 2, K, Sept 2, dia. c.
7833 Stolz, 7, K, Sept 4, dia. c.
8296 Smitzer, J, 1, D, Sept 9, scs.
8716 Segar, Chas, 6, F, Sept 14, scs.
9309 Snyder, F, 2, K, Sept 20, dia.
9451 Stratten, J A, 1 art, C, Sept 21, dia.
10215 Shafer, J N, 1 cav, A, Oct 22, dia.
11159 Samon, L W, 1, I, Oct 19, dia. c.
11160 Speaker, H, 1, F, Oct 19, scs.
12195 Spaulding, J, 4, C, Nov 29, dia.
12704 Smith, G C, 1, I, Feb 26, scs.

149 Tyson, J T, 9, D, March 25, pna.
1022 Tysen, J T, 9, I, May 11, dia. c.
677 Turner, Wm F, 1 cav, D, April 22, dys.
1029 Turner, A, 1 cav, B, May 11, pna.
1356 Tindle, E,‡ 9, G, May 25, dia. c.
1377 Turner, C, 9, E, May 26, dia. c.
7872 Thompson, J, 13, I, Sept 5, scs.
8659 Thompson, John, 2, S, Sept 14, dia.
9246 Tucker, 2, D, Sept 19, scs.
9325 Tindell, Wm, 11, B, Sept 20, scs.
11450 Tilton, J, 1 cav, F, Oct 25, dia.

1583 Ulrich, Daniel, 9, I, June 3, dia.

1305 Veach, Jesse, 2, H, May 23, dia. c.
8269 Viscounts, A J, 1 art, E, Sept 9, dia. c.

78 Wise, John, 9, D, March 20, dia.
21 White, Wm, 9, C, March 7, dys.
553 Widdons, D, 1, E, April 14, dia.
597 Webster, Samuel,‡ 9, G, April 17, dia.
1171 Wharton, Samuel, 2, F, May 17, dia. c.
2275 Worthen, Wm, 9, C, June 20, dia. c.
4748 West, M, 4, D, Aug 5, scs.
9409 Weaver, George, 1, B, Sept 21, dia.
11578 Witman, D, 13, D, Sept 28, scs.
12147 Wolfe, H, 1, B, Nov 24, scs.

455 Yieldhan, R, 9, C, April 9, pna.

1060 Zeck, Wm J,‡ 7, E, May 13, des.
3223 Zimmerman, Chas, 9, E, July 12.

MASSACHUSETTS.

11288 Adams, I B, 16, G, Oct 22, scs.
9561 Adams, S B, 18, G, Sept 23, scs.
6360 Akers, H H, 2, I, Aug 21, scs.
4290 Aldrich, H, 36, G, July 30, dia.
10973 Aldrich, H W, 27, I, Oct 15, scs.
5650 Alger, W A,‡ 15, D, Aug 14, dia.
8730 Allen, Francis, 1 art, M, Sept 14, scs.
5334 Allen, G H, 2, E, Aug 11, dys.
9748 Allen, John, 19, B, Sept 25, dia.
2286 Ames, H, 35, A, June 25, ana.
8349 Ames, M L, 32, G, Sept 10, dia. c.
8373 Analstine, ——, 54, Sept 10, scs.
1084 Anchey, J, 61, F, May 4, dia.
8589 Armington, H, 18, C, Sept 12, scs.
10693 Armstrong, G, 28, A, Oct 11, scs.
9781 Atmore, C, 2 cav, A, Sept 25, dia.
4065 Avery, John W, 1 art, G, July 27, dys.
5372 Avigron, F, 56, I, Aug 11, dys.

10767 Bacey, Wm, 27, H, Oct 12, scs.
7116 Baggard, F, 1 art, B, Aug 28, scs.
8338 Baice, G A, 27, G, Sept 10, dys.
6624 Barley, R, 20, A, Aug 23, scs.
6785 Baker, E E, 34, C, Aug 25, dia.
11435 Baldwin, W, 35, A, Oct 24, scs.
9078 Banner, M, 20, B, Sept 17, scs.
642 Barge, Henry, 20, E, April 20, ts. f.
6974 Barnes, L A, 19, F, Aug 27, ana.
1697 Barnes, W L, 2 cav, M, June 7, dia. c.
7858 Barlen, E F, 18, E, Sept 5, scs.
3841 Barnsh, John, 17, H, July 28, dia.
6952 Barnett, G H, 25, G, Aug 26, dys.
8848 Bassett, B C, 1 art, I, Sept 15, dia.
4355 Batten, Geo C,§ 2 art, G, July 31, dia.
8603 Baxten, H, 2 art, G, Sept 12, scs.
2525 Bear, G W, 56, I, June 26, dia.
6386 Beannian, Wm, 2 art, G, Aug 21, dys.
6499 Beavey, Henry, 59, B, Aug 22, dia.
3801 Beels, H, 59, C, July 22, dia.
8110 Bell, Wm, 2 cav, M, Sept 7, scs.
8442 Bemis, Albert, 57, B, Sept 11, scs.
11955 Berry, George, 18, K, Nov 10, dia.
6403 Besson, Wm, 2 cav, H, Aug 21, dys.
8657 Biglow, G, 34, E, Sept 13, scs.
5321 Biglow, John, 22, F, Aug 11, r. f.
2908 Black, James, 9, E, July 5, dia.
109 Blanchard, Oscar, 2 cav, E, March 23, dia.
4067 Blanchard, O S, 52, G, July 27, dys.
3337 Blair, J W, 27, C, July 15, dia.
8973 Blair, D, 27, B, July 25, dys.
10753 Blake, Wm, 19, K, Oct 12, scs.
7166 Blodgett, A Z, 34, A, Aug 29, des.
137 Blood, T B, 18, F, March 24, ana.
44/0 Bodge, S D, 18, D, Aug 1, dys.
3030 Bosworth, H, 25, B, July 8, dia.
7466 Bowler, H A, 1 art, C, Sept 10, scs.
12013 Boyd, F, 18, A, Nov 10, dia.
1796 Boynton, Henry, 32, A, June 10, dia.
1857 Bracketts, L, 23, C, June 12, pls.
4059 Brackin, Denis, 46, July 27, dia.
6512 Bradford, J, 2 cav, F, Aug 22, wds.
3178 Brady, F, 27, G, July 11, dia.
11902 Bradish, F, 19, B, Nov 11, scs.
12030 Branagan, C, 2 art, H, Nov 15, scs.
4070 Brand, S C, 57, K, Oct 12, scs.
2565 Briggs, W, 2 art, G, July 2, brs.
993 Briggs, W W, 36, H, May 10, ts. f.
8799 Bromley, A, I, K, Sept 15, dys.
465 Broadley, James, 17, A, April 9, scs.
5587 Bronagan, M, 17, E, July 19, dys.
11932 Brotherton, W H,‡ 29, G, Aug 26, dys.
2641 Brown, A, 56, D, June 29, dia.
5057 Brown, D, 18, K, Aug 18, dia.
6177 Brown, I, 25, A, Aug 19, scs.
3660 Brown, J, 11, E, Sept 24, dia.
10819 Brown, John,‡ 57, E, Oct 12, dys.
7440 Brown, L, 27, I, Sept 1, dys.

8780 Brown, Samuel, 56, E, Sept 14, dia.
5339 Brown, Wm, 2 art, H, Aug 11, dia.
6842 Brownell, A G, 58, B, Aug 25, scs.
6903 Bryant, W A, 2 art, H, Aug 26, scs.
7758 Buchanan, J, 27, A, Sept 4, dia.
5775 Buldas, L, 56, I, Aug 9, dia.
10746 Bullen, J W, 60, C, Oct 11, dia.
11517 Bubler, J W, 40, C, Oct 26, scc
1784 Bullock, W D, 24, K, July 22, dia.
11154 Burns, W H,‡ 2 art, H, Oct 19, scs.
2007 Burt, C E,‡ 2 art, K, July 5, dia.
7134 Burgan, L, 25, G, Aug 28, scs.
3699 Burgess, W F, 16, H, July 21, scs.
5540 Burnham, J, 12, I, Aug 13, scs.
7777 Burton, John, 19, E, Sept 4, dys.
2429 Butler, A, 72, H, June 24, dia.
4956 Buxton, Thomas, 1 art, G, Aug 7, dys
9868 Byerns, I, 1 art, I, Sept 27, scs.

7230 Callihan, J, 57, B, Aug 29, dia.
3158 Callihan, P, 57, A, July 11, brs.
12663 Campbell, D A, 15, G, Feb 16, dia.
4081 Carr, Wm,‡ 1 art, H, July 27, scs.
4456 Carroll, J, 2 art, D, Aug 1, dia.
4366 Carroll, O J, 2 art, G, July 31, dys.
4168 Casey, M, 28, C, July 23, dia.
4509 Casey, M, 17, H, Aug 2, scs.
4226 Castle, M, 22, H, July 29, dys.
6724 Caughlin, B, 56, E, Aug 24, dia.
7070 Caswell, James, 18, F, Aug 18, dia.
7313 Chase, John, 25, F, Aug 30, dia.
8086 Chase, M M, 2 art, G, Sept 13, scs.
6230 Child, A F, 1 cav, E, Aug 20, ces.
3344 Chiselson, P, 1 cav, B, July 15, scs.
1684 Church, W H, 1 cav, E, June 6, dia.
2416 Churchill, F J, 39, G, June 24, dia.
7674 Chute, A M, 23, B, June 11, dia.
4516 Claflin, F G, 1 art, F, Aug 1, dia.
11178 Clang, J H, 1 art, E, Oct 19, scs.
3016 Clansky, J,‡ 17, E, July 7, dia.
10099 Clark, ——,‡ 27, A, Sept 30, dia.
3648 Clark, E, 27, H, July 20, dia.
4295 Clark, George, 16, I, July 30, dia.
6492 Clark, S, 27, I, Aug 27, dia.
7928 Clemens, J, 19, B, Sept 5, dia.
12825 Cloonan, P, 1 art, E, April 7, dia.
5315 Coffin, A R, 2 cav, M, Aug 11, dia.
11590 Cohash, John, 23, I, Oct 28, scs.
8099 Cole, W H, 16, K, Sept 7, dys.
8 Coleman, Leonard, 1 cav, A, Mar 5, pna
10773 Coalman, C S, 37, I, Oct 12, scs.
11853 Collins, A J, 2 art, D, Nov 6, scs.
6714 Collins, C R, 27, D, Aug 24, dia.
5409 Colt, J, 20, K, Aug 12, ana.
9081 Colyer, B, 1 art, G, Sept 18, scs.
6062 Coney, C W, 1 art, L, Aug 18, ts. f.
6591 Congden, E, 2 cav, G, Aug 23, ana.
9332 Connell, J D, 24, E, Sept 19, scs.
1848 Conner, D, 17, H, June 11, dia.
6673 Conner, John, 11, F, Aug 24, scs.
11892 Conner, P, 2 cav, H, Nov 7, scs.
11575 Conner, F, 9, C, Oct 28, scs.
4547 Conlin, Tim, 1 art, L, Aug 2, dys.
7593 Cook, W H, 37, H, Sept 2, scs.
8841 Coombs, George, 2 art, Sept 15, dia.
1088 Coones, J M, 1 cav, E, May 14, dia.
11174 Copeland, J, 15, D, Oct 19, scs.
7802 Corbet, W M, 1 art, M, Sept 4, dia.
4210 Cox, D O, 59, F, July 29, dia.
637 Cox, Joseph, 7, G, May 23, dia.
11030 Cox, P,§ 1 art, G, Oct 16, dia.
4483 Crockett, A W, 17, K, Aug 1, dia.
174 Crofts, E P, 17, E, March 26, pna.
7619 Cromian, John, 1 art, E, Sept 2 dia.
9026 Crominshield, T, 37, I, Sept 17, scs.
6812 Crosby, E, 40, A, Aug 25, dia
15 Cross, Ira M, 16, G, March 6, dys.

****

3592 Cross, George W, 1 art, L, July 19, dys.
5248 Crosser. E P, 9, C, Aug 10, dia.
5150 Crossman, E, J, 20, L, Aug 9, scs.
1290 Cummings, A B,§ 29, C, May 22, dys.
3746 Culligan, Joseph, 2 cav, A, July 22, dia. c.
574 Cunell, H G, 39, C, April 16, dia.
7853 Curren, F, 58, I, Sept 5, dia.
1869 Cushing, C E, 12, June 12, dia.
10172 Cutler, C F, 2 art, G, Oct 1, dia.

3579 Dalber, S A, 17, B, July 19, dia.
787 Daly, John, 28, F, April 28, dia.
9421 Davis, C, 27, B, Sept 21, dia.
7180 Davis, C A, 58, I, Aug 29, dia.
1518 Davis, Thomas, 1 cav, H, May 31, dia.
12037 Davidson, W, 27, H, Nov 16, scs.
7239 Day, D B, 25, Aug 29, des.
2390 Decker, C, 1 art, E, June 24, dia.
11763 Delano, E, 19, E, Nov 3, scs.
7848 Densmore, Wm, 9, F, Sept 4, scs.
6883 Dewry, L A, 27, C, Aug 26, dys.
4042 Dexter, G, 2 cav, M, July 27, scs.
7069 Dill, Z, 58, A, Aug 28, dys.
10964 Dimmick. George H, 27, I, Oct 15, scs.
8430 Dodge, Thomas A, 1 cav, A, Sept 11, scs.
3059 Downing, G, 14 bat, July 9, dys.
5501 Doggett, L, 22, L, Aug 13, dia.
9577 Dolan, J, 1 cav, D, Sept 23, dia.
8732 Dole, Charles H, 10, H, Sept 4, dia.
6676 Dones, S M, 58, A, Aug 24, dys.
12004 Douglass, B, 10, H, Sept 14, dia.
12829 Dow, H A,‡ 1 art, E, April 10, dia.
3678 Dowlin, J, 27, H, July 20, scs.
1677 Downey, Joel, 2 art, M, June 6, dia.
2676 Drake, E C, 57, E, June 30, dia.
12773 Drake, T, 4, D, March 14, rhm.
7115 Dansfield, John, 19, E, Aug 28, scs.
5856 Drawn, George, 32, C, Aug 16, mas.
2717 Drickarm, L, 1 cav, K, July 1, dys.
8294 Dromantle, W, 25, G, Sept 9, scs.
3570 Drum, R, 19, G, July 19, dia.
9251 Duffey, J, 2 art, H, Sept 19, scs.
1512 Duffey. James, 18, A, May 31, dia.
4613 Dull, W, 2 art, H, Aug 31, dys.
11666 Dunmett, S, 4, D, Oct 30, dia.
10660 Dunn, J, 2 art, G, Oct 11, scs.
11319 Dunn, I, 20, H, Oct 22, scs.
4471 Dunn, P, 2 art, H, Aug 1, scs.
4964 Dyer, G W, 2 art, H, Aug 7, dys.

8212 Eaff, N, 56, H, Sept 8, dia.
8616 Earl, G W,§ 1 art, I, Sept 13, scs.
8157 Eastman, D, 35, I, Sept 8, dys.
10000 Eaton, F W, 5, D, Sept 29, scs.
7284 Edes, W,‡ 11, F, Aug 20, scs.
11809 Edwards, C, 19, A, Nov 4, scs.
6354 Edwards, C F, 2 art, H, Aug 21, dia.
171 Egan, Charles, 17, K, March 26, pna.
10822 Eibers, Henry, 19, Oct 12, scs.
6994 Emerson, G W, 57, A, Aug 27, dia.
418 Emerson, Wm, 12, D, April 7, pls.
5619 Emery, J, 1 art, F, Aug 14, scs.
5539 Emmerson, F F, 1 art, B, Aug 13, dia.
3300 Empay, Robert, 25, E, July 14, dia.
10542 Emusin, D G, 21, B, Oct 5, dia.
5236 Evans, H, 1 cav, K, Aug 10, scs.
2785 Evans, J, 17, H, July 2, dia.
7889 Ester, W A, 1 art, A, Sept 5, dys.
4399 Everts, T P, 2 art, G, July 31, dia.

8556 Farmer, G S,§ 1 art, H, Sept 12, scs.
11908 Farralle, G, 19, K, Nov 7, scs.
9443 Farisdale, H, 1 art, G, Sept 21, dia.
3926 Fearing, J I, 1 art, F, July 25, dia.
4987 Fearnley, Wm, 25, E, Aug 7, scs.
6450 Fegan, John, 2 art, H, Aug 21, dia.
12812 Fellows, H, 15, E, March 19, scs.
7803 Felyer, Wm, 20, E, Sept 4, dia.
7611 Fenis, J, 1 cav, C, Sept 2, scs.
5795 Fields, E, 37, F, Aug 15, dia.
11401 Finjay, W, 1 cav, K, Oct 24, scs.
6723 Finigan, B, 19, Aug 24, dia.

3974 Fisher, C B, 2 art, G, July 25, dia.
441 Fisher, John 2 cav, E, April 9, pna.
3451 Flanders, Charles, 1 art, E, July 17, scs
286 Fleming, M, 17, E, April 1, pna.
2476 Floyd, George E, 2 art, H, June 25, dia
4187 Forbs, H, 1 art, B, July 28, dia.
70 Fosgate, Henry S, 17, K, March 19, dia
5649 Fowler, Samuel, 1 art, M, Aug 14, scs.
10601 Frahar, P, 2 art, D, Oct 10, scs.
11135 Fraier, L, 20, C, Oct 18, dys.
3848 Fray, Patrick, 17, C, July 24, scs.
4267 Frederick, C, 20, A, July 29, scs.
8186 Frisby, A, 12, G, Sept 8, scs.
9502 Frost, B, 16, H, Sept 21, dia.
10205 Frost, B, 16, H, Oct 2, scs.
7170 Fuller, A, 2 cav, G, Aug 29, des.
12681 Fuller, H, 15, E, Feb 20, rhm.
5467 Fuller, S, 27, D, Aug 13, dys.
7392 Fuller, Geo A, 2 art, G, Aug 31, dys.
7154 Funold, C G, 23, G, Aug 29, dia.

9304 Gadkin, G H, 21, H, Sept 22, dia.
4333 Gaffering, John, 11, F, July 30, dia.
8927 Galligher, F, 18, B, Sept 19, dia.
2787 Galse, I E,‡ 27, B, July 2, dia. c.
7569 Gardner, D, 25, E, Sept 2, dia.
12630 Garland, W, 1 art, M, Feb 10, scs.
8882 Garman, E, 2 art, Sept 16, dia. c.
11470 Gay, C, 1 cav, K, Oct 6, scs.
7910 Gay, George C, 2 art, G, Sept 5, dia.
8312 Gibson, D E, 33, F, Sept 10, dia.
8364 Gibson, H H, 25, B, Sept 10, scs.
4464 Gifford, J, 40, A, Aug 1, dia.
4250 Gilbert, S, 2 art, H, July 29, dia.
159 Gilchrist, J R,‡ 17, A, March 25, r. f.
11157 Gilliland, J, 17, H, Oct 19, scs.
7110 Gilsby, P, 36, G, Aug 28, dia.
10918 Glancey, P, 59, A, Oct 18, scs.
9471 Goanney, G, 2 art, G, Sept 21, dia.
2414 Godbold, F A, 29, K, June 24, scs.
3585 Gooding, N, 54, C, July 19, wds.
9202 Goodman, J, 25, Sept 18, scs.
5983 Goodman, S, 2 art, B, Aug 17, dia.
9817 Goodrich, G J, 1 art, F, Sept 25, dia.
12844 Gonier, D, 4, D, April 23, dia.
179 Gordon, Charles, 17, C, March 26, pna.
3486 Gordon, W L, 2 art, H, July 17, dys.
10501 Goriche, H, 2 art, G, Oct 8, scs.
893 Gould, Wm, 17, G, May 5, dia.
8092 Gove, J, 2 art, G, Sept 7, dys.
8339 Gowen, J, 11, C, Sept 10, dys.
7885 Grant, George W, 1 art, E, Sept 5, dia.
8277 Grant, J, 15, E, Sept 9, scs.
10491 Grant, Wm, 15, E, Oct 7, dia.
8898 Gray, C, 28, D, Sept 16, scs.
2018 Green, John, 18, A, June 15, dia.
9417 Gayson, C W, 25, I, Sept 21, dia.
5166 Guild, C, 2 art, C, Aug 9, dia.
12568 Guilford, J, 1 art, I, Feb 1, des.
10108 Gutherson, G, 1 art, B, Sept 30, scs.

8056 Haggert, P,‡ 2 cav, M, Sept 7, scs.
7408 Haley, Wm, 16, F, Aug 31, scs.
151 Halstead, J W,‡ 2 cav, M, March 25, pna
11086 Hall, G H, 1 art, E, Oct 18, scs.
1742 Hanlin, H P, 2 cav, M, June 8, dia.
9342 Hammond, George,‡ 77, G, Sept 19, scs.
7374 Handy, George, 1 art, K, Aug 31, dia.
10126 Handy, Moses, 59, A, Oct 1, scs.
8273 Hane, J H, 1 art, I, Sept 9, dia.
8804 Hanks, Nelson, 98, D, Sept 15, scs.
6582 Hanley, M, 1 cav, L, Aug 23, ana.
12276 Hare, F, 27, H, Dec 13, scs.
8697 Harding, C, 58, G, Sept 14, scs.
556 Harrison, Henry, 12, I, April 14, dia.
7626 Hamesworth, F, 27, A, Sept 2, dia.
3901 Harrington, F, 12, H, July 24, dys.
7957 Hart, W, 15, G, Sept 6, dia.
6923 Hartret, M, 34, I, Aug 26, ana.
766 Harty, John,‡ 2 cav, M, April 27, dia.
3505 Harvey, S J, 2 art, G, July 7, ana.
10024 Hash, Wm, 1 art, H, Sept 29, scs.

****

8241 Hay, Wm, 2 art, H, July 13, ts. f.
5781 Haymouth, N, 2 cav, M, Aug 15, scs.
4209 Haynes, Charles E, 2 art, H, July 29, dia.
9604 Hayes, P, 37, A, Sept 23, dia.
3508 Heart, John, 28, G, July 18, dia.
7416 Hebban, Thomas, 28, B, Aug 31, dia.
3163 Henrie, E W, 17, H, July 14, dia.
5606 Henry, D, 16, H, Aug 14, dys.
4604 Henry, J, 2 art, K, Aug 3, dia.
1093 Hermans, John, 11, G, May 24, dys.
7297 Hervey, George W, ‡ 33, I, Aug 30, scs.
6242 Higgin, A, 23, B, Aug 20, ts. f.
4906 Hill, F, 9, I, Aug 6, dia.
1740 Hills, J B, 2 cav, G, June 8, dia.
11762 Hillman, G, 16, H, Nov 3, scs.
6056 Hines, S, 59, C, Aug 10, dys.
9223 Hitchcock, J C, 27, C, Sept 19, dia.
6907 Hogan, Pat, 2 art, G, Aug 26, dys.
6067 Hogan, S, 19, E, Aug 18, dia.
9260 Holt, D, 19, B, Sept 19, scs.
4811 Hoitt, J F, 2 art, D, Aug 5, dia.
6228 Holbrook, Charles, 2 art, H, Aug 20, ana.
6826 Holden, Pat, 2 art, G, Aug 25, r. f.
1986 Holland, P, 17, I, June 15, dia.
905 Holland, Pat, 11, C, May 5, dia.
4816 Holmes, S, 12, I, Aug 5, scs.
8712 Holt, E K, 1 art, Sept 14, scs.
6716 Holt, T E, 22, H, Aug 24, ana.
8575 Howard, C, 24, C, Sept 12, dia.
10864 Howard, James, 59, D, Oct 13, scs.
7025 Howe, C H, 36, G, Aug 27, scs.
222 Howe, E H, 36, H, May 29, dia.
3871 Howe, John W, 24, B, July 24, scs.
5973 Hubbard, E, 34, B, Aug 17, dia.
11045 Hubert, G W, 27, I, Oct 17, scs.
11960 Hunt, J, 84, D, Nov 11, scs.
4323 Hunting, John W, 25, I, July 30, dia.
12299 Hartshaw, L E, 56, A, Dec 16, dia.
6161 Hyde, N L, 2 cav, B, Aug 19, scs.
5470 Hyde, Richard, 39, E, Aug 13, scs.

3487 Jackson, N S, 1 art, K, July 17, dys.
3501 Jackson, N S, 17, K, July 17, dia.
8429 Jackson, Wm R, 2 cav, B, Sept 11, scs.
5733 Jaquirius, C, 57, D, Aug 13, dia.
2308 Jaynes, H, 59, G, June 22, ana.
10561 Jeff, M, 16, I, Oct 9, scs.
5915 Jeffrey, A, 58, B, Aug 17, des.
9951 Jewett, E, 27, I, Sept 28, dia.
12820 Jewett, G, 4, A, April 11, dia.
5473 Johnson, M, 34, G, Aug 13, scs.
5850 Johnson, R A, 19, G, Aug 16, dys.
3684 Johnson, Wm, 2 art, H, July 21, dia.
10702 Jones, J, 59, E, Oct 11, dia.
603 Jones, John, 2 cav, M, April 18, dys.
8875 Jones, N P, 32, F, Sept 16, dia.
6054 Jones, Thomas, 11, A, Aug 18, scs.

6183 Kavanaugh, Jas, 32, K, Aug 19, des.
8658 Kelley, Charles, 3 art, C, Sept 13, scs.
6579 Kelley, Henry, 20, E, Aug 23, scs.
9983 Kelley, M, 2 art, H, Sept 17, scs.
6275 Kelsey, E, 27, D, Aug 20, mas.
6712 Kempton, E, 2 art, G, Aug 24, pls.
5708 Kennedy, Wm, 59, F, Aug 15, scs.
6529 Kenny, J, 3 cav, G, Aug 23, scs.
8252 Kent, S, 27, H, Sept 9, dia.
12490 Kerr, Wm, § 56, D, Jan 20, scs.
6036 Keyes, J C, 2 art, G, Aug 18, scs.
868 Kice, Thomas, 2 cav, B, May 3, r. f.
296 Kilan, M, § 17, I, April 1, pna.
4544 Kimball, A, 1 art, B, Aug 2, des.
1754 Kinnely, F, § 17, E, June 9, dia.
12815 Kluener, F, 27, A, March 25, des.
554 Knapp, David, 2 cav, M, April 14, dia.
3842 Knight, —, 25, A, July 23, wds.
11119 Keephart, A, 2 art, E, Oct 18, scs.
5037 Kuppy, H, 1 art, K, Aug 8, dia.
8648 Krote, Huer, 20, G, Sept 13, scs.

12849 Langley, L F, § 28, B, Jan 28, scs.
8735 Lain, S, 12, I, Aug 24, dia.

10885 Lane, J H, § 23, Oct 13, scs.
9738 Latham, W, 25, K, Sept 25, dia.
8835 Lathrop, W O, 58, C, Sept 15, scs.
2175 Laurens, John, 23, E, June 15, dia.
9621 Leach, C W, 20. I, Sept 23, dia.
2781 Leary, D, 2 cav, A, July 2, dia.
7707 Leavey, W H, 12, A, Sept 3, dys.
7210 Lecraw, W P, 1 art, G, Aug 29, dia.
7548 Leonard, W E, 59, H, Sept 2, dia.
7725 Leonard, I G, 1 art, K, Sept 3, scs.
7798 Lewin, Charles, 19, I, Sept 3, dys.
2448 Lewis, F, 2 art, G, June 25, dia.
10068 Lewis, G G, 2 art, G, Sept 30, scs.
4082 Lewis, L, 5 cav, L, July 27, dia.
10750 Lewis, L, 1 art, A, Oct 12, dys.
5401 Lindsay, J, 18, A, Aug 12, scs.
12413 Liswell, L, 27, F, Jan 8, dia.
8748 Livingston, R, 39, C, Sept 14, dia.
1156 Lochlen, Joel, 1 cav, E, May 16, dia.
480 Lohem, E D, 18, H, April 9, dys.
3163 Lombard, B K, 58, A, July 11, cah.
12256 Loring, G, 20, A, Dec 10, scs.
10744 London, Ed, 22, G, Oct 11, scs.
8437 Lovely, Francis, 25, I, Sept 11, scs.
3217 Lovett, A W, 39, E, July 12, scs.
3175 Lowell, George, 22, E, July 11, dys.
9957 Lucier, J, 2, G, Sept 28, dia.
4090 Lugby, Z, 2 art, G, July 27, dia.
8593 Lyons, E, 27, I, Sept 12, scs.
3683 Lynch, John, 56, K, July 21, dia.

7521 Macey, Charles, 18, I, Sept 1, dys.
4264 Macomber, J, 20, H, July 29, dia.
4034 Mahan, E, 56, I, July 26, dia.
3383 Marintine, G H, 18, I, July 18, dys.
9940 Mann, N C, 16, saddler, F, Sept 28, scs.
6220 Mansfield, D R, 58, G, Aug 20, ces.
503 Marden, G O, 17, I, April 12, r. f.
1350 Mariland, W H, 17, D, May 25, dia.
7147 Marchet, C, 28, F, Aug 29, dia.
8450 Martin, C M, 2 art, H, Sept 11, ana.
6272 Maxwell, M, 1 art, I, Aug 20, mas.
5060 McAllister, J, ‡ 17, Aug 8, dys.
7823 McCaffrey, J, 27, E, Sept 4, dia.
3835 McCloud, J, 56, K, July 23, dia.
9942 McCord, J G, 32, H, Sept 28, scs.
12176 McCorner, J, 19, F, Nov 27, scs.
8905 McDavle, J, 8 art, M, Sept 15, dia.
6162 McDermott, J, 2 art, B, Aug 19, scs.
4409 McDevitt, Wm, 25, E, July 31, dia.
9439 McDonald, R, 18, D, Sept 21, dia.
430 McDonnell, P, 2, B, April 8, pna.
7459 McDonough, P, ‡ 25, E, Sept 1, dia.
1984 McGiven, J, 22, K, June 15, dia.
6375 McGovern, B, 34, D, Aug 21, dia.
2652 McGowen, John, 2 art, H, June 29, dys.
5280 McGowen, Wm, 12, A, Aug 11, dys.
4260 McGoneyal, R, 16, K, July 29, dia.
5124 McGuire, A, 58, D, Aug 9, dys.
6460 McHenry, James, 2 art, G, Aug 21, scs.
6544 McIntire, H, 1 art, K, Aug 23, dia.
11531 McKarren, E, 1 art, I, Oct 26, scs.
11849 McKenny, B, 34, A, Nov 5, dys.
6358 McKinzie, George, 27, I, Aug 5, scs.
5223 McKnight, B, 3 cav, G, Aug 10, scs.
3174 McLaughlin, E, § 9, C, July 11. ts. f.
10030 McMasters, 57, A, Sept 29, dia.
3675 McMillan, Jas, 24, B, July 20, dys.
522 McNamara, 17, I, April 13, dys.
5185 McNaury, R, 27, I, Aug 9, dia.
11381 McNulty, P, 2 art, G, Oct 24, scs.
5194 McWilliams, W, 77, D, Aug 10, scs.
7586 Medren, W, 20, G, Sept 2, scs.
5808 Mehan, B, 2 art, H, Aug 16, ana.
1434 Melan, A, 18, F, May 28, dia.
9735 Melvin, S, 1 art, K, Sept 25, dia.
2269 Meritt, M, 27, C, June 20, pna.
1358 Merriman, W H, 17, D, May 25, dia. c
9117 Messers, W, 1 art, B, Sept 18, dia.
9597 Mesters, E, 34, H, Sept 23, scs.
6286 Meyer, J, 1 cav, K, Aug 20, dia.
8631 Miland, John, 2 art, H, Sept 13, scs.

11514 Millard, P S, 19, G. Oct 26, scs.
1219 Miller, A, 28, F, May 19, dia.
4329 Miller, J M, 11, A, July 30, ts. f.
10169 Miller L, 20, Oct 1, scs.
4050 Miller, Joseph,§ 57, C, July 27, dia.
7178 Millrean, M W,‡ 2 cav, E, Aug 29, ana.
9539 Milton, C, 21, A, Sept 22, dia.
8506 Mitchell, W C, 23, A, Sept 11, scs,
11867 Mitchell, F, 14, A, Nov 6, scs.
11771 Mitchell, John, 19, C, Nov 3, dia.
8343 Mittance, L, 20, G, Sept 10, scs.
4053 Mixter, G L, 1 cav, E, July 27, dia.
6235 Monroe, J, 2 art, M, Aug 20, dia.
2456 Morgan, C H, 27, H, June 25, r. f.
8077 Morgan, Pat, 23, B, Sept 7, scs.
3160 Moore, A, 56, C, July 11, dys.
5490 Moore, C A, mus, 2 art, N, Aug 13 dia.
10593 Moore, M, 57, A, Oct 10, dia.
3411 Moore, P, 18, F, July 16, dia.
3990 Morris, N G, 1 art, July 26, dys.
1004 Morris, R,§ 28, F, May 10, dys.
9627 Mortimer, L, 19, E, Sept 24, scs.
8272 Morton G H, 42, C, Sept 9, dia.
5360 Morton J, 34, A, Aug 11, dia.
6982 Moss, Charles, 2 art, H, Aug 27, dia.
12516 Moulton, H, 15, F, Jan 23, dia.
12619 Murdock, A B,‡ 27, D, Feb 8, dia.
321 Murley D, 9, D, April 2, dia.
7862 Murphy, C, 17, D, Sept 5, ana.
5488 Murphy, F, 17, D, Aug 13, scs.
1680 Murphy, Michael, 12, K, June 6, des.
12783 Murphy, P, 27, H, March 15, scs.
5041 Murray, Thomas, 19, A, Aug 8, scs.

9241 Needham, J A, 1 art, B, Sept 19, scs.
9278 Nelson, J, 2 art, Sept 19, scs.
7006 Newcomb, John E, 2 art, G, Aug 27, scs.
9694 Nitchman, A, 19, B, Sept 24, scs.
1282 Noble, David, 17, D, May 22, dia.
12439 Norman, E, 1 art, E, Jan 12, pls.
350 Norton, F F, 39, H, April 14, dia.
10058 Nottage, I L, 2, F, Sept 30, scs.

7193 O'Brien, James, 2 art, G, Aug 29, dys.
2509 O'Brien, John, 36, K, June 26, dia.
5117 O'Connell, J, 9, C, Aug 9, scs.
12189 O'Connell, J, 15, H, Nov 28, wds.
9789 O'Connell, M, 2, H, Sept 26, dia.
11080 O'Conner, Wm, 29, K, Oct 17, dia.
11493 O'Donnell, W, 11, G, Oct 26, scs.
10592 Oliver, J, 39, E, Oct 10, scs.
4640 Oliver, S E, 27, B, Aug 3, dia.
7161 O'Neil, Charles, 25, B, Aug 29, dia.
4884 O'Neil, D, 25, E, Aug 6, dia.
4975 Osborn, W, 19, K, Aug 7, scs.

5340 Packard, N M, 27, C, Aug 11, scs.
6629 Page, Wm, 16, D, Aug 23, dia.
598 Paisley, Wm, 17, D, April 17, dia.
10695 Palmer, T, 59, E, Oct 11, dia.
4714 Panier, J M, 17, K. Aug 4, dys.
11059 Pantins, A J. 15, H, Oct 17, scs.
6899 Pandes, L, 3 art, G, Aug 26, dia.
7811 Parrish, Charles, 1 cav, C, Sept 4, dys.
5380 Pains, F, 2 art, E, Aug 12, scs.
1074 Parker, D H, 36, C, May 13, dia.
2327 Parsons, W D, 23, E, June 22, dia.
6860 Pasco, J M, 58, D, Aug 26, scs.
1231 Patterson, H W, 33, G, May 20, dia.
8888 Payne, G A, 57, H, Sept 16, scs.
4967 Payne, Wm A, 1 art, M, Aug 7, dys.
7556 Peabody, W F, 37, Sept 2, dia.
6471 Peckham, A P, 15, B, Aug 21, dia.
5441 Peeto, A, 36, A, Aug 12, td. f.
4003 Pennington, R A, 1 art, July 26, dys.
9602 Perry, N, 1 art, F, Sept 23, dia.
274 Perry, Samuel K, 39 D, March 31, c. f.
4986 Pettie, C, 2 art, H, Aug 7, dia.
7671 Phillbrook, J E, 56, F, Sept 3, des.
7708 Phillips, A, 50, B, Sept 3, scs.
10889 Phillips, L M,§ 17, D, Oct 5, scs.
6906 Phipps, H B,‡ 1 art, B, Aug 20, dys.

4763 Phipps, M M, 27, C, Aug 4, dia.
11079 Pierson, R,§ 2 art, H, Oct 17, dia.
20 Pilhuton, John, 11, E, April 14, s. 1k
5128 Piper, Charles, 28, G, Aug 9. dia.
6740 Piper, F, 25, E, Aug 24, dia.
7080 Polshon, F B, 17, D, Aug 28, scs.
703 Poole, Charles,‡ G, April 23, dys.
6583 Pratt, Daniel, 27, I, Aug 27, dys.
12135 Pratt, D W, 2 art, G, Nov. 23, scs.
5742 Pratt, Henry, 23, C, Aug 15, scs.
2008 Price, Edward, 2 art, M, June 15, dia.
12475 Prichard, J,‡ 2, G, June 18, scs.
5404 Prior, Michael, 56, I, Aug 12, ana.
11975 Puffer, E D, 34, A, Nov 12, scs.

4218 Quinn, James, 15, M, July 29, ana.
12804 Quirk, M J, 1, D, March 20, dia.

12094 Ragan, C,‡ 27, H, Nov 19, scs.
10156 Ramstell, H, 37, H, Oct 1, dia.
5500 Rand, M, 2 art, G, Aug 13, scs.
3358 Randall, J, 2, F, July 15, dia. c.
54 Raymond, C, 20, I, June 12, s. p.
8072 Reed, Charles, 2 art, H, Sept 7, dia.
1725 Rensseller, C N, 54, C, June 8, dia.
6122 Rapp, James, 28, A, Aug 19, dys.
2970 Reynolds, N A, 36, C, July 7, dia.
3272 Rice, C A, J, 2 art, G, July 13, dia.
1285 Rich, C, 2, D, May 22, dia.
4233 Rich, Samuel, 27, B, July 29, dia.
4918 Richards, G, 16, I, Aug 6, brs.
3156 Richards, James, 27, C, July 11, dia.
11553 Richardson, L, 1 art, G, Oct 27, scs.
4167 Richardson, S R, 1 art, M, July 28, dia.
7546 Richard, Thomas, 20, B, Sept 2, dia.
7199 Ridlam, James, 19, C, Aug 29, dia.
10638 Riley, H J, 2 art, G, Oct 10, dia.
8642 Riley, M, 56, K, Sept 13, ana.
7200 Ripley, M A, 32, F, Aug 29, dia.
6650 Rippon, Wm, 58, G, Aug 23, scs.
6166 Roach, J, 35, F, Aug 19, mas.
11552 Roberts, J H, 18, I, Oct 27, scs.
9448 Roberts, Joseph, 1 cav, K, Sept 21, dia.
12505 Roberts, L, 13, F, Jan 22, pls.
11699 Robinson, J, 19, H, Oct 31, scs.
3833 Robinson, R, 27, F, July 23, dys.
5659 Roe, Wm, 2 art, H, Aug 14, scs.
4875 Roferty, John, 2, K, Aug 6, dia.
12393 Rome, R, 1, I, Jan 4, scs.
4219 Rover F, 4, E, July 29, dia.
6654 Rope, A R, 11, I, Aug 23, dys.
5336 Rowe, Asa, 1 art, K, Aug 11, i. f.
11521 Rowley, Charles, 19, K, Oct 26, scs.
3455 Russell, ——, 27, C, July 17, td. f.
9349 Rustar, R, 27, A, Sept 19, dia.
5987 Ruth, F, 36, C, Aug 17, dys.
6036 Ryes, J C, 2 art, G, Aug 18, scs.

5276 Sabines, Edward, 19, K, Aug 11, dia.
9465 Samlett, P V, 1, A, Sept 21, scs.
8074 Sanborn, G B, 2 cav, B, Sept 7, dia.
392 Sanborn, T, 17, D, April 6, dia.
8281 Sanders, F, 2 art, G, Sept 9, dys.
10637 Sandwich, J, 1, G, Oct 10, dia.
3405 Sanford J D, 40, A, July 16, dia.
10406 Savin, J H, 34, C, Oct 6, scs.
11888 Sawer, John, 33, F, Nov 7, scs.
4180 Sawyer, S F, 1 art, D, July 28, dia.
11203 Sayer, G D, 11, I, Oct 20, dys.
5834 Schalster, S, 25, G, Aug 16, mas.
5623 Seeley, Charles H, 2 art, G, Aug 14, dia.
11731 Sergeant, J C, 19, E, Nov 2, scs.
11338 Shamrock, I, 19, H, Oct 23, scs.
6782 Shaw, Andrew, 25, K, Aug 25, dia.
12303 Shaw, C L,‡ 15, E, Dec 18, scs.
7827 Shea, J, 2 art, H, Sept 4, dia.
7481 Shehan, James, 2 art, G, Sept 1, scs.
2324 Sherman, P H, 37, E, June 23, i. f.
8822 Sherwood, F, 76, B, Sept 15, dia.
4950 Shindler, John, 1 art, I, Aug 7, dia.
6602 Shore, J J, 1, F, Aug 23, dia.
10946 Short, J, 2, B, Oct 14, scs.

Federal Soldiers who Died at Andersonville, Georgia Confederate Prison   27

****

7735 Shultes, A M, 23, B, Sept 3, scs.
10415 Shults, George, 28, H, Oct 6, scs.
1458 Simmonds, E, 17, D, May 29, dia.
6957 Simons, A, 2 art, M, Aug 26, scs.
4186 Simpson, D O, 34, D, July 28, dia.
9842 Simpson, W, 2 art, H, Sept 27, scs.
6141 Sinclair, A, 1, G, Aug 19, dia.
11189 Sloan, S, 20, K, Oct 19, i. f.
8375 Small, Z, 1 art, G, Sept 11, scs.
10404 Smalley, J H, 2, G, Oct 6, scs.
9 Smith, Warren, 12, F, March 5, phs.
10256 Smith, C, 27, D, Oct 3, scs.
8002 Smith, C A, 1 art, C, Sept 6, td. f.
4952 Smith, D H, 1, I, Aug 7, scs.
12499 Smith, E, 27, G, Jan 21, dia.
11904 Smith, E M, 1, D, Nov 4, dys.
7158 Smith, H, 57, D, Aug 29, dia.
7443 Smith, J,‡ 20, E, Sept 1, dia.
967 Smith, John, 17, K, May 8, dia.
7538 Smith, J P, 1 art, A, Sept 2, dia.
5780 Smith, J H, 19, G, Aug 15, des.
8184 Smith, W, 23, B, Sept 8, scs.
154 Smith, W H, 12, I, March 25, phs.
2304 Smith, Wm, 54, June 22, dys.
12748 Smith, V, 57, K, March 6, pls.
3745 Snow, W, 16, E, July 21, scs.
12063 Somers, F, 19, G, Nov 17, dia.
5316 Switzer, L, 16, E, Aug 11, dia.
8280 Southworth, J, 18, G, Sept 9, dys.
2469 Southworth, John, 18, E, June 25, dys.
2188 Spalding, J, 2, E, June 19, dia.
12160 Spar, H, 19, H, Nov 25, scs.
10342 Spellman, B F, 2 art, Oct 4, scs.
6179 Spence, David, 19, D, Aug 19, ces.
4153 Spooner, C L, 27, H, July 28, ana.
5600 Spooner, E O, 27, A, Aug 14, scs.
4652 Spooner, F, 18, A, Aug 3, dys.
3397 Stalder, E P,§ 17, H, July 16, pna.
9873 Stauf, J, 20, D, Sept 27, scs.
6501 Steadson, W, 16, G, Aug 22, dia.
5028 Stelle, F, 1 art, I, Aug 8, scs.
7991 Stevens, Henry, 28, F, Sept 6, scs.
9183 Stevens, N, 1, E, Sept 18, ana.
2381 Stevens, Thomas, 2, M, July 4, ts. f.
1758 Steward, J, 11, H, June 9, des.
11291 Stewart, E, 52, D, Oct 22, dia.
12420 Stone, F P, 27, A, Jan 9, des.
10181 Stone, A, 2 art, H, Oct 1, dia.
5957 Sullivan, John, 16, A, Aug 17, scs.
7401 Sullivan, John, 2, K, Aug 31, scs.
10890 Sullivan, M, 2, D, Oct 4, scs.
8203 Sullivan, P, 9, Sept 8, dia.
10792 Sullivan, P, 15, I, Oct 12, rhm.
11671 Sullivan, F, 59, B, Oct 30, scs.
12788 Sylvester, D, 1, B, March 17, dia.
3325 Sylvester, E, 2 art, H, Sept 10, dia.
12053 Sylvester, J, 4, A, Nov 16, scs.

11957 Tabor, B, 35, C, Nov 11, scs.
10697 Tabor, F,§ 16, E, Oct 11, scs.
2067 Taggerd, John, 17, E, June 19, dia.
3368 Taylor, N, 37, D, July 15, scs.
2515 Taylor, Thomas, 2 cav, G, June 26, dys.
8805 Teinerts, T J,§ 110, D, Sept 15, scs.
4386 Tenney, William, 3, G, July 31, td. f.
3812 Thayer, J, 27, A, July 23, dys.
8612 Thomas, J, 2 art, H, Sept 13, dia.
11123 Thomas, J A, 32, G, Oct 18, scs.
2421 Thomas, J W, 56, I, June 24, dia.
12527 Thompson, C, 1 art, B, Jan 26, scs.
1890 Thompson, George, 16, June 13, pna.
4536 Thompson, George, 58, F, Aug 2, scs.

3908 Thompson, J M, 27, H, July 24, dys.
3596 Thompson, W W, 58, G, July 19, scs.
4634 Tibbett, A, 23, F, Aug 3, scs.
7468 Tiffany, J, 4, F, Sept 1, dia.
6549 Tilden, A, 27, B, Aug 23, dia.
3898 Tillson, Chas E, 29, E, July 24, dia.
3549 Tooma, John, 28, E, July 18, dia.
407 Torey, L, 12, H, April 7, dys.
6019 Torrey, C L, 7, G, Aug 17, dia.
10131 Townley, J J, 1, F, Oct 1, scs.
9108 Travern, W, 2 art, G, Sept 18, dia.
7860 Travis, H C,‡ 59, C, Sept 5, dia
7996 Trescutt, W M, 15, I, Sept 6, dia.
8132 Turner, H, 34, F, Sept 8, c. f.
12161 Tuith, F, 20, F, Nov 25, scs.
5428 Twichell, J, 17, K, Aug 12, dia.
6332 Twichell, ——, 36, C, Aug 21, des.

9517 Usher, Samuel, 17, I, Sept 22, dia.

8466 Wade, A D L, 2 art, G, Sept 11, scs.
5959 Waldon, William, 36, B, Aug 17, dia.
12444 Walker, A, 19, F, Jan 12, scs.
3377 Wallace, P, 57, B, July 16, scs.
11494 Walsh, M, 4, C, Oct 26, dys.
5191 Walton, E A, 57, H, Aug 10, dys.
8724 Walton, Nathaniel, 59, E, Sept 14, scs.
8304 Wanderfelt, ——, 6, C, Sept 10, dia.
1733 Wardin, H, 17, I, June 8, ana.
5217 Ware, Samuel, 1, H, Aug 10, dia.
8664 Warffender, J W, 27, C, Sept 15, dia.
12131 Warner, A F,‡ 19, D, Nov 22, scs.
6454 Washburne, W E, 27, I, Aug 21, dia.
4721 Weidan, H, 17, H, Aug 4, ana.
1066 Welch, Frank, 17, B, May 13, dia.
6224 Weldon, Charles, 1 art, D, Aug 29, dys
11796 Wells, S, 1, A, Nov 14, scs.
5214 Wellington, G W, 2, G, Aug 10, scs.
3547 Welwarth, C W, 18, D, July 18, dia
3247 Werdier, W, 58, G, July 13, dia.
1334 West, E, 24, A, May 24, rhm.
7002 West, J G, 1 art, E, Aug 27, dys.
4577 White, F, 15, K, Aug 2, dia.
6807 White, Joseph, 2 art, G, Aug 25, dys.
7188 White, Joseph, 2, G, Aug 29, dia.
7902 Whiting, A, 27, H, Sept 5, dia.
6867 Whitney, F P, 1, G, Aug 26, scs.
635 Whittaker, S, 17, D, April 20, dia.
1115 Wiggard, George, 22, A, May 15, dia
6715 Wilber, E, 27, G, Aug 24, ana.
4539 Wilcox, Allen, 14 art, C, Aug 2, dia.
5519 Wilder, L E, 2, G, Aug 13, dia.
7318 Wilkins, S O, 1, G, Aug 30, dia.
6661 Williams, Chas, 27, G, Aug 24, dia.
8668 Williams, J, 58, G, Sept 13, dia.
3469 Willis, C, 17, K, July 17, dys.
7549 Wilson, J, 2 art, H, Sept 2, dia.
6769 Wilson, Robert, 34, A, Aug 25, scs.
6742 Wilson, S, 2 art, G, Aug 24, r. f.
10545 Wilson, W, 18, B, Oct 9, dia.
6213 Witherill, O, 47, C, Aug 20, dia.
6483 Woodbury, B, 17, A, Aug 21, des.
6564 Woodward, W A, 27, B, Aug 23, i. s.
6368 Wright, C E, 27, B, Aug 21, scs.
6288 Wright, M E, 27, C, Aug 20, dia.
4923 Wyman, H C, 2 art, H, Aug 6, dia. c.
3562 Wright, W M, 3 art, G, July 18, dia.

8882 Young, E, 2, Sept 16, dia.
6922 Young, G W, 2 art, H, Aug 26, dia.
7152 Young, N C, 1, I, Aug 29, dia.

MICHIGAN.

2198 Ayres, J B,§ 22, C, June 17, dys.
2247 Acker, J 22, K, June 20, dia.
2461 Atkinsor, P, 22, C, June 22, dia. c.
2546 Anderson, George, 23, E, June 27, des
8257 Abbott, C M, 5, E, July 13, dys.

4947 Ammerman, H H, 23, A, Aug 7, scs.
5472 Aulger, Geo, 10, F, Aug 13, scs.
5601 Ackler, W, 3 cav, C, Aug 14, ana.
6119 Austin, D, 8, C, Aug 19, scs.
6713 Allen, A A, 14, I, Aug 24, des.

9156 Anderson, F, 1 cav, G, Sept 18, scs.
12350 Arsnoe, W, 7, E, Dec 27, dia.
12571 Allen, J, 9, H, Feb 2, rhm.
12606 Adams, A, 4, B, Feb 7, pls.

121 Brockway, O, 11, K, March 23, ts. f.
1154 Banghart, J, 9 cav, G, May 16, dia. c.
1288 Broman, C, 4, H, May 22, paralysis.
1511 Beckwith, E,‡ 6 cav, I, May 31, ana.
1513 Bishop, C, 27, F, May 31, rhm.
1664 Beard, J, 6, E, June 6, dia.
2004 Bostwick, R S,‡ 2, F, June 15, pna.
2025 Bowerman, R,‡ 22, H, June 17, dia. c.
2201 Bryant, Geo, 6 cav, H, June 17, dys.
2271 Bush, Thomas, 8, A, June 20, dia. c.
2303 Brigham, David, 22, D, June 22, dia. c.
2381 Bowlen, J, 27, E, June 23, dys.
2478 Briggs, I, 6, E, June 25, dia. c.
2595 Berry, Henry, 15, E, June 28, scs.
2700 Broo, F, 22, I, June 30, dia. c.
2946 Bailey, John, 4 cav, M, July 6, dia.
3149 Briggs, W H, 20, G, July 11, dia.
3215 Bibley, J, 3, C, July 12, dia. c.
3479 Brannock, F, 3, C, July 17, dia.
3517 Brush, J, 16, K, July 18, dia.
3531 Bradley, Geo, 17, B, July 18, dia. c.
3591 Bulit, F, 3 art, A, July 19, dia.
3777 Bohnmiller, J, 10 cav, H, July 22, scs.
3798 Beardslee, M A,§ 22, D, July 22, dys.
4109 Billiams, Jno, 2, K, July 27, dia.
4339 Binder, John, 2, A, Aug 30, dia. c.
4395 Brown, G, 4 cav, E, July 31, dia.
4810 Baker, A, 5 cav, F, Aug 5, dia.
5573 Betts, P, 1, C, Aug 14, dys.
8333 Brookiniger, F, 7, D, Sept 10, scs.
5950 Bertan, I, 8 cav, B, Aug 16, mas.
5970 Burnett, J, 7, G, Aug 17, ens.
6013 Burkhart, C,‡ 22, G, Aug 17, scs.
6065 Brower, L F,‡ 17, H, Aug 18, dys.
6290 Bilbey, Geo, 9, E, Aug 20, scs.
6388 Burcham, J, 5, B, Aug 21, scs.
6990 Burdick, Theo, 6 cav, I, Aug 27, dia.
7148 Beirs, S, 18, B, Aug 29, scs
7227 Billingsby, J, 1 bat, Aug 29, dia.
7536 Bradley, B, 9 cav, E, Sept 1, dia.
7796 Blair, John, 7, E, Sept 4, dys.
7932 Barr, W,§ 8 cav, L, Sept 5, brs,
8391 Brown, H S, 8 cav, I, Sept 10, dia. c.
8505 Bradley, E,§ 11, K, Sept 12, dia.
8814 Blanchard, Jas, 7, G, Sept 15, scs.
8869 Brown, A, 3, G, Sept 15, dia.
9226 Beckley, W, 1 cav, E, Sept 19, wds.
9240 Brown, H, 13, A, Sept 19, scs.
9305 Beebe, John,‡ 1, A, Sept 20, dia. c.
9430 Baker, John, 1 cav, H, Sept 21, scs.
9545 Birdsey, J, 7, D, Sept 23, scs.
9553 Barber, J M,‡ 26, C, Sept 23, scs.
9637 Baxter, S, 6 cav, L, Sept 24, scs.
9890 Batt, W H, 6 cav, L, Sept 27, dia. c.
9834 Bunker, R B, 1, D, Sept 27, scs.
9853 Barnard, G,‡ 7 cav, M, Sept 27, scs.
9866 Beekley, L, 10, F, Sept 27, scs.
10044 Barney, H, 17, D, Sept 29, scs.
10340 Blackburn, Jas, 5, G, Oct 4, dia.
10490 Bentley, H, 24, I, Oct 7, scs.
10835 Bittman, J, 1 cav, C, Oct 13, scs.
11275 Baldwin, L A, 24, B, Oct 22, scs.
12130 Beck, G, 1 cav, H, Nov 23, scs.
12162 Bennett, W L, 26, G, Nov 26, scs.
12187 Barnett, I, 2, E, Nov 28, dia.
12745 Bearves, M, 15, G, Oct 7, dia. c.

34 Colan, Fred, 17, F, Feb 9, pna.
210 Chilcote, Jas C, 20, G. Feb 28, dia. c.
398 Chambers, J R,§ 5 cav, ..., April 5, dia. c.
439 Cowill, Ed, 8 cav, G, April 8, nes.
593 Cowell, John, 10 cav, H, April 15, des.
937 Conrad, Edson, 8 cav, G, May 12, dys.
1077 Cripper, G F, 5 cav, C, May 14, ana.
1164 Coastner, J D, 5 cav, L, May 16, dys.
1330 Chapman, H, 5 cav, E, May 24, pna.
1351 Cameron, Jas,§ 27, H, May 25, scs.

1505 Constank, John, 9, B, May 21, dia.
1692 Cronkwhite, John, 22, K, June 7, dia. c.
1711 Cook, J, 4 cav, D, June 7, dia. c.
1811 Churchward, A R, 9, C, June 10, dia. c.
1943 Clear, James, 22, F, June 14, dia. c.
2617 Cussick, B, 7, C, June 28, dys.
3071 Collins, James, 5, I, July 9, dia. c.
3462 Cartney, A, 2 cav, E, July 17, ana.
3595 Cameron, D,§ 1 cav, L, July 19, dys.
3800 Cummings, W, 2, F, July 22, ana.
3989 Clements, Wm, 1 s s, C, July 26, dys.
4032 Cook, J, 10, F, July 26, dia. c.
4620 Cronk, James, 5 cav, G, Aug 3, dia.
4920 Cooper, J, 7, K, Aug 6, dia. c.
4956 Curtis, M D, 8, C, Aug 7, scs.
5201 Crunch, J, 1 cav, Aug 10, ses.
5685 Cummings, D, 5 cav, I, Aug 15, scs.
5686 Churchill, G W, 3, A, Aug 15, dia.
5905 Carr, C B, 25, K, Aug 16, dia. c.
6263 Coft, James, 20, F, Aug 20, scs.
6285 Cobb, G, 4, D, Aug 20, dia. c.
6446 Cook, George, 10 cav, H, Aug 22, des.
6904 Cahon, W J, 1, H, Aug 26, ana.
7094 Carp, J S,§ 1, K, Aug 28, phs.
7164 Caten, M, 7 cav, E, Aug 29, dys.
7496 Cling, Jacob, 2, K, Sept 1, scs.
7534 Campbell, S B, 2, H, Sept 1, dia.
7883 Coldwell, W,‡ 124, H, Sept 5, dia.
8406 Cope, J B, 17, A, Sept 11, dia. c.
8993 Cornice, J D, 7, F, Sept 17, dia.
9341 Carver, J H, 4 cav, Sept 20, scs.
10644 Cooley, G, 3, A, Oct 9, dys.
10759 Clago, S,§ 7, C, Oct 12, scs.
10788 Crain, R O, 17, A, Oct 12, scs.
10871 Cooley, Henry, 34, G, Oct 13, scs.
11743 Collins, C, 2, K, Nov 2, scs.
11903 Clark, G W,§ 1 art, C, Nov 7, scs.
12143 Cameron, F, 17, E, Nov 24, scs.
12258 Cook, N, 1, K, Dec 10, scs.
12391 Case, S,‡ 5 cav, L, Jan 4, scs.
12474 Coras, E, 6 cav, C, Jan 17, dia.
12634 Chambers, W, 8 cav, G, Feb 10, dia. c.

1345 Davis, Wilson, 8, A, May 24, pna.
43 Diets, John, 6 cav, I, Feb 14, dia.
195 Dunay, John, 6, C, Feb 27, brs.
315 Deas, Abe, 7 cav, L, April 2, dia.
716 Decker, L, 10, H, April 24, dia.
1270 Drummond, John, 27, E, May 21, dia.
1292 Dolf, Sylvanus, 27, G, May 23, dia.
1296 Dentor, W A, 5 cav, E, May 23, dia. c.
1683 Dougherty, D, 8, C, June 6, dia.
2090 Demerie, D, 1 bat, June 17, dia.
2248 Dillingham, W O,‡ 20, I, June 20, ana.
2683 Dennison, H, 5 cav, G, June 30, des.
2882 Dreal, D, 2 cav, B, July 4, ts. f.
3207 Dusalt, A, 17, H, July 12, dia. c.
3314 Dyre, Wm, 17, B, July 14, dys. c.
3610 Davy, R, 22, C, July 19, dia. c.
3619 De Realt, F, 5, C, July 20, dys.
4660 Decker, G S,‡ 5 cav, K, Aug 3, dys.
4669 Darct, S, 5, I, Aug 4, dys.
4670 Dugan, D, 21, I, Aug 4, dia.
5070 Dawson, D, 17, H, Aug 8, dia. c.
5351 Dalzell, Wm, 6, A, Aug 10, dia.
5666 Dolph, S, 8, B, Aug 14, scs.
6225 Duinz, G W, 5 cav, I, Aug 20, dys.
6401 Denton, G, 5, E, Aug 21, dys.
7654 Derfly, Wm, 1, H, Sept 3, dia.
7769 Dumont, W, 36, H, Sept 4, dys.
8651 Daly, A,‡ 7 cav, E, Sept 13, dia.
9995 Dyer, J, 5, I, Sept 29, scs.
10161 Doap, M, 1 cav, L, Oct 1, scs.
10922 Dixon, John, 5 cav, L, Oct 14, scs.
11125 Dennis, C, 1, H, Oct 18, dia. c.
12124 Dunroe, P I, 24, H, Oct 22, scs.
12574 Drake, O, 22, D, Feb 2, dia.

2850 Egsillim, P H, 22, K, July 4, brs.
5318 Eggleston, Wm, 7 cav, E, Aug 10, dia. s
3981 Elliot, J, 24, G, July 26, scs.
1210 Eaton, R, 22, H, May 19, scs.

1240 El is, E, 2 cav, B, May 20, dia. c.
2788 Ensign, J, 11, A, July 2, dia.
7901 Edwards, S, 6, E, Sept 5, dia.
8255 Edmonds, B, 1, H, Sept 9, dia.
11065 English, James, 17, B, Oct 17, scs.
5817 Everett, J, 77, K, Aug 16, dia.

890 Force, F, 27, D, May 5, dia. c.
1064 Fitzpatrick, M, 1 cav, B, May 13, brs.
1367 Folk, C, 14, E, May 25, des.
2197 Fitse, T, 1 cav, C, June 19, dia. c.
2252 Fairbanks, J, 15 cav, G, June 20, dia. c.
2343 Face, W H, 6, June 23, dia.
4194 Fisher, F, 22, G, June 29, dip.
5081 Farmer, M, 22, D, Aug 8, dia. c.
5861 Flanigan, John, 5, D, Aug 16, mas.
6135 Farnham, A, 5, A, Aug 19, dia.
6363 Fox, James, 3, H, Aug 21, dia.
6680 Fritchei, M, 22, G, Aug 24, scs.
6983 Fitzpatrick, M, 8, E, Aug 27, dia.
7027 Fox, Charles, 1, B, Aug 27, dia.
7060 Forsythe, H, 5, F, Aug 28, phs.
7171 Forbs, C, 1 cav, B, Aug 29, scs.
8586 Fethton, F, 1 cav, G, Sept 12, scs.
10275 Fliflin, H, 27, F, Oct 3, scs.
11500 Freeman, B, 1 s s, Oct 26, scs.
11709 Fredenburg, F, 7, Nov 1, dia. c.
12688 Findlater, H, 7 cav, C, Feb 22, dia.
12845 Frederick, G, 9, G, April 23, dia.
8250 Face, C, 1 s s, B, Sept 9, scs.
11509 Fox, W, 22, E, Oct 26, scs.

145 Goodenough, G M, 23, K, Mar 25, dia. c.
566 Grover, James, 20, H, April 15, des.
784 Grippman, J, 5 cav, M, April 28, ts. f.
956 Graham, Geo W, 5, C, May 8, dys.
1049 Goodbold, Wm, 2 cav, L, May 12, dia.
1131 German, E, 13, H, May 16, asc.
1234 Garrett, S H, 2 cav, G, May 20, dia. c.
1927 Grimley, James, 22, D, June 14, dys.
2192 Ganigan, J, 9 cav, L, June 19, dia. c.
2614 Gorden, Jas, 1, D, June 28, dia.
2862 Gilbert, F, 3, K, July 3, scs.
2928 Gibbons, M, 6, C, July 5, dia. c.
3863 Goodman, W, 5, I, July 24, ana.
4092 Griffin, G, 11, H, July 27, scs.
4225 Green, E, 11, H, July 29, dys. c.
5716 Galrin, M, 23, I, Aug 15, scs.
6482 Greek, C H, 1 cav, K, Aug 22, dia. c.
6866 Gillis, Jno, 4 cav, F, Aug 26, dia. c.
7476 Gaines, A, 22, F, Sept 1, scs.
7518 Guilz, H, 1, A, Sept 1, scs.
7624 Griens, G D, 8, I, Sept 2, dia. c.
7659 Graff, Jacob, 17, H, Sept 3, dia.
7741 Gibson, J, 1, K, Sept 3, scs.
7968 Grant, A H, 7, D, Sept 6, scs.
8628 Gray, George, 1 cav, E, Sept 13, scs.
10671 Gallett, L, 22, F, Oct 9, scs.
10726 Gibbs, J, 7, B, Oct 11, scs.
11207 Gask, I, 8 cav, C, Oct 20, wds.
11302 Gray, James, 6 cav, A, Oct 22, scs.
11352 Groucher, J, 6 cav, B, Oct 23, scs.
11647 Grabaugh, J, 5, G, Oct 30, scs.
12164 Gifford, L, 6, 1, Nov 26, scs.
12443 Gowell, N, 19, F, Jan 12, scs.
12573 Goodel, M, 5, C, Feb 2, dia.
5818 Gurmane, B S, 77, K, Aug 16, dia.
4511 Grasman, E, 23, I, Aug 1, dia. c.
12207 Gabulison, J, 5 cav, F, Dec 1, dia. c.

6 Hall, William, 2 cav, M, Feb 5, pna.
339 Holton, S M, 1, B, April 20, dys.
367 Henry, James, 8, A, April 5, pna.
409 Hartsell, Geo, 7 cav, B, April 6, dia. c.
818 Hutton, S, 9 cav, G, April 30, dia. c.
860 Hood, Jas D, 22, H, May 3, dia.
947 Hart, J R, 6, E, May 7, ana.
1452 Hannah, Jno, 22, C, May 29, ana.
1519 Hunter, F A, 22, F, May 31, ana.
1656 Herriman, D, 22, D, June 6, dia.
1738 Huntley, W, 5 cav, E, June 8, dia. c.
1813 Haines, R, 9 cav, G, June 10, dia. c.

1904 Hough, M, 22, June 13, dia. c.
1910 Harty, J S, 16, F, June 13, dia. c.
2660 Hays, C, 6, H, June 29, dia.
3015 Hardy, Jno, 4, H, July 7, dia.
3040 Hughey, James, 17, B, July 8, dia c.
3206 Hopkins, N, 6 cav, E, July 12, dia c.
4 Halson, David, 8 cav, A, March 27, s. p.
3343 Heil, H, 9, G, July 15, scs.
3483 Honsigner, W L, 7, C, July 17, dia. c.
3889 Hance, C, bugler, 7, D, July 24, dia. c.
3927 Hawkins, George, 12, H, July 25, dia.
4166 Hunter, M W, 22, D, July 28, dys.
4286 Heron, Jno, 5, F, July 30, dia.
4426 Heath, M, 21, C, July 31, dia.
4674 Hale, S B, 7 cav, D, Aug 4, dys.
5332 Hollen, Geo, 1 cav, L, Aug 11, dia.
5370 Haynes, P, 1 cav, H, Aug 11, dys.
5376 Husted, J, 10, C, Aug 10, dia.
5556 Henrich, J, 3, C, Aug 13, scs.
5931 Hall, W, 26, I, Aug 17, dia. c.
6110 Holmes, J F, 42, H, Aug 18, scs.
6276 Hibler, A, 9 cav, D, Aug 20, mas.
6992 Henry, A, 27, B, Aug 27, dia.
6998 Hungerford, C, 20, E, Aug 27, dia.
6999 Hunt, L, 2, C, Aug 27, dia. c.
8100 Holcomb, J, 6 cav, K, Sept 7, dys.
8624 Harrington, G, 6 cav, D, Sept 13, dia. c.
9233 Hawley, C, 4, F, Sept 19, dia.
9686 Hartman, H, 29, A, Sept 24, dia.
9968 Hinkley, G C, 20, F, Sept 28, dia.
10348 Hoag, J M, 20, H, Oct 5, scs.
11027 Hankins, E, 5, E, Oct 16, scs.
11057 Hayes, James, 1, E, Oct 17, scs.
11070 Haywood, J B, 1 cav, H, Oct 17, scs.
11260 Hamlin, J H, 1 s s, K, Oct 20, scs.
11336 Hoag, J M, 20, H, Oct 23, scs.
11412 Hill, W, 1 s s, Oct 24, scs.
11480 Howard, F S, 8, E, Oct 26, scs.
11593 Hawk, H L, 24, I, Oct 28, scs.
11757 Hodges, M, 22, 1, Nov 3, scs.
11835 Hilmer, C, 6 cav, M, Nov 5, scs.
12067 Howe, J, 7 cav, F, Nov 17, scs.
12612 Hicks, C, 8, B, Feb 8, dia. c.
9718 Harper, D, 3, E, Sept 25, dia.

5141 Ingraham, W L, 5 cav, B, Aug 9, scs.

1817 Jackson, James, 7, I, June 7, dia. c.
2576 Jones, A, 6, E, June 27, scs.
3564 Jagnet, E B, 7 cav, C, July 19, dia. c.
3621 Jackson, Geo G, 22, F, July 20, scs.
4736 Johnson, J H, 7, G, Aug 4, scs.
6578 Johnson, J, 24, I, Aug 23, dia. c.
7520 Jump, D O, 1, A, Sept 1, dys.
7753 Johnson, H, 9 cav, L, Sept 2, dia. c.
9746 Jackland, C, 8 cav, E, Sept 25, dia. c.
12010 Jamieson, H, 5 cav, H, Nov 14, scs.
12396 Jondro, M, 1, K, Jan 5, dia.
12463 Johnson, A, 5, C, Jan 16, dia.

368 King, Leander, 8, G, April 5, dia. a.
488 Keintzler, R, 5 cav, F, April 12, dys.
706 Karl, Wm, 2, A, April 24, dys.
4140 Klunder, Charles, 5 cav, F, July 28, dia
4397 Kennedey, H, 27, H, July 31, scs.
4424 Kinney, Jno, 17, H, July 31, dia.
4728 Kendall, W, 6, D, Aug 4, dia.
8289 Kessler, J, 11, G, Sept 9, dys.
10789 Kinsell, George, 5 cav, B, Oct 12, scs.
10908 Kenkham, H C, 5 cav, H, Oct 14, scs.
12431 Kenney, C, 5 cav, H, Jan 11, scs.

1882 Lewis, F L, 9 cav, June 12, dia. c.
223 Lossing, Jno, 8 cav, B, March 29, pna.
960 Loring, Jno, 27, E, May 8, hep.
1187 Lewis, P, 5, D, May 18, dys.
1301 Lancreed, M, 14, B, May 23, dia. c.
37 Lumer, Jno, 17, F, March 28, s. p.
3303 Lanning, H B, 22, H, July 14, dia.
3700 Lyon, A D, 5 cav, G, July 21, ana.
4243 Lonsey, L, 1 cav, L, July 29, dia. c.
4913 Luce, F, 1 art, A, Aug 6, scs.

30   **Federal Soldiers who Died at Andersonville, Georgia Confederate Prison**

****

VIEW OF THE ANDERSONVILLE GRAVEYARD,

As the Rebels left it, containing the remains of nearly 14,000 victims to rebel barbarity. Taken from Rebel Photographs in possession of the publishers.

"Carrying away the dead to their final rest was but a horror in keeping with the scenes described, and a fitting climax to the life of misery which ended in the prison."

4992 Lu Duk, Jas, 17, G, Aug 7, dia.
5142 Larke, J A, 23, F, Aug 9, scs.
5216 Lowell, Jas, 7 cav, E, Aug 10, dia. c.
5776 Laribee, L, 8, H, Aug 15, brs.
5923 Lofler, E E, 1 , H, Aug, 17, dia.
6667 Lord, M,§ 3, M, Aug 24, dys.
8085 Leamon, G, 8 cav, H, Sept 7, scs.
9685 Lard, H O, 22, D, Sept 24, dia.
9760 Lund, Jas, 6 cav, H, Sept 25, scs.
10877 Laidham, G, 1, D, Oct 13, dia.
11969 Lutz, Wm, 6 cav, F, Nov 11, scs.

218 McCartney, H, 6 cav, K, March 29, dia. c.
268 McGuire, Jno, 20, A, March 31, ts. f.
542 Markham, D, 5 cav, B, April 14, pna.
612 McCarter, Jas, 22, H, April 14, dia.
1059 Mum, A F, 27, F, May 13, dia.
1062 Miller, Charles, 5 cav, D, May 13, dia.
1710 Miller, J, 3, C, June 7, dia. c.
2255 Maby, Ed, 8 cav, K, June 20, des.
2586 McDowell, J, 8 cav, F, June 28, scs.
2759 McSpoulding, W, 22, E, July 2, dia. c.
2828 Manwaring, Wm, 22, D, July 3, dia. c.
2976 Man, Thos G, 5, A, July 7, dia.
3090 Marshall, H E, 27, B, July 9, ana.
3150 Morris, A T, 14, K, July 9, dia.
3537 Marvey, Andrew, 17, G, July 18, dys.
3697 Miller W E, 2, K, July 21, ts. f.
3936 McCabe, F, 22, H, July 25, dys.
3954 Morgan, M, 2, E, July 26, scs.
4078 McFall, H, 17, E, July 27, dia. c.
4144 Miller, G, 5, I, July 28, dia.
4204 Mouny, Jno, 5 cav, L, July 30, dia.
4783 Monroe, D, 6 cav, A, Aug 4, dia.
4942 Morgan, E C, 23, G, Aug 7, scs.
5153 Miller, L, 7, F, Aug 9, scs.
5630 Mench, C,§ 20, I, Aug 14, dia.
6249 McCarty, Charles, 26, I, Aug 20, dys.
6229 Meyers, J, 6, H, Aug 21, dia.
6820 Myer, J, 4, I, Aug 25, scs.
7114 Moore, J, 27, B, Aug 28, i. f.
7269 Merrill, S B, 5, G, Aug 30, scs.
7279 McLaine, Thos, 1, I, Aug 30, dia.
7473 McCloud, A, 21, I, Sept 1, scs.
7513 Mason, F, 7 cav, L, Sept 1, scs.
7918 Martin, Peter, 17, H, Sept 5, dys.
7936 Musket, J, 4 cav, K, Sept 5, dia.
7962 Miller, F, 22, G, Sept 6, dia.
8025 Mundy, E, 17, G, Sept 6, ts. f.
8387 McClure, R, 7, D, Sept 9, dia.
8518 Miles, C S,‡ 1 cav, F, Sept 12, scs.
8590 McGinis, P, 16, Sept 12, scs.
8650 McKay, K, 10, Sept 6, dia.
8876 Munson, H C, 30, E, Sept 16, scs.
8897 Morrison, J, 21, F, Sept 16, scs.
8994 Maher, S L, 7 cav, I, Sept 17, dia.
9185 Marine, Wm, 22, E, Sept 18, ana.
9750 McArthur, W,§ 7 cav, D, Sept 25, scs.
9791 Moore, John, 6 cav, G, Sept 26, scs.
10011 Moses, C, 5 cav, I, Sept 29, scs.
10134 Moses, A, 6 cav, M, Oct 1, dia.
10423 Migele, J, 9, A, Oct 6, scs.
10575 Mays, Thos, 6 cav, H, Oct 9, dia.
10958 McMillen, Alex, 5 cav, M, Sept 14, scs
11126 Miller, Jno A, 10, F, Oct 13, dia. c.
11536 Molosh, F, 3, D, Oct 27, scs.
11548 McMann, W, 17, A, Oct 27, scs.
11582 Mongby, D, 22, C, Oct 28, scs.
11798 Merrill, C, 4, K, Nov 4, scs.
12085 Miller, H, 9, A. Nov 18, scs.
12093 Magram, J, 1 s s, Nov 19, dia.
12252 McCame, W, 7, B, Dec 9, scs.
12458 Morton, J, 1, I, Jan 15, dia.
11511 Mackswarer, W, 1 s s, K, Oct 26, scs.
12674 Marshall, G, 4, M, Feb 19, dia. c.
12733 McNiell, C, 8 cav, M, March 5, dia. c.
3790 Major, Wm, 22, D, July 22, scs.
7916 Monroe, Jno, 7, I, Sept 5, dys.
9791 Moor, Jno, 6 cav, G, Sept 26, scs.
9985 McClary, W, 7 cav, H, Sept 28, dia.

513 Nicholson, E, 6 cav, G, April 12, dia. c.

1209 Newbury, Jas, cav, A, May 19, td. f.
2077 Nash, Charles, 22, H, June 17, dia. c.
3343 Nail, H,§ 9, F, June 15, pna.
4102 Neck, H, 4, K, July 27, dia.
5092 Nirthhammer, J, 20, D, Aug 8, scs.
5400 Nagle, C, 11, G, Aug 11, scs.
5493 Narrane, A, 17, E, Aug 13, scs.
11011 Noyes, Jas E, 1, Oct 16, dia. c.
11911 Niland, H, 8, D, Nov 9, dia.
1005 Nurse, H W, 5 cav, L, May 10, dia.
9812 Northam, O H, 6, M, Sept 26, dia.

285 O'Brien, Austin, 9 cav, H, April 1, pna.
499 Oliver, Alex, 8 cav, G, April 12, dia. c.
1189 Orrison, George, 9 cav, M, May 18, dys
2267 Olney, G W, 4, A, June 20, dia. c.
4384 Osborn, S, 27, B, July 31, scs.
4874 Overmeyer, J F, 6 cav, E, Aug 6, scs.
5574 O'Neil, J, 22, K, Aug 14, dys.
5846 Orcutt, C, 3, F, Aug 16, ens.
8141 Ornig, S W, 20, C, Sept 8, dia.
8511 O'Brian, W H,§ 7 cav, A, Sept 12, dia.
9041 Ogden, E S, 5 cav, M, Sept 17, scs.
11940 O'Leary, J,‡ 1 s s, H, Nov 9, dia.
11999 Osborn, J L, 6, E, Nov 13, scs.
12500 Oathart, D, 18, C, Jan. 17, dia. c.

443 Parsons, G, 7, I, April 9, dia.
515 Pullman, Geo, 5, I, April 12, dia. c.
1033 Parker, B C,§ 8 cav, C, May 12, dys.
1276 Perigo, John, 2 cav, D, May 22, pls.
1374 Parish, Thos, 6, I, May 26, dys.
1892 Paisley, A G,§ 22, June 13, dia.
1997 Payne, R H, 6, I, June 15, dia. c.
2533 Piffer, J, 6 cav, I, June 26, dia.
3546 Pierson, Daniel, 3 cav, C, July 18, dia.
3594 Palmerly, J, 7 cav, C, July 19, dia. c.
4100 Post, R L, 10, H, July 27, dia.
4253 Pratt, M, 22, E, July 29, scs.,
4486 Pelton, A,‡ 21, A, Aug 1, pna.
4662 Philbrook, F, 1 art, Aug 3, phs.
5056 Podroff, D, 13, D, Aug 8, ana.
5546 Peck, J H,‡ 1 cav, D, Aug 13, ana.
5612 Pond, C, 1, I, Aug 14, dia.
5745 Pettibone, E E, 7, D, Aug 15, dys.
4584 Porter, L, 1 s s, C, Aug 2, phs.
5760 Pentecost, W G, 18, Aug 15, scs.
5852 Palmer, D, 5, D, Aug 16, mas.
7389 Parks, V, 7, C, Aug 31, scs.
7354 Perrin, N, 8 cav, B, Aug 31, c. f.
7960 Parks, F, 5 cav, E, Sept 6, wds.
8195 Pearmell, J,‡ 23, B, Sept 8, scs.
8636 Pike, B H,‡ 2 cav, C, Sept 13, dia.
8986 Plant, Wm, 16, G, Sept 16, dia. c.
9331 Pharrett, Wm, 22, D, Sept 20, scs.
11046 Platt, R, 22, A, Oct 17, scs.
11177 Palmer, P, 5, H, Oct 19, scs.
11986 Preston, B, 7, K, Nov 13, scs.
12273 Plins, Wm, 5 cav, C, Dec 12, scs.
12409 Preston, J, 6, C, Jan 7, scs.
12578 Pratt, L, 8 cav, C, Feb 3, dia. c.
12762 Parmalee, C,‡ 8 cav, M, Feb 12, pls.

77 Roloff, Jno, 5 cav, E, March 20, ts. f.
324 Russell, Peter, 23, G, April 2, dia.
623 Rowland, B, 6, M, April 19, dia.
922 Robinson, Wm, 2, H, May 6, dia,
1804 Rhinehart, D, 5 cav, C, June 16, dia. c
2291 Rolland, J, 6, G, June 21, dia.
2402 Ruggles, O, 32, H, June 24, dia. a.
3296 Rassan, A, 28, I, July 14, dys.
3732 Riley, Charles, 6, I, July 21, dia.
3740 Riggs, J, 22, I, July 21, dia.
3876 Russ, W J,‡ 22, C, July 24, dia.
5176 Rood, C, 22, C, Aug 9, dia.
5885 Roman, John, 5, C, Aug 16, dia. c.
6154 Relu, A, 17, G, Aug 19, scs.
5707 Ryan, W, 1, E, Sept 1, dia.
7750 Robinson, H, 5 cav, L, Sept 2, dia.
7955 Rich, A, 11, B, Sept 6, dia.
8617 Riley, Miles,‡ 7 cav, F, Sept 13, scs.
9254 Rimer, J C, 1 cav, C, Sept 19, scs.

****

9914 Ryan, T, 22, I, Sept 28, scs.
10136 Robinson, T, 27, F, Oct 1, scs.
10380 Randall, H D, 6, D, Oct 5, dia.
11151 Riley, R,§ 24, H, Oct 19, dys.
11457 Ramsey, J,§ 5, H, Oct 25, scs.
11675 Raley, H, 24 cav, L, Oct 30, scs.
11705 Ricott, S, 1 s s, K, Nov 1, scs.
12553 Richardson, M B, 1, L, Jan 29, scs.
12589 Rodgers, W, 26, G, Feb 5, des.
12740 Robbins, A, 4 cav, H, March 6, pls.
12745 Reaves, M, 15, G, March 8, **dia.** z.

134 Snyder, E, 17, F, March 24, brs.
172 Smith, Wm, 7 cav, L, March 26, pna.
236 Soper, Calvin, 27, H, March 29, ts. f.
330 Sheldon, H S, 1, A, April 2, dia.
520 Shannon, Jno, 20, H, April 13, dia. c.
842 Smith, W W,‡ 5 cav, D, May 2, dia.
854 Stillman, L D, 6, M, May 3, dys.
1082 Stuck, L H, 2 cav, B, May 14, dia. c.
1328 Schemerhorn, J, 7 cav, C, May 24, dia.
1406 Samborn, H, 22, K, May 27, dia.
1446 Snow, Levi, 20, H, May 28, ana.
1626 Smith, A, 1 cav, L, June 4, ana.
1801 Smith, S, 17, C, June 10, dia. c.
1741 Stevens, S,‡ 22, K, June 8, dia.
1948 Shafer, W, 22, G, June 14, **dia.**
1966 Strickland, Thos, 10, E, June 14, dia.
2239 Sanburn, H, 22, K, June 20, dia.
2507 Smith, C, 1 art, E, June 26, dia.
2651 Sarmyes, C, 24, C, June 29, dia. c.
2664 Stevens, L, 6 cav, M, June 29, dia.
2685 Stewart, C A, 7, F, June 30, dia.
2807 Sprague, W B, 11, I, July 3, dys.
2986 Shaw, F N, 2, K, July 7, ana.
3001 Steele, E,§ 2 cav, C, July 7, dia. c.
3085 Sibley, J E, 1, G, July 9, dia.
3353 Stubbs, J, 9 cav, L, July 15, pna.
3518 Simpson, E T, 6 art, G, July 18, dia.
3524 Shultz, C, 5, B, July 18, dia. c.
3544 Shummay, Wm, 8 cav, L, July 18, scs.
3942 Shaw, F F, 7, D, July 25, scs.
3951 Sharp, Jas, 6, July 25, scs.
4103 Stines, H, 4, K, July 27, dia.
4311 Sprague, B, 7 cav, E, July 30, dia.
4433 Sale, Thos, 17, G, July 31, ana.
4859 Smith, Wm, 17, H, Aug 6, dys.
5193 Swain, D, 6 cav, H, Aug 10, dys.
5972 Stow, George, 10, C, Aug 17, ens.
6323 Simpson, T, 8, I, Aug 21, dia.
6506 Simons, A, 17, B, Aug 22, dia. c.
6686 Smoke, H B, 6, H, Aug 24, dia.
7014 Sullivan, Jno, 27, E, Aug 27, sys.
7303 Sherman, Fred, 22, G, Aug 30, dia.
7350 Sayrrer, J M, 1, G, Aug 31, dia.
7528 Schofield, C, 27, G, Sept 1, dys.
7676 Satterley, H J, 6 cav, E, Sept 2, dia. c.
8000 Sutherand, J, 1, I, Sept 6, scs.
8580 Stanning, G W,‡ 5 art, G, Sept 12, dia. c.
9100 Suthphar, H W, 15, F, Sept 18, dia.
9469 Stewart, F, 6 cav, E, Sept 21, scs.
9481 Steward, W V, 5, E, Sept 21, ana.
9629 Snyder, J, 5 cav, M, Sept 24, dia.
10080 Straut, C A, 5 cav, F, Sept 30, dia.
10117 Spencer, George, 21, H, Oct 1, scs.
10254 Sammonds, A,§ 7, E, Oct 3, scs.
10285 Spencer, Jno, 2, I, Oct 3, scs.
10417 Skull, Wm, 7, B, Oct 6, dia.
10444 Simpson, J P, 22, A, Oct 7, scs.
11138 Swart, M M, 3, F, Oct 19, scs.
11148 Swesler, C,§ 5, K, Oct 19, scs.
11234 Sutton, H, 22, I, Oct 21, wds.
11265 Strander, A, 6, G, Oct 21, dia.
11354 Stoddard, S, 5 cav, F, Oct 23, scs.
11701 Steadman, S, 10, H, Oct 30, scs.
11717 Smith, S, 7, H, Nov 1, scs.
11773 Sickles, M, 14, I, Nov 3, dia. c.
12020 Seeley, H, 6 cav, B, Nov 15, scs.
1225 Spondle, C, 1 cav, C, Dec 5, dys.
12229 Sumner, H, 27, B, Dec 6, scs.
12261 Stedman, S D, 10, H, Dec 11, scs.

12310 South, Peter, 1 s s, K, Dec 19, **dia.**
12678 Smith, C B, 8 cav, L, Feb 19, dia. c.
12803 Smith, Geo, 8, B, March 20, dia.
12254 Stickner, J, 16, D, Dec 10, scs.
11508 Sockem, A, 1 s s, K, Oct 26, scs.
11510 Springer, J, 7 cav, K, Oct 26, scs.

1304 Turrell, Henry, 22, H, May 23, dia. c.
2945 Tubbs, P, 7, K, July 6, dia.
48 Tilt, George, 2 cav, D, May 24, s. p.
3498 Thatcher, E H, 6 cav, F, July 18, **dia.**
6703 Tompkins, N R, 1, B, Aug 24, dia.
7009 Tift, H, 5 cav, M, Aug 27, dia.
7544 Thompson, W, 8, F, Sept 2, dia. c.
7599 Tracy, D, 7 cav, K, Sept 2, dia.
7797 Thompson, M C, 5 cav, I, Sept 4, dys.
9103 Taylor, H, 32, F, Sept 18, dys.
11118 Taylor, J M, 11, A, Oct 18, scs.
11148 Twesler, C,§ 5, K, Oct 19, scs.

3945 Udell, W O, 2, D, July 25, dia.

731 Vanderhoof, Jas, 6 cav, G, April 25, dys.
1126 Vangieson, L,§ 5 cav, D, May 15, nes.
1467 Vogle, Jacob, 27, D, May 29, dia.
2270 Van Dyke, Jno, 6 cav, D, June 20, pna.
2994 Van Brant, W H, 9 cav, E, July 7, dia. c.
3278 Vanlin, C,§ 6, F, July 14, dia.
6864 Vanshoten, W H, 6 cav, K, Aug 26, **dia.** c
7595 Vansickle, L,§ 5 cav, G, Sept 2, dys.
8958 Vanmaker, F, 16, G, Sept 15, dia. c
9536 Vork, C, 5, K, Sept 22, dia.
9936 Vleight, A, 22, D, Sept 28, scs.
12166 Vanallen, C, 27, K, Nov 26, dys.
12690 Vincient, J, 8, K, Feb 22, dia. c.

340 Whittaker, J, 7, B, April 2, dia.
733 Whipple, G, 4, A, April 25, dia.
741 Wilson, Byron, 5 cav, D, April 26, **dia.**
749 Wright, Wm A, 7, K, April 26, dys. c.
957 Wilson, J, 22, K, May 8, dys.
2102 Wilson, W, 11, I, June 17, dia. c.
4961 Winegardner, A S, 1 cav, K, Aug 7, dys.
12723 White, C, 5, F, March 3, dia. c.
12796 Whitmore, C, 8 eav, M, March 18, scs.
6781 Wiley, E T,‡ 1, E, Aug 25, dys.
749 Wright, Wm A, 7, K, April 26, dys. c.
1089 Woolsey, R, 22, E, May 14, dia. c.
1701 Walker, J, 22, C, June 7, dia.
1920 Wolf, F, 13, E, June 14, dia.
3301 Wentdarbly, ——, 5, G, July 14, **dia.** c.
2899 Whitlock, M, 2, B, July 5, scs.
3180 Willet, S,§ 22, K, July 11, dys.
3269 Wright, W, 5 cav, K, July 13, **dia.**
3437 Wolverton, C, 6, B, July 17, dys.
3992 Woodruff, H, 1 cav, K, July 26, **dia.**
4419 Warren, H, 4, B, July 31, dia.
4860 Walker, Geo, 22, G, Aug 6, scs.
5051 Williams, M, 1, A, Aug 8, dia.
5786 Williams, T, 2 cav, L, Aug 15, **dia.**
11323 Wolfinger, J M, 20, H, Oct 23, scs.
12307 Windlass, S, 8 cav, K, Dec 18, scs.
5559 Warner, C, 5, F, Aug 13, scs.
11096 Warner, J, 5 cav, K, Oct 18, des.
12723 White, C, 5 cav, F, March 3, dia. c.
9844 Wheeler, E, 24, A, Sept 27, scs.
5930 Wisner, Jno,‡ 6 cav, I, Aug 17, dia.
8331 Wood, A O,§ 8 cav, M, Sept 10, scs.
8076 Wilder, H S, 23, K, Sept 7, scs.
6996 Wolverton, J S, 5 cav, A, Aug 27, dia. c
7362 Way, F, 7, C, Aug 31, dia.
7812 Whalen, H,§ 6, I, Sept 4, dys.
7882 Wells, F, 7, F, Sept 5, dia.
9022 Wing, A, 17, G, Sept 17, dia.
9525 Whitworth, W G, 6 cav, A, Sept 22, **dia.**
12796 Whitmore, C, 8 cav, M, March 18, scs.

2910 Yacht, E,§ 22, E, July 5, dys.

2626 Zett, J, 22, D, June 28, scs.

MINNESOTA.

5964 Atkinson, Geo ꓤ, F, March 17, scs.
6567 Adcock, as, 9 B, March 23, i. s.
11977 Abrian, ᴄ, 1, B, Nov 12, scs.

4224 Becker, G, 9, E, July 29, scs.
5715 Barnard. H A, 9, A, Aug 15, scs
6630 Buzton, M, 9, H, Aug 23, dia.
7841 Brese, D, 9, E, Sept 4, dia.
7892 Brayton, J M, 9, B, Sept 5, scs.
8053 Buckley, J F, 9, G, Sept 7, scs.
8253 Burrows, H, 9, K, Sept 9, dia.
9474 Babcock, L A, 9, D, Sept 21, cah.
9800 Besgrove, Isaac, 9, E, Sept 26, dia.
12778 Baker, J G, 1, A, March 15, dia. c.

2747 Conner, P, 11, A, July 1, dia.
3575 Clabaugh, J, 9, D, July 19, r. f.
4111 Conklin, S, 9, I, July 27, dia. c.
6970 Conklin, E, 9, C, July 27, dia.
10724 Cassady, J, 9, F, Oct 6, dia.

7692 Dunham, R H, 9, K, Sept 3, dia. c.
10971 Davis, E J, 9, E, Oct 15, scs.

8517 Fitch, W F, 9, F, Sept 12, dia.
12656 Fuchs, H, 9, D, Feb 14, dia. c.
9905 Freeschelz, F, 9, F, Sept 27, dia. c.

3287 Geer, O, 9, F, July 14, scs.
10401 Goodfellow, E C, 9, D, Oct 6, dys.
10579 Goodwin, Geo, 9, A, Oct 9, dia. c.
4130 Gordon, W C, 17, I, July 28, dys.

6033 Higly, M F, 9, G, Aug 18, dia.
6064 Hill, C J, 9, K, Aug 18, dys.
6605 Handy, J, mus, 9, I, Aug 23, des.
9144 Hearvay, J E, 9, K, Sept 18, dia.
4176 Holts, A, 9, F, July 23, dia.

7809 Johnson, N, 9, H, July 4, dys.

1211 Kerrick, Samuel, 4, K, May 19, dia.
9127 Kloss, L, 9, H, Sept 18, dia.

5079 Lindley, C, 9, B, Aug 8, dia.
7795 Large, M, 9, G, Sept 4, dia.
12165 Lewis, L, 9, K, Nov 26, dys.
12510 Latimore, W H, 9, D, Jan 22, dys.
9312 Lenyer, M, 9, G, Aug 30, dia.

5460 Myers, J, 3, I, Aug 13, dia.
7288 Mander, J W, 9, A, Aug 30, dia.
8180 McDougal, J, 9, A, Sept 8, dia.
9195 Montenary, J, 9, G, Sept 18, dia.

2829 Nichols, John, 15, A, July 3, dia.

7789 Ollman, Wm, 9, B, Sept 4, dia.
8384 Orcutt, J,‡ 2, C, Sept 10, dia.

2841 Pitcher, E, 5, B, July 3, dia.
4813 Packett, C, 9, K, Aug 5, dia.
5506 Pericle, Jacob, 9, H, Aug 13, dys.
5909 Pence, Geo, 9, H, Aug 16, dys.
8353 Poinder, T, 9, B, Sept 10, dys.
8823 Pettijohn, S W, 9, H, Sept 14, dia. c.

4277 Roberts, J G, 9, E, July 29, dia.
5588 Roovin, J, 1, H, Aug 14, scs.
10327 Robertson, John, 9, B, Oct 4, dia.
10715 Reese, Wm, 9, E, Oct 11, dia. c.

5941 Short, M, 9, K, Aug 17, scs.
6216 Sperce, C, 9, G, Aug 20, scs.
6276 Sontor, C, 9, H, Aug 20, mas.
7185 Scheffer, H, 9, G, Aug 20, dia.
12058 Shiver, F,‡ 9, E, Nov 17, scs.
12808 Sarf, Henry, 5, E, March 22, dia.

8408 Thompson, W, 9, A, Sept 11, dia.
10186 Tiltam, N M, 9, B, Oct 1, dia.
11603 Thomas, W R, 9, E, Oct 28, scs.

12106 Ulrin, A,‡ 9, E, Nov 20, scs.

11505 Vanhouse, B A,‡ 9, C, Oct 26, dia. c.
11568 Vittum, E W, 9, B, Oct 27, dys.

986 Wood, Ashley, 2, B, May 9, dia.
3867 Walrich, P, 1, C, July 24, dia. c.
4498 Wheeler, A, 9, C, Aug 1, dia.
4588 Woodbury, Jas, 9, C, Aug 2, dia.
5637 Wilson, F C, 9, E, Aug 14, dia.
8233 Winter, G, 9, H, Sept 9, dys.
8416 Whipple, O C, 9, F, Sept 11, dia.
8459 Westorer, J, 9, E, Sept 11, des.
8777 Warren, E F, mus, 9, A, Sept 14, dia. c

5006 Young, D S, 9, I, Aug 8, dia.

MISSOURI.

28! Burns, John, 17, I, April 1, pna.
1251 Burk, J H, 2, H, May 2, ana.
1464 Buel, J, 4, C, May 29, des.
2217 Bishop, P, 15, I, June 20, dia.
2306 Bloomker, Wm, 2, F, June 22, dia.
4269 Broyer, J, 2, E, July 29, dia. c.
5855 Birley, Peter, 29, I, Aug 16, mas.
8664 Berger, J, 2, I, Sept 13, dia.
8772 Bitter, H, 29, F, Sept 14, dys.
11223 Bullard, James, 19, D, Oct 20, scs
12795 Bates, P, 44, F, March 18, dia. c.

2861 Cling, C, 2, I, July 4, cah.
4328 Clemants, Jas, 2 cav, A, July 30, dia. c.
6532 Cornell, James, 9 cav, H, Aug 23, dia.
12351 Coon, F, 15, K, Dec 28, scs.
12776 Chapman, R, 24, B, March 14, pls.

5260 Dicksen, D, 18, Aug 10, scs.
1641 Daley, M, 10 cav, H, June 5, dia. c.

345 Eddington, G W, 29, A, April 2, dia. c.

3963 Engler, John, 15, B, July 25, dia.

6987 Fogg, B F,§ 1 cav, H, Aug 27, dia.
8633 Folk, L,‡ 18, C, Sept 13, dia.
11266 Fay, J W,‡ 2, K, Sept 21, dia.
12805 Fry, M,‡ 12 cav, L, March 21, scs.
6914 Frick, S,‡ 2, E, Aug 26, dia.

2770 Guffy, R, 18, E, July 2, dia.
3725 Gallegher, F, 2, G, July 21, dia.

226 Houston, W E, 18, E, March 29, pna.
4505 Hunter, W, 1 cav, H, Aug 1, scs.
4568 Hartman, V, 29, G, Aug 2, scs.
4727 Huntsley, A,§ 22, H, Aug 4, scs.
7064 Haginey, F, 2, K, Aug 28, scs.
226 Houston, W E, 18, E, March 29, pna.
1552 Head, B J, 26, B, June 2, ana.
2655 Heltgen, G, 12, E, June 29, dys.
8026 Hasse, John, 14 cav, L, Sept 6, td. f.
9042 Hamilton, W,‡ 31, A, Sept 17, dia. c.
11941 Hanahan, A, 29, B, Nov 9, scs.

4440 Isenhour, J, 9, I, July 31, dys.

5709 Keyan, M, 2, D, Aug 15, dia.
7414 Keller, A, 29, H, Aug 31, dia.
8178 Kline, C S,§ 2, F, Sept 8, scs.
10546 Kaunst, H, 18, G, Oct 9, scs.
12221 Keller, I, 40, H, April 1, dia. c.
7713 Kuhn, Jacob, 15, E, Sept 3, des.

8249 Lowe, John, 18, E, July 13, dia.
4803 Lewilley, Wm, 29, K, Aug 5, scs.
7035 Lang, C, 10 cav, B, Aug 27, dia.
12232 Litch, J, 4, A, Dec 6, scs.
5401 Lindsay, J, 18, A, Aug 12, scs.

7438 Miller, W, 4 cav, E, Sept 1, dia.
8913 Morgan, E,‡ 12 cav, F, Sept 16, td. f.
11035 Manning, S H,§ 30, A, Oct 16, scs.
12459 Menzt, W, 15, G, Jan 15, scs.
12706 Martin, J, 44, H, Feb 27, des.
12754 McGuire, O, 2 cav, I, March 12, dia. c.
12760 McDowell, J, 2, F, March 12, dia. c.

3456 Newkirk, Charles, 15, F, July 17, dia. c.
3539 Neclout, W, 2, E, July 18, dia. a.
4169 Nelson, John, 29, A, July 28, dia.

12774 O'Dell, E, 44, B, March 14, des.

12823 Purcell, J R, 44, G, April 5, dia.
755 Phillips, Pat, 11, E, April 27, dys.
25 Payne, Joseph,‡ 29, A, April 16, s. p.
4978 Perkins, A H, 29, L, Aug 7, scs.
6732 Plasmine, A, 26, D, Aug 24, dia.
10539 Plumer, E D, 24, B, Oct 8, dia.

1348 Reilly, P, 29, B, May 25, rhm.
3540 Riddle, F, 8, D, July 18, dia.
5110 Ritteman, Jno, 15, F, Aug 9, scs.
6915 Remers, J, 4, G, Aug 26, dia.
2422 Robertson, J C, 10 cav, F, June 25, dia. c.

1424 Schenck, Philip, 15, B, May 26, dia.
1478 Seebel, A, 12, G, May 30, dia.
1623 Search, Henry, 15, D, June 4, dia.
2464 Stickle, D, 4, D, June 24, scs.
2480 Stofacke, F, 15, D, June 25, dia. c.
28 Stiner, Gotlieb, 29, A, April 17, s. p.
5239 Stormn, F, 58, E, Aug 9, dia.
5667 Schmas, G, 15, G, Aug 14, nes.
6856 Segin, C,§ 2, H, Aug 26, dia.
6930 Shuman, Joseph, 1, B, Aug 26, dia.
7535 Sherman, H, 15, G, Sept 1, scs.
9821 Schaat, D B, 18, E, Sept 26, dia. c.

536 Trask, Geo K, 29, A, April 14, dia.
770 Terrill, Christian, 27, E, April 27, dys. s.
1509 Terrell, J, 12, A, May 31, dia.
5672 Tresler, H W, 4, I, Aug 14, dys. c.
12730 Turman, D, 44, B, March 4, des.

2803 Vance, H J, 26, B, July 3, dys.

373 Walham, H,§ 4, C, April 5, dia.
678 Watson, J J, 18, A, April 22, dia.
3106 Wigan, M, 2, F, July 10, dia.
7494 Williams, J M, 31, H, Sept 1, scs.
10889 Weidam, J,‡ 2 B, Oct 14, dia.
12550 Ware, J B, 40, K, Jan 29, scs.
12739 West, J, 40, K, March 6, dia. c.

NEW HAMPSHIRE.

26 Ames, John G,§ 2, F, March 8, pna.
29 Allen, E S, 2, H, March 9, pna.
4656 Allen, S, 9, C, Aug 3, scs.
4746 Abbott, C, 7, K, Aug 5, dia.
7130 Arches, J L, 9, A, Aug 28, dia.
9518 Atmore, G W, 3, G, Sept 22, scs.
9832 Anderson, J N, 7, E, Sept 24, scs.
11765 Avery, J, 1 cav, M, Nov 3, dia. c.
5721 Austendalph, I, 3, D, Aug 15, ens.

833 Bushby, N, 7, C, May 1, dia.
3346 Bailey, A D, 7, C, July 15, dia.
3380 Bush, A, 4, H, July 16, dia.
4447 Bachelor, J R, 1, Aug 1, dia.
4965 Baker, Wm, 4, H, Aug 7, dys.
4988 Babb, Jas, 7, D, Aug 7, wds.
6871 Brown, W F, 2, B, Aug 26, nes.
6765 Breakman, A, 12, I, Aug 25, dia.
7857 Baker, D W, 3, G, Sept 5, dia.
8463 Bell, Geo, 5, C, Sept 11, scs.
10294 Bond, J, 12, F, Oct 4, scs.

2228 Clark, G M,‡ 7, C, May 20, ana.
3326 Combs, John, 7, B, July 14, dia. c.
4230 Coon, Charles, 7, G, July 29, scs.
5137 Colby, John N, 13, D, Aug 9, dia.
7072 Cooney, Thomas, 9, C, Aug 28, dia.
6551 Connelly, M, 4, C, Sept 12, scs.
2796 Chadwick, C E, 7, F, July 2, dia. c.
11192 Carr, P, 1, H, Oct 20, dys.

1370 Downs, E, 7, I, May 25, r. f.
2086 Doer, S, 7, D, June 17, dia. c.,
8663 Dodge, C F,§ 7, K, July 20, scs
5577 Drake, Charles C, 1 cav, B, Aug 14, scs.

3566 Eschoymer, H, 1 cav, B, July 19, dys.
5337 Estey, E E, 4, C, Aug 10, dia.
8426 Edwards, John, 9, F, Sept 11, scs.
12841 Elliott, A, 7, I, April 21, dia.

1396 Fuller, Geo, 7, B, May 26, dia.

5240 Faucett, J, 7, C, Aug 10, dia.
6678 Flanders, O, 9, F, Aug 24, dys.
6894 Ford, W, 7, K, Aug 26, dia.
9460 Faggerty, Jackson, 1 cav, A, Sept 21, scs
12440 Felch, G P, 7, H, Jan 12, pls.

2838 Guingoelett, H, 2, E, July 3, phs.
4413 Gill, N, 7, A, July 31, scs.
4687 Gooley, J,‡ 7, G, Aug 4, dia. c.
11905 Goodwin, A, 1, I, Nov 7, dia.
9671 Gardiner, A, 4, C, Sept 24, dia.
6516 Gray, G H, 4, E, Aug 22, i. f.

6143 Hunter, C, 4, K, Aug 19, dia.
6875 Hurd, Wm, 6, I, Aug 26, dia.
7869 Hartford, H, 4, A, Sept 5, dia.
8537 Hally, H, 7, C, Sept 12, ers.
10269 Huse, W,‡ 11, H, Oct 3, dia.
11156 Hamlin, G W, 1 cav, I, Oct 19, scs.
11439 Holmes, J,‡ 7, Oct 24, scs.
11468 Holmes, J, 7, Oct 26, scs.

7733 Jones, J B, 9, K, Sept 3, scs.
9198 Johnson, O O, 5, F, Sept 18, scs.
11216 Juntplute, F, 12, E, Oct 20, scs.
11758 Johnson, P, 9, E, Nov 3, scs.

4314 Keyes, C, 1 cav, K, July 30, dia.
5114 Kemp, C H, 7, A, Aug 9, dia.,
5151 Kingsbury, H R, 9, K, Aug 9, dia.
5444 Karson, H B,‡ 2, C, Aug 12, ana.
7397 Kreaser, M, 4, I, Aug 31, dia.
11877 Klinsimth, J,‡ 10, I, Nov 6, scs.
11994 Kingsbury, J H,§ 1 cav, A, Nov 13, scs.

6144 Lawrence, A, 1 cav, C, Aug 19, des.
6787 Lenert, D, 9, K, Aug 25, dia.
8048 Libby, A G, 4, H, Sept 6, gae.
11415 Leport, J, 3 cav, L, Oct 24, scs.
11484 Lucht, P, 5, C, Oct 26, scs.

2687 Mumford, A, 12, A, June 30, brs.

****

3652 Mantove, J, 4, H, June 20, dys.
4284 Miller, F, 11, G, July 30, dia.
4629 Miller, R, 11, H, Aug 3, dia.
7203 Milliot, P, 5, I, Aug 29, des.
7423 Morrison, O P, 9, C, Aug 31, scs.
7948 Marten, J, 4, C, Sept 6, dia. c.
8573 McCann, M, 9, G, Sept 12, dia.
9931 Matheson, F, 7, B, Sept 28, scs.
11207 McCann, O, 13, E, Oct 20, scs.
12234 Montegan, P, 35, F, Dec 6, scs.

1658 O'Brien, Charles, 7, I, June 6, dia. c.
11698 Osmore, J, 1 cav, C, Oct 31, scs.

6185 Patch, John, 3, F, Aug 19, dys.
819 Poore, Samuel,‡ 2, H, April 30, dia. c.
3260 Puny, J, 3, G, July 13, dia.
4764 Place, J K, 7, F, Aug 5, dia.
7011 Patterson, N, 9, L, Aug 27, scs.
11121 Parsons, Samuel, 5, H, Oct 18, scs.
11828 Pewen, H A, 7, A, Nov 5, scs.
11837 Phelps, M F, 9, D, Nov 5, scs.
5383 Pascal, E, 7, E, Aug 12, dia.

1572 Reed, F K, 2, H, June 3, dia. c.
2771 Ramsay, Wm, 7, G, July 2, dia. c.
3406 Richards, W R, 7, C, July 16, dys.
11300 Ringer, J K, sergt major, 11, Oct 22, scs.

1336 Smith, John, 7, K, May 24, dys.
2330 Sanburn, W, 7, H, June 22, dia. c.
2505 Sanlay, E, 9, E, June 26, dia.
2708 Simms, S, 9, C, June 30, dia. c.
2925 Searle, J R, 7, E, July 5, dia. c.
3472 Smith, L F, 13, C, July 17, dia. c.
4779 Steward, Geo, 10, A, Aug 5, dia.
5140 Smith, J, 7, B, Aug 9, dia. c.
5198 Schean, W, 7, A, Aug 9, dia.
5405 Shorey, Ed, 1, C, Aug 12, dia.
5438 Salsbur, J, 4, K, Aug 12, ana.

5621 Stanley, Jno, 9, A, Aug 14, scs.
6547 Smith, J, 11, E, Aug 23, dys.
7040 Swain, C, 7, D, Aug 27, scs.
8629 Smith, C, 3, F, Sept 13. dia. c.
8652 Stark, S, 15, A, Sept 13. dia.
8980 Smith, John, 3, F, Sept 17, scs.
9412 Smith, L, 12, B, Sept 21, scs.
10503 Shantz, J, 11, G, Oct 8, scs.
11887 Spaulding, T C, 4, K, Nov 7, scs.

3396 Taylor, A B, 5, H, July 16, ana.
3431 Tobine, T, 6, A, July 17, dia. c.
4072 Tilton, D B, 7, G, July 26, dia.
8098 Thompson, A, 9, K, Sept 8, scs.
10734 Tilton, L G, 11, B, Oct 11, dia. c.

10493 Upkins, A, 1 cav, B, Oct 7, dia. c.

5491 Valley, John, 10, K, Aug 12, dia.

794 Woodard, L A, 7, K, April 29, dia. c.
1991 Williams, J, 7, I, June 15, dia. c.
2345 Woodbury A, 7, H, June 23, dia. c.
2545 Whipple, John,‡ 11, C, June 27, des.
4156 Webster, J, 6, I, July 28, dia.
2710 Welson, W, 4, F, July 1, dia. c.
4104 Whalen, M, 9, M, July 27, dys.
4749 Welch, James, 7, I, Aug 5, scs.
4750 Weston, W W, 8, A, Aug 5, dys.
5702 Wagner, John, 7, H, Aug 15, scs.
7559 Welsh, J, 7, C, Sept 2, ana.
7834 Wolf, John D, 3, F, Sept 4, dia.
8083 Weilztramsen, F, 9, L, Sept 7, dia. c.
11278 Williams, P, 3, H, Oct 22, scs.
11472 Wingerd, D, 3, G, Oct 26, dys.
11768 Wilson, J, 11, I, Nov 3, scs.
11873 Warren, E, 1 cav, M, Nov 6, dia.
12734 Whitman, G E,§ 1 cav, B. March 6, scs.

8736 York, Charles, 1 cav, B, Sept 14, dia.

NEW JERSEY.

3347 Aaron, Thomas, 2, B, July 15, dia. c.
3354 Aney, G, 1, K, July 15, dia.
4098 Austin, D B, 2, I, July 27, dia.
7138 Anderson, T, 2, E, Aug 28, dys.
8513 Allbright, ——,‡ 3 cav, I, Sept 12, dia.
11389 Alexander, W L, 3, C, Oct 24, scs.
12646 Amps, C, 33, I, Feb 13, v. s.

909 Broderick, J S, 2, A, May 5, dia.
1548 Beach, J, 11, E, June 1, scs.
2181 Brannan, Pat, 11, B, June 19, des.
2260 Bells, J H, 2, M, June 21, dia. c.
2577 Buckley, John, 1, G, June 27, i. f.
2980 Bloon, Adam, 2, I, July 4, dia.
3099 Buffman, A C,‡ 1 art, B, July 10, dia. c.
5761 Bailey, L, 7, A, Aug 9, scs.
5272 Brunn, Geo, 1 cav, B, Aug 10, dia. c.
5357 Burns, P, 3 cav, C, Aug 11, dia.
5379 Baker, Wm, 1 cav, K, Aug 12, scs.
5483 Blanchard, G, 7, K, Aug 13, ana.
5934 Bennett, C, 14, B, Aug 17, scs.
11682 Brant, Charles,§ 1, E, Oct 31, scs.
12238 Buyer, A, 6, I, Dec 7, scs.
12640 Brewer, W H, 10, D, Feb 12, scs.

715 Corley, Daniel, 11, A, April 24, dia.
1437 Creamer, E, 35, A, May 28, dia.
6929 Creamer, E, 10, B, Aug 26, dia.
3209 Chamberlain, R, 1 cav, D, July 12, dia. c.
5730 Clark, C H, 2, C, Aug 15, scs.
8240 Coonan, J, 2, C, Sept 9, scs.
10552 Collar, H, 2, D, Sept 9, r. f.
11990 Clayton, L, 10, B, Nov 13, scs.
3476 Curtis, W O,§ 1 cav, L, July 17, phs.
8041 Coykendall, D, 15, K, Sept 6, dia.

335 Disbrow, J P, 14, K, April 2, dia.

2473 Davenport, J, 7, I, June 25, td. f.
3444 Davis, H, 12, F, July 17, dys.
4926 Dayton, C, 2, C, Aug 6, ana.
5148 Dorland, A H, 10, I, Aug 9, dys.
6306 Dewinger, J, 2, G, Aug 20, des.
7076 Dunham, L, 35, H, Aug 28, dys.
7304 Dilan, Edward, 9, G, Aug 30, dia.
7469 Dermer, J L, 9, G, Sept 1, scs.
7734 Doremus, C, 2 cav, A, Sept 3, scs.
7804 Duncan, H P, 2, G, Sept 4, scs.
8440 Doyle, H, 16, C, Sept 11, scs.
10533 Dunn, G, 1, F, Sept 3, dia.

1426 Ebner, Charles, 1 cav, K, May 28, dia.
1715 Egbert, James, 15, B, June 8, dia.
4303 Esl{gh, Jacob, 10, D, July 30, dia.

1522 Farrell, J H, 5, G, May 31, dia. c.
3938 Foliand, M,‡ 1 cav, K, July 25, scs.
4693 Fitch, F,§ 35, F, Aug 4, dia.
5327 Fry, John, 9, G, Aug 4, scs.
6737 Fisher, Wm, 9, C, Aug 24, dia.
7285 Farren, J, 3, Aug 30, dia.
9972 Fairbrother, H, 35, D, Sept 28, scs.
11584 Ford, A, 7, K, Oct 28, scs.
7338 Fisher, N O, 9, I, Aug 30, dys.

5900 Gale, B,‡ 9, D, Aug 16, dia.
7039 Galloway, F C, 12, K, Aug 27, scs.
11165 Glenn, C H, 4, I, Oct 19, scs.
11120 Guier, G, 7, D, Oct 20, scs.

1508 Hallman, H, 6, C, May 31, dia. c.
3072 Hemis, Daniel, 1 cav, B, July 9, dia. c.
3819 Hick, James, 9, G, July 23, dia.
4151 Hegamann, J, 14, K, July 28, dia.
4189 Hammle, A, 1 cav, July 28, dia.

****

4744 Huber, C, 9, G, Aug 5, dia.
4862 Herbert, J S, 2 cav, I, Aug 6, dia. c.
4911 Halmann, M, 1 cav, A, Aug 6, r. f.
7821 Hull, Alexander, 7, C, Sept 4, dia.
7870 Howell, J, 1, K, Sept 5, dia.
7900 Hilgard, P F,‡ 10, A, Sept 5, dys.
10761 Hatter, W, 3, I, Oct 12, scs.
12302 Humes, E M, 2, M, Dec 17, scs.
12416 Hook, J M, 2 cav, D, Jan 8, scs.

5252 Jennings, G H, 2 cav, A, Aug 10, dia.
9519 Jone, A, 1 cav, A, Sept 22, dys.
11117 Jay, H,‡ 5, K, Oct 18, scs.
11399 Jomson, G W, 6, G, Oct 24, scs.
12244 Johnson, A F, 9, D, Dec 26, scs.

3762 Krouk, Peter, 2 cav, H, July 22, dys.
5085 Kuhm, R, 9, A, Aug 8, dia.
8649 Kitchell, S, 7, K, Sept 13, scs.
12023 King, C, 15, G, Nov 15, dia. c.

1985 Lyons, D, 1 cav, K, June 15, dia. c.
795 Layton, Stephen, 11, A, April 29, dia.
1769 Lindsley, Samuel, 10, H, June 9, td. f.
3622 Lewis, S, 3 cav, G, July 20, dia.
4095 Leadbeater, J H, 6, B, July 27, dia.
5944 Leighton, Wm, 5, H, Aug 17, scs.
6157 Luney, Ed, 8, G, Aug 19, dia.
12102 Larime, C, 15, C, Nov 20, scs.

2019 Mennu, Jacob, 11, H, June 15, des.
2852 Miller, J, 1 cav, K, July 4, dia.
3323 McIntire, R, 8, I, July 14, dia. c.
3548 Marks, Charles, 2 cav, G, July 18, dys.
4594 Mulrany, I, 4, B, Aug 3, dys.
4645 Miller, S S, 2 cav, G, Aug 3, dys.
5250 Morell, A, 5, K, Aug 10, scs.
5882 Mahler, John, 35, I, Aug 16, dys.
6986 Munn, Charles, 4, K, Aug 27, dia.
8019 McElroy, E, 10, I, Sept 6, scs.
8332 Meunt, C H, 9, D, Sept 10, scs.
8592 Miller, J, 7, K, Sept 13, scs.
10959 Mullan, A, 39, B, Oct 14, scs.
11252 Mills, F, 2, I, Oct 21, dia.
11564 Millington, J, 1 cav, H, Oct 27, scs.

6780 Noll, M, 9, A, Aug 25, dys.
4983 Nichols, J, 1 s s, C, Aug 7, dys.

7131 Osborne, E, 14, E, Aug 28, dia. c.
10463 Osborn, J M, 9, H, Oct 7, scs.

1071 Pratt, J F, 1, M, May 13, td. f.
1072 Purdee, Charles, 11, C, May 13, dia. c.
5206 Peterson, Henry, 3 cav, H, Aug 10, dia.
6298 Peer, T, 9, K, Aug 20, dia.
6962 Pelger, M, 10, G, Aug 27, dia.
7451 Peterson, G, 12, I, Sept 1, dia.

8017 Post, C J, 4, I, Sept 6, dia.
9990 Parker, W, 2, I, Sept 29, scs.
12221 Prink, J, 2, Dec 4, scs.

2145 Rooks, H, 5, H, June 18, dia. c.
2821 Riley, M, 1 cav, L, July 3, ana.
4066 Robinson, Jacob, 1 cav, B. July 27, td. f.
4358 Radford, Wm, 13, B, Aug 6. des.
8282 Reed, A, 9, D, Sept 9, scs.
10461 Ray, J, 10, A, Oct 7, dia.
10708 Regan, D O, 8, C, Oct 11, scs.
11292 Reevis, F, 2, I, Oct 21, dia.

2548 Starr, N, 5, H, June 27, dia.
5087 Simonds, J, 9, K, Aug 8, dys.
5807 Shanahan, W, 9, C, Aug 16, scs.
7364 Stout, L,§ 2, C, Aug 31, dys.
7565 Street, John J, 9, D, Sept 2, scs.
7577 Stiffin, H, 3, M, Sept 2, dia. c.
7729 Skell, C W, 3 cav, M, Sept 3, gae.
8687 Swetser, P, 9, G, Sept 13, scs.
8751 Stevenson, W, 2 cav, M, Sept 14, dia.
9328 Shay, H H, 7, I, Sept 19, scs.
10846 Smith, A, 5, G, Oct 13, dys.
11615 Sutton, T, 12, K, Oct 28, scs.
11653 Stimmell, I, 5, A, Oct 30, scs.
11793 Sullivan, I, 8, C, Nov 4, scs.
11882 Steele, Geo, 2, B, Nov 6, scs.
10882 Sweet, B F, 10, K, Oct 13, dys.

1853 Tindel, E,§ 1, B, June 11, dia. c
5112 Taylor, Peter, 9, Aug 9, dia.
6131 Townsend, J, 35, I, Aug 19, dia.
7937 Turner, B, 4, G, Sept 5, gae.
9398 Townsend, F, 10, C, Sept 21, dys.
11364 Thompson, S, 4, I, Oct 21, scs.
12451 Thatcher, J, 8, H, Jan 14, scs.
12705 Toy, J, 7, G, Feb 27, des.
10212 Thomas, Henry,§ 10, B, Oct 2, scs.
6448 Traittman, Jas, 9, D, Aug 22, dia. c.

2634 Utter, Stephen, 1 art, B, June 29, scs.

12100 Vallett, W, 5 art, A, Nov 19, scs.

1955 Weed, Wm,‡ 15, I, June 14, dia. c.
2246 Wood, W J, 12, E, June 20, ana.
4643 Widder, W, 5, G, Aug 3, dys.
4998 Wainwright, 9, C, Aug 7, dia.
5031 Wolverton, 1, I, Aug 8, dia.
5099 Warner, A, 4, A, Aug 9, dia.
5333 Willey, J, 2 cav, M, Aug 10, ana.
6168 Wynard, Wm, 2, I, Aug 19, mas.
7560 Willis, A, 35, I, Sept 2, ana.
8142 Wright, S M, 7, K, Sept 8, dia.
8307 Ward, J, 1 cav, H, Sept 10, dia.
12157 Williams, W, 1, D, Nov 20, scs.
12658 Wells, G, 10, C, Feb 15, dia. c.

NEW YORK.

2038 Abbey, O,‡ 174, June 15, dia. a.
2141 Abbey, W H, 85, E, June 18, dia. c.
4719 Abel, C, 15 art, C, Aug 4, dia.
4612 Aber, J, 104, I, Aug 3, dys. c.
5629 Ackerman, Sam'l, 97, K, Aug 14, scs.
64 Ackheart, David, 20, A, March 19, pls.
8497 Adams, H, 98, G, Sept 11, scs.
4581 Adams, J A, 10, F, Aug 2, pna.
6467 Adams, O, 61, C, Aug 22, dia.
8559 Adams, S,§ 100, Sept 12, scs.
8226 Adams, T R, 85, H, July 12.
1700 Ades, Ed, 8 cav, C, June 7, des.
5047 Adeler, A, 8, D, Aug 8, dys.
6575 Adney, F, 85, K, Aug 23, dia.
4382 Ahearn, Daniel, 170, July 31, dia.
3349 Aiken, J W, 85, H, July 15, pna.
8001 Akerman, M, 7 art, L, Sept 6, dia.
7062 Albarson, J, 42, C, Aug 28, dia.
6698 Albert, William, 24 bat, Aug 24, dys.

7007 Alderman, F, 15 cav, F, Aug 27, dia.
1755 Alexander, J, 125, C, June 9, dia. c
11212 Alford, B C, 152, F, Oct 20, scs.
3293 Allen, A W, 14 art, M, July 14, dia.
12452 Allen, J I, 82, A, Jan 14, scs.
5568 Allen, W, 1 cav, H, Aug 13, dys.
5844 Allenberger, J, 39, B, Aug 16, ts. f.
7478 Allenberens, E, 39, D, Sept 1, scs.
11479 Allinger, L, 48, I, Oct 26, wds.
7587 Allman, Charles, 7 art, C, Sept 2, scs.
6941 Almy, F, 111, K, Aug 26, scs.
5938 Alphord, J, 75, G, Aug 17, scs.
7739 Alsaver, S, 47, H, Sept 3, scs.
800 Ambler, Fred, 47, H, April 29, dia. c.
2344 Ambrose, Jacob, 9 cav, C, June 23, sca
10642 Ames, Henry, 2 art, Oct 10, scs.
4654 Ames, J R,§ 14 art, I, Aug 3, dia.
7743 Amgere, G, 47, E, Sept 3, scs.
1954 Amigh, A, 162, K, June 14, ana.

8739 Anderson, A, 100, I, July 21, i. f.
4890 Anderson, A, 99, F, Aug 6, scs.
 537 Anderson, H, 20 cav, M, April 14, des.
8819 Anderson, J, 39, E, Sept 15, gae.
4110 Anderson, L, 14, D, July 27, dia. c.
1389 Andrews, G, 111, 1, May 26, dia. c.
7533 Andrews, W, 85, K, Sept 1, dia. c.
8717 Anson, Robert, 1 cav, K, Sept 14, scs.
6548 Answell, J, 15 cav, A, Aug 23, dys.
8720 Antisdale, George, 5 cav, Sept 14, scs.
6976 Appleby, S W, 85, K, Aug 27, dia.
9741 Argt, C, 6, Sept 25, dys.
11172 Armond, W, 7, F, Oct 19, scs.
9475 Armstrong, H, 140, G, Sept 21, dia. c.
10818 Armstrong, J, 164, C, Oct 12, dys.
11571 Armstroug, W, 24 bat, Oct 27, scs.
7470 Arnold, R B, 7 art, L, Sept 1, dia. c.
6951 Arnott, C, 47, C, Aug 26, dia.
1580 Ashley, C G, 146, G, June 3, dia. c.
12202 Auster, F, 39, B, Dec 1, scs.
12622 Ashley, S, citizen, Feb 9, scs.
5544 Ashtan, ——,‡ 10, I, Aug 13, dia.
7207 Atwood, G S, 24 bat, Aug 29, dia.
 950 Aubray, K,§ 14, A, May 8, dia. c.
11748 Augh, J, 66, D, Nov 2, scs.
5027 Augustine, F, 52, A, Aug 8, dys.
1736 Austin, A, 147, H, June 8, dia.
3094 Austin, J, 7 art, M, July 10, dia.
8218 Austin, G, 147, H, Sept 3, dia.
12820 Ayers, G S, 147, G, March 29, scs.

12347 Babcock, J M, 140, I, Dec 27, scs.
1712 Babcock, H, 111, G, May 7, ana.
3066 Babcock, J, 72, E, July 9, scs.
5335 Babcock, J, 55, E, Aug 11, td. f.
4638 Babcock, J S, 140, D, Aug 3, dia.
4893 Babcock, R, 9, L, Aug 6, dys.
11831 Babcock, W H, 13 cav, L, Nov 5, scs.
5692 Babst, M, 9, D, Aug 15, dia.
 754 Bacon, E P, 154, B, April 27, dys. c.
9101 Bacon, J, 154, E, Sept 13, dia.
2870 Bacchus, A, 169, A, July 4, dys.
11272 Bacchus, E R, 15 art, F, Oct 22, scs.
3447 Bachelder, B F, 24 bat, July 17, c. f.
3115 Backley, C, 24 bat, July 10, ts. f.
3771 Badger, P, 47, E, July 22, des.
7890 Bailey, A, 5, K, Sept 5, dia.
10163 Bailey, C, 76, K, Oct 1, scs.
5697 Bailey, G W,‡ 154, G, Aug 15, scs.
7493 Bailey, John, 12 cav, A, Sept 1, dia. c.
8215 Baker, J, 24 bat, Sept 8, pls.
10636 Baker, A, 93, B, Oct 10, dia. c.
4468 Baker, Charles, 52, G, Aug 1, dia.
3550 Baker, E, 85, E, July 18, dys.
12376 Baker, George, 40, H, Jan 1, scs.
8759 Baker, H, 146, F, Sept 14, dia. c.
8052 Baker, Ira, 85, H, Sept 7, scs.
11848 Baker, J, 24, F, Nov 5, dia.
11660 Baker, J,‡ 16 cav, K, Oct 31, scs.
  61 Baker, Wm, 7, D, March 18, pna.
7591 Baldwin, C, 24 cav, M, Sept 2, dia.
6853 Baldwin, G, 154, C, Aug 25, scs.
4457 Ballard, Robert B, 85, C, Aug 1, con.
4364 Barnard, Wm, 85, K, July 31, dia.
5347 Bancroff, A H, 85, Aug 11, dia.
8192 Barrett, G M, 184, E, Sept 8, dia.
11605 Banigan, A, 82, A, Oct 28, scs.
5536 Banker, J M, 118, K, Aug 13, dys.
9819 Banker, J T, 152, G, Sept 26, ts. f.
8443 Bannan, H, 39, H, Sept 11, scs.
11056 Bannyer, F, 126, K, Oct 17, scs.
12315 Barber, H,‡ 96, D, Dec 20, scs.
1689 Barge, H,§ 120, A, June 6, dia. c.
3748 Barnes, J, 12 cav, F, July 22, dys.
6771 Barnes, J S, 10 cav, K, Aug 25, scs.
11343 Barnes, M,‡ 115, F, Oct 23, wds.
6963 Barnes, A C, 85, D, Aug 27, dia.
8821 Barnes, R W, 24 bat, Sept 15, scs.
10418 Barnes, Thomas, 76, B, Oct 6, ana.
1835 Barrett, J, 132, C, June 11, dia. c.
8361 Barnum, H, 39, H, Sept 10, dia.
7877 Barklett, H, 24 bat, Sept 5, dia.

8192 Barrett, G M, 184, 1 Sept 8, dia.
10153 Barratt, G, 22, A, Oct 1, dia.
 588 Barrett, D, 13, H, April 16, dia.
9979 Barron, C L, 12 bat, Sept 28, dia.
3580 Barrows, M, 14, G, July 19, dia.
11612 Bartill, R, 164, F, Oct 28, scs.
4769 Bartlett, L, 118, I, Aug 5, des.
8409 Barton, D, 85, I, Sept 11, dia. c.
6552 Bass, Charles, 7 art, B, Aug 23, dia.
8217 Bass, George, teamster, 63, Sept 8, dia.
8097 Bassford, J, 12 cav, G, Sept 7, dia.
5555 Bates, G, 5, A, Aug 13, dys.
 520 Bates, J, 97, A, April 13, dia. c.
3845 Bates, John,‡ 14, I, July 24, dia.
1069 Bates, Lester, 97, A, May 13, dia.
10556 Baters, W, 139, G, Oct 9, dys.
10999 Baty, A, 132, K, Oct 16, dia. c.
  61 Bayne, Daniel, 57, D, July 4, s. p.
9380 Baywood, J,§ 1 cav, I, Sept 20, scs.
6021 Beam, B, 2 cav, M, Aug 17, dys.
4302 Beck, John, 97, H, July 30, scs.
6034 Beckham, F B, 10 cav, A, Aug 18, i. f.
9216 Beckshire, J,‡ 12 cav, F, Sept 19, dys.
8472 Beckwith, C, 14 art, D, Sept 11, scs.
5012 Bee, George, 119, F, Aug 8, dia.
8992 Beebe, J E, 11, Sept 17.
3843 Beekman, J, 43, A, July 23, dys.
11933 Beers, W, 82, B, Nov 8, scs.
8010 Belden, Wm, 82, E, Sept 6, dia.
3267 Bell, D S, 20, state mil, D, July 13, scs
9136 Bell, J, 6, B, Sept 13, scs.
11124 Bell, J C, 120, D, Oct 18, scs.
8942 Bell, Wm,‡ 39, K, Sept 16, dia.
11604 Belwea, C, 179, F, Oct 31, dia. c.
3089 Bennett, I H, 85, E, July 9, dia.
3138 Bennett, 146, B, July 10, pls.
5945 Bentley, C, 22 cav, L, Aug 17, cah.
6670 Bentner, Joseph, 100, I, Aug 24, scs.
6979 Benway, C, 6 art, K, Aug 27, dys.
10955 Berges, E, 146, B, Oct 14, dys.
6598 Benall, M L, 125, A, Aug 23, dia. c.
5749 Beat, Isaac, 42, G, Aug 15, scs.
6039 Bertin, F, 69, G, Aug 13, scs.
6137 Besrha, John, 15 art, B, Aug 19, mas.
8234 Beull, J,§ 85, B, Sept 9, ana.
5230 Beyers, H, 24, K, Aug 10, scs.
 351 Bidon, S, 52, A, April 2, ts. f.
10635 Bidwell, J, 5 cav, G, Oct 10, dia. c.
3232 Bigelow, L, 85, D, July 12.
10505 Billings, J, 2 cav, M, Oct 8, scs.
 601 Billings, W W, 52, G, April 17, des.
10945 Bings, G, 5 art, B, Oct 14, scs.
10005 Bingham, C E, 5 cav, D, Sept 29, dia.
12881 Bird, M, 7 art, K, April 14, dia. c.
4780 Bird, P,‡ 7 art, K, Aug 5, pna.
6590 Bishop, C, 7 art, M, Aug 23, dys.
5786 Bissell, J S, 85, D, Aug 15, dia.
11018 Black, J, 42, G, Oct 16, scs.
2574 Black, L, 9, A, June 27, dia.
11971 Black, H C, 42, F, Nov 12, scs.
1885 Blackman, J, 85, June 13, des.
4076 Blackwood, W, 115, G, July 27, ts. f.
7889 Blair, D, 15, C, Sept 5, dys.
12469 Blair, James,‡ 8 cav, K, Jan 16, scs.
 498 Blaize, H, 3 art, H, April 12, dia.
3236 Blake, W D, 24 bat, July 22.
2439 Blake, George, 100, I, June 25, dia. c.
6129 Blanchard, E, 12 cav, F, Aug 19, dys.
8340 Blanchard, L, 100, K, Sept 10, scs.
10083 Blancolt, Wm, 95, B, Sept 30, dia.
1861 Blank, J M, 95, A, June 12, dia. c.
4933 Bliss, James H, 22 cav, I, Aug 7, dia.
8959 Block, J P, 100, F, Sept 16, dia. c.
7206 Blood, L, 7, C, Aug 29, scs.
2777 Blyme, S, 85, G, July 2, dia.
12521 Boaman, J, 1 cav, D, Jan 25, scs.
6371 Boares, A, 178, D, Aug 21, scs.
5285 Bode, A, 85, B, Aug 11, scs.
2989 Bodishay, J, 7, F, July 1, ana.
 474 Boermaster, J, 14, A, April 9, ana.
3073 Bolll, H, 10 cav, E, July 9, ana.
6018 Bolan, E,§ 35, F, Aug 17, dia.

11718 Bolby, O, 14 art, D, Nov 1, scs.
8267 Boles, J, 22 cav, D, Sept 9, dia. c.
3606 Bomsteel, S A, 20, G, July 19, scs.
5269 Borst, J, 5 cav, B, Aug 10, ana.
4401 Bodler, D, 7, D, July 31, dys.
51 Boughton, H, 77, A, March 16, pna.
7627 Boulton, T, 43, G, Sept 2, dia. c.
11066 Bowden, P, 16 cav, M, Oct 17, scs.
6744 Bowen, J H, 65, D, Aug 24, dia.
4601 Bowin, J, 7 cav, K, Aug 3, dia.
11944 Bowman, H, 84, K, Nov 10, scs.
12521 Bowman, I, 1 cav, D, Jan 25, scs.
3635 Bowman, S, 147, H, July 20, dia.
1275 Box, G, 111, D, May 22, dia. a.
9728 Boyce, A, 3 cav, I, Sept 25, des.
2673 Boyce, R, 6 cav, M, June 30, dia.
10 Boyle, Pat, 63, A, March 5, pna.
8912 Boyle, Pat, 48, F, Sept 16, dia. c.
11974 Boyle, I, 16, D, Nov 12, scs.
4365 Bradford, D B, 7 art, B, July 31, dys.
5232 Bradley, John, 69, K, Aug 10, dia.
16685 Bradshaw, R,‡ 120, E, Aug 24, dia.
12219 Brady, J, 140, E, Dec 4, scs.
3979 Bragg, J C, 2 cav, E, July 26, dia.
12263 Brain, Wm, 5 art, B, Dec 12, dia.
7704 Brandon, O, 15 art, A, Sept 3, dia.
1800 Breny, James, 178, K, June 10, dia. c.
5134 Brewer, Fred, 39, C, Aug 9, dia.
11685 Brewer, Henry,§ 2 cav, G, Oct 31, dia. c
10221 Brewer, J S, 6, B, Oct 2, scs.
1365 Brewer, S, 15, K, May 25, dia. c.,
519 Brewer, Thos, 111, F, April 13, dia.
9690 Briant, L A, 146, B, Sept 24, dia. a.
8116 Bright, 104, C, Sept 8, scs.,
11627 Brightman, E, 7, D, Oct 28, scs.,
8415 Brill, C, 140, F, Sept 11, dia.
6953 Brink, C, 109, K, Aug 26, gae.
9787 Britansky, J, 52, E, Sept 26, dia. c.
2997 Brobst, J, 52, B, July 7, dia. a.
9148 Brock, W, 76, F, Sept 18, scs.
6882 Broder, H, 76, F, Aug 26, dia.
12002 Brogan, J M, 85. B, Nov 14, scs.
1324 Brooks, Wm,‡ 10 cav, E, May 24, dia.
1221 Brott, Anthony, 1 cav, K, May 19, ana.
9858 Broscang, C, 150, C, Sept 27, scs.
7517 Brought, Charles, 14 art, I, Sept 1, scs.
51 Broughten, H, 77, H, March 16, pls.
10668 Brown, A, 140, K, Oct 11, scs.
5538 Brown, B M, 85, I, Aug 13, scs.
4112 Brown, C, 103, C, July 27, brs.
9556 Brown, C, 66, K, Sept 23, scs.
11953 Brown, C, 39, H, Nov 10, scs.
11928 Brown, C, 1 cav, M, Nov 8, dia. c.
6623 Brown, Charles, 97, F, Aug 23, dia.
7501 Brown, D, 118, B, Sept 1, dia. c.
3659 Brown, E G, 7 art, L, July 20, pna.
9674 Brown, G H, 85, H, Sept 24, dia.
7985 Brown, G H, 63, C, Sept 6, dia.
2465 Brown, H, 72, C, June 25, dia,
1879 Brown, H, 12 cav, June 12, dys.
7266 Brown, H,‡ 39, F, Aug 30, scs.
1887 Brown, J, 125, June 13, dia.
7658 Brown, J, 16, 3, Sept 3, dia.
6655 Brown, James, 4 cav, E, Aug 24, dys.
6691 Brown, James, 170, K, Aug 24, des.
7526 Brown, John, 66, Sept 1, dia.
7615 Brown, Wm, 5, D, Sept 2, dys.
552 Brown, Warren, 120, K, April 14, dia.
428 Brown, Wm, 42, A, April 8, ana.
7390 Broxmire, Thomas, 15, E, Aug 31, scs.
1559 Brumaghin, T, 125, E, June 2, dip.
4475 Bryant, D, 179, B, Aug 1, dia.
248 Bryant, H, 82, F, Aug 30, ana.
7668 Bryan, Wm, 1 cav, I, Sept 3, scs.
3814 Buck, 24, H, July 23, dia.
9975 Buckbier, J, 7 art, F, Sept 28, dia. c,
10585 Buckley, W, 122, D, Oct 10, scs.
5714 Buel, G W, 115, E, Aug 15, scs.
331 Buel, S, 42, B, April 2, des.
12417 Buffman, L,§ 100, K, Jan 8, dys.
7567 Bulkley, E A, 97, E, Sept 2, dia. c.
12509 Burfield, C, citizen, Jan 22, pls.

5953 Bullier, Wm, 23 cav, B, Aug 17, mas.
9642 Bullock, E,‡ 85, E, Sept 24, scs.
4137 Bundy, Joseph, 7 art, B, July 28, dia. c.
540 Bunn, W H, 132, F, April 14, pna.
9870 Bunnell, W, 59, C, Sept 27., scs.
6452 Burbanks, J, 85, D, Aug 22, dys.
10924 Burdick, A, 85, C, Oct 14, scs.
978 Burdick, C, 47, F, May 9, dys
2134 Burdick, Samuel, 125, A, June 18, dia. c.
7838 Burdock, L, 22 cav, L, Sept 4, dia. c.
10016 Burleigh, L, 6 art, F, Sept 29, scs.
12389 Burley, C, 3, B, Jan 4, dia.
619 Burns, E J,§ 13 cav, D, April 19, asc.
477 Burns, John, 40, I, April 9, dys.
924 Burns, John, 99, H, May 6, i. f.
11881 Burns, J, 118, F, Nov 6, dia.
8745 Burns, W, 3 cav, C, Sept 14, ts. f.
5991 Burns, Daniel, 5 art, D, Aug 17, ces.
7247 Burr, H, 59, C, Aug 30, dia. c.
6171 Bursha, Thomas, 2 art, M, Aug 19, mas
3165 Burshen, F, 54, C, July 11, scs.
2875 Burt, J, 2 cav, A, July 4, des.
7214 Burton, G E, 85, K, Aug 29, dys.
217 Burton, Henry, 140, March 29, dia.
5847 Buserman, E, 97, E, Aug 16, ens.
6457 Bush, E, 20, D, Aug 22, dia.
1415 Bushnell, A, 65, D, May 27, dia. c.
487 Bushan, J R, 132, G, April 11, pna.
11366 Bushley, Wm,‡ 5 art, A, Oct 23, scs.
136C Buskirk, A, 47, A, May 25, dia. c.
2047 Buskirt, O, 13, June 15, dia. a.
721 Butler, Thomas, 132, G, April 25, dia.
4183 Butler, W, 43, D, July 28, dys.
12651 Butoff, R,§ 124, C, Feb 13, dia. c.
10848 Butler, James, 2 cav, D, Oct 13, scs.
9235 Butter, P, 126, D, Sept 19, dia. c.
5805 Button, James, 24 art, B, Aug 16, dys.
3446 Butts, A, 111, C, July 17, dia.
9790 Byron, J,‡ 69, A, Sept 26, dia. c.
1224 Burke, W H, 120, I, May 19, dia. a.
5196 Burk, John, 69, K, Aug 10, dys.
1073 Brower, John A, 5 art, D, Oct 17, dia.

12190 Cademus, C, 48, A, June 19, ana.
0765 Cady, Geo, 66, G, Oct 12, scs.
12377 Cady, J, 77, E, June 23, dia.
0721 Cady, J J, 14, H, Oct 11, scs.
3062 Cain, M, 132, E, July 9, dia. a.
2136 Cale, J, 85, G, June 18, dia. a.
19040 Caldham, L C, 8 cav, L, Sept 17, scs.
11807 Caldwell, A, 42, A, Nov 4, scs.
1530 Caling, Ed, 7, H, Oct 26, scs.
9706 Calkins, S V, 120, D, Sept 25, scs.
8411 Callbrook, J, 147, E, Sept 11, ana.
2848 Cameron, John, 1 cav, H, July 4, dia.
1770 Camp, H, 2 cav, F, June 9, dia. c.
1238 Campbell, D, 8 cav, H, May 20, ana.
7236 Campbell, J, 99, I, Aug 29, scs.
946 Campbell, L R, 104, B, May 7, dys.
8793 Campbell, M, 169, K, Sept 15, scs.
11294 Campbell, W, 2, C, Oct 22, scs.
7378 Campbell, Wm, 76, B, Aug 31, dia.
12178 Card, A, 152, C, Nov 27, scs.
5034 Card, G, 109, F, Aug 8, scs.
8136 Carboines, W,‡ 39, C, Sept 8, dia.
6433 Cardon, E, 115, A, Aug 22, dys.
7555 Carey, D, 57, A, Sept 2, dia. c.
11512 Carey, F, 65, E, Oct 9, scs.
372 Carl, Joseph, 14, A, April 5, dia.
5545 Carl, L, 120, G, Aug 13, cah.
12339 Carle, ——, 1 cav, D, Dec 26, scs.
12268 Carmac, F, 2, D, Dec 12, scs.
7655 Carmer, Andrew, 85, B, Sept 3, ana.
11640 Carney, M, 9 cav, L, Oct 30, scs.
8470 Carnehan, Charles, 24 bat'y, Sept 11 scs
5258 Carney, D J, 132, G, Aug 10, dvs. a.
9879 Carney, Francis, 2 art, C, Sept 27, dia.
3102 Carnes, P, 13 cav, B, July 10, dia.
10806 Carpenter, Frank, 7 art, C, Oct 12, scs.
8854 Carpenter, G, 7, D, Sept 15, dia. c.
4632 Carpenter, H A, 2 art, A, Aug 3, dis
3916 Carpenter, L, 2 art, B, July 25, dia. c.

3977 Carpenter, M B, 85, B, July 26, dia.
6743 Carr, Andrew. 22, Aug 24, dys.
3859 Carr, D, 25, B, July 24, dia. c.
 581 Carr, F, 3 art, K, April 16, dia.
6470 Carr, Geo ‡ A, 3 art, K, Aug 22, dia. c.
5673 Carr, Wm, 125, K, Aug 14, scs.
6304 Carr, Wm, 97, E, Aug 20, gae.
4139 Carroll, James, 69, A, July 28, dia.
10293 Carroll, P,‡ 95, E, Oct 4, scs.
2061 Carroll, F, 132, F, June 15, dys.
12015 Carroll, W, 42, D, Nov 15, scs.
8563 Carson, J G, 100, B, Sept 12, scs.
8023 Cart, M A, 118, F, Sept 6, dia.
1987 Carter, A, 146, E, June 15, brs.
5212 Carter, Ed,‡ 7 art, A, Aug 10, scs.
6433 Carson, E, 115, A, Aug 22, dys.
11640 Carney, M, 9 cav, L, Oct 30, scs.
8479 Case, A F, 8 cav, A. Sept 11, scs.
8377 Case, E, 8 cav, M, Sept 10, scs.
6296 Case, H J, 12 cav, A, Aug 20, scs.
3832 Casey, J, 100, G, July 23, dia.
5271 Casey, P, 174, A, Aug 10, scs.
8421 Cassells, Samuel, 52, D, Sept 11, scs.
2643 Cassine, John S, 24 bat, June 29, pna.
1177 Castano, J, 104, H, May 16, dia. c.
10482 Cashel, C, 7 art, I, Oct 7, dia. c.
1785 Castle, J W, 147, H, June 10, dia. a.
6128 Castle, Wm, 1 art, E, Aug 19, dys.
1534 Cavanaugh, John, 146, H, June 1, ana.
2971 Ceaser, D, 7 art, B, July 7, dia. c.
1466 Centre, A, 16, A, May 29, dia. c.
9682 Chaffe, R A, 5 cav, H, Sept 24, scs.
11101 Chambers, J, 140, F, Oct 18, des.
6557 Chambers, J, 147, E, Aug 23, dia. a.
5860 Chamberlain, C, 154, D, Aug 16, mas.
4768 Champlin, W, 85, E, Aug 5, dia.
4726 Chapel, A, 85, D, Aug 4, dia.
5478 Chapel, R, 6 cav, A, Aug 13, dia.
5881 Chappell, A, 39, E, Aug 16, ens.
10743 Chappell, E, 76, K, Oct 12, dia. c.
3222 Chapin, F, 24 cav, A, July 12.
3286 Chapman, J, 85, K, July 14, r. f.
1593 Chase, A, 111, H, June 3, dia. c.
4856 Chase, D, 98, I, Aug 6, scs.
5469 Chase, N F, 85, K, Aug 13, dia.
7450 Chase, S M, 4 art, D, Sept 1, dia,
2157 Chatbrim, H, 23 bat, June 18, i. f.
8033 Chatman, C, 6 art, I, Sept 6, dia.
6653 Chatman, S M, 2, F, Aug 23, dys.
9919 Chatterton, J, 95, B, Sept 28, scs.
7865 Chagnou, E, 12 cav, F, Sept 25, ts. f.
7189 Chesley, P S, 10 cav, G, Aug 29, scs.
7539 Chestey, John, 174, G, Sept 2, dia. c.
10680 Chickchester, C H, 57, I, Oct 11, dys.
6317 Childs, A, 85, I, Aug 20, dia.
4141 Childs, Wm, 73, A, July 28, dia.
11555 Chile, H,‡ 47, E, Oct 27, scs.
10612 Christy, J, 1 drag, I, Oct 10, scs.
5824 Church, C L, 5 cav, C, Aug 16, mas.
5413 Church, F M, 2 cav, D, Aug 12, dia. c.
4257 Churchill, C, 99, I, July 29, dia. c.
3449 Clancey, Robert, 164, E, July 17, dia.
2114 Clark, A, 85, E, June 17, dia. c.
5167 Clark, Chas, 12 cav, F, Aug 19, ts. f.
2947 Clark, F, 8 cav, B, July 6, dys. a.
12114 Clark, J, 8 cav, K, Nov 21, scs.
12403 Clark, J B,§ 7 art, L, Jan 6, scs.
2154 Clark, John, 48, D, June 18, dia. a.
11304 Clark, L, 100, G, Oct 22, scs.
10611 Clark, P, 42, B, Oct 10, scs.
5802 Clemens, A, 15 cav, F, Aug 15, dia
6909 Clemments, H, 65, F, Aug 26, dia.
11023 Cleever, W, 43, F, Oct 16, dia. c.
 813 Clifford, Chas, 16, B, April 30, dia. c.
 740 Clifford, Geo, 132, K, April 26, dys.
6494 Cline, B, 85, K, Aug 22, scs.
11437 Cline, J W, 85, K, Oct 24, scs.
12021 Cline, S M, 1 drag, H, Nov 15, scs.
9721 Cline, W, 76, F, Sept 25, dia.
6243 Clingman, J, 150, L, Aug 20, scs.
12471 Clinton, R 102, D, Jan 17, dia.
1497 Clute, H V 24 bat, May 31, ana.

5955 Clyem, J P, 147, B, Aug 17, dia. c.
7343 Coanas, W, 73, D, Aug 31, wds.
5365 Coburn, C, 122, E, Aug 11, r. f.
10129 Coburn, A, 116, H, Oct 1, ana.
 933 Coddington, Wm, 99, H, May 7, dys.
7992 Cochran, John, 126, K, Sept 6, dia.
11775 Cochran, M, 42, A, Nov 3, scs.
9237 Cochson, J, 140, C, Sept 19, dia.
10651 Cogger, M, 125, B, Oct 11, scs.
3715 Cogswell, L, 6 art, M, July 21, dia.
10062 Cole, E B, 14 art, B, Sept 30, scs.
8456 Cole, Geo, 12 cav, A, Sept 11, dia. c.
6241 Cole, John J, 5 cav, M, Aug 20, scs.
5890 Cole, M, 15 art, M, Aug 16, dia. c.
4142 Cole, R S, 152, H, July 28, pls.
11589 Cole, F, 109, K, Oct 28, scs.
4519 Cole, Wm, 61, H, Aug 2, dia.
7855 Coleby, A, 1 cav, M, Sept 5, dys.
10553 Coleman, I, 2 art, I, Oct 9, scs.
3070 Collins, A, 98, B, July 9, dia. c.
7557 Colwell, D C,§ 2 art, E, Sept 2, scs.
5743 Colwell, J, 120, A, Aug 15, dia.
6069 Comstock, G E, 2 art, A, Aug 27, dia. c
3509 Condon, Thos, 22 cav, F, July 18, pna.
4320 Cone, R, 8, A, July 30, dys.
9619 Conely, John, 125, K, Sept 23, dia.
5528 Conely, Pat, 164, G, Aug 13, dia.
8919 Conger, Jas,‡ 49, A, Sept 16, scs.
11347 Corvier, Chas, 1 cav, C, Oct 25, scs.
2160 Conkin, A, 69, A, June 19, dia. c.
10699 Conlin, Daniel, 5, A, Oct 11, dia. c.
11513 Connell, T, 139, C, Oct 26, scs.
2033 Connelly, F, 52, June 15, dia. c.
10006 Conners, E, 43, D, Sept 29, scs.
4025 Connor, Henry, 52, D, July 26, dys. a.
 936 Conners, John, 99, D, May 7, dia. c.
7842 Cosgrove, F, 76, H, Sept 4, des.
11093 Cook, C H, 6 cav, E, Oct 18, scs.
11240 Cook, Geo, 66, E, Oct 21, scs.
7485 Cook, G W, 146, E, Sept 1, dys.
5228 Coombs, B, 69, A, Aug 10, dia.
10626 Coombs, J, 96, I, Oct 10, scs.
2195 Coons, F, 52, B, June 19, dia. a.
11418 Coon, Geo F, 65, K, Oct 24, scs.
3692 Cooney, F, 14, G, July 21, dys.
10723 Cooney, T, 82, E, Oct 11, dia. c.
5816 Cooper, James, 22 cav, G, Aug 16, dia. a
12274 Cooper, N, 22 cav, F, Dec 13, scs.
1150 Copeland, J, 106, I, May 16, dia.
1778 Corbit, B F,§ 24 bat, June 9, dys.
10529 Corbit, John, 64, C, Oct 8, scs.
6662 Corless, R, 7 art, A, Aug 24, dia.
7182 Cornelius, J, 12 cav, F, Aug 29, dys.
1995 Coroy, P, 99, A, June 15, dia. c.
6729 Corrall, O B, 1 cav, D, Aug 24, dys.
11331 Correll, P, 100, C, Oct 23, scs.
11347 Corrier, Chas, 1 cav, C, Oct 23, scs.
7471 Costin, J, 22 cav, C, Sept 1, dia. c.
12767 Corselman, G, 152, K, March 13, dia. c
7786 Cottin, Z T, 85, E, Sept 4, ana.
5329 Countryman, 120, A, Aug 11, dys.
3899 Courtney, W, 12 cav, A, July 24, dia. a.
8976 Cowen, J, 4, I, Sept 17, dia. c.
7058 Cox, D, 1 cav, H, Aug 28, scs.
7675 Coy, John H, 1 cav, L, Sept 3, dia.
11158 Coyne, M, 98, H, Oct 19, scs.
7274 Cozin, J, 82, E, Aug 30, dys.
3691 Craft, B, 48, D, July 21, dia.
8221 Craig, J, 139, H, Sept 8, dys.
8328 Crandall, D, 85, E, Sept 10, dys.
8399 Crandall, J,‡ 85, C, Sept 10, dia.
2950 Crandall, R, 115, I, July 6, scs.
3061 Crandle, J F, 120, K, July 9, ts. f.
 334 Craven, J, 134, E, April 2, dys.
3432 Crawford, John, 61, B, July 17, dia. c.
12649 Cripman, S, 2, K, Feb 13, scs.
8783 Crissman, Joseph, 140, F, Sept 14, scs.
11471 Crine, C, 6 cav, K, Oct 26, scs.
2311 Criswell, J, 12 cav, F, June 22, dia. a
2822 Crocker, J, 93, E, July 3, dia.
5886 Cromark, J,§ 77, B, Aug 16, dia. c.
2644 Crompter, Jas,§ 14, F, June 29, dia.

8695 Cromwell, T, 6 art, Sept 14, scs.
3324 Crosby, M, 24 bat, July 14, ts. f.
2273 Crouse, George, 24 bat, June 21, dys.
11297 Crowley, S, 2, B, Oct 22, dia. c.
5993 Cuff, S, 14, E, Aug 17, mas.
7159 Culbert, Wm, 39, D, Aug 29, dia.
4119 Culver, N L, 24 bat, July 28, dia.
8966 Cummings, ——, 22, D, Sept 16, dia. c.
11269 Cron, F, 115, D, Oct 21, scs.
5476 Cunningham, J, 170, E, Aug 13, dia.
6721 Cunningham, J, 42, I, Aug 24, des.
1447 Cunningham, Wm, 45, B, May 29, dia. c.
1204 Curley, P, 125, E, May 19, scs.
3627 Currey, John, 146, B, July 20, dia.
4458 Custerman, F, 47, G, Aug 1, dia.
9540 Cute, A, 8 cav, A, Sept 22, dia.
9611 Cutler, C F,‡ 2, G, Sept 23, dia.
12434 Cutler, J P, 99, B, Jan 11, dia.
4846 Cutler, Wm, 59, B, Aug 6, dia.

8193 Daher, G, 66, D, Sept 8, dia.
8650 Daley, T, 42, I, Sept 13, pna.
10741 Damon, J D, 7 art, K, Oct 11, scs.
3577 Dailey, Wm, 5 cav, I, July 19, scs.
11122 Daniels, W O, 76, K, Oct 18, scs.
5599 Daratt, Louis, 111, G, Aug 14, cah.
1480 Daly, John, 99, 8, May 30, ana.
6641 Dawson, J, 47, K, Aug 23, dia. a.
8095 Darley, J,§ 14 art, D, Sept 7, dia. c.
6726 Darling, G H, 18 cav, F, Aug 24, dys.
5083 Darling, J, 4 cav, C, Aug 8, dia.
7562 Dart, Charles W, 85, C, Sept 2, dys.
6404 Davidson, M, 15 cav, M, Aug 21, dia.
6391 Davis, D, 164, G, Aug 21, dia.
6037 Davis, G, 1, H, Aug 18, scs.
1383 Davis, H, 85, I, May 26, dia. c.
7670 Davis, H, 1 art, D, Sept 3, scs.
8089 Davis, H J, 85, C, Sept 7, scs.
961 Davis, H R,‡ 99, I, May 8, dia. c.
12652 Davis, H T, 5 cav, G, Feb 14, dia. c.
5129 Davis, J, 85, H, Aug 9, brs.
7894 Davis, J J,‡ 43, B, Sept 5, scs.
11817 Davis, John, 47, E, Nov 4, scs.
10241 Davis, P,‡ 94, I, Oct 3, scs.
10018 Davy, J J, 2 cav, A, Sept 29, scs.
5338 Day, J W, 32, D, Aug 11, pna.
3866 Dean, C, 43, E, July 24, dia.
9400 Dean, J, 3 cav, G, Sept 21, dia.
2305 Dean, John, 6 art, K, June 22, dia. c.
10523 Debras, J, 9, A, Oct 8, dia. c.
9958 Decker, A, 82, I, Sept 28, dia.
3660 Deckman, J G, 104, B, July 20, dys.
7505 Declercy, W E, 22 cav, E, Sept 1, dia. c.
10555 Dedrich, P, 9, K, Oct 9, scs.
12320 Deman, W, 66, E, Dec 22, scs.
7059 Dessotell, J, 98, D, Aug 28, scs.
7935 Deet, F, 90, D, Sept 5, dia.
4400 Deffer, Louis, 40, H, July 31, ana.
4914 Degammo, J, 48, E, Aug 6, scs.
6283 Degroff, C, 115, H, Aug 20, dia. c.
12074 Degrout, W, 7 art, I, Nov 18, scs.
12228 Devit, Charles, 7 art, G, Dec 5, scs.
7261 Delane, M, 111, C, Aug 30, des.
11206 Delany, C, 52, H, Oct 20, scs.
12271 Demara, John, 108, M, Dec 12, scs.
5689 Demerest, D, 5, A, Aug 15, scs.
10103 Demerest, H V, 2 cav, M, Sept 30, dia.
8761 Demhart, W, 111, F, Sept 14, scs.
9592 Demming, F M, 85, H, Sept 23, dia.
278 Dempsey, John, 85, B, Aug 30, dia.
1623 Demuning, L,‡ 85, D, Sept 2, scs.
9930 Dennis, A A, 106, H, Sept 28, dia.
1489 Dennis, Thomas, 132, G, May 31, r. f.
4099 Dennison, J, 12 cav, A, July 27, dia.
12257 Dennison, J,§ 155, I, Dec 10, scs.
7461 Dennison, W, 14 art, M, Sept 1, dia.
13259 Denorf, F, 147, B, July 13, wds.
2320 Densamore, S F, 115, G, June 22, dia. c.
6324 Densmore, E,§ 85, K, Aug 21, ana.
12603 Desmond, D,‡ 82, C, Feb 6, scs.
1799 Deveny, H, 99, I, June 10, dia. c.
7598 Devlin, A, 1 art, M, Sept 2, dia.

5502 Devlin, J, 12 cav, F, Aug 13, dia. c.
10077 Dewire, Dennis, 7, E, Sept 30, ana.
2839 De Witt, S C,§ 120, E, July 3, ts. f.
9334 Dewitt, J S,§ 48, H, Sept 20, scs.
9855 Dickinson, N, 152, K, Sept 27, dia. c.
10597 Dickerman, W B, 6 art, A, Oct 10, scs.
11854 Difendorf, R, 2 art, L, Nov 6, dia.
2234 Dykeman, F, 47, C, June 20, dia. c.
10089 Dingle, J,§ 122, G, Sept 30, scs.
1821 Dingley, C, 4 cav, A, June 10, dia. c.
8588 Dighard, F, 15 cav, A, Sept 12, scs.
8245 Doan, A, 85, C, Sept 9, dia.
3773 Dodson, E, 85, C, July 22, scs.
1959 Dolan, J, 48, E, June 14, dia. a.
11805 Dolan, M, 6 cav, F, Nov 4, scs.
5658 Dolan, P, 30, I, Aug 14, dia.
11884 Domick, E, 4 art, E, Nov 6, dia.
4886 Donaghen, J, 16, A, Aug 6, dia.
2809 Dond, Daniel, 155, I, July 3, dia. a.
6149 Dondall, B, 111, G, Aug 19, dia. a.
11357 Donely, M, 10, F, Oct 23, dia.
3081 Donovan, J, 14 art, July 9, dia.
229 Donley, E J, 2 M Rifles, K, Mar 29, dia. c
12718 Donnell, W, 4 art, A, March 2, pls.
655 Donnelly, Jas C,§ 2 cav, D, April 21, des.
10102 Doolittle, W, 76, D, Sept 30, dia.
3533 Dorchester, H S, v s, 12 cav, July 18, ana
12715 Dormity, M, citizen, March 1, des.
10320 Dotsey, J, 139, E, Oct 4, scs.
9416 Dougherty, E S, 85, I, Sept 21, dia.
4650 Dougherty, J, 9, C, Aug 3, dys.
2052 Dougherty, O, 99, I, June 16, dia. c.
10992 Doughty, E S, 48, A, Oct 16, dia.
9298 Downey, H, 11, I, Sept 19, uls.
5705 Downey, J A, 85, H, Aug 15, i. f.
7275 Douglass, M, 48, D, Aug 30, ts. f.
10356 Douglass, P, 147, C, Oct 5, dia.
6149 Dondall, B, 111, G, Aug 19, dia. a.
2561 Doyle, John, 5 cav, G, June 27, dys.
4827 Doyle, James, 120, H, Aug 5, scs.
9142 Doyle, W, 7 art, I, Sept 18, dys.
9308 Dow, M, 125, H, Sept 20, dia.
3929 Drake, D W, 2 art, H, July 25, dys.
2347 Drake, D B, 158, F, June 23, des.
699 Driscoll, ——, 52, B, April 23, dia. c.
2826 Drum, A, 155, A, July 3, dia. c.
9357 Druse, I, 15 art, D, Sept 20, dia.
394 Durfee, James, 99, H, April 6, dia.
3063 Dumfrey, Dennis, 100, I, July 9, dia.
3490 Dudley, J C,§ 10 cav, H, July 17, dia. c
3957 Duell, R, 6 art, F, July 25, dia.
5264 Dumond, A, 85, E, Aug 10, i. f.
5810 Dumond, C, 120, A, Aug 16, dia. c.
6773 Dumond, S, 5, B, Aug 25, dia.
10144 Dumond, F, 146, A, Oct 1, scs.
9116 Dunlap, C, 85, B, Sept 18, dia.
8669 Duane, T, 95, E, Sept 13, dia.
8453 Dritman, William, 42, C, Sept 11, dia. c.
6905 Duble, Henry, 61, F, Aug 26, dys.
6087 Dule, Levi, 5, B, Aug 18, dia.
10948 Duger, P, 67, A, Oct 14, scs.
11104 Dunham, R, 14 art, G, Oct 18, dys.
7621 Dunn, J, 40, G, Sept 2, dia. c.
8244 Dunn, L H, 50 Eng, E, Sept 9, dia.
5732 Dunn, James, 88, D, Aug 15, scs.
1695 Dunn, J H, 99, I, June 7, dia. c.
10948 Dwire, P, 67, A, Oct 14, scs.
123 Dunbar, Thomas, 2, F, March 23, ts. f.
3234 Dunn, M, 90, I, July 12.
919 Dunn, Owen, 126, H, May 6, dia.
1033 Dunn, Pat, 149, A, May 11, ana.
3584 Dunning, Wm, 132, G, July 19, dys.
2972 Dunsham, Abr, 120, C, July 7, dia. c.
7554 Durand, H, 82, K, Sept 2, scs.
4832 Durand, Jas E, 10 cav, E, Aug 6, dia. c
9716 Dyer, S, 7 art, D, July 27, dia.
4086 Dyer, John S, 10 cav, M, Sept 25, scs.
3574 Dykeman, D, 22 cav, F, July 9, pna.
12271 Dunaram, John, 108, F, Dec 12, scs.

9033 Earl, C, 85, D, Sept 17, scs.
2443 Earl, H, 174, H, June 25, dia. c

****

VIEW OF THE MANNER IN WHICH THE DEAD WERE INTERRED.

Taken from a Rebel Photograph. The bodies were laid in rows of one hundred to three hundred, and after the earth was thrown over them, a stake was thrust down to mark the place of burial.   Page 144.

VIEW OF THE KITCHEN,

Which was a one-story shed, built of rough boards, one hundred feet in length, and less than fifty in width; it contained in the interior two medium-sized ranges, and four boilers of fifty gallons' capacity each.

8203 Eastern, Thos, 5 cav, L, July 12, dia.
3919 Eastman, Wm, 10, C, July 25, scs.
4239 Easton, E E, 52, F, July 29, dia.
4410 Eastwood, E, 24 bat, July 31, dia. c.
7449 Eber, James, 76, B, Sept 1, dys.
3552 Edmonds, L, 5 cav, M, July 18, dys.
4288 Edwards, S, 52, F, July 30, dia.
7309 Edsen, John, 64, D, Aug 30, dia.
7850 Edsen, W, 105, E, Sept 5, scs.
2728 Egan, John, 125, D, July 1, dia. c.
9454 Egerton, H, 14 art, L, Sept 20, dia.
2319 Elberson, J, 10 cav, E, June 21, brs.
7420 Eldery, B, 146, E, Aug 31, dia.
6507 Eldred, H, 125, K, Aug 22, dia. c.
3597 Eldred, I, 76, F, July 19, dia.
10339 Ellis, J, 2, H, Oct 4, scs.
12071 Ellis, P M, 2, E, Nov 17, scs.
9736 Ellis, C, 85, G, Sept 25, dia.
7204 Ellis, R H, 76, F, Aug 29, dia.
8960 Elliott, F P, 76, B, Sept 16, scs.
8163 Elliott, L, 3 cav, I, Sept 8, i. f.
1107 Ellis, William, 119, F, May 15, dia. c.
3526 Ellis, Perry, 106, I, July 18, scs.
8274 Ellison, W, 95, F, Sept 9, dia.
6343 Elster, James, 7 art, E, Aug 21, dia.
9564 Elwell, W, 47, B, Sept 23, scs.
8152 Emery, C Z,‡ 48, G, Sept 8, scs.
6096 Engal, W, 39, B, Aug 18, scs.
9086 English, G, 7 cav, I, Sept 18, dia.
9961 Eagh, John, 7 art, E, Sept 28, dia.
2454 Easley, W H, 2 cav, H, June 25, dys. a.
10375 Erst, J, 51, H, Oct 4, scs.
2731 Ethear, J, 13 cav, E, July 1, dia. c.
9459 Evans, Franklin, 140, D, Sept 21, scs.
12365 Evans, L, 7 art, I, Dec 31, scs.
6786 Evens, B, 66, B, Aug 25, dia.
6429 Everett, J, 58, K, Aug 22, dia. c.
11263 Everly, G, 108, I, Oct 21, dia.

11362 Faggerty, C, 2 cav, C, Oct 23, scs.
1622 Fallam, Pat, 3 art, K, June 3, dia.
11576 Famcle, E, 43, D, Oct 28, scs.
7666 Fairfax, Charles, 111, A, Sept 3, dia.
12091 Farland, T, 6, I, Nov 19, dia.
11247 Farley, W, 14 art, F, Oct 21, dia. c.
10259 Farrell, James, 100, C, Oct 3, scs.
5840 Farn, C, 169, G, Aug 16, scs.
5946 Fairman, H B, 6 art, M, Aug 17, scs.
6905 Fawry, John, 2 art, C, Aug 27, dia. c.
7415 Face, J, 115, E, Aug 31, dia.
10057 Fareclough, R, 2, F, Sept 30, scs.
9609 Ferris, C, 100, E, Sept 23, scs.
8439 Ferris, Robert, 14 art, I, Sept 3, scs.
3452 Ferris, John, 5, E, July 17, dia.
4760 Felter, F, 69, C, Aug 5, dys.
7260 Ferguson, H C, 14, C, Aug 30, dia.
7498 Ferguson, M, 39, G, Sept 1, dia.
7412 Felton, George, 164, C, Aug 31, dia.
8407 Feasel, H, 7 art, F, Sept 3, dys.
9779 Ferguson, J M, 15 cav, M, Sept 26, scs.
12507 Finnerty, P, 155, G, Jan 22, dia. c.
247 Fich, John, 8, M, March 30, dia.
3869 Fincucum, John, 96, E, July 24, dia. c.
6192 Fields, F, 2 art, L, Aug 19, dia.
6656 Finch, Henry, 22 cav, L, Aug 24, dys.
8699 Finch, James, 22 cav, M, Sept 14, scs.
10072 Findley, Andrew, 70, D, Sept 30, dia.
11482 Finley, A, 7 art, D, Oct 26, scs.
6215 Fish, L V, 7 art, B, Aug 20, cah.
4412 Fish, JI, 179, A, July 31, dys.
5752 Fish, F, 52, K, Aug 15, ens.
9723 Fish, J W,§ 12 cav, C, Sept 25, dia.
279 Fish, William, 17, H, April 1, ts. f.
11651 Fisher, C P, 124, C, Oct 30, td. f.
10049 Fisher, Conrad, 1 cav, E, Sept 29, dia.
5104 Fisher, Daniel, 45, F, Aug 9, dia.
2389 Fisher, D, 125, K, June 24, dia. c.
12542 Fisher, H, 59, K, Jan 27, uls.
10966 Fisher, L, 39, D, Oct 15, scs.
10171 Fitch, A, 3, F, Oct 1, dia.
4819 Fitch, C, 24 bat, Aug 5, dia.
8569 Fitzgerald, N, 111, C, July 19, scs.

6453 Fitzgerald, Tho, 24 art, D, Aug 22, dia.
12400 Fitzpatrick, ——, 10 cav, G, Jan 5, scs.
6961 Fitzpatrick, O, 100, E, Aug 27, dia.
6500 Flagler, William, 7 art, M, Aug 22, dia. c
7452 Flanigan, Ed, 7 art, C, Sept 1, dia.
5558 Flanigan, P, 40, D, Aug 13, dys.
8583 Fleming, P, 22 cav, E, Sept 12, i. f.
190 Fletcher, Wm,‡ 13 cav, G, March 27, ts. f
12537 Flintkoff, F, 102, E, Jan 27, scs.
774 Florence, B, 99, H, April 28, dia. c.
7690 Fluke, J, 76, K, Sept 3, scs.
8378 Flynn, J, 24 bat, Sept 10, scs.
11958 Flynn, J, 13, K, Nov 11, dia.
9242 Flynn, Wm, 71, E, Sept 19, scs.
9283 Fohnsbelly, C, 169, A, Sept 19, dia.
8042 Folden, H, 7 art, B, Sept 6, dia.
3987 Folet, D, 1 cav, A, July 26, dys.
10841 Follard, James, 1 cav, I, Oct 13, scs.
4807 Foulke, Peter, 100, F, Aug 5, ana.
175 Ford, E V, 132, K, March 26, dys.
7344 Foreber, A, 12 cav, F, Aug 31, ana.
11736 Foley, F, 77, B, Nov 2, scs.
1589 Forget, G H,‡ 85, K, June 3, dia. c.
2470 Foster, H, 1 cav, B, June 25, scs.
759 Foster, J, 5 cav, G, April 27, dys. c.
408 Foster, James, 2 cav, D, April 6, dia. c.
6115 Fox, A, 49, K, Aug 19, ana.
11173 Fox, D, 152, A, Oct 19, scs.
2830 Fox, M, 15 art, K, July 3, dys.
9432 Fruhworth, F, 57, I, Sept 21, wds.
8393 Frake, S, 11, G, Sept 10, scs.
2863 Francis, P L, 2 cav, H, July 4, dia. c.
9917 Franklin, J, 39, I, Sept 28, scs.
4227 Franklin, J C, 22 cav, L, July 29, dia.
10484 Fraser, J H, 73, C, Oct 7, scs.
11353 Freilander, C, 2 cav, B, Oct 23, scs.
4820 Freburg, E, 52, F, Aug 5, dia.
6619 Fredinburg, James, 85, H, Aug 23, ana.
6668 Free, C, 30, B, Aug 24, scs.
11363 French, J, 2 cav, H, Oct 23, scs.
10968 French, James, 22 cav, G, Oct 15, scs.
6989 French, John C, 5 cav, H, Aug 27, dys.
1395 Freiser, John, 111, K, May 26, dys.
5125 Frisby, W L,‡ 111, B, Aug 9, dys. c.
11421 Frositer, F, 16 cav, L, Oct 24, scs.
3806 Fuller, A, 49, K, July 22, brs.
11638 Fuller, C, 52, H, Oct 30, scs.
3713 Fuller, J B, 85, F, July 21, dia. c.
11050 Fuller, N, 18, C, Oct 17, scs.
10295 Fuller, W, 122, A, Oct 4, dia.
10328 Funday, F, 39, B, Oct 4, dia.
10140 Fricks, A, 62, L, Oct 1, scs.

2472 Gagan, Thomas, 85, C, June 25, ts. f.
5773 Gale, George,‡ 2, A, Aug 15, scs.
1148 Gallagher, G, 5 cav, D, May 16, dia.
6106 Gallagher, P, 47, D, Aug 18, scs.
4699 Gallewin, Thomas 20 art, F, Aug 4, dia
10489 Galush, W, 5 cav, F, Oct 7, dia. c.
7678 Gaudley, J, 3 cav, F, Sept 3, dia. c.
6993 Gannon, S, 7 art, E, Aug 27, dia.
385 Gansey, ——, 94, B, April 5, pna.
11153 Gardner, H,§ 52, A, Oct 19, scs.
5251 Gardner, R, 155, K, Aug 10, dia.
982 Gardner, H, 132, E, May 9, dys.
1323 Gardner, O, 104, C, May 24, dys.
9206 Gardner, Wm, 7 cav, I, Sept 18, scs.
7926 Garlock, John, 46, B, Sept 5, dys.
8982 Gaman, J, 126, H, Sept 17, scs.
8383 Garney, C, 40, A, Sept 10, dia.
7033 Garoy, James, 95, C, Aug 27, dia.
2688 Garrison, J, 65, H, June 30, i. f.
7216 Gartill, H, 22 cav, L, Aug 29, dys.
7044 Gartland, ——, 169, Aug 27, dia.
94 Garvey, John, 32, K, March 22, dia. c.
10539 Gatiff, H, 82, D, Oct 8, dia.
5270 Gavette, C, 134, G, Aug 10, dys.
6868 Gear, James, 142, A, Aug 26, dia.
7120 Gees, A, 95, I, Aug 28, dia.
7930 Geiser, Charles, 39, D, Sept 5, dia.
8878 Gemninge, J, 6 art, Sept 16, scs.
7650 Gesler, James, 65, E, Sept 3, scs.

6728 Gian, Benjamin, 11, Aug 24, dys.
10967 Gibbs, Charles, 4 art, B, Oct 15, scs.
6259 Gibbs, M H, 22 cav, E, Aug 20, ces.
3218 Gibson, J, 170, A, July 12.
12017 Gibson, J, 82, I, Nov 15, scs.
6942 Giddings, J, 115, H, Aug 26, dia.
2042 Gifford, H N, 111, June 15, ana.
4185 Gilbert, E,§ 43, D, July 28, scs.
10925 Gilbert, E, 22 cav, B, Oct 14, scs
1834 Gilbert, J, 111, K, June 11, dia. c.
11270 Gillis, G, 85, G, Oct 21, scs.
10160 Gill, John F, 1 cav, B, Oct 1, scs.
2413 Gill, James, 111, K, June 24, ana.
3339 Gillen, M, 107, E, July 15, dia.
7898 Gillett, Wm, 85, F, Sept 5, scs.
12345 Gilmore, M,‡ 17, B, Dec 27, scs.
3106 Gimrich, P, bugler, 2 cav, K, July 10, des.
1678 Gleick, Wm,§ 1 cav, A, June 6, dia. c.
3946 Gleason, Thomas, 97, D, July 25, dia. c.
10336 Goaner, F, 16, K, Oct 4, scs.
2553 Goffney, J, 104, D, June 27, dia. a.
8639 Goldsmith, Wm, 2, F, Sept 13, dia. c.
2962 Gond, E, 104, C, July 6, dia. a.
7088 Goodbread, J F, 147, B, Aug 28, dys.
12529 Goodell, F,‡ 122, K, Jan 26, scs.
4145 Goodenough, Jas,‡ 140, D, July 28, dia. c
7342 Goodman, J A, 154, A, Aug 31, scs.
3042 Goodrich, F, 154, B, July 8, dia. c.
4561 Goodrich, George,‡ 2 cav, D, Aug 2, scs.
1415 Gorman, G, 3 art, K, June 17, dys. c.
8228 Goodnow, J, 64, I, Sept 9, scs.
12604 Golt, C, 49, D, Feb 7, rhm.
2203 Goss, James, 132, G, June 19, dia. a.
3322 Gould, Richard, 61, D, July 14, dia. c.
11985 Gough, H, 146, B, Nov 13, scs.
3765 Gower, J, 147, B, July 22, dia.
10499 Graff, F, 14 cav, M, Oct 8, scs.
9347 Graham, J, 15 cav, L, Sept 20, dia.
7089 Graham, Wm, 12 cav, F, Aug 28, ana.
10093 Grampy, M J, 52, D, Sept 30, dia.
2640 Grandine, D S, 111, E, June 29, brs.
3638 Granger, A, 93, I, July 20, brs.
5798 Granger, John, 107, H, Aug 15, dys.
4131 Granner, H, 62, I, July 28, dia.
3212 Grant, C, 96, B, July 12, dia.
3875 Grant, James,§ 125, K, July 24, dys.
6449 Grant, J K, 9, D, Aug 22, dia. c.
9511 Grass, H, 42, G, Sept 22, dys.
12200 Graves, E, 2 cav, I, Dec 1, scs.
4787 Graves, W F, 2, H, Aug 5, dys.
5354 Gray, John, 6 art, H, Aug 11, scs.
1342 Green, E, 85, C, May 24, dia. a.
12522 Green, H W, 146, E, Jan 26, scs.
10277 Green, J H, 109, K, Oct 3, dia.
6863 Greer, John, 76, B, Aug 26, dia.
5202 Green, O, 154, G, Aug 10, dys.
2184 Greenman, J S,§ 2 cav, D, June 19, dia. c.
7634 Gregory, A D L, 120, E, Sept 2, dia. c.
4322 Gregory, John, 61, E, July 30, dia.
7492 Gregory, L, 7 art, M, Sept 1, dia.
7201 Grenals, H, 70, F, Aug 29, dia.
11502 Griffin, J B, 7 cav, D, Oct 26, scs.
3816 Griffin, John, 40, H, July 23, dia.
5766 Griffin, N, 52, F, Aug 15, scs.
3101 Griffith, A, 24 bat, July 10, dia.
11185 Griffith, E P, 85, D, Oct 19, dia. c.
8351 Grilmartin, A, 69, Sept 10, scs.
3815 Griswold, B F,‡ 109, F, July 23, dia.
1220 Groncly, M, 47, E, May 19, dia.
10944 Gross, C, 68, E, Oct 14, scs.
9653 Gross, J, 140, I, Sept 24, gae.
9981 Gross, —, 151, B, Sept 29, brs.
3092 Groven, Joseph, 49, F, July 10, dia. c.
10997 Grundy, R J, 73, G, Oct 16, scs.
10813 Gunan, Wm, 8 cav, D, Oct 12, dia. c.
5867 Gundaloch, F, 95, A, Aug 16, ens.
1459 Gunn, Calvin, 12 cav, G, May 29, dia. c.
6651 Gunnahan, J, 85, G, Aug 23, dia.
2372 Gunnell, John, 2 cav, B, Sept 20, scs.
8317 Guile, A L,§ 154, C, Sept 10, dia. c.
12145 Guyer, F, 15 art, A, Nov 24, scs.
12328 Gwin, Charles, 69, H, Dec 24, scs.

6495 Hack, J, 12, K, Aug 22, scs.
10194 Hackett. C, 43, C, Oct 2, scs.
2623 Hackett, , 12 cav, F, June 25, td. £
7113 Hackett, J, 7 art, D, Aug 28, dys.
6876 Hagate, Jacob, 10 cav, F, Aug 26, dia.
4677 Hager, —, 52, H, Aug 4, scs.
3646 Hager, J, 59, B, July 20, dia.
6869 Hagerty, Wm, 147, E, Aug 26, des.
8275 Hadden, C, 20, Sept 9, dia.
473 Haddish, J, 14, A, April 9, dia.
7721 Hadsell, F, 2 art, L, Sept 3, dia. c.
8924 Haight, J E, 8 art, H, Sept 16, dys.
2887 Hair, G, 89, A, July 4, des.
11036 Halbert, A H,‡ 85, D, Oct 16, scs.
3342 Halbert, L, 1, D, July 15, dia.
170 Haline, Gotfried, 12 cav, K, March 26, ts. £
11310 Hall, C, 1 drag, H, Oct 28, scs.
2214 Hall, Charles, 12 cav, K, June 20, ana.
5003 Hall, Charles, 109, G, Aug 8, dia. c
12370 Hall, C W, 40, I, Jan 1, wds.
870 Hall, Ed, 111, C, May 3, dys.
2846 Hall, James, 9 cav, E, July 3, dia. c.
4459 Hall, John, 109, E, Aug 1, dia.
9661 Hall, S, 14 cav, L, Sept 24, dia.
7731 Hall, W C, 8 cav, K, Sept 3, scs.
7819 Hall, Wm, 2, K, Sept 4, ana.
10865 Hallenbeck, S, 145, B, Oct 13, scs.
4175 Halloway, J, 146, D, July 28, dia. c.
9253 Halpin, P, 68, Sept 19, scs.
11049 Halper, John, 134, F, Oct 17, dia. c.
8213 Hamilton, H, 132, D, Sept 8, dia.
12405 Hamilton, J, 111, G, Jan 6, scs.
10032 Hamilton, John, 6 art, L, Sept 29, dia.
6601 Hamilton, Thomas, 6 art, L, Aug 23, dia
5634 Hammond, N, 66, G, Aug 14, scs.
1104 Hand, L, 5 cav, C, May 15, pna.
9862 Hanlon, Thomas, 180, F, Sept 27, scs.
11076 Hand, H S, 169, A, Oct 17, scs.
3589 Hanks, J, 1 cav, L, July 19, dys. c.
3857 Hanley, D, 22, B, July 24, ana.
12448 Hanley, Wm, 29, D, Jan 13, scs.
6009 Hancock, R, 2 cav, D, Aug 17, dia. c
1207 Hanor, Frank, 12, G, May 19, dia. c.
6432 Hansom, C, 67, F, Aug 22, dia. c.
11149 Hardy, J, 95, C, Oct 19, scs.
9363 Hardy, I,§ 5 cav, I, Sept 20, dia.
10101 Hardy, W, 95, E, Sept 30, scs.
7929 Hannom, John,‡ 164, I, Sept 5, dia.
1411 Haines, Philip, 85, I, May 27, dia. c.
2383 Harp, M, 95, I, June 23, dia. c.
8323 Harper, J, 126, G, Sept 10, dia. c.
10115 Harren, F J, 52, C, Oct 1, scs.
5550 Harris, C, 63, E, Aug 13, dys.
5482 Haines, H, 5 cav, I, Aug 13, dia.
6784 Harris, Thomas, 85, C, Aug 25, dys.
4056 Harris, V S, 8 cav, M, July 27, dys.
1378 Harrington, Pat, 71, D, May 26, ana.
10384 Harrison, Henry, 76, K, Oct 5, dia.
8362 Harrison, O, 14, K, Sept 10, dia.
2526 Harry, A, 143, K, June 26, dys.
4705 Hart, D R, 109, D, Aug 4, scs.
5748 Hart, J, 12 cav, F, Aug 15, i. s.
11524 Hart, J, 7 art, K, Oct 26, scs.
8287 Hart, S,‡ 146, B, Sept 9, scs.
8337 Hart, S, 22 cav, M, Sept 10, ana.
7432 Hartman, I N, 40, H, Aug 31, des.
766 Harty, John, 2 cav, M, April 27, dia. c
10812 Hasket, A, 39, I, Oct 12, dia. c.
8758 Hasler, M, 119, C, Sept 14, dia. c.
11947 Hass, J F, 49, F, Nov 10, scs.
1891 Hathaway, Charles, 24 bat, June 13, dia
10878 Hause, Jno, 1 cav, L, Oct 13, dia.
2262 Haveland, H, 6 art, June 21, dia. c.
11461 Havens, George, 22, G, Oct 25, scs.
3826 Havens, H, 141, A, July 23, dys.
4814 Havens, S,§ 104, A, Aug 5, dys.
3523 Haverslight, H, 66, E, July 18, dia. c.
11629 Hawley, W L, 2 cav, D, Oct 28, scs.
10646 Hawley, F, 76, E, Oct 11, scs.
5355 Hayatt, L P,‡ 1 cav, A, Aug 11, scs.
11786 Hayes, C, 2, F, Nov 4, dia.
8022 Hayes, Edward, 69, G, Sept 6, scs.

9080 Hayes, J, 6, A Sept 18, dia.
10904 Hayes, James 39, E, Oct 14, scs.
11264 Hayes, P, 35, H, Oct 21, dia.
9134 Head, Thomas, 6 art, A, Sept 18, scs.
3394 Haynes, W C, 6 art, G, July 16, ana.
10220 Hayner, L, 125, H, Oct 2, scs.
10662 Heacock, R,§ 66, H, Oct 11, scs.
3581 Hecker, C, 47, C, July 19, dia.
6181 Heddle, Wm, 5 cav, M, Aug 19, ces.
3155 Hefferman, D, 132, C, July 11, dia.
8135 Helafsattan, J, 63, K, Sept 8, scs.
11382 Helf, J C, 1 cav, G, Oct 24, scs.
6828 Heller, D, 14 art, Aug 25, dia.
7330 Henderson, N J, 85, K, Aug 30, dys.
10206 Hendfest, J B, 100, K, Oct 2, scs.
11380 Henertes, B, 15, I, Oct 24, scs.
11733 Hilbert, G, 5, E, Nov 2, scs.
8336 Hennesy, M, 3 art, K, Sept 10, scs.
7196 Henyon, W, 85, H, Aug 29, dia.
10870 Heratage, Thomas, 8, C, Oct 13, scs.
196 Herget, John, 111, A, March 27, brs.
3119 Hermance, F C,‡ 20, st m, A, July 10, ana.
11996 Hermance, J, 100, C, Nov 13, scs.
4495 Herrick, Charles, 39, M, Aug 1, scs.
6627 Henning, C, 140, I, Aug 23, scs.
10566 Hestolate, John, 69, Oct 9, dia.
12104 Hewes, J, 1 cav, A, Nov 20, scs.
11193 Hewes, R,‡ 100, C, Oct 20, dys.
7605 Hicks, W H, 99, I, Sept 2, scs.
99 Hietzel, C, 52, B, March 22, dia.
9937 Higgins, J, 43, G, Sept 28, dia.
888 Higgins, Wm, 99, B, May 4, dia.
4058 Higley, George, 85, F, July 27, dia.
7652 Hildreth, H, 85, K, Sept 3, dia.
3698 Hildreth, L C, 88, D, July 21, scs.
777 Hill, A A, 44, G, April 28, i. f.
8643 Hill, A J,‡ 2, F, Sept 13, dia. c.
3970 Hill, Frank, 2 cav, K, July 25, scs.
11998 Hill, L, 22, B, Nov 13, scs.
11912 Hill, William, 24 cav, E, Nov 8, scs.
3316 Hillman, George, 85, B, July 14, dys.
4454 Hines, J, 126, G, Aug 1, scs.
9060 Hingman, A, 140, G, Sept 17, scs.
31 Hinkley, B, 9 cav, E, March 9, pna.
6255 Hinkley, D, 1 cav, E, Aug 20, scs.
5331 Hinton, J, 14 art, D, Aug 11, dia. a.
2967 Hinton, Thomas,‡ 12 cav, E, July 6, dia.
7192 Hoag, I, 169, A, Aug 29, dys.
395 Hoag, John A, 21 cav, L, April 6, dia.
11670 Hoar, H J, 120, I, Oct 30, scs.
2085 Hobbs, J, 8, H, June 17, dia. c.
2984 Hobson, Wm, 14 cav, F, July 7, dia. a.
6556 Hodge, John, 22 cav, A, Aug 23, dia. a.
6977 Hodgekiss, A, 8 cav, M, Aug 27, dys.
1027 Hoffaud, John, 132, E, May 11, dia. c.
5010 Hoffman, Fred, 48, B, Aug 8, scs.
3811 Hoffman, H, 47, E, July 23, dys.
4932 Hoffman, H, 7 art, L, Aug 7, scs.
6248 Hoffman, N, 5 cav, F, Aug 20, dia. c.
7718 Hofyenneck, T, 21 cav, 1, Sept 3, dia.
11317 Hogan, J, 63, F, Oct 22, scs.
5489 Hogan, John J, 6 art, M, Aug 13, dia.
162 Horsenton, E L, 94, B, March 26, dia.
6465 Holbrook, G, 76, K, Aug 22, dia. c.
6327 Holbrook, J E, 85, E, Aug 21, dia.
5013 Holcomb, M D, 95, F, Aug 8, dys.
2204 Holcomb, Theo, 44, K, June 19, dia. a.
11662 Holfe, J, 48, E, Oct 30, scs.
6475 Holiday, S, 85, E, Aug 22, scs.
2510 Hollands, H, 115, E, June 26, dia. c.
7218 Hollen, M, 152, A, Aug 29, scs.
2573 Hollenbeck, H J, 120, G, June 27, des.
7051 Holliday, S,‡ 85, K, Aug 28, dys.
10624 Holmen, J, 50, C, Oct 10, scs.
7952 Holmes, C, 85, A, Sept 6, dia.
7104 Holmes, E, 7 art, K, Aug 28, dia.
5531 Holmes, Henry, 99, H, Aug 13, scs.
12467 Holmes, J, 4 art, K, Jan 16, scs.
1504 Holstenstein, H, 48, E, May 31, dia. c.
12298 Holtcamp, B, 96, F, Dec 16, scs.
7826 Homvighansen, F, 140, B, Sept 4, dys.
7127 Hooker, T, 111, D, Aug 28, t. f.

5369 Hoover, A, 15 art, H, Aug 11, dia.
514 Hoppock, A, 15 art, H, April 12, dia.
8040 Honstead, H, 22, A, Sept 6, dia.
6114 Hore, R,‡ 15 cav, L, Aug 19, dia. c.
2445 Hosford, W F, 24 bat, June 25, td. f.
6094 Houghtalinger, M, 120, D, Aug 18, dia.
10817 Houghteling, C, 5 art, A, Oct 12, dia.
5652 Hour, James, 119, E, Aug 14, ana.
7457 Hous, A R, 96, C, Sept 1, dia.
11099 Houslin, E, 95, G, Oct 18, des.
11693 Howard, A, 2 art, M, Oct 31, dia.
8477 Howard, J, 12 cav, F, Sept 11, scs.
4387 Howard, Wm, 39, A, July 31, dia.
10114 Howe, G, 16 cav, M, Oct 1, dia. c.
12292 Howe, S, 59, C, Dec 15, scs.
11064 Howell, C R, 2 cav, C, Oct 17, scs.
6622 Hoye, J, 9 art, I, Aug 23, dia.
7301 Hubbard, A, 76, B, Aug 30, scs.
10666 Hudson, J A, 148, A, Oct 11, scs.
9562 Hudson, S R, 15 cav, L, Sept 23, scs.
9337 Hull, J E, 24 cav, E, Sept 20, dia.
1482 Huff, W S, 140, C, May 29, dia. c.
7931 Huganer, A,§ 85, K, Sept 5, dys.
16 Huganer, D M, 64, I, March 6, dys.
7805 Hughes, John, 93, K, Sept 4, scs.
11191 Hughes, M,§ 82, K, Oct 20, dys.
7287 Hughes, Thomas, 61, G, Aug 30, dys.
2562 Hulet, W, 22 cav, L, June 27, ts. f.
7584 Hulse, G, 99, I, Sept 2, scs.
1474 Hulse, W S, 47, G, May 30, dia. c.
7153 Humphrey, H,‡ 85, F, Aug 29, dia. c.
2618 Humphrey, Jas, 155, I, June 28, dia. c.
2898 Hunnell, J, 100, A, July 5, dys.
476 Hunt, F J, 46, D, April 9, dia. c.
3365 Hunter, E,§ 24 bat, July 15, ts. f.
10978 Hunter, J, 115, Oct 15, scs.
9862 Hanlon, Thomas, 180, F, Sept 27, scs.
5841 Huntsmore, G, 66, E, Aug 16, dia.
5497 Hurlburt, S B, 100, E, Aug 13, scs.
4430 Hurley, John, 52, A, July 31, dia.
12614 Hurrell, J, 10 cav, E, Feb 8, dia.
11851 Hutchings, H W, 1 cav, D, Nov 1, dia.
3112 Hutchings, S A, 5 cav, B, July 10, dia.
5024 Hutchings, Wm, 6 art, G, Aug 8, dys.
898 Hutchinson, T, 13 cav, D, May 4, dia.
8585 Hutchinson, J, 82, A, Sept 12, scs.
11019 Hutchinson, M,‡ 52, G, Oct 16, scs.
9173 Huleson, Wm E, 2 art, B, Sept 18, scs.
8955 Hyde, C, 14, F, Sept 16, scs.
11083 Hyde, G, 42, C, Oct 18, scs.
8770 Hyde, J F, 76, B, Sept 14, dia.
7625 Hyland, O, 5, D, Sept 2, dia. c.
2106 Hyman, J, 45, E, June 17, dia.

2187 Imhoff, R, 2 cav, G, June 19, dys.
4019 Imlay, E,§ 95, A, July 26, dia.
4359 Inman, J P, 1 cav, A, July 31, dia.
10549 Ingerson, S, 14 art, G, Oct 9, dys.
4685 Ingraham, C B, 85, B, Aug 4, dia.
3428 Inier, I, 1 cav, H, July 16, dia. c.
4587 Irish, G, 85, C, Aug 2, dys.
11781 Ivespack, W, 15 cav, E, Nov 3, scs.

8159 Jaquays, R, 9, L, Sept 8, pls.
7596 Jack, J W, 95, H, Sept 2, dia.
6558 Jackson, A, 5 cav, E, Aug 23, dia.
9048 Jackson, J, 43, K, Sept 17, dia.
11391 Jackson, T A, 122, E, Oct 24, scs.
5402 Jackson, John S, 100, F, Aug 12, dia.
7253 Jackson, William, 85, F, Aug 30, dia.
6966 Jarmine, James, 115, I, Aug 27, scs.
4795 Jamison, A, 51, A, Aug 5, scs.
3645 Jarvis, E, 106, H, July 20, dia.
11704 Jasper, C, 7 art, D, Oct 31, scs.
6671 Jay, John, 8 art, Aug 24, scs.
9389 Jay, John, 2 art, G, Sept 20, dia.
3984 Jeffrey, B, 9 art, D, July 26, dys.
1120 Jelley, John, 99, K, May 15, dia. c.
29 Jenner, Henry, 3 art, K, April 19, s. p.
10757 Jennings, C, 149, K, Oct 12, wds.
744 Jewell, Jas R, 3 art, K, April 26, dys.
9934 Johnson, A, 74, C, Sept 28, scs.

11182 Johnson, A, 7 art, A, Oct 19, wds.
12121 Johnson, B, 63, D, Nov 22, scs.
12477 Johnson, B F, 82, H, Jan 17, pls.
10118 Johnson, H S, 85, D, Oct 1, scs.
5916 Johnson, H, 115, I, Aug 17, dia. c.
6232 Johnson, H, 10 cav, C, Aug 20, dia. a.
7712 Johnson, J, 89, I, Sept 3, dia.
12546 Johnson, J, 146, A, Jan 27, dys.
10043 Johnson, L W, 14 art, C, Sept 29, dia.
5935 Johnson, M, 96, H, Aug 17, scs.
9495 Johnson, P B, 24 bat, Sept 21, dia. c.
8054 Johnson, R, 111, A, Sept 7, scs.
3427 Johnson, R, 120, I, July 16, dia.
4047 Joice, Thomas, 22, C, July 27, ts. f.
7413 Jolley, F, 93, E, Aug 31, dia.
5980 Jones, C N, 10 cav, C, Aug 17, mas.
6898 Jones, David, 85, H, Aug 26, dys.
10769 Jones, E C, 147, E, Oct 12, dia. c.
3650 Jones, E, 134, F, July 20, dys.
4373 Jones, G C, 20, July 31, dia.
3282 Jones, G W, 47, F, July 14, scs.
5753 Jones, H, 10 cav, I, Aug 15, dia.
5582 Jones, John, 76, K, Aug 14, r. f.
11855 Jones, John, 6 cav, A, Nov 6, scs.
2487 Jones, R, 99, B, June 26, dia. c.
4403 Jones, Thos, 116, B, July 31, ana.
5042 Jones, Wm, 52, B, Aug 8, dia.
8867 Jones, Wm, farrier, 5 cav, C, Sept 15, dia.
8771 Jones, J B, 22, F, Sept 14, scs.
9528 Jourdan, Barry, 7 art, E, Sept 22, dia.
4188 Jule, H, 51, E, July 28, dia.
9107 Jump, O, 8 cav, Sept 18, dia. c.

5198 Kahbaun, E, 12 cav, F, Aug 10, scs.
12170 Kane, F, 82, A, Nov 26, scs.
792 Kane, Peter, h s, 20 cav, April 28, dia. c.
8868 Kanope, C, 49, Sept 15, dia.
9194 Kapp, D, 100, F, Sept 18, dia.
10222 Kearney, W, 16 cav, A, Oct 2, scs.
8452 Keating, M, 146, A, Sept 11, dia. c.
4484 Keating, Thos, 83, L, Aug 1, dia.
11075 Keean, W, 47, I, Oct 17, scs.
7387 Keers, M, 49, A, Aug 31, scs.
11756 Kehoe, T, 155, A, Nov 3, scs.
10341 Kelley, M, 2 art, L, Oct 4, dia.
10649 Kellar, John, 140, E, Oct 11, scs.
6739 Kelley, D,‡ 45, C, Aug 24, dys.
11100 Kelley, J, 4 art, K, Oct, 18, des.
10675 Kelley, Jas, 146, K, Oct 11, scs.
6997 Kelley, James, 40, F, Aug 27, dia. c.
10388 Kelley, M, 63, Oct 5, scs.
9676 Kelley, P, 106, D, Sept 24, scs.
12209 Kelley, T,§ 82, F, Dec 2, dia.
10960 Kenarm, Alfred, 70, K, Oct 14, scs
11425 Kennedy, M E, 82, K, Oct 24, scs.
9865 Kennedy, W, 132, D, Sept 27, scs.
11244 Kennion, F, 8, H, Oct 21, scs.
3572 Kenny, A W, 85, D, July 19, dys.c
1250 Kenny, G W, 24 bat, May 21, ts. f.
3671 Kenny, M, 2, F, July 20, dia. c.
4398 Kent, E L, 85, I, July 31, dia.
7403 Kenwell, R, 5 cav, D, Aug 31, scs.
1079 Keogan, Peter, 132, C, May 14, dia.
5952 Kerrit, Jacob, 132, D, Aug 17, mas,
5310 Kerr, C L, 85, B, Aug 11, scs.
2434 Kerr, H, 2 cav, L, June 25, ana.
3915 Kertser, T, 178, K, July 25, dia. c.
2797 Kester, Chas,§ 141, F, July 2, dia. c.
1622 Kettle, Sol, 2 art, K, Oct 28, scs.
9015 Keys, R, 95, C, Sept 17, dia.
650 Keyes, O S, 5 cav, E, April 20, dia.
1932 Kidd, Owen, 126, K, June 14, dia. c.
4608 Killner, Sanford, 125, F, Aug 3, dys. c.
1864 Kilmer, J, 5, I, June 12, dys.
10614 Kilson, J, 115, E, Oct 10, scs.
12026 Kimball, S,§ 7 art, F, Nov 15, scs.
3262 Kimberly, C, 76, B, July 13, dia.
7999 King, ——, 99, I, Sept 6, dia.
9816 King, N, 21 cav, G, Sept 26, dia.
8738 King, Sylvanus, 24 bat, Sept 14, dia.
8787 King, Richard,§ 99, H, July 22, ana.
8085 Kingsley, D, 12 cav H, July 10, dia.

9689 Kingsley, James, 5 cav, Sept 24, dia.
239 Kinney, Lucas, 99, H, March 30, dia. c.
11558 Kinney, M, 42, C, Oct 27, scs.
8400 Kinnie, J, 76, F, Sept 10, scs.
564 Kinsey, B B,§ 132, K, April 15, dia.
7977 Kinsman, John E, 14 art, I, Sept 6, dia.
12839 Kinsman, W S, 86, I, April 20, dia.
4297 Kirby, Charles, 12 cav, F, July 30, ana.
7087 Kirkland, I, 2 art, D, Aug 28, dys.
12742 Kirkpatrick, ——, 12 cav, D, Mar 6, dia. e
5589 Kittle, E N,‡ 125, E, Aug 14, scs.
8873 Kizer, G W, 76, B, Sept 15, scs.
4525 Knapp Henry, 24 cav, A, Aug 2, scs.
5233 Knapp, Phillip, 10 cav, C, Aug 10, dia.
2604 Knabe, E, 48, C, June 28, dia. c.
7949 Knight, Wm, 142, C, Sept 6, dia. c.
12318 Knowl, H, 66, C, Dec 21, scs.
11976 Kossuth, W, 54, F, Nov 12, dia. c.
8860 Krasipars, K, 65, L, Sept 15, dia. c.
9211 Krautz, H,‡ 54, E, Sept 19, scs.
12215 Kreit, J K,§ 1 cav, L, Nov 21. scs.
11948 Krelar, A, 13 bat, Nov 10, wds.
3892 Kroom, C E, 64, G, July 24, dia. c.
1208 Krouser, G R, 178, K, May 19, dia. c.

8956 Lahey, P, 1, D, Sept 16, dia. c.
8447 Lacey, P, 12 cav, F, Sept 11, scs.
3601 Lacey, Wm,‡ 85, K, July 19, dia.
10736 Lackley, P I, 1 cav, Oct 11, scs.
10879 Lacks, Lee, 22, G, Oct 13, scs.
8372 Lacoster, H, 85, Sept 10, scs.
11527 Lader, A, 9, E, Oct 26, scs.
7156 Lagay, Frank, 118, B, Aug 29, scs.
41 Lahey, Daniel, 82, I, March 13, pna.
12775 Lahiff, D, 42, K, March 14, dia. c.
12100 Lake, Wm, 146, K, Nov 21, scs.
6487 Laman, C, 39, H, Aug 22, dia.
6381 Lamareux, J, 76, K, Aug 21, scs.
11893 Lambright, A,‡ 7 art, K, Nov 7, dia. e.
11599 Lambly, J, 1, I, Oct 28, scs.
11318 Lampman, W S, 6 art, M, Oct 22, scs
11213 Lampert, R, 98, D, Oct 20, des.
9836 Larrabee, E,‡ 15, D, Sept 27, scs.
3283 Landers, C, 7 art, July 14, dia.
12214 Lane, C, 146, E, Dec 3, scs.
7462 Lane, Chas, 3 cav, E, Sept 1, ana.
2678 Lane, G W, 85, C, June 30, dys.
11499 Lane, J W, 15 cav, M, Oct 26, dia. c.
2288 Lang, A,‡ 85, F, June 21, ts, f.
13 Lang, Wm W, 1 drag, March 6, pna.
8238 Langdon, A M, 85, B, Sept 9, scs.
4375 Lansing, Wm, 12 cav, B, July 31, scs.
3788 Lansop, J, 85, D, July 22, dia.
10096 Langeu, A, 39, I, Sept 30, dia.
4871 Lappan, L H, 24 bat, Aug 6, dia.
8087 Larcks, G, 85, F, Sept 7, scs.
6631 Larkins, M C, 100, A, Aug 23, wds.
14 Lasar, Benjamin, 6 cav, F, March 6, r. §
8956 Latey, P, 1, D, Sept 16, dia. c.
851 Lattaretta, J,‡ 1 cav, A, May 3, dia. c.
4107 Langha, W, 1 art, M, July 27, dia. c.
8162 Lawton, J, 69, E, Sept 8, cah.
10095 Lawrence, J, 7 art, G, Sept 30, dia.
4101 Lawson, John, 2 cav, D, July 27, dys.
6434 Layman, C, 120, K, Aug 22, dys.
2374 Leabrook, John, 157, B, June 23, pna.
2119 Leach, S, 10 cav, E, June 17, dia. c.
1737 Lean, W H, 21 cav, C, June 8, dys.
7142 Ledderer, Wm, 132, G, Aug 29, dia. e.
1944 Lee, A, 24 bat, June 14, dia. c.
2169 Lee, F, 15, F, June 19, scs.
2572 Lee, P, 2 art, A, June 27, r, f.
9696 Lee, Wm, 6 cav, L, Sept 24, scs.
8514 Legrist, W, 11, E, Sept 10, dia.
6399 Leichinger, J, 3 cav, D, Aug 21, ana.
3565 Leiner, A, 39, B, July 19, dys.
11697 Lenot, V, 47, I, Oct 31, dia.
2686 Lent, A, 24 bat, June 30, pna.
7499 Leonard, A, 52, B, Sept 1, dia. c.
12076 Leonard, C H, 7 art, A, Nov 18, scs.
8987 Leonard, J W, 85, K, Sept 17, dia.
10065 Lestraff, C, 7 art, A, Sept 30, dia.

6150 Letch, John, 5 cav, C, Aug 19, ces.
8774 Levalley, C, 140, A, Sept 14, scs.
9045 Lewis, C, 85, F, Sept 17, dia. c.
3727 Lewis, C F, 52, E, July 21, dia. c.
1329 Lewis, F A, 9, G, May 24, ts. f.
11515 Lewis, G W, 146, G, Nov 8, scs.
8297 Lewis, J, 1 art, E, Sept 9, brs.
5115 Lewis, P W, 85, B, Aug 9, dia.
10365 Lickley, P, 1 cav, E, Oct 5, scs.
11551 Limbach, S, 7, D, Oct 27, scs.
8419 Linch, J H, 76, I, Sept 11, ts. f.
5845 Linchler, F, 1 cav, E, Aug 15, dia.
10559 Lindlay, D, 147, E, Oct 9, dia.
7815 Lineham, Thomas, 125, C, Sept 4, dia.
6759 Ling, John, 4 art, F, Aug 25, dia. a.
38 Link, Gotlieb, 54, K, March 12, dys. c.
10073 Little, C, 76, F, Sept 30, scs.
10933 Livingston, A, 1 cav, C, Oct 14, dia.
4543 Locher, Conrad, 15 art, Aug 2, dys.
5565 Lock, A, 98, B, Aug 13, dia. c.
2142 Lodge, T, 12, A, June 18, dia. a.
8246 Loftern, H, 12 cav, F, Sept 9, dia. c.
9722 Loftus, M, 11 cav, E, Sept 24, dia.
7010 Longs, R, 2 art, A, Aug 27, scs.
11591 Long, J, 75, A, Oct 28, scs.
7924 Long, L, 40, I, Sept 5, ana.
4514 Longle, William, 4 art, B, Aug 1, scs.
5434 Loomis, John, 14 art, M, Aug 12, scs.
9712 Loony, C, 40, A, Sept 25, dia.
9988 Lorzbrau, J, 64, E, Sept 20, dia.
11906 Louis, C, 16 cav, C, Nov 7, scs.
12329 Love, J, 125, A, Dec 24, scs.
7146 Lovejoy, F, 1 cav, I, Aug 29, scs.
10248 Lovering, F, 14 art, I, Oct 3, scs.
12313 Lowery, G, 7, A, Dec 20, scs.
2568 Lowery, James F, 140, A, June 27, dys. a.
9663 Lows, H, 22 cav, E, Sept 24, dia.
8395 Loyd, S, 47, D, Sept 10, dys.
9354 Luce, V, 140, D, Sept 20, scs.
10311 Lucia, A, 95, H, Oct 4, scs.
7268 Lurcock, E, 14 art, M, Aug 30, scs.
9002 Lutton, O, 14 art, H, Sept 17, scs.
5772 Lynch, D, 164, A, Aug 15, dia.
6895 Lynch, F,‡ 43, K, Aug 26, ana.
931 Lynch, Pat, 99, H, May 7, dia. c.
12633 Lyons, Charles, 2 cav, M, Feb 10, des.
1427 Lyons, Michael, 99, E, May 28, dia. c.
8419 Luch, J H, 76, I, Sept 11, ts. f.
6151 Lucah, John, 5 cav, C, Sept 19, ces.
8542 Lyons, J H, 5 art, Sept 10, scs.
6156 Lyons, Thomas, 6 art, G, Aug 19, dia. a.
7913 Lyons, W,‡ 47, A, Sept 5, dia. c.

37 Mace, Jeff, 134, I, March 12, dia.
6665 Mace, L, 43, H, Aug 24, scs.
10850 Mack, J, 39, D, Oct 13, dia.
5016 Mackin. Wm, 85, F, Aug 8, dia. c.
3933 Madder, P, 155, E, July 25, dia. c.
10506 Madden, F,§ 122, E, Oct 8, dia. c.
4822 Madden, ——, 1 cav, D, Aug 5, dys.
11257 Madezan, John, 125, B, Oct 21, scs.
9798 Madison, D, 75, D, Sept 26, scs.
11714 Magrath, G H, 61, D, Nov 1, dys.
4028 Mahon, E, 170, G, July 26, tonsilitis.
122 Mahon, James,§ 132, K, March 23, ts. f.
1422 Mahon, Thomas, 120, C, May 28, dia. c.
5842 Mailer, J R,§ 134, B, Aug 16, ers.
11679 Maine, F O, 85, A, Oct 31, scs.
11580 Mainhart, F, 39, B, Oct 28, scs.
12069 Makay, J, 5, E, Nov 17, scs.
7942 Malleck, M,‡ 6 cav, D, Sept 5, dia. c.
9427 Malley, S S, 16, K, Sept 21, dia.
9457 Malone, Pat, 123, F, Sept 21, scs.
3284 Maloney, C, 6, C, July 14, dia. c.
11447 Maloney, J, 73, G, Oct 25, scs.
7600 Mandeville, Wm, 85, F, Sept 2, scs.
2802 Mangin, M, 7 art, F, July 3, scs.
10624 Manning ——, 33, Oct 9, scs.
7138 Manning M, 6 art, D, Aug 28, scs.
10540 Manning Thomas, 125, B, Oct 8, scs.
2952 Mannilly J, 74, C, July 6, dia. a.
2856 March, J 22 cav, C, July 4, dia. c.

4000 Marley, John, mus, 53, E, July 28, dia.
1123 Marron, J, 99, I, May 15, dys.
11764 Martaugh, J, 6 cav, A, Sept 3, scs.
3824 Marsh, Ira, 6 art, M, July 23, scs.
5407 Marsh, J, 104, D, Aug 12, dia.
11997 Marston, A, 65, G, Nov 13, scs.
3441 Martin, A, 12 cav, F, July 17, dys.
435 Martin, C, 10 cav, A, April 8, ana.
6543 Martin, Charles, 42, G, Aug 23, dia.
11600 Martin, E A, 5 cav, C, Oct 28, scs.
12208 Martin, J, 39, G, Dec 2, dia.
4321 Martin, H, 76, H, July 30, dys.
5086 Martin, J C, 24 bat, Aug 8, dia. c.
9164 Martin, P, 99, H, Sept 18, scs.
6293 Martin, John, 16 cav, L, Aug 20, scs.
1256 Martin, Peter, 40, I, May 21, dia. a.
8003 Martin, W, 142, F, Sept 6, scs.
3939 Martin, W B, 12, I, July 25, scs.
8746 Martin, W H, 24 art, M, Sept 14, dia.
1073 Martin, Wm, 13 cav, D, May 13, dia. c.
676 Marvoney, James, 132, G, April 22, pha
10483 Mason, F,‡ 14 art, I, Oct 7, scs.
2315 Martin, Samuel, 85, I, June 22, dia. c.
11290 Masterson, E, 2, D, Oct 22, scs.
11296 Massen, H L, 86, C, Oct 22, scs.
10498 Maxwell, J, 85, D, Oct 8, scs.
1477 Maxwell, Robert, 48, D, May 30, wds.
11788 Matthews, W, 155, I, Nov 4, scs.
4472 Matthews, H, 12 cav, M, Aug 1, dia.
2100 Mattice, H C, 134, E, June 17, dia. c.
5651 Mattison, R, 85, D, Aug 14, scs.
4946 Maxum, S G, 12 cav, A, Aug 7, dia. c.
10519 McAllister, J, 125, I, Oct 8, scs.
7995 McBride, ——, 52, K, Sept 6, scs.
4508 McCabe, James, 88, D, Aug 1, dia.
2517 McCabe, P,§ 12 cav, F, June 26, dia. c.
732 McCabe, Peter,§ 2 cav, E, April 25, dys.
2196 McCabe, J, 44, C, June 19, dia. a.
8324 McCafferty, W, 100, C, Sept 10, dia. c.
10716 McCain, L, 18, C, Oct 11, scs.
9864 McCardell, W, 15 cav, H, Sept 27, scs.
7620 McCarten, L, 9 art, B, Sept 2, dia. c.
3413 McCarty, D, 155, G, July 16, dia. a.
4480 McCarty, Denis, 2 art, D, Aug 1, dia. c.
5122 McCarty, I, 99, H, Aug 9, dys. c.
9633 McCarty, I, 2, m r, K, Sept 24, dia.
4759 McCarty, John, 69, K, Aug 5, dia.
6136 McCarty, John, 104, E, Aug 19, ces.
1035 McCarty, P, 132, K, May 11, dia.
2965 McCarty, S, 99, C, July 6, dia. a.
6227 McCarty, W, 9 cav, L, Aug 20, dys.
8242 McClusky, F, 173, E, Sept 9, dia.
1344 McColigan, Pat, 99, F, May 24, dia. a.
9266 McCauley, J H, 47, G, Sept 19, scs.
6440 McCloud, John, 97, A, Aug 22, scs.
4416 McConnell, E, 9 art, July 31, dia.
6012 McCord, H, 7 art, G, Aug 17, dia.
11110 McCormic, M, 93, K, Oct 18, dia. c.
6697 McCormick, H, 69, K, Aug 29, scs.
9018 McCormick, H, 173, F, Sept 17, dia.
3629 McCormick, J, 155, H, July 20, dys.
6203 McCormick, J, 24 bat, Aug 19, dia.
7441 McCormick, J, 43, F, Sept 1, dys.
10258 McCormick, P, 43, D, Oct 3, scs.
1433 McCormick, Peter, 39, I, May 28, dia. s
5203 McCormick, W, 2, I, Aug 10, dia.
7730 McCracker, B, 7 art, B, Sept 3, scs.
8644 McCrass, J, 148, Sept 13, scs.
2279 McCrember, M, 85, I, June 21, dia. c.
8507 McCullen, D, 57, F, Sept 12, dia.
10778 McDavid, J, 5, D, Oct 12, scs.
6912 McDermott, P, 164, H, Aug 26, scs.
8969 McDonald, A, 24 bat, Sept 16, dia. c
7745 McDonald, A H, 85, E, Sept 3, dia.
7140 McDonald, B, 52, D, Aug 29, dia.
4013 McDonald, John, 164, E, July 26, dys.
12138 McDonald, F, 16 cav, L, Nov 23, scs.
10002 McDonald, F,‡ 95, A, Sept 29, dia.
7259 McDonnell, Wm, 14 art, D, Aug 30, scs.
8126 McDurie, C, 71, Sept 8, scs.
4089 McElray, John, 43, I, July 27, dia.
9581 McErmany, P, 7 art, G, Sept 23, ta.

****

838 McFarland, A, 72, I, April 2, pna.	8080 Mitchell, J, 125, E, Sept 7, dia.
12478 McGiben, I, 170, B, Jan 17, scs.	9939 Mitchell, John, 129, I, Sept 28, dia.
11116 McGowan, Wm, 6 art, L, Oct 18, scs.	7396 Milty, Samuel, 12 cav, L, Aug 30, dia.
4001 McFadden, Jas, 39, F, July 26, dys.	2486 Moe, John, 120, I, June 25, dia.
2665 Mcgain, I, 99, H, June 29, dia. c.	4121 Moffat, J, 7 art, C, July 28, dia.
354 McGeatte, 52, D, April 2, pna.	5720 Monaghan, ——, 66, D, Aug 15, dia.
8551 McGibney, H, 85, E, July 18, phs.	4441 Monihan, J, 85, C, July 31, dia.
2756 McGiven, Wm, 158, B, July 1, scs.	4392 Monohan, J, 73, D, July 31, dia.
8225 McGowan, F, 170, H, Sept 9, dia.	11537 Monohan, P, 88, D, Oct 27, scs.
248 McGowan, John, 132, K, March 30, dia.	4658 Monroe, J R,‡ 111, G, Aug 3, scs.
1112 McGrath, M, 12 cav, E, May 15, dia. c.	11961 Monroe, A J, 22, G, Nov 11, scs.
4709 McGucker, A,§ 1 cav, C, Aug 4, dys.	7453 Morgan, M, 76, B, Sept 1, dys.
4995 McGuire, P, 140, C, Aug 7, dia. c.	8241 Monschitz, J, 65, D, Sept 9, scs.
6827 McGuire, P, 10, C, Aug 25, dia.	1933 Monson, Wm, 11, G, June 14, dia.
3220 McGuire, Pat, 101, F, July 12.	7830 Monson, Geo, 6, Sept 4, dys.
8354 McHarty, M, 69, A, Sept 10, scs.	5635 Monta, Henry, 52, B, Aug 14, dys.
3233 McKabe, J, 12 cav, F, July 12.	3512 Montag, Geo, 39, B, July 18, scs.
1168 McKenley, J, 99, I, May 16, dia.	11650 Moran, D G, 40, G, Oct 30, dia.
12664 McKenna, H,‡ 12, F, Feb 16, uls.	6565 Moran, Thos, 85, A, Aug 22. i. s.
5359 McKerchay, J H, 85, F, Aug 11, dia.	7732 Moram, M J, 3 cav, Sept 3, scs.
9390 McKinney, John, 82, D, Sept 20, dia.	11621 Morearty, I, 1, M, Oct 28, scs.
10392 McLain, R, 42, F, Oct 6, scs.	10308 Morgraff, Wm, 64, H, Oct 4, dia.
10055 McLaughlin, O, 9, F, Sept 30, scs.	8461 Moody, C R, 100, B, Sept 11. scs.
4268 McLorens, R, 20 cav, M, July 29, dia.	6423 Moody, Thos, 147, B, Aug 22, scs.
6850 McLaughlin, J,‡ 63, D, Aug 25, dys.	3108 Moony, P, 3 art, K, July 10, dia. c.
3611 McMahon, C L, 3 cav, E, July 19, dia,	3651 Moony, I, 188, D, July 20, dia.
6814 McMurrier, Wm, 2 cav, L, Aug 25, dia.	8417 Mooney, J, 52, D, Sept 11, dia.
9969 McNamara, Wm, 2 art, L, Sept 28, dia.	10886 Mooney, Thos, 139, F, Oct 14, scs.
10728 McNamirin, B F, 14, A, Oct 11, scs.	2766 Moore, A, bugler, 22 cav, E, July 12, dia. s.
5406 McNulty, 85, E, Aug 12, dia.	7656 Moore, C C, 1 cav, B, Sept 3, dia.
3724 McPeak, W, 2 cav, B, July 21, dia.	11829 Moore, C, 2 art, B, Nov 5, scs.
7271 McPherson, Wm, 14 art, M, Aug 30, scs.	658 Moore, Martin, 74, C, April 21, dia.
5868 McQuillen, A, 6 art, L, Aug 16, dia.	1694 Moore, S, 46, H, June 7, dia. c.
8889 McSorley, G W, 20, M, Sept 16, scs.	442 Moore, T H, 5 cav, M, April 9, pna.
3127 Mead, P, 1 art, C, July 10, dia.	457 Moore, W H, 125, F, April 9, dia.
150 Megrawe, W H, 99, E, March 25, pna.	7767 Moore, John, 39, H, Sept 4, dys.
10599 Melin, A, 14 art, L, Oct 10, dia.	9778 Moore, W S, 85, D, Sept 26, scs.
11167 Melins, W, 82, B, Oct 10, dys.	10781 Morgan, E, 14 art, 8, Oct 12, scs.
2068 Menzie, A, 3 art, K, June 16, dia. c.	7563 Morgan, E J, 179, C, Sept 2, dys.
6042 Meritt, H D, 76, F, Aug 18, dys.	10631 Mortross, D H, 7 art, L, Oct 10, dia. c.
9353 Merkle, J, 15, A, Sept 20, scs.	624 Morland, H, 21 cav, H, April 19, dia.
11204 Merwin, A, 2 cav, A, Oct 20, dia. c.	4686 Morris, E, 7 art, K, Aug 4, scs.
11214 Merz, F A, 5, I, Oct 20, scs.	9944 Morris, T, 65, C, Sept 28, scs.
8906 Messing, I, 39, A, Sept 16, scs.	3780 Morris, H, 71, F, July 22, dia.
10116 Messinger, C, 1 cav, L, Oct 1, scs.	8031 Morris, J, 5 cav, D, Sept 6, scs.
6462 Messirie, J M,§ 1 cav, A, Aug 22, scs.	11226 Morris, J, 99, A, Oct 20, scs.
2523 Metcalf, A, 85, G, June 26, dia. c.	5865 Morris, J A, 7 art, G, Aug 16, ens.
3134 Meyers, F, 45, G, July 10, pna.	6069 Morris, John, 70, B, Aug 18, ts. f.
8852 Meyer, H, 66, F, Sept 10, dia.	12387 Morris, R, 66, G, Jan 3, scs.
11723 Meyers, I, 57, F, Nov 1, scs.	9373 Morris, L R, 85, B, Sept 20, scs.
2896 Meyers, W, 54, C, July 5, ana.	7703 Morris, T A,§ 111, E, Sept 3, dia.
4520 Michael, ——, 66, A, Aug 2, dia.	4880 Morris, Wm,§ 102, G, Aug 6, scs.
11780 Michello, W, 2 cav, B, Nov 3, i. f.	8638 Morrison, W, 5, I, Sept 13, gae.
3750 Midlam, F,‡ 12 cav, A, July 22, ana.	9371 Morrison, W, 5 cav, I, Sept 20, scs.
2709 Migner, F,§ 54, D, June 30, dia. c.	7958 Morse, E,‡ 5 cav, L, Sept 6, dia.
6202 Milard, F J,§ 12 cav, A, Aug 19, dia.	12511 Morse, I, 1, L, Jan 23, scs.
168 Millens, Adam, 125, E, March 26, dia.	617 Martin, Chas, 47, A, April 18, dia.
5520 Miller, A W, 52, D, Aug 13, dia.	10625 Martin, G H, 7 art, L, Oct 10, scs.
4647 Miller, C, 111, I, Aug 3, ana.	3181 Martin, Henry, 61, C, July 11, scs.
6469 Miller, Chas B, 24 cav, E, Aug 22, dia.	7672 Mortimer, Wm, 5 art, A, Sept 3, dia.
3521 Miller, F, 182, D, July 18, dys.	7079 Mosher, E, 9 art, D, Aug 28, dia.
5155 Miller, F,§ 99, Aug 9, dia.	10152 Mosier, E, 9 art, E, Oct 1, dia.
6865 Miller, F, 15 art, D, Aug 26, dia.	11016 Mosier, M W, 4, G, Oct 16, scs.
1516 Miller, G A, 152, C, Oct 26, scs.	2872 Moses, L, 85, E, July 4, dia.
6585 Milen, Geo, 61, F, Aug 23, dia.	12003 Motts, C, 24 bat, Nov 14, scs.
11522 Miller, Geo, 1, G, Oct 26, scs.	8711 Moss, W S,‡ 7 art, Sept 14, scs.
3131 Miller, H, 1 cav, L, July 10, scs.	11466 Mulcaby, W,§ 42, E, Oct 26, dia.
10627 Miller, H W, 96, E, Oct 10, dia. c.	7997 Mulcohy, D D, 76, F, Sept 6, scs.
8278 Miller, J, 95, E, Sept 9, scs.	11368 Mulgrave, James, 2, C, Oct 23, scs.
5521 Miller, Jacob, 39, I, Aug 13, scs.	12240 Mullen, Charles, 7 art, I, Dec 7, scs.
628 Miller, J E, bugler, 2 cav, M, Apr 19, pna.	11324 Muller, P, 7, H, Oct 23, scs.
9505 Miller, John, 12, A, Sept 22, scs.	6985 Mulligan, J, 34, H, Aug 27, scs.
708 Miller, O, 126, G, April 24, dys. c.	11485 Mulish, R, 48, A, Oct 26, scs.
9986 Miller, Wm, 2 art, C, Sept 29, scs.	12155 Mullin, J, 82, G, Nov 25, scs.
8063 Millerman, G, 22 cav, B, Sept 7, dia.	4720 Mullington, C,‡ 6 art, H, Aug 4, bra.
8862 Mills, J J, 85, Sept 15, scs.	8370 Munger, D, 2 art, C, Sept 10, dia.
2844 Mills, S, 12 cav, A, July 3, ana.	8404 Murchison, D,§ 4 cav, D, Sept 11, dia. a.
4854 Millspaugh, Fred, 6 art, A, Aug 6, scs.	146 Murphy, John, 99, H, March 25, dia.
79 Miline, John, 95, G, March 20, pna.	5804 Murphy, F, 61, B, Aug 16, dys.
1889 Mindler, Peter, 1 cav, June 13, dia. c.	5918 Murphy, L, 170, E, Aug 17, dys.
4771 Miner, J G, 24 bat, Aug 5, dia.	6550 Murphy, W S, 40, K, Aug 23, dia.
618 Mirie, F, 99, F, July 20, dys.	11803 Murphy R,‡ 85, E, Nov 4, scs.

10200 Murphy, Martin, 2 cav, D, Oct 2, scs.
12118 Murray, J, 23 cav, F, Nov 22, scs.
11273 Murray, J, 47, I, Oct 22, scs.
3389 Murry, A, 118, C, July 16, dia.
8947 Murry, J, 39, C, Sept 16, scs.
11519 Murry, M, John, 63, F, Oct 26, scs.
6218 Murny, 11 bat, Aug 20, dys.
11954 Murrey, M,‡ 98, D, Nov 10, scs.
1560 Murville, S, 1, C, June 2, dia.
12494 Muselman, J, 2, K, Jan 20, scs.
1384 Myers, E, 154, D, May 26, dia. c.
4958 Myers, H, 47, A, Aug 7, dia. c.
9913 Myers, H, 2 cav, G, Sept 28, scs.
5000 Myers, H L, 147, H, Aug 7, dys.
8970 Myers, J, 20 cav, M, Sept 16, dys.
6221 Myers, Jas, 66, K, Aug 20, dys.

8973 Neal, J, 22, E, Sept 16, dia. c.
10587 Nedden, J, 82, A, Oct 10, scs.
7922 Nellman, A, 66, I, Sept 4, dia.
2541 Nelson, B, 39, A, June 27, dia.
6051 Nelson, John, 82, D, Aug 18, dia.
11062 Nelson, John, 2 art, D, Oct 17, scs.
3022 Nevens, C, 100, F, July 7, dia.
2985 Newton, L C, 14 art, I, July 7, pna.
4469 Newton, R J, 24 bat, Aug 1, dia.
4943 Newton, Sam'l D, 85, G, Aug 7, dia. c.
5227 Newton, C W,‡ 85, K, Aug 10, con.
2258 Nichols, A S, 2, C, June 20, dia. c.
5109 Nichols, D A, 125, D, Aug 9, dia.
7050 Nichols, F E,‡ 7 art, F, Aug 27, dia.
9017 Nobles, E, 14, A, Sept 17, dia.
11533 Nolan, M, 5, I, Oct 26, dys.
11356 Nolan, Pat, 88, D, Oct 23, scs.
5050 Noonan, E,§ 16 cav, L, Aug 8, scs.
4683 Norman, J, 15 art, H, Aug 3, dys.
633 Northrop, D, 125, H, April 19, dia.
5928 Northrop, V, 10, G, Aug 17, ens.
17 Norton, Alonzo, 154, A, March 7, pna.
4451 Norwood, D F, 85, E, Aug 1, ana.
4735 Nostrand, C, 2 art, I, Aug 4, scs.
12241 Nott, S A, 15 cav, E, Dec 7, scs.
2549 Nutt, M, 126, D, June 27, dia. a.
11681 Nutterville, W, 8, G, Oct 31, scs.

5439 O'Brien, D, 63, F, Aug 12, dia.
9765 O'Brien, M, 1 cav, A, Sept 25, scs.
3036 O'Brien, S, 5 cav, L, Sept 6, dia.
1553 O'Brien, W, 8 cav, A, June 2, dia.
6270 O'Carrell, F, 69, A, Aug 20, mas.
7359 Och, S, 46, D, Aug 31, dys.
3530 O'Connell, Thomas, 72, B, July 18, dia. c.
2755 O'Dougherty, J, 51, F, July 1, dys.
12397 O'Kay, Peter, 140, E, Jan 5, scs.
9737 O'Keif, C, 146, C, Sept 25, dia.
9916 Olahan, A, 65, F, Sept 23, scs.
10069 Olmstead, F H, 2 art, I, Sept 30, scs.
6435 Older, W M, 16 cav, L, Aug 22, dys.
1448 Omat, M, 178, B, May 28, dia. c.
12150 Omma, James, 7 art, B, Nov 24, scs.
11404 O'Neil, J, 39, H, Oct 24, scs.
1988 Ostenhal, L,§ 73, C, June 15, dia. c.
12 Osterstuck, W, 154, I, March 5, dys. c.
6456 Osborne, R H, 22, E, Aug 22, dia.
2714 Osterhardt, B S, 120, C, July 1, dia.
12269 Ostrander, J, 86, A, Dec 12, scs.
108 Ostrander, J H, 120, F, March 23, c. f.
6326 Otis, John, 94, A, Aug 21, scs.
8768 Otto, Charles, 100, F, Sept 14, scs.
656 Otto, James L,‡ 10 cav, E, April 21, dia.
5447 Owens, Ed, 47, G, Aug 12, dys.
12227 Owens, Wm, 49, I, Dec 5, scs.
7504 O'Reilly, Philip, 2 art, I, Sept 1, dia. c.

9319 Page, O D, 146, F, Sept 20, dia.
2325 Palmer, P H, 85, D, June 22, dia. c.
2582 Palmer, F, 17, F, June 27, dia.
6753 Pallette, D, 15 cav, K, Aug 24, dys.
20 Palmiter, R,‡ 86, D, March 7, dys. c.
5958 Pamperin, Wm, 71, H, Aug 17, ens.
3350 Pardy, E,§ 85, K, July 15, dia. c.
710 Parish, D, 146, E, Aug 15, scs.

12180 Parker, F,‡ 128, C, Nov 27, scs.
2092 Parker, I, 85, I, June 17, dia. c.
2819 Parker, Isarc, 124, G, J uly 3, dia.
1392 Parker, J, 8 I, May 26, dia. c.
2953 Parker, J, 154, G, July 6, dia.
3386 Parker, J, 15 cav, F, July 16, dia.
4732 Parkinson, A, 4 art, C, Aug 4, dia. c.
11956 Parks, Wm, 109, K, Nov 11, scs.
11218 Parsons, W, 64, E, Oct 20, scs.
9487 Patterson, D, 76, D, Sept 21, scs.
5880 Patterson, E, 6 art, M, Aug 16, scs.
3440 Patterson, Geo W, 15 art, M, July 17, dys
6165 Patterson, H, 1 cav, C, Aug 19, ces.
5279 Patterson, I H, 85, F, Aug 11, dia. c.
4708 Patterson, J H, 85, G, Aug 4, dys.
10368 Paul, P, 39, L, Oct 8, scs.
6696 Pease, Martin, 2 cav, C, Aug 24, scs.
2166 Peck, J G, 22 cav, F, June 19, dia. c.
11630 Peckins, L, 2 cav, A, Oct 28, dys.
11673 Pedro, Francis, 12 cav, E, Oct 30, scs.
1542 Pellett, Ed, 15 cav, I, June 1, dia.
3781 Pen, R, 2 cav, F, July 22, dys.
2763 Penablin, John, 69, F, July 12, dys.
11348 Pen, Charles, 6 art, D, Oct 23, scs.
7398 Perkey, D, 85, B, Aug 31, dia.
7172 Perkins, J P, 24 bat, Aug 29, scs.
10562 Perry, A,‡ 39, G, Oct 9, scs.
4527 Perry, John, 84, D, Aug 2, scs.
7866 Perry, W, 2 cav, B, Sept 5, dia.
3721 Perry, William, 99, E, July 21, phs.
12182 Perry, William, 79, A, Nov 27, scs.
4517 Person, A, 61, H, Aug 2, dia.
3082 Persons, W B, 64, B, July 9, dia.
5224 Peters, Fritz, 52, C, Aug 10, dys. c.
3914 Peters, J, 114, F, July 25, dia. c.
5684 Peterson, C, 178, I, Aug 15, scs.
9120 Peterson, H, 48, B, Sept 18, dia.
3302 Pettis, L P, 100, F, July 14, dia.
5527 Petrie, Joseph, 81, I, Aug 13, scs.
486 Phelps, Mortin, 132, G, April 9, pna.
4235 Phillips, Geo A, 85, B, July 29, dia.
12481 Phillips, I, 6 cav, E, Jan 17, scs.
7637 Phillips, H,§ 100, H, Sept 2, scs.
3318 Phillips, R,‡ 85, B, July 14, dia. c.
4152 Pierce, Albert, 2 art, M, July 28, dia.
2459 Pierce, Charles, 73, F, June 25, pna.
5371 Pierce, H,‡ 85, D, Aug 11, dys.
6027 Pierce, J, 85, D, Aug 18, dia.
11663 Pierce, J H, 8 cav, 8, Oct 30, scs.
6005 Pierson, J, 76, B, Aug 17, dys.
9422 Pilseck, E, 61, I, Sept 21, dia.
1532 Pinmon, John, 99, I, May 31, dia.
9994 Pitts, G, 97, K, Sept 29, dia.
11441 Pivant, M, 61, D, Oct 25, scs.
6086 Place, E, 47, F, Aug 18, dia.
815 Plass, H, 120, G, April 30, dys.
11379 Plunkett, J, 146, A, Oct 24, scs.
9549 Polack, J, 85, C. Sept 23, dys.
4432 Pollock, R, 16 cav, L, July 31, ana.
1843 Pomroy, C, 21 cav, G, June 11, dia. c.
4531 Ponteis, G, 16 cav, K, Aug 2, scs.
1830 Popple, W G, 85, B, June 11, ts. f.
11120 Pope, James E, 15 art, A, Oct 18, scs.
12291 Post, H E, 125, G, Oct 15, scs.
12425 Post, J A, 94, E, Jan 10, des.
6385 Potter, H, 48, E, Aug 21, dys.
1582 Potter, W H,§ 85, F, June 3, dia. c.
5116 Powell, George, 7 art, H, Aug 9, dys.
2948 Powers, J, 24 cav, H, July 6, dys. c.
3367 Powers, J, 10, K, July 15, dys.
6390 Powers, O, 6 art, I, Aug 21, dia.
5435 Pratt, B F, 146, G, Aug 12, dia.
1394 Presselman, C, 4 cav, M, May 26, dia. c.
5523 Preston, H G, 9, G, Aug 13, dia.
1096 Price, David, 154, A, May 14, ana.
12346 Price, J, cit, Dec 27, scs.
6455 Pratt, P, 24 bat, Aug 22, dia.
1651 Priest, W, 132, E, June 5, pna.
1479 Pratt, G B, 10 cav, D, May 30, dia.
7964 Pringler, Thomas W,‡ 148, A, Sept 6, dia
6914 Prow, John, 14 art, L, Aug 26, dia.
9668 Prowman, S H, 149, H, Sept 24, dia.

9937 Puff, I, 15 art, Sept 28, dia.
2321 Puley, Daniel, 115, I, June 22, ts. f.
729 Pullers, U H, 132, E, April 25, dia. c.
2395 Putnam, L, 14 art, L, June 24, las.
1515 Purkey, Jacob, 84, B, May 31, dia. c.
4063 Purstle, S, 49, A, July 27, dys.
1432 Prunan, L,‡ 147, H, Oct 24, dia.

3046 Quackenbuss, P, 11, K, Sept 17, dia. c.
8227 Quigley, J, 99, I, Sept 9, dys.
8064 Quinn, Edser, 10 cav, B, Sept 7, dia.

4305 Randolph, ——, 9, E, July 30, des.
11648 Rafbrun, W, 59, C, Oct 30, scs.
512 Rafferty, M, 132, G, April 12, dys.
2534 Rafferty, P, 5 cav, M, June 26, dys. a.
11330 Rafferty, T, 5 art, B, Oct 23, scs.
4593 Raker, L, 1 cav, E, Aug 3, dia.
3751 Ranch, J, 100, D, July 22, dia.
9875 Randall, John, 99, A, Oct 13, dia.
6503 Ralinger, J, 47, D, Aug 22, scs.
6794 Rangheart, John, 100, A, Aug 25, dia.
7778 Rastifer, John, 100, A, Sept 4, dys.
4216 Rattery, John, 104, I, July 29, dys.
10987 Ray, C, 3 cav, B, Oct 14, dia. c.
10246 Ray, R S, 154, A, Oct 3, dia.
4336 Raynard, F, 125, F, July 30, dia. c.
3435 Rattersboom, J, 3 art, K, July 17, scs.
2880 Ramsay, Isaac, 86, I, July 4, dia.
1265 Ramsay, Hiram, 31, K, May 21, dia.
2186 Reamer, W C, 111, B, June 19, dia. c.
2820 Redman, J, 3 art, K, July 3, dia. c.
11695 Reddo, D V, 8 cav, M, Oct 31, dia. c.
7232 Reed, F A, 64, E, Aug 30, scs.
8574 Reed, J, 140, H, Sept 12, dia.
406 Reed, S G, 13, D, April 6, dia. c.
6041 Reed, W D, 146, H, Aug 18, scs.
10232 Reed, W J, 41, I, Oct 2, dia.
8492 Reed, William, 14 art, I, Sept 11, scs.
7369 Reetz, John, 52, A, Aug 31, dia.
5694 Reeve, G, 152, C, Aug 15, scs.
1680 Reeves, John, 57, H, June 6, scs.
10467 Redmond, J, 43, C, Oct 7, scs.
10911 Regler, W H, 22 cav, M, Oct 14, dia. c.
9122 Reiley, P O, 164, B, Sept 18, dia.
7195 Renback, C, 29, Aug 29, dia.
12455 Rebman, J, 59, C, Jan 15, dia. c.
8431 Rencermane, J R, 5 cav, B, Sept 11, scs.
9320 Randall, A B, 76, F, Sept 20, dia. c.
3352 Remsen, C, 2 cav, M, July 15, scs.
8209 Reynolds, O, 155, E, Sept 8, scs.
6799 Reynolds, O S, 85, E, Aug 25, dia.
10265 Reynolds, Samuel, 92, H, Oct 3, dia.
6350 Reynolds, William, 140, I, Aug 21, dys.
6546 Reidy, J D, 65, I, Aug 23, dys.
4318 Rice, F,‡ 39, I, July 30, dia. c.
3077 Rich, T D, 24 bat, July 9, dia.
12289 Rich, J, 82, C, Dec 15, scs.
3561 Richey, R, 66, C, July 18, dia.
2427 Rider, E, 178, E, June 24, dia. c.
8005 Rhenevault, R H, 21, B, Sept 6, dia.
11904 Rehm, W, 7 art, C, Nov 7, scs.
3891 Richistine, C,‡ 132, D, July 24, dia. c.
5317 Richards, A, 52, D, Aug 11, dia.
3674 Richards, A, 41, E, Aug 14, gae.
12243 Richards, A, 9, C, Dec 7, scs.
3682 Richards, H, 47, E, July 21, dys.
7578 Richards, N J,§ 146, C, Sept 2, dia. c.
4240 Richardson, H M, 20 cav, M, J'ly 29, dia.c.
12193 Ricker, M, 2 art, M, Nov 29, scs.
8155 Rickhor, J, 85, E, Sept 8, dys.
415 Rikel, Robert, 125, G, April 7, dia. c.
12382 Riley, I, 73, E, Jan 2, dys.
2885 Riley, J, 99, C, July 4, dys.
5021 Riley, John, 176, C, Aug 8, scs.
6347 Riley John, 39, D, Aug 21, dia.
11163 Ripley, F A, 152, C, Oct 19, scs.
11760 Ripp, W, 42, B, Nov 3, scs.
3514 Rising, C, 75, B, July 18, dia.
10810 Risley, Geo W, 46, G, Oct 4, dia.
2558 Ritcher, F,§ 132, D, June 27, dys.
7245 Ritson, S, 18 cav, E, Aug 29, dys.

9224 Ritzmillin, John, 115, Sept 1, scs.
1775 Roach, F, 99, F, June 9, ana.
1842 Roach, Chas, 85, E, June 11, dia. c.
2354 Robberger, P H, 46, B, June 23, dia. c.
11195 Roberson, C A, 122, B, Oct 20, dys.
2346 Robertson, W H, 134, B, June 23, dia. c.
8554 Robertson, W M, 96, B, Sept 12, scs.
9970 Robinson, H, 39, K, Sept 28, dia.
7607 Robinson, A, 111, I, Sept 2, dia.
3680 Robinson, H C, 95, I, July 21, scs.
6419 Robinson, John, 115, A, Aug 22, dia.
27 Robins, L, 154, K, March 8, pna.
7663 Roberts, A, 173, C, Sept 3, dys.
7585 Rockwell, N C, 14 art, D, Sept 2, scs.
3813 Rockfellar, R E, 85, D, July 23, dia.
11342 Rockfellar, H, 15 art, M, Oct 23, scs.
3959 Rock, F, 6 art, F, July 25, dys.
4350 Rogers, A, 7 art, I, July 31, scs.
6059 Rogers, A, 125, H, Aug 18, scs.
5791 Rogers, G, mus, 85, F, Aug 15, rhm.
3011 Rogers, James, 132, H, July 7, dia.
4287 Rogers, H C, 85, C, July 30, dia.
8363 Rogers, H J, 2 art, E, Sept 10, scs.
4912 Rogers, M, 43, D, Aug 6, ana.
7208 Rogers, O S,§ 85, C, Aug 29, scs.
6824 Rogers, Thomas, 12, F, Aug 25, dia.
11772 Romer, F, 9, A, Nov 3, dia. c.
8468 Rook, G, 6 art, E, Sept 11, scs.
9963 Rooney, John, 152, G, Sept 28, dia.
9102 Rooney, M, 132, F, Sept 18, scs.
8922 Rooney, P, 2 art, C, Sept 16, dys.
5569 Root, A N, 85, C, Aug 14, ana.
2999 Roots, W T, 120, H, July 7, dia.
1735 Root, Legrand, 24 bat, June 8, pna.
10278 Rose, A, 16, L, Oct 2, scs.
9550 Rosecrans, J E, 125, H, Sept 23, dys.
8171 Ross, C, 23 cav, A, Sept 8, dys.
3874 Ross, E F, 111, I, July 24, ts, f.
5591 Ross, David, 27, D, Aug 14, scs.
6741 Ross, G, 76, K, Aug 24, dia.
9751 Ross, A, 1 cav, M, Sept 25, scs.
11963 Ross, J H, 121, G, Nov 11, scs.
5929 Rosenberger, John, 4, D, Aug 17, ens.
3618 Rosser, Lewis, 84, A, July 20, dys.
2924 Rosenburg, J, 30, A, July 5, dia. c.
8737 Rosson, Chas, 24 cav, E, Sept 14, dia.
12259 Roswell, J, 93, K, Dec 10, scs.
727 Ross, Jacob, 151, A, April 25, dia. c.
1940 Row, W J, 120, B, June 14, dia. c,
5097 Roth, Louis, 39, D, Aug 9, scs.
8504 Rothwell, M,‡ 20 cav, M, Sept 12, scs.
3722 Rouge, Wm, bug, 12 cav, F, July 21, dia
7709 Rowbotham, R, 11 cav, L, Sept 3, scs.
5857 Rowell, J E, 70, G, Aug 16, mas.
3492 Rowell, L N, 99, H, July 17, dia.
59 Roberts, A B,§ 8 cav, B, March 18, pna.
2609 Ruddin, C, 120, H, June 28, dia.
867 Rudler, William, 120, M, May 3, dys.
40 Rue, Newton,§ 5 cav, A, March 13, dia. q
8667 Runey, F, 69, H, Sept 13, dia.
12635 Russ, John, 2, K, Feb 10, dia. c.
8856 Russell, J,‡ 7 art, A, Sept 15, dia. c.
5094 Ryan, D, 106, D, Aug 8, dia.
8599 Ryan, J, 95, E, Sept 12, scs.
8741 Ryan, J, 22 cav, E, Sept 14, ts. f.
7258 Ryan, Owen, 12, A, Aug 30, dia.
4762 Ryonch, John, 66, I, Aug 5, scs.
6413 Ryson, John, 7 art, L, Aug 22, scs.
6206 Ryne, J M, 39, E, Aug 9, dia. c.
684 Rush, John, 111, E, April 23, dys. q.

7234 Sackett, R S, 85, G, Aug 29, dia. c.
1929 Sadley, M, 77, H, June 14, dia. c.
1880 Safford, B J, 24 bat, June 12, dys.
11870 Salsbury, H, 1 art, M, Nov 6, dia.
10652 Salisbury, E, 16, D, Oct 11, scs.
10923 Samlett, ——, 13 cav, I, Oct 14, scs.
10880 Samet, W, 15, H, Oct 13, scs.
3769 Sampson, J, 106, K, July 22, dia.
346 Sanders, Charles,‡ 9 mil, A, April 2, r f
3818 Sanders, J, 99, C, July 23, dia. c.
9857 Sanders, J, 12 cav, A, Sept 27, scs.

4423 Sandford, P O, 7 art, L, July 31, dia. c.
2341 Sanghin, J, 12 cav, F, June 23, r. f.
7740 Sawyer, J, 2 cav, L, Sept 3, dia.
11232 Sayles, A, 22 cav, E, Oct 21.
3612 Seaman, A,‡ 85, H, July 19, dia.
10856 Seaman, A, 2 art, Oct 13, dia.
1372 Sears, F, 2 cav, H, May 25, dys.
6120 Seagher, J, 8, M, Aug 19, dys.
4325 See, Henry, 11, K, July 30, dys.
8824 Seeley, A J, 140, A, Sept 15, dia.
11374 Seeley, C B, 15, H, Oct 24, scs.
4256 Seeley, Thomas, 100, F, July 29, dys.
10027 Segam, Ed, 5 cav, K, Sept 29, dia.
4204 Seigler, George, 10, July 29, dia.
7458 Seigle, John R, 120, K, Sept 1, dia.
11586 Selson, H, 59, C, Nov 6, scs.
3457 Serrier, R, 40, C, July 17, scs.
1746 Serine, C, 4 cav, M, June 8, dia. c.
629 Settle, Henry, 99, H, April 19, dia.
9828 Seyman, F, 1 cav, A, Sept 27, dia.
5951 Seard, Louis, 77, E, Aug 17, mas.
6888 Schayler, J W, 21 cav, M, Aug 26, pna.
10794 Schadt, Theodore, 160, A, Oct 12, scs.
3557 Scheck, B, 2 cav, G, July 18, dia.
3190 Schemerhorn, H, 120, G, July 12, dia.
11965 Schempp, M, 7 art, F, Nov 11, scs.
2795 Schermashie, B, 170, A, July 2, dys.
1325 Schlotesser, J, 91, H, May 24, dys.
11515 Schlotesser, J,§ 1, L, Oct 26, scs.
9578 Schmaker, John, 39, B, Sept 23, dia. c.
10291 Schmaley, J, 1, G, Oct 16, scs.
10550 Schmeager, A, 39, A, Oct 9, scs.
5311 Schneider, Charles, 39, A, Aug 11, dia.
8595 Schockney, T T, 24 bat, Sept 12, scs.
8796 Schofield, J, 7, H, Sept 15, dia.
2441 Scholl, John, 54, D, June 25, scs.
11422 Schriber, H, 59, I, Oct 24, scs.
7814 Schroder, G, 7 art, E, Sept 4, dia.
8550 Schrum, J, 15 art, K, Sept 12, scs.
1070 Schrimer, Wm, 20, B, May 13, dia.
4280 Schware, F, 12 cav, K, July 30, dia.
6613 Schwick, A, 66, G, Aug 23, dia.
4849 Scott, J C,§ 85, K, Aug 6, dia. c.
6857 Scott, P C, 14 cav, G, Aug 26, dys.
8622 Scott, W W, 2 cav, F, Sept 13, scs.
8290 Sibble, W, 148, G, Sept 9, dia.
4362 Sick, R, 5, E, July 31, dia.
4557 Sickler, E, 7 art, E, Aug 2, dia.
3210 Sickles, A, 120, D, July 12, dia.
11950 Siddell, G, 40, H, Nov 10, scs.
12284 Simmons, A, 8 art, H, Dec 13, scs.
6364 Simmons, C G,§ 85, B, Aug 21, dia.
8316 Simon, H, 146, B, Sept 10, dia.
6284 Simons, H L,§ 85, E, Aug 20, dia. c.
142 Simondinger, B, 155, I, March 24, dys.
242 Simpson, D, 99, H, March 30, c. f.
6345 Sisson, P V,§ 22 art, M, Aug 21, dia.
10067 Shaat, J, 50, A. Sept 30, scs.
201 Shae, Pat, drummer, 61, M, Mar 28, dia. c.
4801 Shaffer, M, 7 art, Aug 5, ana.
4584 Shaffer, J, 66, E, Aug 2, dia.
782 Shafer, H, 103, F, April 28, dia. c.
6747 Shaughnessey, J, 6 cav, A, Aug 24, dia.
4446 Shannan, E, 6 art, H, Aug 1, ana.
5645 Shank, S W, 24 bat, Aug 14, dia.
290 Shaw, Alexander, 3 art, K, April 1, pna.
9667 Shaw, T I, 15 cav, M, Sept 24, dia.
12814 Shaw, W, 7 art, F, March 25, dia. c.
7660 Shay, John, 69, B, Sept 3, dia.
3360 Sheldon, M, 7 art, B, July 15, dys.
4247 Shepardson, L,‡ 22 cav, E, July 29, dia.
5474 Shaw, J, 2 cav, E, Aug 13, dia.
7798 Shuler, Chas, 52, G, Sept 4, dia.
6335 Shaw, M, 76, D, Sept 10, scs.
9924 Sheppard, W H, 9, F, Sept 28, scs.
8205 Shever, H, 5 cav, Sept 8, dia.
10930 Sheridan, J, 2 cav, F, Oct 14, scs.
4676 Sherwood, J E, 76, G, Aug 4, dia. c.
720 Shields, Richard, 132, F, April 25, dia. c.
701 Shilts, E, 52, K, April 23, cah.
10495 Shidler, George, 97, F, Oct 8, scs.
8206 Shindler, J, 15 art, E, Sept 8, dia.

7437 Shirlock, R, 85, K, Sept 1, dia.
5837 Shippey, F, 85, D, Aug 16, dia.
2340 Shirley, P, 24 bat, June 23, dys.
2151 Shats, C, 111, F, June 18, dia. c.
5755 Shorty, Robert, 164, B, Aug 15, dia.
5343 Shotliff, J,§ 7 art, L, Aug 11, dia.
2975 Shults, John, 118, F, July 7, scs.
6633 Shultz, F, 76, F, Aug 23, dys.
12194 Shultz, Wm, 7 art, C, Nov 29, scs.
11822 Shultz, C,‡ 66, F, Nov 5, scs.
11813 Shumaker, P, 100, K, Nov 4, scs.
11280 Shuhps, P D, 125, K, Oct 22, gae.
2462 Shuster, ——, 54, C, June 25, dys. a.
2922 Slater, F, 48, F, July 5, dia. c.
700 Slater, John, 120, H, April 23, des.
12534 Slater, Jas,§ 7, K, Jan 27, scs.
11162 Slater, Richard, 2, E, Oct 19, scs.
12811 Sleight, C, 32, I, March 24, dia. c.
10377 Sloat, Wm, 140, E, Oct 5, scs.
6819 Sloates, F, 76, F, Aug 25, dia.
10125 Slimp, W, 146, A, Oct 11, scs.
7628 Smades, W, 9, D, Sept 2, dia.
12083 Small, S, 53, F, Nov 18, scs.
7783 Smarty, John, 22 cav, G, Sept 4, dia.
7406 Snead, L, 18 art, D, Aug 31, dys.
762 Smalley, Geo, 140, H, April 27, hyx.
12503 Smith, A, 7 art, F, Jan 21, scs.
11371 Smith, A, 9, A, Oct 23, scs.
7326 Smith, A J, 85, D, Aug 30, dia. c.
802 Smith, Bernard,‡ 132, B, April 29, dia. c.
1310 Smith, Benjamin, 2 cav, H, May 23, td.
2659 Smith, Chas, 61, A, June 29, dia. c.
3735 Smith, Chas, 52, E, July 21, dys. c.
4534 Smith, Chas, 100, B, Aug 2, dys.
7612 Smith, Chas, 15 art, K, Sept 2, scs.
10052 Smith, Chas, 9, G, Sept 30, scs.
11283 Smith, E, 61, D, Oct 22, scs.
1819 Smith, F, 48, F, June 10, dia. c.
1246 Smith, Frank, 99, I, May 20, dia.
11839 Smith, G R, 2 cav, H, Nov 5, dia.
3372 Smith, N, 9 cav, C, July 15, dia. c.
1247 Smith, Henry, 132, C, May 20, dys.
3238 Smith, J, 5 cav, July 12.
3504 Smith, J, 4 cav, B, July 18, dia.
4834 Smith, J, 115, G, Aug 6, dia. c.
9300 Smith, J, 52, A, Sept 20, dia.
10456 Smith, J,‡ 13 cav, D, Oct 7, scs.
12627 Smith, J, 46, E, Feb 10, des.
1245 Smith, Jas, 20 cav, M, May 20, dia.
7004 Smith, James, 6, A, Aug 27, dia.
11787 Smith, Jas, 57, B, Nov 4, scs.
7610 Smith, Jackson, 85, I, Sept 2, dia.
11210 Smith, J, 52, A, Oct 20, scs.
305 Smith, John, 71, C, April 1, dia. c.
534 Smith, John, 3 cav, E, April 14, dya. c.
5496 Smith, John, 41, E, Aug 13, dia.
5602 Smith, John, 66, F, Aug 14, scs.
6428 Smith, John, 95, D, Aug 22, scs.
10547 Smith, John, 69, G, Oct 9, scs.
5882 Smith, John J, 109, C, Aug 16, dys.
11454 Smith, J M, 59, A, Oct 25, scs.
10079 Smith, K, 22 cav, K, Sept 30, scs.
5009 Smith, L A, 115, F, Aug 8, scs.
9973 Smith, Levi, 125, B, Sept 28, dia.
7706 Smith, John C,‡ 48, E, Sept 3, dys.
2780 Smith, S, 11, I, July 2, pna.
5854 Smith, S A, 132, F, Aug 16, mas.
6709 Smith, T, 147, E, Aug 24, scs.
6361 Smith, Thomas, 47, C, Aug 21, scs.
9499 Smith, T R, 2, E, Sept 21, gae.
139 Smith, Wm, 99, H, March 24, dys.
325 Smith, Wm, 3 art, K, April 2, dia.
532 Smith, Wm, 104, A, April 14, dia. a.
812 Smith, Wm, 106, B, April 30, dia. c.
7550 Smith, Wm, 2, L, Sept 2, dia. c.
10164 Smith, Wm, 76, K, Oct 1, scs.
12394 Smith, H, 7, C, Jan 5, dia.
3708 Snedegar, A J, 111, D, July 21, dia.
7173 Snyder, A, 25, E, Aug 29, ts. f.
4448 Snyder, B, 2, B, Aug 1, scs.
10076 Snyder, Wm, 1 drag, E, Sept 30, scs.
1319 Sombeck, Geo, 52, I, May 24, ana.

5169 Somers, John, 2, E, Aug 9, des.
2773 Sopher, Jas, 132, F, July 2, dys.
2403 Sopher, S, 102, K, June 24, des.
4352 Sotter, J M, 47, C, July 31, dia.
3534 Southard, H, 5 cav, C, July 18, des.
10526 Southard, N, 2, H, Oct 8, scs.
11346 Southard, W A, 18, I, Oct 23, gae.
2877 Souther, Henry, 69, K, July 4, dys.
8124 Southworth, R, 22 cav, E, Sept 8, dia.
10488 Skall, S, 7 art, L, Oct 7, dia.
12029 Skeeley, T, 66, H, Nov 15, scs.
9954 Spark, G,§ 16 art, C, Sept 28, scs.
6975 Sparks, E, 10, B, Aug 27, dia.
5421 Spaulding, H, 1 cav, F, Aug 12, scs.
5567 Spellman, John, 66, B, Aug 13, scs.
10712 Spencer, A, 93, D, Feb 28, scs.
10999 Sperry, A, 51, F, Oct 16, scs.
3532 Span, Jas, 147, H, July 18, dia. c.
5982 Spanbury, S, 14 art, C, Aug 17, dia. c.
5821 Sprague, E H, 10 bat, Aug 16, scs.
3593 Sprague, J, 85, I, July 19, dia.
10730 Sprig, Jas A, 24 cav, E, Oct 11, scs.
4877 Sprink, A, 146, F, Aug 6, dys.
9035 Strats, John, 15, A, Sept 17, scs.
889 Stacey, John, 99, I, May 4, td. f.
4574 Stadler, J,§ 39, A, Aug 2, scs.
10078 Stancliff, A B, 106, H, Sept 30, scs.
2570 Stanton, H H, 22, E, June 27, dia. c.
5187 Stark, J D,‡ 100, A, Aug 9, dia.
11740 Starkweather, L, 146, E, Nov 2, dys.
12650 Star, C, 15, D, Feb 13, des.
7381 Stanton, L H, 7 art, K, Aug 31, dys.
2520 Stark, J H, 121, A, June 26, dia. a.
1698 Stanley, J C,‡ 85, C, June 7, pna.
10290 St Dennis, L, 16, F, Oct 4, scs.
9903 Stewart, Peter, 5, B, Sept 27, scs.
7636 Stevens, E, 120, C, Sept 2, dia. c.
95 Stevenson, Wm, 132, G, March 22, ts. f.
3782 Sternhoff, A, 15 art, C, July 22, ana.
4678 Stevens, John S, 100, F, Aug 4, dia. c.
5530 Steiner, C, 7 art, 1, M, Aug 13, cah.
7028 Stevens, Wm, 99, I, Aug 27, scs.
2543 Stead, J, 115, F, June 27, ts. f.
6531 Stebins, C, 85, C, Aug 23, ana.
3872 Stevenson, W, 10, F, July 24, dys.
6443 Stead, J, 15, D, Aug 22, scs.
2094 Stewart, John, 89, June 15, dys.
1863 Stebbins, H, 85, B, June 12, dys.
6049 Stelrocht, D, 22 cav, C, Aug 18, ces.
10149 Stickler, E, 169, A, Oct 1, scs.
11755 Stivers, R, 111, F, Nov 2, scs.
7075 Still, D, 132, D, Aug 28, dys.
6102 Stump, W, 6, K, Aug 18, dia.
4193 Still, James, 164, E, July 29, phs.
4385 Stillwell, S, 2 art, E, July 31, dys.
915 Stone, John, mus, 5 cav, C, May 6, dys.
11043 Stoddard, I, 111, F, Oct 17, dia. c.
6722 Stone, L, 24, E, Aug 24, dia.
2053 Stoup, J, 15, A, June 16, dia.
3415 Strue, G N, 1 art, B, July 16, dia. c.
3997 Storing, A, 54, B, July 26, dia. c.
8520 Strain, N W, 2 cav, I, Sept 12, dia.
3905 Streeter, F, 76, F, July 24, scs.
4665 Storms, A N, 7 art, I, Aug 4, dia. c.
4798 Strale, J, 178, B, Aug 5, scs.
5342 Strater, Geo, 85, K, Aug 11, scs.
6988 Stratten, J H, 140, H, Aug 27, dys.
11967 Strip, W,‡ 42, E, Nov 11, scs.
116 Streight, Lewis, 127, A, March 23, pna
2401 Stratten, Chas. 125, K, June 24, dia. c.
7845 Sturdevant, G, 5 cav, I, Sept 4, dia.
5994 Stutzman, r, 39, D, Aug 17, mas.
6102 Stump, W, 60, K, Aug 18, dia.
1832 Styler, G W, 7 art, I, Nov 5, scs.
9953 Sughem, I, h a, B, Sept 28, scs.
640 Sullivan, Ed, 69, A, April 20, dia.
6048 Sullivan, M, 69, K, Aug 18, ces.
1492 Sullivan, Pat,‡ 99, H, May 31, des.
7728 Sullivan, P C,‡ 155, E, Sept 3, dia.
5440 Susear, Fred, 39, I, Aug 12, ts. f.
10431 Sutliff, E,‡ 15 cav, M, Oct 11, dia c.
1 Swarner, J H, 2 cav, H, Feb 27, p a.

4005 Swarner, J, bugler, 2 cav, H, July 26, ana.
6466 Swartz, M, 2 cav, M, Aug 22, dia.
12267 Swager, G, 103, F, Dec 12, dys.
2322 Sweeney, James, 155, I, June 22, dia. a.
5835 Sweeney, M, 122, C, Aug 16, mas.
3527 Sweet, E, 93, F, July 18, scs.
2921 Sweet, L, 4 art, M, July 5, dia.
4960 Sylurs, S, 140, E, Aug 7, dia. c.
12765 Swancoil, J, 2, A, March 13, dia. c
10559 Stratton, E, 76, E, Oct 10, scs.

1934 Taylor, A, 2 cav, F, June 14, dia. c.
4867 Taylor, C, 115, F, Aug 6, dia.
551 Taylor, Charles B, 154, April 14, dia.
11321 Taylor, D, 149, D, Oct 22, scs.
2742 Taylor, R H, 125, F, July 1, dia. c.
493 Taylor, Thos B, 10 cav, E, April 11, rhm
9993 Taylor, L R,‡ 147, K, Sept 29, scs.
12290 Taylor, W, 12 cav, A, Dec 15, scs.
12480 Taylor, W, 42, B, Jan 17, scs.
10370 Taylor, W H, 7 art, C, Oct 5, scs.
10738 Taylor, W H, 7 cav, C, Oct 11, dia. c.
10157 Taylor, Wm, 22 cav, C, Oct 1, dia.
8961 Taylor, W W,§ 2, I, Sept 16, scs.
8988 Tarvis, G W, 1 drag, K, Sept 17, dia.
9480 Tare, W, 115, D, Sept 21, dia.
3681 Tambrick, A, 16 cav, A, July 21, scs.
3976 Tanner, M, 1, E, July 25, dia.
4326 Tanschivit, Ed, 15 art, E, July 30, dys.
7019 Tell, William, 59, C, Aug 27, dys.
9143 Thompson, A, 9, D, Sept 18, dia.
133 Terry, Aaron,§ 12, K, March 24, brs.
9064 Teneych, M, 14 art, E, Sept 17, dia.
4909 Tewey, J, 99, H, Aug 6, scs.
6445 Terwilliger, D R, 85, D, Aug 22, i. f.
10352 Thomas, J, 2 cav, D, Oct 5, dys.
3598 Thomas, H,§ 88, D, July 19, dys.
3711 Thomas, W, 3, H, July 21, dia. c.
4619 Thomas, J, 85, G, Aug 3, ts. f.
10361 Thearer, J, 1 bat, Oct 5, scs.
8161 Thompson, C W, 85, K, Sept 8, dia.
4781 Thompson, J, 39, H, Aug 5, dia.
5510 Thompkins, Ira, 6 art, Aug 13, scs.
5524 Thompson, P, 10, E, Aug 13, scs.
6730 Thompson, N B, 146, A, Aug 24, scs.
5734 Thompson, J, 104, G, Aug 15, dia.
2613 Thompson, T, 12 cav, F, June 28, dia. c.
320 Thompson, Daniel, 142, E, April 2, dia.
3538 Thresh, G, 5 cav, K, July 18, dys.
5147 Thruston, N E, 85, C, Aug 9, dia.
11235 Thornton, J, 14 art, L, Oct 21.
6309 Thorpe, W C, 82, I, Aug 20, dia.
4393 Thurston, G W, 85, E, July 31, dys.
12843 Thayer, G, 70, E, April 22, dia. c.
679 Thierbach, P M, 39, D, April 22, ts. f.
11230 Tilton, H, 24 art, Oct 20, scs.
8283 Tillitson, N P, 51, A, Sept 9, dia. c.
8849 Timerson, Wm, 2 art, I, Sept 15, dia.
2680 Timmish, ——, 85, C, June 30, dia. a.
659 Tiner, David, 79, E, April 21, des.
10422 Townsend, W, 111, B, Oct 6, scs.
8068 Townsend, L, 22 cav, G, Sept 7, dys.
3883 Townsend, John, 52, A, July 24, dia. c.
535 Townsend, Geo M, 111, F, April 14, dia.
9050 Tohnson, E, 22, Sept 17, dia.
4774 Toney, L, 100, D, Aug 5, scs.
10727 Tolal, Pat, 164, K, Oct 11, scs.
5833 Tonner, L, 5 cav, G, Aug 16, ens.
6047 Tobias, A, 120, G, Aug 18, dys.
2112 Toomey, J F,‡ 85, I, June 17, dia. c.
12465 Tourney, P, 99, B, Jan 16, dia. c.
12636 Tocdt, H, 1, K, Feb 10, dia.
12708 Tomlinson, W F, 22, G, Feb 28, dia. c.
3193 Tripp, Ira,§ 77, B, July 12, dia.
10442 Tripp, O S, 3 art, K, Oct 7, scs.
9507 Truman, A M, 2 art, D, Sept 22, scs.
7629 Trueman, R, 7 art, G, Sept 2, dia. c.
8544 Tremor, M, 76, F, Sept 12, scs.
7317 Trumpp, E, 22 cav, F, Aug 30, des.
3882 Trumbull, H, 115, I, July 24, dia. c.
7187 Travis, T, 8 cav, G, Aug 29, dia.
4052 Truesdale, W J, 85, H, July 27, dia.

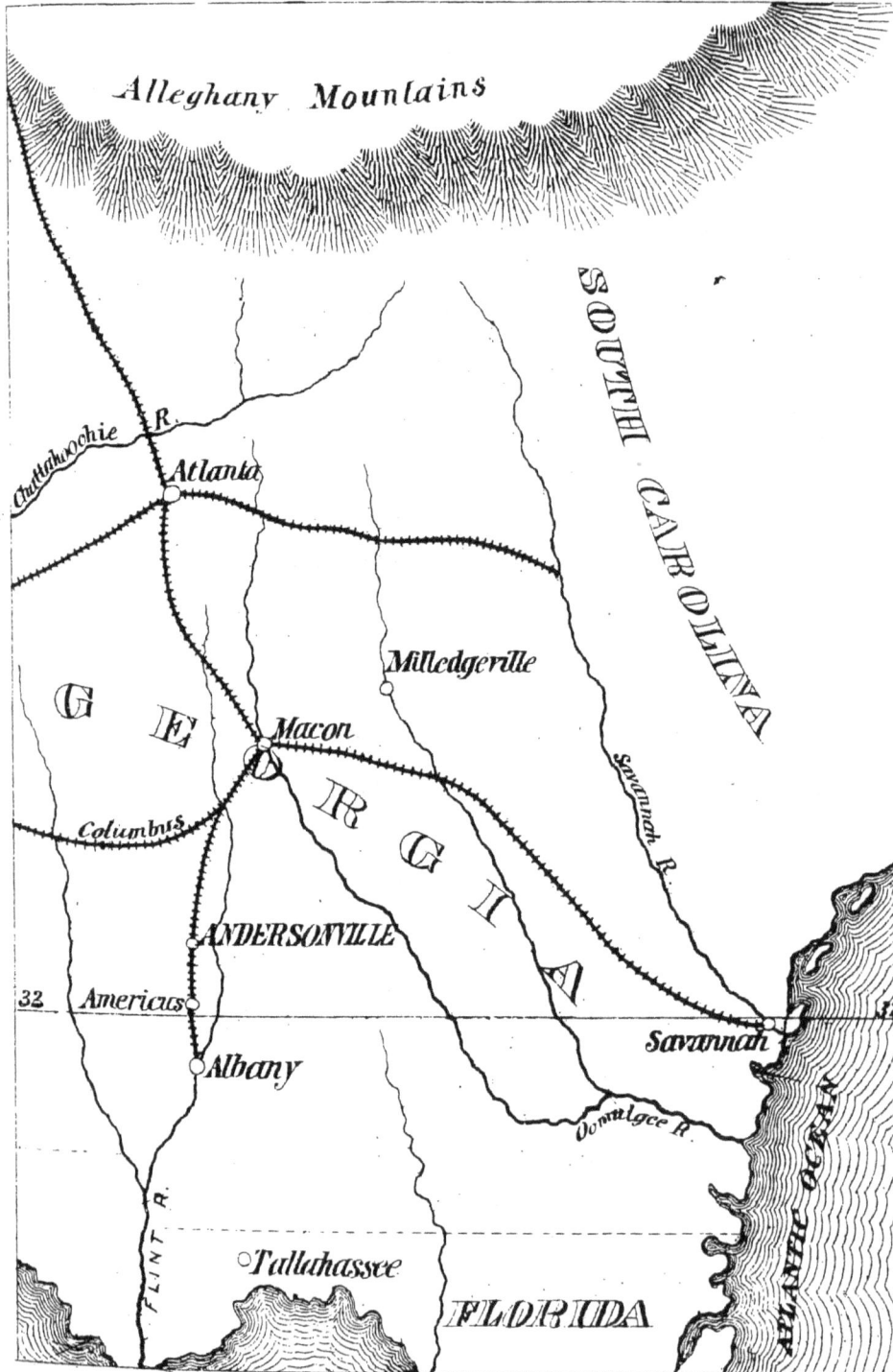

3425 Trompter, F.§ 140, B, July 16, wds.
100 Tracey, Pat, 99, 1, March 22, ts. f.
707 Turner, Wm,‡ 5 cav, G, April 24, dys. c.
7970 Turner, John, 49, A, Sept 5, scs.
11376 Turner, J, 22 cav, M, Oct 24, scs.
1688 Turner, Thomas, 16 cav, B, June 6, dia.
2120 Turner, J B, 85, C, June 17, dia. c.
10535 Tuthill, C, 22 cav, G, Oct 8, scs.
9687 Tuthill, S D, 2 art, M, Sept 24, dia.
.0604 Tuft, E, 29, C, Oct 10, dys.
7915 Turden, E S,·15 cav, D, Sept 5, dia.
7421 Turton, W F, 2 art, I, Aug 31, dia.
3796 Tubbs, W H, 85, D, July 22. dia. c.
3084 Tupple, H,§ 154, H, July 9, pna.
3129 Tucker, L, 120, D, July 10, dia.
2893 Tuttle, W, 48, K, July 4, ts. f.
10494 Tyrrell, I, 22 cav, A, Oct 8, dia.

4217 Uncer, James, 15, H, July 29, dia. c.
416 Uber, Charles,§ 14, A, April 7, dia. c.
12401 Udell, J, 7 art, H, Jan 5, scs.
10887 Ulmer, H, 15 art, K, Oct 14, scs.
2317 Underburg, L W, 77, G, June 22, des.
254 Underhill, H, 47, E, March 30, i. f.
1495 Underwriter, A, 62, F, May 21, pna.

1091 Van Clarke, Wm, 106, D, May 14, dia.
9087 Van Allen, C, 7, E, Sept 18, dys.
1025 Van Buren, J W, 3 art, K, May 11, dia. c.
664 Van Buren, Henry, 3 art, K, April 21, dia.
10071 Van Bethysen, H, 7 art, I, Sept 30, scs.
12539 Van Bramin, T, 71, K, Jan 27, dia. c.
1577 Van Derbreck, A, 132, B, June 3, dys.
3463 Van Dugen, 24 cav, M, July 17, dys.
6560 Van Hosen, C, 95, A, Aug 23, dia.
10656 Van Housen, B, 12 bat, Oct 11, scs.
3371 Van Haughton, J, 124, C, July 15, dia.
1418 Vanderbrogart, W, 104, F, May 27, dia. c.
8957 Vanarsdale, P, 1, G, Sept 16, dia.
8782 Vanalstine, H, 152, A, Sept 14, scs.
8806 Vanclack, F, 5, D, Sept 15, scs.
7564 Vanvelzer, J M, 85, I, Sept 2, dys.
7635 Vanburen, J, 15 cav, B, Sept 2, dia.
11446 Vanscott, L, 59, C, Oct 25, scs.
11596 Vanarnum, J, 8 cav, E, Oct 28, scs.
7054 Vanwagner, C, 2 art, F, Aug 28, dia.
7244 Vanesse, M, 2 cav, K, Aug 29, dys.
7252 Vanzart, Wm, 7 art, E, Aug 30, dia.
6472 Varney, C, 169, E, Aug 22, dia.
6634 Vanalstine, C, 7 art, C, Aug 23, dys.
3333 Vanest, J H, 14 art, B, July 15, dia.
83 Vanvelsen, J, 120, A, March 21, brs.
2089 Vaughan, W H, 8 cav, K, June 17, dia. c.
973 Vespers, Jas W, 85, D, May 9, dia. c.
7506 Van Osten, C, 52, H, Sept 1, dia.
5661 Vencot, L, 2 cav, H, Aug 14, scs.
4196 Veil, Wm, 6 art, F, July 29, dia. c.
1539 Vernon, S, 2 cav, M, June 1, scs.
7846 Vincent, R, 178, I, Sept 4, dia.
2782 Vincent, Richard, 1, K, July 2, dia. c.
2879 Vinsant, G, M, 14 art, I, July 4, dia.
2715 Vish, O, 178, E, July 1, dia. c.
6525 Vibbard, Geo, 22 cav, E, Aug 22, dia.
10023 Voerling, H, 15 art, C, Sept 29, dia.
4623 Vogle, Anton, 10, C, Aug 3, dys.
5503 Voorhies, A H, 1 cav, H, Aug 13, dia. c.
11507 Voorhies, E R, 85, C, Oct 26, scs.
6682 Voorhies, Geo, 85, C, Aug 23, dia. c.

1184 Walls, Peter, 4 cav, D, May 18, dia. c.
5001 Wall, Jas,§ 15, G, Aug 7, scs.
1398 Wallace, John, 11 cav, B, May 26, dia.
10211 Watt, H, 12 cav, A, Oct 2, scs.
9977 Watts, C, 6, C, Sept 28, dia. c.
10313 Waters, A L, 8 cav, F, Oct 4, dys.
10477 Warner, Chas L, 2 cav, D, Oct 7, dia. c.
4026 Warrer, L, 95, I, July 26, dys.
7351 Warner, P P, 14 art, M, Aug 31, dia.
7444 Warner, A J, 76, F, Sept 1, dia.
12449 Warner, Luther, 12 cav, A, Jan 9, dia. c.
10543 Ward, Patrick, 88, C, Oct 8, dia.
5127 Ward, J, 99, G, Aug 9, asc.

10920 Ward, , 40, H, Oct 14, sua.
2238 Ward, , 95, I, June 2(, des.
400 Ward, W A, 99, B, April 6, dia.
12816 Warden, H B, 5, B, March 25, dia. c
9858 Walters, D, 125, E, Sept 27, scs.
1557 Walters, Nelson,§ 120, K, June 2, dia. c
3381 Walterhouse, Ed, 9, I, July 16, dys.
2827 Wallace, J, 2 cav, M, July 3, pna.
8939 Watson, G, 6 art, C, Sept 16, scs.
10965 Watson, Jas, 15 art, M, Oct 15, scs.
6947 Watson, T, 99, I, Aug 26, dys.
9356 Wade, M, 14 art, D, Sept 20, dia.
8146 Walker, J, 2 art, D, Sept 8, dia.
8198 Wall, J, 64, I, Sept 8, dia.
7276 Warhurst, Samuel, 7 art, I, Aug 30, dia
3731 Washington, I, 76, G, July 21, scs.
5679 Washburn, H, 5 cav, D, Aug 14, scs.
2023 Wagner, C, 39, E, June 15, dia. c.
10686 Wagner, C, 93, K, Oct 11, scs.
11001 Warren, P, 7 art, G, Oct 16, uls.
6537 Warren, E, 22 cav, L, Aug 23, scs.
4120 Warren, Geo R, 2, F, July 28, scs.
11082 Warrell, E C,§ 57, I, Oct 17, scs.
11945 Waterman, S, 169, K, Nov 10, scs.
6978 Waldron, N, 146, A, Aug 27, dys.
7249 Walz, M, 14 art, I, Aug 30, dia.
6425 Walling, Geo, 76, B, Aug 22, scs.
6046 Watchler, J,§ 119, G, Aug 18, scs.
4060 Walls, C H, 109, K, July 27, dia.
3336 Walser, John, 15 art, D, July 15, dia.
1564 Walcott, G P, 67, D, June 2, des.
2294 Wales, J,§ 85, D, June 22, dia. c.
1537 West, James, 3 art, H, June 1, dia.
9572 West, T, 13 cav, F, Sept 23, dia.
3964 West, Wm, 152, E, July 25 scs.
739 West, Jas.§ 2 cav, E, April 25, dys.
10303 Weston, L, 115, F, Oct 4, dia.
9731 Webster, G, 29, C, Sept 25, dia.
5593 Webster, E, 76, E, Aug 14, scs.
1598 Webster, Jas, 137, C, June 4, dia. c.
9889 Wendle, John, 7 art, E, Sept 27, scs.
9941 Wellstraff, C, 100, D, Sept 28, scs.
10013 Welch, W, 76, G, Sept 29, scs.
5030 Welch, C, 3 cav, B, Aug 8, dia.
8555 Welber, E G, 120, K, Sept 15, dia.
8208 Weil, E C, 164, B, Sept 8, dys.
7561 Welson, James H, 74, K, Sept 2, dys.
8177 Welch, C, 39, H, Sept 8, dia.
5181 Welch, E, 24 bat, Aug 9, dys.
6692 Welch, J, 5 cav, K, Aug 24, scs.
2310 Welsh, L, 146, B, June 22, dia. c.
8855 Welber, E G, 120, K, Sept 15, dia. c.
9428 Weaver, J, 1 cav, E, Sept 21, dia.
7078 Weaver, B S, 96, I, Aug 28, dia.
9448 Webber, C H, 85, C, Sept 21, dia.
9506 Westerfield, P S, 7 art, B, Sept 22, scs.
8731 Werting, John, 52, D, Sept 14, scs.
7987 Wellington, G R,§ 12 cav, A, Sept 6, dia.
8204 Weeks, J, 7, G, Sept 8, dia.
7472 Wells, Jeff, 9, H, Sept 1, dia.
12036 Wells, E, 69, K, Nov 16, scs.
7667 Weismere, H, 32, I, Sept 3, ts. f.
4915 Wedder, N C, 184, E, Aug 6, dys.
11061 Wellder, C M, 22 cav, G, Oct 17, dys
11397 Westbrook, D, 155, H, Oct 24, des.
6927 Weafer, Chas, 115, A, Aug 26, dia.
7256 Wertz, Jas, 12 cav, I, Aug 30, des.
6370 Webb, M E, 14 art, F, Aug 21, scs.
11127 Welch, J, 5 cav, D, Oct 18, dia. c.
6002 Weiber, J, 6 art, E, Aug 17, dia.
4272 Weller, W H, 85, E, July 29, dia.
3235 Westfall, John, 151, H, July 12.
265 Weldon, Edson, 20 cav, M, M'ch 31, dys. c
507 Westhrop, H, 125, B, April 12, dia. c.
6755 Webster H, 22 cav, A, Aug 24, scs.
10303 Weston, L, 115, F, Oct 4, scs.
7543 Whitmore, D, 140, I, Sept 2, dys.
10423 Wharton, J R, 5 cav, L, Oct 6, scs.
9743 Whittle, J C, 85, E, Sept 25, dys.
9878 Whertmour, M, 15 art, M, Sept 13, dia.
8611 Whipple, M, 22 cav, D, Sept 13, dia. c.
8680 White, Jas, 1 drag, D, Sept 13, scs.

54   **Federal Soldiers who Died at Andersonville, Georgia Confederate Prison**

****

11879 White, L, 8 art. G, Nov 6, dia.
3034 White, E, 10 cav, D, July 8, dys.
8792 Whiting, M, 85, D, Sept 15, scs.
7417 Whitney, John,§ 39, K, Aug 31, dia.
5207 Whitney, J, 104, E, Aug 10, dia. c.
10972 Whitman, J, 16, H, Oct 15, scs.
12049 Whitmans, P, 66, E, Nov 16, scs.
11724 Whitbeck, J,‡ 20, D, Nov 1, dia. c.
2611 Wheeler, D, 147, H, Aug 23, dia. c.
5770 Whitmore, O B, 40, A, Aug 15, dys.
4155 Whitlock, Wm, 14 art, I, July 28, dia.
1133 Wilson, Jas, 132, K, May 16, pna.
3757 Wilson, John, 95, A, July 22, dia.
6832 Wilson, M, 2 art, H, Aug 25, scs.
11983 Wilson, W, 155, H, Nov 13, dys.
5870 Wilson, A J, 57, A, Aug 16, dia. c.
1645 Wilson, D, 48, H, June 5, dys.
6233 Windness, A, 15 art, C, Aug 20, wds.
4080 Williams, F, 125, A, July 27, dia.
4522 Williams, Ed, 42, A, Aug 2, dia.
11130 Williams, H, 2 cav, M, Oct 18, scs.
12697 Williams, S, 94, I, Feb 23, scs.
9516 Williams, L D, 85, G, Sept 22, dia.
8478 Wilcox, T E, 85, B, Sept 11, scs.
7945 Williams, Jas, 63, G, Sept 5, dia.
4603 Williams, Geo,‡ 1 cav, K, Aug 3, scs.
4701 Williams, John, 52, K, Aug 4, scs.
3947 Williams, O,§ 24 bat, July 25, dia.
1567 Williams, H, 9 s m, A, June 2, pna.
6861 Williams, L, 16, A, Aug 26, scs.
7112 Williams, J B, 24 cav, C, Aug 28, dys.
6219 Williams, C R, 85, E, Aug 20, ana.
3069 Winn, P, 20 cav, M, July 9, dia.
3273 Wicks, D, 63, D, July 13, dia. c.
1938 Wilcox, Geo, 12 cav, F, June 14, r. f.
2044 Wilcox, R, 14, June 15, dia.
9496 Wilcox, W, 43, G, Sept 21, dia. c.
3576 Wilcox, J, 85, D, July 19, scs.
11111 Wilcox, H R, 55, C, Oct 18, scs.
11428 Wilcox, C,§ 5 cav, G, Oct 24, dia. c.
12607 Wiley, I, 59, B, Feb 7, dia. c.
10122 Willis, J, 121, G, Oct 1, scs.
9057 Willsey, D, 7 art, Sept 17, scs.
8729 Wiggins, James, 52, D, Sept 14, scs.
7980 Winn, James, 7 art, I, Sept 6, scs.
8208 Will, E C, 164, B, Sept 8, dys.
7622 Wiley, W, 115, G, Sept 2, dia. c.
3728 Wilkey, S, 8, B, July 21, dys.

10977 Wilkinson, J N,‡ 42, A, Oct 15, scs.
5663 Wicks, Frank, 1 art, K, Aug 14, dia.
11474 Winney, G A, 100, D, Oct 25, dys.
11520 Winter, G, 10 cav, L, Oct 26, scs.
11689 Wilds, J, 154, B, Oct 31, dia. c.
7122 Winser, J, 117, I, Aug 28, dia.
7581 Wood, E G, 24 bat, Sept 2, dia.
3607 Wood, F, 5 cav, I, July 19, dia.
9874 Wood, H, 115, G, Sept 27, scs.
10063 Wood, H, 15, D, Sept 30, scs.
9715 Wood, J, 10 cav, M, Sept 25, scs.
7686 Wood, John, 97, D, Sept 3, dia.
3881 Wood, M, 111, H, July 24, dia
5039 Wood, J S, 6 art, A, Aug 8, dia. c.
9132 Woodmancy, D M, 3 cav, M Sept 18, **dia**
10141 Wood, W J, 95, H, Oct 1, scs.
8382 Woodworth, B, 56, D, Sept 10, **dys**.
7884 Woodand, H, 1, I, Sept 5, ana.
5696 Woodhull, D F, 8 cav, E, Aug 15, scs.
12356 Wooley, G C, 7 art, K, Dec 30, scs.
11821 Wolf, T, 88, D, Nov 5, scs.
11031 Wolfe, W, 2 art, M, Oct 16, scs.
6130 Wolfe, Fred,‡ 24 cav, E, Aug 19, des.
591 Wolfran, A, 52, C, April 16, dia. c.
4847 Wright, Charles, 118, E, Aug 6, **dia. c.**
10941 Wright, D, 4 G, Oct 14, scs.
5126 Wright, J J, 148, I, Aug 9, scs.
4281 Wuag, C, 39, E, July 30, dia.
7784 Wulslager, John, 85, G, Sept 4, dia.
4589 Wyatt, James, 147, G, Aug 2, dia.
7334 Wyncoop, G,§ 12 cav, H, Aug 30, scs.
2104 Winegardner, L, 18, G, June 17, dia. c.

7433 Yales, W G, 71, H, Sept 1, dia.
4984 Yencer, J D, 24 bat, Aug 7, dys.
12501 Yeomand, G, 7, A, Jan 21, dia.
6539 Young, C, 41, D, Aug 23, scs.
5598 Young, Charles, 15, C, Aug 14, **scs.**
8224 Young, E, 2 art, L, Sept 8, dia. c.
1306 Young, Eugene, 111, G, May 23, **dia.**
8733 Young, George, 22, H, Sept 14, dia.
6946 Young, J,§ 1 cav, B, Aug 26, dia.
7411 Young, T B, 148, A, Aug 31, dia.
10481 Youker, W, 10 art, B, Oct 7, dia.

7480 Zaphan, H P, 7 art, E, Sept 1, scs.
12204 Zolber, F W, 40, D, Dec 1, scs.
12617 Zeigler, S, 145, G, Feb 9, scs.

NORTH CAROLINA.

1596 Barker, J, 2, F, June 3, dys.
849 Briggs, Wilson, 1, A, May 3, dys. c.

275 Collowill, B, 2, F, March 31, c. f.
475 Cox, William C,§ 2, F, April 9, i. f.
864 Check, W F,‡ 2, F, May 8, dia. c.

144 Dunbar, Alex, 2, F, March 25, dia. c.

1057 Miller, J, drum, 2, D, May 13, phs.
10705 Masey, Henry, 7, Oct 11, dia.
11844 Moss, Wm, 1, F, Nov 5, scs.

8690 Norfield, Warren, 1, G, Sept 14, **dia.**

370 Stone, Jno A, 2, F, April 5, dia. a.
2636 Smith, Jas, 2, F, June 29, dia. c.
4899 Smith, Geo, 2, E, Aug 5, scs.

333 Turner, F, 2, I, April 2, dia. a.
798 Turner, H, 1 col'd, I, April 29, **dia. c.**

204 Weeks, Nathan, 2, F, March 28, dia. c.
712 Williams, Thos, 2, D, April 24, **dia.**

OHIO.

12846 Akers, J W, 4, B, April 24, dia.
251 Arther, George, 7, B, March 30, dia.
789 Arrowsmith, W R, 45, K, April 23, dia. c.
1118 Ames, George, 100, K, May 15, dys.
1550 Allen, W, 45, B, June 1, dia. c.
1569 Alinger, D, 51, C, June 2, dia. c.
1724 Anderson, D, 111, B, June 8, dia.
1779 Augustus, T, 89, K, June 9, pna.
1805 Akers, A A, 94, F, June 10, ana.
2040 Aldridge, C W, 33, June 15, pna.
2935 Adam, Miller, 103, I, July 5, des.
3046 Anderson, R, 93, C, July 8, dia.

3197 Aldbrook, C W, 60, July 12, dia.
3485 Arthur, J C,§ 89, A, July 17, dia.
3852 Armebrish, A, 21, A, July 24, scs.
3932 Almond, A, 72, A, July 25, dia.
4529 Arnold, Charles, 9 cav, G, Aug 2, **dia.**
4990 Ailes, T G, 20, I, Aug 7, dia.
5048 Andrews, Samuel, G, Aug 8, dia. c.
6422 Adams, E, 2 cav, C, Aug 22, scs.
7429 Allen, A B,‡ 121, C, Aug 31, scs.
7482 Alward, A, 135, B, Sept 1, i. s.
7736 Arthur, J, 69, I, Sept 3, des.
7843 Arne, I, 64, D, Sept 4, dia.

9818 Alown, A, 34, D, Sept 26, dia.
10393 Andrews, J R, 63, K, Oct 6, dia. c.
10425 Adams, J, 122, I, Oct 6, dia.
10874 Allen, James C, 91, F, Oct 13, scs.
11198 Andermill, John, 24, K, Oct 20, scs.
12495 Allen, J W,‡ 1, G, Jan 20, scs.

188 Baiel, W T,§ 45, F, March 27, dia.
207 Bodin, Thomas S,§ 44, March 28, dys. a.
691 Beaver, George E, 111, B, April 23, ts. f.
829 Beeman, Richard, 125, E, May 1, dys.
861 Biddinger, M, mus, 94, K, May 3, dia. c.
952 Branigan, James, 82, F, May 8, dia.
1094 Blangy, S, 70, B, May 14, dia. c.
1212 Botkins, A S, 45, G, May 19, des.
1226 Black, G W, 99, F, May 20, dia.
1366 Bates, L B, 1 cav, A, May 25, dys.
1368 Bodkin, W, 45, K, May 25, ana.
1376 Baldwin, N, 9 cav, F, May 26, dys.
1385 Bowers, James, 89, A, May 26, mas.
1468 Boyd, H J, 7, H, May 30, dia.
1602 Boman, John, 2, C, June 4, dia. c.
1609 Bryan, R, 16, C, June 4, dia. c.
1781 Balcom, D, 19, F, June 9, pna.
1919 Brownles, John, 7, I, June 14, ana.
1937 Brooks, J, 135, I, June 14, dia. a.
1970 Bothin, W J, 45, F, June 15, ana.
1993 Bartholomew, E W, 205, C, June 15, des.
2065 Belding, F, 105, D, June 16, dia. c.
2067 Brookheart, W, 45, I, June 16, dia. c.
2087 Benor, H, 100, E, June 17, scs.
2110 Bishop, S, 49, K, June 17, dia. c.
2170 Berry, J C, 90, E, June 19, dia. c.
2264 Beers, A, 45, A, June 20, dia.
2292 Burnham, W, 1 art, K, June 21, ana.
2415 Bird, J, 45, A, June 24, dia. c.
2492 Bratt, G,§ 21, G, June 26. r. f.
2599 Boughfman, J, 39, C, June 28, ana.
2696 Brandon, John, 15, F, June 30, pna.
3053 Barnes, V H, 92, H, July 9, dia.
3245 Brown, Charles, 23, D, July 13, dia.
3299 Burns, M G, 111, B, July 13, dia.
3608 Brackneck, H, 7 cav, A, July 19, dia.
3656 Bogart, John, 9, G, July 20, scs.
3706 Buntrell, C, 6, G. July 21, dia.
3756 Batch, O, 45, I, July 22, dia.
3831 Bowman, S, 51, K, July 23, dys.
4073 Brockway, M, 2 art, D, July 27, dys.
4279 Boyle, W H, 11, H, July 30, dia.
4684 Britton, B H, 125, H, Aug 4, rhm.
4968 Berdy, M J, 45, D, Aug 7, scs
5138 Buckle, John J, 126, E, Aug 9, dia.
5219 Brabham, George, 9 cav, B, Aug 10, scs.
5498 Baldwin, George, 9 cav, G, Aug 13, dia. c
5653 Bonestine, W H,‡ 107, I, Aug 14, cah.
5656 Burna, J M, 121, K, Aug 14, dia.
5758 Balmet, J, 19, I, Aug 15, scs.
5771 Brutch, E, 10 cav, I, Aug 15, dys.
5819 Bond, S F, 123, B, Aug 16, mas.
5825 Boyle, H, 130, B, Aug 16, mas.
5937 Bower, F, 61, I, Aug 17, dys.
5985 Birch, L F, 31, H, Aug 17, mas.
6008 Bowman, A, 104, E, Aug 17, dia.
6020 Bright, N, 6, E, July 17, dys.
6152 Brown, G S, 111, F, Aug 18, scs.
6839 Baren, T J,‡ 89, A, Aug 25, scs.
7280 Barrett, S C, 26, F, Aug 30, dia.
7283 Bell, A, 70, B, Aug 30, dia.
7484 Baxter, P D, 121, D, Sept 1, scs.
7490 Brenning, C, 14, G, Sept 1, dys.
7529 Brown, W, 26, G, Sept 1, scs.
7806 Bear, E, 33, A, Sept 4, dys.
7983 Bender, C, 54, C, Sept 6, dia.
7993 Brown, M,‡ 110, F, Sept 6, dys.
7994 Barnes, T S, 31, B, Sept 6, scs.
8365 Benear, W A, 135, F, Sept 10, scs.
8376 Barston, G H, 135, F, Sept 10, scs.
8476 Brenner, N, 60, F, Sept 11, scs.
8496 Barnes, A, 36, G, Sept 11, dia.
8508 Blythe, C, 1, I, Sept 12, ana.
8509 Brinhomer, J, 65, C. Sept 12, dia.
8676 Brown, H H, 41, A, Sept 13, scs.

8693 Bell, James, 135, B, Sept 14 scs.
8872 Buckley, J G, 126, A, Sept 1 , dys.
8939 Blessing, C, 9, F, Sept 16, scs.
9287 Baker, W C, 94, Sept 19, dia.
9446 Brookover, Geo, 135, B, Sept 21, dia.
9473 Briace, J R, 122, C, Sept 21, dia.
9625 Bradley, A, 101, A, Sept 24, dia.
9679 Blackman, S, 72, G, Sept 24, scs.
9897 Burchfield, Eli, 14, Sept 27, dia.
9949 Beant, H T, 34, m i, D, Sept 28, dia.
10120 Brewer, D C, 43, K, Oct 1, wds.
10199 Brown, E N, 21, E, Oct 2, scs.
10281 Brum, W H,§ 20, B, Oct 4, dia.
10591 Briggs, F, 17, G, Oct 10, dia.
11072 Baymher, L G, 153, A, Oct 17, scs.
11307 Boles, G, 112, H, Oct 22, scs.
11308 Brunker, J, 11, K, Oct 22, scs.
11313 Burns, M, 12, K, Oct 22, scs.
11626 Bricker, J J,§ 126, H, Oct 28, dia.
11920 Bumgardner, Joel, 3, C, Nov 8, scs.
11939 Barber, B, 10 cav, D, Nov 9, dia. c
12296 Bissel, J, 2 cav, E, Dec 16, scs.
12383 Beckley, G, 102, F, Jan 3, dia. c.
12524 Barnes, E H, 2, D, Jan 26, scs.
12641 Bower, A, 27, F, Feb 12, dia. a.
517 Blackwood, J, 92, I, April 12, dia. c.
12772 Bowens, W H, 100, A, March 13, pls.

5 Carpenter, White,‡ 92, D, March 4, pna
458 Copeland, C, 1, A, April 9, wds.
561 Coates, Geo H, 7 cav, I, April 15, dia.
563 Campbell, James, 7 cav, H, April 15, dia
723 Callaway, Wm, 7 cav, F, April 25, dia. c
763 Coleman, G, 101, A, April 27, dia.
911 Chapman, Geo, 75, A, May 1, phs.
928 Crosser, M, 111, B, May 7, dia.
965 Corley, W C, 111, B, May 8, dia.
1269 Cruct, Wm, 89, C, May 21, dia.
1291 Collins, Thomas,‡ 21, G, May 22, dia. c.
1521 Capeheart, H, 70, I, May 31, dia.
1587 Clark, H S, 62, E, June 3, dia. c.
1631 Conklin, W, 121, B, June 5, pna.
1679 Clark, D V, 111, B, June 6, dia.
1900 Childers, Wm, 89, B, June 13, dia.
1945 Crocker, Geo, 1 art, A, June 14, dia.
1992 Christy, W, 89, K, June 15, dia. c.
2017 Curtis, N, 45, D, June 15, ana.
2025 Careahan, G M, 65, F, June 15, dia. c.
2101 Caldwell, J,§ 15, D, June 17, dia. a.
2162 Cornelius, L C,‡ 89, C, June 19, cas.
2207 Cochrane, James,§ 22, G, June 20, dia s
2468 Church, E, 2, G, June 25, dia.
2578 Combston, J, 7 cav, L, June 27, dia. c.
2963 Cameron, H, 69, B, July 6, dia. c.
3002 Callahan, H, 34, C, July 7, dys.
3241 Coyner, Geo M, 89, D, July 13, dia.
3307 Canard, J Q A, 14, G, July 13, dia.
3356 Cruer, J W, 60, B, July 15, dia. c.
3541 Cole, B, 82, A, July 18, dia.
3578 Collins, T, 15, I, July 19, dia.
3604 Cook, L B, 2 cav, C, July 19, dia.
3617 Clark, J C,§ 31, H, July 20, scs.
3774 Clayton, D J, 9 cav, D, July 22, scs.
3937 Cover, L, 49, B, July 25, dia. c.
4128 Clayton, J, 89, G, July 28, dia.
4342 Conway, J, 103, A, July 30, dia.
4493 Cordray, J J, 89, G, Aug 1, scs.
4865 Cahill, J N, 90, C, Aug 6, dia.
5105 Charles, F, 100, A, Aug 9, dia. c.
5451 Collyer, J, 11, G, Aug 12, dia.
5548 Chandler, M, 124, E, Aug 13, dia.
5922 Clark, James, 89, I, Aug 17, des.
6022 Cline, K, 111, B, Aug 17, dia.
6108 Church, Geo E,§ 14, C, Aug 18, dia.
6188 Chambers, R S, 89, A, Aug 19, scs.
6258 Copir, S A,‡ 33, C, Aug 20, ana.
6281 Conklin, J R, 45, L, Aug 20, dia. c.
6562 Craig, D,§ 2, D, Aug 23, cah.
7483 Caswell, G, 21, C, Sept 1, dys.
7486 Coons, David, 57, C, Sept 1, scs.
7495 Crooks, J M, 92, K, Sept 1, dia.
7695 Chard, C W, 2, H, Sept 3, dia.

7800 Cregg, J,§ 49, K, Sept 4, dia.
7835 Cline, M, 2, E, Sept 4, dia.
7919 Clark, George, 60, D, Sept 5, r. f.
7998 Clokie, J W, s major, 49, Sept 6, dia.
8130 Cummings, W S, 35, I, Sept 8, dia.
8454 Cattlehock, F, 35, A, Sept 14, dia. c.
8457 Campbell, W C, 5, I, Sept 11, dia.
8694 Chapin, James, 135, F, Sept 14, scs.
8701 Crooke, W B, 135, B, Sept 14, scs.
8810 Clark, J R, 135, F, Sept 15, scs.
9243 Corstein, W,‡ 98, C, Sept 19, scs.
9288 Cramblet, A J, 123, H, Sept 19, dia. c.
9452 Campbell, Samuel, 74, G, Sept 21, dia.
9476 Cadwell, A F, 3, E, Sept 21, dia.
9491 Clay, O, 122, D, Sept 21, dia.
9582 Cort, W, 11, D, Sept 24, dia.
9770 Cummings, A, 6 cav, E, Sept 25, scs
9772 Clark, S, 24, H, Sept 26, scs.
9895 Conner, J B, 9 cav, G, Sept 27, dia.
9971 Castable, I, 51, A, Sept 28, dia.
10381 Coates. Rufus, 2 cav, Oct 5, dia.
10796 Colts, R E, 2, C, Oct 12, scs.
10834 Cepp, J, 14, I, Oct 13, scs.
10986 Carey, A, 21, E, Oct 16, scs.
11103 Carter, John B, 89, I, Oct 18, scs.
11224 Craven, A J,‡ 15, C, Oct 20, dys.
11262 Cromwell, W H, 59, H, Oct 21, dia. c.
11403 Cutsdaghner, W J, 95, D, Oct 24, scs.
11540 Crominberger, J C, 23, I, Oct 27, scs.
11567 Cantwright, L, 51, F, Oct 27, scs.
11587 Chapin, J A, 135, F, Oct 28, scs.
11618 Clark, H M, 21, A, Oct 28, scs.
11641 Clingan, A P, 26, K, Oct 30, scs.
11766 Cohagen, J H, 6, K, Nov 3, dia.
12082 Cahill, Wm, 51, A, Nov 18, scs.
12385 Calvington, R, 72, C, Jan 3, r. f.
12435 Chambers, J C, 15, C, Jan 11, scs.
12691 Crampton, A, 79, C, Feb 22, dia. c.
12798 Conover, S, 175, B, March 19, dia. c.

690 Davis, Wm E, 7, H, April 23, brs.
930 Downing, George, 45, C, May 7, r. f.
981 Dumar, R,§ 45, B, May 9, des.
1267 Dugan, Thomas, 1 cav, B, May 21, ts. f.
1748 Davis, I,§ 7 cav, F, June 9, dys.
2251 Decker, B F, 111, B, June 21, des.
2296 Dumas, J P, 2, H, June 21, dys.
2351 Douglass, W, 24, F, June 23, dia. c.
2674 Davis, B, 22, B, June 30, scs.
2909 Davis, G W, 45, E, July 5, dia.
2973 Dandelion, T, 3d Co, ind cav, July 7, ana.
3703 Dodson, E, 7 cav, H, July 21, dia.
3802 Dille, Charles, 23, I, July 22, dia. c.
4455 Dodge, ——, 2, I, Aug 1, dia.
4501 Diecy, C, 26, G, Aug 1, dia.
4772 Denton, John, 7 cav, E, Aug 5, scs.
5020 Desselbem, M, 1, I, Aug 8, des.
5268 Dorson, L,‡ 12, I, Aug 10, dys.
5299 Doty, E E, 41, H, Aug 11, dia.
5368 Dyke, F, 5 cav, K, Aug 11, dia.
5465 Donly, James, 1 cav, F, Aug 13, scs.
5620 Davis, W H, 33, D, Aug 14, dia.
6043 Decker, J, 111, B, Aug 18, dia. c.
6223 Durant, B, 95, D, Aug 20, dia.
6312 Downer, A P, 52, B, Aug 20, ana.
6708 Dougherty, W H, 15, H, Aug 24, gae.
7229 Dildine, J, 33, K, Aug 29, dia.
7376 Deming, W,‡ 111, B, Aug 31, ana.
7419 Daley, S, 33, D, Aug 31, dia.
7427 Dick, Charles,§ 53, G, Aug 31, wds.
7479 Drake, M, 59, D, Sept 1, scs.
7500 Doran, James, 60, A, Sept 1, dia.
7609 Ditto, John, 51, A, Sept 2, dia.
7631 DeMastoris, J, 54, B, Sept 2, wds.
8034 Davidson, P S, 21, K, Sept 6, scs.
8483 Donley, M, 59, G, Sept 11, scs.
8498 Drake, John F, 135, C, Sept 11, scs.
8779 Diver, J, 4, Sept 14, scs.
8820 Davere, J, 49, D, Sept 15, scs.
9293 Diver, John, 123, H, Sept 19, dia. c.
9605 Decker, S, 12, C, Sept 23, scs.
9702 Dobson, J R, 99, H, Sept 25, dia.

9849 Duffy, G, 45, C, Sept 27, dia.
10112 Dunbar, J, 122, F Oct 1, dys
10113 Diven, J, 135, F, Oct 1, dys.
10130 Duncan, A, 49, K, Oct 1, scs.
10190 Dunham, James, 8 cav, M, Oct 1, dia.
10424 Dewitt, Joseph, 65, G, Oct 6, scs.
10596 Dibble, F, 101, H, Oct 10, scs.
11017 Diper, O, 128, I, Oct 16. scs.
11102 Danton, W H, 105, E, Oct 18, dia.
12159 Donahue, P, 72, K, Oct 25, scs.
12224 Drith, C, 33, K, Dec 4, scs.
12675 Dunken, T, 20, K, Feb 19, dia. c.
12738 Deputy, W, 21, H, Feb 6, dia. c.
7431 Davis, G W,‡ 21, G, Aug 31, scs.
1629 DeRush, Samuel, 94, F, June 5, dia. c.

327 Elijah, Baker, 45, B, April 2, dys.
341 Evalt. E J, 10, M, April 2, dia. c.
1047 Eppert, Samuel, 9, B, May 12, ana.
2221 Earles, William, 4 cav, G, June 20, lia c
3376 Ellis, Charles, 29, B, July 16, scs.
4504 Elliott, W,‡ 20, F, Aug 1, ana.
5304 Evans, Samuel, 33, C, Aug 11, scs.
5349 Eastman, J, 18, C, Aug 11, dys.
5717 Evens, Charles, 1 art, D, Aug 15, ens.
5887 Ensley, Wm, 135, F, Aug 16, dia.
6015 Eckhart, J, 2, B, Aug 17, scs.
7448 Elmann, A, 28, F, Sept 1, scs.
8981 Entulin, B C, 104, K, Sept 17, scs.
11051 Evans, W, 51, I, Oct 17, uls.
11169 Evans, E M,§ 20, I, Oct 19, scs.
11452 Elha, D, 8, A, Oct 25, scs.
11654 Ewing, D, 135, D, Oct 30, scs.
12321 Ellerman, N, 59, K, Dec 22, scs.

75 Falman, A, 82, H, March 20, pna.
176 Fairbanks, Alph, 45, A, March 26, dys.
246 Ferris, Joseph, 2 cav, H, March 30, dia.
311 Foster, A M, 100, A, April 2, ts. f.
572 Frayer, Daniel, 99, I, April 5, dia.
636 Facer, Wm, 111, K, April 20, f.
830 Fisher, Charles, 3 cav, C, May 1, dys.
1054 Free, M, 22 bat, May 13, dys.
1381 Freenough, George, 3 cav, May 26, dia. c
1786 Fraiser, James,§ 2, E, June 10, dia.
2457 Fry, W L, 123, H, June 25, dia.
2479 Fenton, J M,§ 35, I, June 25, scs.
2761 Finlan, James, 18, K, July 2, dia. c.
4231 Fry, Jacob, 99, I, July 29, dia.
4317 Fitch, E P, 40, G, July 30, dia.
4337 Fulkinson, H, 2, I, July 30, dia.
4651 Fife, J, 33, E, Aug 3, dia.
4868 Fling, T J, 27, A, Aug 6, scs.
5249 Ferce, R S, 2, C, Aug 10, dia.
5626 Falk, W, 82, D, Aug 14, dys.
5864 Fullerston, W,‡ 18, K, Aug 16, ana.
6212 Foreman, A, 64, E, Aug 19, dys.
6308 Fisher, D, 89, I, Aug 20, scs.
6891 Futers, John H, 82, F, April 26, contag
7373 Franks, R L, 122, E, Sept 5, scs.
7976 Forney, W O, 123, D, Sept 6, dia.
9158 Firman, V, cav, Sept 18, dia. c.
9225 Ferguson, H, 3 cav, D, Sept 19, gae.
9530 Fowler, C, 100, A, Sept 22, scs.
9557 Finch, C, —, B, Sept 23, dia.
9976 Frankinburg, C, 72, C, Sept 28, dia.
10045 Farshay, A, 116, F, Sept 29, dia.
10915 Freeley, P, 10, G, Sept 14, scs.
11819 Flowers, W F, 116, D, Nov 5, scs.
11914 Forest, Wm, 21, K, Nov 8, scs.
12108 Fargrove, M B, 135, F, Nov 21, scs.
12637 Fussieman, J, 20, H, Feb 11, rhm.
12781 Foults, M, 183, D, March 15, dia. c.
12427 Fike, W P, 95, H, Jan 9, pls.

197 Griling, Daniel, 13, A, March 27, brs.
245 Gardner, A, 100, H, March 30, dia.
386 Grescaust, S,‡ 6 cav, G, April 2, des.
611 Gillinghar, B, 7 cav, L, April 13, dia.
681 Godfrey, Amos, 45, C, April 23, dys. c
693 Greek, Samuel, 100, C, April 23, dia.
906 Gibson, Collins, 46, H, May 5, dia. c.

1465 Greer, R J, 6 cav, C, May 29, dia.
2542 Gilanni, J, 35, K, June 27, dys.
2926 Garner, C, 1 cav, K, July 5, dia.
3130 Goffe, P E, 19, K, July 10, dia. c.
3251 Gaunt, Wm,‡ 14, I, July 13, dia.
3327 Gibson, R, 40, B, July 15, dia. c.
3962 Gingeng, P S,‡ 21, E, July 25, dia.
4037 Gillette, G W, 6, G, July 26, scs.
4242 Gilbert, J, 19, B, July 29, dia. c.
4301 Grafton, D, 118, D, July 30, brs.
4383 Graham, J W, 31, C, July 31, dia.
4445 Goffy, P, 113, G, Aug 1, ana.
4655 Gragrer, H, 125, H, Aug 3, scs.
4802 Greer, G G, 49, D, Aug 5, cah.
4902 Granbaugh, 85, E, Aug 6, scs.
6023 Gordon, Wm, 45, B, Aug 17, dia.
6075 Gallagher, James, 30, F, Aug 18, scs.
6207 Green, E, 4 cav, D, Aug 19, ts. f.
6346 Gordon, W, 10, G, Aug 21, dia.
6408 Gruff, A J, 13, E, Aug 22, cah.
6486 Gates, H, 13, G, Aug 22, dia.
6821 Groovs, L, 12, C, Aug 25, scs.
7111 Gilland, A, 27, F, Aug 28, wds.
8330 Goodrich, J S, 9, A, Sept 10, dia.
8367 Ganold, L, 60, A, Sept 10, scs.
9566 Gould, J M, 124, A, Sept 23, dia. c.
9813 Graft, P, 20 bat, Sept 26, dia.
9927 Galbraith, J S,§ 6 cav, M, Sept 28, dia.
11215 Ginther, J, 60, B, Oct 20, scs.
11850 Gardner, G, 1, K, Nov 5, scs.
12033 Glissin, A,§ 2 cav, M, Nov 15, scs.
12064 Gillenback, J, 77, E, Nov 17, scs.
12109 Goodbrath, C, 28, G, Oct 21, scs.
12560 Griffith, J H, 58, C, Jan 31, dia. c.
12842 Gassler, P, 64, A, April 22, dia. c.

35 Hall, J W, 4, A, March 9, pna.
295 Hochenburg, N, 45, C, April 1, dia.
420 Hanney, W F, 45, A, April 7, dia. c.
424 Hill, J,§ 7 cav, L, April 7, dia. c.
427 Henry, James, 7 cav, L, April 8, dia. c.
464 Haner, Jacob, 45, B, April 9, dia. c.
527 Hickcox, M R, 2 cav, B, April 13, pls.
580 Holdman, F, 1 bat, D, April 16, pna.
748 Hanning, Mark, 7 cav, I, April 26, dia.
748 Harvey, Charles, 76, E, April 26, dys. c.
875 Henry, G W, 95, E, May 4, dia.
949 Hawkins, W W,‡ 103, G, May 8, ts. f.
1129 Hudsonpilfer, R L, 7 cav, L, May 15, dia. c.
1354 Hend, George, 103, H, May 25, dia.
1390 Holloway, G W, 1, C, May 28, dia. c.
1524 Harrison, J, 21, I, May 31, dys. c.
1666 Hazlett, Wm, 2, K, June 6, i. f.
1822 Hull, S,§ 21, E, June 10, dia. c.
1979 Harris, E D,§ 99, I, June 15, dia.
2029 Hugle, John, 1 cav, C, June 15, dys.
2185 Humphreys, Wm, 45, C, June 19, pls.
2263 Hanley, C, 15, F, June 20, dia.
2300 Henderson, S W,§ 40, H, June 22, dia. c.
2369 Howard, J, mus, 70, D, June 23, dia. c.
2424 Hayford, A E, 125, C, June 24, dia.
2597 Harrington, S J, 103, I, June 28, brs.
2671 Hurles, I, 126, C, June 30, i. f.
2775 Hurlburt, O, 14, H, July 2, dia. c.
2842 Hudison, J,‡ 111, B, July 3, dia.
3185 Hall, T,§ 2, H, July 11, dia.
31 Heaton, Ames, 45, F, April 20, s. p.
3388 Hudsen, Wm, 74, July 16, dia.
3420 Hunt, W H, 113, G, July 16, dys.
3736 Harman, L, 9, F, July 21, dia. c.
4030 Hansbury, E A, 6, G, July 26, scs.
4408 Hendershot, John, 45, D, July 31, scs.
4411 Harris, J, 1, E, July 31, dia.
4506 Hartman, H, 13, K, Aug 1, dia. c.
4599 Harrison, J M, 105, M, Aug 3, dia. c.
4993 Hendrickson, O, 19, F, Aug 7, scs.
5293 Holibaugh, J A, 23, E, Aug 11, dia.
5296 Hatfield, George W, 126, K, Aug 11, dys.
5396 Holman, A, 68, K, Aug 12, wds.
5554 Honnill, F R, 9, G, Aug 13, dia.
5630 Hany, B F, 89, C, Aug 14, scs.
5818 Hicks, F, 40, H, Aug 16, dia.

5853 Hibbet, Wm, 21, D, Aug 19, mas.
5858 Hoit, P, 116, B, Aug 16, mas.
6058 Hamm, E J,‡ K, Aug 18, ces.
6123 Higgins, J W,§ 14, C, Aug 18, dia.
6174 Houser, W R, 89, K, Aug 18, ces.
6522 Hicks, J, 11, D, Aug 22, dys.
6625 Hughes, Henry, 33, A, Aug 23, scs.
6639 Henricks, E, 34, H, Aug 23, scs.
6647 Hartman, J, 2, K, Aug 23, scs.
6793 Herrig, N, 7 cav, D, Aug 25, cah.
6802 Hine, T E, 2 cav, D, Aug 25, dia.
7022 Hull, O, 89, B, Aug 27, dia.
7388 Hubbell, W A, 23, A, Aug 31, scs.
7446 Hurdnell, O, 72, C, Sept 1, ts. f.
7825 Holley, V H,§ 100, B, Sept 4, scs.
7946 Hughes, J, 12, E, Sept 5, dia.
8060 Herbolt, Daniel, 115, F, Sept 7, dia.
8067 Harper, J H, 60, I, Sept 7, dia.
8284 Halshult, A, 12, C, Sept 9, dia.
8481 Hechler, John, 36, G, Sept 11, scs.
8696 Hitchkock, G, 34, G, Sept 14, scs.
8725 Hifner, G, 86, C, Sept 14, dia.
9189 Hoyt, R, 7, K, Sept 18, scs.
9210 Hart, E, 10, H, Sept 19, scs.
9538 Hall, S, 126, F, Sept 20, scs.
9415 Hood, F, 13, F, Sept 21, dia.
9510 Hamilton, J, 13, A, Sept 22, dia.
9582 Hoover, J, 18, K, Sept 23, dia.
9622 Hurley, John C, 124, C, Sept 23, dia.
10094 Holmes, Wesley, 135, F, Sept 30, dia.
10207 Harrison, J, 2 cav, A, Oct 2, scs.
10208 Holcomb, L, 7, L, Oct 2, scs.
10225 Harkins, M, 60, D, Oct 2, dia.
10390 Hinton, Wm, 72, A, Oct 5, dia.
10492 Hererlin, B, 32, Oct 7, dia.
10518 Herbert, Wm, 4, L, Oct 8, scs.
10524 Honich, C, 110, D, Oct 8, scs.
10647 Herman, R, 135, F, Oct 11, scs.
11029 Hilyard, J, 98, F, Oct 16, dia.
11032 Hubber, D, 5, A, Oct 16, scs.
11053 Heyners, B, 2, G, Oct 17, scs.
11209 Hanard, J B, 123, C, Oct 20, dys.
11228 Hoyt, W B, 29, A, Oct 20, scs.
11335 Henderson, D, 122, H, Oct 23, scs.
11588 Hintz, D, 1, B, Oct 28, scs.
11592 Hutchins, G W, 135, A, Oct 28, scs.
11696 Hutchins, J W, 153, A, Oct 31, dia.
11856 Hayner, B, 135, A, Nov 6, scs.
11938 Hatfield, A G, 114, E, Nov 9, des.
12353 Hume, J A,‡ 32, F, Dec 29, mas.
12371 Haines, N S,‡ 72, E, Jan 1, scs.
12404 Hill, W L, 54, A, Jan 6, scs.
12446 Hill, E P, 89, G, Jan 13, scs.
12512 Hagerman, R, 33, B, Jan 23, dia.
12569 Hart, H C, 2, C, Feb 1, scs.
12611 Hagerly, D G, 72, E, Feb 7, des.
12743 Holtz, W, 101, I, March 7, des.
1129 Hudson, R L,‡ 7 cav, L, May 15, dia. c.
1132 Hauk, George B, 7 cav, L, May 16, pna.
2607 Handa, L C, 92, E, June 28, dia. c.

1280 Irving, Ester, 114, H, May 22, f.
1967 Ingler, Wm, 31, C, June 14, dia. c.
7489 Imboden, J, 44, E, Sept 1, dys.
8744 Irwin, A, 1, I, Sept 14, des.
10700 Idold, A,§ 7 cav, C, Oct 11, dia.
12579 Isham, D, 89, G, Feb 3, scs.

354 Justice, George W, 45, B, April 2, dia. c.
1637 Johnson, J H, 98, D, June 5, ts. f.
3590 Jacobs, P O, 45, E, July 19, scs.
3754 Jones, R, 45, C, July 22, scs.
3903 Jones, S, 111, B, July 24, i. f.
4381 Jewell, I, 99, F, July 31, dys.
5120 Johnston, John W, 89, H, Aug 9, dia.
5508 Johnson, M, 126, C, Aug 13, dys.
5583 Jones, H, 40, G, Aug 14, dys. c.
5624 Jewell, W A, 126, G, Aug 14, dia.
5839 Jolly, G, 21, K, Aug 16, scs.
6265 Jeffries, H, 36, I, Aug 20, i. s.
6810 Jones, John,‡ 40, G, Aug 25, scs.
7308 Johnson, E, 124, I, Aug 30, dia.

****

7861 Jones, R, W, 118, F, Sept 5, dia.
8647 Jenkins, Wm, 3 bat, Sept 13, scs.
8757 Johnson, D, 43, B, Sept 14, dia.
8760 Johnson, I, 51, A, Sept 14, dia.
9306 Jordan, A, 103, G, Sept 20, scs.
9700 Jones, I B, 30, M, Sept 25, dia.
9744 Johnson, I B, 2, C, Sept 25, dia. c.
9850 Jones, Wm,‡ 84, B, Sept 27, dia.
11014 Jones, S D, 135, F, Oct 16, dys.
11203 Jennings, John,‡ 24, K, Oct 20, scs.
11942 Jones, G L, 105, G, Nov 9, scs.
12126 Jarvitt, W, 15, A, Nov 22, scs.
12231 Johnson, A S,§ 45, I, Dec 6, dia. c.
12335 Jones, W H, 2, C, Dec 26, scs.
12428 Jackson, S, 72, E, Jan 10, pls.
7947 Jacobs, H,‡ 26, F, Sept 6, dia.

836 Kelley, Josiah, 45, C, May 1, pna.
4615 Kimble, S, 98, A, Aug 1, des.
4715 Knight, J, 21, E, Aug 4, ana.
5381 Kelley, E, 21, D, Aug 12, dia.
5448 Knidler, J W, 33, H, Aug 12, dys.
5576 Kelly, H, 1, I, Aug 14, dys.
6195 Kelsey, John,‡ 3, I, Aug 19, des.
7177 Kenedy, S J B, 45, E, Aug 29, scs.
7424 Kelley, G, 15, E, Oct 31, ana.
9377 Kelly, Wm, 46, C, Sept 20, ana.
9436 Kerr, J H, 122, C, Sept 21, dia.
9680 Knapp, J, 54, E, Sept 24, dia.
10139 Killar, J, 15, D, Oct 1, scs.
10607 Kirby, A, 4 cav, A, Oct 10, scs.
10853 Keanshoff, L, 28, I, Oct 13, dia.
11055 Kerr, A, 13, I, Oct 17, dia. c.
11732 Kingkade, S, 18, C, Nov 2, scs.
12661 Kennedy, J, 70, K, Nov 16, brs.
12746 Kaler, J, 72, B, March 8, dia. c.
12802 Karch, J, 183, B, March 20, pls.
765 Kinney, John,‡ 67, E, April 27, dia. c.
2406 Knowlton, E, 6 cav, B, June 24, dia. c.
13 Kiger, J H,‡ 45, E, April 9, s. p.

834 Lowry, James, 49, I, May 1, dia.
935 Lewis, Frank, 103, D, May 7, dia. c.
1286 Larme, Charles, 45, K, May 22, dia. c.
1364 Larkin, Joseph, 1 art, May 25, dia. c.
1470 Logan, Frank, 89, F, May 30, dia.
1615 Logan, H, 6 cav, E, June 4, dia. c.
1828 Leonard, John, 21, A, June 11, scs.
2173 Lever, H B, 2, C, June 19, dys.
2372 Lisure, Samuel, 7, A, June 23, ts. f.
2426 Lemons, M, 89, E, June 24, ts. f.
3495 Lutz, M,‡ 14, C, July 18, scs.
3497 Love, John, 96, E, July 18, dia.
3649 Linsay, J, 21, D, July 20, dia.
4097 Lyon, L L, 1 art, E, July 27, dia.
4354 Law, S S, 124, I, July 31, dia.
4262 Lawsen, J,‡ 2, E, July 29, ana.
4641 Lucas, J, 89, H, Aug 3, ana.
4628 Legrand, D, 111, B, Aug 3, scs.
4692 Long, John, 45, H, Aug 4, dia.
5195 Lightfoot, Wm,‡ 9 cav, G, Aug 10, scs
5246 Latta, W H, 89, H, Aug 10, dia. c.
5449 Lehigh, W, 22, B, Aug 12, dys.
5665 Lamphare, G W, 125, K, Aug 14, dia.
5676 Larisen, A, 63, D, Aug 14, wds.
6066 Lowe, G H, 72, C, Aug 18, ces.
6344 Leasure, Isaac, 122, K, Aug 21, wds.
7123 Leasure, F, 45, K, Aug 28, scs.
7744 Linway, J, 2, H, Sept 3, scs.
8016 Lambert, James, 89, A, Sept 6, dia.
8739 Lickliter, Henry, 135, B, Sept 14, scs.
8874 Lindsley, A K, 99, K, Sept 16, dia.
9336 Leonard, T M, 12, H, Sept 20, scs.
9358 Lovely, John, 100, K, Sept 20, dia.
9361 Lawyer, J B, 89, L, Sept 20, dia.
9419 Lefarer, W E, cit, Gardner, Athens Co.
10039 Laley, ——, 28, Sept 29, dia.
11161 Lepe, A, 7, K, Oct 19, scs.
11196 Lantz, A W, 45, A, Oct 20, scs.
11344 Lochner, M, 72, E, Oct 23, scs.
11440 Laughlin, M W, 1, I, Oct 24, scs.
11490 Lips, F,‡ 2, H, Oct 26, scs.

11816 Lane, D, 91, D, Nov 4, scs.
12007 Lay, John, 123, K, Nov 19, scs.
12201 Lohmeyer, H, 35, K, Nov 30, shot by g'rd
12297 Livingood, C B,‡ 35, G, Dec 16, scs.
12525 Longstreet, W F, 31, A, Jan 26, scs.
12698 Lewis, D, 7, A, Jan 23, dia. a.
12826 Little, Wm, 175, D, April 7, dia.

66 Metcalf, Milo R, 100, E, March 19, c. f.
96 Malsbray, Asa, 40 cav, A, March 22, ts. f
113 Moore, T J,§ 2, D, March 23, pna.
141 McKeever, James, 8, G, March 24, scs.
165 Mickey, Samuel, 45, E, March 26, dia.
215 Murphey, John, 7 cav, B, March 28, dia.
412 Mitchell, J, 120, F, April 7, dia.
444 McKindry, M, 7, I, April 9, dia.
575 Malone, R J,§ 40, H, April 16, dia.
880 McCormick, J W E, 33, B, May 4, c. f.
984 Musser, D, 45, B, May 9, dia.
998 Meek, David, 111, K, May 10, dia.
1262 McKnight, H, 11, G, May 21, dia.
1283 McMunny, George,§ 21, G, May 22, dia
1630 Moore, Charles, 19, H, June 5, dia. c.
1849 Masters, Samuel, 17, I, June 11, ana.
1930 Martin, G, 105, F, June 14, ana.
2075 McCling, B, 7 cav, I, June 17, dia.
2139 Maloney, A, 4, H, June 18, dys.
2150 Mitchell, W H, 31, D, June 18, dia. c.
2290 Massey, J C, 33, A, June 21, dia. c.
2471 Mullin, J, 65, K, June 25, ana.
2667 McCloud, A, 35, G, June 29, dia.
2682 Miller, T, 4 cav, A, June 30, dys.
2743 McFarland, L, 2, I, July 1, dia.
2806 McInness, A, 45, B, July 3, dia.
2873 Moriatt, Joseph, 5, K, July 4, scs.
2991 Mitchell, James, 17, D, July 7, ana.
3104 Malone, L B, 7 cav, L, July 10, dia.
3122 Mitchell, C, 1, K, July 10, dia.
3137 Minshall, R, 45, C, July 10, ana.
3290 Mahin, B, 51, I, July 13, dys.
3491 Master, J, 13, A, July 17, dia.
3718 Miller, E, 4, E, July 21, dia.
4040 Marshall, T,‡ 21, G, July 26, dys.
4199 Myer, C, 21, I, July 29, dia.
4252 Meck, J, 19, E, July 29, dys.
4298 McKell, M J,§ 89, D, July 30, ana.
4361 Mooney, James, 50, D, July 31, dia.
4421 Morris, C E, 11, H, July 31, scs.
4591 McCann, A, 33, C, Aug 3, dys.
4657 Maher, P, 7, E, Aug 3, dia.
4789 Martin, D, 3 cav, L, Aug 5, scs.
5738 McCabe, H, 12, C, Aug 15, dia.
5777 Mansen, W, 9, G, Aug 15, brs.
5883 McIntosh, D, 50, D, Aug 16, dia.
6026 Manahan, Thos, 21, D, Aug 18, dia.
6040 McKee, James, 51, A, Aug 18, des.
6055 McHugh, W S, 2, D, Aug 18, ces.
6063 McClair, P M, 27, A, Aug 18, dys.
6478 McCabe, J, 66, C, Aug 22, scs.
6841 McCormick, W P, 2, G, Aug 25, dia.
6855 McSorley, D, 49, F, Aug 26, dia.
6862 McCoy, J B, 98, A, Aug 26, dia.
6920 McDell, Wm, 89, K, Aug 26, dys.
7108 McDonald, J, 99, H, Aug 28, dia.
7133 Mason, J, 45, D, Aug 28, scs.
7136 More, John H, 60, D, Aug 28, dys.
7515 Myers, L H, 135, B, Sept 1, scs.
7896 Morris, J, 105, A, Sept 5, dia.
8021 Meek, Robert, 111, K, Sept 6, scs.
8044 Myers, A, 51, I, Sept 6, wds.
8385 Maymer, R, 68, D, Sept 10, ts. f.
8408 McCabe, J, 70, C, Sept 11, scs.
8482 Morens, H, 51, A, Sept 11, scs.
8638 Moore, T H, 59, C, Sept 12, scs.
8726 Miller, Samuel, 135, F, Sept 14, scs.
8838 Mackrill, R, 50, I, Sept 15, scs.
8885 Manlig, S, 60, A, Sept 16, dia.
9039 Miller, C, 28, I, Sept 17, scs.
9096 McMillan, J F, 123, A, Sept 18, dia.
9241 McComb, J S, 14, K, Sept 19, scs.
9348 Maxwell, P, 12, A, Sept 20, dia.
8236 Moor, D D, 2, A, Sept 9, dia.

9659 Manley, J, 7, M, Sept 24, scs.
9867 Mitchell, R C, 10 cav, Sept 27, scs.
10064 Morgan, R O, 12 cav, H, Sept 30, dia.
10081 McIntosh, Wm,§ 23, I, Sept 30, scs.
10106 Morais, Wm, 135, F, Sept 30, dia.
10517 Montgomery, J, 2, G, Oct 8, scs.
10563 Myer, L, blacksmith, 1, A, Oct 9, dia.
10936 Martin, F, 10 cav, A, Oct 14, scs.
11156 McElroy, John, 92, B, Oct 18, scs.
11200 Martin, W, 15, A, Oct 20, scs.
11341 McQuilken, F, 1, I, Oct 23, scs.
11400 Mark, J, 135, B, Oct 24, scs.
11811 Miller, J, 135, I, Nov 4, scs.
12050 Moore, R F, 101, C, Nov 16, scs.
12054 Mills, G W, 60, F, Nov 16, des.
12184 Morrison, J H, 21, H, Nov 28, scs.
12535 McDonald, H H, citizen, Jan 27, dia.
12717 Millholand, R, 183, B, March 1, dia.
12872 McGrath, D,‡ 115, G, March 15, scs.
12875 Martin, M,‡ 135, B, March 16, dia.

983 Neal, John, 45, C, May 9, dia.
2328 Nash, C D, 45, B, May 22, dia. c.
4994 Nelson, J, 1 cav, K, Aug 7, scs.
5897 Neff, B, 95, H, Aug 16, dia.
7103 Nelson, Thomas, 1 cav, Aug 28, dia.
10584 Nelder, S, 89, G, Oct 10, dys.
11012 Nott, J, 153, H, Oct 16, dia.
11448 Norman, G L, 135, B, Oct 25, scs.
12815 Norris, E J, 102, K, March 25, dia. c.
2183 Niver, Edward, 3 cav, I, June 19, dia.

2245 Ostrander, E W, 100, A, June 20, dia. c.
2442 Ott, C, 51, C, June 25, dia.
4552 O'Neil, James, 126, F, Aug 2, dys.
12024 O'Connor, F, 103, F, Nov 15, dia.
12247 Oliver, J, 122, C, Dec 8, scs.
12429 Olinger, J, 63, F, Dec 10, scs.
12835 Ornig, J B, 101, I, April 17, dia.
11349 O'Brien, John, 2, D, Oct 23, scs.

65 Pusey, James, 45, H, March 19, c. f.
724 Parker, Wm E, 45, H, April 23, ts. f.
913 Penny, A,‡ 59, C, May 6, dia. c.
1326 Prouty, Wm, 9 cav, L, May 24, dia. c.
2692 Phenix, A H. 21. H, June 20, scs.
9 Price, Barney, 20, I, April 5, s. p.
3391 Pile, Wilson,‡ 33, F, July 16, scs.
3555 Pierce, H, 100, A, July 18, dia.
4020 Perkins, W B, 89, G, July 26, scs.
5190 Piffer, G, 123, A, Aug 9, ts. f.
5377 Parker, W,‡ 124, H, Aug 11, scs.
5426 Perrin, N, 72, A, Aug 12, dia.
6463 Parlice, Geo W, 94, H, Aug 22, scs.
6589 Potter, H, 72, E, Aug 23, des.
6690 Pullen, Samuel, 33, B, Aug 24, dia.
6717 Post, J, 1 art, D, Aug 24, dia.
6984 Palmer, Samuel, 135, I, Aug 27, dia.
7021 Pease, G E, 10 cav, I, Aug 27, dia.
7157 Plunket, M,‡ 124, E, Aug 29, dia.
7329 Peltersen, F, 113, G, Aug 30, wds.
7368 Purcell, John, 72, D, Aug 31, dia. c.
7384 Pierson. J, 125, B, Aug 31, scs.
4399 Palmer, F G, 2 cav, D, Aug 31, dia.
7519 Patten, W, 21, D, Sept 1, pna.
7644 Pierce, Wm, 75, H, Sept 3, dia.
7701 Prnser, H, 1, B, Sept 3, dia.
7724 Payne, J, 89, E, Sept 3, dia.,
8109 Potts, James, 122, E, Sept 7, dys.,
8288 Phillips, H, 33, I, Sept 9, scs.
8534 Powell, F, 9, G, Sept 12, scs.
8597 Pror, A M,§ 135 cav, B, Sept 12, scs.
8620 Pinert, F, 21, C, Sept 13, dia. c.
8753 Parker, Z, 124, E, Sept 14, dia. c.
9111 Parks, J W, 6 cav, G, Sept 18, scs.
9327 Parker, J, 40, H, Sept 20, scs.
9470 Perrin, G, 3, B, Sept 21, dia. c.
9768 Pipenbring, Geo, 13, K, Sept 25, scs.
9822 Preston, Wm, 34, m i, B, 27, dia.
10056 Parks, E F, 36, D, Sept 30, scs.
11221 Piper, E A, 23, B, Oct 20, scs.
11453 Patterson, F, 28 cav, F, Oct 25, scs.

11676 Prouse, P I, 1, I, Oct 30, scr
11779 Preshall, J A, 116, C, Nov 3, scr
12033 Peasley, J,§ 65, H, Nov 16, + s.
12040 Porter, W C, 40, H, Nov 16, scs.
12352 Powers, J, 21, K, Dec 23, scs.
12551 Poistan, J, 183, F, Jan 29, scs.
12645 Piper, I, 64, F, Feb 13, dia. c.

344 Ricker, Henry, 2 cav, E April 2, dia
908 Rush, D, 107, H, May 5, dia. c.
1642 Radabaugh, W H, 33, A, June 5, dia.
2030 Ralston, W J,§ 89, C, June 15, dia.
2124 Rawlings, S, 45, E, June 17, dia. c.
2156 Rancey, A K, 111, B, June 18, dia.
2281 Rickards, W V, 33, B, June 20, dia. c
2410 Rowe, A, 124, F, June 24, dia. c.
2878 Rees, Thomas,‡ 98, C, July 4, scs.
3074 Rix, Wm, 2, K, July 9, dys.
49 Reed, Harmon, 103, E, May 25, s. p.
3400 Rogers, T, 51, C, July 16, dia. c.
3426 Ralston, J M, 89, C, July 16, dys.
3613 Russell, L F, 111, B, July 20, dia.
3862 Regman, O, 2, D, July 24, dys.
3961 Robinson, H H,§ 110, H, July 25, dia.
4061 Reiggs, H, 21, F, July 27, dia. c.
4235 Rex, J W, 3 cav, K, July 30, dia.
4777 Robbins, A, 6 cav, D, Aug 5, rhm.
5570 Reichardson, G, 82, G, Aug 14, scs.
5631 Russell, J G, 116, G, Aug 14, scs.
5639 Read, Geo H, 21, H, Aug 14, scs.
5641 Redder, G, 45, G, Aug 14, scs.
6488 Robbins, D B, 89, I, Aug 22, dia.
6511 Ross, J, 59, A, Aug 22, dia. c.
6835 Reidgway, John, 23, D, Aug 25, dys.
6948 Redd, C, 122, H, Aug 26, dia.
7174 Ross, A, 45, H, Aug 29, scs.
7353 Roberts, Ed, 75, K, Aug 31, dia.
7639 Rutain, E B, 44, E, Sept 2, dia.
7844 Russell, James, 9, E, Sept 4, dia.
8521 Rhotin, W, 2, C, Sept 12, scs.
8747 Riley, W M,‡ 89, B, Sept 14, dia.
8818 Robertson, R, 120, D, Sept 15, dys.
9614 Robinson, J, 65, D, Sept 23, scs.
9617 Rose, John, 72, H, Sept 23, dia.
10165 Riper, O H, 110, G, Oct 1, scs.
10354 Rogers, C, 13, H, Oct 5, scs.
10658 Rochelle, John,‡ 135, F, Oct 11, ts. f.
11279 Romain, J, 59, H, Oct 21, dia.
11360 Reece, A, 80, C, Oct 23, scs.
11413 Reese, R, 59, D, Oct 24, scs.
11646 Rapp, N, 10, A, Oct 30, scs.
11657 Robins, P, 122, H, Oct 30, scs.
11672 Robinson, C J, 2 cav, E, Oct 30, scs.
11859 Rourk, J, 6, G, Nov 6, scs.
12366 Repan, A, 47, A, Dec 31, scs.
12647 Rapp, D C, 2, C, Feb 13, dia.
12692 Rawsbottom, A F, 99, D, Feb 22, dia. c.
1763 Rei, J, 124, K, June 6, dia. c.

33 Smith, J E, 7 cav, C, March 9, pna.
44 Smith, H B, 82, B, March 14, ts. f.
58 Strill, Michael, 100, K, March 18, diz.
231 Sears, Samuel, 2 cav, F, March 29, des.
260 Stephen, H, 100, B, March 31, dia.
263 Shields, Geo, 7 cav, L, March 31, dia. c.
284 Saughessy, John, 45, B, April 1, dia.
481 Steel, Abraham, 80, H, April 9, dia.
504 Swench, W, 45, A, April 16, dia.
653 Snyder, Lewis, 89, C, April 20, dia. c.
726 Sweeny, Samuel, 7 cav, G, April 25, dia
771 Shannon, Charles, 45, I, April 28, ii. c
804 Starbuck, F, 62, E, April 29, dia.
937 Storer, John, 17, A, May 7, dia.
962 Smith, John, 7 cav, F, May 8, dia
994 Smith, Wm, 103, E, May 10, ana.
1160 Samse, Wm, 14, H, May 17, dia.
1179 Smith, Conrad, 100, A, May 18, dia
1183 Smith, Wm, 2, G, May 18, scs.
1229 Spangler, A, 45, E, May 20, i. f.
1281 Swineheart, J W, 111, B, May 22, i. f.
1404 Seyman, Aaron, 89, D, May 27, scs.
1672 Sprague, W L, 6 cav, K, June 6, dys.

1773 Simmons, John, 22 bat, June 9, dia.
2220 Shannon, E, 35, A, June 20, scs.
2230 Stanett, J, 45, C, June 20, dia. c.
2376 Stiver, J, 93, C, June 23, dia. c.
2524 Smith, G W, 11, K, June 26, dia.
2575 Sampson, C, 89, D, June 27, scs.
2638 Stults, P, 45, F, June 29, dia.
2783 Shiver, L, 31, B, July 2, pna.
2792 Smith, N H, 1, H, July 2, dia. c.
3116 Smith, G,§ 21, I, July 10, dia.
42 Sabine, Alonzo, 100, A, May 11, s. p,
3252 Short, James,§ 4 cav, A, July 13, dia.
3288 Smith, D, 7, H, July 13, scs.
3361 Saffle, J, 2, E, July 15, scs.
3536 Steward, C S, 33, K, July 18, dia.
3602 Stevenson, D, 111, B, July 19, scs.
3298 Squires, Thomas, 49, C, July 20, dia.
3744 Snyder, Thomas,§ 9, G, July 21, dia. c.
3770 Smith, D,‡ 2, I, July 22, dia. c.
3794 Sever, H H, 2, C, July 22, dys.
4249 Shephard, J H,‡ 2, E, July 29, dia.
4275 Smith, J B,§ 1, B, July 29, dia. c.
4294 Steward, J,§ 2, K, July 30, dia. c.
4745 Steiner, M J, 72, F, Aug 5, dia.
5018 Smock, A, 93, D, Aug 8, dys.
5054 Smarz, A, 93, E, Aug 8, scs.
5066 Shipple, John, 6 cav, G, Aug 8, ana.
5133 Scott, S E, 4, I, Aug 9, scs.
5287 Stevenson, John, 111, B, Aug 11, scs.
5330 Spegle, F, 14, D, Aug 11, scs.
5373 Schem, J, 101, K, Aug 11, dys.
5455 Stevens, G W, 101, K, Aug 12, scs.
5896 Sullivan, W, 78, D, Aug 16, dia. c.
6010 Staley, G, 89, A, Aug 17, dia.
6032 Smith, Wm, 9 cav, G, Aug 18, dia.
6178 Simpson, W J, 32, F, Aug 19, wds.
6199 Sheddy, G, 2, K, Aug 19, dys.
6214 Shaw, George W, 105, A, Aug 20, dia.
6253 Shoulder, E, 24, F, Aug 20, scs.
6779 Soper, P, 72, G, Aug 25, dys.
6870 Scarberry, O, 89, D, Aug 26, dia.
7034 Sutton, J, 4, A, Aug 27, dia.
7065 Shoemaker, J,§ 47, E, Aug 28, dys.
7436 Stinchear, F E,§ 101, A, Sept 1, dia.
7475 Shafer, J, 9, G, Sept 1, scs.
7540 Sell, Adam, 125, E, Sept 2, dia.
7788 Stewart, John S, 19, B, Sept 4, dia.
7897 Smith, H H, 2 cav, A, Sept 5, dia.
7986 Selb, Jacob, 28, Sept 6, dia.
8014 Shriver, George, 45, K, Sept 6, dia.
8015 Snider, James, 4, C, Sept 6, ana.
8156 Sturdevant, W, 72, A, Sept 8, des.
8197 Shrouds, J, 6 bat, Sept 8, dia.
8200 Stroufe, A, 7, E, Sept 8, scs.
8229 Shaw, W, 15, I, Sept 9, dia.
8300 Smith, N, 121, H, Sept 9, scs.
8319 Sheldon, W, 49, E, Sept 10, dia.
8422 Sullivan, John, 135, F, Sept 11, scs.
8728 Sisson, P B, 18, H, Sept 14, scs.
8752 Sickles, J, 51, I, Sept 14, dia.
8914 Simmonds, S P, 1, A, Sept 16, uls.
8931 Stull, G, 15, G, Sept 16, scs.
9009 Sharp, F S, 63, K, Sept 17, dia.
9244 Scmall, J D, 12, E, Sept 19, dia.
9386 Smith, L, 153, H, Sept 20, scs.
9645 Scott, J H, 33, H, Sept 24, gae.
9649 Skiver, J, 114, H, Sept 24, dia.
10250 Sheets, W, 81, A, Oct 3, ana.
10312 Spencer, S M,‡ 89, E, Oct 4, scs
10434 Shingle, D, 2 cav, L, Oct 6, dia.
10437 Stanford, P W,§ 2 cav, A, Oct 6, dia.
10576 Stonehecks, J D, 51, F, Oct 9, scs.
10618 Schafer, P, 101, I, Oct 10, dia.
10703 Stouts, Samson, 2, F, Oct 11, scs.
10833 Sheppard, John, 34, D, Oct 13, scs.
11139 Shork, H, 72, F, Oct 17, scs.
11146 Smith, G A,‡ 45, F, Oct 19, scs.
11249 Sullivan, F, 76, C, Oct 21, dia.
11433 Swaney, E, 124, A, Oct 24, scs.
11579 Smith, P, 69, I, Oct 28, scs.
11595 Sapp, W N,§ 20, E, Oct 28, dia.
11711 Spiker, J, 122, Nov 1, scs.

11797 Shaler, F,‡ 72, E, Nov 4, scs.
12105 Sly, F, 89, G, Nov 20, scs.
12281 Singer, J, 6, G, Dec 13, scs.
12305 Sweet, M,§ 49, F, Dec 18, scs.
12441 Shoemaker, C, 8, F, Jan 12, pls.
12538 Stewart, A F, 2, D, Jan 27, dia. c.
12562 Sponcerlar, George, 71, B, Jan 31, dia
12668 Shorter, W, 89, K, Feb 17, dia. c.
12769 Sloan, L, 123, D, March 13, dia. c.
12789 Stroup, S, 50, B, March 17, dia. c.
12793 Seeley, N, 132, D, March 18, dia.
12810 Scott, R, 75, G, March 24, dia.

730 Tweede, R, 1 cav, A, April 25, dia.
743 Trescott, Samuel, 2, C, April 26, dia.
999 Trimmer, Wm, 40, H, May 10, dys.
1196 Turney, U S, 2 cav, G, May 18, dys.
1496 Thomas, Wm, 10 cav, M, May 30, r.
2860 Thomas, W B, 89, C, July 4, dia.
4784 Thompson, J, 2, E, Aug 5, dia.
4951 Toroman, W R, 13, E, Aug 7, scs.
5356 Tierney, W, 1 art, L, Aug 11, dia.
5552 Tensley, M, 90, B, Aug 13, scs.
5668 Terilliger, N, 12, C, Aug 14, scs.
6330 Tanner, A,§ 32, G, Aug 21, wds.
7224 Thompson, V B, 26, C, Aug 29, dia.
7246 Turner, S B, 45, B, Aug 30, cah.
7640 Thomas, James, 44, C, Sept 2, dia.
8850 Talbert, R, 135, F, Sept 15, ts. f.
9774 Thomas, N, 103, B, Sept 26, scs.
9945 Townsend, J, 26, C, Sept 28, dia.
10471 Tattman, B, 153, C, Oct 7, dia.
10800 Tinway, P, 93, Oct 12, dia.
11820 Townsley, E M,§ 89, B, Nov 5, r .s.
12577 Tensdale, T H, 2 cav, E, Feb 2, pls.

12251 Uchre, S, 12, E, Dec 9, scs.

2194 Vining, W H H, 45, G, June 1, dia. c
3902 Valentine, C, 123, H, July 24, scs.
4450 Vaugh, B, 125, F, Aug 1, dia.
4497 Vangrider, H, 103, H, Aug 1, dia.
5263 Vatier, J F, 6 cav, Aug 10, dia.
6170 Vail, John L,§ 17, C, Aug 19, ces.
6859 Vanaman, M, 21, E, Aug 26, scs.
6985 Vanderveer, A, 6, H, Aug 27, dia.
7756 Victor, H, 1 art, D, Sept 4, gae.
9576 Volis, J, 34, H, Sept 23, scs.
10252 Vail, N, 12, K, Oct 3, scs.
10389 Vail, G M, 7, D, Oct 5, scs.
10472 Van Fleet, H, 14, I, Oct 7, scs.
11095 Vankirk, G, 135, B, Oct 18, scs.
11097 Van Malley, J M, 89, G, Oct 18, des.
1255k Vanhorn, S, 9 cav, C, Jan 30, scs.

7 Wiley, Samuel, 82, A, March 5, pna.
185 Wickman, Wm, 111, B, March 27, ts.
779 Wooley, John, 45, B, April 28, dia. c.
807 Werts, Louis, 45, D, April 30, dip.
1085 Wood, William, 89, A, May 14, dia. c.
1449 Wentling, Joseph, 100, K, May 29, ans
1604 Wood, Joseph, 15, B, June 4, dys.
1836 Wilkinson, W,‡ 89, D, June 11, dys.
1913 Wilson, James, 93, I, June 13, dia. c.
2020 Way, John, 44, I, June 15, dia.
2041 Windgrove, S R, 15, June 15, dia. c.
2172 Webb, E, 45, A, June 19, dia.
2358 Walters, F, 9, E, June 23, dia. c.
2536 Wing, F, 2 cav, M, June 26, dia. c.
2815 Willis, A, 89, A, July 3, dia.
2840 Wroten, L, 89, H, July 3, dys. c.
3188 Williams, D, 90, A, July 12, ana.
34 Wright, Wm, 7, H, April 24, s. p.
3310 White, H, 15, A, July 15, r. f.
3325 Whitton, G, 75, K, July 14, dia. c
4214 West, J B, 89, B, July 29, dia
4681 Witt, John T, 93, G, Aug 4, dys
4688 Wou, J,‡ 111, B, Aug 4, scs.
4695 Wile, A,‡ 33, D, Aug 4, dys.
5121 Winder, P, 70, D, Aug 9, scs.
5211 Wood, N L, 4 cav, L, Aug 16, dia
5726 Winters, George, 145, E, Aug 15, scs

6314 Wainwright, S G, 89, G, Aug 20, scs.
6318 Wisser, F J, 35, A, Aug 20, dia.
6362 Wistman, N, 9 cav, G, Aug 21, dia.
6397 Wilson, E, 4, A, Aug 21, des.
6700 Watson, G, 21, A, Aug 24, dys.
6761 Wood, S, 123, A, Aug 25, dia.
7056 Wood, W H, 59, E, Aug 28, dia.
7373 Wyatt, J, 90, B, Aug 31, dia.
7582 Wentworth, L 72, A, Sept 1, dia. c.
8298 Wright, J S, 89, E, Sept 9, dia. c.
8396 Warner, 7, 14, C, Sept 10, scs.
8907 Wyckman, D, 73, G, Sept 16, scs.
9284 Worte, J, 116, Sept 20, scs.
9527 Woodruff, J M, 135, F, Sept 22, dia.
9691 Wagner, J, 93, F, Sept 24, dia.
0007 Whitney, E, 21, K, Sept 29, ana.
0220 Williams, Orland, 7 cav, K, Oct 2, dia.
10309 Weaver, M, 72, H, Oct 4, gae.
10402 Ward, Francis, 21, H, Oct 6, dys.
10464 Whitehead, A B, 33, E, Oct 7, scs.
10528 Wiley, A, 26, I, Oct 8, scs.
10733 White, I, 73, E, Oct 11, scs.
10844 Westbrook, R L,‡ 135, F, Oct 13, dia.
11013 Walker, C, 65, I, Oct 16, scs.

11034 Waldron, H, 14, A, Oct 16, scs.
11418 Williams, S M, 60, F, Oct 24, dia. c.
11770 Worthen, D, 122, B, Nov 3, scs.
11874 Weason, J, 36, F, Nov 6, scs.
12042 Wickham, J, 14, H, Nov 16, scs.
12073 White, R M, 15, D, Nov 18, scs.
12158 Warner, B F, 35, E, Nov 25, scs.
12584 Whitaker, E, 72, A, Feb 4, rhm.
12722 Wella, E, 57, A, March 3, rhm.
12759 Winklet, T, McL's sq'n, March 12, scs.
12786 Warner, M, 102, G, March 16, dia. a.
4833 Webricks, Joseph H, 9, G, Aug 6, dys.

638 Yuterler, W A, 45, E, April 20, dia.
5477 Younker, S, 80, F, Aug 13, scs.
6068 Young, John, 7, E, Aug 18, dys.
7816 Yeager, John, 7 cav, B, Sept 4, dia.
7876 Young, J, 9, F, Sept 5, dia.
10583 Young, W, 6, G, Oct 10, dys.
12659 Young, W, 15, A, Feb 16, pls.

3225 Zubers, J M, 100, B, July 12.
11253 Zink, A J, 72, E, Oct 21, scs.

PENNSYLVANIA.

224 Attwood, Abr'm, 18 cav, I, March 29, dia.
250 Armidster, M, 4 cav, A, March 30, dia.
468 Ackerman, C, 8, B, April 9, dia. c.
758 Arb, Simon, 4 cav, C, April 27, dys.
846 Allbeck, G B,§ 52, F, May 3, wds.
975 Algert, H K, 54, F, May 9, brs.
1382 Arble, Thomas, 13 cav, A, May 26, dia. c.
1837 Ait, M, 21, K, June 11, i. s.
2348 Akers, George, 90, H, June 23, dia. c.
2398 Allison, E, 55, K, June 24, dys.
2547 Anderson, D,§ 103, K, June 27, ts. f.
2648 Able, J, 54, F, June 29, dys.
2956 Amagart, Eli,‡ 103, F, July 6, dia. c.
3018 Ackley, G B, 3 art, B, July 7, dia.
3317 Alexander, M, 1 cav, F, July 14, dys.
3967 Ardray, J F,§ 13, F, July 25, dia.
4055 Anderson, J,‡ 79, I, July 27, dys.
4143 Aches, T J, 7, H, July 28, dia.
4149 Alcorn, George W, 145, F, July 28, dia.
4195 Archart, H, 51, C, July 29, dia. c.
4673 Allen, C, 8 cav, K, Aug 4, scs.
4973 Andertin, J, 4 cav, L, Aug 7, dia.
5286 Aler, B, 103, D, Aug 11, dia. c.
5511 Ault, J L, 101, C, Aug 13, scs.
5862 Armstrong, Chas,§ 4 cav, C, Aug 16, dia.
6029 Anersen, John, 91, C, Aug 18, mas.
7163 Arnold, Daniel, 184, C, Aug 29, dia.
7887 Angstedt, Geo W, 1, F, Sept 5, dys.
8185 Allen, J L, 101, I, Sept 8, scs.
8232 Ambler, C, 13 cav, D, Sept 9, dia. c.
8388 Alexander, W, 2 reserve, I, Sept 10, dia.
8653 Armstrong, A. 7, K, Sept 13, dia. c.
8655 Arnold, L, 73, A, Sept 13, scs.
8765 Altimus, Wm, 7, E, Sept 14, dia.
1743 Ainley, Wm, 3 cav, E, June 8, ana.
9150 Alcorn, J W, 18 cav, D, Sept 18, scs.
9896 Allison, D B, 55, K, Sept 27, dia.
10487 Andersen, A, 135, F, Oct 7, dia.
10570 Allen, D, 126, A, Oct 9, dia. c.
10823 Allin S, 7 cav, H, Oct 13 wds.
11419 Applebay, T M, 149, K, Oct 24, scs.
11607 Antill, J, 61, I, Oct 28, st.s.
11710 Anger, W, 118, Nov 1, scs.
11852 Afflerk, T, 2, F, Nov 6, scs.
11860 Amandt, J, 184, D, Nov 6, scs.
12520 Atchinson, W P, 142, F, Jan 25, scs.

228 Bull, Frank, 4 cav, H, March 29, dia. c.
249 Burton, Lafayette, 18 cav, D, M'ch 30, dys.
332 Briggs, Andrew, 13 cav, H, April 2, dia. c.
427 Beagler, A, 27, C, April 8, dia. c.
543 Breel, Jacob, 27, H, April 14, pna.
569 Black, James A, 14 cav, D, April 15, pna

661 Bradley, Alex, 3 cav, F, April 21, dia.
671 Burns, Samuel, 73, K, April 22, ts. f.
673 Barra, J, 54, F, April 22, dia.
822 Bayne, Wm, 145, I, May 1, dys.
874 Bradley, M, 3 art, A, May 4, dys.
897 Brown, Henry, 90, H, May 5, dia. c.
938 Brown, D, 4, C, May 7, dia. c.
974 Batting, Isaac,‡ 8 cav, H, May 9, dia.
1046 Baker, J D, 57, F, May 12, dia. c.
1188 Butler, Wm, 90, B, May 18, scs.
1300 Boyd, Thomas, 9, D, May 23, dia. c.
1309 Bryson, J, 2 cav, D, May 23, dys.
1327 Brining, J, 13 cav, B, May 24, dys.
1375 Burney, J, 13 cav, G, May 26, dys.
1393 Brown, J B, 4 cav, K, May 26, dia. c.
1576 Boman, Samuel, 3 art, B, June 3, dia.
1601 Berfert, R, 103, B, June 4, ts. f.
1654 Brumley, Geo, 4 cav, I, June 5, dia.
1790 Butler, J D, 76, B, June 10, dia.
1859 Berkhawn, H, 73, G, June 12, scs.
1872 Brooks, D S, 79, June 12, dia.
1923 Brian, Charles, 183, F, June 14, dia. c.
1999 Bixter, R, 73, C, June 15, dia.
2026 Burns, Owen, 13 cav, C, June 15, dia.
2046 Bigler, M, 4 cav, June 15, dia.
2127 Brown, C, 3 cav, B, June 17, dia.
2134 Buckhannan, W, 3 art, B, June 18, des.
2180 Ball, L, 26, K, June 19, dia.
2236 Barr, J T, 4 cav, K, June 20, dia. c.
2323 Baker, Henry, 18 cav, I, June 22, dia.
2483 Bisel, John,§ 18 cav, K, June 25, dia. c.
2538 Balsley, Wm, 20 cav, F, June 26, dia. a.
2610 Brown, M, 14 cav, C, June 28, dia.
2727 Brenn, J, 73, K, July 1, dys.
2733 Bolt, J H,§ 18 cav, E, July 1, dia. c.
2741 Beam, John, 76, E, July 1, scs.
2816 Burns, John, 13 cav, A, July 3, dia. c.
2913 Bish, J, 103, F, July 5, dys.
2918 Belford, John, 145, F, July 5, dia.
3005 Bryan, P, 3 art, A, July 7, dia.
3019 Barr, S, 103, G, July 7, dia.
3027 Braney, J, 48, E, July 7, dia.
3051 Barnes, W,‡ 101, H, July 8, scs.
3097 Butler, L J, 118, E, July 10, pna.
3109 Brunt, A, 119, G, July 10, ana.
3216 Beraine, A A, 101, B, July 12.
3294 Burns, James, 103, F, July 14, dia.
3442 Brinton, J, 157, D, July 17, dys.
3477 Baker, Wm, 103, F, July 17, dia.
3535 Burnside, J,§ 57, H, July 18, dia.
3600 Black, W O, 103, G, July 19, dia. c.
3693 Billig, J L, 3 cav, L, July 21, scs.
3716 Brenlinger, Wm R,§ 4 cav, D, July 21, scs.

****

8808 Butler, C P, 148, A, July 22, scs.
3821 Batchell, D, 55, D, July 23, dia.
3917 Bright, E, 90, I, July 25, dia.
3988 Bradford, L, 10, I, July 26, dys.
4002 Berkley, M, 50, I, July 26, dys.
4084 Backner, Adam, 116, G, July 27, i. f.
4330 Barrett, J, 6, K, July 30, dia. c.
4360 Brown, J, 53, G, July 31, dia. c.
4402 Butler, D, 53, G, July 31, i. f.
4494 Barton, James, 4 cav, B, Aug 1, scs.
4500 Burke, J, 90, A, Aug 1, dia.
4610 Baker, E,‡ 4, K, Aug 3, dia.
4667 Behreas, A, 7, E, Aug 4, scs.
4752 Bennett, George, 55, D, Aug 5, scs.
4959 Bowers, J, 2 art, I, Aug 7, wds.
5040 Bammratta, ——, 73, D, Aug 8, dia.
5071 Barber, C, 6, D, Aug 8, scs.
5084 Buck, B F, 2 cav, K, Aug 8, dia.
5113 Brown, M, 50, D, Aug 9, scs.
5324 Berlingame, A J, 141, K, Aug 11, scs.
5391 Bear, John, 79, D, Aug 12, scs.
5416 Bruce, John, 101, C, Aug 12, r. f.
5526 Bower, Benjamin, 6 cav, L, Aug 13, scs.
5587 Burnham, H, 143, F, Aug 14, scs.
5592 Broadbuck, Adam, 11 cav, A, Aug 14, cah.
5662 Buck, B F, 2 cav, K, Aug 14, dys.
5877 Browning, Thomas, 103, A, Aug 16, ens.
5948 Bohnaberger, A, 115, G, Aug 17, mas.
5969 Boyer, F, 43, E, Aug 17, dia.
6061 Baker, James, 101, C, Aug 18, dia.
6074 Bower, G W, 103, K, Aug 18, dys.
6099 Bailey, J F, 18, D, Aug 18, dia.
6127 Benhand, J A, 103, D, Aug 19, dys.
6229 Bear, Samuel, 55, G, Aug 20, dia.
6244 Boles, M S,‡ 4 cav, K, Aug 20, ts. f.
6279 Bower, C, 101, C, Aug 20, scs.
6319 Birney, J, 4 cav, C, Aug 20, scs.
6359 Bennett, A, 67, K, Aug 21, scs.
6542 Blackman, W, 18, D, Aug 23, dia.
6551 Brannon, P, 7, A, Aug 23, dys.
6554 Baldwin, C H, 2 cav, K, Aug 23, scs.
6604 Barnett, E T, 149, I, Aug 23, dia.
6621 Bell, Thomas, 11, E, Aug 23, dia.
6660 Blair, John G, 46, F, Aug 24, dia.
6663 Breckinridge, W, 73, K, Aug 24, dia.
6688 Bowman, A, 63, B, Aug 24, scs.
6701 Boyd, J W, 101, C, Aug 24, dys.
6704 Beemer, Wm, 145, K, Aug 24, scs.
6887 Brown, T,‡ 11 cav, I, Aug 26, dys.
6928 Bryan, L, 106, F, Aug 26, dia.
7125 Bridaham, H W, 55, H, Aug 28, scs.
7181 Bemer, S, 184, E, Aug 29, dia.
7347 Ball, P, 49, H, Aug 31, dia. c.
7460 Barnes, W, 119, G, Sept 1, dia.
7477 Bennett, J, 55, D, Sept 1, scs.
7541 Barnett, M, 145, K, Sept 2, dia.
7684 Black, J, 143, I, Sept 3, dia.
7747 Blair, J G, 49, E, Sept 3, dys.
7775 Brink, F, 11 cav, M, Aug 4, dia.
7940 Browers, J A, 184, F, Sept 5, des.
7963 Brumley, Frederick, 54, K, Sept 6, dia.
8073 Bright, Adam,‡ 101, K, Sept 7, dys.
8075 Boland, Daniel, 183, I, Sept 7, dia. c.
8256 Barr, P, 103, C, Sept 9, dia.
8286 Brown, L, 8 cav, C, Sept 9, dia.
8356 Brown, A, 101, H, Sept 10, dia. c.
8358 Brickenstaff, W, 101, I, Sept 10, dia.
8363 Bruce, J B,§ 101, F, Sept 10, dia.
8413 Blosser, Jonas, 7 reserve, H, Sept 11, dia.
8434 Bowsteak, T D,§ 106, H, Sept 11, scs.
8499 Bicklet, E H, 57, K, Sept 11, scs.
8606 Boots, E N, 101, H, Sept 12, scs.
8719 Beatie, Robert, 95, D, Sept 14, scs.
8769 Boyer, J M,§ 7 cav, F, Sept 14, scs.
8795 Bentley, T, 54, H, Sept 14, dia. c.
8794 Brown, P, 55, A, Sept 15, scs.
8902 Baker, J, 184, C, Sept 16, scs.
8917 Baker, Wm, 11 cav, Sept 16, scs.
9147 Blake, E, 69, K, Sept 18, scs.
9520 Boyler, James, 7, E, Sept 22, scs.
9632 Baldwin, A, 51, K, Sept 24, dia.
9745 Bowers, F, 5 cav, A, Sept 25, dia.

5809 Bonewell, W W, 14 cav, C, Sept 28, dia.
9952 Blair, George, 7 art, Sept 28, scs.
10201 Burdge, H L, 3 cav, D, Oct 2, als.
10226 Byers, J, 22, E, Oct 2, scs.
10260 Burns, J, 103, E, Oct 3, scs.
10292 Brown, G M, 10, I, Oct 4, scs.
10357 Burgess, H, 27, C, Oct 5, scs.
10534 Buck, D C, 2 cav, L, Oct 8, dia.
10577 Ballinger, George, 87, D, Oct 9, scs.
10674 Blackman, W, 84, A, Oct 11, scs.
10758 Beightel, J F, 51, G, Oct 12, scs.
10779 Boies, J M, 145, G, Oct 12, dia.
10783 Bonling, J, 3, A, Oct 12, dia. c.
10943 Barthart, I, 116, H, Oct 14, scs.
10980 Baney, George, 4, I, Oct 15, scs.
10983 Banyar, J S, 55, E, Oct 15, scs.
11024 Bunker, F, 55, K, Oct 16, scs.
11087 Boman, G, 149, E, Oct 18, gae.
11322 Bisel, B, 142, F, Oct 22, scs.
11329 Bruce, A, 11, I, Oct 23, scs.
11434 Berk, G, 51, A, Oct 24, scs.
11445 Ball, J,‡ 19, K, Oct 25, gae.
11504 Bain, G, 183, G, Oct 26, scs.
11528 Baney, I, 4 cav, I, Oct 26, scs.
11556 Baker, B H, 148, B, Oct 27, scs.
11563 Brock, C, 46, A, Oct 27, scs.
11569 Beighley, W, 103, C, Oct 27, scs.
11597 Blair, John, 106, H, Oct 28, scs.
11611 Boyer, T, 11, F, Oct 28, scs.
11635 Burr, E, 145, K, Oct 28, scs.
11674 Bolinger, G, 87, D, Oct 30, scs.
11818 Bayley, H, 66, K, Nov 4, scs.
11894 Burch, W, 2 art, F, Nov 7, scs.
11929 Burke, J D, 22 cav, D, Nov 9, gae.
11972 Bupp, L, 149, G, Nov 12, scs.
12039 Bailey, J J, 2 art, F, Nov 16, scs.
12059 Bogar, David,§ 184, C, Nov 17, dia. c.
12079 Bond, C C, 20, K, Nov 18, scs.
12096 Brady, N, 5 cav, M, Nov 19, dia. c.
12188 Brubaker, B P,‡ 79, D, Nov 26, scs.
12177 Braddock, T, 77, C, Nov 27, scs.
12418 Barrens, J, 5 cav, G, Jan 9, scs.
12812 Barnett, J, 6, D, March 25, dia.
2917 Brinn, James, 56, I, July 5, dia.
12665 Bennett, J, 184, E, Feb 16, pls.

45 Carter, William, 139, H, March 14, dys. a
97 Chase, Wm B,§ 15 cav, C, March 22, pna.
156 Compsey, James, 14 cav, H, Mar 25, dys.
355 Carman, F H, 54, F, April 2, dia. c.
445 Coyle, P, 45, A, April 9, pls.
466 Crouch, Levi, 40, I, April 9, pna.
479 Croghan, John,§ 3 cav, A, April 9, dia. c.
548 Case, Daniel, 8 cav, M, April 14, dia.
734 Conner, Andrus, 4 cav, L, April 25, dia.
837 Cravener, S P, 14 cav, K, May 1, dia.
869 Curry, A, 119, E, May 3, ana.
1015 Campbell, Wm, 8 cav, E, May 10, dys.
1099 Case, Silas,‡ 2 cav, L, May 14, dia.
1138 Carmicheal, Geo, 18 cav, K, May 16, ana
1186 Crisholm, J H, 150, H, May 18, scs.
1206 Caldwell, S A, 14 cav, E, May 19, ana.
1232 Coburg, M C, 6 cav, L, May 20, dia. c.
1490 Coon, J H, 18 cav, K, May 31, dia.
1498 Campbell, H B, 103, E, May 31, pna.
1530 Clatter, F, 18 cav, C, May 31, dia.
1702 Calihan, Thos, 14 cav, H, June 7, dia. c.
1731 Cephas, L, 145, I, June 8, dia.
1829 Carter, Wm, 101, K, June 11, pna.
1832 Calvert, R R,§ 6, B, June 11, ana.
1871 Coombs, John, 3 art, June 12, dia.
1873 Cox, J A, 113 cav, June 12, dia. c.
2069 Cooper, T, 18 cav, K, June 16, dys.
2349 Curry, R, 73, F, June 23, dia. c.
2399 Coyle, H, 8 cav, F, June 24, ana.
2455 Crouse, E, 141, A, June 25, dia.
2695 Copple, F, 54, H, June 30, dia. c.
2713 Chapman, J, 7, H, July 1, dia.
2849 Carron, James, 4 cav, C, July 4, dia.
2884 Calean, Samuel, 103, K, July 4, dys.
2995 Coleman, J,§ 18 cav, K, July 7, dys.
3320 Chase, F M, 72, G, July 14, pna.

3362 Clark, N, 8 cav, D, July 15, dia.
3417 Caton, W T, 49, D, July 16, dia. c.
3430 Couch, Benjamin, 50, H, July 17, ana.
3948 Coyle, Ed, 58, E, July 25, dys.
3993 Curtey, L, 10, I, July 26, dys.
4045 Carpenter, L, 12, K, July 27, dia. c.
4117 Cantrill, M, 6, B, July 28, dia.
4263 Conklin, N, 90, K, July 29, scs.
4331 Chapman, J, 3 art, B, July 30, dia.
4353 Crawford, M, 14 cav, G, July 31, dia.
4357 Cox, James, 103, A, July 31, dys.
4369 Claybaugh. G W, 2 art, F, July 31, cah.
4512 Crock, H,‡ 45, A, Aug 1, dia.
4682 Croup, W S, 103, L, Aug 4, dys.
4729 Cochran, C, 103, I, Aug 4, dia.
4903 Chew, John,‡ 18, F, Aug 6, dia.
5177 Cranes, E, 4 cav, M, Aug 9, scs.
5375 Campbell, James, 3 cav, F, Aug 11, dia.
5417 Cregy, J G, 54, I, Aug 12, scs.
5423 Cumberland, Thos, 14 cav, B, Aug 12, dia.
5484 Conahan, M, 115, B, Aug 13, scs.
5578 Carpenter, W C, 145, G, Aug 14, dia.
5584 Campbell, R D, 11, E, Aug 14, scs.
5623 Cox, H,‡ 7 cav, B, Aug 14, dia.
5828 Cummings, Benj, 3, A, Aug 16, ens.
5979 Connor, J N, 184, C, Aug 17, mas.
6237 Corbin, W, 49, C, Aug 20, scs.
6209 Campbell, R G, 11, C, Aug 20, mas.
6320 Coon, George, 2, F, Aug 21, dia.
6336 Cameron, Wm,‡ 101, A, Aug 21, dia.
6395 Connelly, Wm, 55, C, Aug 21, dys.
6430 Conner, J, 6, D, Aug 22, dia.
6502 Cline, J, 3, H, Aug 22, dia.
6615 Crawford, J, 77, E, Aug 23, dia.
6645 Coleman, C, 19, E, Aug 23, dys.
6746 Comly, John, 101, A, Aug 24, dia.
6913 Craft, A, 90, G, Aug 26, scs.
7045 Cobert, F C, 11 cav, L, Aug 27, dia.
7095 Carr, J, 51, G, Aug 28, scs.
7116 Cathcart, Robt, 103, H, Aug 29, dia.
7209 Crain, J, 4 cav, H, Aug 9, scs.
7456 Craig, Wm, 103, D, Sept 1, scs.
7463 Clay, Henry, 184, A, Sept 1, scs.
7617 Curry, S, 140, C, Sept 2, scs.
7632 Carroll, A, 2 cav, A, Sept 2, dia.
7669 Campbell, Geo T, 3 art, A, Sept 3, scs.
7696 Criser, M, 54, F, Sept 3, dia.
8117 Crawford, J A, 103, B, Sept 8, dia.
8121 Collins, M, 101, K, Sept 8, scs.
8169 Cole, J C, 118, K, Sept 8, dia.
8260 Chapman, ——, 18, A, Sept 9, dia.
8512 Coyle, M,‡ 79, B, Sept 12, scs.
8594 Culver, J, 60, Sept 12, scs.
8665 Clutler, L, 11, C, Sept 13, scs.
8700 Cavender, J L, 149, E, Sept 14, scs.
8884 Cysey, A, 3 hvy art, Sept 15, dia.
9094 Coffman, Wm, 13, F, Sept 18, scs.
9134 Cramer, E, 55, F, Sept 18, dia.
9141 Church, C H,‡ 45, B, Sept 18, dia. c.
9269 Clark, J, 101, Sept 19, ana.
9396 Coats, S R, 135, C, Sept 20, scs.
9410 Combs, S, 1, H, Sept 21, dia.
9508 Clonay, J, 145, F, Sept 22, scs.
9554 Crum, C, 149, G, Sept 23, dia. c.
9639 Cline, J, 118, A, Sept 24, dia. c.
9773 Coulter, G, 45, K, Sept 25, scs.
9823 Cummings, R, 65, K, Sept 27, dia.
9886 Callahan, M, 52, D, Sept 27, scs.
9931 Conrad, W, 14 cav, M, Sept 28, dys.
10104 Campbell. Wm, 13 cav, D, Sept 30, dia.
10120 Coats, L R, 139, H, Oct 1, scs.
10274 Crawford, George, 1, F, Oct 3, scs.
10276 Cantler, J L, 13, A, Sept 3, scs.
10283 Cromich, F, 7, H, Oct 4, scs.
10386 Cornelius, Wm, 7 cav, Oct 5, dia.
10399 Cullingford, P, 55, C, Oct 6, dia.
10443 Clarke, W, 5 cav, K, Oct 7, dia. c.
10462 Canby, G C, 2 cav, E, Oct 7, scs.
10497 Coperhewer, Wm,‡ 1, D, Oct 8, dia.
10541 Culberton, Louis, 73, B, Sept 9, scs.
10842 Corbin, M, 184, D, Oct 13, scs.
10847 Clark, G, 1 cav, H, Oct 13, scs.

11005 Coe, George W, 145, E, Oct 16, scs.
11025 Clark, J, 3, D, Oct 16, scs.
11250 Clark, H, 184, F, Oct 21, dia. c.
11309 Clark, E B, 101, B, Oct 22, scs.
11370 Carol, W, 145, B, Oct 23, scs.
11436 Crawford, L, 184, B, Oct 24, pls.
11438 Cole, H O, 2 cav, L, Oct 24, scs.
11477 Campbell, C A, 11 cav, C, Oct 26, scs.
11565 Creagan, G, 1 cav, F, Sept 27, dia. c.
11614 Crawford, M, 14, K, Sept 28, scs.
11656 Coyle, H, 54, K, Oct 30, scs.
11659 Craney, George, 20 cav, L, Oct 30, scs.
11800 Cregger, W H, 5 cav, G, Nov 4, scs.
11815 Chacon, A W, 106, B, Nov 4, dia. c.
11826 Colebaugh, W, 60, K, Nov 5, scs.
11876 Crandall, L, 145, I, Nov 6, scs.
11922 Cleaveland, E, 10 cav, I, Nov 8, dia. c.
11993 Crampton, A B, 143, B, Nov 13, scs.
12120 Cullen, T P, 31, I, Nov 22, gae.
12141 Conway, C C, 2 art, A, Nov 23, scs.
12253 Crompton, F G, 71, F, Dec 10, scs.
12295 Cone, S, 115, E, Dec 16, scs.
12301 Cuip, P K, 138, B, Dec 17, scs.
12368 Connor, S, 112, H, Jan 1, shot by the guard
12424 Clark, J, 89, D, Jan 9, brs.
12487 Collins, G, 118, E, Jan 19, scs.
12509 Cassell, D, 20, E, Feb 6, pls.
12672 Clark, F D, 7, C, Feb 20, rhm.
12818 Copeland, B, 14 cav, D, March 29, scs.
1961 Culbertson, John, 13 cav, B, June 14, dia.

152 Davidson, H, 57, I, March 25, dia.
866 Dorr, Phineas, 119, K, May 3, dys.
1020 Doran, McK, 63, D, May 11, dia.
1161 Duntler, Henry,‡ 51, K, May 16, dia.
1338 Dooner, M, 2, K, May 24, dys.
1463 Davis, Richard, 3 cav, L, May 29, rhm.
1541 Deamott, J K, 45, C, June 1, dia. c.
1545 Davis, Isaac, 8 cav, H, June 1, dia. c.
2630 Dun, R B, 101, B, June 29, pna.
2657 Donovan, J, 139, K, June 29, brs.
2716 Deily, William, 53, H, July 1, dia. c.
2938 Davis, M, 22 cav, B, July 6, dia. c.
3338 Degret, N, 15 cav, M, July 15, dia.
3363 Davidson, Charles, 100, M, July 15, dia.
3741 Dallin, James, 8 cav, H, July 21, dia. c.
3795 Davis, J, 103, A, July 22, dys. a.
3873 Davis, M H, 103, E, July 24, dia.
3985 Dougherty, J, 7, E, July 26, dys.
4087 Deron, Robert P, 149, B, July 27, dys.
4202 Drenkle, J A, 79, K, July 29, scs.
5232 Dechman, John, 184, G, July 29, dia.
4481 Dodrick, Louis, 50, 1, Aug 1, des.
4491 Denton, M, 9 cav, B, Aug 1, dia.
4497 Day, Wm, 97, A, Aug 1, dia.
4625 Davis, J, 101, E, Aug 3, dia.
4711 Dort, C R, 4 cav, H, Aug 4, dia.
4786 Dondle, Robert, 101, A, Aug 5, dia.
4792 Davy, H,‡ 68, K, Aug 5, i. f.
4806 Davenbrook, J J, 101, G, Aug 5, ana.
4885 Delaney, J, 101, A, Aug 6, dia.
4897 Dunbar, John, 14 cav, M, Aug 6, dia.
4910 Dean, J, 148, F, Aug 6, scs.
5023 Dawlin, L, 110, D, Aug 8, dia.
5256 Ditztell, L, 73, I, Aug 10, ana.
5431 Davidson, George, 57, C, Aug 12, dia. a
5468 Dougherty, 101, I, Aug 13, dia. c.
5664 Decker, J, 45, B, Aug 14, dia.
5740 Day, And H, 2 cav, H, Aug 15, dia.
5746 Doran, P, 99, I, Aug 15, dys.
6017 Deal, F, 63, A, Aug 17, dys.
6045 Degroot, H,§ 13 cav, A, Aug 18, dia.
6176 Defree, James, 15, G, Aug 19, ces.
6226 Dodd, J, 18, F, Aug 20, ana.
6316 Davis, Wm, 153, A, Aug 20, dia. c.
6568 Dawney, George, 148, B, Aug 23, i. f.
6679 Donovan, D, 90, B, Aug 24, dys.
6678 Dunn, Johnes, 69, F, Aug 25, dia.
6797 Dailey, M, 7, I, Aug 25, dia.
6879 Dunn, John, 184, A, Aug 26, dia.
7053 Dakenfelt, J, 55, D, Aug 28, dia.
7077 Deets, R, 3, A, Aug 28, dia.

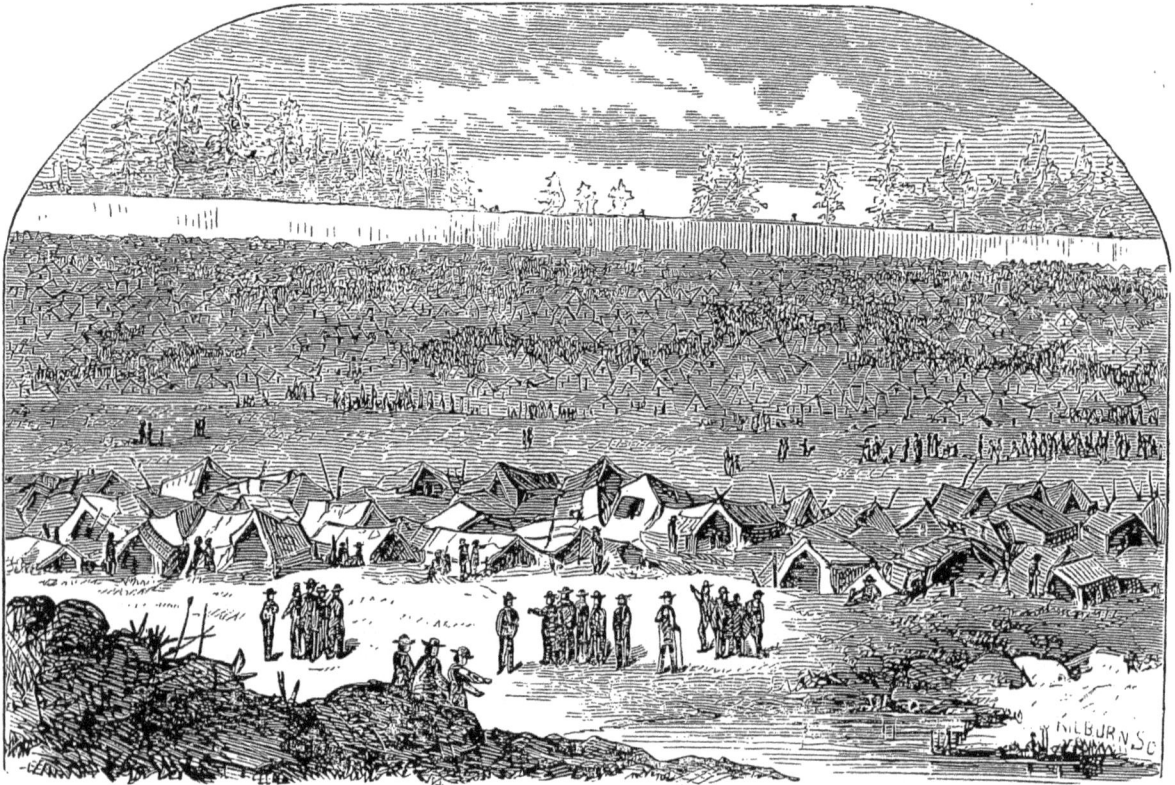

VIEW OF THE INTERIOR OF THE PRISON,

With the quagmire, and crowds of huts and men beyond.   Taken from rebel photographs.

"The space thus filled in was occupied, almost to the very verge of the sink, by the prisoners, gathered here for the conveniences of the place, and for obtaining water."   Page 90.

7282 Day, S,‡ 13, A, Aug 30, gae.
7360 Dively, J, 110, C, Aug 31, dys.
7488 Dilks, C, 1, K, Sept 1, dia.
7651 Dewell, Samuel, 50, G, Sept 3, dia.
7828 Dougherty, J, 184, D, Sept 4, dia.
8211 Dixon, J, 105, B, Sept 8, ts. f.
8334 Doherty, J,§ 73, F, Sept 10, scs.
8569 Duff, J,§ 4 cav, B, Sept 12, dia.
8579 Dougherty, F, 90, C, Sept 12, dia.
8718 Durharse, B, 11 cav, G, Sept 14, scs.
8828 Donnelly, J, 97, H, Sept 15, scs.
8887 Dean, R, 2 cav, M, Sept 15, scs.
9109 Davidson, C, 90, G, Sept 18, dia.
9146 Driscoll, N C, 26, I, Sept 18, scs.
9191 Duffie, J, 52, F, Sept 18, ts. f.
9289 Delaney, E, 7, G, Sept 19, scs.
10004 Davidson, G,‡ 12, K, Sept 29, scs.
10193 Dougherty, M, 3 cav, D, Oct 2, uls.
10436 Durkale, John, 1 cav, F, Oct 6, dia.
10917 Dalzell, J G, 139, I, Oct 14, scs.
11295 Derry, Frederick, 20, C, Oct 22, scs.
11350 Dichell, Espy, 55, D, Oct 23, scs.
11394 Dewitt, M, 1 cav, E, Oct 24, scs.
11628 Davidson, S, 184, A, Oct 28, scs.
11988 Dickens, Charles, 2 art, A, Oct 13, dia.
12136 Dalrysuffle, J E, 145, K, Oct 23, scs.
12399 Donley, P, 120, G, Jan 5, wds.
12575 Deeds, J, 13 cav, H, Feb 2, dia.
11181 Dixon, B, 145, K, Oct 19, scs.

972 Ellers, Henry, 13 cav, H, May 9, dia.
1081 Eisley, John, 18 cav, K, May 14, dia.
1436 Engle, Peter, 14 cav, K, May 28, dia.
2105 Elliott, John, 13 cav, F, June 17, dys.
2794 Elliott, J, 69, D, July 2, dia. c.
3038 Erwin, C, 78, D, July 8, des.
3052 Epsey, James,§ 145, H, July 9, r. f.
3295 Elliott, J P, 103, D, July 14, dia.
3823 Ebright, Benj, 9 cav, A, July 23, scs.
4278 Eaton, Nat, 1 rifle, E, July 30, dia.
4761 Elenberger, P, 145, D, Aug 5, dia.
5687 Ennies, Andrew, 145, K, Aug 15, scs.
6424 Ewetts, James, 103, G, Aug 22, scs.
6607 Ellis, F, 53, G, Aug 23, dia. c.
6872 Eckles, E, 77, E, Aug 26, dys.
6889 Ensley, C, 184, A, Aug 26, dys.
7300 Ellis, H H, 18 cav, I, Aug 30, dia.
7657 Egan, John, 55, C, Sept 3, des.
8064 Exline, Jacob, 55, K, Sept 7, dia.
8543 Eichnor, C, 143, F, Sept 12, scs.
8964 Earlman, J, 7, K, Sept 16, dia.
10009 Elfrey, B S, 7, K, Sept 29, dia. c.
10694 Elliott, John H, 83, D, Oct 11, dia.
10731 Erdibach, C,‡ 5 cav, B, Oct 11, dia.
10799 Ervingfelts, Jacob, 187, D, Oct 12, dia. c.
11834 Edgar, W H,§ 7, G, Nov 5, scs.
11838 Erebedier, J,§ 5, B, Nov 5, scs.
12001 Etters, D, 145, D, Nov 14, scs.
12673 Ebhart, J,‡ 87, E, Feb 18, dia. c.
5490 English, J C, 100, K, Sept 21, dia.

200 Fluhr, John, 73, D, March 28, dia.
511 Fich, John, 83, B, April 12, dia. c.
791 Fry, L,§ 4 cav, D, April 28, dia. c.
1010 Fuller, H, 13 cav, H, May 10, dia. c.
1098 Fifer, Charles, 27, I, May 14, ers.
1431 Fry, Alexander,‡ 4 cav, B, May 28, dia. c.
1728 Fink, Peter, 73, C, June 8, scs.
1957 Freeman, W M,§ 4 art, A, June 14, dys. a.
2078 Fulton, Thomas A, 103, H, June 17, dia.
2099 Friday, S D, 101, H, June 17, dia. c.
2147 Fish, Charles W, 101, B, June 18, dia. c.
2155 Farley, James, 54, F, June 18, dia. c.
2261 Fox, George, 78, E, June 21, dia.
2477 Flay, L, 26, G, June 25, dia.
2530 Funkhanna, Jas, 101, C, June 26, ts. f.
2537 Fatleam, A, 50, D, June 26, dia. c.
2594 Fagartus, T, 90, K, June 28, scs.
2853 Faney, George, 13 cav, F, July 4, scs.
3088 Ford, M, 53, K, July 9, scs.
3258 Fisher, B M,‡ 101, H, July 13, dia.
3582 French, A, 2 art, G, July 19, dys.

3742 Forsyth, J, 18 cav, H, July 21, dia. c.
3870 Fingley, John, 14 cav, D, July 24, dia.
4307 Flick, L, 184, G, July 30, dia.
4439 Filey, J H, 53, E, July 31, wds.
4452 Foreman, G S,‡ 1 cav, B, Aug 1, pna.
4521 Flasharse, B, 12 cav, A, Aug 2, dia.
4586 Flynn, M, 13 cav, B, Aug 2, dia.
4642 Fewer, E, 87, H, Aug 3, dys.
4668 File, C, 145, D, Aug 4, scs.
5062 Fish, J, 85, Aug 8, dys.
5172 Fleming, W‡, 97, E, Aug 9, scs.
5586 Flickinger, Jno, 50, B, Aug 14, scs.
5788 Ferry, W, 79, A, Aug 15, ana.
5873 Fee, George M, 103, G, Aug 16, scs.
6092 Faiss, A, 145, E, Aug 18, ces.
6134 Farman, E, 57, E, Aug 19, ces.
6155 Feltharsen, 145, G, Aug 19, scs.
6180 Fantlenger, F, 53, K, Aug 19, scs.
6365 Faneu, James F, 7 reserve, G, Aug 21, dia.
6396 Finlaugh, S, 14 cav, G, Aug 21, dy
6649 Fox, R, 155, H, Aug 23, scs.
6675 Fritzman, J W,§ 18, K, Aug 24, scs.
6694 Finliu, Thomas, 143, G, Aug 24, dia.
6881 Fuller, G, 2 cav, A, Aug 26, dia.
6884 Frederick, L, 148, B, Aug 26, scs.
6890 French, James, 101, H, Aug 26, dys.
6892 Ford, Thomas, 7, I, Aug 26, dys.
7041 Fullerton, E, 99, E, Aug 27, scs.
7097 Fester, John, 103, B, Aug 28, des.
7169 Fisher, W, 54, I, Aug 29, dia. c.
7198 Fry, S, 101, E, Aug 29, dia. c.
7575 Fitzgerald, M, 145, K, Sept 2, dia. c.
7588 Fahy, John, 13 cav, B, Sept 2, dys.
7776 Fritz, D,‡ 18 cav, K, Sept 4, dys.
8006 Felter, H M,§ 13 cav, K, Sept 6, dys.
8149 Fullerton, J, 118, I, Sept 8, ana.
8175 Fetterman, J, 48, H, Sept 8, dia.
8321 Francis, N, 69, G, Sept 10, dia.
8631 Fagan, R, 118, F, Sept 13, scs.
9062 Fisher, C, 4 cav, Sept 17, dia.
9099 Floyd, B, 67, K, Sept 18, dia.
9232 Farr, J C, 107, H, Sept 19, scs.
9869 Faith, Alexander, 183, C, Sept 27, scs.
10176 Fessenden, N E, 140, F, Oct 1, dia.
10408 Fingley, S, 14, B, Oct 6, dia.
10639 Fisher, W, 101, E, Oct 10, dys.
10667 Flynn, S,‡ 76, C, Oct 11, scs.
10688 Free, J, 145, H, Oct 11, dia.
11026 Flemming, J, 97, E, Oct 16, scs.
11112 Flanney, J, 106, K, Oct 18, scs.
11164 Ferguson, J R, 11 cav, D, Oct 19, scs
11367 Fox, M, 8 cav, H, Oct 23, scs.
11378 Frill, D, 55, C, Oct 24, scs.
11601 Ferguson, John, 134, A, Oct 28, scs.
11802 Frishi, H, 115, E, Nov 4, scs.
11916 Freed, S, 53, B, Nov 8, scs.
11962 Fairbanks, E, 140, A, Nov 11, scs.
12000 Fagley, C,‡ 14 cav, I, Nov 14, scs.
12025 Foust, S L, 149, I, Nov 15, scs.
12207 Foster, C W, 76, B, Dec 1, scs.
12244 Falkenstine, F, 148, C, Dec 8, scs.
12336 Fruce, J, 52, A, Dec 26, scs.
12445 Fisk, J, 67, H, Jan 13, scs.
12605 Faile, W D, 20 cav, A, Feb 7, des.

71 Goodman, Robt, 13 cav, M, March 19, dia
131 Gesse, Christian, 54, F, March 23, c. f.
314 Graffell, Wm, 73, B, April 2, pna.
529 Guley, J, 145, G, April 12, dia.
573 Green, Wm, 3 cav, A, April 16, dia. c.
968 Garman, B, 18 cav, E, April 9, dys.
1001 Greer, J A,‡ 3 cav, E, May 10, dys.
1008 Graham, W J, 4, C, May 10, dia.
1063 Goodman, Henry, 27, I, May 13, pna.
1302 Gray, M, 7, B, May 23, dia. c.
1373 Gilbert, John, 29, G, May 25, dia. c.
1399 Gilroy, Berney, 73, F, May 26, scs.
1528 Getts, B, 84, G, May 31, ana.
1649 Griffil, G W, 13 cav, L, June 5, dia.
1761 Genst, J W, 57, I, June 9, dia. c.
1793 Gardner (negro), 8, F, June 10, dia
1911 Gensle, John, 19 cav, F, June 13, dia. a.

****

1939 Gerlt, E, 73, H, June 14, dia.
2060 Galliger, F, 13 cav, B, June 16, dys.
2084 Gilmore, James, 110, E, June 17, dia. c.
2297 Gunn, Alex, 4 cav, D, June 21, dia.
2356 Greenwald, G,§ 27, H, June 23, dia.
2531 Gumbert, A,‡ 103, B, June 26, dia.
3587 Gettings, J H, 1 rifle, C, June 28, dia. c.
2944 Gross, Samuel, 51, E, July 6, dia.
2955 Gotwalt, H,‡ 55, D, July 6, dia.
2988 Griffin, J, 103, I, July 7, dia.
2992 George, A, 149, G, July 7, dia.
2996 Gists, H, 103, H, July 7, dia, c.
3037 Gilleland, Wm, 14 cav, B, July 8, dia. c.
3528 Gorsuch, M A, 110, B, July 18, scs.
3599 Gibbs, E, 18 cav, K, July 19, dia.
4944 Gost, W H, 5 cav, K, Aug 7, dys.
5422 Gregg, T, 139, K, Aug 12, dys.
5655 Gross, John, 62, K, Aug 14, dia. c.
5735 Gregg, D, 142, A, Aug 15, dys.
5737 Graham, Wm, 103, F, Aug 15, dia. c.
5803 Graham, D,‡ 4 cav, K, Aug 16, dia. c.
5881 Grouse, G, 145, C, Aug 16, dia. c.
5888 Gettenher, D M, 103, I, Aug 16, dys.
6006 Geand, C,‡ 4 cav, M, Aug 17, scs.
5288 Gladen, A, 21, C, Aug 11, scs.
6140 Garrett, James, 51, K, Aug 19, dys.
6158 Gunn, J W, 101, H, Aug 19, dia.
6384 Gamble, O J,‡ 77, A, Aug 21, scs.
6389 Gallagher, E, 48, A, Aug 21, dia.
6897 Green, J C, 13 cav, D, Aug 26, dys.
7223 Gibson, D, 56, A, Aug 29, dia.
7320 Graham, J, 56, B, Aug 30, scs.
7340 Geary, D, 184, G, Aug 30, scs.
7357 Groves, A T, 45, A, Aug 31, scs.
7352 Glass, Wm, 55, C, Aug 31, dia.
7527 Griffith, A, 54, F, Sept 1, dia.
7589 Granger, E H, 55, C, Sept 2, dia.
7679 Geslin, E H, 4, G, Sept 3, dia.
7773 Giles, C, 7, K, Sept 4, dia.
7839 Gross, G W,‡ 79, A, Sept 4, ana.
8109 Galbraith, C,§ 11, K, Sept 6, dia.
8311 Garrison, W, 8, K, Sept 10, scs.
8448 Gallagher, Wm, 5 cav, F, Sept 11, scs.
8735 Griffin, J C, 5 cav, D, Sept 14, dia.
9005 Gearhan, S, 142, C, Sept 17, scs.
9210 Griffin, D, 11, E, Sept 19, scs.
9326 Gilbert, H, 53, F, Sept 20, scs.
9437 Gorby, F J, 19 cav, M, Sept 21, ana.
9503 Goodman, F, 55, H, Sept 21, dia.
9764 Grubbs, J, 103, F, Sept 25, scs.
9776 Gibson, J, 11, D, Sept 26, scs.
9792 Glenn, Wm, 101, C, Sept 26, scs.
9811 Grear, R, 73, H, Sept 26, dia. c.
9986 Gilbert, D, 138, B, Sept 28, dia.
9989 Garrett, F, 139, G, Sept 29. scs.
10051 Gibson, D G, 16 cav, A, Sept 30, ana.
10127 Gemperling, Wm, 79, A, Oct 1, scs.
10468 Grant, M, 18 cav, I, Oct 7, dys.
10615 Griffin, J, 56, A, Oct 10, scs.
10706 Ginberling, I, 184, F, Oct, 11, dia.
11060 Greathouse, E, 14, B, Oct 17, scs.
11197 Grabb, M P, 83, H, Oct 20, scs.
11299 Gilbert, A F, 14 cav, F, Oct 20, scs.
11496 Grant, J, 6, E. Oct 26, dys.
11573 Ganse, R, 22, B, Oct 27, dys.
11806 Gordon, R, 65, F, Nov 4, scs.
11901 Green, W S, 12, I, Nov 7, dia.
12181 Giher, P, 73, H, Nov 27, scs.
12237 George, F,§ 18 cav, D, Dec 6, dia.
12337 Garrety, Ths, 106, C, Jan 2, froze to death.
12411 Gates, J, 11 cav, E, Jan 7, dia.
12432 Grunnell, John, 26, H, Jan 11, dys.
5846 Gillespie, J, 11, A, Aug 16, dia.
5118 Gibbons, Wm, 11, H, Aug 9, dia.
6228 Gallagher, T,‡ 101, A, Aug 21, scs.
5971 Gray, L,§ 163, D, Aug 17, dia.

423 Hanson, T R, 119, E, April 7, dia.
470 Herbert, Otto, 73, A, April 9, pna.
555 Hoffmaster, L, 16, H, April 14, dia.
654 Hamilton, J G,‡ 4 cav, L, April 20, dia.
711 Hall, J (negro), 8, E, April 24, dia. c.

769 Hessimer, P, 73, E, April 27, dia.
988 Hammons, J, 3 art, A, May 10, dys.
990 Heager, J, 2, B, May 10, dia.
1080 Huff, Arthur, 54, F, May 14, dia.
1113 Hates, Charles, 2, H, May 15, dia. c,
1225 Henderson, Rob't, 18 cav, D, May 20, dia
1311 Heckly, M,§ 4 cav, M, May 23, dia.
1420 Hill, H C,§ 18, K, May 28, dia. c.
1483 Holtenstein, G W, 18 cav, I, May 30, dia. c
1502 Henen, Pat, 145, E, June 2, dia. c.
1650 Hendricks, N, 4 cav, D, June 5, dys.
1768 Holmes, Robert, 12 cav, H, June 9, dia. c
2011 Hannah, Thos,§ 4 cav, D, June 15, dia.
2153 Hammer, P C, 18 cav, D, June 18, dia. c.
2189 Harts, John, 51, H, June 19, dia.
2387 Hooks, T, 103, D, June 24, ts. f.
2450 Hiler, H, 50, C, June 25, dys.
2551 Hammer, John,§ 73, G, June 27, dia. c.
2707 Howard, James, 83, I, June 30, dia.
2723 Henderson, A, 58, F, July 1, scs.
2786 Hollibaugh, W, 57, C, July 2, ana.
2800 Hastings, J, 118, D, July 2, dys.
2916 Homer, D,‡ 13 cav, F, July 5, dia.
3020 Holley, E F,‡ 57, A, July 7, dia.
3201 Harrington, John, 55, C, July 12, scs.
2 Headley, J D, 18, G, March 15, s. p.
3379 Height, S C, 55, H, July 16, dia.
3439 Hughes, John, 118, A, July 17, phs.
3525 Heenan, John, 14 cav, F, July 18, scs.
3554 Hazlet, J, 4 cav, G, July 18, dys.
3563 Hester, I P, 7, H, July 18, dia.
3626 Heth, R, 2, A, July 20, dia.
3785 Harrington, J W, 3 cav, A, July 22, dia.
3792 Haller, Peter, 139, K, July 22, scs.
3836 Harvey, P D, 57, B, July 23, dia.
3853 Hollenbeck, J A, 55, B, July 24, scs.
3920 Hall, Henry, 53, H, July 25, scs.
3953 Haller, A, 73, A, July 25, scs.
4105 Hartlick, C, 99, E, July 27, dia.
4136 Hiffefinger, V, 14, K, July 28, dia.
4147 Hobbs, A, 141, H, July 28, dia.
4154 Hill, P,‡ 101, B, July 28, dia.
4222 Hoover, John, 18 cav, E, July 29, dia. c
4332 Holland, J, 143, I, July 30, dia.
4370 Hilt, John, 73, I, July 31, dia.
4379 Hardinger, W, 147, B, July 31, scs.
4431 Hill, Thomas, 18, L, July 31, dia.
4474 Hans, John, 116, K, Aug 1, dia.
4790 Haffinger, J, 91, C, Aug 5, dia.
4921 Hick, G, 12, G, Aug 6, dia.
5045 Haher, C, 14 cav, B, Aug 8, scs.
5080 Hall, H, 149, I, Aug 8, dia.
5082 Hunter, L, 63, C, Aug 8, dia. c.
5131 Hardis, J L, 11, A, Aug 9, dys.
5178 Harden, M, res. home g'ds, F, Aug 9, sca
5281 Huffman, Charles, 7 cav, K, Aug 11, scs.
5284 Hickey, D C, 3 cav, C, Aug 11, scs.
5289 Hanson, J, 76, B, Aug 11, dys.
5486 Harder, ——, 184, C, Aug 13, scs.
5575 Hoffmaster, G,§ 20, F, Aug 14, ana.
5688 Heinback, S, 116, H, Aug 15, dia.
5954 Holinbeck, D, 101, E, Aug 17, mas.
6175 Honigan, C, 55, C, Aug 19, dys.
6302 Henry, R W, 4 H, Aug 20, dia.
6367 Hill, J E, 2 cav, L, Aug 21, scs.
6481 Hollingworth, J (neg), 8, A, Aug 22, dia
6597 Hofmaster, L, 73, I, Aug 23, dia. c.
6685 Hazenfflucey, J, 26 bat, A, Aug 23, scs.
6711 Hoch, John, 103, K, Aug 24, scs.
6752 Haden, R, 119, A, Aug 24, pna.
6792 Hogan, Thos, 103, K, Aug 25, scs.
6845 Hurling, A, 57, C, Aug 25, dys.
6901 Hammer, John, 3 art, B, Aug 26, dia.
7000 Hoy, J, 101, F, Aug 27, dys.
7102 Houseman, G, 118, I, Aug 28, dia.
7286 Holloman, Wm, 102, G, Aug 30, dys.
7328 Hopes, W, 2 art, A, Aug 30, dys.
7422 Havert, B, 52, I, Aug 31, scs.
7491 Halliger, C, 63, D, Sept 1, dia.
7531 Hill, E, 110, Sept 1, dys.
7537 Henry, A B, 103, E, Sept 1, ana.
7568 Hobson, B F, 7, G, Sept 2, dys.

7571 Harman, John, 14, H, Sept 2, dia.
7588 Harris, A, 2 cav, K, Sept 2, scs.
7613 Homiker, J, 119, H, Sept 2, scs.
7661 Hockenbroct, J, 2 art, F, Sept 3, scs.
7665 Hughes, J, 11 cav, B, Sept 3, dia.
7682 Hoover, S P, 7, H, Sept 3, dia.
7687 Hunter, Charles, 3, A, Sept 3, dia.
7881 Holmes, S,‡ 140, B, Sept 5, dia.
7965 Hutton, James, 118, I, Sept 6, dia.
7990 Hazel, George, 2 cav, D, Sept 6, dia.
8254 Hecker, G, 6 reserves, C, Sept 9, dia. c.
8462 Henry, O H, 2 cav, L, Sept 11, scs.
8526 Heselport, J F, 68, G, Sept 12, dia.
8532 Hopkins, G R,§ 50, K, Sept 12, dia.
9088 Hansey, ——, 90, C, Sept 18, dia. c.
9118 Hooker, Wm, 8, G, Sept 18, dia.
9123 Holdhans, C, 63, E, Sept 18, dia.
9404 Houghbough, J, 143, D, Sept 21, dia. c.
9434 Hanks, J, I, A, Sept 21, dia. c.
9433 Hartzel, J, 7, I, Sept 21, dia. c.
9532 Houston, D, 4, B, Sept 22, scs.
9579 Harmony, J, 169, H, Sept 23, dia.
9843 Heninshalt, W, 149, E, Sept 27, scs.
9884 Hibbane, J, 99, H, Sept 27, scs.
9904 Hughly, John, 69, D, Sept 27, scs.
10022 Hamilton, B, 183, Sept 29, dia.
10070 Holden, Isaac, 7, G, Sept 30, dia.
10109 Harper, R, 103, B, Sept 30, scs.
10239 Hicks, J F, 14 cav, A, Oct 2, dia.
10349 Hammond, J, 10, D, Oct 5, scs.
10385 Hill, S M, 14, D, Oct 5, scs.
10430 Haldwell, P, 7 cav, E, Oct 6, wds.
10448 Hiller, S, 64, D, Oct 7, gae.
10474 Howe, M A, 12 cav, B, Oct 7, dys.
10538 Hand, H, 58, Oct 8, dia.
10571 Holden, P, 12 cav, B, Oct 9, dia.
10574 Hayes, J,§ 15 cav, G, Oct 9, dia.
10640 Hands, J, 106, A, Oct 10, dia.
10670 Hull, Ed, 77, G, Oct 11, scs.
10804 Hennesy, P, 49, H, Oct 12, scs.
10814 Hunbach, J, 116, G, Oct 12, dia.
10862 Hoberg, A J, 2 cav, M, Oct 13, dia.
10903 Hannesay, A, 55, I, Oct 14, scs.
10906 Hall, A, 118, E, Oct 14, scs.
10952 Hoover, S, 79, G, Oct 14, dia.
10962 Huffman, S, 64, C, Oct 15, scs.
11033 Happy, G, 101, K, Oct 16, scs.
11092 Harty, James, 148, I, Oct 18, scs.
11113 Horton, S, 106, I, Oct 18, scs.
11183 Hess, G, 118, D, Oct 19, scs.
11194 Hepsey, M, 73, K, Oct 20, dys.
11383 Hunter, T, 5 cav, M, Oct 24, scs.
11481 Hart, J, 7, I, Oct 26, scs.
11219 Hunter, J, 14 cav, M, Oct 20, scs.
11495 Hardinivick, J, 2, C, Oct 26, dys.
11609 Hosaflock, H A, 6 cav, E, Oct 28, dia. c.
11643 Hacket, J, 30, D, Oct 30, scs.
11702 Hoover, J, 90, A, Oct 31, scs.
11799 Hagerty, W R, 7, G, Nov 4, scs.
11897 Hart, M, 11, K, Nov 7, scs.
12215 Hyatt, F, 118, F, Dec 3, dia.
12260 Healy, J B, 100, M, Oct 11, scs.
12306 Hammond, W, 20, K, Dec 18, scs.
12610 Heneman, E L, 5, C, Feb 7, des.
12632 Healey, J,‡ 143, K, Feb 10, dia.
12719 Hummell, J, 87, B, March 2, dia. c.
7020 Hazen, M J, 101, H, Aug 22, dys.
3474 Hall, B, 105, F, July 17, scs.
10227 Haman, I, 118, E, Oct 1, dia.

124 Isheart, N, 18 cav, G, March 23, dys.
1401 Illy, Tobias, 27, C, May 27, dys.
10504 Irvin, T,§ 15 cav, M, Oct 8, ana.
10616 Ireton, S R, 138, I, Oct 10, dys.
11560 Irwin, W, 184, A, Oct 27, scs.
831 Ingersoll, Sam'l, 3, D, May 1, dia.

233 Johnson, John J, 45, I, March 29, des.
463 Johnson, Charles, 90, C, April 9, dia.
565 Johnson, John, 2 cav, G, April 15, dia.
976 Jacobs, Jacob, 2 cav, M, April 9, dia.
1303 Jones, William, 145, A, May 23, dia. c.

1595 Jones, J, 147, C, June 3, dia.
1840 Jones, Wm, 26, C, June 11, dia. c.
2108 Jones, O, 4 cav, D, June 17, dia. c.
2312 Johnston, Wm, 3 art, A, June 22, dia.
2593 Jones, R. 103, D, June 28, dia.
2914 Jordan, D W, 103, B, July 5, dia.
3499 Johnson, D, 45, I, July 18, pna.
3510 Jennings, H, 45, G, July 18, pna.
3885 Jones, Wm, 55, C, July 24, dia.
4057 John, Thomas, 54, E, July 27, wds.
4093 Jones, J, 79, A, July 27, dia. c.
4540 Johnson, J W, 50, G, Aug 2, dia.
4590 Jameson, Wm, 103, H, Aug 3, dia.
4817 Johns, Robert, 101, I, Aug 5, dia.
5295 Johnson, H, 2 art, I, Aug 11, scs.
5516 Jacobs, B G, 150, F, Aug 13, dia.
5871 Jones, Robert, 100, A, Aug 16, ens.
6197 Jones, T, 101, I, Aug 19, dia.
6200 Jones, W E, 27, B, Aug 19, scs.
6317 Jones, S, 49, G, Aug 22, i. f.
6760 Joslin, J, 145, I, Aug 25, ana.
6817 Jober, J, 77, B, Aug 25, dys.
6931 Jarmter, C. 7, A, Aug 26, scs.
7566 Johnson, Charles, 53, G, Sept 2, scs.
8318 Johnson, J, 45, I, Sept 10, dia.
8853 Jolly, James, 101, H, Sept 15, dia.
9303 Jones, P, 63, F, Sept 20, dia.
9351 Jordan, J M, 149, D, Sept 20, scs.
9378 Jacobs, J S, 6 cav, F, Sept 20, ana.
9982 Jeffres, C, 4, B, Sept 29, dia.
9999 Jones, T, 101, B, Sept 29, scs.
10735 Jabin, James, 55, E, Oct 11, scs.
10987 Jones, A, 27, D, Oct 16, dia. c.
11058 Johnson, Wm, 184, D, Oct 17, scs.
11430 Jordan, Thomas, 148, Oct 24, scs.
11539 Jenks, J C, 115, H, Oct 27, dys.
12007 Jobson, L, 118, C, Nov 4, scs.
12331 Jack, J P, 7, E, Dec 24, scs.
2889 Johnson, A G,‡ 103, I, July 4, r. f.

2 Kelley, Charles H, 71, H, March 1, pha.
238 Kelley, H S,§ 13 cav, H, March 30, dia.
266 Kuntyelman, J, 63, E, March 31, ts. f.
1024 Kenny, Wm, 12, F, May 11, dia. c.
1824 Kyle, Wm, 5, H, June 10, dia.
1875 Kelly, Peter, 73, June 12, ana.
2076 Knight, John, 7 cav, K, June 17, dia.
2335 Kehoe, Moses, 8, H, June 22, dia. c.
2639 Kenoan, M A, 14 cav, L, June 29, dia.
3048 King, C, 6, C, July 8, des.
3187 Keich, N,‡ 54, A, July 12, ana.
3265 Klink, A, 101, C, July 13, des.
3471 Kemp, E, 103, A, July 17, dia. c.
3634 Keeston, E, 103, I, July 20, dia.
4162 Kagman, J T, 45, B, July 28, dia.
4293 Kuffman, S D, 45, E, July 30, dys.
4545 Kanf, J, 2 art, B, Aug 2, scs.
4895 Kelley, O F, 148, B, Aug 6, dys. c.
5058 Kock, K, 21, H, Aug 8, dia.
5145 Kawell, John H, 18 cav, E, Aug 9, scs.
5154 Keys, Alex C,‡ 10 cav, H, Aug 9, dia.
5208 Kester, L, 149, F, Aug 10, brs.
5443 Kelley, T, 13 cav, H, Aug 12, ana.
5851 Kalm, R, 96, K, Aug 13, dys.
5718 Keister, John M, 103, A, Aug 15, dys.
5744 Keeley, Wm, 13 cav, A, Aug 15, scs.
6028 Kauffman, B F, 45, K, Aug 18, dia.
6084 Kemper, J, 73, D, Aug 18, scs.
6459 Kiger, Wm, 3 cav, C, Aug 22, scs.
6497 Kenter, A W, 67, B, Aug 22, dia. c.
6514 Kniver, S, 184, F, Aug 22, ts. f.
6638 Krigle, H, 11, K, Aug 23, dia.
6965 Krader, W O, 55, H, Aug 27, scs.
7005 King, M, 3 cav, A, Aug 27, dia.
7372 Keller, A, 9, M, Aug 31, dia.
7553 Keller, M, 105, G, Sept 2, scs.
7781 Kyle, Wm, 118, F, Sept 4, dia.
8210 Kinsman, F P, 184, F, Sept 8, ts. f.
8734 Kanfard, John C, 8 m, 5 cav, Sept 14, dia.
8799 Kaufman, J, 45, E, Sept 17, ana.
9139 Kipp, W, 12 cav, D, Sept 18, dia. c.
9563 Kinmick, T,‡ 145, K, Sept 23, scs.

****

9630 Kearney, L, 50, F, Sept 24, scs.
10335 Kerr, B, 149, B, Oct 4, dia.
10367 Kirby, J A, 101, E, Oct 5, scs.
10439 Kline, Ross, 184, F, Oct 6, scs.
10502 Kennedy, J, 152, A, Oct 8, dia.
10698 King, M, 11, K, Oct 11, dia. c.
11747 Kirkwood, H, 101, C, Oct 11, scs.
10926 Kneiper, C, 89, F, Oct 14, scs.
11238 Kurtz, J, 55, K, Oct 21, scs.
11332 King, J R, 55, K, Oct 23, scs.
11384 Kelley, E, 7 cav, F, Oct 24, scs.
11463 King, R, 6, E, Oct 26, scs.
11645 Kramer, George, ‡ 116, G, Oct 30, scs.
12695 Knox, J,§ 184, A, Feb 23, dia. c.
3676 Kerer, H N, 63, E, July 20, scs.

88 Liesen, Lewis, 13 cav, A, March 21, brs.
243 Lancaster, E, 14 cav, F, March 30, c. f.
297 Luck, W, 11 cav, H, April 1, pna.
549 Lynch, Adam, 6 cav, L, April 14, dia.
1403 Levy, Frank, 3 cav, H, May 27, dia.
1429 Liesine, Wm,‡ 13, E, May 28, dia. c.
1579 Lindine, J, 3 art, A, June 3, dia.
1588 Little, M, 106, F, June 3, dia.
1621 Luhars, Melter, 145, A, June 4, dia.
2250 Lackey, James, 183, D, June 21, des.
2379 Leach, J, 3 cav, D, June 23, dia. c.
3091 Larimer, J, 11, E, July 9, r. f.
3734 Ladbeater, Jas, 7, K, July 21, dia. c.
3305 Link, P, 98, H, July 14, scs.
3306 Long, A, 118, H, July 14, scs.
3369 Lanigan, N,§ 13 cav, L, July 15, ana.
3403 Lewis, Ed, 101, I, July 16, dys.
3448 Leonard, Geo, 49, G, July 17, r. f.
3489 Logan, B, 90, B, July 17, dia. c.
3545 Lee, Jas, 13 cav, B, July 18, dia.
4312 Long, D F B, 101, I, July 30, dia.
4434 Lambert, W, 4 cav, K, July 31, dia.
4696 Larrison, Wallace, 14 cav, C, Aug 4, dia.
4818 Lewis, A, 3 cav, D, Aug 5, pna.
4857 Laughlin, J,§ 101, E, Aug 6, dia.
4907 Lahman, C, 73, C, Aug 6, dia.
4929 Livingston, J K, 2 B, Aug 6, ana.
5199 Long, Augustus, 55, H, Aug 10, dia.
5225 Loudin, H N, 14, H, Aug 10, scs.
5314 Lacock, Hugh, 116, E, Aug 11, scs.
6252 Lodiss, H, 96, A, Aug 20, ces.
6636 Leach, Jas, 49, E, Aug 23, ana.
6783 Light, S,‡ 143, H, Aug 25, dys.
7145 La Bolt, J, 21, F, Aug 29, dys.
7938 Lemou, John E, 4 cav, I, Sept 5, ana.
7950 Lockhard, J, 145, B, Sept 6, dia.
8405 Lepley, Chas, 103, E, Sept 10, dia.
8754 Layman, F, 49, B, Sept 14, dia.
8833 Laughlin, J L, 1, H, Sept 15, scs.
8895 Lester, W H, 7 cav, I, Sept 16, dia.
8904 Lippoth, J, 5, E, Sept 16, dia.
9085 Logne, S, 26, A, Sept 18, dia.
9291 Leary, C, 83, K, Sept 19, dys.
9647 Lolen, J, 4 cav, C, Sept 24, des.
10066 Laytin, P, 110, D, Sept 30, scs.
10086 Lutz, P M, 21, G, Sept 30, scs.
10091 Lebos, C, 116, D, Sept 30, scs.
10273 Limar, W, 140, Oct 3, scs.
10298 Long, W, 67, G, Oct 4, dys. c.
10372 Long, P,‡ 11 cav, C, Oct 5, dys.
10548 Lancaster, C, 119, B, Oct 8, scs.
10572 Lynch, W J, 3 cav, I, Oct 9, dia.
10580 Labor, R, 7, F, Oct 10, dia.
10687 Luchford, R, 143, F, Oct 11, scs.
10873 Lang, I, 110, C, Oct 13, scs.
11004 Lenchlier, J, 5, Oct 16, scs.
11255 Lantz, Wm, 7, C, Oct 21, dia.
11465 Lewis, J, 4 cav, L, Oct 26, dia. c.
11728 Luther, I, 4 cav, L, Nov 1, scs.
11869 Lego, Geo, 12, A, Nov 6, dys.
11907 Ladd, A, 53, M, Nov 7, dia. c.
12192 Lape, J, 18, K, Nov 28, dia.
12210 Lewis, D S, 53, K, Dec 2, scs.
12489 Linsey, D, 77, G, Jan 19, scs.
5699 Ledwick, F M, 139, C, Aug 15, scs.
7084 Latchem, David, 4 cav, K, Aug 28, dia.

7307 Lochery, A, 14 cav, E, Aug 30, dia.
5985 Logan, W, 97, A, Aug 17, dys.
6030 Loudon, S, 101, A, Aug 18, mas.
6053 Layton, Samuel, 181, A, Aug 18, scs.
6071 Lamb, C, 71, B, Aug 18, dia.
6082 Lane, Amos, 6 cav, E, Aug 18, ces.
6152 Lehnich, John, 2 art, F, Aug 19, mas.
753 Lenard, M, 13 cav, D, April 26, dys.
761 Lord, G W, 141, E, April 27, rhm.
871 Loudon, Samuel,‡ 2, F, May 4, brs.

183 Maynard, John, 105, G, March 27, pna.
208 Missile, Val, 47, C, March 28, dys.
225 Miller, Daniel, 13 cav, H, March 29, pna.
361 Martin, J F, 14 cav, K, April 2, dia.
461 McEntire, W, 51, F, April 9, dia. c.
538 Mine, Joseph,‡ 54 F, April 14, dia.
586 Marple, S L, 14, A, April 17, rhm.
605 McKissick. John, 23, F, April 18, dia.
667 Myers, G, 1 cav, E, April 22, dia.
736 McKeever, E L,§ 71, F, April 25, dia.
773 McDonald, R, 23, C, April 28, dia. c.
780 McCartny, Jas, 18 cav, E, April 28, dia. 2
969 McQueeny, W, 79, B, May 9, dys.
1006 Moyer, John, 2 cav, E, May 10, dia.
1128 McKey, J, 1 cav, I, May 15, ana.
1139 McMahon, J, 73, F, May 16, dia. c.
1147 McKnight, J E, 57, B, May 16, dia.
1151 McHale, J, 14 cav, D, May 16, dia.
1185 Moser, John, 13 cav, B, May 18, scs.
1273 McCollen, W,§ 4 cav, L, May 22, dys.
1287 Milligan, J, 61, F, May 22, dia.
1308 McCartney, M, 73, B, May 23, ana.
1460 Murray, John, 13 cav, E, May 29, dia. c.
1586 Miles, Lewis, 4 cav, I, June 3, dia. c.
1643 Myers, J R,‡ 13 cav, M, June 5, dia. c.
1722 Marshall, M M, 78, E, June 8, dia. c.
1748 Moyer, Thos, 103, E, June 9, dia. a.
1792 Mifler, M, 118, A, June 10, ts. f.
1858 McHose, J; 4 cav, A, June 12, dia. c.
1907 Miller, Henry, 8, G, June 13, , dia. c.
1962 Mucholians, J, 101, K, June 15, dia. c.
2056 Mouny, W H, 3 cav, A, June 16, pna.
2058 Matchell, J J, 101, K, June 16, pna.
2159 Monan, J, 101, C, June 19, scs.
2265 McCutcheon, J, 4 cav, C, June 21, dia.
2278 Milton, Wm, 19 cav, H, June 21, dia.
2333 Myers, F,§ 27, H, June 22, dia. c.
2364 Myers, Peter, 76, G, June 23 dia.
2388 Morton, T, 79, I, June 24, dia. c.
2409 McCabe, J, 3 cav, L, June 24, pna.
2411 McKay, M J, 103, B, June 24, ts. f.
2493 Merry, Jas, 67, E, June 26, dys.
2503 Martin, A J,‡ 4 cav, E, June 26, dys.
2508 Morris, J, 18 cav, A, June 26, dys.
2653 McManes, 77, B, June 29, des.
2684 Mipes, J, 101, B, June 30, dia. c.
2690 Morris, G, 77, G, June 30, dia.
2798 Marsh, D, 50, D, July 2, dia.
2831 McCane, Charles, 14, C, July 3, dia.
3017 McRath, J, 48, C, July 7, dia. c.
3065 Morris, Calvin, 53, D, July 9, scs.
3133 McCalasky, J E,§ 4 cav, K, July 10, dia.
3151 Mattiser, B, 57, F, July 11, dia.
3172 Madden, Daniel, 149, G, July 11, pna.
3250 Myers, M, 103, E, July 13, dia.
3374 Mink, H, 3 art, A, July 16, dia.
3467 Meaker, E N, 155, H, July 17, dys. c.
3481 McKeon, John, 101, H, July 17, dia.
3483 Mihan, J, 138, D, July 17, dys.
3939 Marony, John, 1 cav, D, July 20, dys.
3690 McCarron, J, 4 cav, A, July 21, ana.
3766 Myers, John, 116, D, July 22, scs.
3971 Martin, G, 45, I, July 25, dia.
4016 McDermott, J M, 70, F, July 28, dia.
4123 McGee, James, 103, I, July 28, ana.
4197 Moore, M G, 1 art, A, July 29, cah.
4341 Marquet, M, 6, M, July 30, dia.
4407 McKever, John, 100, A, July 31, cah.
4414 McFarland, Jas, 55, E, July 31, dys.
4546 Moan, Jas, 101, K, Aug 2, dia.
4607 Martin, Bryant, 7, F, Aug 3, scs.

4535 McKeral, James, 14, K, Aug 3, dia.
4710 Mathews, C W,‡ 145, B, Aug 4, scs.
4734 Moore, M, 71, I, Aug 4, scs.
4796 McDevitt, J, 3 art, D, Aug 5, dia.
4824 Miller, H, 14 cav, I, Aug 5, dia.
4876 Mills, Wm, 150, G, Aug 6, scs.
4898 Muldany, M, 96, K, Aug 6, dia.
5068 Martain, John, 103, E, Aug 8, dys.
5069 Measler, James, 103, E, Aug 8, scs.
5139 McCaffrey, John, h s, 3 art, A, Aug 9, dia.
5159 Martin, C, 8 cav, A, Aug 9, scs.
5266 Marey, H F, 103, F, Aug 10, dys.
5291 Mohr, J R, 14, G, Aug 11, dia.
5415 McCarty, Dennis, 101, K, Aug 12, i. f.
5433 McGee, J, 14, H, Aug 12, ana.
5595 Mickelson, B, 16 cav, B, Aug 14, dys.
5642 McClough, L C, 18, C, Aug 14, ana.
5704 Miller, John, 101, G, Aug 15, dys.
5723 McCann, John, 3 art, A, Aug 15, scs.
5781 Miller, S, 143, B, Aug 15, dia.
5809 Montgomery, R, 62, A, Aug 16, ana.
5868 McQuillen, A, 6 art, L, Aug 16, dia.
5893 McCuller, S, 4 cav, B, Aug 16, dia.
5926 Mulchy, J A, 50, D, Aug 17, dia.
5988 Mann, James,‡ 119, G, Aug 17, dia. c.
6014 McPherson, D, 103, F, Aug 17, scs.
6038 Moore, C, 103, G, Aug 18, scs.
6143 McCracker, J, 53, K, Aug 19, r. f.
6294 McLaughlin, Jas, 4 cav, A, Aug 20, scs.
6441 McWilliams, H, 82, I, Aug 22, scs.
5480 Martin, John, 103, D, Aug 22, dia.
6532 McGan, J, 18 cav, Aug 23, dia.
6664 McKee, ——, 144, C, Aug 24, scs.
6689 Manner, M, 73, K, Aug 24, dia.
6910 McGlann, H, 143, B, Aug 26, dia.
6925 McGuigan, H C, 7, K, Aug 26, dia.
7026 Marks, P, 143, B, Aug 27, dys.
7061 Moore, M J, 107, Aug 28, dys.
7107 Moyer, Wm M, 55, H, Aug 28, dia.
7119 Miller, John L, 53, K, Aug 28, i. f.
7127 McAfee, Jas, 72, F, Aug 28, scs.
7175 Moore, Thomas, 69, D, Aug 29, scs.
7283 Martin, John, 77, C, Aug 30, dia.
7265 Musser, John, 77, D, Aug 30, scs.
7305 Moser, S, 103, E, Aug 30, dys.
7333 Morris, John, 183, G, Aug 30, dia.
7407 Marchin, Wm, 50, E, Aug 31, scs.
7512 Millinger, John H, 7, C, Sept 1, dys.
7602 Moorhead, J S, 103, D, Sept 2, dia.
7719 Myers, H, 9, A, Sept 3, scs.
7875 Mayer, W, 8, M, Sept 5, dia.
7925 Mays, N J, 103, H, Sept 5, dia.
8027 Murphy, A, 13 cav, I, Sept 6, ts. f.
8047 McKnight, J, 18 cav, I, Sept 6, dia. c.
8122 Miller, J,‡ 101, C, Sept 8, scs.
8123 Mullings, W, 145, G, Sept 8, scs.
8128 Munager, W, 13 cav, L, Sept 8, dia.
8134 Mehaffey, J M, 16 cav, B, Sept 8, scs.
8153 McCantley, W, 2 art, A, Sept 8, dia.
8158 McLane, T, 12, E, Sept 8, scs.
8194 McKink, J,‡ 119, D, Sept 8, dia.
8216 Mansfield, J, 101, G, Sept 8, dia.
8322 Myers, A, 118, I, Sept 10, dia.
8469 Magill, H, 103, I, Sept 11, scs.
8596 Morrison, J, 146, E, Sept 12, scs.
8627 McKinney, D, 90, C, Sept 13, scs.
8691 Moritze, A, 118, D, Sept 14, dia. c.
8802 McCulloyt, ——, 101, E, Sept 15, scs.
9071 Maynard, A, 3 art, Sept 17, dia.
9090 McCall, Wm, 22 cav, B, Sept 18, dia.
9228 McCullough, S, 138, K, Sept 19, wds.
9270 Mayhan, F, 20 cav, Sept 19, ana.
9315 Marsh, W, 149, K, Sept 20, scs.
9339 Meyers, J A, 138, C, Sept 20, scs.
9526 McQuigley, John, 101, C, Sept 22, scs.
9583 Mead, H J, 184, B, Sept 23, scs.
9598 Martin, J, 17 cav, C, Sept 23, scs.
9644 Morris, J, 54, I, Sept 24, scs.
9646 Morgan, J E, 2, A, Sept 24, gae.
9651 McCook, B, 118, A, Sept 24, scs.
9761 McMurray, Wm, 1 cav, I, Sept 25, scs.
9871 Masen, John, 112, A, Sept 27, scs.

4578 McKern, S, 73, K, Ar 2, ana.
10050 Mesin, James,‡ 9, K, Sept 30, scs.
10060 Morgan, C, 45, A, Sept 30, scs.
10119 McClany, J, 101, C, Oct 1, scs.
10154 McElroy, Wm, 13 cav, L, Oct 1, dia.
10306 Meese, J, 48, A, Oct 4, dia.
10396 McGraw, John, 3 art, A, Oct 6, scs.
10407 Miller, H, 79, K, Oct 6, scs.
10486 Miller, Washington, 18 cav, C, Oct 7, dia.
10610 McKearney, J W, 118, K, Oct 10, scs.
10620 McClief, Wm, 7, A, Oct 10, dia.
10641 Marker, W H, 118, D, Oct 10, dia.
10678 Martin, J P, 7, I, Oct 11, scs.
10684 Miller, James, 7, I, Oct 11, dia.
10803 Mattis, Aaron, 138, Oct 12, scs.
10825 Moore, C H, 13 cav, C, Oct 13, dys.
10929 Mortin, Geo H, 108, I, Oct 14, scs.
10981 Maxwell, S, 14 cav, B, Oct 15, scs.
10991 Moses, W, 16 cav, H, Oct 16, scs.
10993 McKnight, Jas, 118, K, Oct 16, scs.
11081 Mitchell, J O, 55, H, Oct 18, scs.
11142 Mansfield, George, 101, I, Oct 19, r. f.
11229 McClay, J, 11 cav, D, Oct 20, scs.
11305 McBride, J, 2 cav, H, Oct 22, scs.
11326 Marshall, L, 184, A, Oct 23, scs.
11387 Moore, S, 101, F, Oct 24, scs.
11459 Moore, J, 13 cav, B, Oct 25, scs.
11464 McNelse, J H,‡ 100, E, Sept 26, scs.
11542 Miller, F, 54, K, Oct 27, scs.
11655 Midz, J, 20 cav, A, Oct 30, scs.
11658 Menk, W, 12 cav, F, Oct 30, scs.
11683 Morrow, J C, serg maj, 101, E, Oct 31, scs.
11684 McCann, J, 11 cav, L, Oct 31, scs.
11686 Moore, W, 184, B, Oct 31, dia.
11692 Muligan, J, 7, H, Oct 31, pna.
11909 McCune, J, 67, E, Nov 8, scs.
11913 McClush, N, 97, E, Nov 8, scs.
11982 Manee, M, 53, H, Nov 13, scs.
12008 McCray, J, 145, A, Nov 14, scs.
12068 Maher, D, 118, E, Nov 18, scs.
12103 Miller, W, 31, I, Nov 22, gae.
12248 Murray, W, 14 cav, H, Dec 8, scs.
12326 McIntire, J, 55, C, Dec 24, scs.
12334 Myers, A D, 52, A, Dec 26, scs.
12554 Matthews, J, 6 cav, F, Jan 30, scs.
12595 Maloy, J M, 184, D, Feb 5, scs.
12625 McGenger, J, 20, C, Feb 9, dia. c.
12696 Myers, H, 87, E, Feb 23, dia. c.
12771 McDonald, ——, 9, G, March 13, des.
12806 McGarrett, R W, 103, F, Feb 21, dia. c.

1134 Nicholson, John, 3 cav, H, May 16, des.
1298 Nelson, Wm, 76, H, May 23, dia. c.
2332 Nolti, Wm, 6, F, July 3, dia. c.
3653 Newell, G S, 183, A, July 20, ana.
4246 Nicholson, W, 1 cav, H, July 29, dys.
4489 Nelson, George, 2, K, Aug 1, scs.
4936 Nayler, G W,§ 13 cav, L, Aug 7, dia.
5109 Nichols, D A, 125, D, Aug 9, scs.
6001 Neal, H G, 90, B, Aug 17, dia.
6011 Nickle, C, 37, G, Aug 17, dia.
6702 Nickem, James, 77, G, Aug 24, scs.
8154 Naylor, S, 20 cav, H, Sept 8, dia.
8907 Noble, J, 73, D, Sept 16, scs.
9424 Nice, Isaac, 11, L, Sept 21, dia.
9463 Neff, J, 4 cav, D, Sept 21, scs.
10146 Nelson, G, 55, A, Oct 1, dia.
10286 Nelson, J A, 145, G, Oct 4, dia.
10764 Newberry, John, 20 cav, A, Oct 2, gae.
11107 Nelson, A, 160, E, Oct 18, dia. c.
11254 Noble, Thomas, 19 cav, G, Oct 21, dia. c.
11776 Nichols, G, 20, C, Nov 3, dia.

414 Osborne, S R, 4, K, April 7, dys.
622 Ogelsby, J, 4 cav, K, April 19, dia.
1318 O'Brien, P, 13, A, May 23, dia. c.
1409 Ottinger, I, 8 cav, I, May 27, dia.
1897 O'Neil, John,§ 69, June 12, dia. c.
2589 Oswald, Stephen, 55, G, June 28, dia. c.
3161 O'Conor, ——, 83, July 11, scs.
3199 O'Neil, J, 63, I, July 12, ana.
3704 Olmar, H,§ 2 cav, H, July 21, dia.

****

3861 O Connor, H, 49, E, July 24, dys.
4161 Owens, G ll, 7, A, July 28, dia.
5119 Offleback, Z, 90, K, Aug 9, dia. c.
5184 Oliver, W, 103, D, Aug 9, dia.
5939 O'Hara, M, 101, E, Aug 17, scs.
6254 O'Connell, Wm, 183, G, Aug 20, scs.
6535 O'Hara, John, 150, E, Aug 23, scs.
6658 Oiler, Samuel, 103, G, Aug 24, dys.
6908 O'Rourke, Charles, 109, C, Aug 26, dys.
7105 Otto, John, 5 cav, B, Aug 28, dia.
7552 ———, J M,§ 101, I, Sept 2, scs.
——— ———, 184, A, Sept 18, scs.
——— ———, N V B, 149, K, Sept 20, dia.
9330 Owens, E, 50, D, Sept 20, scs.
10805 Osborn, E,‡ 11 cav, A, Oct 13, s s.

30 Peck, Albert, 57, K, March 9, pna.
62 Patterson, Robt, 2 res, E, March 18, ts. f.
125 Parker, Jas M,‡ 76, B, March 23, dys. c.
500 Petrisky, H, 54, F, April 12, dia.
1110 Patterson, Thos, 3 cav, A, May 15, dia. c
1119 Patent, Thos, 73, G, May 15, dia.
1258 Powell, Wm, 14 cav, D, May 21, dia.
1556 Powers, John, 26, I, June 2, dia. c.
1780 Preso, Thomas, 26, E, June 9, pna.
1884 Powell, Frank, 18, June 12, dia. c.
2566 Page, J, 183, G, June 27, ts. f.
2590 Porter, David, 101, H, June 28, dia.
2903 Parsons, J T, 103, D, July 5, dia.
3197 Painter, J G, 26, F, July 11, dia.
3445 Painter, S, 63, A, July 17, scs.
4049 Patterson, R, 101, H, July 27, dia.
4157 Pickett, J C, 3 cav, A, July 28, dia.
4177 Pratt, F, 14 cav, I, July 28, dys.
4191 Plymeer, W, 20 cav, B, July 28, dia.
4415 Page, John, 112, A, July 31, dia.
4473 Powell, H, 102, H, Aug 1, scs.
5823 Prosser, J, 63, Aug 11, scs.
5579 Pyers, Isaac, 72, G, Aug 14, dia.
5610 Phillips, Jas B, 101, I, Aug 14, dia.
5947 Parish, J A, 184, Aug 17, scs.
6241 Preans, H, 149, K, Aug 21, scs.
6439 Palmer, H, 140, D, Aug 22, scs.
6527 Poole, G, 52, B, Aug 22, dia.
6536 Pifer, M, 13, G, Aug 23, scs.
6574 Phillips, J W, 1 cav, F, Aug 23, scs.
6843 Peterson, G, 103, D, Aug 25, scs.
6844 Penn, John, 5 cav, E, Aug 25, scs.
6885 Pattin, H W, 2 art, F, Aug 26, dia. c.
7118 Potts, Edward, 183, H, Aug 28, brs.
7232 Perkins, N, 103, D, Aug 29, dia. c.
8020 Powell, A T, 149, C, Sept 6, dia.
8160 Pricht, F, 87, H, Sept 8, scs.
8763 Peck, C W, 145, H, Sept 14, dia.
8877 Persil, Frederick, 101, Sept 15, scs.
9220 Palmer, A, 143, D, Sept 19, ts. f.
9684 Perego, W, 143, G, Sept 24, scs.
9754 Phipps, J H, 57, E, Sept 25, scs.
10074 Price, G, 106, H, Sept 30, dia.
10573 Penstock, A, 144, B, Oct 9, dia.
10858 Powell, I, 101, I, Oct 13, scs.
11168 Price, O, 109, C, Oct 19, scs.
11261 Phay, M, 69, C, Oct 21, scs.
11637 Phillips, F, 61, K, Oct 28, scs
11737 Pees, M T, 145, H, Nov 2, dia.
11883 Penn, J, 18 cav, I, Nov 6, scs.
11918 Phelps, W, 4 cav, G, Nov 8, scs.
11328 Porterfield, J K, 5 cav, M, Oct 23, scs.
12075 Pemer, W, 18, C, Nov 18, scs.
12191 Pryor, Wm, 11, C, Nov 28, scs.
12359 Poleman, H, 1 cav, F, Dec 30, scs.
12378 Perry, H, 121, C, Jan 2, dys.
12388 Pritchett, J, 72, C, Jan 3, des.
12479 Potter, B F, 148, I, Jan 17, scs.

6756 Quinby, L C, 76, E, Aug 24, scs.

47 Reed, Sam'l, 4 cav, D, March 15, pna.
126 Robertson, J, 119, K, March 23, dia.
132 Rosenburg, Henry, 49, K, March 24, dia.
171 Reign, John, 83, K, March 26, ana.
308 Richpeder, A, 13, B, April 2, dia.

610 Ray, Wm, 8 cav, F, April 18, dia.
847 Rhinehart, J, 3 cav, D, May 3, ana.
895 Russell, F, 4, D, May 5, dia.
907 Rhinebolt, J, 18 cav, I, May 5, dia. c.
940 Robinson, C W,§ 150, E, May 7, dia. c.
1152 Randall, H, 4 cav, H, May 16, dia. c.
1218 Rigney, Chas, 4 cav, G, May 19, dys.
1454 Raleigh, A, 51, G, May 29, dia. c.
1485 Rudolph, S,‡ 13 cav, K, May 30, dia. c.
1599 Rhine, George, 63, I, June 4, dia.
1624 Rosenburg, H, 13 cav, H, June 4, dia. 3,
1719 Raymond, John,§ 18 cav, H, June 8, scs.
1803 Rheems, A,§ 73, I, June 10, des.
1833 Ramsay, J D, 103, F, June 11, scs.
1922 Rush, S, 18, G, June 14, dia.
1942 Robinson, Wm, 77, D, June 14, dia. c.
2225 Roush, Peter, 101, E, June 20, dia. c.
2528 Rupert, F, 2 cav, H, June 26, scs.
2602 Roat, J, 54, F, June 28, scs.
2735 Rhodes, F, 79, E, July 1, dia.
2911 Rock, J E, 5, M, July 5, brs.
2979 Regart, John, 13 cav, E, July 7, dia.
2103 Ray, A,§ 77, E, June 17, dia. c.
3024 Rugh, M J, 103, D, July 7, scs.
3270 Robins, R, 69, B, July 13, dia.
3468 Ransom, H, 148, I, July 17, dys.
3827 Rinner, L, 5 cav, A, July 23, dys.
4074 Ringwalk, F J, 79, H, July 27, dys.
4241 Roger, L, 115, L, July 29, ts. f.
4309 Rogers, C, 73, C, July 30, dia.
4476 Ray, James R, 184, B, Aug 1, dys.
4507 Riese, S, 103, D, Aug 1, dia. c.
4844 Riche, James, 103, B, Aug 6, dia.
4940 Ruthfer, J, 2 art, F, Aug 7, dia.
5319 Rice, Sam'l, 101, K, Aug 11, cah.
5389 Ross, David, 103, B, Aug 12, dia.
5430 Robinson, John, 99, D, Aug 12, dia.
5537 Rose, B, 13, I, Aug 13, dys.
5800 Robins, J, 2 cav, M, Aug 15, ts. f.
5879 Reider, H, 7 cav, L, Aug 16, dia.
5894 Richards, E, 143, E, Aug 16, dia.
5912 Rease, Jacob, 103, B, Aug 17, dia.
5940 Richards, John,‡ 1 cav, G, Aug 17, scs.
6321 Robbins, G, 106, G, Aug 21, pna.
6373 Roger, John L, 110, H, Aug 21, scs.
6520 Reynolds, J, 14, H, Aug 22, scs.
6725 Rowe, E,‡ 103, A, Aug 24, dia.
6777 Rangardener, J, 149, H, Aug 25, dia.
6789 Richards, G, 13 cav, A, Aug 25, dia.
6790 Runels, John, 6 cav, L, Aug 25, dys.
6822 Rum, A, 188, C, Aug 25, scs.
6838 Reese, D, 148, K, Aug 25, gae.
6896 Raiff, T, 1, A, Aug 26, scs.
6933 Richardson, ———, 61, Aug 26, dia.
7067 Reese, D, 143, F, Aug 28, dys.
7202 Rueff, J, 103, F, Aug 29, dia.
7292 Redmire, H, 98, D, Aug 30, dia.
7293 Robins, George, 62, A, Aug 30, dia.
7410 Richardson, H, 103, K, Aug 31, dia.
7467 Richard, D, 18 cav, D, Sept 1, scs.
7716 Rice, E, 7, B, Sept 3, dia.
7738 Roads, Frederick, 101, E, Sept 3, dys.
8139 Rathburn, K, 2, F, Sept 8, scs.
8540 Russell, S A,‡ 79, A, Sept 12, scs.
8545 Ray, A, 149, D, Sept 12, dys.
8602 Richards, J, 106, H, Sept 12, scs.
8635 Rhangmen, G,§ 138, D, Sept 13, scs.
8742 Root, D, 48, B, Sept 14, dia.
9019 Ret, George, 18, A, Sept 17, dia.
9272 Ramsay, J I, 149, Sept 19, ana.
9585 Richie, H, 11, F, Sept 3, scs.
9590 Renamer, W H, 87, H, Sept 23, dia.
9612 Richards, John, 113, D, Sept 23, dia.
9653 Reed, R, 103, A, Sept 24, dia.
9766 Ramsay, R, 84, D, Sept 25, scs.
9882 Richards, J, 53, K, Sept 27, dia.
10174 Reed, J, 55, A, Oct 1, dia.
10863 Ramsay, Wm, 87, B, Oct 13, scs.
10622 Reedy, E T,§ 87, B, Oct 10, dia. c.
10935 Roundabush, H B, 55, A, Oct 14, dia.
10947 Rockwell, A, 2 cav, L, Oct 14, scs.
11071 Raeff, J B, 72, E, Oct 17, scs.

11115 Rinkle, John A, 20, A, Oct 18, scs.
11293 Rolston, J, 18, F, Oct 22, scs.
11147 Rudy, J, 13, F, Oct 19, scs.
11444 Riffle, S G,‡ 189, C, Oct 25, scs.
11566 Richardson, A, 144, E, Oct 27, scs.
11868 Rowland, N, 111, F, Nov 6, scs.
12008 Rapp, A E, 18 cav, I, Nov 15, scs.
12048 Ruth, B S, 23, I, Nov 16, scs.
12206 Rothe, C, 101, A, Dec 1, scs.
12355 Reese, D, 7, A, Dec 29, dia.
12372 Reed, W S, 128, H, Jan 1, des.

377 Smith, M D, 18, B, April 5, dia. a.
788 Smith, Geo, 5 cav, H, April 28, dia. c.
851 Smith, Wm, 4, A, May 4, dia. c.
882 Smith, T, 19, G, May 4, dia.
921 Steffler, W J,§ 12 cav, G, May 6, dia.
1014 Serena, H, 4 cav, D, May 10, dys.
1030 Shebert, Gotlieb, 73, C, May 11, dys.
1058 Spilyfiter, A, 54, F, May 13, ana.
1105 Sullivan, D, 101, K, May 15, dia. c.
1114 Shindle, S R,§ 140, K, May 15, dia.
1155 Stearnes, E K, 14 cav, A, May 16, dia. c.
1169 Sloat, D, 76, I, May 16, dia.
1175 Scott, Wm, 4, B, May 16, dia. c.
1216 Severn, C, 139, A, May 19, dia.
1256 Sammoris, B,§ 2 cav, B, May 21, dia.
1349 Smith, Charles, 26, A, May 24, ana.
1453 Schlenbough, C, 4 cav, G, May 29, dia. c.
1503 Smith, Martin, 18 cav, H, May 31, dia. c.
1535 Stone, Samuel, 26, F, June 1, des.
1543 Shoemaker, M,§ 13 cav, H, June 1, dia.
1605 Swearer, G, 13, H, June 4, dia. c.
1620 Schiefeit, Jacob, 54, F, June 4, dia.
1632 Schmar, R, 45, F, June 5, dia.
1963 Smith, D, 11 cav, H, June 14, dys.
2039 Slough, H, 53, June 15, ts. f.
2070 Stevens, A, 13 cav, M, June 16, dys.
2121 Sherwood, C H,§ 4 cav, M, June 17, dia. c.
2123 Stall, Samuel, 75, D, June 17, pna.
2126 Say, J R, 4 cav, K, June 17, dia. c.
2163 Steel, J S, 7 cav, F, June 19, dia.
2259 Scoles, M, 27, K, June 21, dia. c.
2331 Sims, B, 14 cav, G, June 22, dia. c.
2412 Shoop, Jacob, 2, M, June 24, ts. f.
2622 Springer, John, 101, E, June 28, ts. f.
2650 Stewart, J B, 103, A, June 29, dia. c.
2725 Scott, Allen, 150, H, July 1, dys.
2738 Schimgert, J, 73, G, July 1, scs.
2791 Shimer, J A, 13 cav, A, July 2, dia. c.
2864 Scott, Wm (negro), 8, D, July 4, dia.
2905 Stump, A, 11, I, July 5, dys.
2941 Smith, Jacob, 51, H, July 6, dia.
2982 Shaw, W, 140, B, July 7, dia. c.
2999 Smulley, Jno, 112, K, July 7, r. f.
3057 Sutton, R M, 103, I, July 9, dia.
3113 Sweet, H, 57, K, July 10, dys.
3136 Shoemaker, M, 148, G, July 10, scs.
3154 Sillers, Wm, 77, D, July 11, scs.
3214 Stone, W F, 53, G, July 12, scs.
3480 Swelser, J, 103, D, July 17, dia. c.
3567 Smalley, L, 58, K, July 19, dia.
3568 Stevens, S G, 150, H, July 19, scs.
3586 Sickles, Daniel, 116, K, July 19, dys.
3632 Serders, J S, 142, K, July 20, dys.
3670 Stopper, Wm, 16, B, July 20, ana.
3763 Stillenberger, F, 172, F, July 22, dys.
3775 Strance D, 11, H, July 22, scs.
3855 Smith, J, 19, F, July 24, dia. c.
3906 Smith, O C,§ 77, G, July 24, dia. c.
3956 Seilk, A, 144, D, July 25, dys.
3960 Sullivan, T, 7, F, July 25, dia.
4006 Smith. F, 64, K, July 26, ana.
4009 Shafer, J H, 84, E, July 26, dia. c.
4012 Shapley, Geo, 103, G, July 26, dys.
4043 Strichley, C. 53, H, July 27, dia.
4064 Shrively, E S, 19 cav, M, July 27, dys.
4113 Sheppard, E, 145, G, July 28, dia.
4164 Smith, S W, 101, B, July 28, dia. c.
4213 Shaffer, Peter, 52, F, July 29, dia.
4223 Shister, F, 3 cav, A, July 29, scs.
4228 Stein, J, 7, G, July 29, dia.

4274 Sloan, J, 11, E, July 29, ana.
4285 Shone, P, 4 cav, D, July 30, scs.
4345 Stobbs, W W,‡ 101, E, July, 30, dia.
4348 Scott, A, 22 cav, F, July 31, des.
4351 Scundler, J, 67, A, July 31, dia.
4372 Smith, P, 72, C, July 31, dia.
4566 Sale, Thomas, 15, M, Aug 2, scu
4775 Shink, James, 81, F, Aug 5, scs.
4791 Sullivan, Ed, 67, H, Aug 5, scs.
4797 Sear, C, 14 cav, L, Aug 5, dia.
4845 Shember, Jno, 11 cav, D, Aug 6, dia.
4928 Slicker, J, 77, D, Aug 6, scs.
4931 Sheit, P, 61, G, Aug 7, dia.
4945 Swarts, P,‡ 27, I, Aug 7, dys.
5180 Stiner, John, 22 cav, G, Aug 9, scs.
5189 Striker, F, 14 cav, C, Aug 9, scs.
5215 Sworeland, Wm, 184, A, Aug 10, dia.
5232 Speck, A, 118, A, Aug 10, dys.
5411 Shaffer, Daniel, 13 cav, F, Aug 12, pna
5529 Shangrost, A, 103, D, Aug 12, dia.
5437 Shears, J S, 149, K, Aug 12, dia.
5463 Stibbs, W, 56, H, Aug 13, dys.
5494 Shape, F, 18 cav, A, Aug 13, dia.
5603 Somerfield, W, 69, E, Aug 14, dia.
5700 Stineback, A, 150, C, Aug 15, dia.
5750 Spears, W M,§ 2 cav, K, Aug 15, pna
5874 Sheppard, N, 79, F, Aug 16, scs.
5965 Shultz, F, 13 cav, K, Aug 17, dia.
6205 Shoop, G, 103, K, Aug 19, scs.
6289 Smith, H, 26, K, Aug 20, ts. f.
6337 Smith, W, 18 cav, B, Aug 21, des.
6382 Swager, M, 101, F, Aug 21, dia.
6436 Spain, Thos, 118, H, Aug 22, dia.
6523 Stover, J, 49, F, Aug 22, scs.
6526 Stahler, S, 149, G, Aug 22, ana.
6534 Suyder, John, 118, C, Aug 23, scs.
6584 Sloate, E, 50, D, Aug 23, dys.
6595 Shirley, Henry, 105, I, Aug 23, dia. c.
6669 Sherwood. P, 84, I, Aug 24, dys.
6776 Shellito, R, 150, C, Aug 25, dys.
6823 Spain, Richard, 118, H, Aug 25, ana.
6829 Sturgess, W A ‡ 79, G, Aug 25, scs.
6880 Stahler, D, 4 cav, A, Aug 26, ana.
7029 Strickler, J W, 11, F, Aug 27, dys.
7106 Smith, John F, 55, C, Aug 28, ics.
7137 Sloan, J M, 18 cav, D, Aug 28, dys.
7141 Springer, J, 103, F, Aug 29, dys.
7262 Shriver, B, 13 cav, K, Aug 30, dia.
7302 Siuger, J, 2 art, A, Aug 30, dia.
7358 Scoleton, J, 53, F, Aug 31, scs.
7363 Sweeney, D, 14 cav, E, Aug 31, dia. c.
7379 Scott, W B, 4 cav, D, Aug 31, dia.
7631 Streetman, J, 7, E, Sept 2, dia.
7638 Steele, J, 62, M, Sept 2, dia.
7648 Spencer, Geo, 20, C, Sept 3, dia.
7662 Snyder, M S, 183, A, Sept 3, dys.
7705 Swartz, Geo, 5 cav, A, Sept 3, r. f.
7770 Stockhouse, D,‡ 18 cav, I, Sept 4, dia.
7905 Sellers, H, 149, G, Sept 5, dia.
7939 Shultz, John, 4 cav, I, Sept 5, ana.
7969 Smith, A C, 7, F, Sept 6, dia.
8038 Simpson, T, 53, K, Sept 6, dia.
8103 Stump, J, 105, I, Sept 7, dia.
8112 Slade, E,‡ 150, H, Sept 7, scs.
8444 Shirk, M B, 142, A, Sept 11, scs.
8567 Simous, Wm H, 76, K, Sept 12, scs.
8659 Spould, E, 90, E, Sept 13, scs.
8773 Smith, Wm, 2, K, Sept 14, gae.
8795 Stella, J F, 1, B, Sept 15, dia.
9296 Signall, —— ‡ 79, H, Sept 19, scs.
9012 Steadman, W, 54, F, Sept 17, dia.
9123 Schably, J, 54, A, Sept 18, dia. c.
9138 Shoup, S, 16 cav, B, Sept 18, dia. c.
9310 Smith, Charles, 7, H, Sept 20, dia.
9365 Stebins, Z, 7, H, Sept 20, dia.
9411 Scott, D, 149, G, Sept 21, scs.
9567 Snyder, A, 148, I, Sept 23, dia.
9593 Sternholt, Wm, 38, Sept 23, dia.
9742 Supple, C M,‡ 63, B, Sept 25, dys.
9780 Surplus, W,§ 13 cav, L, Sept 26, dia
9890 Siherk, Christian, 145, Sept 27, scs.
9898 Sweeny, W P, 13 cav, Sept 27, scs.

****

9912 Sanford, C, 69 H, Sept 28, ana.
9985 Sheppard, C,§ 118, E, Sept 29, scs.
10088 Sloan, P, 115, A, Aug 30, scs.
10132 Smith, J S, 22 cav, B, Oct 1, dia.
10299 Strong, H, 55, E, Oct 4, scs.
10323 Smith, E, 10, H, Oct 4, scs.
10516 Snyder, Wm, 54, H, Sept 8, dys.
10525 Stones, T, 121, K, Oct 8, dys.
10530 Smallwood, C, 7, F, Oct 8, scs.
10609 Small, H, 101, H, Oct 10, scs.
10720 Smallman, J W, 63, A, Oct 11, dia.
10808 Steele, F F, 20 cav, A, Oct 12, scs.
10837 Shank, A. 184, C, Oct 13, scs.
11044 Smith, Andrew, 22 cav, B, Oct 17, dia.
11069 Stevens, C P, 11, A, Oct 17, scs.
11233 Smith, H W, 53, B, Oct 21, scs.
11246 Smith, James, 57, E, Oct 21, ts. f.
11355 Silvy, David, 18 cav, I, Oct 23, scs.
11368 Seyoff, H, 81, C, Oct 23, scs.
11488 Sunderland, E, 11, D, Oct 26, scs.
11529 Stevenson, John, 111, I, Oct 26, scs.
11661 Speck, Olive, 67, H, Oct 30, scs.
11741 Smith, H, 183, D, Nov 2, scs.
11785 Snodgrass, R J, 145, H, Nov 4, scs.
11792 Sellentine, M, 145, C, Nov 4, scs.
11825 Seltzer, D, 20, K, Nov 5, scs.
11885 Smith, W B, 14 cav, E, Nov 6, scs.
11890 Shure, J P, 184, F, Nov 7, scs.
11895 Snively, G W, 20 cav, F, Nov 7, scs.
11923 Scover, J H, 79, G, Nov 8, scs.
11951 Shefiley, W, 118, G, Nov 9, scs.
12057 Stitzer, G, 2, E, Nov 16, scs.
12081 Stensley, D,‡ 184, A, Nov 18, scs.
12217 Smith, J S, 118, F, Dec 3, dia.
12218 Skinner, S O,‡ 77, A, Dec 4, scs.
12282 Shafer, T, 184, E, Dec 13, scs.
12308 Stafford, W, 67, H, Dec 19, scs.
12384 Sourbeer, J E, 20, A, Jan 3, scs.
12590 Sipe, F, 87, C, Feb 5, dia. c.
12598 Stauffer, J, 1, K, Feb 6, dia. c.
12648 Stain, G W, 20 cav, K, Feb 13, des.
12669 Slough, E B,‡ 1 cav, D, Feb 17, pls.
12670 Scott, A J, 14, D, Feb 17, dia. c.
12676 Sheridan, M, 103, F, Feb 19, dia. c.
12817 Sharks, J N, 14, D, March 27, dia.
12824 Shultz, H H, 87, A, April 5, dia.

778 Thistlewood, J, 73, E, April 23, c. f.
785 Tolland, D, 13 cav, D, April 28, las.
1144 Taylor, J F, 13, E, May 16, ts. f.
1145 Tull, D,‡ 4, D, May 16, pna.
1153 Toner, Peter, 19, A, May 16, dia. c.
1814 Thompson, H, 57, C, June 10, dia. c.
2182 Thompson, A, mus, 4 cav, C, June 19, des.
2302 Townsend, D, 18 cav, D, June 22, dia. c.
2635 Tyser, L, 145, D, June 29, dia. c.
2897 Terwilliger, E,§ 103, H, July 5, dys.
3003 Thompson, R, 103, F, July 7, dia.
47 Taylor, C W, 84, D, May 24, s. p.
2329 Titus, W, 171, D, July 14, des.
3473 Todd, Wm, 103, K, July 17, scs.
3571 Thompson, J S, 183, H, July 19, dys.
3768 Terrell, A, 12 cav, B, July 22, dia.
3968 Trumbull, H, 3, E, July 25, scs.
4116 Thompson, Jas,§ 13 cav, G, July 28, dia.
4160 Tinsdale, ——, 149, E, July 28, dia.
4713 Thompson, J, 3 art, A, Aug 4, scs.
5179 Thompson, W W, 101, E, Aug 9, scs.
5345 Thomas, F, 7, F, Aug 11, scs.
5966 Thompson, J B, 100, H, Aug 17, scs.
6146 Thompson, F A B, 69, I, Aug 19, ces.
6447 Tubbs, E, 143, I, Aug 23, scs.
6476 Toll, Wm, 11 res, I, Aug 22, scs.
6791 Turner, John, 118, H, Aug 25, dia.
7250 Thomas, E, 23, F, Aug 30, dia. c.
7409 Thorpe, L, 61, E, Aug 31, dia.
7904 Trash, Seth, 81, A, Sept 6, dia.
8231 Truman, E W, 9, G, Sept 9, scs.
8531 Tilt, W, 115, A, Sept 12, dia.
8619 Tutor, C, 184, A, Sept 13, scs.
9027 Tits, P, ——, C, Sept 17, scs.
9212 Thorpe, D, 18, D, Sept 19, dia.

9302 Thompson, H, 18 cav, I, Sept 20, dia.
9726 Tonson, J, 99, B, Sept 21, dia.
9775 Thuck, I, 7, C, Sept 26, scs.
9981 Tones, E, 145, F, Sept 26, dia.
10008 Thompson, J, 90, H, Sept 29, scs.
10725 Tibbels, Geo,‡ 69, K, Oct 11, scs.
11002 Thatcher, R, 14, C, Oct 16, dia. c.
11407 Thompson, J, 12 cav, E, Oct 24, dia.
11754 Trespan, P, 67, H, Nov 2, scs.
12080 Townsend, C,‡ 103, E, Nov 18, scs.

971 Ulrick, John, 17, E, May 9, ts. f.
4184 Urndragh, W, 4, B, July 28, dia.
12133 Utler, Wm, 45, H, Nov 23, dia.

1369 Ventler, Chas,§ 75, G, May 25, rhm.
7739 Vogel, L,‡ 150, A, June 8, dia. c.
2428 Vernon, S, 7, K, June 24, des.
4265 Vanholt, T, 13, A, July 29, dia.
5392 Vandeby, B,§ 7, A, Aug 12, dia.
6877 Vanderpool, F, 57, B, Aug 26, dia.
7716 Vancampments, George, 52, I, Sept 4, dia.
8270 Vail, G B, 77, G, Sept 9, dia.
8791 Vaughan, J, 108, A, Sept 15, dia.
8948 Varndale, J, 112, A, Sept 16, dia.
9688 Vandier, Wm, Phila, Sept 24, scs.

57 Wilkins, A, 12 cav, L, March 17, c. f.
123 Waterman, John, 88, B, March 23, dys.
193 Wise, Isaac, 18, G, March 27, pls.
496 Wheeler, J, 150, I, April 12, dia.
516 Warren, J, 76, A, April 12, dia.
587 Weed, A B, 4, K, April 17, dys.
657 Wentworth, Jas, 83, G, April 21, ts. f.
665 Watson, F F, 2, B, April 22, dys.
686 Wahl, John, 73, C, April 23, rhm.
764 Wilson, John, 14 cav, H, April 27, dia.
852 Williams, S, 18 cav, I, May 3, dia. c.
941 Wolf, J H, 13 cav, H, May 7, dia. c.
1021 Wright, J, 12 cav, B, May 11, dia. c.
1067 Whitton, Robt, 145, C, May 13, dia. c.
1093 Wright, Wm, 16 cav, A, May 14, dia. c.
1386 Wymans, Jas,‡ 150, C, May 26, dia. c.
1387 Wilson, James, 13 cav, D, May 26, dia. s
1443 Williams, F, 3 cav, B, May 28, dia. c.
1494 Williams, Fred, 101, K, May 30, dia.
1525 Wallace, H, 13 cav, H, May 31, pna.
1563 Waltermeyer, H, 76, H, June 2, dia. c.
1721 Whitney, W, 83, A, June 8, dia.
1749 Woodsides, W I, 18, E, June 9, dia. c.
1791 Wolf, Samuel, 77, A, June 10, dia.
1903 Woodward, G W, 3 cav, June 13, dia.
1977 Wyant, H, 103, G, June 15, dia. c.
2338 Walters, C, 73, B, June 22, dia. c.
2616 Williams, J, 83, F, June 28, dys.
2699 Wike, A, 96, B, June 30, dia.
2790 Whitaker, —— (negro), 8, July 2, dia.
2987 Winsinger, S, 96, E, July 6, dia.
3023 Weider, L, 50, H, July 7, dia. c.
3135 Wallace, A, 116, I, July 10, dia. c.
3277 Wright, W A, 20 cav, G, July 14, dia.
3384 Woodruff, W D, 103, B, July 16, dia.
3392 Wait, Geo, 1 cav, G, July 16, dia. c.
3605 Walker, E, 7, A, July 19, dys.
3694 White, E D,§ 2 cav, H, July 21, dia.
4181 Wisel, M, 18 cav, K, July 28, dip.
4338 Ward, Daniel, 138, E, July 30, dia.
3880 White, M, 7, C, July 24, dia.
3822 Wilson, Andrew, 103, H, July 23, dia.
4069 Wolf, A, 146, D, July 27, dia.
4046 Winegardner, A, 73, G, July 27, dia.
3921 Wilson, Wm, 43, July 25, dia.
4428 Williams, George, 54, H, July 31, dia.
4702 Willebough, E, 148, I, Aug 4, scs.
4828 Ward, P, 103, B, Aug 6, dia.
4966 Wetherholt, C, 54, F, Aug 7, des.
4981 Waserun, G, 4 cav, I, Aug 7, dia.
4996 White, S, 14 cav, B, Aug 7, dia.
5106 Weaver, James, 90, K, Aug 9, scs.
5353 Wilks, S, 77, G, Aug 11, pls.
5458 Wilson, Wm, 7, K, Aug 12, dys.
5677 Weeks, D, 53, G, Aug 14, dys. c.

6050 Williams, J, 7, A, Aug 18, dia.
6052 Waterhouse, W, 3 cav, L, Aug 18, ces.
6133 Workman, A, 118, D, Aug 19, dia.
6305 Whipple, H,‡ 18, B, Aug 20, des.
6427 Wart, C, 143, E, Aug 22, scs.
6530 Winerman, Jas, 77, A, Aug 23, scs.
6563 Wible, Paul, 57, A, Aug 23, i. s.
6626 Walker, S A, 103, I, Aug 23, scs.
6808 Wick, R C, 103, E, Aug 25, dys.
6980 Woolslaer, W H,‡ 77, C, Aug 27, scs.
8981 White, Jas P, 149. D, Aug 27, des.
7023 Woodford, J A, 101, E, Aug 27, dia.
7277 White, Ed, 103, K, Aug 30, dia.
7382 Webb, J S, 69, K, Aug 31, dys.
7386 Walton, A,§ 4 cav, A, Aug 31, scs.
7680 Wallwork, T, 118, D, Sept 3, dia.
7714 Warner, L, 5 cav, C, Sept 3, dia. c.
7799 Wynn, H, 101, F, Sept 4, dia.
7809 Wiggins, D, 2 art, D, Sept 5' dia. c.
7914 Weekland, F, 101, K, Sept 5, dia.
7933 Wade, Geo W, 118, E, Sept 5, dia.
8081 Weber, W, 116, F, Sept 7, dia.
8360 White, D, 2 art, F, Sept 10, dia. c.
8879 Wheeler, J, 7, C, Sept 15, scs.
9091 Wheeler, C C, 14 cav, M, Sept 18, dia.
9343 Williams, W, 20 cav, Sept 20, scs.
9434 Wilson, W H, 3, I, Sept 21, dia.
9534 Woolman, H, 18 cav, A, Sept 22, scs.
9573 Wingert, C, 111, I, Sept 23, wds.
9634 Wismer, J, 100, A, Sept 24, dia.
9657 Wilson, G M, 7 cav, M, Sept 24, dia.
9825 Walke, G, 4 cav, K, Sept 27, dia.
9909 Wentley, J, 155, G, Sept 28, dia.
10092 Watson, Wm, 99, I, Sept 30, dia.
10217 Weeks, C, 76, F, Oct 2, dia.
10229 Waltz, J, 7, H, Oct 2, dia.
10236 Weekly, John, 14, A, Oct 2, dia.
10253 Weeks, C, 76, F, Oct 3, scs.
10315 Wolfhope, J, 184, A, Oct 4, dys.
10400 Wilson, G, 55, C, Oct 6, dia.
10426 Wilson, J, 118, D, Oct 6, dia.
10521 Williams, W, 46, K, Oct 8, dys.
10568 Walk, W, 87, E, Oct 9, dia. c.
10632 Welry, John M,‡ 116, E, Oct 10, dia. c.
10659 Watts, A J, 12 cav, I, Oct 11, scs.

10729 White, J M, 21, G, Oct 11, scs.
10797 Walker, Wm, 148, B, Oct 12, scs.
9464 Warner, Cyrus W, 184, B, Oct 21, scs.
10840 Wright, Wm, 16, I, Oct 13, scs.
10902 Wolford, D, 54, K, Oct 14, scs.
10974 Watson, C, 184, E, Oct 15, scs.
11048 Wilderman, E, 14, D, Oct 17, scs.
11108 Walker, A, 45, D, Oct 18, dia.
11129 Wilson, G, 140, F, Oct 18, scs.
11498 Warrington, J H, 106, H, Oct 26, dia.
11503 Waiter, W, 184, F, Oct 26, scs.
11557 Wood, J,§ 19, C, Oct 27, scs.
11722 Woodburn, D J, 7, G, Nov 1, scs.
11750 Wyncoop, F P, 7, I, Nov 2, scs.
11899 Webster, J,§ 20 cav, L, Nov 7, dia. c.
11978 Wilkinson, C,§ 104, I, Nov 12, scs.
11987 Weaver, J, 53, K, Nov 13, dia.
12095 Walder, John, 5 cav, L, Nov 19, scs.
12098 Wider, N H, 184, F, Nov 19, scs.
12123 Weatherald, H W, 7, H, Nov 22, scs
12129 Webb, C M,§ 101, H, Nov 23, scs.
12222 Williams, J, 145, A, Dec 4, scs.
12137 Wood, J M, 2, A, Nov 23, scs.
12380 Watson, H, 184, A, Jan 2, dia. c.
12485 Williams, B, 75, B, Jan 19, dia.
12493 Walker, N C, 87, B, Jan 20, des.

10158 Van Dyke, D L, 103, A, Oct 1, dia.
11810 Vanmarkes, D, 6, E, Nov 4, scs.
12154 Vanhatterman, I, 4, G, Nov 25, scs.
3958 Vogle, V, 78, D, July 25, scs.

3799 Yocumbs, W B, 93, B, July 22, dia. c.
4900 Yocum, D, 1 cav, M, Aug 6, dia. c.
6103 Yingling, E, 78, E, Aug 13, dia.
6545 Yeager, Samuel, 158, D, Aug 23, dia.
10204 Young, J B, 49, G, Oct 2, dys.
11040 Young, W H, 145, F, Oct 17, dia. c.
11872 Yeager, J, 49, C, Nov 6, dys.

1806 Zerphy, J, 79, E, June 10, dia. c.
4255 Zimmerman, B, 148, B, July 29, dia.
6573 Zane, Wm, 19, K, Aug 23, i. s.
6818 Zerl, S, 103, F, Aug 25, scs.
11327 Zane, M, 118, E, Oct 23, scs.

VIEW OF THE HUTS

Occupied by a few of the more fortunate Prisoners.

"The common shelter was, however, constructed with blankets, old shirts, &c.; while a great number had no shelter at all, or burrowed, for the want of one, in the ground."   Page 76.

VIEW OF THE BAKERY,

Which was one story high, and contained two rooms, one of which communicated with two ovens; these two ovens, fourteen feet in length by seven feet in width, supplied the prisoners with all the bread they obtained.

RHODE ISLAND.

3266 Austin, J A,§ 1 cav, H, July 13, dia.
6231 Allen, Chas, 1 cav, D, Aug 21, dia. c.

1744 Bonley, Wm, 1 cav, M, June 8, dia. c.
1958 Bidmead, Jas, 1 cav, G, June 14, dys.
2521 Blake, J F, 1 cav, M, June 26, dia.
3647 Bürk, Jas, 1, C, July 20, dys.
4261 Bether, J, 2, C, July 29, scs.
4576 Baine, H, 5, A, Aug 2, dia. c.

1339 Carpenter, P, 1 cav, E, May 24, ana.
1413 Carson, B F, 1 cav, K, May 27, dys.
3810 Carnahan, Jas, bat, July 23, dys.
7966 Colvin, E O,‡ 5 art, A, Sept 6, scs.
12832 Collins, J H, 1 cav, A, April 16, dia. c.

651 Delanah, E B,§ 1 cav, G, April 20, dia.
1217 Dix, Geo, 1 cav, M, May 19, pna.
1435 Dickinson, Jacob,§ 1 cav, K, May 28, dia.
3086 Dearborn, G, 1 cav, July 8, r. f.
4742 Durden, Robert, 1 cav, F, Aug 5, scs.
4927 Doolittle, G S, 2 art, B, Aug 6, dia.
5670 Doyle, Jas, 5 art, A, Aug 14, dia.

827 Eustace, Geo C, 1 cav, M, May 1, dia.
10203 Eaton, A, 5 art, A, Oct 1, scs.

939 Freelove, H, 1 cav, H, May 7, dia.
4533 Farrell, Jas F, 1 art, A, Aug 2, dia.
4672 Fay, John, 2, G, Aug 4, ts. t.
7356 Fey, A, 5 art, A, Aug 31, scs.

1366 Goudy, John, 5 art, A, June 12, dia. c.
4866 Gallagher, C, 5, A, Aug 6, dys.
5561 Garvey, Wm, 5 art, A, Aug 13, ana.
8308 Green, R, 2, B, Sept 10, dia. c.
9978 Green, Daniel, 2, H, Sept 29, dia.,

1075 Henry, T, 1 cav, F, May 13, dia.
2656 Healy, A, 1 cav, D, June 29, ts. f.
2746 Hunt, C W, 1 cav, A, July 1, dia.
3904 Harmpstead, J, 5 art, F, July 24, scs.
7032 Hooker, A, 1 cav, G, Aug 27, dia.
11843 Hawkins, D F, 5, A, Nov 5, wds.
12016 Hanley, T, 5 art, A, Nov 15, scs.

1962 Ide, S R, 1 cav, H, June 14, dys.

3049 Johnson, A G, 5 art, A, July 8, dia.

2968 Kettell, Jas, 1 cav, B, July 6, dia.
3096 Kiney, J, 2, B, July 10, dys. c.

4215 Lewis, Edward, 5 art, A, July 29, dys.
5827 Littlebridge, W H,‡ 5 art, A, Aug 16, dia
6798 Lee, Cornelius, 5 art, A, Aug 25, dia.
7849 Leach, L D, 1 cav, F, Sept 5, dia.
11688 Livingston, J'n, mus, 5 art, A, Oct 31, dia

1750 Miner, S, 1 cav, D, June 9, dia. c.
7393 McKay, Thos, 2, F, Aug 31, dia.
8306 McKenna, J, 3 art, Sept 10, dia.

3192 Northorp, E, 1 cav, H, July 12, dia
7904 Navoo, G, 5, K, Sept 5, dia.

607 Peterson, John, 1, D, April 18, dys.

7219 Ruthburn, J, 1 cav, A, Aug 29, des.

2382 Sweet, M, 1 cav, D, June 23, dia.
2563 Spink, J, 1 cav, H, June 27, dia.
2859 Slocum, Geo T, 2d lt, 1 cav, A, July 4, ts. f.
4153 Smith, P, 1 cav, A, July 28, dia.
4949 Stalord, J, 1 bat, A, Aug 7, scs.
6186 Sisson, Charles T, 5 art, A, Aug 19, dys.
6187 Seymour, H, 5 art, A, Aug 19, dia.
6351 Sullivan, J, 5 art, A, Aug 21, dia. c.
7129 Sander, Charles, 5 art, A, Aug 28, ana.

7425 Slocum, C A,‡ 5 art, A, Aug 31, ana.

3075 Turner, Charles, 7, E, July 9, dia.
8522 Thomas, J, 5, Sept 12, scs.

19 Wright, Moses, 2 cav, A, March 7, r. f.
1788 West, H, 1, A, June 10, dia. c.
3173 Wallace, Wm, 5 art, A, July 11, dia. c.
5908 Wood, J B, 5, A, Aug 16, dia.
6222 West, J, 2 cav, A, Aug 21, dia. c.
6766 Wayne, S, 1 cav, A, Aug 25, dia.
7831 Wilson, J, 5, A, Sept 4, ana.
9273 Witham, B, 1 light art, Sept 19, ana.

TENNESSEE.

883 Allen, James W, 11, B, May 4, dia. c.
987 Amos, F G, 2, C, May 10, dia.
2213 Allison, B F, 13 cav, D, June 22, dia. c.
2631 Andrewson, Joseph, 2, C, June 29, dia.
3167 Anderson, S, 8 cav, B, July 11, dia.
3194 Aber, A, 7 cav, A, July 12, dia.
3334 Anglon, Wm, 7 cav, A, July 15, dia.
4004 Athens, J H, 2 east, C, July 26, ana.
6411 Aikin, George W,‡ 7, K, Aug 22, scs.
6474 Ashby, J F, 7 cav, B, Aug 22, ts. f.
6541 Antoine, P, 13 cav, H, Aug 23, dys. c.
7572 Aspray, Wm,§ 13, B, Sept 2, dia.
7907 Anderson, C S,§ 10, D, Sept 5, dys.
9151 Achley, A, 3, A, Sept 18, scs.
9910 Atkins, L, 2, D, Sept 28, scs.
1895 Arrowood, James, 8 cav, June 13, dia.
8493 Alexander, P S, 13 cav, D, Sept 11, dia.
12710 Allen, G W, 7, I, Feb 28, pls.

539 Boling, Wm, 11, E, April 14, dia.
585 Beason, Benjamin, 2, E, April 17, pna.
663 Bond, Jas J T, 2, F, April 21, dia.
695 Baker, T K, 5 cav, April 23, dys. c.
705 Batey, W H, 2, B, April 24, dys. c.
772 Burton, Wm, 1 art, A, April 28, dia. c.
808 Brannin, Ellis, 2, F, April 30, dia. c.
845 Browden, H V, 2, K, May 1, dia.
859 Byerly, W H, 1, A, May 3, dia.
920 Brewer, M, 2, E, May 6, dia.
1053 Boyden, A L, 2, B, May 13, dia.
1137 Beatty, Thomas, 2, B, May 16, dia.
1242 Bryant, James A, 8, I, May 20, pna.
1244 Barnard, W H, 2, A, May 20, dia.
1248 Boyd, A D,‡ 2, F, May 20, dia. c.
1527 Butler, J J,§ 7, B, May 31, dys.
1538 Bradshaw, A G, 2, B, June 1, dia.
1610 Browning, J, 2, F, June 4, dia. c.
1625 Brown, J, 13 cav, E, June 5, dia.
1847 Branon, Wm, 2, F, June 11, ana.
1876 Birket, W D,‡ 7, June 12, dia.
1883 Burchfield, W R, 2, June 12, dia. c.
1976 Berger, W, 2, B, June 15, dia. c.
2037 Berger, W M, 2, June 15, dia.
2555 Boutwright, A,§ 7, A, June 27, dia.
2744 Brewer, W T, 7 cav, D, July 1, dia.
2939 Bibbs, Alexander, 7 cav, D, July 6, dia. a.
2983 Bright, John, 8, G, July 7, dys.
3176 Blalock, H, 2, D, July 11, abs.
3198 Brown, J B,§ 2, F, July 12, ana.
6 Brandon, C, 4, D, April 4, s. p.
16 Burke, John, 2, D, April 12, s. p.
52 Brummell, A D, 2, H, June 3, s. p.
57 Broits, S, 4, F, June 20, s. p.
58 Beeler, Daniel, 5, D, June 25, s. p.
3328 Barton, F F, 13 cav, A, July 14, dia. c.
3330 Bynom, J W, 13 cav, C, July 14, dia. c.
3414 Brennan, James, 2, I, July 16, dia.
3636 Burris, D B, 13, B, July 20, ana.
3643 Brannan, J, 2, A, July 20, dia. c.
3726 Billings, W, 6, I, July 21, dia.
3786 Bowman, J, 7 cav, C, July 22, dia. c.
3934 Boles, H, 13, C, July 25, dia.
4108 Boyd, W H, 9 cav, C, July 27, dia.
4221 Barnes, A C, 15, H, July 29, wds.

4770 Bryant, Wm, 2, D, Aug 5, dia.
5017 Butler, W W, 7 cav, B, Aug 8, ana.
4371 Bradfield, E L, 7 cav, C, July 31, ana.
5049 Brummetti, B, 11 cav, C, Aug 8, scs.
5277 Barnhart, D F, 7 cav, B, Aug 11, dia.
5294 Baker, Isaac, 13, B, Aug 11, dys.
5313 Blackwood, G W, 11, B, Aug 11, pls.
5533 Boles, G W, 13 cav, B, Aug 13, scs.
5617 Baker, M A, 13 cav, E, Aug 14, dys. c.
6003 Boles, W G, 13 cav, B, Aug 17, ana.
6142 Bayles, K, 2, C, Aug 19, dys.
6194 Burnett, S H, 6, H, Aug 19, ana.
6287 Butler, W J, 7, B, Aug 20, dia. c.
6569 Barnes, Wm, 7 cav, M, Aug 23, i. s.
6672 Bishop, W, 7 cav, H, Aug 23, ts. f.
7430 Brewer, J, 2, D, Aug 31, gae.
7664 Bales, Henry, 2, K, Sept 2, dia.
7943 Boyer, D, 15, D, Sept 5, scs.
8222 Bird, S H, 13 cav, D, Sept 8, ana.
8998 Blackner, Thomas, 7 cav, L, Sept 17, ana
9023 Bill, F, 5, I, Sept 17, dia.
9079 Boyle, R C, 7 cav, I, Sept 17, scs.
9149 Bean, C S, 3 cav, E, Sept 18, scs.
9478 Bowlen, C F, 13, B, Sept 21, scs.
9543 Bromley, H,§ 7, Sept 23, scs.
4888 Brannon, L, 2, A, Aug 6, scs.
10098 Byerly, James, 1, e c, A, Sept 30, scs.
10452 Bible, W, 8, D, Oct 7, dia.
10617 Blackney, B, 7, E, Oct 10, dia. c.
10826 Bartholomew, John, 7 cav, H, Oct 13, scs
11015 Bosworth, W H, 7 cav, E, Oct 16, scs.
11298 Brogan, John,‡ 2, C, Oct 22, dia.
11372 Brown, J B,‡ 2, K, Oct 23, scs.
12171 Bradford, H A, 7, E, Oct 26, scs.
12565 Brown, J W, 13, B, Jan 31, scs.
12613 Barnhart, G, 7, C, Feb 8, dia. c.
12662 Barnes, F B, 7 cav, D, Feb 16, dia. c.
462 Bell, E S, 4, C, April 9, dia. c.
4782 Barnes, G, 10, D, Aug 5, con.

189 Cardwell, W C, 6, C, March 27, dia.
216 Conaster, Philip, 2, D, March 28, dys. c.
230 Chimney, Jesse,§ 2, A, March 29, dia. a.
375 Colwell, J H, 2, C, April 5, dia. c.
436 Croswell, Samuel, 2, K, April 8, dia. c.
459 Childers, J M, 2, D, April 9, dia.
482 Clark, Lewis, 2 cav, B, April 9, dia. a.
615 Covington, A, 2, K, April 18, dia.
717 Chitwood, J H, 2, G, April 24, dia.
811 Carden, Robert, 2, C, April 30, dia. c.
840 Cardwell, W C, 6, G, May 2, dia.
1050 Cooper, C, 2, B, May 12, dia.
1213 Clark, Alexander, 2, C, May 19, ana.
1425 Cross, M C, 2, F, May 28, dia.
1574 Childers, J, 13, A, June 3, rua.
1636 Clemens, J D, 7 cav, D, June 5, dia. c
1751 Campbell, W, 2, A, June 9, dys. a.
1839 Carden, A K, 7 cav, E, June 11, dia. c
2031 Covington, J B, 2, K, June 15, dia.
2062 Carwin, James, 1, June 16, dia.
2071 Crow, J,§ 2, F, June 16, scs.
2289 Crawford, A, 13 cav, B, June 21, dia.
2466 Childers, Thos L, 2, G, June 25, con.
2632 Cooper, E, 1, A, June 20, ana.

****

2789 Cook, W P, 2 e, A, July 1, dia.
2858 Cooper, G W, 7, B, July 4, dia.
2886 Collins, W, 2, H, July 4, scs.
2940 Carter, H C, 13 cav, E, July 6, dia. c.
3687 Cross, N, 2, H, July 21, dia. c.
3983 Corwine, J, East Tenn, G, July 26, dia.
4691 Cornish, A, 13 cav, C, Aug 4, ana.
5298 Chase, A P, 7 cav, I, Aug 11, scs.
5829 Collins, R, 7 cav, K, Aug 16, mas,
5895 Clyne, E T,§ 11 cav, E, Aug 16, dys.
6810 Crews, G, 7 cav, B, Aug 20, dia.
7523 Childers, E, 13, E, Sept 1, scs.
7525 Clark, James, 13, A, Sept 1, ana.
7601 Cunise, E, 7 cav, I, Sept 2, dia.
7702 Childers, W E, 7 cav, E, Sept 3, dia.
7857 Cothrain, S, 13, E, Sept 5, gae.
7871 Camp, W W, 7, K, Sept 5, dys.
7880 Cotterell, G W, 7, C, Sept 5, dia.
8219 Creesy, S P, 7 cav, K, Sept 8, ana.
9021 Crum, A, 4, F, Sept 17, dia.
9208 Cooley, J, 7 cav, L, Sept 18, ana.
9698 Chadwick, M, 16, I, Sept 24, scs.
10137 Cole, Geo M,§ 9, C, Oct 1, scs.
10268 Clay, H, 13, H, Oct 3, dia.
10403 Cleaver, W, 7, G, Oct 6, dys.
10654 Churchill, E, 13, A, Oct 11, scs.
11239 Cheek, R, 6 cav, D, Oct 20, scs.
11312 Carter, W B, 11, E, Oct 22, scs.
12643 Camway, H, 6, K, Feb 13, rhm.

302 Dodd, Benjamin, 2, D, April 1, dia. c.
399 Doss, J W, 2, C, April 6, dia. c.
485 Dudley, Samuel, 1 cav, A, April 9, dys.
645 Dutrom, Irdell, 2, G, April 20, dys. c.
759 Duncan, G W,‡ 2, B, April 27, dia. c.
856 Doak, I V, 2, F, May 3, dia.
894 Davis, Leroy, 7, K, May 5, pna.
1016 Diggs, J G, 2, C, May 9, dys.
43 Dykes, Pleasant, 2, K, May 11, s. p.
1182 Duff, I W, 16, B, May 18, dia.
1581 Davis, J W, 2, C, June 3, dia. c.
2266 Dabney, B, 1, A, June 20, dia. c.
2366 Daniel, Suttrell, 2, K, June 23, dys.
2449 Diggs, John G, 2 east, C, June 25, dia. c.
3513 Deer, H, 7, M, July 18, scs.
3667 Davis, J, 3, A, July 20, scs.
5398 Disney, E W,§ 11 cav, C, Aug 12, scs.
6261 Dunn, R, 19, I, Aug 20, scs.
6991 Dyn, Wm, 7 cav, K, Aug 27, dia.
4821 Draan, R H, 10, I, Aug 5, scs.
8423 Davis, Levi, 7 cav, K, Sept 11, scs.
7219 Davis, James, 7, C, Aug 30, des.
7608 Diel, S F,§ 7 cav, B, Sept 2, dia.
8329 Dyer, W, 7 cav, K, Sept 10, dys.
9373 Dodd, Chas, citizen, Dec Co, Sept 20, scs.
9453 Dort, R, 7, G, Sept 21, dia.
9701 Duke, Wm, 7, E, Sept 25, dia.
10014 Dyer, H, 4 cav, A, Sept 29, dia.
10244 Davis, Wm, 7, D, Oct 3, scs.
12119 Dodd, J A, 1 cav, M, Nov 22, scs.
12379 Dykes, L, 2, K, Jan 2, scs.
12498 Delf, E, 8, C, Jan 21, dia.
12794 Doty, I, citizen, Jan 18, dia.

293 Edwards, I, 5, B, April 1, dia. c.
360 Everitt, A T, 2, A, April 2, dia.
510 Evans, S D, 8, C, April 12, dia. c.
557 Everitte, John, 2, G, April 14, dia.
848 Evans, W,§ 7, C, May 3, pna.
873 Edwards, C S, 5, B, May 4, i. f.
970 Evans, J M, 7, M, May 9, pna.
979 Etler, Valentine, 11, D, May 9, dia.
1886 Emmert, J C,§ 4, June 13, ana.
55 Eddes, James C, 2, E, June 16, s. p.
3761 Ellison, Isaac, 2 east, F, July 22, scs.
4785 Ellis, C O, 13 cav, C, Aug 5, scs.
5904 Ethridge, Wm, 13, B, Aug 16, dia.
7402 Elder, P, 2, F, Aug 31, scs.
9075 Escue, H,‡ 6 cav, Sept 17, dia.
10560 Elliott, Wm, 4, A, Oct 9, dia. c.
10985 Easton, J, 13 cav, B, Oct 16, scs.
11639 Ellington, J, 13 cav, B, Oct 30, scs.

353 Fairchilds, Jesse, 2, B, April 2, dia.
683 Fryer, W L,§ 2, H, April 23, dia.
697 Fagen, Parker, 8, I, April 23, dia.
1445 Fannon, G H, Tenn St Gd, April 28, ana
2408 Fisher, C N, 2, K, June 24, cah.
2506 Francisco, R, 7 cav, B, June 26, dia.
62 Friar, John, 2, n, July 9, s. p.
2835 Fox, E, Tenn State Guard, July 3, dia. c.
5320 Firestone, ——, 1 cav, M, Aug 11, i. f.
5997 Frazier, John, 8, H, Aug 17, dia. c.
6299 Flowers, W P,§ 13 cav, B, Aug 20, dia. c.
7244 Franks, W W, 2, B, Aug 29, des.
7782 Fields, R G, 1, Sept 4, dia.
8555 Finch, A, 7 cav, L, Sept 12, scs.
10133 Finch, J B, 7, B, Oct 1, scs.
12502 Franshier, J D, 8, K, Jan 21, des.
3006 Fowler, I, 4, A, July 7, dia. a.
3733 Finch, H, 7 cav, I, July 21, dia.

578 Goddard, John, 2, B, April 16, dia.
1831 German, P, 2, C, June 11, dia.
2043 Gorman, James, 6, June 15, dia.
2571 Graham, J D, 7 cav, D, June 27, dia. c.
2891 Gooding, James, 2, D, July 4, dia.
3 Guild, James, 11, B, March 18, s. p.
15 Graves, Henry, 2, E, April 11, s. p.
59 Gray, John W, 2, I, June 29, s. p.
3291 Gorman, F, 6, B, July 14, scs.
3357 Grays, L, 12, F, July 15, scs.
9238 Gamon, I A, 7 cav, A, Sept 19, scs.
3620 Grundee, Alex, 4, D, July 20, dys.
3719 Grier, J O,‡ 7, B, July 21, dia. c.
3887 Gilson, C G, 1, B, July 24, dia. c.
4531 Grevett, S P, 7 cav, C, Aug 1, brs.
5182 Given, I A, 9, I, Aug 9, dia.
5146 Griswell, Thos J, 7 cav, H, Aug 9, dia.
5374 Garrett, M T, 7 cav, L, Aug 11, dia.
5388 Green, S G, 7 cav, I, Aug 12, dia.
6376 Grims, Wm, 2, A, Aug 21, dia. c.
6490 Graves, J C, 2, E, Aug 21, dys.
6498 Grisson, C, 8, B, Aug 22, dia. c.
7221 Green, J C, 7, I, Aug 29, scs.
7454 Gunter, R C,§ 13, A, Sept 1, dys. c.
7908 Griswold, W H, 7 cav, K, Sept 5, dia.
8012 Gibbs, J A, 7 cav, L, Sept 6, dia. c.
8093 Griffin, W A, 2 cav, C, Sept 7, scs.
8946 Gill, G W, 1 cav, L, Sept 16, scs.
9271 Gaff, R, 1 cav, C, Sept 19, ana.
9875 Gibson, James, 13 cav, Sept 27, scs.
10334 Gardner, H, 14 cav, C, Oct 4, dia.
10590 Garrison, A,‡ 7, E, Oct 10, scs.
11063 Galbraith, G W, 7 cav, E, Oct 17, scs.
11632 Grier, J, 7, B, Oct 28, scs.
11925 Giles, M C, 7, I, Nov 8, scs.
12402 Ganon, T, 4 cav, I, Jan 6, scs.
12438 Gilbert, Wm, 7 cav, C, Jan 12, scs.
12464 Golden, J H, 7 cav, C, Jan 18, scs.
1000 Grey, Thomas, 11, E, May 19, dia.
433 Graves, James, 2, E, April 8, pna.

58 Hampton, I A, 8, D, March 16, pna.
85 Heniger, Peter, 11, I, March 21, dia.
163 Hoover, Samuel, 2, B, March 26, dia.
316 Huff, Benjamin, 2, K, April 2, dia. c.
357 Huckleby, Thomas, 2, C, April 2, dia.
467 Hickson, George, 11, E, April 9, pna.
616 Hurd, William, 2, B, April 18, dia.
660 Head, Daniel, 12 cav, B, April 21, dia.
682 Hixton, John, 2, F, April 23, dys. c.
714 Henderson, Robert, 2, B, April 24, brs
805 Hayes, J, 7, E, April 29, dia. c
844 Hughes, E, 2, I, May 2, dia. c.
958 Hickley, Thomas, 2, K, May 8, dys.
1036 Hickson, Henry, 2, I, May 12, dys.
1124 Hall, John, 2, B, May 15, ana.
1159 Heatherby, John, 1, C, May 19, ana.
1491 Hickson, Daniel, 2, F, May 31, dia. c
1551 Hopkins, A, 1 art, A, June 2, dia. c.
1554 Hunt, J, 2, B, June 2, des.
1766 Harris, Wm, 8, I, June 9, dia. c.
1774 Hodges, I M, 2, F, June 9, dia. c.
1846 Harman, A B, 4, A, June 11, des.

1925 Hendson, J S, 2, K, June 14, dia. c.
1950 Hickerman, T, 9 cav, B, June 14, dia.
2276 Hilton, A F,§ 2, H, June 20, dia. a.
2375 Hugely, C W, 13 cav, D, June 23, dys. a.
2491 Hawa, E A, 2, B, June 26, dia. a.
2642 Hale, R H, 3, F, June 29, rua.
2851 Hall, B A, 2, A, July 4, ts. f.
2949 Hudson, J A, 8 cav, F, July 9, dia.
3012 Haines, J A, 13, E, July 7, dia.
4855 Hall, J J, 13 cav, E, Aug 6, dia. c.
4836 Hermsen, Wm, 13 cav, B, Aug 6, dia. c.
4805 Haywood, J G, 7, I, Aug 5, dia.
3098 Hawkins, S D, 3, E, July 10, dia.
3121 Hodgen, ——, 7, K, July 10, dia. c.
8248 Hopson, Thomas, 3 cav, E, July 13, dia.
3421 Howard, A, 2, F, July 16, dys.
3672 Heckman, Wm,‡ 2 east, G, July 20, dys.
3712 Henderson, J R, 6, B, July 21, dia. c.
3729 Hendlay, J, 9, A, July 21, dia. c.
3807 Hayes, J C, 7 cav, C, July 22, ana.
4535 Henry, Wm, 7, C, Aug 1, i. f.
5278 Hudson, John, 55, I, Aug 11, dia.
5326 Harvey, Morgan, 2, F, Aug 11, scs.
5535 Hensley, James M, 3, E, Aug 13, scs.
5604 Hicks, M, 2, I, Aug 14, dia.
5607 Hasborough, J H, 13 cav, E, Aug 14, scs.
6393 Haines, G, 13 cav, A, Aug 21, dys.
6553 Hughes, Wm, 2, F, Aug 23, dia.
6581 Hibbrath, M H, 7 cav, I, Aug 23, i. s.
6648 Harris, A G, 5, E, Aug 23, ana.
6681 Horton, W C, 7 cav, H, Aug 24, dia.
7808 Hinson, John, 7 cav, H, Sept 4, dys.
8094 Hallford, J A, 13, A, Sept 7, scs.
8115 Hicks, E, 9, F, Sept 7, scs.
8486 Hale, Ira, 7 cav, C, Sept 11, scs.
8529 Hayewood, A J,§ 7, I, Sept 12, scs.
9044 Henderson, A G, 13, C, Sept 17, dia. c
9788 Hodges, John, 13, E, Sept 26, dia. c.
9797 Herbs, D, 1 cav, D, Sept 26, scs
9805 Haney, H, 7 cav, A, Sept 26, scs.
9892 Hanks, A,§ 11, D, Sept 27, dys.
10003 Hall, W R, 2, D, Sept 29, scs.
10145 Halliwarke, ——, 7, E, Oct 10, scs.
10329 Hooks, John L, 7 cav, A, Oct 4, dia.
10810 Holler, W, 6 cav, E, Oct 12, scs.
10956 Holloway, H B, 2, G, Oct 14, scs.
11377 Herman, H, 4, K, Oct 23, scs.
11791 Hickman, D, 2, I, Nov 4, scs.
11801 Howard, ——, 16, Nov 4, scs.
11861 Higgs, L, 7, D, Nov 6, scs.
12028 Hazzle, Wm, 7, C, Nov 13, scs.
12146 Hall, J M, 1, A, Nov 24, scs.
12212 Hanley, T, 2, E, Dec 2, scs.
12423 Hoag, B F, 7, E, Jan 9, scs.
12655 Huffaker, J, 2, K, Feb 14, scs.
12693 Hanbuck, J, 7, K, Feb 22, rhm.

1941 Israel, S, 21, B, June 14, ana.
9515 Irwin, P P, 49, F, Sept 22, dia.

52 Jones, Rufus, 2, I, March 16, dys.
291 Jones, Warren T, 11, C, April 1, dia.
358 Jeffers, J, 2, C, April 2, dia.
491 Jones, J E, 2, G, April 11, dia.
584 Jack, Benjamin S, 2, B, April 17, dys
668 Jones, H D, 4, F, April 22, dia.
1181 Johnson, E A,§ 2, A, May 18, ana.
1227 Johnson, S L, 2, A, May 19, dia.
1536 Jones, John J, 13 cav, C, June 1, dia.
3805 Jones, H, 2, H, July 22, scs.
3980 Johnson, A, 10, C, July 26, dia. c.
4571 Jones, D, 6, C, Aug 2, ana.
5517 Johnson, C F, 7, K, Aug 13, dia.
5921 Jones, J M, 2, K, Aug 17, dia. c.
7447 Jones, Albert,§ 13 cav, B, Sept 1, dys
8013 Joiner, J M, 7 cav, B, Sept 6, ts. f.
8503 Jones, J, 13 cav, B, Sept 12, scs.
8560 Johnson, J,‡ 3 east, Sept 12, scs.
8764 Johnson, C M, K, Sept 14, scs.
8552 Jones, D, 11, E, Sept 23, scs.
9618 Jones, Wm T,‡ 11 cav, Sept 23, dia.
10479 Johnson, M, 11 cav, G, Oct 7, scs.

12319 Johnson, E W, 7 cav, C, Dec 21, scs.
12702 Johnson, W, 13, D, Feb 26, scs.

32 Kirby, James, M, March 11, pna.
434 Kilpatrick, R, 2, E, April 8, dia. c.
595 Kelsey, John,§ 2, A, April 17. dys. c.
600 Kentzler, Henry, 2, G, April 17, dys. a
35 King, James T, 2, D, April 25, s. p.
3702 Kirk, B J, 7 cav, B, July 21, dia. c.
3749 Keene, Hoza, 7 cav, C, July 22, dys.
7367 Keen, J S, 7 cav, C, Aug 31, dia.
7641 Kirk, J P, 3, D, Sept 2, dia.
8183 Kingsley, S, 2, D, Sept 8, dys.
8714 Kenser, Joseph, 2 cav, Sept 14, scs.
9407 Kelley, J W,§ 2, E, Sept 21, dia.
11241 Kissinger, F, 7, I, Oct 21.
12570 Kidwell, J, 4, C, Feb 2, scs.
1157 Kuner, E B, 3, E, May 16, dia.

627 Long, Jonathan, 2, H, April 19, ts. f.
688 Lane, L E, 2, I, April 23, pna.
713 Lofty, R J, 2, I, April 24, dia.
1223 Lovette, W T, 13 cav, A, May 19, rua.
1252 Langley, E G, 11, B, May 21, scs.
1352 Long, C C, 2, C, May 25, ana.
1597 Long, John, 2, C, June 3, dia. c.
2193 Looper, E, 2, D, June 19, dia. a.
8 Lanen, Thomas, 2, H, April 5, s. p.
45 Lingo, James, 2, C, May 17, s. p.
53 Levi, J N, 2, I, June 3, s. p.
3696 Lamphey, J, 7 cav, C, July 21, dia.
3760 Little, E D, 7, A, July 22, scs.
3830 Lemmar, J E,§ 13 cav, A, July 23, dia.
4114 Lawrence, J C, 13 cav, I, July 28, dia. a
4292 Lewis, R, 1 bat, B, July 30, dys.
4575 Long, John, 13, H, Aug 2, scs.
8640 Lawson, M, 8, H, Sept 13, dia. c.
8926 Lawson, H G, 8, I, Sept 14, scs.
9594 Lester, James, 7 cav, M, Sept 23, dia.
9641 Lewis, J, 3, G, Sept 24, dia. c.
11827 Laprint, J, 11, K, Nov 5, scs.
1352 Long, C C, 2, C, May 25, ana.
11979 Leonard, J, 7, C, Nov 12, dia.

388 McCune, Robert, 2, E, April 5, dia. c.
405 Meyers, W J, 12, F, April 6, i. f.
558 Miller, W H, 2, F, April 15, dia.
562 Macklin, John, 2, H, April 15, dia.
583 Malcolm, S A, 4, B, April 16, dia.
722 Maines, Wm, 1, D, April 27, dia. c.
801 McCart, Wm, 2, B, April 29, dia. c.
845 McDowell, G I, 2, D, April 26, dia.
1051 Mynck, Eli, 2, A, May 12, dia.
1176 May, W, 10, C, May 16, dia.
1289 Meyers, D, 2, H, May 22, dia.
1402 Martin, F A, 2, A, May 27, dia.
1451 McLane, H C, 2 east, I, May 29, dia. c.
1561 Massie, Eli, 2, C, June 1, dia. c.
1668 Myers, John,‡ 2, H, June 6, dia. c.
1703 Moulden, Wm, 2, A, June 7, scs.
1723 Mecart, J, 2, B, June 8, rhm.
1960 McDonald, L M,§ 2, G, June 14, pna
2050 Meyers, Wm,§ 2, H, June 16, dia. c.
2171 Matheny, D C, 7, D, June 19, ana.
2224 Melterberger, M, 2, G, June 20, dia. a.
2277 Morris, J,‡ 2 cav, E, June 20, dia. c.
2475 Mitchiner, H, 13, H, June 25, ts. f.
2500 Mackin, W, 7 cav, K, June 26, r. f.
2516 Moss, J, 2, A, June 26, dia. c.
3124 McAllister, W H, 4 cav, H, July 10, dia. a
24 Mayes, William, 2, E, April 15, s. p.
38 Mee, Thomas, 2, F, April 29, s. p.
46 Mergen, H S, 2, G, May 18, s. p.
3243 McGee, Wm, 7 cav, B, July 3, scs.
3642 Maynard, W J, 13, A, July 20, dys.
4567 Miller, J W, 8 cav, G, Aug 2, dia.
4523 McLean, A G, 3, C, Aug 1, scs.
3897 McCoy, W C, 2, G, July 24, dia. c.
4236 McDover, H, 2, C, July 29, dia. c.
4237 Montgomery, Wm, 4, C, July 29, dia.
4751 McCrum, M, 7 cav, C, Aug 5, scs.
4905 Mussurgo, M, 9 cav, H, Aug 6, brs.

4496 Mulanox, A C,‡ 2, B, Aug 1, scs.
5608 Myers, A, 13 cav, C, Aug 8, dia.
5064 Miles, Samuel, 2, A, Aug 8, cah.
5282 Morris, H S, 13 cav, C, Aug 11, dia.
5594 Mitchell, Jas, 7 cav, K, Aug 14, dia.
5782 Miflin, Wm, 13, B, Aug 15, dia.
6555 Maddro, Jas, 2, C, Aug 23, scs.
7435 Mefford, J,‡ 8 cav, C, Sept 1, dia.
7574 Moore, Jas, 13, Sept 2, dia.
7764 McGee, A 13, B, Sept 4, dia.
8059 Mayher, J W, 2, E, Sept 7, dia.
8174 Martin, J S, 7 cav, H, Sept 8, td. f.
8954 Mackey, S, 7, D, Sept 16, dia. c. ,
9140 McKeese, Samuel, 8 cav, G. Sept 17, dia. c.
9542 McDonald, W, 7, D, Sept 23, dia.
9559 Montgomery, C F, 1 cav, L, Sept 29, dys.
9783 Metheney, V V, 13 cav, A, Sept 26, scs.
9861 Macart, R, 2, B, Sept 27, scs.
10795 Martin, S, 7 cav, G, Oct 12, scs.
10976 Meare, J H, 7 cav, I, Oct 15, ts. f.
11532 Mays, L, 9 cav, A, Oct 26, scs.
11544 McCaslin, M C, 7, D, Oct 27, scs.
11649 Myracle, C, 7, C, Oct 30, scs.
11667 Morris, Wm, 7 cav, I, Oct 30, dia.
11845 Moore, Wm P, 11, D, Nov 5, scs.
12277 McNealy, W, 7 cav, C, Dec 3, scs.
12338 Moore, T, 7 cav, I, Dec 26, scs.

7497 Norton, J, 10, K, Sept 1, scs.
160 Newman, Jesse, 2, K, March 25, ts. f.
828 Norris, Thomas, 2, D, May 1, dys.
1237 Norman, Jas,‡ 13 cav, C, May 20, rua.
3191 Newport, H, 11 cav, E, July 12, scs.
50 Nicely, A, 8, H, June 2, s. p.
6262 Nichols, W T, 7 cav, A, Aug 20, i. s.
7818 Newman, T A,§ 4, Sept 4, dia.
9068 Norwood, Wm, 7 cav, I, Sept 17, scs.
9447 Norris, P W, 7 cav, B, Sept 21, dia.
9640 Needham, F, 13, C, Sept 24, dia. c.
9996 Neighbour, M, 7, E, Sept 29, scs.
10223 Norris, W, 2, D, Oct 2, dia.
12642 Neighbors, A, 7, B, Feb 13, rhm.

4689 Odorn, John,§ 8, B, Aug 4, scs.
1753 Owen, A, 2, D, June 9, dia. c.
10743 Oliver, L, 13, C, Oct 11, dia.
923 Ollenger, John, 2, I, May 6, dys.
2697 Overton, J S, 2, C, June 30, pna.

689 Palmer, Wm, 2, K, April 23, brs.
806 Perkins, G W,§ 7, M, April 29, dys.
1141 Penix, John, 5, G, May 16, i. f.
1363 Perry, Jas, 6 cav, L, May 25, dia. c.
1517 Proffett, Jas, 13, C, May 31, dia. c.
1638 Powers, H,§ 7 cav, A, June 5, dia.
2146 Parder, E H, 11, K, June 18, dia. c.
2748 Perry, Thomas, 13, B, July 1, dys.
2767 Pursly, W B,§ 13 cav, C, July 2, dia.
3170 Pankey, A J, 13, B, July 11, dia.
506 Pilot, Joseph, 2, K, April 12, dia. c.
4592 Piscall, J B, 13, B, Aug 3, dia.
4572 Powell, A N,§ 7, K, Aug 2, dia.
8605 Pavies, S, 7 cav, C, Sept 12, scs.
1 Polivar, Martin, 2, E, March 12, s. p.
10 Phillips, N, 2, H, April 5, s. p.
32 Parker, Wiley, 3, B, April 25, s. p.
4041 Parmer, E, 7, I, July 26, des.
4380 Palmer, D P, 7 cav, I, July 31, scs.
6190 Parks, R T, 7 cav, I, Aug 19, scs.
6335 Prison, E T, 7, B, Aug 21, ts. f.
6485 Prices, Nelson, 15, B, Aug 22, des.
6600 Phillips, T, 2, G, Aug 23, ana.
7290 Park, Jas, 7 cav, E, Aug 30, des.
9020 Penn, W H, 2, E, Sept 17, dia.
9121 Paddock, D W,‡ 2 cav, I, Sept 17, dia.
9606 Pennington, G W,‡ 11, Sept 23, dia.
10304 Pegram, W, 7, A, Oct 4, scs.
10318 Powers, H M,‡ 7, A, Oct 4, scs.
10364 Poster, N P,§ 13, E, Oct 4, scs.
10655 Pomeroy, John, 7, K, Oct 11, scs.
10852 Pierce, Wm, 8, A, Oct 13, scs.
10907 Parham, F, 7, K, Oct 14, scs.

11285 Pickering, E, 4 cav, G, Oct 22, scs.
11406 Pinkley, J, 7, B, Oct 24, dia.
11501 Powers, J, 7 cav, A, Oct 26, scs.
12644 Powers, R, 7 cav, H, Feb 13, dia. c.
675 Perry, Wesley, 2, I, April 22, brs.
1978 Pope, F, 7 cav. D, June 15, dia. c.

2232 Quiller, T, 7 cav, D, June 20, dia. c

271 Ragan, J, 2, B, March 28 dia. c.
380 Ronden, Wm, 2, A, April 5, dia. c.
382 Reynolds, Henry, 11 cav, L, Apr 5, dia. c
454 Russell, R, 2, K, April 9, dia. c.
4644 Roberts, John, 2, F, Aug 3, dys..
5815 Rouser, A,‡ 1, A, Aug 16, dia.
2519 Reed, John C, 7, A, June 26, dia. c.
523 Robinson, Jas M, 3, A, April 13, dia.
646 Robinson, Isaac, 3, A, April 20, des
951 Robinson, Wm, 1, G, May 8, pna.
1438 Rayle, F, 1 art, C, May 28, dia. c.
1450 Reice, James, 13, C, May 29, dia. c.
1783 Ralph, J F, 13, E, June 10, dia. c.
1924 Reed, G W, 7, A, June 14, dia. c.
2005 Ringoland, W H, 2, D, June 15, ana.
2006 Rabb, G W, 13, A, June 15, dia. c.
2093 Ryan, Wm, 3, K, June 17, dia. c.
2219 Robinson, J C, 2, B, June 20, dia. c.
2314 Roberts, T, 2, H, June 22, brs.
2691 Riley, J M, 6, G, June 30, dia.
2750 Ryan, C P, 2, G, July 1, dia.
17 Riddle, Robert, 2, F, April 12, s. p.
3752 Ritter, John, 3, C, July 22, dia. c.
3755 Robins, T, 2, D, July 22, des.
3772 Reeves, Geo W, 4, F, July 22, des.
4086 Robinson, A, 2, B, July 27, dys.
4254 Renshaw, H G, 7 cav, C, July 29, ts. f
4368 Rainwater, A, 7, F, July 31, dia.
5974 Riter, Henry, 7 cav, E, Aug 17, dia. c
4616 Roberts, Chas, 7, A, Aug 3, scs.
6267 Reeves, A, 11 cav, B, Aug 20, i. s.
6409 Rider, W R,§ 13, C, Aug 22, dia.
6837 Rogers, A G, 7 cav, B, Aug 25, gae.
7082 Russell, J S, 7, E, Aug 28, scs.
7090 Ross, John, 7 cav, B, Aug 28, dia.
7099 Roach, J W, 7 cav, K, Aug 28, ana.
7190 Riter, John, 7, E, Aug 29, scs.
7774 Reynolds, W, 3, G, Sept 4, dia.
7978 Reogan, Geo W, 3, G, Sept 6, dia.
8137 Rose, M L, 2 east, A, Sept 8, dia.
8523 Ramsay, W, A, Sept 12, scs.
9513 Renmeger, Jeff, 13 cav, Sept 22, dys.
10107 Richardson, R, 13 cav, E, Sept 30, scs.
10869 Rushing, W R, 7, B, Oct 13, scs.
11995 Roberts, J G, 7, I, Nov 13, scs.
12101 Risley, J, 6, E, Nov 20, scs.
12753 Robins, W, 7, B, March 12, dia. c.
8968 Reeder, C, sutler, 51, Sept 16, i. f.

298 Stinger, A E, 2, K, April 1, dia. c.
319 Sane, Joseph, 8, B, April 2, des.
374 Sukirk, J F, 2, B, April 5, dia. a.
390 Smith, John, 2 cav, I, April 6, dia. c.
776 Scott, R S, 2, April 28, dia. c.
985 Smithpater, Eli, 11, K, May 9, dia.
1140 Seals, John, 2, D, May 16, dia.
1191 Stepp, Preston, 2, D, May 18, dia. c.
1254 Stafford, Wm, 13 cav, C, May 21, rus.
1278 Sisson, James, 2, E, May 22, dia.
1284 Smith, T A, 2, C, May 22, pna.
1313 Short, L H, 7 cav, C, May 23, dia. c.
1353 Smith, C, 2, B, May 25, dia.
1408 Simpkins, Thomas, 9, A, May 27, dia. c
1475 Smith, Joel, 2, A, May 30, dia.
1481 Stransberry, A, 8, A, May 30, dia.
1488 Sutton, John, 2, I, May 31, dia. c.
1526 Stover, A, 2, C, May 31, ers.
1670 Smith, Wm, 2, D, June 6, dia. c.
2280 Stevens, R, 2, D, June 20, dia. c.
2284 Smith, J, 13 cav, E, June 21, dia. c.
2958 Smith, J B, 20, I, July 6, dia.
11 Stanton, W, 4, E, April 5, s. p.
12 Sutton, Thomas, 2, I, April 8, s. p.

39 Sandusky, G, 2 B, April 29, s. p.
56 Stout, D D, 2, F, June 18, s. p.
3035 Scarbrough, S N, 13, E, July 8, dys.
3276 Shrop, J B, 2 east, E, July 14, dia.
3298 Sells, W, 2 east cav, D, July 14, dys.
3332 Swappola, O B, 4, A, July 15, dia.
3520 Slaver, A, 11 cav, C, July 18, dia.
3865 Smith, John M, 12, M, July 24, dia. c.
4038 Sapper, S, 8, H, July 26, dia.
4170 Snow, W, 7 cav, M, July 28, dia.
5462 Smith, L, 13, L, Aug 13, scs.
5625 Sutton, Andrew, 13 cav, E, Aug 14, dia.
5859 Swan, John, 2, D, Aug 16, mas.
5962 Scott, John, 13, B, Aug 17, dia. c.
6643 Sutton, D, 1 cav, H, Aug 23, scs.
7056 Smith, J, 6, M, Aug 28, gae.
7296 Stewart, J W, 13 cav, B, Aug 30, dys.
7314 Smidney, E, 1 cav, E, Aug 30, dia. c.
7787 Scobey, L A H, 13 cav, B, Sept 2, dys.
7923 Sarret, Jas D, Tenn State Gd, Sept 5, dys.
8637 Smith, J, 3 cav, E, Sept 13, dia.
9192 Smith, T A, 13, C, Sept 18, dia.
9381 Southerland, J, 13 cav, C, Sept 20, scs.
9395 Stewart, E, 13 cav, D, Sept 20, scs.
9555 Smith, W H, 7, B, Sept 23, dia. c.
9719 Swatzell, W L, 8 cav, E, Sept 25, scs.
9803 Stratten, J L, 7 cav, M, Sept 25, scs.
10409 Stafford, S, 13, A, Oct 6, ana.
10454 Shonall, John, 13, C, Oct 7, scs.
11594 Shay, D, 11, E, Oct 28. dia.
12558 Smith, H, 2, E, Jan 30, scs.
12749 Stevens, J F, 2 cav, E, March 8, scs.
12756 Smith, J D, 4, C, March 12, dia. c.
12784 Stewart, R H, 7, C, March 15, pls.
12800 Shook, N A, 7, B, March 19, rhm.
12836 Smith, George, 2, B, April 18, dia. c.
36 Stiner, W H, 2, E, April 28, s. p.
3995 Slover, A W, 2, C, July 26, dia.

211 Tompkins, T B, 2, F, March 28, dys. c.
258 Thompson, W D, 2, F, March 31, dia. c.
793 Thompson, Charles, 2, April 29, dia. c.
932 Thomas, W H, 2, K, May 7, ana.
1657 Tomlin, A, 7 cav, M, June 6, dia. c.
1704 Thauton, S A, 1 art, H, June 7, dia.
2229 Tice, S J, 7, B, June 20, dia. c.
2718 Tipton, W H, 2, I, July 1, dys. c.
3460 Taylor, J, 13, D, July 17, scs.
4122 Tyrrle, John, 1 cav, A, June 28, dys.
4778 Templeton, G W, 2, C, Aug 5, dia.
5646 Tite, W S, 13, C, Aug 14, dia.
7052 Thomas, W H, 7 cav, A, Aug 28, des.
9203 Tolley, D, 8, H, Sept 19, scs.
9375 Terry, D, 9 cav, D, Sept 20, scs.
10780 Thinn, R A, 7 cav, B, Oct 12, dia. c.
12694 Tidwell, T, 13, D, Feb 22, pls.
4825 Tidwell, J W, 13, C, Aug 5, r. f.

2592 Usley, T R, 2, A, June 28, brs.
4518 Undergrate, A, 2, I, Aug 2, scs.

885 Vaugh, I, 8, H, May 5, des.
1203 Vanhorn, J, 2, H, May 19, dia. c.
2915 Varner, T W, 11 cav, E, July 5, scs.
7217 Vanhook, J M, 11 cav, H, July 29, ana.
4530 Vaughry, Frederick, 2, D, Aug 1, rhm.

60 Wolfe, John, 11, E, March 18, dia.
259 Woolen, I, 2, A, March 31, dia. c.
339 Webb, Robert, 2, B, April 2, ts. f.

359 Wuas, M, 2, I, April 2, pna.
501 Watts, C C, 2, A, April 12, dys
570 Ward, Jordan, 2, A, April 15, ana.
810 White, John, 2, B, April 30, dia. c.
902 William, C, 7, B, May 5, phs.
1052 Ward, A, 3, I, May 12, des.
1756 Watts, J W, 7, M, June 9, ts. f.
1794 White, I, 2, D, June 10, dys.
1865 Wallace, L, 2 east, C, June 12, ana.
2057 Ward, C, 2, H, June 16, dia. c.
2066 Watts, T, 2, I, June 16, dia. c.
2132 Wray, Samuel, 13, C, June 18, scs.
2496 Wilson, A, 8 cav, June 26, dys. a.
2764 Winningham, J, 2, B, July 2, dia. c.
2810 Wells, E, 8, H, July 3, scs.
3021 Watkins, J M, 4, I, July 7, scs.
3031 Woodsend, T, 7, K, July 8, scs.
3189 Webb, D, 8 cav, G, July 12, scs.
21 Winchester, J D, 1 cav, E, April 15, s. p
19 Weaver, P, 2, D, April 13, s. p.
4554 West, W F, 2, H, Aug 2, ana.
4869 Ward, John, citizen, Aug 6, dia.
22 Whitby, R B, 2, C, April 15, s. p.
33 Weese, W, 2, I, April 23, s. p.
3297 Weir, I, 1 cav, B, July 14, dia. c.
3304 Wilson, H, 2, B, July 14, scs.
3319 Wolf, A, 10, C, July 14, pna.
3458 Williams, A, 3 cav, E, July 17, scs.
3615 Willis, James, Tenn St Gd, July 20, dys
3714 Webbe, J, 2, B, July 21, des.
3737 Wilson, J, 12, F, July 21, dia.
3982 Wilson, S L, 2, D, July 26, scs.
4033 Walford, W, 7, A, July 26, dia. c.
4704 Wallace, L, 2, C, Aug 4, con.
5267 Wright, J W, 7 cav, B, Aug 10, con.
5572 Withyde, S, 1, A, Aug 14, scs.
6108 Wood, P D, 3, B, Aug 19, dia.
6580 Webb, Robert, 2, B, Aug 23, dia.
6608 Wortell, H H, 7 cav, I, Aug 23, dia. c.
7618 White, R O M, 13, B, Sept 2, dia. c.
8740 Whicks, N, 7, H, Sept 14, dia.
7231 Wood, J, 7, C, Aug 29, ana.
9193 Woolsey, J, 2, F, Sept 18, des.
9479 Walker, John, 13 cav, C, Sept 21, dia.
9658 Williams, C S, 9 cav, B, Sept 24, scs.
9670 Whittle, H W, 7 cav, C, Sept 24, dia.
9730 Webb, T, 6, G, Sept 25, dia.
9929 White, L S, 11 cav, D, Sept 28, dia.
10337 Wiggins, G W, 11 cav, C, Oct 4, dia.
10338 White, H, 7 cav, A, Oct 4, scs.
10739 Warrell, J W, 7 cav, Oct 11, dia.
10605 Webb, W, 3, A, Oct 10, scs.
11386 Worden, J W, 7, E, Oct 24, uls.
12107 Winelug, J, 7, M, Nov 21, scs.
12125 White, Wm, M, 11, D, Nov 22, scs.
12139 Watson, I C, 7 cav, C, Nov 23, scs.
12576 Walker, C H, 6, H, Feb 3, scs.
12699 Woodruff, J, 4 cav, B, Feb 24, des.
12779 Woods, Thomas, 13, B, March 15, scs.
8190 White, J, 7 cav, A, Sept 8, dia.
5669 Wilson, Wm A, 6, A, Aug 14, dia.
4717 Westbrook, J H, 6 cav, A, Aug 4, dia.
4793 Wilson, J M, 13 cav, D, Aug 5, scs.

383 Yarbor, Wiley, 5, I, April 5, dia. c.
878 Young, James, 2, D, May 4, dia. c.
1142 Young, James, 2, F, May 16, ana.
14 Yeront, Samuel, 3, E, April 10, s. p.
5682 Yarnell, J E, 8, E, Aug 14, scs.

VERMONT.

3975 Averill, T E, 9, I, July 25, dia.
4579 Adams, Daniel, 1 cav, L, Aug 2, i. f.
8301 Albee, S, 11, G, Sept 9, dia. c.
9960 Atwood, A, 1, C, Sept 23, dia.
10664 Aldrich, L E, 11, A, Oct 11, dia.
11259 Aldrich, H B, 1 art, A, Oct 21, scs.
12092 Aiken, M A, 1, A, Nov 19, dia.

12766 Avery, B F, 3, C, March 13, dia. c.

2035 Bloomer, J, 2 bat, June 15, dia. c.
3166 Bailey, James, 2, A, July 11, dia. c.
4036 Brown, George, 16, B, July 20, scs.
4173 Bailey, S P, 1 cav, H, July 28, dia. a.
4200 Beadle, H H, 9, G, July 29, dys

****

4500 Bucker, James, 1, M, Aug 1, dia. c.
4637 Boyd, A M, 1 cav, L, Aug 3, dia.
4954 Bentley, M W, 6, A, Aug 7, dia.
5671 Bacom, A M, 8, G, Aug 14, dia.
5728 Bliss, J H, 1 cav, L, Aug 15, scs.
6334 Burchard, C, 11, L, Aug 21, des.
6349 Benson, A, 1, C, Aug 21, dia. c.
6416 Bennvils, J, 4, D, Aug 22, scs.
6594 Barnes, W, 1 cav, F, Aug 23, dys.
7886 Barton, W, 11, K, Sept 5, dia.
8029 Beady, Wm, 9, I, Sept 6, dys.
8086 Barker, F, 1 art, A, Aug 7, dia.
8315 Burrows, H, 11, F, Sept 10, dia. c.
8591 Brainard, J B, 1 cav, L, Aug 12, scs.
10305 Brown, G, 9, D, Oct 4, dia.
10371 Bowles, L H, 7, A, Oct 5, scs.
10431 Burton, C, 4, A, Oct 6, dys.
10745 Barker, C, 4, D, Oct 11, dia. c.
11068 Brown, J B, 1, A, Oct 17, dia.
11225 Batch, B F, 4, C, Oct 20, dys.
11375 Bohamar, J, 9, I, Oct 24, scs.
11469 Baker, John, 11, E, Oct 26, scs.
11747 Boulon, A, 2, B, Nov 2, scs.
11841 Babcock, T, 1, K, Nov 5, dia.
12055 Barber, W H, 1, C, Nov 16, dia.
12185 Burns, J, 7, B, Nov 28, scs.
12239 Butter, A F, 1 art, L, Dec 7, scs.
12406 Baxter, G, 4, A, Jan 6, scs.
12412 Bishop, E, 11, E, Jan 8, rhm.
12585 Bailey, E, 4, B, Feb 4, scs.

1044 Corey, C A, 1 cav, F, May 12, dia. c.
1170 Clifford, Jas, 4, F, May 17, dys.
1228 Chatfield, Wm,‡ 10, F, May 20, dia.
1973 Collitt, Jas, 1 cav, H, June 15, dia. c.
2675 Caswell, F, 9, June 30, dia.
2694 Clough, B, 9, A, June 30, dys.
2811 Chase, M, 6, H, July 3, brs.
3351 Cole, A H, 9, H, July 15, scs.
3817 Crocker, D, 5, D, July 23, dia.
3918 Clough, John D, 11, A, July 24, dia. c.
4205 Chamberlain, ——, 6, A, July 29, dia.
4883 Crouse, N, 5, C, Aug 6, wds.
5103 Chester, A, 11, K, Aug 9, dia.
5480 Carey, Thos, 1 art, Aug 13, scs.
6806 Carmine, P, 1 art, L, Aug 25, dia.
6952 Conner, W A,§ 4, A, Aug 26 dia.
7345 Clark, M L, 11, F, Aug 31, dia.
7361 Clark, John, 11 art, M, Aug 31, scs.
7698 Cunningham, J, 1 cav, F, Sept 3, scs.
8320 Cook, J J,‡ 1 cav, I, Sept 10, dia. c.
8923 Chase, E L, 1 art, C, Sept 16, dys.
9724 Crowley, D, 11, F, Sept 25, dia.
11738 Cross, E F, 11, L, Nov 2, scs.
11769 Carter, J, 11, A, Nov 3, scs.
10330 Colburn, W, 1 art, M, Oct 4, scs.

3068 Drew, F, 1 cav, F, July 9, dia.
5927 Donohue, P, 1 cav, D, Aug 17, dys.
6104 Dunn, G E,‡ 1, G, Aug 18, scs.
6338 Doying, F W, 1 art, F, Aug 21, dia.
6840 Darcy, F, 4, D, Aug 25, scs.
7974 Day, Geo, 11, H, Sept 6, r. f.
8271 Davis, O F, 9, I, Sept 9, dia. c.
10420 Dunn, W W, 1 cav, G, Oct 6, dia.
10458 Day, J D, 1 cav, A, Oct 7, dys.
12375 Dragoon, N, 1 cav, G, Jan 1, dia. c.

6353 Ennison, G, 11, A, Aug 21, dia. c.
10316 Eliot, C, 4, F, Oct 4, scs.

821 Farmer, E L, 14, H, May 1, dia.
3464 Freeman, C R, 9, H, July 17, scs.
4077 Farnsworth, M, 1, B, July 26, dia.
5851 Farnham, L B, 1 art, A, Aug 16, mas.
5914 Foster, A, 17, K, Aug 17, dia.
6758 Fuller, W, 1 cav, G, Aug 25, dia.
7165 Forrest, S, 3, I, Aug 29, ana.
8096 Fox, W, 11, K, Sept 7, dia.
8201 Foster, H B, 11, L, Sept 8, dia. c.
10784 Feast, Geo, 1 art, K, Oct 12, dia.
9969 Fisk, W P, 4, K, Oct 15, dia. c.

11314 Farrell, J H, 4, D, Oct 22, scs.
11351 Flint, C B, 4, D, Oct 23, scs.
11458 Foster, H C, 1 art, D, Oct 25, scs.
12317 Ferand, A, 1 art, B, Dec 21, scs.
12322 Ferrett, J, 1, K, Dec 23, scs.
12065 Fairchild, G L, 1 art, A, Nov 17, scs.
6264 Farnham, L D,§ 11, A, Aug 20, i. s.

1730 Gelo, A, 3, B, June 8, dia. c.
5273 Green, E, 2 bat, Aug 10, dia. c.
8572 Gleason, C W, 1 art, H, Sept 12, dys.
9799 Gillman, S A, 4, G, Sept 26, dia.
11598 Graves, J, 11, E, Oct 28, scs.
12531 Gerry, E B,‡ 4, H, Jan 26, dia. c.

2176 Hubbard, F, 2 bat, June 19, dia. c.,
3851 Humphrey, J, 1 cav, A, July 24, dia. c.
5218 Hall, Benj, 11, A, Aug 10, scs.
6145 Hyde, E,‡ 11, L, Aug 18, dia.
6657 Havens, E W, 9, H, Aug 24, dys.
7394 Hazen, W, 9, H, Aug 31, dys.
10824 Hines, L, 11, A, Oct 13, dia.
10843 Hart, S L, 2, Oct 13, dia. c.
10910 Hudson, J B, 11, A, Oct 14, scs.
10996 Hudson, J M, 11, A, Oct 16, dia. c.
11442 Howard, J, 1 cav, K, Oct 25, scs.
11730 Holmes, Joseph, 1 art, K, Nov 2, scs.
11814 Howard, J, 11, A, Nov 4, dia. c.
1206 Hall, C A, 1, A, Nov 17, scs.
12300 Hodges, J, 1 cav, H, Dec 17, scs.

3309 Jones, H L, 6, B, July 14, dia.
3858 Joslin, H, 1, B, July 24, dia. c.
3886 Jordan, A E, 17, A, July 24, scs.
4690 Johnson, D W, 11, H, Aug 4, scs.
10183 Johnson, John, 1 art, K, Oct 1, dia.

4007 Knapp, L, 1, G, July 25, ana.
6968 Kelsey, L C, 1 art, F, Aug 27, scs.
7762 Kingsley, S, 1, D, Sept 4, scs.
8901 Knowles, C W, 4, H, Sept 16, scs.
6239 Knight, Chas, 1 art, K, Aug 26, scs.

4597 La Boney, H, 1, M, Aug 3, dia.
4664 Laraway, H, 5, A, Aug 3, dys.
7653 Lapcam, A, 1 cav, Sept 3, des.
7891 Laddenbush, J, 17, A, Sept 5, dia.
8355 Leoport, C, 11, L, Sept 10, dia.
10180 Lungershan, W C, 1 cav, F, Oct 1, dia.
11074 Lacker, H, 11, A, Oct 17, scs.
12916 Lumsden, C, 4 cav, D, Feb 8, scs.

1335 Mitchell, Jacob, 2 bat, May 24, ana.
1544 Mosey, A, 1 cav, K, June 1, dia. c.
2088 McIntire, John, 7, F, June 17, dia. c.
2394 Manian, P, 9, June 24, dia.
4617 Morse, W, 1, F, Aug 3, dia.
5073 Martin, Jas, 1, M, Aug 8, c. f.
5949 Mills, Wm, 1, E, Aug 17, mas.
7324 Merrill, B J, 1, B, Aug 30, dys.
8475 Mayhim, J, 6, C, Sept 11, dia.
8965 Manchester, J M, 1 cav, I, Sept 16, dia.
9352 McGager, J, 2, G, Sept 20, scs.
9405 Montgomery, O A, 10, A, Sept 21, dia. c.
11227 McAllister, W B, 3, I, Oct 20, scs.
11735 Martin, M, 1 art, A, Nov 2, dia.
12631 Monroe, A, 11 art, L, Feb 10, dia. c.
9901 Morgan, Chas, 11 art, M, Sept 27, scs.
4473 McCrillis, Edw, 1 cav, C, Aug 1, ana.
7289 Milcher, Wm, 9, F, Aug 30, dia.

6559 Nownes, Geo H, 1 cav, C, Aug 23, dia.
11067 Nichols, H, 1 art, A, Oct 17, dia. c.
12283 Nelson, S H, 4 art, I, Dec 13, scs.

704 O'Brien, Wm, 1, H, April 23, cah.
4300 O'Neil, J M, 10, A, July 30, dia.

3183 Plude, John, 2 bat, July 11, rhm.
3213 Pev, Jas, 17, D, July 12.
4981 Preston, F, 1 art, Aug 7, dia.
5135 Phelps, H W, 9, H, Aug 9, dia.

5605 Poppins, Frank, 3, I, Aug 14, dia.
6586 Parmor, E, 4, C, Aug 23, dia.
7290 Park, Jas, 7 cav, E, Aug 30, des.
10040 Pillsbury, F, 4 cav, C, Sept 29, dia.
10237 Paul, John C, 4 cav, G, Oct 2, scs.
11041 Page, E, 4, I, Oct 17, scs.
11307 Powers, A, 4, H, Oct 22, scs.
11992 Packard, M G,‡ 1 art, A, Nov 13, dia.
12198 Pike, N N, 4, I, Nov 30, dia. c.
12721 Perry, A B, 4, H, March 3, dia. c.

1888 Reed, D W, 1 cav, June 13, dia. c.
6699 Ransom, Geo W, 1 art, L, Aug 24, dys.
7697 Rascoe, C, 11, H, Sept 3, dia.
8138 Roberts, J M, 11, K, Sept 8, dia.
8173 Richards, J, 1 cav, L, Sept 8, dia.
9462 Raynor, Louis, 4 cav, C, Sept 21, scs.
9894 Ross, H E, 11 bat, K, Sept 27, dia.
11009 Raynolds, F, 11, F, Oct 16, scs.
11426 Raney, A. 4, A, Oct 24, scs.
11691 Rice, F W, 14, F, Oct 31, dys.
12519 Rouncervee, E T, 9, D, Jan 25, scs.

648 Spoore, W O, 1 cav, B, April 20, dia.
2943 Smith, J C, 1, H, July 6, pna.
3382 St John, A, 11, A, July 16, dys.
4580 Seward, O, 5, C, Aug 2, dia.
5707 Skinner, F A, 4, H, Aug 15, scs.
5963 Stone, Jas A, 1 art, H, Aug 17, dia.
6640 Simons, L, 1, G, Aug 23, dia.
7509 Seaton, T B, 4, F, Sept 1, dia.
7810 Sweeney, Henry, 11, C, Sept 4, dys.
7813 Sprout, A, 17, F, Sept 4, dia.
8444 Stockwell, A, 11, H, Sept 11, scs.
10696 Sanburn, H, 4, G, Sept 11, dia. c.
10811 Styles, A B,‡ 4, K, Sept 12, dia. c.
10897 Sheldon, H, 1 cav, M, Sept 14, scs.
11282 Sarlett, L, 1, M, Oct 22, scs.
11476 Swaddle, W, 4, G, Oct 26, scs.
11966 Sanborn, M L, 1 art, A, Nov 11, dia.
12266 Scott, R O, 4, F, Dec 12, dys.

12514 Shay, J, 1 cav, K, Jan 23, dia. c.
12552 Sheldon, G, 1, K, Jan 29, scs.
12567 Stewart, E W, 11, A, Feb 1, scs.
5911 Scott, Geo W, 1 cav, C, Aug 17, dia.
8436 Suppes, T E, 1 cav, K, Sept 11, scs.

3784 Tuttle, C S, 1 cav, F, July 22, dia. c.
5833 Tatro, Alfred, 9, F, Aug 16, mas.
6587 Taylor, H C, 1 art, L, Aug 23, dia.
6659 Trow, H, 17, D, Aug 24, des.
9374 Tanner, H,‡ 11, I, Sept 20, scs.
9574 Talman, W C,§ 11, F, Sept 23, dys.
11171 Taylor, J W, 1 art, A, Oct 19, scs.
11220 Thompson, W A, 1 art, I, Oct 20, scs.

5693 Varnum, E G J, 11, F, Aug 15, scs.

3177 Weller, D, 9, B, July 11, ts. f.
4376 Whitehall, Geo, 6, B, July 31, dia.
4435 Wilson, A, 6, B, July 31, dia. c.
4585 Wilder, L F, H, H, Aug 2, wds.
5075 Whitney, A, 9, D, Aug 8, dia.
5307 Warner, Geo O, 10, E, Aug 11, scs.
5751 Woodard, S P, 1 art, H, Aug 15, ens.
7063 Wells, Geo A, 4, F, Aug 28, dia.
7322 Wright, E S, 11 art, A, Aug 30, des.
7689 Witt, T, 1 cav, F, Sept 3, scs.
7920 Ward, Alfred, 11, A, Sept 5, dia.
8239 Watkins, G C, 1, C, Sept 9, dys.
9264 Woodmance, G, 11, F, Sept 9, scs.
9178 Welles, C, 11, H, Sept 18, dia.
10510 White, A, 11, A, Oct 8, scs.
10711 Webster, W A,§ 4, A, Oct 11, dia. c.
11289 Wakefield, J W, 4, H, Oct 22, scs.
11398 Woods, J M, 1, F, Oct 24, scs.
11783 Wheeler, B, 11, K, Nov 3, dia. c.
11840 Warden, G, 3, B, Nov 5, dia.
11865 Worthers, S T, 1 cav, D, Nov 6, dys.
12156 Willey, J S, 1 art, A, Nov 25, scs.
4533 Washburn, Tru, 1 cav, D, Aug 2, dys.

VIRGINIA.

824 Anderson, A, 2, H, May 1, dys.
876 Armstrong, ——,§ 8 mil, C, May 4, dia.
942 Ayers, S V, 11, C, May 7, dia. c.
1968 Armstrong, G B, 8, C, June 14, ana.
2769 Armhult, W H,‡ 10, I, July 1, dia. c.
5011 Armstrong, J, 3, C, Aug 8, scs.
5341 Arbogast, C W, 1 art, C, Aug 11, scs.
8865 Abercrombie, W H, 12, C, Sept 15, scs.
11525 Allison, G, 1, F, Oct 26, dys.

221 Burns, S A,§ 8, C, March 29, dia. c.
255 Brooks, Samuel F, 10, I, March 30, i. f.
448 Boone, Jas, 1 cav, L, April 9, dia. c.
756 Bennett, L J, 11, C, April 27, dys. c.
943 Brake, J,§ 6, C, May 7, pna.
980 Blackburn, Geo, 10, I, May 9, dia.
1705 Bates, T E, 11, F, June 7, dia.
2518 Brown, M. 14, E, June 26, dia c.
2627 Bowermaster, S R, bu, 3 cav, D, Jn 28, scs.
3407 Bateman, D P, 2, B, July 16, dys.
4427 Barber, Jas, 1 cav, F, July 31, dia. c.
5495 Bishop, J C, 3, C, Aug 12, dia.
6706 Bearer, P, 10, I, Aug 24, scs.
10297 Boutnell, O, 4, F, Oct 3, dia.
7126 Beasley, P, 9, G, Aug 28, scs.
7909 Bogard, Jno R,‡ 14, A, Sept 5, scs.
8539 Batt, M, 18, E, Sept 12, ana.
9796 Butcher, Peter, 14, F, Sept 26, dia.
10198 Broom, J, 1 cav, B, Oct 2, r. f.
11090 Blessing, P, 15, K, Oct 18, scs.
11337 Bush, H H, 14, B, Oct 23, scs.
11411 Burton, W B, 6 cav, A, Oct 24, dia.
11669 Barnett, J, 6 cav, K, Oct 30, scs.
11924 Beach, J F, 14, K, Nov 8, scs.
12045 Boggs, H C,‡ 6 cav, E, Nov 16, scs.
12414 Burton, F. 3 cav, B, Jan 8, rhm.

110 Corbett, L B, W Va mil, C, Mar 23, dia.
403 Carr, Wm. 8, B, April 6, ts. f.
835 Clendeman, C L, 4 cav, D, May 1, dia.
1032 Caste, Jesse, 8, E, May 11, dia.
1100 Coon, Nathan, 14, K, May 14, dia. c.
2013 Carrington, Jas, 2, A, June 15, ana.
2235 Coffman, F, 3 cav, A, June 20, phs.
2569 Cunderson, ——, 8, D, June 27, dys.
2661 Carnes, H, 10, E, June 29, dia.
2817 Conrad, H, 3, F, July 3, dia. c.
2930 Cunningham, J, 8, E, July 5, dys.
3315 Cox, T A,§ 3 cav, A, July 14, dia.
4363 Cool, J B,‡ 3 cav, H, July 31, dia.
4741 Crook, E H,§ 7, I, Aug 5, ana.
5174 Cuppett, J, 3, H, Aug 9, dys.
5384 Covil, Wm, 3, I, Aug 12, des.
6674 Clements, L, 3 cav, A, Aug 24, dys.
6809 Curtin, B, 4 cav, B, Aug 25, dia. c.
7091 Clark, ——, 7, E, Aug 28, dia.
7179 Cremones, D, 9, D, Aug 29, scs.
8990 Cook, J, 7 cav, I, Sept 17, dia.
9406 Campbell, O H, 14, F, Sept 21, dia.
9755 Christian, J, 15, C, Sept 25, scs.
9762 Catnill, L, 9, B, Sept 25, scs.
9967 Cobin, J M, 14, B, Sept 28, dia.
10598 Childs, S P, 1 cav, C, Oct 10, dia.
11561 Castle, C H, 1, A, Oct 27, scs.
11830 Cooper, A H,‡ 7 cav, I, Nov 5, dia.
12174 Campbell, B, 12, I, Nov 26, scs.

24 Deboard, H A, 5, G, March 8, ts. f.
202 Douglas, Geo, 8, C, March 28, dia. c.
347 Dean, Samuel, 5, H, April 2, dys.
632 Defibaugh, W R,‡ 1 art, G, April 19, dia
647 Davis, S, 3, D, April 20, pna.
843 Duncan, J M, 5, D, May 2, dys.

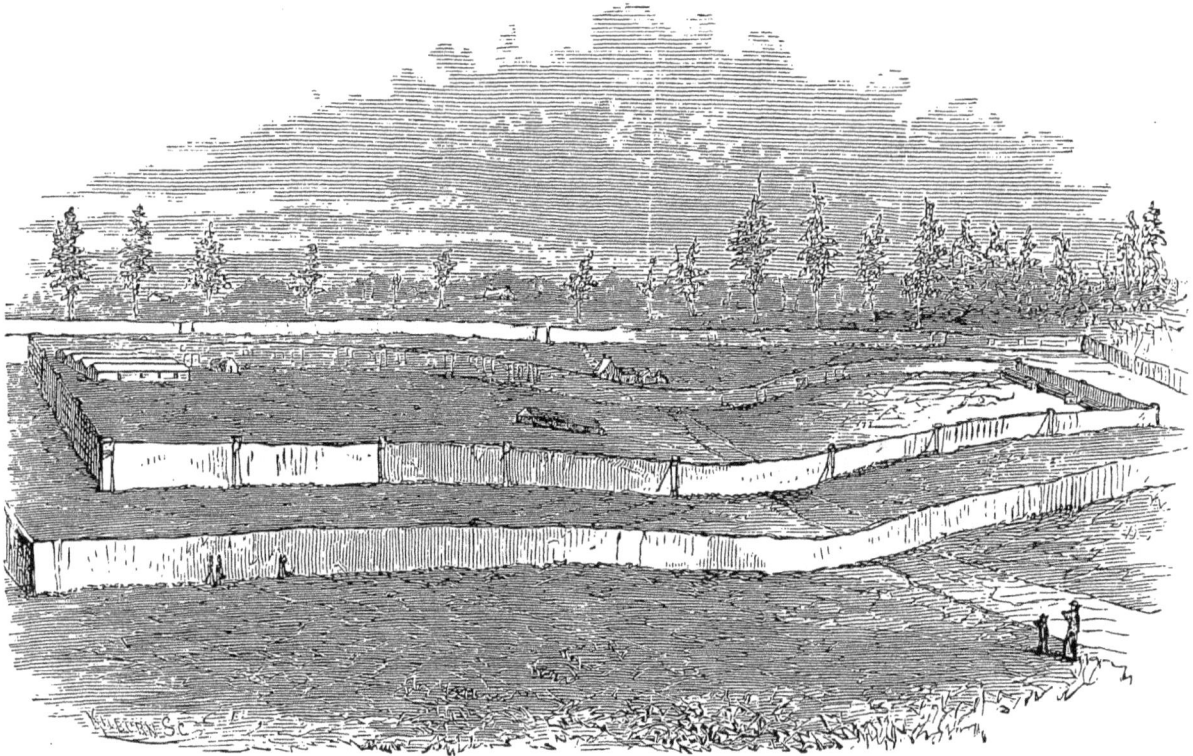

VIEW OF THE STOCKADE, — as the Rebels left it.

"The prison at Andersonville was situated on two hill-sides, and through the centre ran a sluggish brook, branch, as it was commonly called. There were no signs of vegetation in the pen; it had all been trampled out." Page 74.

2081 Daly, Jas, 3 cav, A, June 17, dys.
3105 Duckworth, W B, 14, A, July 10, dia.
3246 Dyer, James, 10, I, July 13, pna.
5507 Drake, Samuel, 9, B, Aug 13, scs.
6588 Dorsey, A L, 15, K, Aug 23, dia.
6745 Daner, J, 10, I, Aug 24, ts. f.
6936 Darsey, M, 9, L, Aug 26, scs.
6949 Dodd, S,§ 9, F, Aug 26, scs.
7092 Dunberger, Geo, 9, C, Aug 28, dia.
8248 Divers, G, 15, D, Sept 9, scs.
8467 Dant, Jno M, 7 cav, H, Sept 10, scs.
8582 Dason, N, 8 cav, L, Sept 12, dys.
9159 Dunn, I, 2, K, Sept 18, dia.
12225 Duncan, W M, 6 cav, C, Dec 6, scs.
12807 Donohue, S, 9, C, March 21, pls.
12508 Doty, John, 6 cav, A, Jan 23, dia.

10975 Estuff, Jno, 1 cav, L, Oct 12, dia. c.

117 Fuller, Irwin, militia, March 23, pna.
613 Foster, Charles K, 9, H, April 18, dys.
955 Fox, H C, 1,‡ D, May 8, dia. c.
5765 Fawkes, Wm, 14, D, Aug 15, wds.
7203 Foster, S, 8, A, Aug 29, dys.
7941 Feather, J B, 14, B, Sept 5, dia. c.
8698 Feasley, Len, 1 art, Sept 14, scs.
8723 Fusner, J E, 6 cav, D, Sept 14, dia.
10206 Freeborn, R L,§ 14, B, Oct 2, r. f.
10709 Furr, E, 10, K, Oct 11, dia.
11022 Fleming, W W, 6 cav, A, Oct 16, scs.
10314 Forth, R, 8, D, Sept 3, scs.

2485 Grey, P, 3 Va, A, June 25, dia.
2649 Greshoe, M, 11, C, June 29, brs.
2712 Golden, J, 2 cav, G, July 1, dia.
4738 Gordon, S, 2, G, Aug 4, scs.
6348 Guenant, A, 2, I, Aug 21, dia.
10581 Garton, Wm,‡ 2, I, Oct 10, scs.
11574 Gluck, A E, 10, D, Oct 28, scs.
11864 Gibson, A, 1, A, Nov 6, scs.

84 Hollingshead, S, 1, G, March 8, ts. f.
294 Harrison, D, 10, I, April 1, dia. c.
365 Henry, Robt O, 8, C, April 2, dia. c.
398 Hunter, G W, 8, A, April 6, brs.
568 Heller, Wm,‡ 3, D, April 15, dia.
839 Halpin, Jno, 2, D, May 2, dys.
997 Hoffman, G W, 8, E, May 10, dia.
1013 Hess, J, 11, C, May 10, dia.
1421 Hatfield, J, 1, B, May 28, dia. c.
1854 Harkins, H, 2, F, June 11, scs.
2702 Hoover, W H, 3, A, June 30, des.
2902 Howell, A, 14, E, July 5, dia. c.
2957 Howe, S, 2, I, July 5, dia. c.
3930 Horant, E A, 3, C, July 25, dia. c.
4739 Hine, Wm, 2, A, Aug 5, dia. c.
5061 Hammer, S, 3 cav, G, Aug 8, dys.
5412 Hartly, Isaac, 3, I, Aug 12, dys.
5649 Hall, Henry, 10, F, Aug 14, scs.
6538 Harper, W, 8, H, Aug 23, ana.
8061 Hushman, W, 10, I, Sept 7, dia.
8268 Hardway, D B, 9, G, Sept 9, dia.
8341 Harden, G W, 6 cav, A, Sept 10, scs.
8344 Hutson, J, 14, A, Sept 10, scs.
9166 Hauslan, B, 6 cav, Sept 18, scs.
9537 Hudgins, J, 14, B, Sept 22, ana.
9794 Handland, H, 1, H, Sept 26, dia.
10990 Hollinbeck, W H,‡ 1 cav, B, Oct 14, dia.
11316 Hubert, W C, 12, G, Oct 22, scs.
11596 Hendershot, F F, 7, E, Oct 24, scs.
11739 Hurn, R, 8, E, Nov 2, scs.
12014 Hartzel, S, 1, D, Nov 15, dys.
12153 Hickman, E, 11, B, Nov 24, scs.

312 Johns, E K, 8 mil, C, April 2, dia. c.
3045 Jake, A R, 8, I, July 8, ana.
3969 Jackson, S E, 2, E, July 25, scs.
6098 Jones, G, 2 cav, D, Aug 18, dia.
7681 Johnston, I A, 1 cav, D, Sept 3, dys.
8371 Jenkins, W, 1 art, D, Sept 10, dia.

823 Kane, J, 4 cav, L, April 2, pna.

5822 Kimball, Jno, 14, K, Aug 16, ens.

589 Ludihing, W, 2, A, April 17, dia.
1565 Langstan, N H, 1 cav, A, June 2, dia c.
1592 Lanham, Henry, 8, C, June 3, des.
1949 Logger, J, 3 cav, B, June 14, dia. c.
2734 Lyshon, Wm, 2, I, July 1, ana.
2739 Loud, Geo, 9, D, July 1, dia. c.
6924 Lansbury, W,§ 15, E, Aug 26, dia.
7237 Lough, H, 1 cav, L, Aug 29, scs.
10564 Liston, David, 6 cav, C, Oct 9, dia.
10569 Lowe, J, 9, C, Oct 9, dia.
11021 Lowe, W G, 13, G, Oct 16, scs.
11325 Laymou, W F, 14, C, Oct 23, scs.
11624 Laughlin, D,‡ 9, E, Oct 28, wds.
11989 Lucas, J, 9, D, Nov 13, scs.
12262 Lowring, J, 1 art, D, Dec 12, dia.

41 Maddons, W L, 4 cav, K, May 3, s p
280 Mason, Peter, 10, G, April 1, dia. c.
387 Magaher, J, 3 cav, A, April 5, dys.
422 McNeily, Jas, 3 cav, A, April 7, ana.
582 McCormick, R, 2, F, April 16, asc.
786 McConnaughy, D, 11, F, April 28, dia. a
820 McGitton, J, 6, G, May 1, dys.
1068 Morris, J M, 3 cav, E, May 13, dia. c.
1419 Murphy, J, 8, D, May 28, dys.
1675 Moore, M, 14, K, June 6, ana.
2932 Milum, Jas, 8, I, July 5, dia.
3955 Mokie, R, 7 cav, July 20, scs.
6960 Miller, C W, 2, C, Aug 27, dia.
7018 Meiner, H, 12, I, Aug 27, dia.
9699 Mencar, L B, 14, B, Sept 24, scs.
9767 Morris, G, 14, A, Sept 25, scs.
9955 Miller, D, 14, C, Sept 28, scs.
10567 Moody, R W, 6 cav, E, Oct 9, scs.
10578 McKinney, Wm, 1 cav, L, Oct 9, scs.
10934 McConkey, A L,‡ 6 cav, B, Oct 14, dia.
10970 McLoughlin, R, 1 art, D, Oct 15, dia.
11546 Monsen, J F, 14, C, Oct 27, scs.
12099 Matt, Henry, 12, E, Nov 19, scs.
12272 McCausland, R, 1, G, Dec 12, scs.
9483 McGregor, P, 1, E, Sept 21, dia.
12068 McWilson, J, 14, F, Nov 17, scs.

2857 Norman, H, 2, I, July 4, dia.
3395 Newman, A, 1 cav, B, July 16, ana.
6442 Nichols, L D, 9, F, Aug 22, scs.
12472 Nicholson, J, 3 cav, B, Jan 17, scs.

241 Oxley, Robert, 14, C, March 30, dia. c.
1767 Osborne, Thos, 5, H, June 9, dys.

39 Packard, Myron C, 2 cav, I, Mar 13, pls
1707 Porterfield, Jno, 4, F, June 7, dia. c.
2433 Porrellson, C D, 10, I, June 24, dys.
2645 Patny, J, 8, G, June 29, dia.
2737 Painter, C,§ 9, F, July 1, ana.
3055 Petit, J,‡ 1 cav, L, July 9, dia.
4707 Paine, M,‡ 8, F, Aug 3, des.
5004 Pugh, L, 3, I, Aug 8, dia.
5213 Polland, Jno, 10, I, Aug 10, scs.
6004 Polley, J, 8, C, Aug 17, ana.
6196 Perkins, James A, 12, K, Aug 19, dia. c.
11267 Palmer, Jno,§ 1 cav, L, Oct 21, scs.

349 Reakes, Wm, 8 m, C, April 2, dia.
521 Rice, A, 4 cav, G, April 13, dys.
560 Randall, Jas A, 9, K, April 15, dys. c.
959 Rinker, F A, 3 cav, A, May 8, dys.
1040 Robb, M, 2, A, May 12, ts. f.
1916 Richards, G L, 14, D, June 14, dia. c.
3459 Rummer, L, 5, A, July 17, scs.
3465 Read, J, 12, B, July 17, scs.
3641 Redden, J, 9, F, July 20, dia.
4163 Ronsey, Wm, 9, C, July 29, dia.
7257 Rutroff, Jacob, 7, H, July 30, dia.
8082 Reush, Jas, 7, B, Sept 7, dia.
10527 Reed, J M,‡ 12, D, Oct 7, scs.
11518 Rock, J H, 12, C, Oct 26, scs.
11794 Raleigh, S, 1 cav, I, Nov 4, scs.
7005 Richardson, W, 14, K, Aug 27, dia.

****

273 Sayre, Michael, 14, I, March 31, dia.
680 Sprague, Geo, 11, F, April 23, dia.
927 Stackleford, S, 3 cav, A, May 7, dys.
1510 Scott, Z,§ 8, D, May 31, dia.
2226 Steward, C, 2 cav, I, June 20, dia.
2259 Stagg, Wm, 10, I, June 23, scs.
2437 Stutter, J N, 3 cav, B, June 25, dia. a.
2931 Skillington, G, 4 cav, D, July 5, dia.
3321 Stephenson, A, 1 cav, B, July 16, ana.
3588 Shilber, C A, 3, A, July 19, dia.
3747 Shaub, F, 2, E, July 22, dia.
3895 Simons, C E, 8, C, July 24, dia. c.
3965 Stewart, Wm A, 14, I, July 25, ics.
4463 Steele, A, 2 cav, C, Aug 1, scs.
4812 Snider, S, 3, K, Aug 5, scs.
4935 Sturn, E E, 12, F, Aug 7, wds.
5130 Smith, ——, 2, F, Aug 8, scs.
5237 Simmons, E, 8, C, Aug 10, scs.
5727 Sprouse, A, 11, F, Aug 15, scs.
5975 Smith, J W, 8, G, Aug 17, ts. f.
6473 Sprouse, W, 11, F, Aug 22, dia.
6610 Squares, Samuel, 6 cav, D, Aug 23, dia.
7091 Stratton, B B, 1 art, F, Aug 28, dia.
7944 Stoker, S, 3 cav, C, Sept 5, dia. c.
8011 Sands, Wm, 10, F, Sept 6, scs.
8164 Scritchfield, W, 16, F, Sept 8, dia.
8390 Stuck, H M, 14, B, Sept 10, dia.
8516 Smith, B, 9, H, Sept 12, dia.
8646 Sturgiss, W T, drum, 14, B, Sept 12, scs.
9217 Smith, G H, 7 cav, G, Sept 19, scs.
9714 Sullivan, E, 2, A, Sept 25, scs.
9786 Snyder, J V,§ 3, D, Sept 26, dia.
9872 Semeir, G S, 4 cav, Sept 27, scs.
9906 Sands, G W, 1, Sept 28, dia. c.
10151 Smith, J, 14, B, Oct 1, scs.

11276 Smith, J A, 9, B, Oct 22, scs.
11625 Slee, R,§ 1 cav, D, Oct 25. dia. c.
11824 Spaulding, F, 1 cav, A, Nov 5, scs.
11836 Stockwell, C H, 3, B, Nov 5, scs.
7291 Saylor, C M, 9, B, Aug 30, dia.

1108 Thatcher, J P, 2, A, April 15, dys.
3404 Trobridge, S, 6, B, July 16, dys.
5136 Tyrm, T, 8, H, Aug 8, scs.
6379 Thurston, C C, 1, I, Aug 21, scs.
8663 Taylor, J, 8, G, Sept 13, dia.
12332 Thorpe, S S, 3, I, Dec 26, scs.
3846 Tomlinson, S,§ 3, I, July 24, dys.
8119 Tatro, L, 11, B, Sept 8, dia.

244 Vincent, Jas, 8, C, March 30, dys.
814 Very, W, 1 cav, C, April 30, dys.
1149 Vauscoy, A,‡ 3 cav, E, May 16, dia. s.
1322 Virts, R, 3 cav, A, May 23, dia. c.

945 Wilson, Walter, 11, F, May 7, dia. c.
1757 Weaver, M, 1 cav, C, June 7, dia. c.
2854 Worp, J, 3, F, July 6, dia. c.
3723 Wich, J, 1 cav, L, July 21, des.
3925 Whitney, W A, 8, F, July 25, dys.
3996 Whit, A, 5, F, July 25, dia.
7542 Wilson, J, 3, B, Sept 2, dys.
7832 Warwicke, E, 2, D, Sept 4, dia.
8598 Wells, E, 7, F, Sept 12, scs.
9626 Wolfe, C, 14, B, Sept 24, gae.
10854 White, J N, 6 cav, C, Oct 13, dys.

148 Young, A, 8, C, March 25, dia.
456 Young, A B, 8, C, April 9, dia.
694 Young, Ed, 8 cav, C, April 23, dia.

WISCONSIN.

2113 Allwise, J R, 24, E, June 17, dia. c.
4477 Austin, Isaac, 25, G, Aug 1, dia.
5241 Abbott, A,§ 21, D, Aug 10, scs.
5453 Allen, C P, 2, G, Aug 12, wds.
8692 Adams, A F, 36, F, Sept 14, scs.
10830 Adams, P, 10, A, Oct 13, scs.
11492 Aultin, E V,‡ 13, E, Oct 26, scs.
12728 Antone, C, 31, D, March 4, dia. c.

1341 Bower, H, 1, A, May 24, dys.
1838 Burk, O, 15, B, June 11, dia.
2009 Bawgarder, B, 2, K, June 15, dia.
2055 Ball, H, 7, A, June 16, dia.
2128 Bowhan, H A,§ 10, F, June 18, ts. f.
2334 Brooks, E, 1 cav, H, June 22, dia. c.
2451 Broomer, B F,‡ 10, I, June 25, dys. a.
2681 Brown, O, 15, G, June 30, dia. c.
3253 Brown, J, 4, H, July 13, dia.
3673 Bruce, H, 24, H, July 20, dia.
4870 Brumsted, G,§ 15, A, Aug 6, dia.
5026 Briggs, H, 1 cav, L, Aug 8, dys.
5100 Budson, John, 1 cav, L, Aug 9, scs.
5164 Bemis, H, 10, C, Aug 9, scs.
5322 Briggs, E, 1 cav, Aug 11, scs.
5564 Bailey, W,‡ 25, E, Aug 13, wds.
6204 Banick, S, 17, I, Aug 19, scs.
7295 Bailey, J, 36, I, Aug 30, dys.
7323 Burk, J, 10 cav, E, Aug 30, gae.
7755 Borden, E,‡ 21, K, Sept 3, dia.
7759 Boyle, P, 25, D, Sept 4, dia.
8576 Batchelder, J, 1, I, Sept 12, dia.
8641 Bushell, C C, 2, B, Sept 13, dys.
9607 Brinkman, J, 2, A, Sept 23, scs.
10686 Britton, H,§ 15, I, Oct 11, scs.
10919 Bohnsen, N, 15, I, Oct 14, scs.
11754 Butler, M, 10, K, Nov 2, scs.
12032 Blakeley, R, 7, F, Nov 15, scs.
11610 Batterson, L, 10, K, Oct 28, dia.

2360 Church, A, 7, H, June 23, ana.
2668 Chapman, J, 2, G, June 29, dys.
2969 Cowles, D, 10, B, July 6, dia. c.

3292 Cummings, S, 21, A, July 14, dia.
3828 Crane, R, drummer, 7, D, July 23, dys.
4390 Chapel, C, 1, E, July 31, dys.
5102 Cavanaugh, John, 1 cav, H, Aug 9, scs.
8105 Chase, F M,‡ 1, A, Sept 7, dia.
9418 Currier, C C, 21, F, Aug 22, wds.
9169 Carlintyre, G, 23, Sept 18, scs.
10752 Castle, C, 1 cav, C, Oct 12, scs.
11020 Cofam, W, 10, A, Oct 16, scs.
11088 Chusterson, F, 15, E, Oct 18, hes.
11535 Chamberlain, J, 21, I, Oct 27, scs.
11744 Clark, W C, 10, E, Nov 2, scs.
10346 Crommings, H, 7, C, Oct 5, scs.

1591 Duffey, E, 1, L, June 3, dia. c.
2522 Damhocker, E, 26, I, June 26, wds.
3244 Daggo, John, 1 cav, L, July 13, scs.
5830 Destler, Fred, 26, G, July 16, dia.
6967 Dick, Benjamin, 36, G, Aug 27, scs.
7455 Davis, J, 36, B, Sept 1, scs.
8530 Decker, G,§ F battery, Sept 12, scs.
8587 Depas, A, 21, A, Sept 12, scs.
8900 Daryson, W, 7, C, Sept 15, scs.
9739 Dacy, G, 12, I, Sept 25, dia.
10771 Davis, John, 1, B, Oct 12, dia. c.
12750 David, D P, 25, B, March 8, dia. a.

2419 Enger, J, 15, K, June 24, dys. c.
5247 Egan, John, 7, A, Aug 10, scs.
6160 Erickson, C, 15, B, Aug 19, dys.
8601 Ellwood, S,§ 10, C, Aug 13, scs.
9537 Erricson, S, 50, D, Sept 20, dys.
11687 Ellenger, P, 21, K, Oct 31, dia.
12286 Enkhart, H, 36, G, Dec 14, scs.

36 Fordrury, G W, 7, C, March 12, dys.
1260 Fuller, C W,‡ 7, E, May 21, dia. c.
2283 Fountain, W F, 10, A, June 20, dia. a.
5007 Forslay, W K, 8, K, Aug 8, scs.
5759 Fleins, Oscar, 1 cav, H, Aug 15, scs.
5811 Fisk, J B,§ 1 cav, H, Aug 16, dia.
6097 Fischnor, D,§ 36, H, Aug 18, ics.

****

6236 Fanon, Wm, 1, A, Aug 20, dys.
8460 Farnham, M B, 4, K, Sept 11, scs.
9664 Ferguson, I,§ 15, G, Sept 24, dia.
10234 Fagan, M, 15, G, Oct 2, dia.
12618 Frost, A, 7, B, Feb 8, scs.
12653 Ferguson, W R, 24, D, Feb 14, rhm.

1529 Gilbert, O,§ 16, K, May 31, dia.
2392 Grush, Fred, 15, I, June 24, dia.
3164 Guth, H, 1, D, July 11, dia.
3390 Greenman, D,§ 21, K, July 16, dys.
5557 Greenwall, M, 1 cav, C, Aug 13, dys.
7355 Grunds, L, 15, I, Aug 31, dia. c.
8326 Groupe, D, 4, F, Sept 10, dia.
10691 Gunduson, H,§ 15, I, Oct 11, scs.
6614 Goon, John E, 36, Aug 23, dia.

303 Helt, Carl, 26, E, April 1, dys.
710 Hale, A C, 21, I, April 24, ts. f.
1002 Haskins, J, 1, E, May 10, dys.
1655 Hoffland, ——, 1 sgt, 15, K, June 5, ana.
1673 Harvey, D M, 1, I. June 6, ts. f.
2384 Hanson, J, 15, K, June 23, dia. c.,
2556 Hough, B J,‡ 10, K, June 27, dia. c.
3720 Henderson, O, 15, F, July 24, i. f.
4542 Hewick, Nelson, 10, B, Aug 2, brs.
4570 Halts, S, 26, C, Aug 2, scs.
5312 Howard, F B, 10, K, Aug 11, pls.
5628 Holenback, A, 25, D, Aug 14, wds.
6468 Hall, A W, 21, I, Aug 22, dia.
7081 Hanley, T, 3 art, D, Aug 28, scs.
7149 Hutchings, B, 1 cav, E, Aug 29, dia. c.
7649 Hanson, L, 15, B, Sept 3, scs.
7791 Harding, W F,§ 21, C, Sept 4, scs.
8584 High, M, 25, E, Sept 12, wds.
9333 Halter, D. 22, D, Sept 20, scs.
10427 Hans, P, 10, D, Oct 6, scs.
11443 Holenbeck, C, 13, A, Oct 25, scs.
11927 Hanson, ——, 1, B, Nov 8, scs.
12167 Harris, N, 12, D, Nov 26, wds.
12586 Hardy, E L, 6, E, Jan 4, scs.
12848 Hanson R, 1, F, April 28, dia.
12468 Hand, G, 10, D, Jan 16, scs.

8614 Ingham, J, 10, K, Sept 13, scs.
9808 Irwin, A, 25, C, Sept 26, scs.

2003 Jacobson, O,‡ 15, D, June 15, dia.
3281 Jackson, T, 4, H, July 13, dia.
3478 Jillett, J, 7, H, July 17, dia.
6938 Jennings, J R,‡ 45, G, Aug 56, dia.
11284 Johnson, W H, 6, H, Oct 22, scs.

1165 Kemmett, J, 1, H, May 17, scs.
2498 Kundson, J, 15, E, June 26, dys. c.
4133 Kellett, John B,‡ 21, B, July 27, i. f.
4405 Kull, L, 24, C, July 31, dia.
4614 Klepps, C H, 1 cav, E, Aug 3, scs.
8592 Kendall, W, 32, Sept 12, scs.
9063 Keerroger, Wm, 36, G, Sept 17, dia.
10536 Kane, F, 26, E, Oct 8, dia.
10692 Knowles, H, 21, D, Oct 11, dia.
8299 Kinds, M O, 21, A, Sept 9, scs.

3009 Lack, Peter, 7, A, July 7, dia. c.
5397 Livingston, J H, 3 art, E, Aug 12, ana.
6642 Lansing, G, 10, A, Aug 23, dia.
7235 Lowe, F, 16, G, Aug 29, scs.
7522 Lawson, M, 15, B, Sept 1, dys.
8944 Laich, F, 26, K, Sept 16, scs.
9997 Latgen, E, 15, A, Sept 29, scs.
8977 Laich, F, 26, K, Sept 17, dia.

1752 Mauger, James,‡ 24, H, June 9, ana.
1896 Mulligan, J, 1, June 13, dia.
2732 McMann, W, 3 bat, July 1, dys.
2951 McCormick, E, 1 cav, L, July 6, dia.
2981 McKenzie, J, 1, F, July 7, dia.
3625 McLaulin, C, 36, I, July 20, dia.
4925 Mathison, E N, 2, E, Aug 6, dia.
5043 Many, J, 24, D, Aug 8, dia.
5163 McFadden, H, 1 cav, F, Aug 9, dia.

5683 Mortes, B, 10, D, Aug 15, scs.
5739 Main, Henry, 30, F, Aug 15, dia.
6231 McClury, A, 10, I, Aug 20, dia.
6377 Messer, F, 5, B, Aug 21, dia.
10289 Myers, S, 15, G, Oct 4, scs.
11936 Mulasky, E, 21, B, Nov 9, scs.

4289 Nelson, R, 15, R, July 30, scs.
4980 Northam, S R,§ 10, C, Aug 7, scs.
6090 Nichols, Wm, 10, 1, Aug 18, dys.
10369 Neff, Wm, 33, I, Oct 6, scs.

3162 Olson, O, 15, B, July 11, dia.
11545 Ochle, F, 26, E, Oct 27, wds.
11931 Olston, M, 15, B, Nov 7, dia.

604 Palmer, John,‡ 7, C, April 18, dia.
2535 Plum, A, 4 cav, K, June 26, dia. c.
2847 Peterson, A,‡ 15, K, July 4, dia.
3511 Picket, T E,‡ 1, F, July 18, dia.
4340 Purdy, M, 10, E, July 30, dia.
6406 Piriris, J, 17, F, Aug 22, wds.
7530 Purdee, J, 10, I, Sept 1, scs.
7893 Peterson, S, 15, K, Sept 5, dia. c.
8515 Pillsbury, A J, 1 cav, H, Sept 12, gas.
8654 Patterson, J, 21, A, Sept 13, scs.
9014 Painter, H,§ 10, F, Sept 17, dia.
9902 Patterson, S,‡ 15, I, Sept 27, scs.
9461 Peterson, C, 15, I, Sept 21, scs.

2028 Roach, A, 21, F, June 15, dia.
3624 Renseler, H, 2, G, July 20, dia.
3665 Reynolers, F S, 10, K, July 20, dys.
4997 Reed, G, 1, K, Aug 7, dys.
5792 Rasmusson, A, 1 cav, L, Aug 15, dys.
6088 Robinson, W M,‡ 10, C, Aug 18, scs.
9860 Rice, J, 7, C, Sept 27, dia.
11812 Randles, J, 25, D, Nov 4, scs.
12233 Richmond, B,§ 1 cav, L, Dec 6, scs.
12242 Randell, P D, 1 cav, K, Dec 7, scs.

68 Schleassen, J J, 7, F, March 19, dys.
440 Shrigley, H, 10, G, April 8, dia.
2814 Stiffus, R, 15, F, July 3, dia. c.
3078 Sirbirth, F, 24, E, July 9, ana.
3503 Shoop, W, 1, G, July 18, dia.
3583 Sutton, J, 10, B, July 19, dia.
4343 Sharp, J W, 2, G, July 30, dia.
4378 Smith, W F, 10, B, July 31, dia.
4436 Shun, J, 24, H. July 31, dia.
4788 Scott, E G,§ 21, D, Aug 5, scs.
4882 Slingerland, John, 1 cav, B, Aug 6, i. f.
6943 Starr, E, 16, F, Aug 26, wds.
7614 Seaman, M,§ 21, D, Sept 2, dys.
8168 Smith, L, 4 cav, K, Sept 8, dia.
9693 Snyder, M, 26, E, Sept 24, scs.
11037 Smith, S,M,‡ 21, F, Oct 17, scs.
11047 Sales, A D, 4, K, Oct 17, ana.

2148 Tung, S W, 21, D, June 18, scs.
2385 Tay, S, 1, K, June 24, dia. a.
2588 Tomlinson, Robt, 6, B, June 28, dia. c.
3120 Thompson, D D, 36, B, June 10, dia.
3375 Tyler, J,‡ 10, A, July 16, dia.
3661 Tucker, C P, 1, I, July 20, dia.
4467 Taylor, A L, 25, E, Aug 1, dia.
6858 Taylor, I, 6, E, Aug 26, dys,
7160 Thorn, P C, 1 cav, L, Aug 29, dia.
8500 Troutman, A, 2, Sept 12, scs.
11236 Thurber, D,‡ 36, G, Oct 21, scs.
11420 Tyler, E P, 10, F, Oct 24, scs.
11475 Thorson, P, 24, G, Oct 26, scs.
12374 Thompson, O, 15, K, Jan 1, scs.

2309 Updell, J S, 15, B, June 22, dia. c.

2954 Vohoss, O H, 1, L, July 6, brs.
3076 Vitter, J, 6, F, July 9, dia.
8359 Vancoster, H, 1 cav, C, Sept 10, gas.
8427 Vanderbilt, J, 36, D, Sept 11, scs.
11390 Voclee, F,‡ 10, E, Oct 24, scs.

****

929 Webster, A C,§ 7, E, May 7, brs.
884 Winleis, P, 1, M, May 5, dia.
1007 Wilder, John, 1 cav, F, May 10, dia. c.
1520 Welcome, E D, 1 cav, L, May 31, dia.
1693 Walter, S P, 21, G, June 7, dia.
1909 Welton, M S, 1 cav, L, June 13, dia. c.
2591 Winchester, Geo, 21, I, June 28, scs.
2894 Weaver, H, 10, F, July 4, dia.
8378 Wens, Charles, 7, B, July 16, dia. c.

4706 Wakefield, D, 25, K, Aug 4, dia.
9484 Woodward, W B, 1, Sept 21, scs.
9938 Wick, J, 1 cav, H, Sept 28, scs.
10213 Willis, E, 7, E, Oct 2, scs.
10395 Winchell, S, 1, D, Oct 6, scs.
12111 Whalen, M, 12, B, Oct 21, scs.
12363 Ward, A, 1 cav, C, Dec 31, scs.

12626 Yessen, A, 24, A, Feb 10, scs.

UNITED STATES ARMY.

1798 Anderson, A, 16, C, June 10, dia. c.
3666 Atwell, Thos,§ 6 cav, M, July 20, phs.
4349 Allen, Chas, 18, H, July 31, scs.
4537 Ashley, D B, 16, C, Aug 2, i. f.
6077 Arnold, H, 18, H, Aug 18, ces.
6089 Adams, G, 14, C, Aug 18, dys.
8069 Austin, Jas,§ 4 cav, K, Sept 7, dys.
11523 Annis, Chas, 8 (colored), I, Oct 26, scs.
9250 Alfka, A H, 2 cav, D, Sept 19, dia.

102 Blossom, Chas, 6 cav, E, March 22, dys.
1122 Boughten, M, 15, E, May 15, ana.
1158 Bailey, Andrew, 16, K, May 16, dia.
1199 Britner, A, 16, K, May 18, ana.
1201 Banks, E E, 17, C, May 19, dia.
1266 Burton, George, 8 (col'd), I, May 21, dia.
1397 Barden, Chas S, 15, E, May 26, scs.
1442 Beal, H, 15, C, May 28, dia. c.
1461 Becker, L, 2, B, May 29, dia.
1762 Brown, C, 16, D, June 9, ana.
2122 Bates, E L, 5 cav, E, June 17, dia.
2434 Brannagan, J, 18, D, June 24, des.
2436 Bigler, N M, 2 cav, B, June 25, dia. c.
2749 Bradshaw, H, marine corps, July 1, dia.
3370 Bush, W, 15, E, July 15, dia. c.
4861 Baldwin, G, 19, A, Aug 6, dys.
4969 Baker, F, signal corps, Aug 7, dia. c.
5657 Boyd, S,‡ 4, C, Aug 14, dia.
5774 Breen, A, 2, F, Aug 15, dys.
6126 Boyd, John B, 4, K, Aug 19, dia.
6628 Bradman, A M,§ 6 cav, M, Aug 23, dia. c.
6652 Burd, W U, 6, E, Aug 23, ana.
6937 Bowers, J, 4, K, Aug 26, ana.
7717 Burk, James, 1, K, Sept 3, dia.
7921 Brossessault, M, 2 art, M, Sept 5, dia.
8909 Banvall, J, 4, F, Sept 16, scs.
9477 Bartlett, E K, 2 s s, D, Sept 21, scs.
9631 Barstow, J, 18, D, Sept 24, dia. c.
9848 Barrett, J, 18, D, Sept 27, scs.
10621 Britzer, L B,‡ 15, C, Sept 10, dia.
11577 Brown, J, 12, H, Oct 28, scs.
11706 Brickley, H, 1, K, Nov 1, scs.
12077 Ball, W, 12, C, Nov 18, scs.
12112 Boyer, J, 1 cav, K, Nov 21, scs.
12564 Bromley, J, 18, G, Jan 31, scs.

760 Chisholm, J M,§ m. corps, Apr 27, dia. c.
1947 Clemens, D, 6, L, June 14, dia. c.
2174 Clemburg, J, 16, D, June 19, dia.
2216 Cassman, A, marine corps, June 20, dia.
2726 Carter, Thos, 15, H, July 1, dia. c.
3126 Cavanaugh, P, 16, A, July 10, dia.
3500 Conden, H, 12, A, July 18, dys.
3911 Crookey, S,‡ 15, H, July 24, dia.
4346 Chase, V, 16, C, July 30, dia.
4930 Campbell, S L, 15, C, Aug 7, ana.
5107 Croy, J, 18, B, Aug 9, dia.
5156 Cussey, Jas, 15, A, Aug 9, dia.
5234 Casey, J, 15, A, Aug 10, ana.
5436 Champney, P A, sig. corps, Aug 12 dys.
6420 Cammell, J, 12, H, Aug 22, dys.
7532 Coolidge, M, 17, B, Sept 1, dia. c.
7722 Connor, H, 15, H, Sept 3, dia.
7906 Corst, James, 14, D, Sept 5, dia. c.
8161 Connell, J, 14, D, Sept 8, scs.
8243 Chamberlain, C, 17, B, Sept 9, dia.
8570 Collins M, 4 cav, H, Sept 12, scs.
8767 Carter, C A, 1, B, Sept 14, scs.

9034 Clifford, J, 6 cav, B, Sept 17, scs.
9113 Chase, L, 10, C, Sept 18, dia. c.
9186 Carroll, L, 2 cav, G, Sept 18, dia. a.
9295 Congreve, E, 5, A, Sept 19, dia.
9482 Cuyler, W, 16, B, Sept 21, ana.
9814 Crocker, Chas, 2, A, Sept 26, dia.
10210 Cargill, C, 12, F, Oct 2, scs.
10557 Clark, R W, 2 s s, Oct 9, dia.
11176 Casey, Jno, 19, A, Oct 19, scs.
11201 Childs, G, 16, B, Oct 20, dys.
11633 Cramer, A,§ 19, C, Oct 28, scs.

914 Dunn, John, 6, A, May 6, dys.
910 Dangler, W G, 5, M, May 5, dia. c.
1255 Doney, J W, 6 cav, D, May 21, dia.
1653 Dunn, Wm, 19, F, June 5, dys.
2274 Dunn, John, 18, I, June 20, dia. c.
2495 Donalan, M, 2 cav, L, June 26, dys.
3025 Deyer, H,§ 18, D, July 7, dys.
4377 Darvin, W W, 2 s s, B, July 31, dia.
4490 Dinslow, B F, 12, G, Aug 1, scs.
4626 Delaney, Jacob, 5 art, F, Aug 3, scs.
5348 Doll, R, 14, C, Aug 11, dia.
5459 Dolan, P, 19, F, Aug 12, phs.
5756 Davis, G,‡ 19, A, Aug 15, scs.
6025 Decker, James, 10, Aug 18, dys.
6210 Davis, J W,‡ 15, E, Aug 19, dia. c.
6297 Doran, J M, 19, E, Aug 20, dia. c.
6770 Doughty, D B, 3 art, C, Aug 25, scs
6805 Davidson, J 11, 15, C, Aug 25, ana.
6955 Delaney, E, 19, F, Aug 26, ana.
7049 Davis, G, 15, F, Aug 27, dia.
7241 Delaney, J, 2, F, Aug 29, dys.
7792 Dean, Samuel, 4 cav, B, Sept 3, scs.
8214 Downing, M, 10, D, Sept 8, dia.
8832 Doule, J, 10, D, Sept 15, scs.
10235 Davis, Clarke, 1 bat, K, Oct 2, dia.
10883 Draper, L, 14, F, Oct 14, scs.
11554 Davy, H, 18, G, Oct 27, scs.
11613 Diller, O M, 5 cav, I, Oct 28, scs.
12140 Drummond, J, 18, F, Nov 23, scs.
12591 Dunn, C, 15, C, Feb 4, scs.

5648 Evans, T, 14, F, Aug 14, dys.
6813 Edwards, Wm (negro), 8, A, Aug 25, dia
7576 Erick, J, 2, K, Sept 2, dys.
7616 Ellerton, N, 16, D, Sept 2, scs.
12689 Emmict, S S, 5, C, Feb 22, scs.

42 Ferguson, J, 6 cav, E, March 15, cah.
1243 Fitzgibbons, Thos, 2, C, May 20, dia.
1509 Ferrell, J, 12, A, May 31, dia. c.
2355 Fiffey, H, 18, E, May 23, dia. a.
2888 French, George, 1st lieut, 37, July 3, r. l
3007 Feed, G, 6 cav, D, July 7, dia.
3256 Frenchy, D, 2, F, July 13, dys.
3543 Fielding, A, 13, E, July 18, dia. c.
5487 Fliestine, S, 16, C, Aug 13, ana.
6804 Felps, Daniel (negro), 8, H, Aug 25, dia
7167 Flanigan, M, 2, I, Aug 29, des.
8536 Fannton, H, 14, F, Sept 12, scs.
9154 Flanery, M, 1 cav, H, Sept 18, dia.
9725 Frum, E, 3 cav, C, Sept 25, dia.
9983 Flarety, O, 16, Sept 29, scs.
10655 Fenall, J, 14, G, Oct 11, dia.
10839 Flanagan, P, 4 cav, D, Oct 13, scs.
11402 Fritz, A,§ 19, A, Oct 24, scs.
12312 Foster, J, 4, H, Dec 19, scs.

272 Gil igan, Mat,‡ 1, I, March 31, dys.
1639 Gardener, C, signal corps, June 5, dia. a.
2801 Gulterman, S,§ 16, D, July 2, dia.
4977 Gray, Wm, 18, C, Aug 7, dia.
6182 Gale, Walter, 11, F, Aug 19, dia. c.
7220 Gulvere, David, 4, C, Aug 29, scs.
8057 Griffith, S, 11, F, Sept 7, scs.
8671 Gunter, John, 4 cav, Sept 13, dia.
8857 Grace, Thos, 1, B, Sept 15, wds.
9851 Gilbert, A, 5, K, Sept 27, scs.
12066 Getts, F, 19, E, Nov 16, dys.
7335 Golton, R, 16, B, Aug 30, dia.

397 Hatch, T C, 11, A, April 6, pna.
533 Halbert, F, 2, H, April 13, dys.
1547 Halpin, P, 5 art, H, June 1, dia. c.
1585 Haney, H, 16, D, June 3, dia. c.
1608 Hurman, J H, 4 cav, E, June 4, dia. c.
2096 Hendricks, J, 16 D, June 17, ana.
2209 Hogan, M, 16, A, June 20, dia. a.
2706 Henry, Wm, 2, B, June 30, dia. a.
2730 Hurley, D, marine corps, July 1, dys.
2987 Hulit, Wm, 16, D, July 7, dia. c.
3753 Hill, Geo, 17, H, July 22, dia. c.
8893 Hopkins, W (negro), 17, C, July 24, ana.
4429 Hill, D S (negro), 16, C, July 31, dia.
7238 Heddington, W, 15, F, Aug 29, dys.
7405 Harsham, J R, 15, G, Aug 31, ana.
8004 Halley, J, 13, B, Sept 6, dia.
9104 Hook, H, 19, F, Sept 18, dia. c.
9155 Heir, J, 14, A, Sept 18, scs.
9665 Hildreth, Jas, 12, Sept 24, dia.
9918 Haney, J, 12, C, Sept 23, scs.
10054 Hasler, C, 13, M, Sept 30, gae.
10439 Hirshfield, G, marine corps, Oct 7, scs.
10857 Harman, J, 15, E, Oct 14, dia.
11136 Hamilton, S, 2 s s, D, Oct 19, dia. c.
12369 Hill, M A, 2, G, Jan 1, des.
12601 Hoit, E (negro), 35, H, Feb 6, dia. c.
10322 Hamman, W H, 15, F, Oct 3, scs.

5532 Imhoff, I, 15, E, Aug 13, pls.
7647 Ireland, Geo, 14, E, Sept 3, dia.
10742 Ireson, I, 4 cav, A, Oct 11, scs.

1111 Johnson, P, 6, C, May 15, dia. c.
8125 Johnson, P, 2 bat, Sept 8, scs.
8866 Jones, W, 1 art, K, Sept 10, scs.
10319 Jones, C B, 1 cav, H, Oct 3, scs.
11923 Jerald, W H,§ 18, F, Nov 8, scs.

495 Kingeny, J, 1, K, April 12, dia.
912 Kelly, John, 16, C, May 5, dia. c.
1662 Kain, P F,§ 15, A, June 6, dys.
3256 Kenley, D, 2, F, July 13, dys.
3341 Kerkney, F, 18, F, July 15, dia.
3685 Kilbride, J, 15, F, July 21, dia.
4245 Kane, Wm, 18, H, July 29, dys.
4266 Kalkrath, C, 3, I, July 29, dia.
4271 Kelly, D, 4, H, July 29, dia.
4694 Kester, J, 15, F, Aug 4, dia.
5640 Kay, Robt, 4, F, Aug 14, scs.
5643 Kelly, J, marine corps, Aug 14, scs.
6271 Kochel, J,‡ 19, G, Aug 20, mas.
6577 Kelly, Wm, 9, I, Aug 23, dys.
6764 King, I, 7, K, Aug 25, dia.
7465 Kinney, G W, 1 bat, D, Sept 1, scs.
8261 Klinty, H, 1 art, K, Sept 9, scs.
8490 Kricks, F, 14, C, Sept 11, scs.
8527 Kripp, J, 16, D, Sept 12, scs.
9082 Knapp, C, 11, A, Sept 18, gae.
11268 Kain, Pat, 15, A, Oct 21, scs.
11767 Kelly, J S, 2, D, Nov 3, cah.
11949 Kennedy, J, 12, A, Nov 10, scs.
12205 Kahl, Chas, 2 art, M, Dec 1, scs.
12532 Kemp, J W, 2, K, Jan 27, dia. c.

55 Love, Wm,§ 6, F, March 17, pna.
2282 Larreby, G, 16, D, June 20, dia.
2774 Little, J, 19, E, July 21, dys.
3999 Lackey, J, 16, B, July 26, dia. c.
4453 Langsaff, R, 10, F, Aug 1, dia.

5711 Lake, Horace, 4 cav, K, Aug 15, dia.
5891 Lynch, B, 18, E, Aug 16, dia.
6116 Lattin, E, 12, A, Aug 19, ces.
6300 Lawrence, C, 11, E, Aug 20, dia.
6352 Lyons, E, signal corps, Aug 21, dia. c.
6561 Little, R, 19, F, Aug 23, scs.
9732 Larqdell, Wm,§ 14, A, Sept 25, dia.
10317 Louby, O, 4 cav, H, Oct 3, scs.
10379 Lockewood, H (negro), 8, D, Oct 5, dia.
11038 Lyons, R, 1 cav, E, Oct 17, scs.,
11543 Lyman, O S, 18, A, Oct 27, scs.
11973 Lewis, Wm P, 8, B, Nov 12, scs.

180 McCoy, Augustus, 6, M, March 26, dia.
267 McClellan, J, 6 cav, D, March 31, ts. f.
828 Mason, C H, 12, I, May 1, dys
948 Murphy, D, 12, B, May 8, dys.
1012 McEvers, T L, 13, C, May 10, dia.
1043 McGuire, J, 3, C, May 12, dia
1332 Murray, Thos, 1 art, I, May 24, dia.
1471 Mulhall, Peter,§ mar corps, May 30, dia.
1823 Marze, Jas, 12, D, June 10, dia.
1946 McLaughlin, J, 2, H, June 14, dia. c.
1965 McConaghy, P, mar corps, June 14, scs.
2444 Meadow, John, 6 cav, E, June 25, scs.
3054 Muller, J, mar corps, June 30, dys.
2920 Miller, C H, 6 cav, E, July 5, scs.
3054 McKinney, J, mar corps, July 9, dia. c.
3083 Maloney, B, 19, B, July 9, dia. c.
3950 Merkill, Peter, 14, H, July 25, dia.
4712 Murch, Wm, 11, C, Aug 4, dia.
4823 McClintock, J S, 18, H, Aug 5, dia. c.
4863 Martin, M, mar corps, Aug 6, dia.
5303 Martin, J, 1 cav, K, Aug 11, dia. c.
5364 McCann, B, 12, B, Aug 11, dia.
5456 Nichols, R, 1 cav, K, Aug 12, scs.
5581 McLean, P, 17, C, Aug 14, scs.
5769 McCoslin, Robt, 1 art, B, Aug 15, ens.
6073 McDonald, 4 cav, E, Aug 18, dys.
6081 McClair, R, 11, G, Aug 18, scs.
6313 Munson, C, 12, D, Aug 20, scs.
6407 Mulhern, C, 4 cav, C, Aug 22, scs.
6515 Mantle, J M,‡ 15, F, Aug 22, ts. f.
6851 Marston, B, 51, s s, G, Aug 25, dia.
6973 McKinley, E W, mar corps, Aug 27, dia.
7341 McGuire, J, 12, D, Aug 30, scs.
8293 Mun, W, 18, H, Sept 9, scs.
8473 McGinness, A, 4 art, E, Sept 11, scs.
9110 Montgomery, C, 13, G, Sept 18, dia.
9231 McCoy, J M,§ mar brigade, Sept 19, dia.
9368 Miller, H, 2 art, Sept 20, dia.
9472 Morris, G J, 18, I, Sept 21, dia.
9830 McDermott, H, 18, E, Sept 26, scs.
10135 Manning, J, 15, A, Oct 1, scs.
10321 McCoy, J, 4, F, Oct 3, scs.
10457 Mills, A, 15, G, Oct 7, scs.
10554 McCord, G, 14, E, Oct 9, scs.
10855 McGee, P,‡ 2, Oct 13, scs.
11008 Murray, Jas, 17, G, Oct 16 scs.
12148 Mizner, W, 1st sig corps, K, Nov 24, scs.
12151 Moran, J, 4 cav, F, Nov 24, scs.
7341 McGuire, J, 12, D, Aug 31, scs.
12364 McGorren, J, 17, C, Dec 31, scs.

2876 Northrup, H E, 4, H, July 3, dia.
6803 Newcombe, John, 18, G, Aug 20, ana.
6954 Nichols, H,‡ 12, A, Aug 26, dia.
10240 North, Jacob, 15, A, Oct 3, scs.
12386 Neise, J, 6, F, Jan 2, des.
12833 Naff, V, bugler, 1 art, B, April 16, dia.
12790 Newel, L, 18, G, March 17, dia. c.

2368 O'Reilly, Theodore,§ 3, K, June 23, scs.
7036 Ott, John, 10, A, Aug 27, scs.
11846 Osrans, J, 4 cav, I, Nov 5, scs.

492 Partridge, J W, signal corps, April 12, dia
1607 Pace, J F, 18, C, June 4, dia.
1893 Pulliam, Wm, 1 cav, June 13, dia. c.
3219 Pigot, J, marine corps, July 12, dia.
3669 Ponter, ——, 1 art, I, July 18, dia.
4631 Pearson, S C, 40, C, Aug 3, dia.

5309 Pratt, C E, 1 art, M, Aug 11, scs.
5729 Pike, Wm,‡ 5 cav, G, Aug 15, scs.
5731 Poulton, Henry, 19, A, Aug 15, scs.
6392 Page, J E, 18, B, Aug 21, dys.
7008 Phillips, C, 14, D, Aug 27, scs.
7267 Pruet, Jas M, 19, A, Aug 30, scs.
7311 Plummer, G, 2 s s, D, Aug 30, dia.
2611 Preston, John, marine corps, June 28, dia.
7752 Pratt, J, 3, B, Sept 3, dia.
9571 Post, A, 1 art, F, Sept 23, dia.
10951 Palmer, Wm E,§ 15, F, Oct 14, scs.
11170 Pattit, J S, 11, F, Oct 19, scs.
12142 Puck, C, 15, G, Nov 24, scs.

4022 Quinback, J, 18, G, July 26, scs.

11 Ross, ——, 19, A, March 5, phs.
194 Rooney, Mark, 14, F, March 27, pna.
404 Reardon, D, 13, G, April 6, dys.
702 Reynolds, Edwd, m corps, April 23, dys. c.
3355 Roney, F J, 18, E, July 15, dia. c.
3820 Ritzer, Geo A, 5 cav, H, July 23, dia.
4276 Robison, W R, 6 cav, H, July 30, dia.
4957 Rhodes, A, 18, B, Aug 7, scs.
5210 Rinkle, George, 2 cav, G, Aug 10, dia.
5984 Rouke, J, 10, D, Aug 17, dia.
7151 Richards, Theod, 2 cav, D, Aug 29, dia.
8438 Rogers, Wm, 18, G, Sept 14, scs.
9268 Reynolds, D, 4 cav, C, Sept 19, ana.
10792 Reilly, J, 3, B, Oct 2, scs.
2701 Rawson, J, 16, K, June 30, dia. c.

363 Striff, John, 2, F, April 2, dia.
1236 Shelton, C, 8, F, May 20, dia.
1253 Spalding, Wm, 3 cav, B, May 21, dia.
1295 Scripter, C E, 5 cav, D, May 23, dia.
1647 Sweitzer, M, 19, H, June 5, scs.
1714 Smith, H W, 15, C, June 7, dia.
2073 Stoltz, ——,§ 16, C, June 17, scs.
2082 Smith, James, 16, D, June 17, ana.
2298 Styles, J N, 13, A, June 22, dia.
2550 Sumser, J, 19, G, June 27, dia.
3110 Spaulding, James, 13, B, July 10, dia.
3114 Skinner, L, 13, C, July 10, dia.
3838 Smartkash, C,‡ 15, C, July 23, dia. c.
3978 Somers, P, 4 cav, C, July 26, dia.
4238 Seybert, J S,‡ 1 s s, H, July 29, dia.
4310 Smith, Allen, 4, H, July 30, ana.
4666 Striper, M, 18, D, Aug 4, scs.
5022 Sutgen, F, 16, C, Aug 8, dia. c.
5305 Sorg, A, 1 art, M, Aug 11, scs.
5393 Swagger, H, 4 cav, D, Aug 12, dia.
5801 Sisson, J, 4, D, Aug 15, scs.
6620 Slaughterback, B, 15, H, Aug 23, ana.
6833 Sutgen, F, 16, C, Aug 25, scs.
7377 Smith, F, 14, E, Aug 31, scs.
7606 Starr, Darius,§ 2 s s, F, Sept 2, dys.
7874 Snider, J, 11, B, Sept 5, dia. c.
8839 Scott, Jas H, 2 cav, B, Sept 15, scs.
9215 Stansbury, E, marine corps, Sept 19, dia.
9514 Souls, J H, 15, F, Sept 22, ana.
10214 Sullivan, T, 11, C, Oct 2, scs.

11144 Schroder, F, 15, C, Oct 19, scs.
11301 Smith, J, 8, D, Oct 22, scs.
11333 Stanton, R, 14, K, Oct 23, scs.
11664 Spencer, J H, 2, D, Oct 30, scs.
11690 Shortman, J, 14, E, Oct 31, dys.
12186 Streeter, J, 16, B, Nov 28, scs.
12211 Stanton, C, 2, I, Dec 2, dia.

92 Tooley, Michael, 13, G, March 21, dia. &
489 Taylor, Amos, 17, H, April 12, dia. c
2603 Thompson, Wm, 18, G, June 28, scs.
2662 Truman, J, 5 cav, D, June 29, dys.
3466 Tyson, E S, 14, D, July 17, pls.
4716 Tredridge, A, musician, 13, Aug 4, ana.
7306 Taylor, M D, 18, E, Aug 31, dia.
7801 Turk, H, 18, H, Sept 4, dia.
8258 Thomas, J, 1 cav, D, Sept 9, dia. c.
8259 Trainer, M, 6, F, Sept 9, dia.
8279 Thomas, L (negro), 8, D, Sept 9, i. f.
9115 Taylor, E,‡ 18, I, Sept 18, dia. c.
11393 Topper, J, 11, B, Oct 24, scs.

7829 Unmuch, C, 1 art, K, Sept 4, dys.

3657 Volmore, J, 3, K, July 18, scs.
7042 Vancotten, Wm, 16, D, Aug 27, scs.
7135 Vickery, Wm, 1, H, Aug 28, dia.
12041 Van Buren, W H, 16, B, Nov 16, scs.

1259 Walker, Wm, 6, D, May 21, dia.
1299 Worster, Chas B, 5 cav, H, May 23, dia. c
2752 White, Thomas, 1, D, July 1, dia.
4023 Williams, D, 18, D, July 26, scs.
4248 Warner, S, 16, E, July 29, dia. c.
4306 Williams, John, 4, D, July 30, dia.
5425 Walmor, ——, 10, D, Aug 12, dia.
6125 Wickham, G H, 16, B, Aug 19, scs.
6637 Wills, S, 15, E, Aug 23, dys.
7048 Wright, C S, 12, C, Aug 27, c. f.
7109 Wadsworth, B H, 12, C, Aug 28, dia.
7254 Warner, H, 2, D, Aug 30, dia.
9105 Whitney, J W,‡ 4 cav, K, Sept 18, scs.
9131 White, Samuel, 8, F, Sept 18, dia.
9677 Walker, John (negro), 8, F, Sept 24, scs.
9854 Walter, I, 17, B, Sept 27, scs.
10355 Wigley, E, 17, C, Oct 5, dys.
10374 Waters, ——,§ 8, C, Oct 5, dia.
10756 Waldo, J M, 1 art, K, Oct 12, scs.
11137 Williams, C, 1 art, K, Oct 19, scs.
11395 Wizmaker, G, 2, M, Oct 24, scs.
12009 Wilson, C W, 15, A, Nov 14, scs.
12027 Wise, G B, 6, F, Nov 15, ana.

6496 Yarger, A, 18, Aug 22, scs.
7101 Young, Robert, 1 cav, K, Aug 28, dia.
10754 Young, F B, 2 art, M, Oct 12, scs.
11373 Young, J C, 19, A, Oct 23, scs.

7793 Zimmerman, J, 17, D, Sept 4, scs.
10428 Zing, P,§ 10, C, Oct 6, scs.
10450 Zimmerman, M, 14, I, Oct 7, scs.

UNITED STATES NAVY.

2619 Akinson, A, Nepsia, June 27, dia.
4698 Anker, George, Norman, Aug 4, dia.
8071 Anderson, Chas, Saithfield, Sept 7, dia.

2919 Bradley, John, Southfield, July 3, dia.
3475 Broderick, W, July 17, dia.
5072 Bowers, W H, Water Witch, Aug 8, dia. c.
12047 Boucher, W, Shawsheen, Nov 16, scs.

1914 Carnes, Wm, June 13, dia. c.
2149 Conant, G S, Southfield, June 18, dia.
2580 Carter, W J, Montgomery, June 27, dia. c.
6201 Collins, Thomas, Southfield, Aug 19, dys.
7144 Corbet, E, Aug 29, des.
7508 Connor, J, Sept 1, scs.

9544 Culbert, J, Sept 23, dia.

164 Dillingham, J N, Housatonic, Mar 26, phs
6437 Duffney, J, Aug 22, dia.

3086 Ellis, J H, Columbine, July 9, ts. f.
4134 Evans, John, Shawsheen, July 28, dia. c.
4462 Earl, Jas H, paym'r steward, Aug 1, scs.

5419 Foley, Daniel, Southfield, Aug 12, dia. c.

4605 Green, G C, Southfield, Aug 3, scs.
8871 Goundy, Thomas, Sept 15, dia.

1087 Heald, Wm, Canandaigua, Apr 14, dia. &

1469 Hunter, John, seaman, May 30, ana.
221. Hilton, John, Johana, June 20, dia.
3444 Hodges, L, Norman, July 17, brs.
3793 Hughes, Benj, Wabash, July 22, ts. f.
5875 Heald, H H, merch'tman, Aug 16, dia. c.
9284 Holas, Thos, Water Witch, Sept 19, dia.

1432 Jones, Wm, Underwriter, May 28, dia. c.
2178 Jones, Theo, Underwriter, June 19, dia. c.
2206 Journeay, John, fireman, June 19, dia. c.
6417 Jackson, J, Shawsheen, Aug 22, scs.
8291 Johnson, G P, Sept 9, dia.
8858 James, F A, Sept 15, dys.
9392 Johnson, M, Sept 20, dia.
10218 Joseph, F, Oct 2, dia.

602 Keefe, John, Housatonic, April 18, dys.
698 Kultz, A, T Ward, April 23, dys.
1546 Kelly, James, Underwriter, June 1, dia. c.
3860 Kinney, J, Water Witch, July 24, dia. c.

7375 Lodi, John, Aug 31, dia.
2843 Lindersmith, E, Montgomery, July 3, dia.
4291 Lawton, James, Ladona, July 30, dys.

235 Mays, A H, mate, Norman, Mar 29, dys.
2452 McDonald, John, June 25, dia.
2581 Moore, A, Anna, June 27, scs.
3128 Malaby, P, Montgomery, July 10, dys.
3348 Murphy, M J, July 15, dia.
3529 McDonald, John, July 17, dia.
3804 Matthews, J, Underwriter, July 22, dia. c.
4208 McHenry, Daniel, Southford, July 29, dia.
4324 McCarty, T, Housatonic, July 30, dia. c.
4396 McVey, K, July 31, dys.
4679 McTier, J, Aug 4, dys.
4800 McLaughlin, E, Aug 5, dys.
5485 Meldon, J, Aug 13, pna.
6355 Marshall, N B, Leipsig, Aug 21, dia.
6571 McDermott, P, Montgomery, Aug 23, des.
6825 Mathews, W C, Aug 25, dia.
6917 McLaughlin, B, Aug 26, scs.
7251 McGowan, J, Powhattan, Aug 30, dia.
11863 Maston, J, Ratler, Nov 6, scs.

7824 Noe, M, Sept 4, i. f.

2227 O'Brien, Wm, June 20, dia.
3208 Ottinger, M, Water Witch, July 12, scs.

3153 Page, Lyman, July 11, scs.
5325 Parkham, Jas C, Shawsheen, Aug 11, dia.
9024 Peterson, J, Sept 17, dia.

2460 Quinlan, N, June 25, scs.
7867 Quade, M, Sept 5, scs.

2237 Ragan, John, T Ward, June 20, i. f.
4661 Raymond, W, T Ward, Aug 3, scs.
5108 Roland, John, Underwriter, Aug 9, scs.
7003 Reynolds, T J, Aug 27, dia.

169 Stark, John, March 26, dia. c.
2010 Sullivan, J, Underwriter, June 15, dia.
2883 Smith, John W, Southfield, July 3, ts. f.
3261 Sampson, J R, nav battalion, July 13, dia.
4611 Smith, B N, Mendota, Aug 3, scs.
6592 Stanley, Wm, Southfield, Aug 23, dia. c.
11299 Smith, Wm, Water Witch, Oct 22, scs.

1713 Thomas, Saml, Southfield, June 7, dia. c.
1851 Thomas, John, Southfield, June 11, dia. c.
3757 Turner, Wm, July 1, r. f.
4159 Trymer, James, Southfield, July 28, dia.
7445 Tobin, Michael, Sept 1, dia.
8302 Ta, B F, Southfield, Sept 10, dia.

1646 Willis, J P, June 5, dia.
3004 Wilson, A, Southfield, July 7, dia. c.
3878 Williams, M W, July 24, dia.
4118 Willis, M, Southfield, July 28, scs.
4198 Williams, C, Aries, July 29, dia. c.
5820 Wordell, G K, Aug 16, mas.
5990 Warren, W H, Aug 17, dia.
6458 Wooley, M, Aug 22, scs.
7503 Walsh, Jas, Sept 1, dia.
8104 Welch, V, Southfield, Sept 7, dia.
10565 West, John, Southfield, Oct 9, dia.

MISCELLANEOUS.

1460 Addley, A, citizen, Oct 25, scs.
887 Amos, J, Ringold bat, F, May 4, ts. f.
2977 Augar, A, July 7, dia.

282 Bane, S, Ringold bat, A, April 1, pna.
2072 Beatty, D, Ring bat, F, June 17, dia. c.
4327 Baker, John, teamster, July 30, dia. c.
4904 Bennmar, L, Aug 6, dia.
5747 Butterfield, James, citizen, Aug 15, dys.
6100 Blair, H, citizen, Aug 18, ana.
6366 Bidwell, C, cit teamster, Aug 21, dys.
8102 Burkhead, W, Prunell's legion, Sept 7, dia.
9344 Blood, G P, Sept 20, scs.
9591 Brogdin, D C, Sept 23, dia.
10500 Burk, C, citizen, Oct 8, scs.
10602 Bishop, J, citizen teamster, Oct 10, dys.
10963 Brown, Geo, Bridge's bat, Oct 15, scs.
12342 Boland, Jas, Prunell's cav, Dec 26, dia. c.

177 Cannon, Wm, teamster, March 26.
389 Campbell, D, Ring bat, E, April 6, dia.
431 Childers, C H, April 8, dia. c.
1195 Cobb, J, citizen teamster, May 18, pls.
1881 Clark, M, citizen teamster, June 12, dia. a.
3399 Cable, C, citizen, July 16, des.
3972 Cregger, J F, musician, July 25, dia.
6315 Crowley, Pat, Aug 20, scs.
9245 Carroll, C, teamster, 19 ar corps, Sept 19, scs.
10485 Corbit, J, Oct 7, wds.
10872 Carey, Thos, Oct 13, scs.
11726 Collins, J, citizen teamster, Nov 1, scs.
12449 Carroll, J, citizen teamster, Jan 13, scs.

752 Deems, P, Ringold bat, E, April 26, dia. c
2620 Delp, Geo, citizen teamster, June 28, dia.
4334 Davis, J, citizen, July 30, dia.
5866 Danfirth, Geo A, Aug 16, dia.
8202 Delmore, W, citizen, Sept 8, dia.
11084 Dubin, M, citizen teamster, Oct 18, scs.
11248 Delhanta, Wm, citizen, Oct 21, dia.

182 England, E, March 27, pna.
3923 Evans, M, citizen, July 25, dia.
——— Everett, T S, citizen, Md, Aug 30, dia.

157 Freeman, John, March 25, dys.
453 Fenley, R, citizen, April 9, dia c.
1116 Fannon, A, citizen, May 15, dys.
2332 Foster, W, tel operator, June 22, dia. c.
2435 Farrell, M, citizen, June 25, ana.
10473 Flickison, J, Oct 7, dia.
4808 Fitzgerald, ———, Aug 5, dia.
5078 Frank, F M, Wilder's bat, Aug 8, scs.
5609 Fox, Henry, cit teamster, Aug 14, scs.
7643 Ford, P, teamster, Sept 3, dia.
9084 Foncks, H C, Keye's ind't cav, Sept 18, dia
11315 Ferrall, M C, teamster, Oct 22, scs.

2729 Gildea, D, citizen, July 1, scs.
4115 Grogran, D, July 28, dia c.
4747 Gishart, J, Aug 5, ts. f.
6139 Graham, E, citizen, Aug 19, dia.
7854 Gorb, S, Sept 5, scs.
9747 Goodman, J O, Sept 25.
10672 Gillman, John, Oct 11, dia. c.

11802 Goodyear, F, citizen, Nov 6, scs.
10717 Graves, Wm E, Oct 11, scs.

219 Heartless, S, March 29.
264 Hammond, S, teamster, March 31, dia. c.
606 Hoffman, Chas, cit teamster, Apr 18, dys.
1274 Harkins, John, teamster, May 22, dia. c.
2370 Hammond, J, cit teamster, June 23, dia.
322f Hudson, G W, cit teamster, July 12, dia.
4244 Hughes, P, July 29, wds.
6070 Harway, D, cit teamster, Aug 18, ts. f.
8055 Heritage, J, teamster, Sept 7, scs.
8756 Harkins, D S,‡ m m b, Sept 14, dia.
9006 Hyatt, J, Sept 17, scs.
9051 Hulbert, J H S, Sept 17, dia.
9297 Hall, M, a a s, Sept 19, scs.
9425 Hart, Isaac, citizen teamster, Sept 21, dia.
10262 Hines, Daniel, Oct 3, dia.
10331 Hopkins, John, Oct 4, dia.
11934 Heckinbridge, ——, Nov 9, scs.
12456 Harrington, J,§ Jan 15, dia. c.

8722 Imhagg, ——, Sept 14, dia.

4794 Jones, Chas, cit teamster, Aug 5, dia. c.
6854 Jacobs, W C, citizen, Aug 25, dys.
12714 Johnson, J, citizen, Canada, Mar 1, dia. c.

2208 Kingland, W H, citizen, June 20, dia.
3515 Kerr, E, citizen teamster, June 18, dia.
6273 Kins, W H, citizen teamster, Aug 20, mas.
7864 Knight, J B, citizen teamster, Sept 5, ana.
9467 Kellogg, E L, cit, S'gfi'ld, Ms, Sept 21, dia.

546 Lee, James, cit teamster, April 14, dys. c.
1772 Lafferty, Wm, Ringgold bat, June 9, scs.
3689 Lummo, Robert, citizen, July 21, scs.
10853 Linton, E, Ringgold bat, Oct 5, dys.

76 Morton, J B, Ringgold cav, A, Mar 20, ts.f.
203 McMahon, Pat, March 28, dia.
220 Morrison, F, cit teamster, March 29, dia.
865 Mower, W, citizen, May 3, des.
2285 McAtie, M, teamster, June 21, dia. c.
2432 Manning, B F, cit teamster, June 24, dia.
2373 McEushon, Peter, June 23, dys.
3450 Moyer, J, July 17, dia.
4017 Messenger, H M, citizen, July 26, dys.
5387 Morland, J S, cit teamster, Aug 12, dia.
5996 McGee, J, Aug 17, dia.
6380 McKenna, F, Aug 21, scs.
8039 McGuire, J, citizen, Sept 6, scs.
9135 Myers, John, Sept 18, dia.
9247 McDonald, J, Sept 19, scs.
9616 Munch, Christian, top eng, Sept 23, dia.
12535 McDonald, H H, cit, Ohio, Jan 27, dia.
6666 Monteith, M, cit teamster, Aug 24, dia.

184 Newton, Wm, teamster, March 27, pna.
7074 Norton, E, citizen, Aug 28, dys.
8510 Nichols, J, teamster, 15 ar c, Sept 12, dia.

4190 Osborne, J, citizen, July 28, dys.
5414 Oliver, W W, Aug 12, scs.

719 Pringle, Wm, cit teamster, April 25, ts. f
1855 Podzas, L, citizen teamster, June 12, dia.
5920 Poole, C, Aug 17, scs.
8893 Powers, G, citizen, Sept 16, scs.
9010 Potter, S D, Sept 17, dia.
9366 Phillips, B B, teamster, Sept 20, dia.
12354 Parker, Jas, cit teamster, Dec 29, dia. c
10100 Parkhurst, W L, 1 m m b, Sept 30, dia.

853 Quinn, James, citizen, May 3, dia. c.
5394 Quinlan, Pat, cit teamster, Aug 12, scs.
5768 Quinn, ——, citizen, Aug 15, scs.

3542 Reed, A R, independent, July 18, dia.
3779 Rand, J, cit teamster, July 22, scs.
5986 Ronley, J, Aug 17, dia.
10111 Rendig, C H, citizen, Oct 1, scs.
10453 Ryan, John, citizen, Oct 7, gae.
11131 Reien, R, citizen, Oct 18.
11703 Richardson, J C, 1 m m b, I, Oct 30, scs.

449 Scott, Blair, citizen, April 9, dia. c.
2431 Smith, P, m m b, June 24, dia.
2440 St Clair, Benj, cit teamster, June 25, dia.
2552 Slater, Chas, cit teamster, June 27, dia.
2959 Spicer, W, citizen teamster, July 6, pna.
3000 Stout, Chas, citizen, July 7, des.
3662 Shunk, J, citizen, July 20, dys.
4008 Smith, H, Bridges bat, July 26, ana.
4843 Sawyer, J D, Aug 6, dys.
9729 Stanton, J, citizen, Sept 25, dia.
10815 Smayo, David, Oct 12, dia.

136 Thompson, Jno, teamster, March 24, pna
1531 Tullis, L B G, citizen, June 1, dia. c.
2693 Thompson, Geo, June 30, scs.
3409 Thomas, J H, cit teamster, July 16, dia.
3896 Taylor, J W, citizen, July 24, con.
12337 Tucer, B, citizen, Indiana, Dec 26, scs.

9397 Ulmgender, G, m m b, C, Sept 21, dia.

9497 Vankirk, W, Ringgold bat, Sept 21, scs.
9688 Vandier, W M, cit, Phila, Pa, Sept 24, dia

799 Wilkins, A,‡ Ringgold bat, Apr 29, dia. c.
1092 Welsh, G L, cit teamster, May 14, dia. c.
1121 White, Geo, citizen, May 15, dys.
2784 Wilson, D E, Ringgold bat, July 2, des.
10953 Weir, J, citizen teamster, Oct 14, dia.
11606 Woods, R C, Knapp's bat, Oct 28, scs.
4730 Wright, Chas, cit teamster, Aug 4, dys.
4869 Ward, John, citizen teamster, Aug 6, dia
9043 Williams, F G, Sept 17, dia. c.
10075 Wentgel, Thomas, Sept 30, dia.

4127 Young, Henry, cit teamster, July 23, dys
12246 Young, D, citizen teamster, Nov 8, scs.

MEN THAT WERE HUNG.

1 Sarsfield, Jno, 144 N Y, July 11.
2 Collins, Wm, 88 Pa, D, July 11.
3 Curtis, Chas, 5 R I art, A, July 11.

4 Delaney, Pat, 83 Pa, E, July 11.
5 Mun, A, U S Navy, July 11.
6 Rickson, W R, U S Navy, July 11.

GRAVES OF UNKNOWN U. S. SOLDIERS.

No.	No.	No.	No.	No.	No.	No.	No.
101	4758	8558	8881	9055	9286	9837	10378
103	4815	8561	8883	9056	9346	9841	10382
104	4837	8564	8889	9058	9355	9863	10387
105	4839	8565	8890	9061	9359	9876	10391
106	4840	8566	8891	9066	9360	9877	10429
107	4841	8600	8892	9069	9364	9881	10432
111	4842	8604	8894	9070	9382	9883	10470
115	4851	8609	8896	9072	9391	9887	10475
120	4852	8610	8915	9074	9393	9891	10507
127	4864	8660	8916	9076	9394	9900	10532
138	4873	8672	8918	9077	9440	9908	10544
140	4891	8673	8920	9124	9442	9922	10628
147	4924	8674	8921	9126	9449	9923	10629
232	4938	8675	8927	9128	9455	9956	10630
326	4939	8677	8928	9130	9466	9959	10633
345	4972	8678	8929	9133	9485	9964	10643
2672	5032	8679	8930	9152	9489	10012	10697
2719	5033	8683	8932	9157	9493	10020	10701
2721	5052	8684	8933	9160	9522	10021	10704
2722	5096	8702	8934	9161	9523	10025	10707
2779	5111	8703	8935	9163	9524	10034	10712
2865	5157	8704	8936	9165	9529	10038	10713
2866	5168	8705	8940	9167	9565	10041	10714
3117	5204	8706	8941	9168	9569	10090	10718
3118	5205	8707	8945	9171	9586	10105	10719
3125	5209	8708	8949	9172	9587	10159	10722
3140	5300	8709	8950	9174	9588	10162	10732
3141	5301	8710	8951	9176	9589	10166	10755
3142	5302	8784	8952	9177	9595	10167	10774
3143	5492	8785	8953	9179	9596	10168	10777
3144	5509	8786	8973	9180	9601	10173	10786
3145	5804	8787	8979	9181	9608	10175	10798
3146	6031	8789	8984	9182	9610	10177	10801
3147	6939	8790	8985	9197	9613	10178	10802
3148	7030	8800	8989	9199	9615	10182	10807
3171	7047	8801	8991	9200	9620	10185	10836
3186	7545	8803	8995	9201	9666	10188	10838
3200	8090	8808	8996	9203	9669	10189	10860
3221	8179	8809	8997	9204	9672	10191	10867
3229	8191	8811	9000	9207	9673	10195	10927
3285	8251	8813	9007	9255	9675	10209	10994
3364	8327	8816	9008	9257	9683	10238	11003
3454	8394	8817	9016	9259	9685	10261	11007
3494	8412	8825	9026	9261	9695	10263	11010
3502	8420	8826	9029	9262	9697	10264	11023
4016	8424	8829	9030	9264	9749	10266	11105
4282	8432	8831	9031	9267	9756	10282	11106
4600	8435	8842	9032	9275	9769	10324	11128
4609	8471	8843	9036	9276	9771	10325	11145
4671	8485	8844	9038	9277	9782	10326	11150
4753	8489	8845	9047	9279	9802	10333	11190
4754	8491	8846	9049	9280	9804	10343	11208
4755	8494	8847	9052	9281	9806	10344	11237
4756	8535	8870	9053	9282	9810	10345	11340
4757	8552	8880	9054	9285	9815	10363	11417

ARTHUR
D., 16
J., 54
J.C., 54
ASHBY
J.F., 75
ASHFORD
A.W., 14
ASHLEY
C.G., 37
D.B., 86
J.M., 16
S., 37
ASHTAN
[BLANK], 37
ASPRAY
WM., 75
ATCHINSON
W.P., 61
ATHENS
J.H., 75
ATKINS
A., 16
E., 4
J.F., 9
L., 75
ATKINSON
GEO., 33
JAMES, 4
P., 27
ATLAND
C., 9
ATMORE
C., 23
G.W., 34
ATTWOOD
ABR'M, 61
ATWELL
THOS., 86
ATWOOD
A., 4, 79
G.S., 37
AUBRAY
K., 37
AUBURN
C., 9
AUGAR
A., 89
AUGH
J., 37
AUGHLIN
J.A., 16
AUGUSTINE
F., 37
J., 4
AUGUSTUS
T., 54
AULGER
GEO., 27
AULT
J.L., 61
J.W., 9
AULTON
E.V., 84
AUSTENDALPH
I., 34
AUSTER
F., 37
AUSTIN
A., 37
ALFRED, 9
D., 27
D.B., 35
G., 37
ISAAC, 84
J., 37
J.A., 74

JAS., 86
WM., 14
AVERILL
T.E., 79
AVERY
B.F., 79
J., 34
JOHN W., 23
AVIGRON
F., 23
AYERS
E., 16
G.S., 37
S., 16
S.V., 81
AYRES
J.B., 27

-B-

BABB
JAS., 34
SAMUEL, 21
BABBITT
JOHN, 4
W.H., 10
BABCOCK
F., 4
H., 37
J., 37(2)
J.M., 37
J.S., 37
L.A., 33
R., 2, 37
T., 80
W.H., 37
BABST
M., 37
BACCHUS
A., 37
E.R., 37
BACEY
WM., 23
BACHELDER
B.F., 37
BACHELOR
J.R., 34
P., 20
BACKLEY
C., 37
BACKNER
ADAM, 62
BACOM
A.M., 80
BACON
E.P., 37
J., 37
BADGER
P., 37
BAGGARD
F., 23
BAGLEY
T., 16
BAICE
G.A., 23
BAIEL
W.T., 55
BAILEY
A., 37
A.D., 34
A.W., 16
ANDREW, 86
C., 37
E., 80
F., 2
F.M., 16
G.W., 37

GEORGE, 10
J., 84
J.F., 62
J.H., 16
J.J., 62
JAMES, 79
JOHN, 28, 37
L., 35
P., 4
S.P., 79
W., 84
BAIN
G., 62
BAINE
H., 74
BAIRD
J.J., 14
SAM'L J., 16
BAKER
A., 28, 37
A.W., 16
B.H., 62
CHARLES, 37
D.W., 10, 34
E., 37, 62
E.E., 23
F., 86
GEORGE, 37
H., 37
HENRY, 61
I.P., 10
IRA, 37
ISAAC, 16, 75
J., 10, 37(3), 62
J.D., 61
J.G., 33
JAMES, 4, 20, 62
JOHN, 4, 28, 80, 89
M.A., 75
T.K., 75
THOMAS, 4
W.C., 55
WM., 16, 34, 35, 37,
61, 62
BALCOM
D., 55
BALCOMB
[BLANK], 2
BALDWIN
A., 62
C., 37
C.H., 62
G., 37, 86
GEORGE, 55
J.W., 16
L.A., 28
N., 55
THOMAS, 2
W., 23
BALES
HENRY, 75
THOMAS, 4
BALL
DAVID, 16
H., 84
H.A., 1
J., 62
J.A., 21
L., 61
P., 62
W., 86
BALLARD
ROBERT B., 37
BALLAST
J., 20
BALLENTINE
ROBERT, 2

BALLINGER
GEORGE, 62
ROBERT, 10
BALMET
J., 55
BALSLEY
WM., 61
BALSON
L., 16
BALSTRUM
J., 10
BAMGROOVER
J.A., 10
BAMMRATTA
[BLANK], 62
BANCROFF
A.H., 37
BANE
S., 89
BANEY
GEORGE, 62
I., 62
BANGHART
J., 28
BANICK
S., 84
BANIGAN
A., 37
BANKER
J.M., 37
J.T., 37
BANKS
E.E., 86
BANNAN
H., 37
BANNER
J., 16
M., 23
BANNING
J.F., 2
BANNYER
F., 37
BANVALL
J., 86
BANYAR
J.S., 62
BARBER
B., 55
C., 62
C.F., 4
H., 37
J.M., 28
JAS., 81
T., 16
W.H., 80
BARCLAY
P., 4
BARDEN
CHAS. S., 86
BAREN
T.J., 55
BARGE
H., 37
HENRY, 23
BARGER
GEORGE, 16
BARKER
C., 80
F., 80
J., 54
BARKLETT
H., 37
BARLEN
E.F., 23
BARLEY
R., 23
BARLOW

O.L., 1
BARNARD
G., 28
H.A., 33
W., 4
W.H., 75
WM., 37
BARNES
A., 55
A.C., 37, 75
E.H., 55
F.B., 75
G., 75
J., 16, 37
J.S., 37
L.A., 23
M., 37
R.W., 37
T.S., 55
THOMAS, 4, 37
THOMAS M., 10
V.H., 55
W., 61, 62, 80
W.L., 23
WM., 75
BARNET
J., 4
BARNETT
A., 16
E.T., 62
G.H., 23
I., 28
J., 62, 81
JAMES, 16
M., 62
BARNEY
G.S., 20
H., 28
BARNHART
D., 75
G., 75
BARNSH
JOHN, 23
BARNUM
H., 37
BARR
J.T., 61
P., 62
S., 61
W., 28
BARRA
J., 61
JOHN, 10
BARRATT
G., 37
BARRENS
J., 62
BARRETT
A., 4
D., 37
E., 10
G.M., 37(2)
J., 37, 62, 86
S.C., 55
BARREY
H., 10
HENRY, 9
BARRON
C.L., 37
BARROWS
M., 37
BARSTON
G.H., 55
BARSTOW
J., 86
BARTCHE
C.P., 14

BARTHART
I., 62
BARTHOLOMEW

E.W., 55
I., 10
JOHN, 75
BARTILL
R., 37
BARTLETT
E.K., 86
H., 20
L., 37
BARTLEY
S., 10
BARTON
D., 37
E., 10
F.F., 75
GEORGE, 10
J.F., 10
JAMES, 62
W., 80
WM., 1
BASHAM
S., 16
BASS
CHARLES, 37
GEORGE, 37
J., 4
BASSETT
B.C., 23
J.B., 2
BASSFORD
J., 37
BASSINGER
H., 10
BASTING
C., 4
BATCH
B.F., 80
O., 55
BATCHELDER
BENJ., 1
J., 84
BATCHELL
D., 62
BATEMAN
D.P., 81
BATES
E.L., 86
G., 37
J., 37
JOHN, 37
L.B., 55
LESTER, 37
P., 33
T.E., 81
W., 37
BATEY
W.H., 75
BATHRICK
J., 4
BATSDORF
M., 4
BATT
M., 81
W., 16
W.H., 28
BATTEN
GEO. C., 23
BATTERSON
L., 84
BATTING
ISAAC, 61
BATY
A., 37

JOHN, 1
BAWGARDER
B., 84
BAXTEN
H., 23
BAXTER
G., 80
P.D., 55
S., 28
BAYER
F., 10
BAYLES
K., 75
BAYLEY
FRANK, 4
H., 62
BAYMHER
L.G., 55
BAYNE
DANIEL, 37
WM., 61
BAYWOOD
J., 37
BEACH
J., 35
J.F., 81
BEADLE
H.H., 79
BEADY
WM., 80
BEAGLER
A., 61
BEAL
H., 86
JOHN, 4
BEALE
R., 21
BEAM
B., 37
JOHN, 61
BEAN
C.S., 75
G.W., 20
BEANNIAN
WM., 23
BEANT
H.T., 55
BEAR
D., 4
E., 55
G.W., 23
JOHN, 62
SAMUEL, 62
BEARD
J., 4, 28
JOHN C., 16
BEARDSLEE
M.A., 28
BEARER
P., 81
BEARVES
M., 28
BEASLEY
P., 81
BEASON
BENJAMIN, 75
BEAT
ISAAC, 37
BEATIE
ROBERT, 62
BEATTY
D., 89
R., 16
THOMAS, 75
BEAVER
GEORGE E., 55
M., 4

BEAVEY
HENRY, 23
BECK
G., 28
J., 4
JOHN, 37
BECKER
G., 33
L., 86
BECKHAM
F.B., 37
BECKLEY
G., 55
W., 28
BECKSHIRE
J., 37
BECKWITH
C., 37
E., 28
BEE
GEORGE, 37
THOMAS, 9
BEEBE
J.E., 37
JOHN, 28
BEEKLEY
L., 28
BEEKMAN
J., 37
BEELER
DANIEL, 75
BEELS
H., 23
BEEMAN
RICHARD, 55
BEEMER
WM., 62
BEERS
A., 55
JAMES C., 2
W., 37
BEHREAS
A., 62
BEIGHLEY
W., 62
BEIGHTEL
J.F., 62
BEIRS
S., 28
BELDEN
WM., 37
BELDING
F., 55
BELFORD
JOHN, 61
BELISKEY
J., 4
BELL
A., 55
D.S., 37
E.S., 75
GEO., 34
J., 37
J.C., 37
J.R., 21
JAMES, 55
P.B., 16
THOMAS, 62
WM., 23, 37
BELLE
ROBERT, 1
BELLINGS
J., 14
BELLS
J.H., 35
BELTZ
W.W., 21

BELWEA
C., 37
BEMER
S., 62
BEMIS
ALBERT, 23
CHARLES, 2
H., 84
J.M., 10
BENALL
M.L., 37
BENDER
C., 55
GEORGE, 4
BENEAR
W.A., 55
BENHAND
J.A., 62
BENNET
A., 4, 10
BENNETT
A., 62
C., 10, 35
C.B., 21
GEORGE, 62
I.H., 37
J., 62(2)
L., 20
L.J., 81
N., 1
R.N., 10
W.L., 28
[BLANK], 37
BENNING
JOHN, 4
BENNMAR
L., 89
BENNVILS
J., 80
BENOR
H., 55
BENSON
A., 80
BENSTILL
JOHN, 4
BENTLEY
C., 37
H., 28
M.W., 80
T., 62
BENTLY
F., 2
JAMES, 2
BENTNER
JOSEPH, 37
BENTON
C.W., 4
L., 10
BENWAY
C., 37
BERAINE
A.A., 61
BERDY
M.J., 55
BERFERT
R., 61
BERGER
J., 33
W., 75
W.M., 75
BERGES
E., 37
BERK
G., 62
BERKHAWN
H., 61
BERKLEY

M., 62
BERLIN
JAS., 21
BERLINGAME
A.J., 62
BERLIZER
B., 4
BERRY
C.H., 20
GEORGE, 23
HENRY, 28
J.C., 55
J.M., 1
BERTAN
I., 28
BERTIN
F., 37
BESANNON
PETER, 2
BESGROVE
ISAAC, 33
BESRHA [SIC]
JOHN, 37
BESSON
WM., 23
BEST
WILLIAM, 4
BETHER
J., 74
BETSON
JAMES, 21
BETTS
P., 28
BEYERS
H., 37
BIBBS
ALEXANDER, 75
BIBLE
W., 75
BIBLEY
J., 28
BICKLET
E.H., 62
BIDDINGER
M., 55
BIDMEAD
JAS., 74
BIDON
S., 37
BIDWELL
C., 89
J., 37
BIGELOW
C., 20
L., 37
WM., 1
BIGLER
A., 16
M., 61
N.M., 86
BIGLOW
G., 23
JOHN, 23
BILBEY
GEO., 28
BILL
B.S., 16
F., 75
BILLIAMS
JNO., 28
BILLIG
J.L., 61
BILLINGS
J., 37
W., 75
W.W., 37
BILLINGSBY

J., 28
BINDER
 JOHN, 28
BINGHAM
 C.E., 37
BINGMAN
 W.H., 14
BINGS
 G., 37
BIRCH
 L.F., 55
 T.A., 10
BIRD
 J., 55
 M., 37
 P., 37
 S.H., 75
 W.T., 16
BIRDSELL
 D., 2
BIRDSEY
 J., 28
BIRKET
 W.D., 75
BIRLEY
 PETER, 33
BIRNEY
 J., 62
BISEL
 B., 62
 JOHN, 61
BISH
 J., 61
BISHOP
 A., 2
 B.H., 2
 C., 28, 37
 D.L., 16
 E., 80
 J., 89
 J.C., 81
 P., 33
 S., 55
 W., 75
BISSEL
 J., 55
BISSELL
 J.S., 37
BITTER
 H., 33
BITTMAN
 J., 28
BIXTER
 D., 10
 R., 61
BLACK
 G.W., 55
 H.C., 37
 J., 37, 62
 J.H., 4
 JAMES, 23
 JAMES A., 61
 JOHN, 4
 L., 37
 W.O., 61
BLACKABER
 WM. H., 10
BLACKBURN
 GEO., 81
 JAS., 28
BLACKMAN
 A., 2
 J., 37
 S., 55
 W., 62(2)
BLACKNER
 THOMAS, 75

BLACKNEY
 B., 75
BLACKWOOD
 G.W., 75
 J., 55
 W., 37
BLAIR
 D., 23, 37
 GEORGE, 62
 H., 89
 J.G., 62
 J.W., 23
 JAMES, 37
 JOHN, 28, 62
 JOHN G., 62
BLAIZDELL
 H., 20
BLAIZE
 H., 37
BLAKE
 E., 62
 GEORGE, 37
 J.F., 74
 W.D., 37
 WM., 23
BLAKELEY
 R., 84
BLAKELY
 GEO., 14
BLAKESLEE
 H., 2
BLALOCK
 H., 75
BLANCHARD
 A., 14
 E., 37
 G., 35
 JAS., 28
 L., 4, 37
 O.S., 23
 OSCAR, 23
BLANCOLT
 WM., 37
BLANGY
 S., 55
BLANK
 J.M., 37
BLESSING
 C., 55
 P., 81
BLISS
 J.H., 80
 JAMES H., 37
BLOCK
 J.P., 37
BLODGETT
 A.Z., 23
BLOOD
 G.P., 89
 L., 37
 T.B., 23
BLOOM
 J., 21
BLOOMER
 H., 16
 J., 79
BLOOMKER
 WM., 33
BLOON
 ADAM, 35
BLOSS
 P., 4
BLOSSER
 JONAS, 62
BLOSSOM
 CHAS., 86
BLUMLY

E., 1
BLYME
 S., 37
BLYTHE
 C., 55
BOAMAN
 J., 37
BOARES
 A., 37
BOBINSON [ROBINSON?]

 J., 26
BOCK
 SAMUEL, 9
BODE
 A., 37
BODGE
 S.D., 23
BODIN
 THOMAS S., 55
BODISHAY
 J., 37
BODKIN
 W., 55
BODKINS
 E.L., 4
 P., 16
BODLER
 D., 38
BOERMASTER
 J., 37
BOGAR
 DAVID, 62
BOGARD
 JNO. R., 81
BOGART
 JOHN, 55
BOGGS
 H.C. [?], 81
BOGLEY
 J.E., 4
BOHAMAR
 J., 80
BOHEM
 J., 4
BOHEMS
 PHILIP, 10
BOHINE
 C., 2
BOHL
 H., 37
BOHNABERGER
 A., 62
BOHNMILLER
 J., 28
BOHNSEN
 N., 84
BOICE
 J., 3
BOIES
 J.M., 62
BOISSONNAULT
 F.M., 4
BOLAN
 E., 37
BOLAND
 DANIEL, 62
 JAS., 89
BOLBY
 O., 38
BOLES
 G., 55
 G.W., 75
 H., 75
 J., 38
 M.B., 14
 M.S., 62

W.G., 75
 WILLIAM, 4
BOLEY
 A.J., 9
 PETER, 16
BOLING
 WM., 75
BOLINGER
 G., 62
BOLT
 J.H., 61
BOLTON
 N.P., 4
BOMAN
 G., 62
 J., 4
 JOHN, 55
 SAMUEL, 61
BOMSTEEL
 S.A., 38
BOND
 C.C., 62
 J., 34
 JAS. J.T., 75
 S.F., 55
BONE
 A., 1
BONESTINE
 W.H., 55
BONEWELL
 W.W., 62
BONLEY
 WM., 74
BONLING
 J., 62
BONLY
 JAMES, 10
BONTRELL
 C., 55
BOOBUR
 WM., 1
BOOK
 C., 21
BOOM
 W.P., 10
BOONE
 JAS., 81
BOOREM
 O., 4
BOOTH
 J., 10
 Z., 16
BOOTS
 E.N., 62
BORDEN
 E., 84
BOREM
 M., 4
BOREN
 W., 20
BORST
 J., 38
BOSTON
 J., 16
BOSTWICK
 R.S., 28
BOSWORTH
 A.M., 2
 H., 23
 W.H., 75
BOTHIN
 W.J., 55
BOTKINS
 A.S., 55
BOTTOMS
 J.M., 16
BOUCHER

W., 88
BOUGHFMAN
 J., 55
BOUGHTEN
 M., 86
BOUGHTON
 H., 38
BOUGIN
 JOHN, 2
BOULON
 A., 80
BOULTON
 T., 38
BOUSER
 G., 4
BOUTNELL
 O., 81
BOUTWRIGHT
 A., 75
BOW
 JAMES, 16
BOWDEN
 P., 38
 W., 4
 [BLANK], 20
BOWEN
 A.O., 4
 J.H., 38
BOWENS
 W.H., 55
BOWER
 A., 55
 BENJAMIN, 62
 C., 62
 F., 55
 G.W., 62
 H., 84
 JOHN, 2
BOWERMAN
 R., 28
BOWERMASTER
 S.R., 81
BOWERS
 A., 21
 F., 62
 J., 62, 86
 JAMES, 55
 W.H., 88
BOWHAN
 H.A., 84
BOWIN
 J., 38
BOWLEN
 C.F., 75
 J., 28
BOWLER
 H.A., 23
BOWLES
 L.H., 80
BOWLIN
 WM., 10
BOWMAN
 A., 55, 62
 E., 4
 G., 16
 H., 38
 HENRY, 16
 I., 38
 J., 75
 JOHN, 10
 S., 38, 55
BOWSTEAK
 T.D., 62
BOX
 G., 38
BOYCE
 A., 38

JOHN, 23, 38
L., 23, 62
M., 55, 61, 62, 81
O., 84
P., 62
SAMUEL, 23
T., 9, 62
W., 55
W.F., 34
WARREN, 38
WILLIAM, 5(2)
WM., 23, 38(2)
BROWNELL
A.G., 23
BROWNING
J., 75
THOMAS, 62
BROWNLES
JOHN, 55
BROXMIRE
THOMAS, 38
BROYER
J., 33
BRUBAKER
B.P., 62
BRUCE
A., 62
H., 84
J.B., 62
J.W., 10
JOHN, 62
BRUM
W.H., 55
BRUMAGHIN
T., 38
BRUMLEY
FREDERICK, 62
GEO., 61
BRUMMELL
A.D., 75
BRUMMETTI
B., 75
BRUMSTED
G., 84
BRUNKER
J., 55
BRUNKISSELL
H., 1
BRUNN
GEO., 35
BRUNT
A., 61
BRUSH
J., 28
BRUTCH
E., 55
BRYAN
L., 62
P., 61
R., 55
WM., 38
BRYANT
C.D., 20
D., 38
GEO., 28
H., 38
JAMES A., 75
W.A., 23
WILLIAM, 5
WM., 75
BRYER
P., 10
BRYSON
J., 61
BUBLER
J.W., 23
BUCHANAN

J., 23
S., 16
BUCHMAN
[BLANK], 5
BUCK
B.F., 5, 62(2)
D.C., 62
H., 21
[BLANK], 38
BUCKBIER
J., 38
BUCKER
JAMES, 80
BUCKHANNAN
W., 61
BUCKHART
E., 10
BUCKLE
JOHN J., 55
BUCKLEY
A.M., 21
GEO., 21
J.F., 33
J.G., 55
JOHN, 35
W., 38
BUCKMASTER
F., 14
J., 5
BUCKNER
GEORGE, 21
BUDSON
JOHN, 84
BUEL
G.W., 38
J., 33
S., 38
BUELL
J., 14, 37
BUFFINGTON
B., 5
BUFFMAN
A.C., 35
L., 38
BULDAS
L., 23
BULIT
F., 28
BULKLEY
E.A., 38
BULL
FRANK, 61
BULLARD
JAMES, 33
BULLEN
J.W., 23
BULLIER
WM., 38
BULLOCK
E., 38
W.D., 23
BULLSEN
E.T., 20
BUMGARDNER
JOEL, 55
[BLANK], 10
BUNDY
JOSEPH, 38
BUNER
A.E., 20
BUNKER
F., 62
R.B., 28
S.A., 20
BUNN
W.H., 38
BUNNELL

W., 38
BUPP
L., 62
BURBANKS
J., 38
BURCH
W., 62
BURCHAM
J., 28
BURCHARD
C., 80
BURCHFIELD
ELI, 55
W.R., 75
BURD
W.H., 86
BURDES
G., 5
BURDGE
H.L., 62
BURDICK
A., 38
C., 38
SAMUEL, 38
THEO., 28
BURDOCK
L., 38
BURFIELD
C., 38
BURGAN
L., 23
BURGEN
A., 20
BURGESS
H., 62
W.F., 23
BURK
C., 89
J., 84
J.H., 33
JAMES, 86
JAS., 74
JOHN, 38
O., 84
BURKE
H., 1
J., 62
J.D., 62
JOHN, 75
W.H., 38
BURKHART
C., 28
BURKHEAD
W., 89
BURLEIGH
L., 38
BURLEY
C., 38
BURNA
J.M., 55
BURNETT
J., 28
S.H., 75
WM., 10
BURNEY
J., 61
BURNHAM
F., 1
H, 62
J., 23
W., 55
BURNS
B., 2
DANIEL, 38
E.J., 38
J., 5, 38, 62, 80
JAMES, 61

JOHN, 1, 5, 33,
  38(2), 61
M., 55
M.G., 55
OWEN, 61
P., 35
S.A., 81
SAMUEL, 61
W., 38
W.H., 23
BURNSIDE
J., 61
BURR
E., 62
H., 38
W.B., 5
BURRIS
D.B., 75
BURRITT
B., 16
BURROWS
H., 33, 80
J., 5
WM., 16
BURSFORD
M., 14
BURSHA
THOMAS, 38
BURSHEN
F., 38
BURT
C.E., 23
J., 38
BURTON
C., 80
G.E., 38
GEORGE, 86
HENRY, 38
JOHN, 23
LAFAYETTE, 61
N. [?], 81
O.L., 5
TILLMAN, 16
W.B., 81
WM., 75
BUSERMAN
E., 38
BUSH
A., 34
DAVID, 9
E., 38
H.H., 81
THOMAS, 28
W., 86
BUSHAN
J.R., 38
BUSHBY
N., 34
BUSHELL
C.C., 84
BUSHLEY
WM., 38
BUSHNELL
A., 38
WM., 2
BUSICK
W.A., 10
BUSKIRK
A., 38
BUSKIRT
O., 38
BUTCHER
PETER, 81
BUTLER
A., 23
C.A., 20
C.P., 62

D., 62
H.J., 5
J., 5
J.D., 61
J.J., 75
JAMES, 38
L.J., 61
M., 84
N., 5
THOMAS, 38
W., 38
W.J., 75
W.W., 75
WM., 61
BUTNER
L.B., 16
BUTOFF
R., 38
BUTTER
A.F., 80
P., 38
BUTTERFIELD
JAMES, 89
BUTTON
A.R., 5
ED, 16
JAMES, 38
BUTTS
A., 38
JOHN, 5
BUXTON
THOMAS, 23
BUYER
A., 35
BUZTON
M., 33
BYERLY
JAMES, 75
W.H., 75
WM., 16
BYERNS
I., 23
BYERS
J., 62
BYNOM
J.W., 75
BYRES
GEORGE, 5
BYRON
H.M., 16
J., 38

-C-

CABBAGE
C.H., 21
CABLE
C., 89
CADDING
J.C., 5
CADEMUS
C., 38
CADWELL
A.F., 56
CADY
GEO., 38
J., 38
J.J., 38
CAFER
J.H., 10
CAHILL
J.N., 55
WM., 56
CAHON
W.J., 28
CAIN
M., 38

THOMAS, 2
CALDHAM
 L.C., 38
CALDWELL
 A., 38
 J., 55
 S.A., 62
 WM., 16
CALE
 J., 38
CALEAN
 SAMUEL, 62
CALIHAN
 THOS., 62
CALING
 ED, 38
CALKINS
 S.V., 38
CALLAHAN
 C., 5
 H., 55
 J., 2
 M., 63
 P., 21
CALLAN
 M., 10
CALLAWAY
 WM., 55
CALLBROOK
 J., 38
CALLIHAN
 J., 23
 JNO., 3
 P., 23
 PAT, 16
CALLINGS
 W., 10
CALVERT
 G.F., 10
 R.R., 62
CALVINGTON
 R., 56
CAMERON
 D., 28
 F., 28
 H., 55
 JAS., 28
 JOHN, 38
 WM., 63
CAMMELL
 J., 86
CAMP
 H., 38
 W.W., 76
CAMPBELL
 B., 81
 C.A., 63
 D., 38, 89
 D.A., 23
 GEO. T., 63
 H.B., 62
 J., 38
 J.M., 5
 JAMES, 55, 63
 L.R., 38
 M., 38
 O.H., 81
 R.D., 63
 R.G., 63
 ROB'T, 2
 S.B., 28
 S.L., 86
 SAMUEL, 56
 W., 38, 75
 W.C., 56
 WM., 38, 62, 63
CAMWAY

H., 76
CANAHAN
 JAS., 74
CANARD
 J.Q.A., 55
CANBY
 G.C., 63
CANDEE
 D.M., 2
CANE
 JOHN, 2
CANNON
 A., 10
 WM., 89
CANTLER
 J.L., 63
CANTRILL
 M., 63
CANTWRIGHT
 L., 56
CAPEHEART
 H., 55
CAPELL
 C., 5
CAPSEY
 J., 5
CARBOINES
 W., 38
CARCUNRIGHT
 [BLANK], 16
CARD
 A., 38
 G., 38
CARDEN
 A.K., 75
 ROBERT, 75
CARDON
 E., 38
CARDONEY
 C., 20
CARDWELL
 W.C., 75(2)
CAREAHAN
 G.M., 55
CAREY
 A., 56
 D., 38
 F., 38
 THOS., 80, 89
CARGILL
 C., 86
CARIRT
 ROBERT, 5
CARL
 C.C., 5
 J.M., 21
 JOSEPH, 38
 L., 38
CARLE
 [BLANK], 38
CARLEN
 M., 20
CARLINTYRE
 G., 84
CARLISLE
 J., 16
CARLTON
 J.S., 20
CARMAC
 F., 38
CARMAN
 F.H., 62
CARMER
 ANDREW, 38
CARMICHEAL
 GEO., 62
CARMINE

P., 80
CARNAHAN
 A.W., 10
CARNEHAN
 CHARLES, 38
CARNES
 H., 81
 P., 38
 WM., 88
CARNEY
 D.J., 38
 FRANCIS, 38
 M., 38, 39
CAROL
 W., 63
CARP
 J.S., 28
CARPENTER
 FRANK, 38
 G., 38
 H.A., 38
 L., 38, 63
 M.B., 39
 O.C., 10
 P., 74
 S., 10
 W.C., 63
 WHITE, 55
 WM., 21
CARR
 ANDREW, 39
 C.B., 28
 D., 39
 F., 39
 GEO., 39
 J., 20, 63
 P., 34
 WM., 21, 23, 39(2),
  81
CARREN
 O., 5
CARRIER
 D.B., 2
CARRINGTON
 JAS., 81
CARROLL
 A., 63
 C., 89
 F., 39
 J., 5, 23, 89
 J.Q., 5
 JAMES, 39
 L., 86
 O.J., 23
 P., 39
 W., 39
CARRON
 JAMES, 62
CARSON
 B.F., 74
 E., 39
 J.G., 39
CART
 M.A., 39
CARTER
 A., 39
 C.A., 86
 ED, 39
 H.C., 76
 HENRY, 10
 J., 80
 JOHN, 21
 JOHN B., 56
 THOS., 86
 W.B., 76
 W.J., 88
 WILLIAM, 62

WM., 21, 62
CARTNEY
 A., 28
CARVER
 J.H., 28
 JOHN G., 2
CARWIN
 JAMES, 75
CASE
 A.F., 39
 DANIEL, 62
 E., 39
 H.J., 39
 S., 28
 SILAS, 62
CASEY
 J., 39, 86
 JNO., 86
 M., 23(2)
 P., 39
CASH
 PHILIP, 16
CASHEL
 C., 39
CASSADY
 J., 33
CASSELL
 D., 63
CASSELLS
 SAMUEL, 39
CASSINE
 JOHN S., 39
CASSMAN
 A., 86
CASTABLE
 I., 56
CASTANO
 J., 39
CASTE
 JESSE, 81
CASTLE
 C., 84
 C.H., 81
 F., 5
 J.W., 39
 M., 23
 WM., 39
CASWELL
 F., 80
 G., 55
 JAMES, 23
CATEN
 M., 28
CATER
 W., 16
CATHCART
 ROBT., 63
CATNILL
 L., 81
CATON
 W.T., 63
CATTLEHOCK
 F., 56
CAUGHLIN
 B., 23
CAULT
 ALBERT, 5
CAVANAUGH
 JOHN, 39, 84
 P., 86
CAVENDER
 J.L., 63
CEASER
 D., 39
CENTER
 E.R., 5
CENTRE

A., 39
CEPHAS
 L., 62
CEPP
 J., 56
CHACON
 A.W., 63
CHADWICK
 C.E., 34
 M., 76
CHAFFE
 R.A., 39
CHAGNON
 E., 39
CHAMBERLAIN
 C., 39, 86
 J., 84
 J.B., 14
 R., 35
 [BLANK], 80
CHAMBERS
 J., 39(2)
 J.C., 56
 J.R., 28
 R.S., 55
 W., 28
CHAMPLAIN
 H., 2
CHAMPLIN
 W., 39
CHAMPNEY
 P.A., 86
CHANCE
 A.J., 16
CHANDLER
 M., 56
CHAPEL
 A., 39
 C., 84
 R., 39
CHAPIN
 F., 39
 J.A., 56
 J.L., 2
 JAMES, 56
CHAPMAN
 GEO., 55
 H., 28
 J., 14, 39, 62, 63,
  84
 M., 2
 R., 33
 [BLANK], 16, 63
CHAPPELL
 A., 39
 E., 39
CHARD
 C.W., 55
CHARLES
 F., 55
 JAMES, 10
 R.J., 5
CHASE
 A., 39
 A.P., 76
 D., 39
 E.L., 80
 E.S., 5
 F.M., 62, 84
 F.W., 20
 JOHN, 23
 L., 86
 M., 80
 M.M., 23
 N.F., 39
 S.M., 39
 V., 86

WM. B., 62
CHATBRIM
H., 39
CHATFIELD
WM., 80
CHATMAN
C., 39
S.M., 39
CHATSIN
W.M., 16
CHATTENAY
S., 5
CHATTERTON
J., 39
CHECK
W.F., 54
CHEEK
R., 76
CHENLY
S., 5
CHENWORTH
WM., 14
CHENY
JAMES, 10
CHESLEY
P.S., 39
CHESTER
A., 80
CHESTEY
JOHN, 39
CHEW
JOHN, 63
CHICKCHESTER
C.H., 39
CHILCOTE
JAS. C., 28
CHILD
A.F., 23
CHILDERS
C.H., 89
E., 76
J., 75
J.M., 75
THOS. L., 75
W.E., 76
WM., 55
CHILDS
A., 39
G., 86
G.A., 21
S.P., 81
WM., 39
CHILE
H., 39
CHIMNEY
JESSE, 75
CHIPPENDALE
C., 16
CHISELSON
P., 23
CHISHOLM
J.M., 86
CHITWOOD
J.H., 75
THOS. C., 5
CHLUNWORTH
WM., 5
CHOATE
WM., 5
CHRICHFULA
S., 10
CHRISTENBURG
R.I., 16
CHRISTIAN
A.M., 2
J., 81
CHRISTIANSEN

J., 5
CHRISTMAN
J.E., 10
CHRISTMAS
J., 16
CHRISTY
J., 39
W., 55
CHUNBERG
A., 5
CHURCH
A., 84
C.H., 63
C.L., 39
E., 55
F.M., 39
GEO. E., 55
W.H., 23
CHURCHILL
C., 39
E., 76
F.J., 23
G.W., 28
CHURCHWARD
A.R., 28
CHUSTERSON
F., 84
CHUTE
A.M., 23
CLABAUGH
J., 33
CLAFLIN
F.G., 23
CLAGO
S., 28
CLAMSON
HENRY, 14
CLANCEY
J.W., 5
ROBERT, 39
CLANE
H., 16
CLANG
J.H., 23
CLANSKY
J., 23
CLARK
A., 10, 39
A.E., 5
A.H., 16
ALEXANDER, 75
C., 5(2)
C.H., 35
CHAS., 39
D.V., 55
E., 23
E.B., 63
F., 39
F.D., 63
F.J., 5
G., 63
G.M., 34
G.W., 28
GEORGE, 23, 56
H., 63
H.H., 2
H.M., 56
H.S., 55
J., 39, 63(3)
J.B., 39
J.C., 55
J.R., 56
JAMES, 20, 55, 76
JOHN, 39, 80
L., 20, 39
LEWIS, 75
M., 10, 89

M.L., 80
N., 63
P., 39
P.M., 20
R., 5
R.W., 86
S., 23, 56
THEODORE, 4
W., 2, 10
W.C., 84
WM., 5
[BLANK], 23, 81
CLARKE
W., 63
CLARKSON
[BLANK], 2
CLATTER
F., 62
CLAY
H., 76
HENRY, 63
O., 56
CLAYBAUGH
G.W., 63
CLAYCOME
S.A., 10
CLAYTON
D.J., 55
E.B., 20
J., 55
L., 35
CLEAR
JAMES, 28
CLEARY
P., 2
CLEAVELAND
E., 63
CLEAVER
M., 5
W., 76
CLEEVER
W., 39
CLEGGETT
M., 5
CLEMANTS
JAS., 33
CLEMBURG
J., 86
CLEMENS
A., 39
D., 86
J., 23
J.D., 75
CLEMENTS
L., 81
WM., 28
CLEMING
THOS., 16
CLEMMENTS
H., 39
CLENDEMAN
C.L., 81
CLIFFORD
CHAS., 39
GEO., 39
H.C., 10
J., 86
JAS., 80
CLINE
B., 39
J., 63(2)
J.W., 39
JOHN, 5
K., 55
M., 5, 56
S.M., 39
T., 5

W., 39
CLING
C., 33
JACOB, 28
CLINGAN
A.P., 56
CLINGE
W.H., 16
CLINGMAN
J., 39
CLINTON
R., 39
CLOKIE
J.W., 56
CLONAY
J., 63
CLOONAN
P., 23
CLOUGH
B., 80
JOHN D., 80
CLUN
W.H., 16
CLUSTERMAN
[BLANK], 5
CLUTE
H., 39
CLUTLER
L., 63
CLYEM
J.P., 39
CLYNE
E.T., 76
COALMAN
C.S., 23
H., 5
COANAS
W., 39
COASTNER
J.D., 28
COATES
GEO. H., 55
RUFUS, 56
COATS
L.R., 63
S.R., 63
COBB
E., 14
G., 28
J., 89
COBERT
F.C., 63
COBIN
J.M., 81
COBURG
M.C., 62
COBURN
A., 39
C., 39
COCHRAN
C., 63
JOHN, 39
M., 39
COCHRANE
JAMES, 55
COCHSON
J., 39
CODDINGTON
M.J., 5
WM., 39
CODER
E., 14
COE
GEORGE, 63
COFAM
W., 84
COFFIN

A.R., 23
COFFMAN
F., 81
WM., 63
COFT
JAMES, 28
COGGER
M., 39
COGSWELL
L., 39
COHAGEN
J.H., 56
COHAN
D., 20
COHASH
JOHN, 23
COLAN
FRED, 28
COLBERN
M., 5
COLBURN
THOMAS, 5
W., 80
WILLIAM, 5
COLBY
JOHN N., 34
COLDWELL
W., 28
COLE
A.H., 80
B., 55
E.B., 39
F., 39
GEO., 39
GEO. M., 76
H.O., 63
J.C., 63
JOHN, 5
JOHN J., 39
M., 39
R.S., 39
W.C., 16
W.H., 5, 23
WM., 39
COLEBAUGH
W., 63
COLEBY
A., 39
COLEMAN
C., 63
G., 55
I., 39
J., 62
LEONARD, 23
COLES
J.W., 14
COLLAGUE
M., 16
COLLAR
E., 10
H., 35
COLLER
JOHN, 5
COLLINS
A., 39
A.J., 23
C., 28
C.R., 23
D., 21
G., 10, 63
HENRY, 14
J., 89
J.H., 74
JAMES, 28
M., 14, 63, 86
R., 76
T., 55

CRAVEN
A.J., 56
J., 39
CRAVENER
S.P., 62
CRAW
H., 20
CRAWFORD
A., 75
GEORGE, 63
J., 63
J.A., 63
JAMES, 2
JOHN, 39
L., 63
M., 63(2)
WM., 5
CRAZEN
J., 10
CREAGAN
G., 63
CREAMER
E., 35(2)
CREESY
S.P., 76
CREGG
J., 56
CREGGER
J.F., 89
W.H., 63
CREGS
WM., 10
CREGY
J.G., 63
CRELLEY
C.W., 5
CREMAN
GEORGE, 5
CREMONES
D., 81
CRESSY
N.F., 20
CREST
J.D., 10
CREWS
E.M., 10
G., 76
CRINE
C., 39
CRIPMAN
S., 39
CRIPPER
G.F., 28
CRISER
M., 63
CRISHOLM
J.H., 62
CRISLE
J., 21
CRISSMAN
JOSEPH, 39
CRISTIAN
JOHN, 16
CRISWELL
J., 39
CROANE
J.J., 10
CROCK
H., 63
CROCKER
CHAS., 86
D., 80
GEO., 55
J., 39
CROCKETT
A.W., 23
CROFTS

E.P., 23
CROGHAN
JOHN, 62
CROMARK
J., 39
CROMIAN
JOHN, 23
CROMICH
F., 63
CROMINBERGER
J.C., 56
CROMINSHIELD
T., 23
CROMMINGS
H., 84
CROMPTER
JAS., 39
CROMPTON
F.G., 63
CROMWELL
G.W., 14
S.R., 20
T., 40
W.H., 20, 56
CRON
F., 40
CRONK
JAMES, 28
CRONKWHITE
JOHN, 28
CROOK
E.H., 81
CROOKE
W.B., 56
CROOKEY
S., 86
CROOKS
J.M., 55
CROSBEY
J., 5
CROSBY
E., 23
M., 40
W., 20
CROSS
E., 5
E.F., 80
GEORGE W., 24
IRA M., 23
J.D., 5
J.T., 5
M.C., 75
N., 76
NOAH, 20
CROSSER
E.P., 24
M., 55
CROSSLEY
B., 2
CROSSMAN
E.J., 24
CROSWELL
SAMUEL, 75
CROUCH
LEVI, 62
CROUP
W.S., 63
CROUSE
E., 62
GEORGE, 40
J., 5
J.A., 21
N., 80
W.A., 21
CROW
B., 14
J., 75

CROWLEY
D., 80
PAT, 89
S., 40
CROY
J., 86
CRUCT
WM., 55
CRUER
J.W., 55
CRUM
A., 76
C., 63
CRUMTON
R., 10
CRUNCH
J., 28
CRUSE
J., 5
CUFF
S., 40
CULBERT
J., 88
WM., 40
CULBERTON
LOUIS, 63
CULBERTSON
JOHN, 63
S., 14
CULLEN
T.P., 63
CULLER
M., 2(2)
CULLIGAN
JOSEPH, 24
CULLIN
JOHN, 21
CULLINGFORD
P., 63
CULP
P.K., 63
CULVER
J., 63
N.L., 40
CUMBERLAND
THOS., 63
CUMMINGS
A., 56
A.B., 24
BENJ., 63
D., 28
J., 16
J.W., 10
R., 63
S., 84
W., 28
W.S., 56
[BLANK], 40
CUNDERSON
[BLANK], 81
CUNELL
H.G., 24
CUNISE
E., 76
CUNNINGHAM
J., 40(2), 80, 81
K., 3
WM., 40
CUPELL
C., 5
CUPPETT
J., 81
CUPSAY
J., 5
CURLEY
P., 40
CURREN

F., 24
CURREY
JOHN, 40
CURRIER
C.C., 84
WM., 10
CURRY
A., 62
J.W., 10
R., 62
S., 63
W.F., 10
CURTEY
L., 63
CURTIN
B., 81
CURTIS
A., 5
CHAS., 90
M.D., 28
N., 55
W.O., 35
CURTISS
JOHN, 20
CURY
W.H., 21
CUSHING
C.E., 24
CUSSEY
JAS., 86
CUSSICK
B., 28
CUSTERMAN
F., 40
CUTE
A., 40
CUTLER
C.F., 24, 40
J.P., 40
WM., 40
CUTSDAGHNER
W.J., 56
CUTTER
A., 20
CUTTS
O.M., 20
CUYLER
W., 86
CYSEY
A., 63

-D-

DABNEY
B., 76
DACY
G., 84
DAFFENDALL
P.H., 10
DAGGO
JOHN, 84
DAHER
G., 40
DAILEY
M., 63
WM., 40
DAKE
G., 5
DAKENFELT
J., 63
DALBER
S.A., 24
DALBY
JAMES, 5
DALEY
M., 33
S., 56

T., 40
DALLIN
JAMES, 63
DALLINGER
W.C., 10
DALRYSUFFLE
J.E., 65
DALY
A., 28
JAS., 83
JOHN, 24, 40
DALZELL
J.G., 65
WM., 28
DAMERY
JOHN, 2
DAMHOCKER
E., 84
DAMON
J.D., 40
DANDELION
T., 56
DANE
ANDREW, 10
DANER
J., 83
DANFIRTH
GEO. A., 89
DANGLER
W.G., 86
DANIEL
R., 16
SUTTRELL, 76
DANIELS
W.O., 40
DANNARD
W., 16
DANSFIELD
JOHN, 24
DANT
JNO. M., 83
DANTON
W.H., 56
DARATT
LOUIS, 40
DARCT
S., 28
DARCY
F., 80
DARKER
WM., 10
DARLEY
J., 40
DARLING
D.W., 5
G.H., 40
J., 40
DARSEY
M., 83
DART
CHARLES W., 40
DARUM
J.J., 5
DARVIN
W.W., 86
DARYSON
W., 84
DASON
N., 83
DAVENBROOK
J.J., 63
DAVENPORT
J., 10, 35
DAVERE
J., 56
DAVID
D.P., 84

DITTENER
  H., 20
DITTO
  JOHN, 56
DITZTELL
  L., 63
DIVELY
  J., 65
DIVEN
  J., 56
DIVER
  J., 56
  JOHN, 56
  O., 10
DIVERS
  G., 83
DIX
  GEO., 74
DIXON
  B., 65
  J., 65
  JOHN, 28
DOAK
  I.V., 76
DOAN
  A., 40
DOAP
  M., 28
DOBSON
  J.R., 56
  M., 5
DOCK
  C., 5
DODD
  BENJAMIN, 76
  CHAS., 76
  G.W., 5
  J., 63
  J.A., 76
  S., 83
DODGE
  C.F., 34
  THOMAS A., 24
  [BLANK], 56
DODRICK
  LOUIS, 63
DODSON
  E., 16, 40, 56
  R.B., 5
DOER
  S., 34
DOGGETT
  L., 24
DOHERTY
  J., 65
DOLAN
  J., 24, 40
  M., 40
  P., 40, 86
DOLE
  CHARLES H., 24
DOLF
  SYLVANUS, 28
DOLL
  R., 86
DOLPH
  S., 28
DOMICK
  E., 40
DONAGHEN
  J., 40
DONAHUE
  H., 3
  P., 56
DONALAN
  M., 86
DOND

DANIEL, 40
DONDALL
  B., 40(2)
DONDLE
  ROBERT, 63
DONELY
  M., 40
DONEN
  C., 5
DONES
  S.M., 24
DONEY
  J.W., 86
DONLEY
  E.J., 40
  M., 56
  P., 65
DONLY
  JAMES, 56
DONNELL
  F., 20
  W., 40
DONNELLY
  J., 65
  JAS., 40
DONOHUE
  P., 80
  S., 83
DONOVAN
  D., 63
  J., 40, 63
DONOWAY
  J., 2
DOOLEY
  JAMES, 5
DOOLITTLE
  G.S., 74
  W., 40
DOONER
  M., 63
DORAN
  J.M., 86
  JAMES, 56
  McK., 63
  P., 63
  W.H., 5
DORCHESTER
  H.S., 40
DOREMUS
  C., 35
DORLAND
  A.H., 35
DORMITY
  M., 40
DORR
  PHINEAS, 63
DORSEY
  A.L., 83
DORSON
  L., 56
DORT
  C.R., 63
  R., 76
DOSS
  J.W., 76
DOTSEY
  J., 40
DOTY
  E.E., 56
  I., 76
  JOHN, 83
DOUGHERTY
  D., 28
  E.S., 40
  F., 65
  J., 40, 63, 65
  M., 65

O., 40
  THOMAS, 20
  W.H., 56
  [BLANK], 63
DOUGHTY
  D.B., 86
  E.S., 40
DOUGLAS
  GEO., 81
DOUGLASS
  B., 24
  M., 40
  P., 40
  W., 56
DOULE
  J., 86
DOUNTY
  P., 16
DOW
  H.A., 24
  M., 40
DOWD
  F., 2
  J.W., 5
DOWDY
  JOHN, 5
DOWELL
  J.W., 5
  W.L., 10
DOWLIN
  J., 24
DOWNER
  A., 5
  A.P., 56
  S., 2
DOWNES
  J., 20
DOWNEY
  H., 40
  J.A., 40
  JOEL, 24
  S.M., 10
DOWNING
  G., 24
  GEORGE, 56
  M., 86
DOWNS
  E., 34
  J.R., 10
DOYING
  F.W., 80
DOYLE
  H., 35
  J., 5
  JAMES, 40
  JAS., 74
  JOHN, 40
  P., 5
  W., 40
  WM., 20
DRAAN
  R.H., 76
DRAGOON
  N., 80
DRAKE
  CHARLES C., 34
  D.B., 40
  D.W., 40
  E.C., 24
  J.H., 16
  JOHN F., 56
  M., 56
  O., 28
  R.R., 5
  SAMUEL, 83
  T., 24
DRAPER

L., 86
DRAWN
  GEORGE, 24
DREAL
  D., 28
DRENKLE
  J.A., 63
DRESSER
  C., 5
DREW
  C., 21
  E., 5
  F., 80
DRICKARM
  L., 24
DRIEKS
  HENRY, 5
DRISCOLL
  N.C., 65
  [BLANK], 40
DRISDALE
  F., 20
DRITH
  C., 56
DRITMAN
  WILLIAM, 40
DROMANTLE
  W., 24
DRUM
  A., 40
  G., 5
  R., 24
DRUMMOND
  J., 86
  JOHN, 28
DRUSE
  I., 40
DUANE
  T., 40
DUBIN
  M., 89
DUBLE
  HENRY, 40
DUCKWORTH
  J., 10
  W.B., 83
DUDLEY
  J.C., 40
  J.W., 5
  SAMUEL, 76
DUELL
  R., 40
DUFF
  CHAS., 21
  I.W., 76
  J., 65
DUFFEY
  E., 84
  J., 24
  JAMES, 24
DUFFIE
  J., 65
DUFFNEY
  J., 88
DUFFY
  A., 20
  G., 56
DUGAN
  CHAS., 2
  D., 20, 28
  THOMAS, 56
DUGEAN
  J.R., 16
DUGER
  P., 40
DUINZ
  G.W., 28

DUKE
  WM., 76
DULAND
  D.W., 16
DULANEY
  H., 16
DULE
  LEVI, 40
DULL
  W., 24
DULREBECK
  H., 16
DUMAR
  R., 56
DUMAS
  J.P., 56
DUMFREY
  DENNIS, 40
DUMMOND
  J.H., 10
DUMOND
  A., 40
  C., 40
  F., 40
  P., 5
  S., 40
DUMONT
  W., 28
DUN
  R.B., 63
DUNARAM
  JOHN, 40
DUNAY
  JOHN, 28
DUNBAR
  ALEX, 54
  J., 56
  JOHN, 63
  THOMAS, 40
DUNBEN
  M., 10
DUNBERGER
  GEO., 83
DUNCAN
  A., 56
  E., 16
  G.W., 76
  H.P., 35
  J.M., 81
  W.M., 83
DUNHAM
  JAMES, 56
  L., 35
  R., 40
  R.H., 33
DUNKEN
  T., 56
DUNLAP
  C., 40
  W., 10
DUNMETT
  S., 24
DUNN
  ALEXANDER, 5
  C., 86
  G., 35
  G.E., 80
  I., 24, 83
  J., 24, 40
  J.H., 40
  JAMES, 40
  JOHN, 21, 63, 86(2)
  JOHNES, 63
  L.H., 40
  M., 40
  OWEN, 40
  P., 24

104

PAT, 40
R., 76
W.W., 80
WM., 86
DUNNIE
G., 20
DUNNING
S.P., 20
WM., 40
DUNROE
P.I., 28
DUNSHAM
ABR., 40
DUNSING
A, 5
DUNTLER
HENRY, 63
DUPON
F., 16
DURAND
H., 40
JAS. E., 40
DURANT
B., 56
DURDEN
ROBERT, 74
DURFEE
JAMES, 40
DURHARSE
B., 65
DURKALE
JOHN, 65
DUROCHIS
WM., 14
DUSALT
A., 28
DUSAN
J., 10
DUTLIN
S., 14
DUTROM
IRDELL, 76
DUTTON
W.H., 2
DWIRE
P., 40
DYE
JOHN, 20
DYER
G.W., 24
H., 76
J., 28
J.C., 5
JAMES, 83
JOHN S., 40
S., 40
W., 76
DYKE
F., 56
DYKEMAN
D., 40
F., 40
DYKES
L., 76
PLEASANT, 76
DYN
WM., 76
DYRE
WM., 28

-E-

EADLEY
LEVI, 5
EAFF
N., 24
EAGH

JOHN, 42
EARL
C., 40
D., 10
G.W., 24
H., 40
JAS. H., 88
EARLES
WILLIAM, 56
EARLMAN
J., 65
EARNEST
H.C., 2
EASINBECK
M., 5
EASLEY
W.A., 5
W.H., 42
EAST
R., 16
EASTERLY
THOMAS, 2
EASTERN
THOS., 42
EASTMAN
D., 24
J., 56
WM., 5, 42
EASTON
E.E., 42
J., 76
EASTWOOD
E., 42
EATON
A., 74
F.W., 24
NAT., 65
R., 28
W., 2
W.H., 10
EBER
JAMES, 42
EBHART
J., 65
EBNER
CHARLES, 35
EBRIGHT
BENJ., 65
ECKER
J., 10
ECKHARD
H., 20
ECKHART
J., 56
ECKLES
E., 65
EDDES
JAMES C., 76
EDDINGTON
G.W., 33
EDES
W., 24
EDGAR
W.H., 65
EDMISTON
J.W., 16
EDMONDS
B., 29
L., 42
EDSEN
JOHN, 42
W., 42
EDWARDS
C., 24
C.D., 5
C.F., 24
C.S., 76

G.H., 10
H.S., 16
I., 76
J.W., 10
JOHN, 34
N.S., 20
O.J., 2
S., 29, 42
WM., 86
EGAN
CHARLES, 24
JOHN, 42, 65, 84
EGBERT
JAMES, 35
EGERTON
H., 42
EGGLESTON
WM., 28
EGSILLIM
P.H., 28
EIBERS
HENRY, 24
EICHNOR
C., 65
EISLEY
JOHN, 65
ELBERSON
J., 42
ELDER
P., 76
ELDERY
B., 42
ELDRED
H., 42
I., 42
ELDRIDGE
E., 10
ELENBERGER
P., 65
ELFREY
B.S., 65
ELHA
D., 56
ELI
W., 22
ELIJAH
BAKER, 56
ELIOT
C., 80
ELIS
C.O., 76
ELLENGER
P., 84
ELLERMAN
N., 56
ELLERS
HENRY, 65
ELLERTON
N., 86
ELLINGTON
J., 76
ELLIOT
J., 28
ELLIOTT
A., 34
ED, 5
F.P., 42
J., 65
J.P., 65
JOHN, 65
JOHN H., 65
L., 42
W., 56
WM., 76
ELLIS
A., 20
C., 22, 42

CHARLES, 56
F., 65
H.C., 10
H.H., 65
J., 42
J.H., 88
P.M., 42
R.H., 42
WILLIAM, 5, 42
ELLISON
ISAAC, 76
W., 5, 42
ELLS
D., 10
PERRY, 42
ELLWOOD
S., 84
ELMANN
A., 56
ELSLIN
JAMES, 5
ELSTER
JAMES, 42
ELSTON
F., 10
ELWELL
W., 42
EL[_]IS E. [?]
E., 29
EMERSON
G.W., 24
H.H., 20
J., 5
WM., 24
EMERY
C.Z., 42
J., 5, 16, 24
EMMERSON
F.F., 24
EMMERT
J.C., 76
EMMETT
W., 2, 3
EMMICT
S.S., 86
EMMONDS
A., 2
EMMONS
W., 10
EMPAY
ROBERT, 24
EMUSIN
D.G., 24
ENCH
W., 5
ENGAL
W., 42
ENGER
J., 84
ENGLAND
E., 89
G., 14
ENGLE
PETER, 65
ENGLER
JOHN, 33
ENGLISH
G., 42
J.C., 65
JAMES, 29
ENKHART
H., 84
ENNIES
ANDREW, 65
ENNIS
WM., 14
ENNISON

G., 80
ENROW
W., 5
ENSIGN
J., 29
ENSLEY
C., 65
WM., 56
ENSWORTH
JOHN, 2
ENTULIN
B.C., 56
EODUS
JAMES, 16
EPPERT
SAMUEL, 56
EPSEY
JAMES, 65
ERB
J., 5
ERDIBACH
C., 65
EREBEDIER
J., 65
ERICK
J., 86
ERICKSON
C., 84
ERMAINS
F., 5
ERRBANKS
J., 16
ERRICKSON
C., 5
ERRICSON
S., 84
ERST
J., 42
ERVINGFELTS
JACOB, 65
ERWIN
C., 65
ESCHOYMER
H., 34
ESCUE
H., 76
ESENTHAL
F., 10
ESKRIDGE
OAKLEY, 10
ESLIGH
JACOB, 35
ESTEFF
J., 16
ESTELLE
E.W., 10
ESTER
W.A., 24
ESTEY
E.E., 34
ESTUFF
JNO., 83
ETHEAR
J., 42
ETHRIDGE
WM., 76
ETLER
VALENTINE, 76
ETTERS
D., 65
EUSTACE
GEO. C., 74
EVALT
E.J., 56
EVANS
E.M., 56
FRANKLIN, 42

G.H., 10
H., 24
J., 5, 10, 24
J.M., 76
JOHN, 88
L., 42
M., 89
N.L., 2
S.D., 76
SAMUEL, 56
T., 86
W., 10, 56, 76
EVENS
B., 42
CHARLES, 56
EVERETT
J., 29, 42
T.S., 89
EVERITT
A.T., 76
EVERITTE
JOHN, 76
EVERLY
G., 42
EVERTS
T.P., 24
EWETTS
JAMES, 65
EWING
D., 56
EXLINE
JACOB, 65
EYDRONER
R., 6

-F-

FACE
C., 29
J., 42
W.H., 29
FACER
WM., 56
FAGAN
M., 85
O., 6
P.D., 2
R., 65
FAGARTUS
T., 65
FAGEN
PARKER, 76
FAGGERTY
C., 42
JACKSON, 34
FAGLEY
C., 65
FAHY
JOHN, 65
FAILE
W.D., 65
FAIRBANKS
ALPH, 56
E., 65
J., 29
J.E., 22
FAIRBROTHER
H., 35
FAIRCHILD
G.L., 80
FAIRCHILDS
JESSE, 76
FAIRFAX
CHARLES, 42
FAIRMAN
H.B., 42
FAISS

A., 65
FAITH
ALEXANDER, 65
FALCONBURG
I.K., 16
FALK
W., 56
FALKENSTINE
F., 65
FALKERSON
J., 10
FALLAM
PAT, 42
FALMAN
A., 56
FAMCLE
E., 42
FANDISH
S., 6
FANEN
JAMES F., 65
FANEY
GEORGE, 65
FANIER
F., 10
FANNON
A., 89
G.H., 76
FANNTON
H., 86
FANON
WM., 85
FANTLENGER
F., 65
FARECLOUGH
R., 42
FAREWELL
E., 20
FARGROVE
M.B., 56
FARISDALE
H., 24
FARLAND
T., 42
FARLEY
JAMES, 65
W., 42
FARMAN
E., 65
FARMER
E.L., 80
F., 6
G.S., 24
M., 29
FARMINGHAM
W.C., 10
FARN
C., 42
FARNHAM
A., 29
C.A., 6
L.B., 80
L.D., 80
M.B., 85
FARNSWORTH
M., 80
S., 14
FARR
J.C., 65
FARRALLE
G., 24
FARRASS
JAS., 22
FARRELL
C., 4
J.H., 35, 80
JAMES, 42

JAS. F., 74
M., 89
FARREN
J., 35
FARSHAY
A., 56
FATLEAM
A., 65
FAUCETT
J., 34
FAWKES
WM., 83
FAWRY
JOHN, 42
FAY
J.W., 33
JOHN, 74
FEAGE
F.J., 22
FEAMLEY
WM., 24
FEARING
J.I., 24
FEASEL
H., 42
FEASLEY
LEN, 83
FEAST
GEO., 80
FEATHER
J.B., 83
FEATHERSTONE
J., 16
FECKER
L., 22
FEE
GEORGE M., 65
FEED
G., 86
FEELY
M., 2
FEGAN
JOHN, 24
FELCH
G.P., 34
FELLOWS
H., 24
FELNICH
H., 10
FELPS
DANIEL, 86
FELTER
F., 42
H.M., 65
FELTHARSEN
[BLANK], 65
FELTON
GEORGE, 42
FELYER
WM., 24
FENALL
J., 86
FENER
J.W., 15
FENIS
J., 24
FENKSTINE
M., 16
FENLEY
R., 89
FENTON
I., 10
J.M., 56
FERAND
A., 80
FERCE
R.S., 56

FERGUSON
A.W., 15
H., 56
H.C., 42
I., 85
J., 86
J.M., 42
J.R., 65
JOHN, 65
LOUIS, 6
M., 42
W.R., 85
FERMER
J., 6
FERRALL
M.C., 89
FERRELL
J., 86
P., 20
FERRETT
J., 80
FERRIS
C., 42
JOHN, 42
JOSEPH, 56
ROBERT, 42
FERRY
W., 65
FESCHER
D., 10
FESSENDEN
N.E., 65
FESTER
JOHN, 65
FETHTON
F., 29
FETTERMAN
J., 65
FEWER
E., 65
FEY
A., 74
FIBBLES
H., 2
FICH
JOHN, 42, 65
FIELD
JACOB, 14
S., 3
FIELDING
A., 86
FIELDS
E., 24
F., 42
N., 10
R.G., 76
FIFE
J., 56
FIFER
CHARLES, 65
FIFLEY
H., 86
FIKE
TOBIAS, 10
W.P., 56
FILBY
A., 2
FILE
C., 65
R., 6
FILEY
J.H., 65
FINCH
A., 76
C. [BLANK], 56
F.M., 6
H., 76

HENRY, 42
J.B., 76
JAMES, 42
FINCUCUM
JOHN, 42
FINDLATER
H., 29
FINDLEY
ANDREW, 42
FINGLEY
JOHN, 65
S., 65
FINIGAN
B., 24
FINJAY
W., 24
FINK
J.P., 6
L., 22
PETER, 65
FINLAN
JAMES, 56
FINLAUGH
S., 65
FINLEY
A., 42
FINLIN
THOMAS, 65
FINNERTY
P., 42
FIRESTONE
[BLANK], 76
FIRMAN
V., 56
FISCHNOR
D., 84
FISH
C., 10
CHARLES W., 65
F., 42
H., 42
J., 6, 65
J.W., 42
L.V., 42
WILLIAM, 42
WM., 20
FISHER
B.M., 65
C., 65
C.B., 24
C.N., 76
C.P., 42
CHARLES, 56
CONRAD, 42
D., 42, 56
DANIEL, 42
F., 29
H., 2, 42
JOHN, 24
L., 42
N.O., 35
S.F., 6
W., 65(2)
WM., 35
FISK
J., 65
J.B., 84
W.P., 80
FITCH
A., 42
C., 42
E.P., 56
F., 35
W.F., 33
FITSE
T., 29
FITTER

B., 10
FITZGERALD
H., 6
I., 10
JOSEPH, 20
M., 65
N., 42
THO., 42
[BLANK], 89
FITZGIBBONS
THOS., 86
FITZPATRICK
M., 29(2)
O., 42
[BLANK], 42
FLAGG
J.B., 20
FLAGLER
WILLIAM, 42
FLANAGAN
J., 6
P., 86
FLANDERS
CHARLES, 24
L.G., 20
O., 34
FLANERY
M., 86
FLANIGAN
ED, 42
JOHN, 29
M., 86
P., 42
FLANNEY
J., 65
FLARETY
O., 86
FLASHARSE
B., 65
FLAY
L., 65
FLEINS
OSCAR, 84
FLEMING
M., 24
P., 42
R., 16
W., 65
W.W., 83
FLEMMING
J., 65
FLETCHER
T., 16
WM., 42
FLICK
L., 65
FLICKINGER
JNO., 65
FLICKISON
J., 89
FLIESTINE
S., 86
FLIFLIN
H., 29
FLING
T.J., 56
FLINT
C.B., 80
FLINTKOFF
F., 42
FLORENCE
B., 42
J.J., 2
FLOWERS
W.F., 56
W.P., 76
FLOYD

A., 6
B., 65
GEORGE E., 24
FLUHR
JOHN, 65
FLUIT
C.W., 2
FLUKE
J., 42
FLYNN
J., 42(2)
M., 65
S., 65
WM., 42
FOGG
B.F., 33
C., 2
FOHNSBELLY
C., 42
FOLDEN
H., 42
FOLET
D., 42
FOLEY
DANIEL, 88
F., 42
JOHN, 20
FOLIAND
M., 35
FOLK
A.P., 6
C., 29
L., 33
FOLLARD
JAMES, 42
FONCKS
H.C., 89
FONKLE
PETER, 42
FORBS
C., 29
H., 24
FORCE
F., 29
FORD
A., 35
E.V., 42
M., 65
P., 89
THOMAS, 65
W., 34
W.J., 6
FORDRURY
G.W., 84
FORDSON
MICHAEL, 15
FOREBER
A., 42
FOREMAN
A., 56
G.S., 65
FOREST
WM., 56
FORGET
G.H., 42
FORNEY
D., 6
JAMES M., 14
W.O., 56
FORREST
S., 80
THOMAS, 20
FORSHUA
W., 10
FORSLAY
W.K., 84
FORSYTH

J., 65
FORSYTHE
H., 29
FORTEEN
JOHN, 16
FORTH
R., 83
FORWARD
S., 10
FOSGATE
HENRY S., 24
FOSTER
A., 20, 80
A.J., 6
A.M., 56
B.B., 6
C.W., 65
CHARLES, 83
E.R., 20
E.S., 6
H., 42
H.B., 80
H.C., 80
J., 42, 86
JAMES, 42
S., 83
SAMUEL C. [?], 20
W., 89
FOULTS
M., 56
FOUNTAIN
W.F., 84
FOUST
S.L., 65
FOWLER
C., 56
I., 76
JOHN, 6
SAMUEL, 24
FOX
A., 42
CHARLES, 29
D., 42
E., 76
GEORGE, 65
H.C., 83
HENRY, 89
JAMES, 29
M., 42, 65
R., 65
W., 29, 80
FRAHAR
P., 24
FRAHWORTH
F., 42
FRAIER
L., 24
FRAISER
JAMES, 56
FRAKE
S., 42
FRAME
W., 6
FRANCELL
OTTO, 2
FRANCIS
F., 10
J., 22
J.F., 6
N., 65
P.L., 42
FRANCISCO
R., 76
FRANK
F.M., 89
FRANKINBURG
C., 56

FRANKLIN
H., 6
J., 42
J.C., 42
FRANKS
R.L., 56
W.W., 76
FRANSHIER
J.D., 76
FRANTZ
F., 22
FRASER
J.H., 42
FRASS
LOUIS, 6
FRAY
PATRICK, 24
FRAYER
DANIEL, 56
FRAZIER
C.R., 16
JOHN, 76
FREAERE
W., 22
FREBURG
E., 42
FRECKS
F., 10
FREDENBURG
F., 29
FREDERICK
C., 24
G., 29
J.A., 15
J.E., 22
JOHN, 2
L., 65
FREDINBURG
JAMES, 42
FREE
C., 42
J., 65
M., 56
FREEBORN
R.L., 83
FREED
S., 65
FREELEY
P., 56
FREELOVE
H., 74
FREEMAN
B., 29
D., 6
F.J., 15
JOHN, 89
W.M., 65
FREEMAN [?]
C.R., 80
FREENOUGH
GEORGE, 56
FREESCHELZ
F., 33
FREILANDER
C., 42
FREISER
JOHN, 42
FREMONT
JAMES, 6
FRENCH
A., 65
GEORGE, 86
J., 6, 42
JAMES, 42, 65
JOHN C., 42
FRENCHY
D., 86

FRIAR
JOHN, 76
FRICK
S., 33
FRICKS
A., 42
FRIDAY
S.D., 65
FRILL
D., 65
FRISBIE
LEVI, 2
FRISBLE
L., 20
FRISBY
A., 24
W.L., 42
FRISHI
H., 65
FRITCHEI
M., 29
FRITZ
A., 86
D., 65
J., 16
P., 6
FRITZMAN
J.W., 65
FROSITER
F., 42
FROSS
JOHN, 10
FROST
A., 85
B., 24(2)
FRUCE
J., 65
FRUL [?]
J., 14
FRUM
E., 86
FRUSSELL
G.W., 15
FRY
ALEXANDER, 65
JACOB, 56
JOHN, 35
L., 65
M., 33
S., 2, 65
W.L., 56
FRYER
W.L., 76
FUCHS
H., 33
FUGET
W., 10
FULKINSON
H., 56
FULLER
A., 24, 42
C., 42
C.W., 84
G., 65
GEO., 34
GEO. A., 24
H., 24, 65
H.S., 2
IRA B., 6
IRWIN, 83
J.B., 42
N., 42
S., 24
W., 42, 80
FULLERSTON
W., 56
FULLERTON

C., 43
G.W., 66
J., 43
JOHN, 66
SAMUEL, 66
[BLANK], 43
GROUCHER
J., 29
GROUPE
D., 85
GROUSE
G., 66
GROVEN
JOSEPH, 43
GROVER
JAMES, 29
GROVES
A.T., 66
GROWER
H., 6
GRUBBS
J., 66
GRUFF
A.J., 57
GRULACH
J., 17
GRUNDEE
ALEX, 76
GRUNDS
L., 85
GRUNDY
R.J., 43
GRUNNELL
JOHN, 66
GRUSH
FRED, 85
GUENANT
A., 83
GUFFY
R., 33
GUIER
G., 35
GUILD
C., 24
JAMES, 76
GUILE
A.L., 43
GUILFORD
J., 24
GUILZ
H., 29
GUINA
H.M., 2
GUINGOELETT
H., 34
GULEY
J., 65
GULK
P., 6
GULLETT
A., 17
GULLSEN
WILLIAM, 12
GULTERMAN
J., 2
S., 87
GULVERE
DAVID, 87
GUMBERT
A., 66
GUNAN
WM., 43
GUNDALOCH
F., 43
GUNDUSON
H., 85
GUNN

ALEX, 66
CALVIN, 43
J.W., 66
GUNNAHAN
J., 43
GUNNELL
JOHN, 43
GUNNEY
C., 20
J.F., 20
GUNSHAW
C., 15
GUNTER
JOHN, 87
R.C., 76
GURMANE
B.S., 29
GURY
J., 17
GUTH
H., 85
GUTHERSON
G., 24
GUTHRIE
J., 1
W.B., 12
GUYEN
WILLIAM, 6
GUYER
F., 43
GWIN
CHARLES, 43

-H-

HACK
J., 43
HACKET
J., 67
HACKETT
C., 43
J., 43
[BLANK], 43
HADDEN
C., 43
HADDISH
J., 43
HADEN
R., 66
HADSELL
F., 43
HAFF
M., 12
HAFFINGER
J., 66
HAGATE
JACOB, 43
HAGEMAN
JAMES, 6
HAGER
J., 43
[BLANK], 43
HAGERLY
D.G., 57
HAGERMAN
R., 57
HAGERTY
W.R., 67
WM., 43
HAGGARD
E., 6
HAGGERT
P., 24
HAGHTON
J., 12
HAGINEY
F., 33

HAGINIS
W., 6
HAHER
C., 66
HAIGHT
J.E., 43
HAINES
G., 77
H., 43
J., 17
J.A., 77
N.S., 57
PHILIP, 43
R., 29
THEODORE, 6
HAIR
G., 43
HAKAION
F., 22
HAKS
WILLIAM, 6
HALBERT
A.H., 43
F., 87
L., 43
HALDWELL
P., 67
HALE
A.C., 85
IRA, 77
R.H., 77
S.B., 29
HALEY
C.H., 6
WM., 24
HALFRE
J.A., 12
HALINE
GOTFRIED, 43
HALL
A., 67
A.W., 85
B., 2, 67
B.A., 77
BENJ., 80
C., 43
C.A., 80
C.W., 43
CHARLES, 43(2)
ED, 43
F., 17
G.H., 6, 24
H., 66
H.C., 6
H.H., 12
HENRY, 66, 83
J., 22, 66
J.H., 17
J.J., 77
J.L., 6(2)
J.M., 77
J.W., 57
JAMES, 43
JOHN, 43, 76
L.S., 12
M., 90
PETER, 6
S., 43, 57
T., 57
W., 29
W.C., 43
W.R., 77
WILLIAM, 29
WM., 43
WM. G., 2
HALLAM
WM., 6

HALLENBECK
S., 43
HALLER
A., 66
PETER, 66
HALLEY
J., 87
HALLFORD
J.A., 77
HALLIGAN
J., 17
HALLIGER
C., 66
HALLIWARKE
[BLANK], 77
HALLMAN
H., 35
HALLOWAY
J., 43
HALLY
H., 34
THOMAS, 2
HALMANN
M., 36
HALPER
JOHN, 43
HALPIN
JNO., 83
P., 43, 87
HALSHULT
A., 57
HALSON
DAVID, 29
HALSTEAD
J.W., 24
HALTER
D., 85
HALTON
S.M., 17
HALTS
S., 85
HALY
W., 2
HAMAN
I., 67
HAMESWORTH
F., 24
HAMILTON
B., 67
D., 12
H., 43
J., 43, 57
J.G., 66
JAMES, 12
JOHN, 43
P.S., 12
S., 87
THOMAS, 43
W., 33
HAMLIN
G.W., 34
H.P., 24
J.H., 29
HAMM
E.J., 57
HAMMAN
W.H., 87
HAMMER
JOHN, 66(2)
P.C., 66
S., 83
HAMMLE
A., 35
HAMMOND
G.W., 12
GEORGE, 24
J., 20, 67, 90

J.W., 17
N., 43
S., 90
W., 67
HAMMONS
J., 66
HAMMONTIUS
P., 17
HAMNER
A., 17
HAMPTON
I.A., 76
HANAHAN
A., 33
HANARD
J.B., 57
HANBUCK
J., 77
HANCE
C., 29
HANCOCK
R., 43
W., 2
HAND
G., 85
H., 67
H.S., 43
L., 43
HANDA
L.C., 57
HANDLAND
H., 83
HANDS
J., 67
HANDY
GEORGE, 24
J., 33
MOSES, 24
HANE
J.H., 24
HANER
JACOB, 57
HANEY
H., 77, 87
J., 87
HANGER
L.S., 12
HANK
GEORGE B., 57
THOMAS, 22
HANKER
R., 17
HANKINS
E., 29
HANKS
A., 77
J., 43, 67
NELSON, 24
HANLEY
C., 57
D., 43
M., 24
T., 74, 77, 85
WM., 43
HANLON
THOMAS, 43, 44
HANNA
P., 6
HANNAH
H., 6
JNO., 29
THOS., 66
HANNESAY
A., 67
HANNEY
W.F., 57
HANNING

110

H., 3
MARK, 57
HANNOM
JOHN, 43
HANNS
J.B., 17
HANOR
FRANK, 43
HANS
JOHN, 66
P., 85
HANSBURY
E.A., 57
HANSEY
[BLANK], 67
HANSOM
C., 43
D., 6
HANSON
F.A., 2
J., 66, 85
L., 85
R., 85
T.R., 66
[BLANK], 85
HANY
B.F., 57
HAPPY
G., 67
HARDEN
G.W., 83
M., 66
HARDER
[BLANK], 66
HARDING
C., 24
W.F., 85
HARDINGER
W., 66
HARDINIVICK
J., 67
HARDIS
J.L., 66
HARDISON
G., 17
HARDWAY
D.B., 83
HARDY
E.L., 85
I., 43
J., 43
JNO., 29
W., 43
HARE
F., 24
HARKEN
JOHN, 6
HARKINS
D.S., 90
H., 83
JOHN, 90
M., 57
HARLAN
J.C., 6
HARLEY
ALFRED, 17
HARLOW
HARVEY, 17
HARMAN
A.B., 76
J., 87
JOHN, 67
HARMAN [?]
L., 57
HARMONY
J., 67
HARMPSTEAD

J., 74
HARNEY
E., 6
HARP
M., 43
HARPER
D., 15, 29
J., 17, 43
J.H., 57
R., 67
W., 83
HARRELL
G., 6
HARREN
F.J., 43
HARRINGTON
C., 17
F., 24
G., 29
J., 90
J.W., 66
JOHN, 66
O., 12
PAT, 43
S.J., 57
S.M., 6
HARRIS
A., 67
A.G., 77
C., 43
E.D., 57
E.K., 6
G.W., 6
J., 15, 57
J.E., 22
J.S., 20
N., 85
THOMAS, 43
V.S., 43
W.C., 12
WM., 76
HARRISON
D., 83
HENRY, 24, 43
J., 57(2)
J.M., 57
O., 43
HARRY
A., 43
HARSHAM
J.R., 87
HARSHMAN
PETER, 6
HART
A., 12
D.R., 43
E., 57
GEORGE, 6
H.C., 57
ISAAC, 90
J., 43(2), 67
J.R., 12, 29
M., 67
S., 43(2)
S.L., 80
W., 6, 24
HARTER
F., 17
HARTFORD
H., 34
HARTLICK
C., 66
HARTLY
ISAAC, 83
HARTMAN
H., 29, 57
I.N., 43

J., 57
V., 33
HARTRET
M., 24
HARTS
JOHN, 66
HARTSELL
GEO., 29
HARTSHAW
L.E., 25
HARTSOCK
I., 12
HARTY
J.S., 29
JAMES, 67
JOHN, 24, 43
HARTZEL
J., 67
S., 83
HARVEY
CHARLES, 57
D.M., 85
MORGAN, 77
P.D., 66
S.J., 24
HARWOOD
G., 2
HASBOROUGH
J.H., 77
HASFLE
J., 12
HASH
WM., 24
HASKET
A., 43
HASKINS
H., 12
J., 85
JAS., 2
HASLER
C., 87
M., 43
HASS
J.F., 43
HASSE
JOHN, 33
HASSEN
H., 20
HASTING
J., 17
HASTINGS
J., 15, 66
HATCH
J.S., 20
S., 20
T.C., 87
HATES
CHARLES, 66
HATFIELD
A.G., 57
GEORGE W., 57
J., 83
L., 17
HATHAWAY
CHARLES, 43
S., 6
HATTER
W., 36
HAUCH
L., 6
HAUSE
JNO., 43
HAUSLAN
B., 83
HAVELAND
H., 43
HAVENS

E.W., 80
GEORGE, 43
H., 43
S., 43
HAVERSLIGHT
H., 43
HAVERT
B., 66
HAWA
E.A., 77
HAWK
H.L., 29
HAWKINS
D.F., 74
GEORGE, 29
J.W., 6
S.D., 77
W.W., 57
HAWLEY
C., 29
F., 43
W.L., 43
HAY
WM., 25
HAYATT
L.P., 43
HAYES
C., 43
EDWARD, 43
J., 44, 67, 76
J.C., 77
JAMES, 29, 44
P., 25, 44
HAYEWOOD
A.J., 77
HAYFORD
A.E., 57
HAYMOUTH
N., 25
HAYNER
B., 57
E., 17
L., 44
HAYNES
CHARLES E., 25
P., 29
W., 12
W.C., 44
HAYS
C., 29
J.F., 17
HAYWARD
W.G., 6
HAYWOOD
J.B., 29
J.G., 77
[BLANK], 2
HAYWORTH
F., 6
HAZEL
GEORGE, 67
J., 22
HAZEN
M.J., 67
W., 80
HAZENFFLUCEY
J., 66
HAZER
JOHN, 17
HAZLET
J., 66
HAZLETT
WM., 57
HAZLEWOOD
J.H., 17
HAZZLE
WM., 77

HA[_]AY [?]
D., 90
HEACOCK
R., 44
HEAD
B.J., 33
DANIEL, 76
THOMAS, 44
HEADLEY
J.D., 66
HEAGER
J., 66
HEAH
JACOB, 12
HEALD
H.H., 89
WM., 88
HEALEY
J., 67
HEALY
A., 74
J.B., 67
HEARNE
JOHN, 12
HEART
JOHN, 25
W., 2
HEARTLESS
S., 90
HEARVAY
J.E., 33
HEATH
B., 20
J., 2
M., 29
HEATHERBY
JOHN, 76
HEATON
AMES, 57
HEBBAN
THOMAS, 25
HECHLER
JOHN, 57
HECKER
C., 44
G., 67
HECKINBRIDGE
[BLANK], 90
HECKLY
M., 66
HECKMAN
WM., 77
HECTOR
E., 12
HEDDINGTON
W., 87
HEDDLE
WM., 44
HEELLER
A., 15
HEENAN
JOHN, 66
HEFFERMAN
D., 44
HEGAMANN
J., 35
HEGENBERG
W., 6
HEGLEN
C., 17
HEIGHT
S.C., 66
HEIL
H., 29
HEINBACK
S., 66
HEIR

JOHN J., 67
JOSEPH, 7
L.W., 45
M., 25, 45, 57, 77, 89
N., 33
O.O., 34
P., 34, 87(2)
P.B., 45
R., 45(2)
R.A., 25
S.L., 77
SAMUEL, 7
W., 2, 77
W.H., 85
WM., 25, 67
JOHNSTON
I.A., 83
JOHN W., 57
WM., 67
JOICE
THOMAS, 45
JOINER
J.M., 77
JOLLEY
F., 45
JOLLY
G., 57
JAMES, 67
JOMSON
G.W., 36
JONDRO
M., 29
JONE
A., 36
JONES
A., 12, 29, 67
ALBERT, 77
C., 15
C.B., 87
C.N., 45
CHAS., 90
D., 17, 77(2)
DAVID, 22, 45
E., 45
E.C., 45
G., 83
G.C., 45
G.L., 58
G.W., 7, 45
H., 3, 45, 57, 77
H.C., 12
H.D., 77
H.L., 80
I.B., 58
J., 7, 12, 15, 17, 25, 67(2), 77
J.B., 34, 45
J.E., 77
J.M., 77
JAMES R., 2
JNO., 1
JOHN, 25, 45(2), 57
JOHN J., 2, 77
N.P., 25
O., 67
P., 7, 67
R., 45, 57, 67
R.W., 58
ROBERT, 67
RUFUS, 77
S., 57, 67
S.D., 58
T., 67(2)
THEO, 89
THOMAS, 7(2), 25
THOS., 45

W., 87
W.E., 67
W.H., 58
WARREN T., 77
WILLIAM, 67
WM., 7, 20, 45(2), 58, 67(2), 77, 89
WM. M., 12
JORDAN
A., 58
A.E., 80
B.W., 7
D.W., 67
J., 17
J.M., 67
M., 7
THOMAS, 67
JORY
G.F., 20
JOSEPH
F., 89
W.C., 3
JOSLIN
H., 80
J., 67
JOURDAN
BARRY, 45
JOURNEAY
JOHN, 89
JOY
B., 7
JOYCE
A., 7
JUDD
HENRY, 12
JULE
H., 45
JULERSO
H., 12
JUMP
D.O., 29
O., 45
JUNTPLUTE
F., 34
JUSTICE
GEORGE W., 57
H., 7
JUSTIN
J., 17

-K-

KAGMAN
J.T., 67
KAHBAUN
E., 45
KAHL
CHAS., 87
KAIBER
JOHN, 7
KAIN
P.F., 87
PAT, 87
KALER
J., 58
KALKRATH
C., 87
KALM
R., 67
KALTY
J., 2
KAMES
J., 12
KANE
F., 45, 85
H., 7
J., 83

PETER, 45
WM., 87
KANF
J., 67
KANFARD
JOHN C., 67
KANGA
J., 12
KANOPE
C., 45
KAPP
D., 45
KAPPEL
H., 7
KARCH
J., 58
KARL
WM., 29
KARSON
H.B., 34
KAUFFMAN
B.F., 67
KAUFMAN
J., 67
KAUNST
H., 34
KAVANAUGH
JAS., 25
KAWELL
JOHN H., 67
KAY
ROBT., 87
KEANSHOFF
L., 58
KEARN
T., 2
KEARNEY
L., 68
W., 45
KEATING
M., 45
THOS., 45
KEEAN
W., 45
KEEF
P., 12
KEEFE
JAMES P., 7
JOHN, 89
LEWIS, 22
KEEN
J.S., 77
KEENE
HOZA, 77
KEEPHART
M., 25
KEERROGER [SIC]
WM., 85
KEERS
M., 45
KEESTON
E., 67
KEHOE
MOSES, 67
T., 45
KEICH
N., 67
KEILER
A., 34
W.J., 12
KEILING
M., 17
KEINTZLER
R., 29
KELAZE
E., 7
KELL

M.R., 7
KELLAR
J., 20
JOHN, 45
KELLER
A., 67
I., 12, 34
M., 67
KELLETT
JOHN B., 85
KELLEY
CHARLES, 25
CHARLES H., 67
D., 45
E., 58, 68
F., 2
G., 58
H.S., 67
HENRY, 25
J., 45
J.W., 77
JAMES, 45
JAS., 45
JOHN, 7, 12
JOSIAH, 58
L., 20
M., 25, 45(2)
O.F., 67
P., 45
T., 45, 67
WILLIAM, 7
WM., 67
KELLOGG
E.L., 90
KELLY
D., 87
H., 58
J., 87
J.S., 87
JAMES, 89
JOHN, 12, 87
PETER, 67
WM., 58, 87
KELSEY
E., 25
JOHN, 58, 77
L.C., 80
KELSO
E.O., 12
KEMMETT
J., 85
KEMP
C.H., 34
E., 67
J.W., 87
KEMPER
J., 67
KEMPTON
B.F., 2
E., 25
KENARM
ALFRED, 45
KENDALL
W., 29, 85
KENEDY
S.J., 58
KENIGGE
A., 7
KENKHAM
H.C., 29
KENLEY
D., 87
KENNEDEY
H., 29
KENNEDY
A., 17
AMOS, 12

B., 15
J., 58, 68, 87
J.W., 12
JAS., 17
M., 7
M.E., 45
S.B., 17
W., 20, 45
WM., 25
KENNEY
C., 29
KENNION
F., 45
KENNY
A.W., 45
G.W., 45
J., 25
M., 45
WM., 67
KENOAN
M.A., 67
KENSER
JOSEPH, 77
KENT
E.L., 45
J., 7
S., 25
KENTER
A.W., 67
KENTZLER
HENRY, 77
KENWELL
R., 45
KEOGH [?]
PETER, 45
KEPLINGER
J., 22
KERBEY
JOHN, 7
KERER
H.N., 68
KERKNEY
F., 87
KERN
W., 12
KERR
A., 58
B., 68
C.L., 45
E., 90
H., 45
J.H., 58
WM., 25
KERRICK
SAMUEL, 33
KERRIT
JACOB, 45
KERSHOFF
B., 2
KERTSER
T., 45
KESITER
JOHN M., 67
KESLER
F., 15
KESSLER
J., 29
KESSMER
JOHN, 17
KESTER
CHAS., 45
J., 87
L., 67
KETCHUM
G.W., 12
KETTELL
JAS., 74

KETTLE
SOL, 45
KEYAN
M., 34
KEYES
C., 34
J.C., 25
O.S., 45
KEYS
ALEX C., 67
R., 45
WM., 12
KEYSER
JOHN, 7
KEYSTONE
C., 17
KICE
THOMAS, 25
KIDD
OWEN, 45
KIDWELL
J., 77
KIGER
J.H., 58
JOHN, 7
WM., 67
KILAN
M., 25
KILBRIDE
J., 87
KILKREATH
J., 7
KILLAR
J., 58
KILLNER
SANFORD, 45
KILMER
J., 45
KILPATRICK
C., 20
R., 77
KILSON
J., 45
KIMBALL
A., 25
H.H., 2
JAMES, 7
JAS., 18
JNO., 83
S., 45
KIMBERLY
C., 45
KIMBLE
S., 58
KINDERMAN
G., 7
KINDS
M.O., 85
KINEY
J., 74
KING
ALEXANDER, 15
C., 36, 67
D., 12
E., 15
I., 87
J.R., 68
JAMES T., 77
LEANDER, 29
M., 67, 68
N., 45
R., 68
RICHARD, 45
SYLVANUS, 45
[BLANK], 45
KINGENY
J., 87

KINGHAM
J., 7
KINGKADE
S., 58
KINGLAND
W.H., 90
KINGSBURY
C., 2
H.R., 34
J.H., 34
KINGSLEY
D., 45
JAMES, 45
S., 77, 80
KINKLE
JOHN, 7
KINMICK
T., 67
KINNAN
A., 12
KINNELY
F., 25
KINNEY
G.W., 87
J., 89
JNO., 29
JOHN, 58
L., 45
M., 4, 45
KINNIE
J., 45
KINS
W.H., 90
KINSELL
GEORGE, 29
KINSEY
B.B., 45
KINSMAN
F.P., 67
JOHN E., 45
W.S., 45
KIPP
W., 67
KIRBY
A., 58
CHARLES, 45
J., 22
J.A., 68
JAMES M., 77
KIRK
B.J., 77
J.P., 77
KIRKLAND
I., 45
KIRKPATRICK
[BLANK], 45
KIRKWOOD
H., 68
KISSINGER
F., 77
KISTNER
GEORGE, 12
KITCHELL
S., 36
KITTLE
E.N., 45
KIZER
G.W., 45
KLEPPS
C.H., 85
KLINE
C.S., 34
ROSS, 68
KLINEHAUS
D., 7
KLINELAND
L., 2

KLINK
A., 67
KLINSIMTH [SIC]
J., 34
KLINTY
H., 87
KLOSS
L., 33
KLUENER
F., 25
KLUNDER
CHARLES, 29
KNABLE
E., 45
KNAPP
C., 87
DAVID, 25
HENRY, 45
J., 17, 58
L., 80
PHILLIP, 45
THOMAS, 17
KNEIPER
C., 68
KNIDLER
J.W., 58
KNIGHT
CHAS., 80
J., 7, 58
J.B., 90
J.H., 15
JOHN, 67
WM., 45
[BLANK], 25
KNIVER
S., 67
KNOBLE
P., 7
KNOTTS
FRED, 17
KNOWL
H., 45
KNOWLES
C.W., 80
H., 85
KNOWLTON
E., 58
KNOX
J., 68
KOAHL
J., 7
KOCHEL
J., 87
KOCHER
T., 12
KOCK
H., 67
KOHLENBURG
C., 2
KOLENBRANDER
H., 15
KOSSUTH
W., 45
KRADER
W.O., 67
KRAIL
J., 7
KRAMER
GEORGE, 68
KRASIPARS
K., 45
KRAUTZ
H., 45
KREASER
M., 34
KREIGER

J., 7
KREIT
J.K., 45
KRELAR
A., 45
KRESSLER
P., 17
KRICKS
F., 87
KRIGLE
H., 67
KRIPP
J., 87
KROOM
C.E., 45
KROTE
HUER, 25
KROUK
PETER, 36
KROUSER
G.R., 45
KUFFMAN
S.D., 67
KUHM
R., 36
KUHN
JACOB, 34
KULING
I., 12
KULL
L., 85
KULTZ
A., 89
KUNDSON
J., 85
KUNER
E.B., 77
KUNTYELMAN
J., 67
KUPPY
H., 25
KURTZ
J., 68
KYLE
WM., 67(2)

-L-

LA BOLT
J., 68
LA BONEY
H., 80
LABOR
R., 68
LACEY
P., 45
WM., 45
LACK
PETER, 85
LACKER
H., 80
LACKEY
J., 87
JAMES, 68
LACKLEY
P.I., 45
LACKS
LEE, 45
LACOCK
HUGH, 68
LACOST
J.M., 7
LACOSTER
H., 45
LADBEATER
JAS., 68
LADD

A., 68
C., 20
LADDENBUSH
J., 80
LADER
A., 45
LADIEN
J., 7
LAFFERTY
WM., 90
LAGAY
FRANK, 45
LAHEY
DANIEL, 45
P., 45
LAHIFF
D., 45
LAHMAN
C., 68
LAICH
F., 85(2)
LAIDHAM
G., 31
LAIN
S., 25
LAIRD
CORBIN, 22
LAKE
HORACE, 87
WM., 45
LAKIN
A., 12
LALEY
[BLANK], 58
LAMAN
C., 45
LAMAREUX
J., 45
LAMB
C., 68
LAMBER
W., 20
LAMBERT
C., 7
CHAS., 15
JAMES, 58
R., 17
W., 22, 68
LAMBLY
J., 45
LAMBRIGHT
A., 45
LAMPERT
R., 45
LAMPHARE
G.W., 58
LAMPHEY
J., 77
LAMPMAN
W.S., 45
LAMSDEN
W.H., 7
LANCASTER
C., 68
E., 68
LANCE
V., 7
LANCREED
M., 29
LANDERS
C., 45
[BLANK], 17
LANE
AMOS, 68
C., 45
CHAS., 45
D., 58

G.W., 45
J.H., 25
J.W., 45
L.E., 77
LANEN
　THOMAS, 77
LANG
　A., 45
　C., 34
　I., 68
　WM. W., 45
LANGDON
　A.M., 45
LANGEN
　A., 45
LANGHA
　W., 45
LANGLEY
　E.G., 77
　G., 7
　L.F., 25
LANGSTAFF
　R., 87
LANGSTAN
　N.H., 83
LANHAM
　HENRY, 83
LANHART
　J., 17
LANIGAN
　N., 68
LANNER
　W.A., 7
LANNING
　A., 15
　H.B., 29
LANNON
　J.S., 12
LANSBURY
　W., 83
LANSING
　G., 85
　WM., 45
LANSOP
　J., 45
LANTZ
　A.W., 58
　WM., 68
LAPCAM
　A., 80
LAPE
　J., 7, 68
LAPPAN
　L.H., 45
LAPRINT
　J., 77
LARAWAY
　H., 80
LARCKS
　G., 45
LARD
　H.O., 31
LARGE
　M., 33
LARGER
　W., 17
LARIBEE
　L., 31
LARIME
　C., 36
LARIMER
　J., 68
LARISEN
　A., 58
LARKE
　J.A., 31
LARKIN

JOSEPH, 58
LARKINS
　M.C., 45
LARME
　CHARLES, 58
LARQDELL
　WM., 87
LARRABEE
　E., 45
LARREBY
　G., 87
LARRISON
　WALLACE, 68
LASAR
　BENJAMIN, 45
LASH
　J., 12
LASPER
　OTTO, 17
LASTRY
　J., 2
LATCHEM [?]
　DAVID, 68
LATEY
　P., 45
LATGEN
　E., 85
LATHAM
　W., 25
LATHROP
　W.O., 25
LATIMORE
　W.H., 33
LATTA
　W.H., 58
LATTARETTA
　J., 45
LATTIN
　E., 87
LAUGHLIN
　D., 83
　J., 68
　J.L., 68
　M.W., 58
　R.M., 4
LAURENS
　JOHN, 25
LAW
　HENRY, 7
　S.S., 58
LAWRENCE
　A., 34
　B.T., 12
　C., 87
　D., 12
　J., 45
　J.C., 77
　R.J., 12
LAWRENE
　L.G., 7
LAWSEN
　J., 58
LAWSON
　H.G., 77
　JOHN, 45
　M., 77, 85
　WILLIAM, 12
LAWTON
　J., 45
　JAMES, 89
LAWYER
　J.B., 58
　JAMES, 12
LAY
　JOHN, 58
　WM., 17
LAYERS

W., 15
LAYMAN
　C., 45
　F., 68
LAYMON
　W.F., 83
LAYTIN
　P., 68
LAYTON
　SAMUEL, 68
　STEPHEN, 36
LEABROOK
　JOHN, 45
LEACH
　C.W., 25
　J., 68
　JAS., 68
　L.D., 74
　S., 45
　W., 7
LEADBEATER
　J.H., 36
LEAMON
　G., 31
LEAN
　W.H., 45
LEARY
　C., 68
　D., 25
LEASURE
　F., 58
　ISAAC, 58
LEATHERMAN
　M., 7
LEAVEY
　W.H., 25
LEBOS
　C., 68
LEBUD
　J., 22
LECRAW
　W.P., 25
LEDDERER
　WM., 45
LEDFORD
　J.A., 17
LEDWICK
　A., 17
　F.M., 68
LEE
　A., 7, 45
　CORNELIUS, 74
　F., 45
　JAMES, 90
　JAS., 68
　JOHN, 12
　P., 7, 45
　S., 17
　THOMAS, 7
　W.E., 7
　WM., 45
　[BLANK], 2
LEES
　W.H., 22
LEFARER
　W.E., 58
LEGO
　GEO., 68
LEGRAND
　D., 58
LEGRIST
　W., 45
LEHIGH
　W., 58
LEHNICH
　JOHN, 68
LEICHINGER

J., 45
LEIGHTON
　WM., 36
LEINER
　A., 45
LEMMAR
　J.E., 77
LEMON
　JOHN E., 68
LEMONS
　M., 58
LENARD
　M., 68
LENCHLIER
　J., 68
LENDON
　H., 2
LENERT
　D., 34
LENNIERT
　L., 17
LENOT
　V., 45
LENT
　A., 45
LENYER
　M., 33
LEONARD
　A., 45
　C.H., 45
　GEO., 68
　I.G., 25
　J., 77
　J.W., 45
　JOHN, 58
　T.M., 58
　W., 2
　W.E., 25
LEOPORT
　C., 80
LEPE
　A., 58
LEPLEY
　CHAS., 68
LEPORT
　J., 34
LESTER
　JAMES, 77
　W.H., 68
LESTRAFF
　C., 45
LETCH
　JOHN, 46
LEVALLEY
　C., 46
LEVANAUGH
　WM. O., 2
LEVER
　H.B., 58
LEVI
　J.N., 77
LEVILLE
　THOMAS, 17
LEVITT
　H., 20
LEVY
　FRANK, 68
LEWILLEY
　WM., 34
LEWIN
　CHARLES, 25
LEWIS
　A., 68
　C., 46
　C.F., 46
　CHARLES, 7
　D., 58

D.S., 68
ED, 68
EDWARD, 74
F., 25
F.A., 46
F.L., 29
FRANK, 58
G.G., 25
G.H., 2
G.W., 46
J., 2, 12(2), 46,
　68, 77
JAMES, 12
L., 25(2), 33
P., 29
P.W., 46
R., 12, 77
S., 36
T., 17
THOMAS, 7
WM. P., 87
LIBBY
　A.G., 34
LICKEY
　J.B., 7
LICKLEY
　P., 46
LICKLITER
　HENRY, 58
LIDAY
　J., 7
LIESEN
　LEWIS, 68
LIESINE
　WM., 68
LIGGETT
　[BLANK], 12
LIGHT
　S., 68
LIGHTFOOT
　WM., 58
LIKEN
　JOHN, 7
LIMAR
　W., 68
LIMBACH
　S., 46
LIMPKINS
　J.H., 4
LINCH
　J.H., 46
LINCHLER
　F., 46
LINCOLN
　A., 20
LINDAY
　B., 7
LINDERMAN
　H.A., 7
LINDERSMITH
　E., 89
LINDINE
　J., 68
LINDLAY
　D., 46
LINDLEY
　C., 33
LINDSAY
　A., 7
　J., 25, 34
LINDSLEY
　A.K. [?], 58
　SAMUEL, 36
LINDUSKY
　G., 17
LINEBERGH
　I., 7

LINEHAM
  THOMAS, 46
LING
  JOHN, 46
LINGO
  JAMES, 77
LINK
  GOTLIEB, 46
  P., 68
LINKER
  C., 2
LINSAY
  J., 58
LINSEY
  D., 68
LINTON
  E., 90
LINWAY
  J., 58
LINWOOD
  J., 7
LIPPOTH
  J., 68
LIPS
  F., 58
LIPSEY
  D., 7
LISTON
  DAVID, 83
LISURE
  SAMUEL, 58
LISWELL
  L., 25
LITCH
  J., 34
LITTLE
  C., 46
  D., 22
  E.D., 77
  J., 17, 87
  J.F., 17
  M., 68
  R., 87
  WM., 58
LITTLEBRIDGE
  W.H., 74
LITTLEFIELD
  C., 20
LITTLEJOHN
  L.D., 15
LITTLETON
  J., 15
LIVINGOOD
  C.B., 58
LIVINGSTON
  A., 46
  J'N, 74
  J.H., 85
  J.K., 68
  R., 25
LOCHER
  CONRAD, 46
LOCHERY
  A., 68
LOCHLEN
  JOEL, 25
LOCHNER
  M., 58
LOCK
  A., 46
LOCKEWOOD
  H., 87
LOCKHARD
  J., 68
LODGE
  T., 46
LODI

JOHN, 89
LODISS
  H., 68
LOFLER
  E.E., 31
LOFTERN
  H., 46
LOFTUS
  M., 46
LOFTY
  R.J., 77
LOGAN
  B., 68
  FRANK, 58
  H., 58
  W., 68
LOGGER
  J., 83
LOGNE
  S., 68
LOHEM
  E.D., 25
LOHMEYER
  H., 58
LOLEN
  J., 68
LOMBARD
  B.K., 25
LONDON
  ED, 25
LONG
  A., 68
  AUGUSTUS, 68
  C.C., 77(2)
  D.F.B., 68
  J., 46
  JOHN, 58, 77(2)
  JONATHAN, 77
  L., 46
  P., 68
  W., 68
LONGLE
  WILLIAM, 46
LONGS
  R., 46
LONGSTREET
  W.F., 58
LONONEY
  B., 17
LONSEY
  L., 29
LOOMIS
  JOHN, 46
LOONY
  C., 46
LOOPER
  E., 77
LORD
  G.W., 68
  GEO. H., 20
  L., 15
  L.B., 7
  M., 31
  WM., 17
LORING
  G., 25
  JNO., 29
LORSAM
  C., 7
LORZBRAN
  J., 46
LOSSING
  JNO., 29
LOSSMAN
  A., 17
LOUBY
  O., 87

LOUD
  GEO., 83
LOUDIN
  H.N., 68
LOUDON
  L., 7
  S., 68
  SAMUEL, 68
LOUGH
  H., 83
LOUIS
  C., 46
  J., 22
LOVE
  J., 46
  JOHN, 58
  WM., 87
LOVEJOY
  F., 46
LOVELY
  FRANCIS, 25
  JOHN, 58
LOVERING
  F., 46
LOVETT
  A.W., 25
LOVETTE
  W.T., 77
LOWDENBECK
  N., 15
LOWE
  F., 85
  G.H., 58
  J., 83
  JOHN, 34
  W.G., 83
LOWELENBUCK
  D., 15
LOWELL
  B., 20
  GEORGE, 25
  JAS., 31
LOWER
  N.G., 12
LOWERY
  D., 12
  G., 46
  JAMES F., 46
LOWRING
  J., 83
LOWRY
  FRANK, 7
  JAMES, 58
  JAS. W., 17
LOWS
  H., 46
LOY
  W.B., 17
LOYD
  S., 46
LU DUK
  JAS., 31
LUBLETT
  M.L., 17
LUCAH
  JOHN, 46
LUCAS
  J., 58, 83
LUCE
  F., 29
  V., 46
LUCH
  J.H., 46
LUCHFORD
  R., 68
LUCHT
  P., 34

LUCIA
  A., 46
LUCIER
  J., 25
LUCK
  W., 68
LUDIHING
  W., 83
LUDOVICE
  F., 20
LUFF
  C., 12
LUGBY
  Z., 25
LUHARS
  MELTER, 68
LUMER
  JNO., 29
LUMMO
  ROBERT, 90
LUMSDEN
  C., 80
LUND
  JAS., 31
LUNEY
  ED., 36
LUNGER
  A., 12
LUNGERSHAN
  W.C., 80
LURCOCK
  E., 46
LUSK
  JOHN, 7
LUSTER
  W., 17
LUTHER
  I., 68
  J., 15
LUTHERLAND
  H., 17
LUTTON
  O., 46
  THOMAS, 17
LUTZ
  JOHN, 7
  M., 58
  P.M., 68
  WM., 31
LYMAN
  J., 7
  O.S., 87
LYNCH
  ADAM, 68
  B. [?], 87
  D., 46
  F., 46
  JOHN, 25
  PAT, 46
  V., 7
  W.J., 68
LYON
  A.D., 29
  L.L., 58
LYONS
  CHARLES, 46
  D., 36
  E., 25, 87
  J., 46
  MICHAEL, 46
  R., 87
  THOMAS, 46
  W., 46
  WM., 12(2)
LYSHON
  WM., 83

-M-

MABY
  ED, 31
McAFEE
  JAS., 69
McALLISTER
  A.P., 15
  J., 25, 46
  W., 80
  W.H., 77
MACART
  R., 78
McARTHUR
  W., 31
MACARY
  C., 17
McATIE
  M., 90
McBETH
  I.C., 13
McBRIDE
  J., 69
  [BLANK], 4, 46
McCABE
  F., 31
  H., 58
  J., 46, 58(2), 68
  JAMES, 46
  P., 46
  PETER, 46
McCAFFERTY
  W., 46
McCAFFREY
  J., 25
  JOHN, 69
McCAIN
  L., 46
McCALASKY
  J.E., 68
McCALL
  THOS., 15
  WM., 69
McCAME
  W., 31
McCAMERON
  W., 15
McCAMPBELL
  D., 7
McCANE
  CHARLES, 68
McCANN
  A., 58
  B., 87
  J., 69
  JOHN, 69
  M., 35
  O., 35
McCANTLEY
  W., 69
McCARDELL
  W., 46
McCARLE
  JAS., 22
McCARRON
  J., 68
McCART
  WM., 77
McCARTEN
  L., 46
McCARTER
  JAS., 31
  W., 17
McCARTNEY
  H., 31
  M., 68
McCARTNY

JAS., 68
McCARTY
  A., 13(2)
  CHARLES, 31
  D., 46
  DENIS, 46
  DENNIS, 69
  E., 17
  I., 13, 46(2)
  JOHN, 12, 17, 46(2)
  P., 46
  S., 46
  T., 89
  W., 46
McCASLIN
  M.C., 78
McCAULEY
  J.H., 46
McCAULLEY
  JAS., 2
McCAUSLAND
  R., 83
McCLAIR
  R., 87
McCLANY
  J., 69
McCLARR
  P.M., 58
McCLARY
  W., 31
McCLAY
  J., 69
McCLEARY
  THOS., 7
McCLELLAN
  J., 87
McCLIEF
  WM., 69
McCLING
  B., 58
McCLINTOCK
  J.S., 87
McCLOUD
  A., 31, 58
  J., 25
  JOHN, 46
McCLOUGH
  L.C., 69
McCLURE
  P., 17
  R., 31
  Z., 15
McCLURY
  A., 85
McCLUSH
  N., 69
McCLUSKY
  F., 46
  JAMES, 7
McCOLIGAN
  PAT, 46
McCOLLEN
  W., 68
McCOMB
  J.S., 58
McCONAGHY
  P., 87
McCONE
  R., 7
McCONKEY
  A.L., 83
McCONNAUGHY
  D., 83
McCONNELL
  E., 46
McCOOK
  B., 69

McCORD
  G., 87
  H., 46
  J.G., 25
  P., 2
McCORMIC
  M., 46
McCORMICK
  E., 85
  H., 46(2)
  J., 46(3)
  J.W., 58
  P., 46
  PETER, 46
  R., 83
  W., 46
  W.P., 58
McCORNER
  J., 25
McCOSLIN
  ROBT., 87
McCOY
  AUGUSTUS, 87
  G.B., 15
  J., 87
  J.B., 58
  J.M., 87
  W., 13
  W.C., 77
McCRACKER
  B., 46
  J., 69
McCRACKLIN
  H., 4
McCRASS
  J., 46
McCRAY
  A., 7
  J., 69
McCREADY
  J., 7
  WM., 7
McCREIETH
  A., 3
McCREMBER
  M., 46
McCRILLIS
  EDW., 80
McCULLEN
  D., 46
McCULLER
  S., 69
McCULLOUGH
  J., 22
  S., 69
McCULLOYT
  [BLANK], 69
McCUNE
  J., 69
  ROBERT, 77
McCUNNE
  H., 7
McCUTCHEON
  J., 68
McDALE
  R., 12
McDAVID
  J., 46
  JAS., 3
McDAVLE
  J., 25
McDELL
  WM., 58
McDERMOTT
  H., 87
  J., 25
  J.M., 68

  P., 46, 89
McDEVITT
  J., 69
  WM., 25
McDONALD
  A., 46
  A.H., 46
  B., 46
  D.B., 15
  F., 46(2)
  H.H., 59, 90
  I., 13
  J., 17, 58, 90
  JOHN, 46, 89(2)
  L.M., 77
  R., 25, 68
  W., 78
  [BLANK], 69, 87
McDONNELL
  P., 25
  WM., 46
McDONOUGH
  P., 25
McDOUGAL
  J., 33
  W.C., 17
McDOVER
  H., 77
McDOWELL
  G., 77
  J., 3, 31, 34
McDURIE
  C., 46
MACE
  JEFF, 46
  L., 46
McELRAY
  JOHN, 46
McELROY
  E., 36
  JOHN, 59
  WM., 69
McELVAIN
  J., 13
McENTIRE
  L., 7
  W., 68
McERMANY
  P., 46
McEUSHON
  PETER, 90
McEVERS
  T.L., 87
MACEY
  CHARLES, 25
McFADDEN
  H., 85
  JAS., 47
McFALL
  H., 31
  I., 13
McFARLAND
  A., 47
  E.S., 20
  G., 20
  JAS., 68
  L., 58
  W., 20
McFARNEY
  J., 13
McGAGER
  J., 80
McGAIN
  I., 47
McGAN
  J., 69
McGARRETT

  R.W., 69
McGEATTE
  [BLANK], 47
McGEE
  A., 78
  J., 69, 90
  JAMES, 68
  P., 87
  THOMAS, 3
  WM., 7, 77
McGENGER
  J., 69
McGIBEN
  I., 47
McGIBNEY
  H., 47
McGINIS
  P., 31
McGINLEY
  J., 20
McGINNESS
  A., 87
McGINNIS
  J.W., 3
McGITTON
  J., 83
McGIVEN
  J., 25
  WM., 47
McGIVENS
  J., 7
McGLANN
  H., 69
McGONEYAL
  R., 25
McGORREN
  J., 87
McGOVERN
  B., 25
McGOWAN
  F., 47
  J., 89
  JOHN, 47
  WM., 47
McGOWEN
  JOHN, 25
  WM., 25
McGRATH
  D., 59
  M., 47
McGRAW
  JOHN, 69
McGREGOR
  P., 83
McGUCKER
  A., 47
McGUIGAN
  H.C., 69
McGUIGEN
  S.K., 22
McGUIN [McGUM?]

  M., 77
McGUIRE
  A., 25
  J., 87(3), 90
  JNO., 31
  O., 34
  P., 47(2)
  PAT, 47
McHALE
  J., 68
McHARTY
  M., 47
McHENRY
  DANIEL, 89
  JAMES, 25

MACHLER
  C.S., 22
McHOSE
  J., 68
McHUGH
  W.S., 58
McINNESS
  A., 58
McINTIRE
  H., 25
  J., 69
  JOHN, 80
  R., 36
McINTOSH
  D., 58
  WM., 59
MACK
  J., 7, 46
McKABE
  J., 47
McKARREN
  E., 25
McKAY
  K., 31
  M.J., 68
  THOS., 74
McKEARNEY
  J., 69
McKEE
  JAMES, 58
  [BLANK], 69
McKEESE
  SAMUEL, 78
McKEEVER
  E.L., 68
  JAMES, 58
McKELL
  M.J., 58
McKENLEY
  J., 47
McKENNA
  F., 90
  H., 47
  J., 74
McKENNY
  B., 25
McKENZIE
  J., 85
McKEON
  J., 3
  JOHN, 68
McKERAL
  JAMES, 69
McKERCHAY
  J.H., 47
McKERN[_] [?]
  S., 69
McKEVER
  JOHN, 68
McKEY
  J., 68
MACKEY
  S., 78
MACKIN
  W., 77
  WM., 46
McKINDRY
  M., 58
McKINK
  J., 69
McKINLEY
  E.W., 87
McKINNEY
  D., 69
  J., 4, 87
  JOHN, 47
  WM., 83

McKINNNEY
G., 20
McKINSAY
JNO., 22
McKINZIE
GEORGE, 25
McKISSICK
JOHN, 68
MACKLIN
JOHN, 77
McKNIGHT
B., 25
H., 58
J., 69
J.E., 68
JAS., 69
MACKRILL
R., 58
MACKSWARER
W., 31
McLAIN
R., 47
McLAINE
THOS., 31
McLAMAS
J., 22
McLANE
H.C., 77
T., 69
McLARENS
B., 7
McLAUGHLIN
B., 7, 89
E., 25, 89
J., 47, 87
JAS., 69
O., 47
McLAULIN
C., 85
McLEAN
A.G., 77
P., 87
WM., 3
McLING
BENJ., 7
McLORENS
R., 47
McLOUGHLIN
R., 83
McMAHON
C.L., 47
J., 68
M., 7
PAT, 90
McMANES
[BLANK], 68
McMANN
W., 31, 85
McMANNUS
SAML., 17
McMASTERS
[BLANK], 25
McMILLAN
J.F., 58
JAMES, 25
W.B., 7
McMILLEN
ALEX, 31
McMILLER
J.A., 22
W.B., 7
McMULLEN
JAMES, 15
McMUNNY
GEORGE, 58
McMURRAY
WM., 69

McMURRIER
WM., 47
McNAMARA
WM., 47
[BLANK], 25
McNAMIRIN
B.F., 47
McNAURY
R., 25
McNEALY
W., 78
McNEIL
J.W., 15
McNEILY
JAS., 83
McNELSE
J.H., 69
McNIELL
C., 31
McNULTY
P., 25
[BLANK], 47
MACOMBER
J., 25
JOHN, 22
MACON
L., 20
McPEAK
W., 47
McPHERSON
D., 69
WM., 47
McQUEENY
W., 68
McQUESTON
J.O., 13
McQUIGLEY
JOHN, 69
McQUILKEN
F., 59
McQUILLEN
A., 47, 69
McRATH
J., 68
McSHAW
B., 7
McSORLEY
D., 58
G.W., 47
McSPOULDING
W., 31
McTIER
J., 89
McVEY
K., 89
McWILLIAMS
H., 69
W., 25
McWILSON
J., 83
McWORTHY
W.M., 7
MACY
C.S., 15
MADDEN
DANIEL, 68
F., 46
L., 7
[BLANK], 46
MADDER
P., 46
MADDOCK
J.W., 7
MADDONS
W.L., 83
MADDRO
JAS., 78

MADEZAN
JOHN, 46
MADISON
D., 46
MADLENER
L., 13
MADRILL
A., 7
MAGAHER
J., 83
MAGESON
J., 12
MAGILL
H., 69
MAGRAM
J., 31
MAGRATH
G.H., 46
MAHAM
JAS., 4
MAHAN
E., 25
MAHER
D., 69
P., 58
S.L., 31
MAHIN
B., 58
MAHLER
JOHN, 36
MAHON
E., 46
JAMES, 46
THOMAS, 46
MAILER
J.R., 46
MAIN
HENRY, 85
MAINE
F.O., 46
MAINES
WM., 77
MAINFOLD
W., 13
MAINHART
F., 46
MAJOR
WM., 31
MAKAY
J., 46
MALABY
P., 89
MALCOLM
H.M., 20
J.R., 7
S.A., 77
MALLECK
M., 46
MALLEY
S.S., 46
MALONE
JOHN, 3
L.B., 58
PAT, 46
R.J., 58
MALONEY
A., 58
B., 87
C., 46
J., 46
MALOY
I., 13
J.M., 69
MALSBRAY
ASA, 58
MALSHY
F., 12

MAN
THOS. G., 31
MANAHAN
THOS., 58
MANCHESTER
J.M., 80
MANDER
J.W., 33
MANDEVILLE
WM., 46
MANEE
M., 69
MANGIN
M., 46
MANIAN
P., 80
MANIHAN
J., 12
MANK
E., 12
MANLEY
J. [?], 59
MANLIG
S., 58
MANN
J., 15
JAMES, 69
N.C., 25
MANNER
C., 4
M., 69
MANNILLY
J., 46
MANNING
A., 7
B.F., 90
J., 87
M., 46
S.H., 34
THOMAS, 46
[BLANK], 46
MANSEN
W., 58
MANSFIELD
D.R., 25
GEORGE, 69
J., 69
MANTLE
J.M., 87
MANTOVE
J., 35
MANTY
P., 7
MANWARING
WM., 31
MANY
J., 85
MAPE
GEORGE, 3
MAPLES
H., 13
MARCH
J., 46
MARCHET
C., 25
MARCHIN
WM., 69
MARDEN
G.O., 25
MAREY
H.F., 69
MARILAND
W.H., 25
MARINE
WM., 31
MARINTINE
G.H., 25

MARK
J., 59
MARKELL
S., 22
MARKER
W.H., 69
MARKHAM
D., 31
MARKIN
W., 22
MARKMAN
WM., 7
MARKS
CHARLES, 36
P., 69
MARLEY
JOHN, 46
MARLIT
J., 12
MARONY
JOHN, 68
MARPLE
S.L., 68
MARQUET
M., 68
MARRITT
H., 7
MARRON
J., 46
MARSH
D., 68
IRA, 46
J., 12, 46
W., 69
MARSHALL
A., 7
B., 3
B.F., 20
G., 31
H.E., 31
L., 3, 17, 69
M.M., 68
N.B., 89
T., 58
WM., 17
MARSTON
A., 46
B., 87
MARTAIN
JOHN, 69
MARTAUGH
J., 46
MARTEN
J., 35
MARTIN
A., 7, 46
A.J., 68
BRYANT, 68
C., 46, 69
C.M., 25
CHARLES, 46
CHAS., 47
D., 58
E.A., 46
F., 59
F.A., 77
F.P., 17
G., 58, 68
G.H., 47
GEORGE, 12
H., 46
HENRY, 47
I., 7
J., 4, 34, 46, 69,
87
J.B., 15
J.C., 46

J., 68
MILLIKEN
 S.L., 12
MILLINGER
 JOHN H., 69
MILLINGTON
 J., 36
MILLIOT
 P., 35
MILLREAN
 M.W., 26
MILLS
 A., 87
 F., 36
 G.W., 59
 GEORGE, 17
 J.J., 47
 JOHN, 17
 M., 21
 MILTON, 13
 N., 7
 S., 7, 47
 W.J., 2
 WM., 69, 80
MILLSPAUGH
 FRED, 47
MILOR
 W., 3
MILSKER
 J., 13
MILTON
 C., 26
 JOHN, 12
 WM., 68
MILTY
 SAMUEL, 47
MILUM
 JAS., 83
MIND
 S., 7
MINDLER
 PETER, 47
MINE
 JOHN N., 13
 JOSEPH, 68
MINER
 J.G., 47
 S., 74
MINK
 H., 68
MINSHALL
 R., 58
MIPES
 J., 68
MISSILE
 VAL, 68
MITCHAN
 A., 7
MITCHEL
 JNO., 1
MITCHELL
 C., 58
 F., 26
 I., 13
 J., 47, 58
 J.H., 13
 J.J., 12
 J.O., 69
 J.R., 7
 JACOB, 80
 JAMES, 17, 58
 JAS., 78
 JOHN, 26, 47
 R.C., 59
 R.M., 17
 W.C., 26
 W.H., 58

MITCHINER
 H., 77
MITTANCE
 L., 26
MIX
 C., 7
MIXTER
 G.L., 26
MIXWELL
 L.B., 7
MIZNER
 W., 87
MI[_]IE [?]
 F., 47
MOAN
 JAS., 68
MODGER
 A., 3
MOE
 JOHN, 47
MOFFAT
 J., 47
MOFFITT
 THOS., 22
MOHR
 J.R., 69
MOKIE
 R., 83
MOLAND
 B., 22
MOLOSH
 F., 31
MOMGOMERY [SIC]

 WM., 77
MONAGHAN
 [BLANK], 47
MONAN
 J., 68
MONAY
 G.W., 13
MONECAL
 J., 7
MONEYHON
 B., 12
MONGBY
 D., 31
MONIHAN
 J., 47
MONNY
 W.H., 68
MONOHAN
 J., 47
 P., 47
MONROE
 A., 80
 A.J., 47
 D., 31
 H.J., 13
 J., 26
 J.R., 47
 JNO., 31
 S., 12
MONSCHITZ
 J., 47
MONSEN
 J.F., 83
MONSON
 GEO., 47
 WM., 47
MONTA
 HENRY, 47
MONTAG
 GEO., 47
MONTEGAN
 P., 35
MONTEITH

M., 90
MONTENARY
 J., 33
MONTGOMERY
 C., 87
 C.F., 78
 J., 59
 O.A., 80
 R., 12, 69
 W., 13
 W.A., 17
MONTJOY
 T., 3
MOODIE
 Z., 12
MOODY
 C.R., 47
 R.W., 83
 THOS., 47
MOON
 J.J., 22
 JAMES, 15
MOONEY
 J., 47
 JAMES, 58
 PAT, 17
 THOS., 47
MOONY
 I., 47
 P., 47
MOOR
 D.D., 58
 JNO., 31
MOORE
 A., 26, 47, 89
 A.P., 3
 C., 47, 69
 C.A., 26
 C.C., 47
 C.H., 69
 CHARLES, 58
 CHARLES W., 21
 FRANK, 22
 G., 13, 21
 J., 31, 69
 J.D., 21
 JAS., 78
 JOHN, 15, 31, 47
 M., 26, 69, 83
 M.G., 68
 M.J., 69
 MARTIN, 47
 P., 26
 PETER, 12
 R.F., 59
 S., 47, 69
 T., 78
 T.H., 47, 58
 T.J., 58
 THOMAS, 69
 W., 69
 W.C., 21
 W.H., 47
 W.S., 47
 WM., 15, 17, 78
MOORHEAD
 J.S., 69
MORAIS
 WM., 59
MORAM
 M.J., 47
MORAN
 D.G., 47
 F., 7
 J., 87
 THOS., 47
 W., 7

MORBLY
 B., 7
MORE
 JOHN H., 58
MOREARTY
 I., 47
MOREHEAD
 J., 7
MORELAND
 H., 17
MORELL
 A., 36
MORENS
 H., 58
MORGAN
 C., 69
 C.H., 26
 CHAS., 80
 E., 34, 47
 E.C., 31
 E.J., 47
 F., 17
 J., 17
 J.E., 69
 M., 31, 47
 PAT, 26
 R.O., 59
MORGRAFF
 WM., 47
MORIATT
 JOSEPH, 58
MORITZE
 A., 69
MORLAND
 H., 47
 J.S., 90
MORLEY
 H., 7
MORRIS
 A.T., 31
 B., 7
 C.E., 58
 CALVIN, 68
 E., 47
 G., 68, 83
 G.J., 87
 H., 47
 H.S., 78
 J., 7, 47(2), 58,
  68, 69, 77
 J.A., 47
 J.M., 83
 JAMES, 7
 JOHN, 47, 69
 L.R., 47
 N.G., 26
 R., 26, 47
 T., 47
 T.A., 47
 WM., 47, 78
MORRISON
 F., 90
 J., 13, 31, 69
 J.H., 59
 O.P., 35
 W., 47(2)
MORROW
 J.C., 69
MORSE
 E., 47
 I., 47
 W., 80
MORTES
 B., 85
MORTIMER
 L., 26
 WM., 47

MORTON
 G.H., 26
 GEO. H., 69
 J., 26, 31
 J.B., 90
 T., 68
 W., 17
MORTROSS
 D.H., 47
MOSER
 JOHN, 68
 S., 69
MOSES
 A., 31
 C., 31
 L., 47
 W., 69
MOSEY
 A., 80
MOSHER
 E., 47
MOSIER
 E., 47
 M.W., 47
MOSS
 CHARLES, 26
 J., 77
 W.S., 47
 WM., 54
MOSSMAN
 S., 7
MOTTS
 C., 47
MOULD
 JAMES, 2
MOULDEN
 WM., 77
MOULTON
 H., 26
MOUNTZ
 R., 7
MOUNY
 JNO., 31
MOWER
 W., 90
MOXWORTHY
 GEO., 4
MOYER
 J., 90
 JOHN, 68
 THOS., 68
 WM. M., 69
MOYES
 F., 21
MUCHOLIANS
 J., 68
MULANOX
 A.C., 78
MULASKY
 E., 85
MULCABY
 W., 47
MULCHY
 J., 12
 J.A., 69
MULCOHY
 D.D., 47
MULDANY
 M, 69
MULFORD
 W.R., 7
MULGRAVE
 JAMES, 47
MULHALL
 PETER, 87
MULHERN
 C., 87

D., 8
W.H., 31
O'BRIEN
  AUSTIN, 31
  CHARLES, 35
  D., 48
  JAMES, 26
  JOHN, 26, 59
  M., 48
  P., 69
  S., 48
  W., 21, 48
  WM., 80, 89
O'CARREL
  F., 48
OCH
  S., 48
OCHLE
  F., 85
OCHLEY
  WM., 8
O'CONNELL
  J., 26(2)
  M., 26
  THOMAS, 48
  WM., 70
O'CONNER
  P., 15
  THOMAS, 13
  WM., 26
O'CONNOR
  F., 59
  M., 8
O'CONOR
  [BLANK], 69
O'DAVID
  J.H., 8
O'DEAN
  THOMAS, 8
O'DELL
  E., 34
ODOM
  W., 8
O'DONNELL
  W., 26
  [BLANK], 8
ODORN
  JOHN, 78
O'DOUGHERTY
  J., 48
OFFLEBACK
  Z., 70
OGDEN
  E.S., 31
OGELSBY
  J., 69
OGLESBY
  D., 8
O'HARA
  JOHN, 70
  M., 70
OILER
  SAMUEL, 70
O'KAY
  PETER, 48
O'KEEFE
  M., 8
O'KEIF
  C., 48
OLAHAN
  A., 48
OLDER
  W.M., 48
OLDERFIELD
  J.R., 8
O'LEARY
  J., 31

OLENA
  R., 3
OLENY
  A., 8
OLEY
  O.S., 8
OLINGER
  E., 13
  J., 59
OLIVER
  ALEX, 31
  H.H., 13
  J., 13(2), 26, 59
  JOHN, 13
  L., 78
  S.E., 26
  W., 70
  W.W., 90
OLLENGER
  JOHN, 78
OLLMAN
  WM., 33
OLMAR
  H., 69
OLMSTEAD
  F.H., 48
OLNEY
  G.W., 31
OLSON
  J., 8(2)
  O., 85
OLSTON
  M., 85
OMAT
  M., 48
O'MINE
  D.J., 8
OMMA
  JAMES, 48
O'NEIL
  CHARLES, 26
  D., 8, 26
  J., 31, 48, 69
  J.M., 80
  JAMES, 59
  JOHN, 69
O'NIEL
  THOMAS, 13
OPEASE
  S., 21
OPER
  L., 17
ORCUTT
  C., 31
  J., 33
O'REILLY
  PHILIP, 48
  THEODORE, 87
ORNIG
  J.B., 59
  S.W., 31
O'ROURKE
  CHARLES, 70
ORR
  A., 3
ORRISON
  GEORGE, 31
ORTELL
  M., 13
ORTON
  H.C., 3
OSBORN
  A.J., 21
  E., 70
  F.L., 15
  J., 13
  J.L., 31

J.M., 36
J.W., 8
S., 31
W., 26
OSBORNE
  E., 36
  J., 90
  R.H., 48
  S.R., 69
  THOS., 83
OSMORE
  J., 35
OSRANS
  J., 87
OSS
  [BLANK], 8
OSTENHAL
  L., 48
OSTERHARDT
  B.S., 48
OSTERSTUCK
  W., 48
OSTRANDER
  E.W., 59
  J., 48
  J.H., 48
OSWALD
  STEPHEN, 69
OTIS
  JOHN, 48
OTT
  C., 59
  JOHN, 87
OTTINGER
  I., 69
  M., 89
OTTO
  CHARLES, 48
  JAMES L., 48
  JOHN, 70
OTTWAY
  D., 8
OUSLEY
  W.I., 13
OVERMEYER
  J.F., 31
OVERTON
  J.S., 78
O'VERTURF
  P.W., 15
OWEN
  A., 78
  W., 17
OWENS
  C., 8
  E., 70
  ED, 48
  G.H. [?], 70
  O.H., 21
  WM., 48
OXLEY
  ROBERT, 83

-P-

PACE
  J.F., 87
  JOHN, 18
PACKARD
  M.G., 81
  MYRON C., 83
  N.M., 26
PACKER
  SAMUEL B., 13
PACKETT
  C., 33
  T.C., 13

PADDOCK
  D.W., 78
PADFREY
  SYLVANUS, 3
PADON
  C., 8
PAGE
  E., 81
  J., 70
  J.E., 88
  JOHN, 70
  LYMAN, 89
  O.D., 48
  WM., 26
PAINE
  M., 83
  S., 8
PAINS
  F., 26
PAINTER
  C., 83
  H., 85
  J.G., 70
  N.P., 3
  S., 70
PAISLEY
  A.G., 31
  F.F., 8
  WM., 26
PALLETTE
  D., 48
PALLY
  S.C., 17
PALMER
  A., 13, 70
  D., 31
  D.P., 78
  F., 48
  H., 70
  JNO., 83
  JOHN, 85
  L.H., 15
  P., 31
  P.H., 48
  SAMUEL, 59
  T., 26
  WM., 78, 88
PALMERLY
  J., 31
PALMITER
  R., 48
PAMPERIN
  WM., 48
PANDES
  L., 26
PANGBURN
  [BLANK], 13
PANIER
  J.M., 26
PANKEY
  A.J., 78
PANNER [?]
  F.G., 59
PANTER
  R., 1
PANTINS
  A.J., 26
PAPPLE
  D., 22
PARDER
  E.H., 78
PARDY
  E., 48
PARHAM
  W. [?], 78
PARISH
  D., 48

J.A., 70
THOS., 31
PARK
  JAS., 78, 81
  JOHN, 13
PARKER
  A., 21
  B.C., 31
  D., 15
  D.H., 26
  E., 13
  F., 48
  I., 48
  ISAAC, 48
  J., 48(3), 59
  JAS., 90
  JAS. M., 70
  S.B., 3
  W., 36, 59
  WILEY, 78
  WM. E., 59
  Z., 59
PARKHAM
  JAS. C., 89
PARKHURST
  B., 8
  W.L., 90
PARKINSON
  A., 48
PARKS
  E.F., 59
  F., 31
  J.W., 59
  R.T., 78
  V., 31
  WM., 48
PARLICE
  GEO. W., 59
PARMALEE
  C., 31
PARMER
  E., 78
PARMOR
  E., 81
PARRISH
  CHARLES, 26
PARSHALL
  J.M., 8
PARSONS
  G., 31
  J.T., 70
  JAMES W., 21
  SAMUEL, 35
  W., 48
  W.D., 26
PARTEN
  D.R., 13
PARTIS
  J.R., 18
PARTRIDGE
  J.W., 87
  W.J., 8
PASCAL
  E., 35
PASCO
  J.M., 26
PASHBY
  JOHN, 13
PATCH
  JOHN, 35
PATCHEY
  J., 3
PATENT
  THOS., 70
PATNY
  J., 83
PATRICK

124

F., 21
PATTEN
W., 59
PATTERSON
D., 48
E., 13, 48
F., 59
F.J., 8
GEO. W., 48
H., 48
H.W., 26
I.H., 48
J., 18, 85
J.H., 48
N., 35
N.S., 13
R., 70
ROBT., 70
S., 85
THOS., 70
W.D., 1
PATTIN
H.W., 70
PATTIT
J.S., 88
PAUL
JOHN C., 81
P., 48
PAVIES
S., 78
PAVY
W., 13
PAYNE
G.A., 26
J., 59
JOSEPH, 34
R.H., 31
WM. A., 26
PEABODY
F.S., 21
W.F., 26
PEACHE
CYRUS, 13
PEARMELL
J., 31
PEARSON
S.C., 87
PEASE
G.E., 59
MARTIN, 48
PEASLEY
J., 59
PECK
ALBERT, 70
C.W., 70
J.G., 48
J.H., 31
PECKHAM
A.P., 26
PECKINS
L., 48
PEDRO
FRANCIS, 48
PEER
T., 36
PEES
M.T., 70
PEETER
H.M., 8
PEETO
A., 26
PEGRAM
W., 78
PEIR
A., 3
PELGER
M., 36

PELLETT
ED, 48
PELTERSEN
F., 59
PELTON
A., 31
PEMER
W., 70
PEN
CHARLES, 48
R., 48
PENABLIN
JOHN, 48
PENAT
ALEXANDER, 13
PENCE
GEO., 33
PENDALTON
W., 3
PENIX
JOHN, 78
PENN
J., 70
JOHN, 70
W.H., 78
PENNINGTON
G.W., 78
R.A., 26
PENNY
A., 59
JAMES, 8
W., 8
PENSTOCK
A., 70
PENTECOST
W.G., 31
PEQUETTE
P., 21
PEREGO
W., 70
PERICLE
JACOB, 33
PERIGO
JOHN, 31
PERKEY
D., 48
PERKINS
A.E., 8
A.H., 34
D., 21
G.W., 78
J.P., 48
JAMES A., 83
N., 70
T., 21
W.B., 59
PERRIN
G., 59
N., 31, 59
PERRY
A., 48
A.B., 81
GEORGE, 8
H., 70
J., 8
JAS., 78
JOHN, 48
N., 8, 26
SAMUEL K., 26
THOMAS, 78
W., 48
WESLEY, 78
WILLIAM, 48(2)
PERSIL
FREDERICK, 70
PERSON
A., 48

PERSONS
W.B., 48
PETERS
FRITZ, 48
H., 21
J., 48
PETERSON
A., 85
C., 48, 85
G., 36, 70
H., 48
HENRY, 36
J., 15, 89
J.B., 8
JOHN, 75
P., 4
S., 85
PETIT
J., 83
PETRIE
JOSEPH, 48
PETRISKY
H., 70
PETTAS
WM., 8
PETTIBONE
E.E., 31
PETTIE
C., 26
PETTIJOHN
J., 8
S.W., 33
PETTIS
H., 13
L.P., 48
PEV
JAS., 80
PEWEN
H.A., 35
PHARRETT
WM., 31
PHAY
M., 70
PHELPS
F.M., 18
H.W., 80
M.F., 35
MORTIN, 48
S.G., 3
W., 70
W.H., 21
WM. E., 17
PHENIX
A.H., 59
PHEPPS
A., 13
PHILBROOK
A., 8
F., 31
PHILLBROOK
F., 21
J.E., 26
PHILLIPS
A., 26
B.B., 90
C., 88
F., 70
GEO. A., 48
H., 48, 59
I., 48
J.I., 3
J.W., 70
JAS. B., 70
L.M., 26
N., 78
PAT, 34
R., 48

T., 78
WM., 8
PHILLPOT
C.P., 15
PHIPPS
H.B., 26
J.H., 70
M.M., 26
PICKERING
E., 78
PICKET
T.B., 85
PICKETT
J.C., 70
PIERCE
ALBERT, 48
CHARLES, 8, 48
H., 48, 59
J., 48(2)
J.H., 48
W.B., 8
WM., 59, 78
PIERSON
DANIEL, 31
J., 59
R., 26
PIFER
M., 70
PIFFER
G., 59
J., 31
W., 4
PIGOT
J., 87
PIKE
B.H., 31
N.N., 81
WM., 88
PILE
WILSON, 59
PILHUTON
JOHN, 26
PILLMAN
JOHN, 4
PILLSBURY
A.J., 85
F., 81
PILOT
JOSEPH, 78
PILSECK
E., 48
PIMBLE
A., 3
PINDIVILLE
M., 22
PINERT
F., 59
PINKHAM
U.W., 21
PINKLEY
J., 78
PINMON
JOHN, 48
PIPENBRING
GEO., 59
PIPER
CHARLES, 26
E.A., 59
F., 26
I., 59
PIRIRIS
J., 85
PISCALL
J.B., 78
PITCHER
E., 33
PITTS

G., 48
J., 15
PIVANT
M., 48
PLACE
E., 48
J.K., 35
S., 8
PLAMERLY
H., 8
PLANT
WM., 31
PLASMINE
A., 34
PLASS
H., 48
PLATT
R., 31
PLINS
WM., 31
PLOUGH
J.W., 13
PLUDE
JOHN, 80
PLUM
A., 85
JAMES, 3
PLUMER
A., 13
E.D., 34
PLUMMER
G., 88
PLUNKET
M., 59
PLUNKETT
J., 48
PLYMAN
WM., 17
PLYMEER
W., 70
PODROFF
D., 31
PODZAS
L., 90
POINDER
T., 33
POISTAN
J., 59
POLACK
J., 48
POLEMAN
H., 70
POLIVAR
MARTIN, 78
POLLAND
JNO., 83
POLLARD
F., 8
POLLEY
J., 83
POLLOCK
R., 48
POLSHON
F.B., 26
POMEROY
JOHN, 78
POMPEY
C., 3
POMROY
C., 48
POND
C., 31
PONDERS
J., 1
PONTEIS
G., 48
PONTER

[BLANK], 87
POOL
  HANSON, 22
POOLE
  C., 90
  CHARLES, 26
  G., 70
POORE
  SAMUEL, 35
POPE
  F., 78
  FRANK, 17
  I.T., 13
  JAMES E., 48
POPPINS
  FRANK, 81
POPPLE
  W.G., 48
PORRELLSON
  C.D., 83
PORTER
  DAVID, 70
  G., 22
  J.F., 17
  L., 31
  W.C., 59
PORTERFIELD
  J.K., 70
  JNO., 83
PORTERLANGE
  WM., 8
POST
  A., 88
  C., 3
  C.J., 36
  GEORGE, 8
  H.E., 48
  J., 59
  J.A., 48
  R.L., 31
POSTER
  N.P., 78
POTACHE
  A., 3
POTT
  J., 17
  SAMUEL, 18
POTTER
  B.F., 70
  H., 48, 59
  S.D., 90
  W.H., 48
POTTLE
  A.E., 21
POTTS
  EDWARD, 70
  I., 13
  JAMES, 59
POULTON
  HENRY, 88
POWELL
  A., 8
  A.N., 78
  A.T., 70
  D., 8
  F., 59
  FRANK, 70
  GEORGE, 48
  H., 70
  I., 70
  WM., 70
POWERS
  A., 81
  G., 90
  H., 78
  H.M., 78
  J., 48(2), 59, 78

JAMES, 8
JOHN, 70
O., 48
R., 78
PRATT
  A.M., 21
  B.F., 48
  C.E., 88
  D.W., 26
  DANIEL, 26
  F., 70
  G.B., 48
  HENRY, 26
  J., 88
  J.F., 36
  L., 31
  M., 31
  P., 48
  W., 8
  WILLIAM, 13
PREANS
  H., 70
PRENTICE
  J.M., 13
PRESCOTT
  C., 21
PRESHALL
  J.A., 59
PRESO
  THOMAS, 70
PRESSELMAN
  C., 48
PRESTON
  B., 31
  C.W., 8
  F., 80
  H.G., 48
  J., 31
  JOHN, 88
  WM., 59
PRETT
  J.R., 1
PRICE
  BARNEY, 59
  DAVID, 48
  EDWARD, 26
  G., 70
  J., 48
  J.M., 8
  O., 70
PRICES
  NELSON, 78
PRICHARD
  J., 26
PRICHT
  F., 70
PRICKETT
  F., 8
PRIEST
  W., 48
PRIME
  D., 8
PRINGLE
  WM., 90
PRINGLER
  THOMAS W., 48
PRINK
  J., 36
PRIOR
  MICHAEL, 26
PRISON
  E.T., 78
PRITCHETT
  J., 70
PROFFETT
  JAS., 78
PROR

A.M., 59
PROSSER
  J., 70
PROUSE
  P.I., 59
PROUTY
  WM., 59
PROW
  JOHN, 48
PROWMAN
  S.H., 48
PRUET
  JAS. M., 88
PRUILS
  W.H., 17
PRUITT
  H.C., 13
PRUNAN
  L., 49
PRUSER
  H., 59
PRYOR
  WM., 70
PUCK
  C., 88
  JOHR., 8
PUFF
  I., 49
PUFFER
  E.D., 26
PUGH
  A., 15
  L., 83
PUHRER
  FRED, 8
PULERMAN
  G., 21
PULEY
  DANIEL, 49
PULLEN
  SAMUEL, 59
PULLERS
  U.H., 49
PULLIAM
  J., 17
  WM., 87
PULLMAN
  GEO., 31
PUNY
  J., 35
PURCELL
  J., 18
  J.R., 34
  JOHN, 59
PURDEE
  CHARLES, 36
  J., 85
PURDY
  M., 85
PURITAN
  O., 3
PURKEY
  JACOB, 49
PURSLY
  W.B., 78
PURSTLE
  S., 49
PUSEY
  JAMES, 59
PUTNAM
  L., 49
  O., 15
PYERS
  ISAAC, 70
PYNER
  T., 8

-Q-

QUACKENBUSS
  P., 49
QUADE
  M., 89
QUEATA
  J., 18
QUIGLEY
  J., 49
QUILLER
  T., 78
QUINBACK
  J., 88
QUINBY
  L.C., 70
QUINLAN
  N., 89
  PAT, 90
QUINN
  EDSER, 49
  JAMES, 26, 90
  P., 8
  [BLANK], 90
QUIRK
  M.J., 26

-R-

RABB
  G.W., 78
RABERIE
  GEO., 18
RACINE
  P., 18
RADABAUGH
  W.H., 59
RADFORD
  WM., 36
RAEFF
  J.B., 70
RAFBRUN
  W., 49
RAFFERTY
  M., 49
  P., 49
  T., 49
RAGAN
  C., 26
  J., 78
  JOHN, 89
RAIFF
  T., 70
RAINS
  G.D., 13
RAINWATER
  A., 78
RAISER
  A., 15
RAKER
  L., 49
RALEIGH
  A., 70
  S., 83
RALEY
  H., 32
RALINGER
  J., 49
RALPH
  G., 13
  J.F., 78
RALSTON
  J.M., 59
  JOHN, 8
  W.J., 59
RAMAY
  LESTER, 18

RAMSAY
  A.B., 8
  HIRAM, 49
  ISAAC, 49
  J.C., 8
  J.D., 70
  J.I., 70
  R., 70
  ROBERT, 18
  T.J., 8
  W.A., 78
  WM., 35, 70
RAMSEY
  J., 32
RAMSTELL
  H., 26
RANCEY
  A.K., 59
RANCH
  J., 49
RAND
  J., 90
  M., 26
RANDALL
  A.B., 49
  C.F., 8
  H., 70
  H.D., 32
  J., 26
  JAS. A., 83
  JOHN, 49
RANDELL
  P.D., 85
RANDLES
  J., 85
RANDOLPH
  [BLANK], 49
RANDSOM
  GEO. W., 81
RANEY
  A., 81
RANGARDENER
  J., 70
RANGHEART
  JOHN, 49
RANKIN
  J.H., 18
  W.A., 8
RANSOM
  H., 70
  J., 8
RAPP
  A.E., 71
  D.C., 59
  JAMES, 26
  N., 59
RASCOE
  C., 81
RASMUSSON
  A., 85
RASSAN
  A., 31
RASTIFER
  JOHN, 49
RATCLIFF
  J., 15
RATHBONE
  B., 3
RATHBURN
  J., 75
  K., 70
RATTERSBOOM
  J., 49
RATTERY
  JOHN, 49
RAWLINGS
  E., 13

RITER
 HENRY, 78
 JOHN, 78
RITSON
 S., 49
RITTEMAN
 JNO., 34
RITTER
 B.B., 18
 BENJAMIN, 13
 D., 8
 JOHN, 78
RITZER
 GEO. A., 88
RITZMILLIN
 JOHN, 49
RIX
 WM., 59
ROACH
 A., 85
 CHAS., 49
 F., 49
 J., 26
 J.W., 78
ROADS
 FREDERICK, 70
ROAT
 J., 70
ROBB
 M., 83
ROBBERGER
 P.H., 49
ROBBINS
 A., 32, 59
 D.B., 59
 G., 70
ROBERSON
 C.A., 49
ROBERTS
 A., 49
 A.B., 49
 ANDREW, 18
 CHAS., 78
 ED, 59
 H., 21
 J.G., 33, 78
 J.H., 26
 J.M., 81
 JOHN, 78
 JOSEPH, 26
 L., 18, 26
 R., 18
 T., 78
 W.W., 8
ROBERTSON
 H., 18
 J., 70
 J.C., 34
 JOHN, 33
 R., 59
 W.H., 49
 W.M., 49
ROBINS
 GEORGE, 70
 J., 70
 L., 49
 P., 59
 R., 70
 T., 78
 W., 78
ROBINSON
 A., 49, 78
 C.J., 59
 C.W., 70
 D., 15
 E.H., 8
 H., 3, 31, 49

H.B., 8
H.C., 49
H.H., 59
ISAAC, 78
J., 22, 59
J.B., 8
J.C., 78
J.W., 3
JACOB, 36
JAS. M., 78
JOHN, 49, 70
L., 13
R., 13, 26
T., 32
W.M., 85
WM., 31, 70, 78
ROBISON
 W.R., 88
ROBUY
 F., 18
ROCHELLE
 JOHN, 59
ROCK
 F., 49
 J.E., 70
 J.H., 83
ROCKFELLAR
 H., 49
 R.E., 49
ROCKWELL
 A., 70
 N.C., 49
 W.W., 18
RODENBERGER
 N., 8
RODER
 F., 8
RODES
 JAMES, 18
RODGERS
 O., 8
 W., 32
RODH
 SIMON, 22
ROE
 WM., 26
ROFERTY
 J.G.[?], 8
 JOHN, 26
ROGER
 JOHN L., 70
 L., 70
ROGERS
 A., 49(2)
 A.G., 78
 C., 59, 70
 G., 49
 GEORGE, 8
 H.C., 49
 H.J., 49
 HENRY, 18
 JAMES, 49
 L., 15
 M., 49
 O.S., 49
 SILAS, 8
 T., 59
 THOMAS, 49
 W., 18
 WM., 18, 88
ROGMAN
 [BLANK], 13
ROLAND
 JOHN, 89
ROLL
 N.C., 13
ROLLA

E.J., 8
ROLLAND
 J., 31
ROLOFF
 JNO., 31
ROLSTON
 J., 71
ROMAIN
 J., 59
ROMAN
 JOHN, 31
ROME
 R., 26
ROMER
 F., 49
RONDEN
 WM., 78
RONEY
 F.J., 88
RONLEY
 J., 90
RONSEY
 WM., 83
ROOD
 C., 31
ROOK
 G., 49
ROOKS
 H., 36
ROONEY
 JOHN, 49
 M., 49
 MARK, 88
 P., 49
ROOT
 A.N., 49
 D., 70
 LEGRAND, 49
ROOTS
 W.T., 49
ROOVIN
 J., 33
ROPE
 A.R., 26
ROPER
 H., 3
ROSE
 A., 49
 B., 49
 JOHN, 59
 M.L., 78
 R.C., 18
ROSECRANS
 H., 8
 J.E., 49
ROSENBERGER
 JOHN, 49
ROSENBURG
 H., 70
 HENRY, 70
 J., 49
ROSMER
 FRANK, 21
ROSS
 A., 49, 59
 C., 49
 D., 3
 DAVID, 49, 70
 E.F., 49
 G., 49
 H.E., 81
 J., 59
 J.H., 49
 J.W., 8
 JACOB, 49
 JOHN, 78
 THOMAS, 8

[BLANK], 88
ROSSER
 LEWIS, 49
ROSSON
 CHAS., 49
ROSWELL
 J., 49
ROTH
 LOUIS, 49
ROTHE
 C., 71
ROTHWELL
 M., 49
ROUGE
 WM., 49
ROUKE
 J., 88
ROUNCERVEE
 E.T., 81
ROUNDABUSH
 H.B., 70
ROUNDBUSH
 DANIEL, 13
ROURK
 J., 59
ROUSER
 A., 78
ROUSH
 PETER, 70
ROVER
 F., 26
ROW
 W.J., 49
ROWBOTHAM
 R., 49
ROWE
 A., 59
 ASA, 26
 E., 70
 L., 21
ROWELL
 J.E., 49
 L.N., 49
ROWLAND
 B., 31
 N., 71
ROWLEY
 CHARLES, 26
RUBLE
 LEANDER, 18
RUDD
 ERAS, 8
 F., 8
RUDDIN
 C., 49
RUDLER
 WILLIAM, 49
RUDOLPH
 S., 70
RUDY
 J., 71
RUE
 NEWTON, 49
RUEFF
 J., 70
RUET
 H., 21
RUGGLES
 O., 31
RUGH
 M.J., 70
RULE
 Y.A., 15
RUM
 A., 70
RUMMER
 L., 83

RUNELS
 JOHN, 70
RUNEY
 F., 49
RUNS
 T., 18
RUPERT
 F., 70
RURVES
 E., 18
RUSBY
 J., 18
RUSH
 D., 59
 JOHN, 49
 S., 70
RUSHING
 W.R., 78
RUSK
 JOHN, 22
RUSS
 JOHN, 49
 W.J., 31
RUSSEL
 E., 15
RUSSELL
 A.P., 22
 F., 70
 G.A., 21
 J., 13, 49
 J.G., 59
 J.S., 78
 JACOB, 18
 JAMES, 59
 L.F., 59
 PETER, 31
 R., 78
 S.A., 70
 T., 4
 W.H., 13
 [BLANK], 26
RUSSMORE
 E., 13
RUSTAR
 R., 26
RUTAIN
 E.B., 59
RUTGER
 W., 13
RUTH
 B.S., 71
 F., 26
RUTHER
 J., 3
RUTHFER
 J., 70
RUTROFF
 JACOB, 83
RYAN
 C.P., 78
 CHARLES, 15
 D., 49
 J., 49(2)
 JOHN, 90
 M., 8
 MARTIN, 13
 OWEN, 49
 T., 32
 W., 18, 31
 WM., 78
RYES
 J.C., 26
RYNE
 J.M., 49
RYNEDOLLAR
 WM., 22
RYONCH

JOHN, 49
RYSON
JOHN, 49

-S-

SABINE
ALONZO, 60
SABINES
EDWARD, 26
SACKETT
I., 13
R.S., 49
SADDLE
M., 8
SADLEY
M., 49
SAFFLE
J., 60
SAFFORD
B.J., 49
ST. CLAIR
BENJ., 90
ST. DENNIS
L., 51
ST. JOHN
A., 81
ST. PETER
F., 21
SALE
THOMAS, 71
THOS., 32
SALER
J.B., 8
SALES
A.D., 85
SALISBURY
E., 49
SALLAC
GEO., 18
SALMOUND
P., 18
SALSBUR
J., 35
SALSBURY
H., 49
SALTS
H.C., 14
SAMBORN
H., 32
SAMET
W., 49
SAMLETT
P.V., 26
[BLANK], 49
SAMMONDS
A., 32
SAMMORIS
B., 71
SAMON
L.W., 22
SAMPSON
C., 60
E., 21
J., 49
J.R., 89
SAMSE
WM., 59
SANBORN
G.B., 26
M.L., 81
T., 26
SANBURN
H., 32, 81
W., 35
SANDER
CHARLES, 75

SANDERS
B., 18
CHARLES, 49
D., 13
F., 26
J., 49(2)
J.S., 18
SANDERSON
H., 13
SANDFER
JNO., 18
SANDFORD
P.O., 50
SANDLER
L., 8
SANDS
G.W., 84
WM., 84
SANDUSKY
G., 79
SANDWICH
J., 26
SANE
JOSEPH, 78
SANFORD
C., 72
J.D., 26
SANGHIN
J., 50
SANLAY
E., 35
SAPP
A.J., 13
B., 18
W.N., 60
SAPPER
S., 79
SARF
HENRY, 33
SARGEANT
M., 8
SARLETT
L., 81
SARMYES
C., 32
SARRET
JAS. D., 79
SARSFIELD
JNO., 90
SATTERLEY
H.J., 32
SATTERSHWAIT
A., 14
SAUGHESSY
JOHN, 59
SAUIN
B., 8
SAUROT
JOHN, 4
SAVAGE
P.P., 8
SAVIN
J.H., 26
SAWER
JOHN, 26
SAWNEY
WM., 18
SAWYER
ENOS, 21
J., 50
J.D., 90
JOHN, 21
S.F., 26
SAY
J.R., 71
SAYER
G.D., 26

SAYLES
A., 50
SAYLOR
C.M., 84
SAYRE
MICHAEL, 84
SAYRES
W., 15
SAYRRER
J.M., 32
SCARBERRY
O., 60
SCARBORO
ROB'T, 22
SCARBROUGH
S.N., 79
SCARFF
F., 14
SCARLETT
JAS., 22
SCHAAT
D.B., 34
SCHABLY
J., 71
SCHADT
THEODORE, 50
SCHAFER
J.E., 18
P., 60
SCHALSTER
S., 26
SCHANNOLTER
C., 8
SCHAYLER
J.W., 50
SCHEAN
W., 35
SCHECK
B., 50
SCHEFFER
H., 33
SCHEM
J., 60
SCHEMERHORN
H., 50
J., 32
SCHEMPP
M., 50
SCHENCK
PHILIP, 34
SCHERMASHIE
B., 50
SCHIEFEIT
JACOB, 71
SCHIMGERT
J., 71
SCHINEDER
J., 22
SCHLEASSEN
J.J., 85
SCHLENBOUGH
C., 71
SCHLOTESSER
J., 50(2)
SCHMAKER [SIC]
JOHN, 50
SCHMAL
ANDREW, 18
SCHMALEY
J., 50
SCHMAR
R., 71
SCHMAS
G., 34
SCHMEAGER
A., 50
SCHNEIDER

CHARLES, 50
S.A., 13
SCHOCKNEY
T.T., 50
SCHOFIELD
C., 32
J., 50
SCHOLL
JOHN, 50
SCHOTTSMAN
F., 18
SCHRAUSBURG
R., 18
SCHRIBER
H., 50
SCHRIDER
D., 8
JOHN, 8
SCHRIMER
WM., 50
SCHRODER
F., 88
G., 50
W., 13
SCHRUM
J., 50
SCHUBERT
K., 3
SCHURTZ
W., 8
SCHWARE
F., 50
SCHWICK
A., 50
SCITAZ
VICTOR, 8
SCMALL
J.D., 60
SCOBEY
L.A.H., 79
SCOLES
M., 71
SCOLETON
J., 71
SCOTT
A., 71
A.J., 72
ALLEN, 71
B., 13
BLAIR, 90
D., 71
E.G., 85
GEO. W., 81
H., 8
J.C., 50
J.H., 60
JAS. H., 88
JOHN, 79
P.C., 50
R., 60
R.O., 81
R.S., 78
S.E., 60
W., 3
W.B., 71
W.W., 50
WM., 71(2)
Z., 84
SCOVER
J.H., 72
SCRIPTER
C.E., 88
SCRITCHFIELD
W., 50
SCUNDLER
J., 71
SCUYNER

N., 8
SEAGHER
J., 50
SEALS
JOHN, 78
SEAMAN
A., 50(2)
M., 85
SEAR
C., 71
SEARCH
C., 13
HENRY, 34
SEARD
LOUIS, 50
SEARLE
J.R., 35
SEARS
F., 50
I., 13
SAMUEL, 59
SEATON
T.B., 81
SEBASTIAN
J.W., 18
SEBERGER
F., 22
SEE
HENRY, 50
L., 3
S., 8
SEEBEL
A., 34
SEELEY
A.J., 50
C.B., 50
CHARLES, 8
CHARLES H., 26
H., 32
N., 60
NORMAN, 15
THOMAS, 50
SEGAM
ED, 50
SEGAR
CHAS., 22
SEGIN
C., 34
SEIGFERD
G.H., 14
SEIGLE
JOHN R., 50
SEIGLER
GEORGE, 50
SEILK
A., 71
SEINS
WM., 15
SELB
JACOB, 60
SELL
ADAM, 60
SELLENTINE
M., 72
SELLERS
H., 71
SELLS
W., 79
SELORS
W.H., 18
SELSON
H., 50
SELTZER
D., 72
SEM
C., 8
SEMEIR

G.S., 84
SERDERS
J.S., 71
SERENA
H., 71
SERENS
R.B., 8
SERGEANT
J.C., 26
L., 4
SERINE
C., 50
SERRIER
R., 50
SETTERS
GEO. H., 8
SETTLE
HENRY, 50
SEVER
H.H., 60
SEVERN
C., 71
SEWARD
G.H., 3
O., 81
R., 8
SEYBERT
A.J., 8
J.S., 88
SEYMAN
AARON, 59
F., 50
SEYMOUR
H., 75
SEYOFF
H., 72
SHAAT
J., 50
SHADRACH
G.H., 8
SHAE
PAT, 50
SHAFER
H., 50
J., 60
J.N., 22
T., 72
W., 32
SHAFFER
DANIEL, 71
J., 50
M., 50
PETER, 71
SHAGGS
I.P., 18
SHALER
F., 60
SHAMROCK
I., 26
SHANAHAN
W., 36
SHANBACH
ED, 8
SHANGROST
A., 71
SHANK
A., 72
S.W., 50
SHANKS
W.L., 18
SHANNAN
E., 50
SHANNON
CHARLES, 59
E., 60
JNO., 32
SHANTZ

J., 35
SHAPE
F., 71
SHAPLEY
GEO., 71
SHARK
L.F., 8
SHARKS
J.N., 72
SHARP
A., 8
A.H., 8
D.M., 14
E.D.T., 8
F.S., 60
J.W., 85
JAS., 32
SHARPLESS
W., 14
SHATER
J.H., 71
SHATS
C., 50
SHAUB
F., 84
SHAUGHNESSEY
J., 50
SHAVER
F., 13
SHAW
ALEXANDER, 50
ANDREW, 26
C.L., 26
F.F., 32
F.N., 32
GEORGE W., 60
J., 8, 50
JOSEPH, 8
M., 50
T.I., 50
W., 50, 60, 71
W.R., 14
W.W., 15
SHAY
D., 79
H.H., 36
J., 81
JOHN, 50
SHEA
J., 26
SHEARS
J.S., 71
SHEBERT
GOTLIEB, 71
SHEDDLE
G., 15
SHEDDY
G., 60
SHEEBY
JOHN, 8
SHEETS
W., 60
SHEFILEY
W., 72
SHEHAN
JAMES, 26
SHEIT
P., 71
SHELDON
G., 81
H., 81
H.S., 32
M., 50
W., 60
SHELLEY
B., 22
SHELLITO

R., 71
SHELTON
C., 88
SHEMBER
JNO., 71
SHEPARDSON
L., 50
SHEPHARD
J.H., 60
SHEPPARD
C., 72
E., 71
JOHN, 60
N., 71
T.L., 18
W.H., 50
SHERIDAN
J., 50
M., 72
SHERMAN
FRED, 32
H., 34
J.W., 15
P.H., 26
SHERWOOD
C.H., 71
D., 3
F., 26
J.E., 50
J.F., 8
P., 71
SHEVER
H., 50
SHICK
ELI, 13
SHIDLER
GEORGE, 50
SHIELDS
GEO., 59
J., 13
J.A., 8
RICHARD, 50
SHIGLEY
T.W., 13
SHILBER
C.A., 84
SHILLING
WM., 22
SHILTS
E., 50
SHIMER
J.A., 71
SHINDLE
S.R., 71
SHINDLER
J., 50
JOHN, 26
SHINGLE
D., 60
SHINK
JAMES, 71
SHIPLEY
W., 22
SHIPPEY
F., 50
SHIPPLE
JOHN, 60
SHIRK
M.B., 71
SHIRLEY
HENRY, 71
JOHN, 18
P., 50
SHIRLOCK
R., 50
SHISTER
F., 71

SHIVER
F., 33
G.H., 22
L., 60
SHOE
G.W., 14
SHOEL
J.P., 13
SHOEMAKER
C., 60
E.W., 13
J., 60
M., 71(2)
SHOLDER
ED, 4
SHONALL
JOHN, 79
SHONE
P., 71
SHOOK
N.A., 79
SHOOP
G., 71
JACOB, 71
W., 85
SHORE
J.J., 26
SHOREY
ED, 35
S., 21
SHORK
H., 60
SHORT
J., 26
JAMES, 60
L.C., 3
L.H., 78
M., 33
SHORTER
W., 60
SHORTMAN
J., 88
SHORTY
ROBERT, 50
SHOTLIFF
J., 50
SHOULDER
E., 60
SHOUP
S., 71
SHOW
J., 18
SHRIGLEY
H., 85
SHRIVELY
E.S., 71
SHRIVER
B., 71
GEORGE, 60
SHROP
J.B., 79
SHROUDS
J., 60
SHUFFLETON
J., 15
SHUHPS
P.D., 50
SHULDS
J., 18
SHULER
CHAS., 50
SHULTES
A.M., 27
SHULTS
C.T., 3
GEORGE, 27
JOHN, 50

SHULTZ
C., 32, 50
F., 50, 71
H.H., 72
JOHN, 71
WM., 50
SHUMAKER
P., 50
SHUMAN
J., 18
JOSEPH, 34
SHUMMAY
WM., 32
SHUN
J., 85
SHUNK
J., 90
SHURE
J.P., 72
SHUSTER
[BLANK], 50
SHUTTER
J., 15
SIBBLE
W., 50
SIBLEY
J.E., 32
SICK
R., 50
SICKLER
E., 50
SICKLES
A., 50
DANIEL, 71
J., 60
M., 32
SIDDELL
G., 50
SIDES
G., 14
SIEBERT
H.C., 8
SIFFLE
H., 8
SIGNALL
[BLANK], 71
SIHERK
CHRISTIAN, 71
SILKWOOD
H.M., 8
SILL
JAMES, 4
SILLERS
WM., 71
SILTER
JOHN, 8
SILVY
DAVID, 72
SIMBLE
WM., 4
SIMMONDS
E., 27
S.P., 60
SIMMONS
A., 50
C.G., 50
E., 84
G.F., 21
J., 14
JOHN, 60
M.A., 8
W.D., 8
SIMMS
S., 35
SIMON
H., 50
SIMONDINGER

F., 84
H., 51
J., 22
JAMES, 88
T.C., 35
SPEAKER
H., 22
SPEARS
J., 15
W.M., 71
SPECK
A., 71
OLIVE, 72
SPEGLE
F., 60
SPELLMAN
B.F., 27
J., 13
JOHN, 51
SPENCE
DAVID, 27
LEVI, 22
SPENCER
A., 51
GEO., 71
GEORGE, 32
J.H., 88
JNO., 32
M., 13
S.M., 60
SPERCE
C., 33
SPERRY
A., 51
SPICER
W., 90
SPIKER
J., 60
SPILYFITER
A., 71
SPINDLER
W., 8
SPINK
J., 75
SPONCERLAR
GEORGE, 60
SPONDLE
C., 32
SPOONER
C.L., 27
E.O., 27
F., 27
SPOORE
W.O., 81
SPOULD
E., 71
SPRAGUE
B., 32
E.H., 51
GEO., 84
J., 51
W., 8
W.B., 32
W.L., 59
SPRIG
JAS. A., 51
SPRINGER
H.W., 21
J., 32, 71
JOHN, 71
M., 9
SPRINK
A., 51
SPROUSE
A., 84
W., 84
SPROUT

A., 81
SPRULOCK
A., 8
SQUARES
SAMUEL, 84
SQUIRES
THOMAS, 60
STACEY
JOHN, 51
STACKLEFORD
S., 84
STADLER
J., 51
STAFFORD
J.W., 13
JOHN, 22
S., 79
W., 72
WM., 78
STAGG
WM., 84
STAHLER
D., 71
S., 71
STAIN
G.W., 72
STALDER
E.P., 27
STALEY
G., 60
G.W., 14
STALL
SAMUEL, 71
STALORD
J., 75
STANCHLEY
WM., 13
STANCLIFF
A.B., 51
STANDISH
M., 13
STANDSFIELD
H., 9
STANETT
J., 60
STANFORD
P.W., 60
STANHOPE
W.H., 4
STANLEY
C.O., 18
J.C., 51
JNO., 35
WM., 89
STANNING
G.W., 32
STANSBURY
E., 88
STANTON
C., 88
H.H., 51
J., 90
L.H., 51
R., 88
W., 78
STAR
C., 51
STARBUCK
F., 59
STARK
F., 9
J.D., 51
J.H., 51
JOHN, 89
S., 35
STARKE
M.S., 14

STARKEY
I., 13
STARKWEATHER
E.M., 3
L., 51
STARR
C.F., 15
DARIUS, 88
E., 85
N., 36
STAUF
J., 27
STAUFF
J., 3
STAUFFER
J., 72
STEAD
J., 51(2)
STEADMAN
S., 32
W., 71
STEADSON
W., 27
STEAMER
F., 14
STEARNES
E.K., 71
STEBBINS
H., 51
STEBINS
C., 51
Z., 71
STEDMAN
S.D., 32
STEEL
ABRAHAM, 59
J.S., 71
STEELE
A., 84
E., 32
F.F., 72
GEO., 36
H., 3
J., 71
JAMES M., 3
SAM, 3(2)
STEFFLER
W.J., 71
STEGALL
J., 9
STEGEWALD
J.M., 13
STEILHOULT
A., 9
STEIN
J., 71
THOMAS, 13
STEINER
C., 51
M.J., 60
STEINHAUS
J., 9
STELLA
J.F., 71
STELLE
F., 27
STELROCHT
D., 51
STEMPF
LEWIS, 18
STENSLEY
D., 72
STEPHEN
H., 59
STEPHENS
B.H., 3

E.W., 3
STEPHENSON
A., 84
STEPP
PRESTON, 78
STERNHOFF
A., 51
STERNHOLT
WM., 71
STEVENS
A., 71
C.P., 72
E., 51
G.W., 60
HENRY, 27
J.F., 79
JOHN S., 51
L., 32
M., 13
N., 27
P.L., 18
R., 78
S., 9, 32
S.G., 71
THOMAS, 27
WM., 51
STEVENSON
D., 60
JOHN, 60, 72
W., 36, 51
WM., 51
STEWARD
C., 84
C.S., 60
F., 9
G., 21
GEO., 35
J., 27, 60
W.V., 32
STEWART
A.F., 60
C.A., 32
E., 18, 27, 79
E.B., 14
E.W., 81
F., 9, 32
J.B., 71
J.W., 79
JOHN, 51
JOHN S., 60
PETER, 51
R.H., 79
WM. A., 84
STIBBS
W., 71
STICKLE
D., 34
STICKLER
E., 51
STICKNER
J., 32
STIFFIN
H., 36
STIFFUS
R., 85
STILL
D., 51
JAMES, 51
STILLENBERGER
F., 71
STILLMAN
L.D., 32
STILLWELL
F.H., 9
JAMES, 9
S., 51
STIMETT

J., 18
STIMMELL
I., 36
STINCHEAR
F.E., 60
STINE
A., 9
C., 18
STINEBACK
A., 71
STINER
GOTLIEB, 34
JOHN, 71
W.H., 79
STINES
H., 32
STINGER
A.E., 78
STINIT
D., 13
STINO
P., 3
STITZER
G., 72
STIVER
J., 60
STIVERS
R., 51
STOBBS
W.W., 71
STOCKHOFF
G., 13
STOCKHOUSE
D., 71
STOCKMAN
L.M., 13
STOCKWELL
A., 81
C.H., 84
STODDARD
I., 51
S., 32
STOFACKE
F., 34
STOFER
L., 13
STOKER
S., 84
STOLTZ
[BLANK], 88
STOLZ
[BLANK], 22
STONE
A., 27
F.P., 27
H.I., 3
JAS. A., 81
JNO., 54
JOHN, 51
L., 51
SAMUEL, 71
W.F., 71
STONEHECKS
J.D., 60
STONES
T., 72
STOPES
S.W., 9
STOPPER
WM., 71
STOREM
A., 9
C., 9
STORER
JOHN, 59
STORING
A., 51

STORM
  L.M., 13
STORMN [SIC]
  F., 34
STORMS
  A.N., 51
STOUP
  J., 51
STOUT
  CHAS., 90
  D.D., 79
  H., 13
  JOHN, 15
  L., 36
STOUTS
  SAMSON, 60
  [BLANK], 13
STOVER
  A., 78
  J., 71
STOW
  GEORGE, 32
STRAIN
  N.W., 51
STRALE
  J., 51
STRANCE
  D., 71
STRAND
  JOHN, 9
STRANDER
  A., 32
STRANSBERRY
  A., 78
STRATER
  GEO., 51
STRATS
  JOHN, 51
STRATTEN
  CHAS., 51
  J.A., 22
  J.H., 51
  J.L., 79
STRATTON
  B.B., 84
  E., 51
STRAUBELL
  L., 3
STRAUM
  JAMES, 3
STRAUT
  C.A., 32
STREET
  JOHN J., 36
STREETER
  F., 51
  J., 88
STREETMAN
  J., 71
STREIGHT
  LEWIS, 51
STRETCH
  J., 4
STRICHLEY
  C., 71
STRICKLAND
  THOS., 32
STRICKLER
  J.W., 71
STRIFF
  JOHN, 88
STRIKER
  F., 71
  J., 9
STRILL
  MICHAEL, 59
STRINGER

P., 9
STRIP
  W., 51
STRIPER
  M., 88
STRONG
  H., 72
  L., 13
  S.M., 9
STROUFE
  A., 60
STROUP
  S., 60
STRUE
  G.N., 51
STUART
  J., 3
STUBBS
  J., 32
  W., 1
STUCK
  H.M., 84
  L.H., 32
STULL
  G., 60
  G.E., 22
STULTS
  P., 60
STUMP
  A., 71
  J., 71
  W., 51(2)
STUNE
  S.L., 9
STURDEVANT
  G., 51
  W., 60
STURGESS
  W.A., 71
STURGISS
  W.T., 84
STURN
  E.E., 84
STUTTER
  J.N., 84
STUTZMAN
  P. [F?], 51
STYLER
  G.W., 51
STYLES
  A.B., 81
  J.N., 88
SUFFECOL
  S., 22
SUGHEM
  I., 51
SUKIRK
  J.F., 78
SULLIVAN
  D., 71
  E., 84
  ED, 51, 71
  F., 27, 60
  I., 36
  J., 9, 75, 89
  JNO., 32
  JOHN, 27(2), 60
  M., 3, 9, 27, 51
  P., 27(2)
  P.C., 51
  PAT, 51
  T., 71, 88
  W., 60
SUMMERS
  W.H., 18
  WM., 18
SUMMERSVOLT

V., 13
SUMNER
  H., 32
SUMSER
  J., 88
SUNDERLAND
  E., 72
SUNN
  C., 9
SUPPES
  T.E., 81
SUPPLE
  C.M., 71
SURPLUS
  W., 71
SUSEAR
  FRED, 51
SUTCLIFF
  B., 3
SUTER
  B.F., 9
SUTGEN
  F., 88(2)
SUTHERAND
  J., 32
SUTHERLAND
  J.E., 18
SUTHIEN
  J.H., 13
SUTHPHAR
  H.W., 32
SUTLIFF
  E., 51
  J., 3
SUTTON
  ANDREW, 79
  D., 79
  H., 32
  J., 60, 85
  JOHN, 78
  M., 9
  R.M., 71
  S., 15
  T., 36
  THOMAS, 18, 78
SWADDLE
  W., 81
SWAGER
  G., 51
  M., 71
SWAGGER
  H, 88
SWAIN
  C., 35
  D., 32
  J.W., 13
SWAN
  F., 21
  H.B., 21
  JOHN, 79
SWANCENT
  J., 51
SWANEY
  E., 60
  P., 21
SWANSON
  P., 9
SWAPPOLA
  O.B., 79
SWARNER
  J., 51
  J.H., 51
SWART
  M.M., 32
SWARTS
  E., 9
  P., 71

SWARTZ
  A., 9
  GEO., 71
  M., 51
SWATZELL
  W.L., 79
SWEARER
  G., 71
SWEENEY
  D., 71
  HENRY, 81
  JAMES, 51
  M., 15, 18, 51
SWEENY
  SAMUEL, 59
  W.P., 71
SWEET
  B.F., 36
  E., 51
  H., 71
  L., 51
  M., 60, 75
  WM., 9
SWEITZER
  M., 88
SWELSER
  J., 71
SWENCH
  W., 59
SWESLER
  C., 32
SWETSER
  P., 36
SWIETZER
  J., 14
SWIFT
  J., 3
SWILLENBARGER

  F., 13
SWINDLE
  T.O., 13
SWINEHEART
  J.W., 59
SWITZER
  L., 27
SWORELAND
  WM., 71
SYLURS
  S., 51
SYLVANUS
  J.J., 13
SYLVESTER
  D., 27
  E., 27
  J., 27

  -T-

TA [SIC]
  B.F., 89
TABOR
  B., 27
  F., 27
TABU
  SILAS, 18
TAGGERD
  JOHN, 27
TAIPING
  WM., 15
TALBERT
  R., 60
TALMAN
  W.C., 81
TAMBRICK
  A., 51
TANNER

A., 60
  H., 81
  J. [BLANK], 9
  M., 51
TANSCHIVIT
  ED, 51
TAPP
  GEORGE, 18
TARE
  W., 51
TARVIS
  G.W., 51
TASNAHET
  CHARLES, 14
TATRO
  ALFRED, 81
  L., 84
TATTMAN
  B., 60
TAY
  S., 85
TAYLOR
  A., 51
  A.B., 35
  A.L., 85
  AMOS, 88
  C., 51
  C.W., 72
  CHARLES B., 51
  D., 51
  E., 14, 88
  G., 21
  GEORGE, 9
  GEORGE H., 14
  H., 9, 32
  H.C., 81
  I., 85
  J., 3, 79, 84
  J.F., 72
  J.M., 32
  J.W., 81, 90
  JAMES, 9
  L.B., 51
  M.D., 88
  M.P., 9
  MOSES, 3
  N., 14, 27
  PETER, 36
  R.H., 51
  ROBT., 4
  THOMAS, 27
  THOS., 18
  THOS. B., 51
  W., 51(2)
  W.H., 51(2)
  W.W., 51
  WM., 51
TELL
  WILLIAM, 51
TEMERTS
  T.J., 27
TEMPLE
  I., 9
TEMPLETON
  G.W., 79
  W.H., 18
TENEYCH
  M., 51
TENHER
  JAMES, 14
TENNEY
  WILLIAM, 27
TENSDALE
  T.H., 60
TENSLEY
  M., 60
TERHUNE

C., 14
TERILLIGER
  N., 60
TERRELL
  A., 72
  J., 34
TERRILL
  CHRISTIAN, 34
TERRY
  AARON, 51
  D., 79
  JOHN, 9
  WM., 18
TERWILLIGER
  D., 51
  E., 72
TEWEY
  J., 51
THATCHER
  E.H., 32
  J., 36
  J.P., 84
  R., 72
THAUTON
  S.A., 79
THAYER
  D., 9
  G., 51
  J., 27
THEARER
  J., 51
THIER
  A.F., 15
THIERBACH
  P.M., 51
THINN
  R.A., 79
THISTLEWOOD
  J., 72
THOMAS
  A., 9
  E., 72
  F., 72
  H., 51
  H.D., 14
  HENRY, 36
  J., 27, 51(2), 75, 88
  J.A., 27
  J.H., 90
  J.W., 27
  JAMES, 60
  JOHN, 89
  L., 88
  M., 14
  N., 60
  SAML., 89
  W., 51
  W.B., 60
  W.E., 18
  W.H., 79(2)
  W.R., 33
  WM., 60
THOMPKINS
  IRA, 51
THOMPSON
  A., 35, 51, 72
  C., 27
  C.W., 51
  CHARLES, 79
  D., 9
  D.D., 85
  DANIEL, 51
  F., 3, 9, 21
  F.A.B., 72
  G.G., 9
  GEO., 90

GEORGE, 27(2)
H., 72(2)
J., 22, 51(2), 60, 72(3)
J.B., 72
J.M., 27
J.S., 72
JAS., 72
JNO., 90
JOHN, 9, 21, 22
M.C., 32
N.B., 51
O., 85
P., 51
R., 72
S., 36
T., 9, 14, 51
V.B., 60
W., 32, 33
W.A., 81
W.D., 79
W.W., 27, 72
WM., 3, 88
THOMSBURG
  N.C., 9
THOPSON
  M., 15
THORN
  E., 21
  H.I., 4
  J., 9
  P.C., 85
THORNBURG
  B., 18
THORNDIE
  W., 21
THORNTON
  J., 51
THORP
  J., 18
THORPE
  D., 72
  L., 72
  S.S., 84
  W.C., 51
THORSON
  P., 85
THRESH
  G., 51
THROPE
  H., 18
THRUSTON
  N.E., 51
THUCK
  I., 72
THURBER
  D., 85
THURMAIN
  J., 9
THURSTON
  C.C., 84
  G.W., 51
TIBBELS
  GEO., 72
  WM., 3
TIBBETT
  A., 27
TICE
  S.J., 79
TIDWELL
  J.W., 79
  T., 79
TIERNEY
  W., 60
TIFFANY
  J., 27
TIFT

H., 32
TILBRICK
  E.L., 4
TILDEN
  A., 27
TILLITSON
  N.P., 51
TILLSON
  CHAS. E., 27
TILT
  GEORGE, 32
  W., 72
TILTAM
  N.M., 33
TILTON
  D.B., 35
  H., 51
  J., 22
  L.G., 35
TIMERSON
  WM., 51
TIMMISH
  [BLANK], 51
TINDEL
  E., 36
TINDELL
  WM., 22
TINDLE
  E., 22
TINER
  DAVID, 51
TINSDALE
  [BLANK], 72
TINWAY
  P., 60
TIPTON
  W.H., 79
TISDALE
  ED F., 3
TITE
  W.S., 79
TITS
  P., 72
TITUS
  W., 72
TIVIS
  C., 15
TOBIAS
  A., 51
TOBIN
  MICHAEL, 89
TOBINE
  T., 35
TOCDT [SIC]
  H., 51
TODD
  T., 14
  WM., 72
TOHNSON
  E., 51
TOLAL
  PAT, 51
TOLL
  WM., 72
TOLLAND
  D., 72
TOLLEY
  D., 79
TOMLIN
  A., 79
TOMLINSON
  ROBT., 85
  S., 84
  W.F., 51
TOMPKINS
  N.R., 32
  T.B., 79

TONER
  PETER, 72
TONES
  E., 72
TONEY
  L., 51
TONNER
  L., 51
TONSON
  J., 72
TONUNE
  B., 15
TOOLEY
  G.W., 14
  MICHAEL, 88
  W.R., 14
TOOMA
  JOHN, 27
TOOMEY
  J.F., 51
TOOTHACRE
  J., 21
TOPP
  A., 9
TOPPER
  J., 88
TOREY
  L., 27
TOROMAN
  W.R., 60
TORREY
  C.L., 27
TOURNEY
  P., 51
TOWNLEY
  J.J., 27
TOWNSEND
  C., 72
  D., 72
  F., 36
  GEO. M., 51
  J., 36, 60
  JOHN, 51
  L., 51
  W., 51
TOWNSLEY
  E.M., 60
TOY
  J., 36
TRACEY
  PAT, 53
TRACY
  D., 32
  JAS., 18
TRAILER
  VAN BUREN, 9
TRAINER
  M., 88
TRAITTMAN
  JAS., 36
TRASH
  SETH, 72
TRASK
  GEO. K., 34
  J.J., 9
TRAVERN
  W., 27
TRAVIS
  GEO., 18
  H.C., 27
  T., 51
TREADWAY
  J.H., 3
TREDRIDGE
  A., 88
TREMOR
  M., 51

TRESCOTT
  SAMUEL, 60
TRESCUTT
  W.M., 27
TRESLER
  H.W., 34
TRESPAN
  P., 72
TRIMMER
  WM., 60
TRIPP
  IRA, 51
  O.S., 51
TROBRIDGE
  S., 84
TROMPTER
  F., 53
TROUT
  E., 9
TROUTMAN
  A., 85
TROW
  H., 81
TROWBRIDGE
  L., 9
TRUEMAN
  R., 51
TRUESDALE
  W.J., 51
TRUMAN
  A.M., 51
  E.W., 72
  J., 88
  L.H., 14
TRUMBLE
  D.A., 27
TRUMBULL
  H., 51, 72
TRUMPP
  E., 51
TRUNEY
  J., 18
TRYMER
  JAMES, 89
TUBBS
  E., 72
  P., 32
  W.H., 53
TUCER
  B., 14, 90
TUCKER
  C.P., 85
  E., 9
  J., 9
  J.A., 18
  J.P., 9
  L., 53
  ROBT., 18
  WM., 18
  [BLANK], 22
TUDOR
  AB'M, 18
TUFT
  E., 53
TUFTS
  J., 21
TUILER
  W., 9
TUITH
  F., 27
TULL
  D., 72
TULLIS
  L.B.G., 90
TULLOR
  G.W., 18
TUNBLORA

B., 14
TUNG
  S.W., 85
TUPPLE
  H., 53
TURDEN
  E.S., 53
TURK
  H., 88
TURMAN
  D., 34
TURNER
  A., 22
  B., 36
  C., 22
  C.C., 21
  CHARLES, 75
  F., 54
  H., 3, 27, 54
  J., 53
  J.B., 53
  JOHN, 53, 72
  S., 9
  S.B., 60
  THOMAS, 53
  WM., 53, 89
  WM. F., 22
TURNERHOLM
  S.H., 9
TURNEY
  U.S., 60
TURRELL
  HENRY, 32
TURTON
  W.F., 53
TUSSEY
  E.D., 18
TUTHILL
  C., 53
  S.D., 53
TUTOR
  C., 72
TUTTLE
  C.S., 81
  D.L., 21
  L.S., 21
  W., 53
TUTUNE
  J., 18
TWEEDE
  R., 60
TWESLER
  C., 32
TWICHELL
  J., 27
  [BLANK], 27
TYFFLE
  JOHN, 79
TYLER
  E.P., 85
  J., 85
TYRM
  T., 84
TYRRELL
  I., 53
TYSEN
  J.T., 22
TYSER
  L., 72
TYSON
  E.S., 88
  J.T., 22

-U-

UBER
  CHARLES, 53

UCHRE
  S., 60
UDELL
  J., 53
  W.O., 32
ULMER
  H., 53
ULMGENDER
  G., 90
ULRICH
  DANIEL, 22
ULRICK
  JOHN, 72
ULRIN
  A., 33
UNCER
  JAMES, 53
UNDERBURG
  L.W., 53
UNDERGRATE
  A., 79
UNDERHILL
  H., 53
UNDERWOOD
  D., 9
  P., 14
UNDERWRITER
  A., 53
UNMUCH
  C., 88
UPDELL
  J.S., 85
UPKINS
  A., 35
UPTON
  F.M., 14
URNDRAGH
  W., 72
USHER
  SAMUEL, 27
USLEY
  T.R., 79
UTLER
  WM., 72
UTTER
  STEPHEN, 36

-V-

VAIL
  G.B., 72
  G.M., 85
  JOHN L., 60
  N., 60
VALENTINE
  C., 60
VALLETT
  W., 36
VALLEY
  F., 21
  JOHN, 35
VALTER
  H., 3
VAN ALLEN
  C., 53
VAN BETHYSEN
  H., 53
VAN BRAMIN
  T., 53
VAN BRANT
  W.H., 32
VAN BUREN
  HENRY, 53
  J.W., 53
  W.H., 88
VAN CLARKE
  WM., 53

VAN DERBRECK
  A., 53
VAN DUGEN
  [BLANK], 53
VAN DYKE
  D.L., 73
  JNO., 32
VAN FLEET
  H., 60
VAN HAUGHTON

  J., 53
VAN HOSEN
  C., 53
VAN HOUSEN
  B., 53
VAN MALLEY
  J.M., 60
VAN OSTEN
  C., 53
VANALLEN
  C., 32
VANALSTINE
  C., 53
  H., 53
VANAMAN
  M., 60
VANARNUM
  J., 53
VANARSDALE
  P., 53
VANBUREN
  J., 53
VANCAMPMENTS

  GEORGE, 72
VANCE
  H.J., 34
VANCLACK
  F., 53
VANCOSTER
  H., 85
VANCOTTEN
  WM., 88
VANDEBY
  B., 72
VANDERBILT
  J., 85
VANDERBROGART

  W., 53
VANDERHOOF
  JAS., 32
VANDERPOOL
  F., 72
VANDERVEER
  A., 60
VANDEVIER
  J., 18
VANDIER
  W.M., 90
  WM., 72
VANESSE
  M., 53
VANEST
  J.H., 53
VANGIESON
  L., 32
VANGRIDER
  H., 60
VANHATTERMAN

  I., 73
VANHOLT
  T., 72
VANHOOK
  J.M., 79

VANHORN
  J., 79
  S., 60
VANHOUSE
  B.A., 33
VANKIRK
  G., 60
  W., 90
VANLIN
  C., 32
VANMAKER
  F., 32
VANMARKES
  D., 73
VANOSE
  J., 14
VANSCOTT
  L., 53
VANSHOTEN
  W.H., 32
VANSICKLE
  L., 32
VANVELSEN
  J., 53
VANVELZER
  J.M., 53
VANWAGNER
  C., 53
VANZART
  WM., 53
VARNDALE
  J., 72
VARNER
  T.W., 79
VARNEY
  C., 53
VARNUM
  E.G.J., 81
VASE
  [BLANK], 9
VATIER
  J.F., 60
VAUGH
  B., 60
  I., 79
  JAMES, 9
VAUGHAN
  J., 72
  W.H., 53
VAUGHRY
  FREDERICK, 79
VAUSCOY
  A., 84
VEACH
  JESSE, 22
VEAZIE
  F., 4
VEIL
  WM., 53
VENCOT
  L., 53
VENILL
  C., 21
VENOME
  JAMES, 14
VENTLER
  CHAS., 72
VERHOUSE
  D., 14
VERNON
  S., 53, 72
VERY
  W., 84
VESPERS
  JAS. W., 53
VIBBARD
  GEO., 53

VICKERY
  WM., 88
VICTOR
  H., 60
VINCENT
  JAS., 84
  L.D., 9
  R., 53
  RICHARD, 53
VINCIENT
  J., 32
VINING
  W.H.H., 60
VINSANT
  G.M., 53
VIRTS
  R., 84
VISCOUNTS
  A.J., 22
VISH
  O., 53
VITTER
  J., 85
VITTUM
  E.W., 33
VLEIGHT
  A., 32
VOCLEE
  F., 85
VOERLING
  H., 53
VOGEL
  L., 72
VOGLE
  ANTON, 53
  JACOB, 32
  V., 73
VOHOSS
  O.H., 85
VOIT
  T., 14
VOKE
  JOHN, 15
VOLIS
  J., 60
VOLMORE
  J., 88
VOLTER
  GEORGE, 9
VOORHIES
  A.H., 53
  E.R., 53
  GEO., 53
VORIS
  ROSS, 9
VORK
  C., 32
VOUGHT
  WM., 9
VOX
  WM., 9

-W-

WADDLE
  J., 9
WADE
  A.D.L., 27
  C., 14
  GEO. W., 73
  M., 53
  W., 14
WADSWORTH
  B.H., 88
WAGNER
  C., 53(2)
  F., 14

www.ingramcontent.com/pod-product-compliance
Lightning Source LLC
Chambersburg PA
CBHW080425270326
41929CB00018B/3167